Allyn & Bacon Antho
of Traditional Literature

Judith V. Lechner

Auburn University

PEARSON

Boston ■ New York ■ San Francisco
Mexico City ■ Montreal ■ Toronto ■ London ■ Madrid ■ Munich ■ Paris
Hong Kong ■ Singapore ■ Tokyo ■ Cape Town ■ Sydney

Editor: Auroa Martínez Ramos
Editorial Assistant: Erin Beatty
Senior Marketing Manager: Elizabeth Fogarty
Composition and Prepress Buyer: Linda Cox
Manufacturing Buyer: Andrew Turso
Editorial-Production Coordinator: Mary Beth Finch
Editorial-Production Service: Barbara Gracia
Copyeditor: Barbara Willette
Electronic Composition: Omegatype Typography, Inc.

For related titles and support materials, visit our online catalog at www.ablongman.com

Between the time Web site information is gathered and published, some sites may have closed. Also, the transcription of URLs can result in typographical errors. The publisher would appreciate notification where these occur so that they may be corrected in subsequent editions.

Library of Congress Cataloging-in-Publication-Data

Allyn and Bacon anthology of traditional literature / [compiled and edited by] Judith Lechner.
    p. cm.
  Includes bibliographical references and index.
  ISBN 0-8013-3097-1
    1. Folk literature—Themes, motives. 2. Tales. 3. Legends. I. Lechner, Judith.

  GR72.5.A55 2004
  398.2–dc22
                                             2003060374

Printed in the United States of America

In memory of my parents,
Andrew and Clara Nosty
who enriched my sister's and my life with
fables and fairy tales, Bible stories and myths,
and to my children and students,
who will pass the stories on

CONTENTS

CHAPTER   4

Myths   179

CHAPTER 5

Legends, Hero Tales, and Epics 229

ILLUSTRATIONS

PREFACE

The *Allyn and Bacon Anthology of Traditional Literature* provides a sampling of oral and written stories from around the world. Introductions to the major narrative genres as well as to the individual stories are designed to help students in undergraduate or graduate survey courses of children's literature to place the stories in their cultural contexts. The introductions also include discussions of some of the issues involved in collecting, translating, retelling, and selecting traditional tales. Whereas other anthologies focus either on folktales or on myths and legends, this anthology presents under one cover fables, folktales, myths, and legends.

The material for this anthology was chosen primarily from written collections of orally transmitted stories from around the world. A primary selection criterion was that the stories reflect the world view of the original tellers rather than superimposed attitudes of collectors and retellers from outside the culture. Because no single person can claim to have expertise in the beliefs of such a wide range of cultures, I have followed an iterative methodology to identify the cultural authenticity of the stories selected. I began by reading the folklore and criticism of the literature of broad cultural regions such as Africa, South America, and China. I then read both older and newer scholarly and popular adult versions of traditional literature, examined current children's versions and the retellers' sources, and read criticism regarding the published versions written for adults and for children. I also read contemporary writings by authors from some, though by no means all, of the cultures to gain a sense of current attitudes, styles, and concerns. This was particularly true for Native American writers. Finally, I have consulted individuals who are from or are familiar with different cultures about the centrality of the stories I selected and the meaning of some puzzling details.

Though this was a distinct challenge, it was much easier to ascertain authenticity in terms of content and attitudes than storytelling style. Until recently, few collectors were interested in or were able to reproduce the performance styles of the storytellers from who the stories were obtained. Researchers collected stories in situations that were not conducive to optimal performance—for instance, when the collector was the only audience—and edited their collections to suit genteel European or American middle-class readers or school children. Selection for the anthology, therefore, also involved an attempt to provide a variety of voices and styles—some literary, others closer to the folk expression of the culture. Most of the non-European stories were selected from current or recent storytellers, if possible from within the culture, whereas many of the European stories were selected from nineteenth century collections.

Additional criteria for selection of stories included variety in styles, themes, genres, lengths, and sources. The narratives' potential for exploring themes that recur across cultures, their centricity to a culture's tradition, and the likelihood of their interesting children as well as adults were also important considerations. Because the stories were selected with the idea that teachers and librarians should be able to visualize using them with children, most of the stories have limited levels of violence or explicitly sexual descriptions. Nevertheless, stories that were clearly intended for an adult audience are included to provide readers the opportunity to compare variants and to observe the range of audiences for these stories.

The anthology includes some stories, particularly in the myths section, that are so central to Western culture that it is important to continue to present them to a new generation of children. Instructors can also use these stories to discuss enduring themes, motifs, story structures, and sociocultural issues. Besides the Greek and Norse myths, variants of familiar tales such as the Russian "Vasilisa the Fair" and the Southwestern U.S. "La Estrellita," which are versions of Cinderella; several versions of the "kind and unkind sisters" theme of which Perrault's "Diamonds and Toads" is best known; and variants of "Beauty and the

Beast," such as the Scottish "The Red Bull of Norroway" and Appalachian "Little Rusty Cookstove," were included to allow for comparisons with the more familiar variants. The process of compiling this anthology has been a journey of discovery, and I hope to have conveyed the sense of excitement I felt in learning about the ways stories work in our lives.

To keep this anthology to a manageable and affordable size, I have placed approximately 36 of the 167 stories on the Web site at www.ablongman.com/lechner. The introductions to the Web site stories are found in the anthology at the end of each chapter in the section "Web Supplement Stories."

I have also identified picture books, illustrated books, and some videos and audio recordings that are versions of the stories within this anthology. These too have been placed in the Web Supplement and are keyed to each story for users' ease.

Finally, the Web Supplement has a searchable bibliographic database of traditional literature in picture book format.

▓ Acknowledgments

Putting together an anthology is, as others have noted, a labor of love. It is at times quite daunting, however, and I would not have been able to complete this collection without the continuous encouragement, support, prodding, questioning, constructive criticism, and help with everything from permissions to proofreading of my husband Nobert Lechner; the intellectual and moral support, advice, and editorial help of Dr. Joan Nist, Professor Emerita at Auburn University; the insights, bibliographic and clerical help of my son Walden Lechner; and the extensive editiorial help of my son Ethan Lechner.

I am thankful for the comments and feedback of several people whom I have consulted about the accuracy and authenticity of some of the stories— Dr. Joseph Bruchac, author, poet, and storyteller for the Native American stories; Dr. Betsy Hearne, Graduate School of Library and Information Science, University of Illinois at Urbana, for the section on fairy tales and trickster tales; Dr. Frank Hugus, Department of Germanic Languages and Literature, University of Massachusetts at Amherst, for the Norse myths; Dr. Ashenafi Kebede, School of Music and Center for African American Culture, Florida State University, for the Ethiopian stories; Ms. Hamae Okamoto, Japanese translator of English language children's books, for details about Japanese culture; Dr. Barbara Walker, Turkish Archives, Texas Tech University, for the introduction to the fairy tales/wonder tales chapter and to the Turkish tales; and Ms. Fangxia Zhao, graduate student at Auburn University, for the Chinese myths. Any mistakes, however, are entirely my own.

The professional support of Auburn University's Department of Educational Foundations, Leadership, and Technology and of the College of Education was essential for the completion of this work, as without their recognition of the value of this undertaking, it would not have been possible for me to devote most of my research time to this anthology for the last four years. I am grateful for this support. I would also like to thank the Auburn University Library reference librarians, especially education librarians Lisa Beall and Dorothy Marcinko, as well as acquisition librarian Barbara Nelson, for keeping a lookout for and ordering works of interest to this project. I am equally grateful to the entire library staff for making Auburn University a great library to work with. I also wish to thank Ms. Margaret Coughlin at the Children's Division of the Library of Congress and the librarians at the International Youth Library in Munich.

I would like to thank my editor Aurora Martínez Ramos and editorial assistant Katrina Freddoso for their valuable advice and help. Finally, I would like to thank the following reviewers of the manuscript: Carol J. Nelson, Lewis-Clark State College; Kathryn Leo-Nyquist, Champlain University; Thomas A. Caron, Marshall University Graduate College; Melise Bunker, Palm Beach Atlantic College; Carol Butterfield, Central Washington University.

Permissions for the use of stories and art are found on the page where the story starts and in the captions for each illustration. Every effort has been made to obtain permissions for each story that is in copyright. The only piece of work for which no copyright holder could be traced was Uili Beier's "How the World Was Created from a Drop of Milk." If there is a copyright holder for this work from Beier's *The Origin of Life and Death*, Heinemann, 1996, please contact the author at lechnjv@auburn.edu.

An Introduction to Traditional Literature

Stories define who we are or who we wish to be and help us make sense of our experiences. Whether we have a fight with a friend, are unfairly punished, or accomplish something we are proud of, it was in the telling and retelling that the meaning of the experience becomes clear. One story I have heard many times is how my Aunt Ilonka risked her life during the liberation of Budapest at the end of World War II to fetch me, a newborn, from the hospital, while my two grandfathers carried my mother home by a different route. Bombs were a constant threat; one demolished the house in which my aunt had taken momentary shelter soon after she stepped out into the street. There were countless acts of heroism by men and women during the war, but for me my aunt personified the concept of the hero.

As a nation too we have our stories. The telling and retelling of American history have shaped how we view ourselves as a people. Consider the story of the First Thanksgiving, which was developed as a holiday and national legend only in the nineteenth century. The telling of how starving Pilgrims were aided by helpful Indians and their sitting down together for a harvest thanksgiving has come to be prized by most of us, immigrants to this continent, as one of our central myths. Through this story we learn that we belong here and we can all live together peaceably. Though this myth has been violated far too often, it holds out hope for us as a nation as year after year we try to be more inclusive and more aware of who is not at the table. (For a Native American perspective, however, see Michael Dorris's essay, reprinted in *Through Indian Eyes: The Native Experience in Books for Children*, 1992).

Although we all have stories, they are not always easy to share with people outside our culture. Perry Nodelman (1992), a children's literature professor, points out that students in his classes seldom remember or retell stories outside of a limited number of German and English folktales and that they frequently report finding folktales from other cultures boring and "disturbingly alien." My own experience as a teacher has been similar. When asked to identify the story they most enjoyed out of a selection from Jane Yolen's *Favorite Folktales from Around the World* (1986), students in my children's literature class invariably choose European stories such as "Catherine, Sly Country Lass" from Italy or "It Could Always Be Worse," an Eastern European Jewish story. No one chooses "Urashima Taro" with its wistful ending or the various trickster stories, whether West African, Turkish, or Apache. What is more, I too have been baffled from time to time at a choice of imagery, the resolution of a conflict or the absence of conflict, and the meanings of themes.

It was this fundamental feeling that I do not sufficiently understand the folk literature that I am introducing to prospective teachers, as well as the desire to make this literature more meaningful for both my students and myself, that impelled me to explore traditional literature from around the world. The purpose of this general introduction is to provide an overview of the various ways in which people have examined folk literature; to make readers aware of the issues involved in the collecting, interpreting, and retelling of folktales; and to suggest some reasons for using international folk literature with children. The introduction to each section provides a closer look at the specific genre and some of the ways in which it varies in different regions of the world; the introduction to each individual story focuses on details of the story and how it relates to its culture or to other stories. The country and, where appropriate, the ethnic origins of the stories are identified, and in most cases picture book versions are indicated on the anthology's Web site at www.ablongman.com/lechner. Through this anthology readers should become more familiar with the cultural contexts of traditional literature from a wide range of cultures. This anthology, however, is only a beginning. Starting with the background provided here, readers should be able to continue to seek further understanding of their own stories and those of other cultures and to select and use in the classroom the rich variety of folk literature. Because the definitions and categorization of traditional literature can be confusing, it is worth defining the terminology used in this anthology.

▨ Definitions

A legend such as that of the First Thanksgiving represents but one of many different types of traditional tales. The terms "traditional literature," "folk literature," and "oral literature" have been used interchangeably to refer to stories that have become the cultural heritage of a community of people, shaped and reshaped through continuous usage to fit the needs of the tellers and audiences of a particular place or time. Strictly speaking, the three terms traditional, folk, and oral literature are not equivalent.

Traditional literature, for instance, may be oral or written. *Sundiata,* the epic of Mali, has been handed down orally for hundreds of years by professional oral historians called griots, but the original author of the epic is not known. Other epics, such as Homer's *Odyssey,* are in many cases the works of known authors and are considered literary works; however, they draw on myths and legends that had a long oral history before the written work was created. Charles Perrault in 1697 began a 300-year tradition of publishing fairy tales for children, fixing them in print, with the result that most people's encounters with folktales and fairy tales today are through books and films. In some cases even the collectors of folktales

have had to rely on written sources, as oral sources were no longer available. In England, for instance, few living sources of fairy tales were found by nineteenth century collectors such as James O. Halliwell. Consequently, collectors had to turn to sixteenth and seventeenth century chapbooks (cheap booklets) and other printed sources for some of their stories (Briggs and Tongue, 1965). Many American tall tales and other folktales were disseminated through newspapers in the nineteenth century. Today many an urban legend is perpetuated via newspapers and the Internet.

Folk literature, once defined as the productions of the common folk, or illiterate/preliterate people, has also been redefined as having diverse sources and diverse audiences. Many of the stories might have begun as courtly tales but became so popular that they were retold and passed along orally as part of a community's stock of stories. Other narratives too, such as ballads, were probably composed by one individual but entered the oral repertoire of stories. One important criterion for defining a story as a folk narrative is that it has been accepted, adopted, and transmitted in many versions or variants, so whether the story began in print or in an oral telling, it has become the common property of all members of the community and continues to be shaped by its members (Georges and Jones, 1995).

Oral literature is actually an oxymoron, as the term "literature" comes from the Latin for "writing," but the expression is often applied to stories that are passed on orally (Dundes, 1992). For the purposes of this anthology the terms "traditional literature" "folk literature," and "oral literature" will be used interchangeably.

There are many genres of verbal communication. For teachers and their students some of the shorter verbal communications, such as jokes, proverbs, and riddles, may prove to be interesting areas to explore and to collect. This anthology, however, deals only with the longer narrative genres: didactic stories or fables, folktales, myths, and legends. These may be differentiated from one another by the attitudes of the traditional tellers and listeners toward the stories and by the characters in the stories (Brunvand, 1978). **Fables,** which frequently feature animal characters, are told with the intention of educating the listener or reader. Although fables can be intended for an entire community, they are often aimed primarily at children to teach them the values of the community. Both the teller and the audience know that the stories are fiction, but the message is considered important.

Folktales too are seen as fiction. Their purpose, however, is less explicitly to teach, at least not in the direct manner of fables, and more to express the individual's and the community's hopes and fears, to provide entertainment and excitement, and to create role models of desirable conduct for individuals and groups of individuals (for instance, young adults). The characters in folktales tend to be humans who encounter adventures and problems much like those of the listeners in the audience, though often the characters and events can be seen as symbolic—heroes battling giants or dragons symbolizing the small person's fight against great odds such as tyrants or human resistance to evil. Folktales come in many varieties. Some are naturalistic, though exaggerated, as are tall tales; others have foolish protagonists, whom folklorists label as noodleheads, or tricky survivors known as tricksters. Folktales also include the familiar fairy tale or wonder tale characterized by enchantments, magical helpers, and heroic quests.

Eve Engle Kneeland, Director of Youth Services Auburn Public Library, Auburn, Alabama, is doing an evening of ghost story swapping with young people.

Photograph © 2002 by Judith V. Lechner. Used with permission by Eve Engle Kneeland.

Myths are considered sacred stories that deal with origins and explanations of natural phenomena and human institutions. Those who first told the specific myths believed them to be true and treated them as sacred. This anthology deals with both classic myths, which no longer hold a sacred status for any tellers or writers, and living myths, which are sacred to the cultures from which they spring. Thus myths are not fictitious stories.

Legends too have an aura of truth attached to them. They are unverified and often unverifiable stories, more closely related to history and biography than the other forms of oral literature. Legends reflect a people's ideals as embodied in the actions and attributes of their heroes, for instance Odysseus for the ancient Greeks, Roland for medieval France, Sundiata for the people of thirteenth century Mali, and the martyrs and saints of Christianity, Islam, and Judaism. Legends also tell of a people's history as recalled through oral tradition and are frequently used to create a cultural and political identity for the group. Finally, verging on the mythic are legends that tell of the significance of specific landmarks such as rock outcroppings, mountains, waterfalls; of plants such as the dogwood, which has ancient Greek, Christian, and Cherokee legends attached to it; and of ghosts and haunted places. Richard Dorson relates several such stories in *America in Legend: Folklore from the Colonial Period to the Present* (1973).

Although the stories in this anthology are grouped into categories, it is important to point out that these are overlapping categories. A legend might veer more toward the historic or more toward the mythic; trickster tales and pourquoi tales, which have been included among the folktales, can be closer to myths depending on the nature of the event the story describes. Coyote, for instance, might just act like a greedy fool in one trickster story, or he might be the one to bring fire to the world or to choose death as people's final lot in a myth.

Traditional literature was never meant just for children. Myths and legends were for the whole community and were often told by religious leaders or professional poets whose function was to recite the great deeds of the leaders or the history of the people. Folktales were told in a much wider range of settings, from

Hiroko Mochizuki, a member of the Hachioji Story-telling Group is telling stories at Minami-Osawa Library of Hachioji, Tokyo.

Photograph © 2002 by Kiyoshi Okamoto. Used with permission by Kiyoshi Okamoto.

formal community functions such as wakes to family gatherings and recreational occasions. An overview provided by Margaret Read MacDonald's *Traditional Storytelling Today: An International Source Book* (1999) demonstrates that these functions continue throughout the world, though in many places the locales for storytelling have shifted. In the twentieth century non-traditional settings have included public libraries, schoolrooms, parks, and storytelling festivals (Stone, 1986).

As long as the stories remain within the culture that shaped them, they are likely to create only a certain level of disagreement over interpretation. Sometimes ambiguities are deliberately built into the story, as in the African dilemma tales, but the basic world views, expectations for styles of expression, and ability to interpret tone (e.g., humor, irony, earnestness) are shared by tellers and audiences. Misunderstandings and at times controversies arise when people outside of the culture collect, interpret, and retell the stories or when the audience shifts from adults to children. Even Paul Goble, reteller of Siksika (Blackfoot) and Lakota (Sioux) myths and legends, though highly respected by Native Americans for his work, has

drawn criticism when he tried to retell humorous stories about Iktomi, the Lakota trickster. Humor is possibly the tone that is most resistant to translation (Hearne, 1999). In the following sections the history of collecting, interpreting, and retelling traditional stories will be discussed, along with some of the controversies attending these activities.

Collecting Folklore: A Historical Overview

Just as there have been many reasons and occasions for telling stories, so the purposes and methods of collecting and retelling traditional tales have varied over time. One early compiler of oral tales was the ancient Greek Hesiod (~700 B.C.E.), a poet who earned his livelihood reciting narrative poetry and also used the new technology of the time—writing—to record the narratives and to use them as commentary on society (Powell, 1998). The oldest known of the Japanese chronicles, dating to the eighth century, is a set of histories, myths, legends, and folk songs (Georges and Jones, 1995). In the Americas the sacred book the *Popol Vuh,* was compiled from memory by a Mayan in 1558 to preserve the myths after their original writings had been destroyed by the Spanish (Montejo, 1999).

The systematic collecting of traditional literature, however, began in the late eighteenth and early nineteenth centuries. In England study and preservation of ancient lore and customs were the primary interest of scholars of antiquities (Georges and Jones, 1995). In Germany, however, the Brothers Grimm started the systematic collection of folklore to create a national identity for the disunited German principalities, which had only recently been dominated by Napoleon. Determined to raise national consciousness, the Grimms collected folktales to demonstrate that Germans had a shared culture, equal in vigor to the classical and modern French cultures (Zipes, 1988). Within a short time after publication of the first edition of their *Kinder-und Hausmärchen* (1812) (*Children's and Household Tales*), which is better known as Grimms' Fairy Tales in English, other European nations began to collect their own stories with the same goal of national consciousness, and by the end of the century countries as far away as Japan had begun to do the same.

To rule more effectively and perhaps more humanely, colonial governments also collected the folklore of "subject races," as a standard handbook of folklore research by Charlotte S. Burns put it (Dorson, 1965; Okpewho, 1992). Not surprisingly, when those "subject races" began to do their own folkloric work and read Burns's *Handbook of Folklore* (1914), they objected to both the designation and the purpose spelled out therein (Dorson, 1965).

The scientific study of the origins of stories and cultures was yet another nineteenth century purpose in collecting folklore. One school of thought, led by German scholar of linguistics Max Müller, proposed that European languages and stories started in one place (monogenesis)—India—and that all European myths and folktales could be traced back to their Indian origins. Others, such as Andrew Lang, a turn of the twentieth century English folklorist who popularized many international folktales in his *Blue* (*Yellow, Green, Red,* etc.) *Fairy Book* series, pointed out that people throughout the world have the same basic psychological and social needs and proposed multiple origins (polygenesis) for similar stories (Georges and Jones, 1995).

Ethnographers and anthropologists also collected oral literature in the nineteenth and twentieth centuries to study different cultures. One group, the **cultural evolutionists,** assumed that humanity evolved at different rates but that all peoples must go through the same stages of cultural evolution from lower to higher levels of abstraction and sophistication. These researchers thought that by studying the beliefs and tales of contemporary "primitive" people, they would be able to understand the beliefs of ancient people such as the Greeks, who were, according this theory, at the same stage of cultural evolution as the African or Native American cultures of the nineteenth and early twentieth centuries. Besides holding the stages of evolution concept, this group operated under the assumption that "primitive" people told stories to explain phenomena they did not understand (a primitive science) or to teach lessons. They believed that "primitives" were unable to think abstractly and symbolically or to create oral art for sheer enjoyment (Okpewho, 1983).

Another group, the **diffusionists**, basing their research on Max Müller's theory that all stories originated in one place, believed that each culture's stories are merely adaptations of others' stories as cultures influenced each other. They debated as to the routes stories took. One French researcher, for instance, identified ancient Egypt rather than India as the source of all other stories. Early diffusionists, however, agreed that literate and more "advanced" cultures influenced "primitive" ones, but not the other way around. One of the debates involved the route of African American stories; some argued that they were adopted from Euro-American sources and came originally from Europe, while others argued that they were adopted from Native American sources. Diffusionists discounted the idea that African American stories might be original or that they were related to African stories. William Bascom (1992), through extensive comparative work, demonstrated that a great many of them had African counterparts and were most likely of African origin (Okpewho, 1983; Dundes, 1992).

Researchers who espoused a diffusionist theory of folklore collected many variants of the same narratives across cultures to identify what they thought might be the oldest, "true" version of a particular story. To make comparisons easier, a Finnish scholar, Antti Aarne, published a classification of tale types in 1910; it was updated by the American scholar Stith Thompson in 1928 and 1961 as more countries analyzed their own stories and more recurrent tale types were identified. It became apparent, however, that the **Aarne-Thompson tale type index** applies best to the Indo-European tales; relatively few tales recur in their entirety throughout the world. What is more common is recurring story elements (**motifs**) in widely varying stories and cultures. For instance, a bird telling the truth about a victim's plight recurs in Africa, Asia, and Europe.

Collectors following either the cultural evolutionist or diffusionist theory of folklore concentrated on the themes and bare outlines of the narratives, ignoring the artistry of performance and the creativity of the performer who told the stories. Since the 1970s, however, researchers worldwide have been focusing on performance and the role of the performer and even of the audience in creating meaning.

Johnny Moses [Whis.tem.men.knee (Walking Medicine Robe)] is a Tulalip Native American storyteller from the west coast of Vancouver Island, Canada. He is just outside one of the storytelling tents at the National Storytelling Festival at Jonesboro, TN.

Photograph © 2002 by Judith V. Lechner. Used with permission by Johnny Moses.

▨ The Study and Interpretation of Folktales

Three of the most influential theories of the meaning of folklore in the twentieth century were the functionalist, psychoanalytic, and structuralist theories. **Functionalism,** established by sociologists Émile Durkheim and Bronislaw Malinowsky, proposes that the role of folktales and other folklore is to meet specific societal needs, such as establishing hierarchies among people; defining relationships between men and women; teaching a group how to plant, hunt, or heal; and so on (Doty, 1986). The Finnish epic *The Kalevala,* for instance, includes many chants that the hero Väinämöinen (*Vay*-nah-moey-nen) recites that

are thought to have been actual healing chants and teachings for novice shamans (medicine men and women) (Pentikäinen, 1989).

Psychoanalytic theories developed by Sigmund Freud and Carl Jung are based on the assumption that stories are symbolic representations of human needs and fears. Freud focused on the psychosexual development of the individual from full dependency of the infant on the mother through stages that ideally culminate in a strong adult ego able to balance personal desires and responsibilities to lead a meaningful life (Bettelheim, 1976). At each stage the developing child must deal with conflicting desires and fears. For instance, the young child's desire for his mother's exclusive attention, which implies eliminating all rivals, conflicts with the need for the father as well. Freud stated that unresolved conflicts, become repressed in the unconscious and cause neurosis in the child or much later in the adult. He believed that dreams and stories symbolically represented these unconscious conflicts, and he developed a set of symbols with which to interpret them. The family structure on which Freud based his theories was the turn of the twentieth century nuclear family, and the stories he relied on for his symbol systems were Greek myths and Grimms' fairy tales. He drew on these stories—for instance, the myth of Oedipus—as metaphors to name his theories, but he and other psychoanalysts, most notably Bruno Bettelheim, also used the stories in psychotherapy (Bettelheim, 1976). According to Alan Dundes, a folklorist who uses Freudian theories to interpret folktales, only a few folklorists have utilized psychoanalytical techniques, which he considers to be a failing because it limits folklorists to a too literal interpretation of folk literature (Dundes, 1989). Literary scholars, on the other hand, have made much use of Freudian analysis of literary works as well as folktales. As an example, a Freudian analysis of the story of Rapunzel would identify the theme as representing a girl's sexual rivalry with her mother.

Carl Jung rejected the idea that all inner conflict was of a personal nature relating to the psychosexual family drama. He also rejected what he called the "personal unconscious." Instead he proposed that humans draw on a collective unconscious in which is stored a universally shared set of images and ideas or archetypes that are part of our genetic heritage from prehistoric times. These images or **archetypes** are so powerful that they recur in stories throughout the world. Archetypes include characters and events such as the figure of the mother, in a range of variations with positive and negative qualities. Mother, grandmother, stepmother, godmother, mother-in-law, the Mother of God, mother earth, alma mater, motherland, any place of safety and perfection such as paradise, and animal helpers and other supportive characters are some of the positive archetypes of the mother. Witch, enchantress, dragon, the grave, deep water, death, nightmares, and bogies represent the negative archetypes of the mother. Jung, like Freud, believed that in reality humans see the mother figure ambivalently, as both positive and negative, not one or the other (Jung, 1969). An analysis of Rapunzel using Jung's archetypes might focus on the enchantress as a good/bad mother—both protector and oppressor of the child. Like Freudian symbols, Jung's set of archetypes were used extensively during the second half of the twentieth century for literary and folklore analysis, most notably by Joseph Campbell, author of *The Hero with a Thousand Faces* (1968). As with Freud's ideas, however, the universal applicability of archetypes, in spite of the recurrence of many of the characters and actions in stories internationally, has been questioned. As for the hereditary nature of the collective unconscious, there is no scientific evidence that would support this construct. Nevertheless, both Freud's and Jung's symbols provide an important way of looking at stories. The symbolic analysis of folk literature, however, is probably best deferred until middle school and above, when children are at a higher level of cognitive development.

The **structuralist** approach looks at the forms folk narratives take rather than at the content and context of specific stories. Claude Levi-Strauss tried to find the most elemental structures of myths, which he identified as "binary opposites," by studying myths as they were changed or transformed among related cultures. He postulated that it is the resolution of the opposites that describes a culture's deeply held beliefs (Doty, 1986). Typical pairs of opposites include young-old, home-exile, innocence-experience, good

twin–evil twin, and creation-destruction. In the Iroquois creation myth, for instance, the creative twin, Good Mind, and the destructive twin, Evil Mind, are set up in opposition. The resolution to their opposition is the full panoply of nature and the hope that good keeps evil in check. Good Mind brought forth elms, which spread their shade-giving crowns, rivers that ran both upstream and downstream so that people could travel with ease, and animals and birds that were always friendly to human beings, but Evil Mind created briars and other prickly undergrowth, fashioned the rapids and falls, making it hard for people to navigate rivers, and created monsters such as the horned serpent to fill people with dread. In the end (in some versions) Good Mind locks up Evil Mind, showing that good is stronger than evil as long as people stay on the path of Good Mind but the perfection that Good Mind tried to achieve is not present in our world (Bruchac, 1985).

Vladimir Propp (1968) took a different approach to structural analysis. Dissatisfied with trying to compare stories by looking at complete plots and categorizing them into tale types, as Antti Aarne did, or looking at specific motifs and using those for cross-cultural comparisons, as Stith Thompson did, Propp tried to identify recurrent action patterns in stories. He examined the functions of characters' actions for furthering the plot of the story. Using Afanas'ev's collection of Russian fairy tales, Propp identified 31 functions for an unvarying sequence of actions. Not all functions are present in every story, but the sequence is constant, according to Propp. The presence or absence of each function depends on whether the hero is a victim hero, that is, a character who responds to having been harmed, as is Beauty in "Beauty and the Beast" when her mean sisters make her forget to go back to the Beast, or a questing hero, that is, a character who goes into the world to accomplish something, as does Jack in "Jack and the Beanstalk." For a victim hero the story begins with function 1, in which a family member leaves the victim hero unguarded, and continues with function 2, in which the victim hero is told not to break a certain interdiction (prohibition), such as opening the door to a secret room, going near a well, or leaving the path in the woods. There might be a long setting of the stage before the action begins, as when Beauty is first promised to the Beast by her father and she begins to discover the Beast's good qualities.

Often the sequence of functions for a questing hero skips functions 1 though 7 and begins at function 8, when he or she discovers a lack, for example, the hero loses something important such as the family cow and must seek his or her own fortune as in "Jack and the Bean Stalk," or a family member has been enchanted or abducted as in "The Seven Ravens," in which a young girl saves her seven brothers who had been transformed into ravens. In analyzing fairy tales, it is apparent that this approach works for some fairy tales, but the 31 functions are seldom all present in any one story.

Although Propp's own analysis has limited use because of the large number of functions, most of which are hard to fit to a wide variety of genres and cultures, other folklorists have modified his functions, reducing them in number so that the stories of cultures that do not have fairy tales could be analyzed. In *Reading and Writing Literary Genres* (2000), Kathleen Buss and Lee Karnowski provide a modified form of this type of analysis for use with elementary school children to help children identify similarities and differences among variants of popular fairy tales such as Cinderella. Besides Propp's functional analysis, Buss and Karnowski use tale type analysis, motif analysis, and stylistic analysis. This kind of comprehensive analysis combines both a universalist approach, stressing cross-cultural similarities, and a culturally specific approach to looking at stories. These two approaches, however, are seldom reconciled. In fact, most of the theories discussed above—evolutionist, diffusionist, psychoanalytical, and structuralist—focus on the universal rather than the culturally specific meanings of stories. Isidore Okpewho, a folklorist from Nigeria, while acknowledging some value in each of these approaches for the study of African folklore, also insists on looking at the particulars of the cultures.

Many scholars have concluded that traditional stories have universal and enduring themes that can be understood by anyone in any era. This idea is expressed in the following statement from Max Lüthi's *The European Folktale: Form and Nature* (1982):

Although in many ways, like everything human, the folktale is to be interpreted historically, I have preferred to search for its lasting truths. Today more than ever I am convinced that, despite increased interest in the functions of tales and in what has been called folktale biology, the tales themselves merit the greatest attention, just as always. Even though much is clarified by their context, the texts themselves take on an ever new life with the passage of time. (p. xv)

In support of this view one might ask, "How can we communicate about, empathize with, and enjoy each other's cultural products if there are no points of commonality?" When I have asked my students to identify an important theme in the myth of Cupid and Psyche, I get a variety of answers, ranging from "trust is necessary for true love" or "don't be too curious" to "don't meddle in other people's business." The story speaks to contemporary readers, even if some of the meanings they draw from it would have been alien to the ancient Greeks. Additionally, when students read Gayle Ross's Cherokee story *How Turtle's Back Was Cracked* (1995), they have little trouble identifying the warning against boasting. A good story has a life of its own. As Donald Haase put it in "Response and Responsibility in Reading Grimms' Fairy Tales" (1993), the fact that the Grimms' fairy tales have been appreciated in so many different cultures and contexts since the early 1800s and the fact that they have provided such rich ground for interpretation and reinterpretation by people with wildly differing perspectives—theologians, psychoanalysts, feminists, Marxists, and Nazis, among others—suggest that each reader gets what he or she wants and needs from them.

The emphasis on the primacy of the text, however, has its limitations. During the late nineteenth and early twentieth centuries interpreters of world folklore relied on European models. Even today Javanese shadow puppet plays, for instance, are interpreted quite differently by Javanese scholars and by Western scholars because they focus on different aspects of the plays. Western scholars focus on the fact that the plays are reenactments and extensions of an **epic** that was first developed in India, and that is closely tied to the Hindu religion. Javanese scholars focus on the moral and ethical themes of the plays. They do not see these plays as reflecting religious beliefs because the majority of Javanese people are Muslim, not Hindu (Keeler, 1992). While differences in focus may be valuable, misinterpretations due to lack of knowledge about specific cultural values have posed serious problem in the past. A typical misinterpretation of Native American stories, for instance, occurred when outsiders brought their own ideas of who is likely to represent the hero in a story. Barre Toelken (1996), a scholar of Navajo folktales and myths, retells a Chinook sun myth from the Northwest, recorded in 1890, to illustrate how easy it is to misinterpret a story from a tradition outside one's own. It is the story of a chief who goes into the world to visit the sun. Once in the sun's house, he is surrounded by riches yet becomes homesick and wishes to return home. But on his way home he destroys each of the five villages and the inhabitants whose chief he had been, and at the end he is totally alone, building a small house. Nothing in the backgrounds of readers or listeners who are steeped in European and American hero tales would prepare them to interpret this story the way a Chinook listener would understand it. What kind of hero comes home to destroy his own villages instead of bringing back gifts or a prize? Toelken explains that in Chinook culture a chief is not supposed to go away on private errands but is supposed to stay home to lead and have goods come through him. In Chinook society it is the giving away of wealth, not the getting of it, that brings honor, and the chief in this story is not considered a hero. The story tells the listener that to act recklessly means to bring on tragedy to your people and to become socially isolated.

Similarly, an entire genre of oral tales, the **pourquoi** or "why" tales, which typically end with expressions such as "even today the turtle's back is cracked," had been misinterpreted by non–Native American scholars as purporting to be literal explanations of nature phenomena rather than teaching stories designed to impart social norms to children. Because early collectors and retellers focused on the **etiological** (explanation of origins) aspect rather than the instructional aspect of the stories, they viewed Native Americans as rather simple-minded observers of nature (Toelken, 1996). Toelken, like other contemporary scholars, says that when people assume that stories can be universally understood, they negate

Ki Anom Soeroto, a Javanese shadow puppeteer, examines a new puppet At his home in Solo, Indonesia. The puppet is of Bima, one of the five Pandawa brothers in the Hindu epic, *The Mahabharata,* on which most Javanese shadow plays are based.

Photograph by Ward Keeler, copyright © 1992, used with permission. From: *Javanese Shadow Puppets* by Ward Keeler. Oxford: Oxford University, 1992.

what makes a culture unique, and this leads to devaluing and even destroying cultures other than the dominant one.

In an attempt to reconcile the two positions, one might propose that there is a continuum of human experiences and values that all people share but that are given different emphases in different cultures or at different times during the history of a culture. Whereas in contemporary American life, for instance, young people are given a great deal of advice on how to prepare job and college applications to place themselves in the best possible light, or, as some people say, "toot their own horn," they are also taught throughout life the somewhat contradictory value of not being too boastful. The injunction against bragging is far weaker than that in traditional Native American societies; nevertheless, it is part of mainstream U.S. culture. What makes it hard to understand each other's stories is lack of knowledge about their context and lack of familiarity with the specific symbols, tone, allusions, and other storytelling conventions with which they

I Made Djimat is performing a Balinese mask dance, a humorous prelude to a comic romance, Putri Cina—The Chinese Queen of Bali. Mr. Djimat is a member of the Master Dancers of Bali, which reenacts myths and romantic narratives, including stories from *The Ramayana*. The performance took place at Duke University, Durham, NC.

Photograph © 2002 by Judith V. Lechner. Used with permission by Master Dancers of Bali; I. Gusti Raka Panji Tisna, director.

are usually told. Retellers, however, can help to bridge the gap between traditional and new audiences.

Retelling Traditional Stories

The question of who can tell whose story has become a politically charged question. Betsy Hearne (1999), folklorist and storyteller, who as children's literature professor focuses on folklore retold for children, lays out the issues. On the one hand, though collected with questionable motives and methods, folklore collections by nineteenth century collectors did preserve many of the traditional stories of Native Americans

and African Americans. She cites Joel Chandler Harris's *Uncle Remus* as an example. Julius Lester gives his own acknowledgment of his indebtedness to Harris's collection in the introduction to his version of *The Tales of Uncle Remus* (1987). Cherokee storyteller Gayle Ross talks of making use of James Mooney's nineteenth century collection of Cherokee stories, which she compares to contemporary versions and then adapts for modern audiences. On the other hand, cultures change, and the unexamined use of nineteenth century folklore misrepresents the way contemporary cultures tell or interpret their traditional stories. Both Julius Lester and Gayle Ross, coming from within the culture whose stories they retell, adapt their stories to reflect changing language and world views. A storyteller or writer outside of the culture who is mining the same nineteenth century resources has a harder time adding the cultural context, nuances, and symbols that someone from within the culture is able to add (Hearne, 1999).

Contemporary storytellers and writers are also divided on the question of intellectual property as it relates to oral tales. One view is that oral stories belong to everyone and can be adapted by anyone, thus enriching the world's reservoir of literature. Others, however, believe that stories are cultural property and resent outsiders profiting from their lore (Hearne, 1999). Joseph Bruchac (1996) explains that Native Americans view oral stories as belonging to specific tellers; others must ask permission from the individual performer to retell their story, just as one would obtain copyright permission for reproducing a written work.

These debates have had positive outcomes for the collecting, interpreting, and retelling of traditional literature. The critics no longer come only from European or Euro-American backgrounds. Native American, African American, African, and Asian collectors and critics have been turning their focus toward their own cultures' stories, using a variety of critical approaches. Among other ways of looking at the stories, they have looked at the function of performers in retelling stories to fit the needs of their audiences.

Another important shift that has come about is in the way scholars in general approach collecting and interpreting stories. They no longer take the stance that the performer is merely a vehicle for the story, nor

A Xhosa storyteller from South Africa

Photograph by Harold Scheub. From: *The African Storyteller: Stories from African Oral Tradition* by Harold Scheub. Copyright © 1999. With permission by Kendall/Hunt Publishing Company, Dubuque, Iowa.

do they believe that interpretation is the province only of the scholar. Collectors record the name of the storyteller and the place and circumstance of the telling. They also engage the storyteller and audience in helping to interpret the story. Kay Stone, who works with contemporary professional U.S. storytellers, involves them in interpreting the stories they tell. (Stone, 1993, 1996).

Increasingly, too, storytellers and writers are aware of the need to give credit to their sources, whether print or oral, to respect the context of the story and the appropriate time for its telling, and to inform the audience or reader of the ways in which they have adapted the story. Conscientious picture book illustrators of traditional literature research the culture from which the story springs, not simply to recreate folk designs but also to interpret the story in the spirit in which it is told (Hearne, August 1993).

Hearne urges teachers and librarians, when selecting picture book and anthologized versions of traditional literature, to learn as much as possible about the people whose stories they are using and to select books that provide adequate information about sources and the way the story has been adapted by the author. She identifies five levels of source notes, from best to worst, to help with the evaluation:

- S1: a citation that gives the source and the context of the story relative to the original source, that is how it was obtained, how author changed it, why, and so on.
- S2: a citation that provides a general cultural note.
- S3: a citation that appears only in fine print—the reader has to search hard to find it.
- S4: no citation, only a general cultural background.
- S5: nonexistent source note: the author/illustrator takes credit for the story (Hearne, July 1993).

Donna Norton reports a case study of the way a student of hers authenticated John Steptoe's *Mufaro's Beautiful Daughter,* a picture book retelling of a folktale from Zimbabwe. Although Steptoe gave background information and his specific sources, he did not say how he altered the story. The student used the information Steptoe gave as to his sources to discover the changes he had made to the story. As a result she was able to conclude that although Steptoe had made several changes in the story, he kept its cultural essence and accurately illustrated thirteenth century Great Zimbabwe (Norton, 2001). The changes Steptoe made are typical of the way authors and illustrators adapt stories to new audiences. He strengthened the "kind and unkind sisters" motif by developing a scene of friendly interaction between the kind sister and a little snake (really the king in disguise). He also eliminated details that would have required too much cultural explanation for the age of the audience and added visual details that gave information for a new audience that the traditional audience would not have required, such as scenery and clothing styles.

▣ Adapting Traditional Literature for Children

Traditional stories, once the primary form of verbal artistic and instructional expression for all members of society, have become the province primarily of children. The change was well on its way for the upper classes by the time Charles Perrault published his first book of seven folk and fairy tales, *Histoires ou Contes du Temps Passé* (1697), popularly known as "Contes de Ma Mere l'Oye" ("Stories of Mother Goose"). Though the lower classes throughout Europe told folk and fairy tales to adults and children alike, the aristocracy and upper bourgeoisie disdained them as literature. Even the *Précieuses*, the group of seventeenth century upper-class women (and some men) who invented elaborate fairy tales for adults, used the traditional tales only as a basis for their stories. Perrault, who was part of the group, did something new by publishing the traditional tales without a complicated framework story and without extensive embellishments (Zipes, 1989); he recognized them as inherently good stories. At the same time he directed them toward a specific audience, young people, though the ironic morals tacked onto the ends of his stories suggest that his true audience included adults. Although Perrault's Mother Goose stories were not meant exclusively for children, it was not long before fairy tales and folktales were published with the express purpose of educating children in the values and manners of eighteenth century polite society (Zipes, 1989).

Although the publishing of oral stories has fixed them in print—we can always return to the original print version for subsequent reprints—in reality each generation also rewrites the stories to suit the mores of its time and its society's views on childhood. Adapters have often chosen to simplify the stories to make them more aesthetic and literary, to clean up explicitly sexual content and other material that a particular era considers indecent, to shape the stories to political ends, and to create versions that the culture considers psychologically more appropriate for children than the oral versions had been.

Children are sometimes the beneficiaries of historic trends in attitudes toward literature. The elegant courtly romances of medieval England, once abandoned by the upper classes as too French and Catholic, became relegated to **chapbook** status. Cut down to readable size and language, these inexpensive booklets contributed to widespread literacy among servants, artisans, and tradesmen. Middle- and upper-class children frequently had to obtain chapbooks surreptitiously (Jackson, 1989). Though despised as vulgar by polite society, these simplified and often crudely written chapbook versions preserved the fairy tales and medieval romances, including those about

Adam Smith, a member of the Hampstead Players, as Merlin in a performance of "The Legend of King Arthur" for first through fifth graders at Yarbrough Elementary School in Auburn, Alabama.

Photograph © 2002 by Judith V. Lechner. Used with permission by Adam W. Smith.

King Arthur and the Knights of the Round Table, through the seventeenth and eighteenth centuries. They served as gold mines of traditional literature for nineteenth century romantic poets and folklorists.

As myths, legends, and medieval romances became accepted children's literature, writers such as Charles Lamb (*Adventures of Ulysses*, 1808), Nathaniel Hawthorne (*Tanglewood Tales*, 1853, a retelling of Greek myths), Howard Pyle (*The Story of King Arthur and His Knights*, 1903), and Sidney Lanier (*The Boy's King Arthur*, 1917) began to produce simplified and lively versions of the stories. The trend of adapting and simplifying the literature of former courtly audiences continues to this day with children's versions of *The Odyssey, Beowulf,* and the Arthurian romances. The epics of non-Western cultures, such as the epic of

Sundiata, twelfth century king of Mali, and the adventures of India's God-hero Rama of *The Ramayana,* have now been added to the repertoire. Some of these adaptations successfully capture the tone and grandeur of the epics; others are mere skeletons of the great poetic originals.

Whereas the epics of the past had to be simplified to become usable for children, the folktales and fairy tales of the oral tradition had to be adapted to suit the literary tastes of adult buyers as well as those of children if they were to be marketable as children's literature. The Grimms found this out when Volume 2 of the first edition of their *Kinder-und Hausmärchen* (1815) languished unsold for years. Volume 2 contained stories that were transcribed in a style that was closer to the folk idiom of country storytellers than that of Volume 1, many of whose stories were told to the Grimms by their highly literate middle class friends (Bottigheimer, 1993). Over several editions of their collection, Wilhelm Grimm not only added more stories but also combined variants to come up with the "best" version. He also edited the stories to be more readable and dramatic in print, where the text on the page alone had to supply all the variations in tone one would observe at a live performance. Wilhelm Grimm did this consciously, as can be seen by comparing different versions of "The Frog King" over several editions of *Kinder-und Hausmärchen* (Neumann, 1993).

The tension between presenting authentic versions of oral tales, without the adornment of literary devices, and the need to provide readers with the same level of interest in the story one would experience during a live performance has continued to challenge writers (Goble, 1992; Esbensen, 1992; Kimmel, 1994). Goble in particular comments on the fact that his stories are sometimes criticized for not being descriptive enough. He says, "But then Indian storytellers were not descriptive. Instead, they would use a lot of movement to conjure up images. Gestures, many of which were connected to a universal sign language, would provide much of what these critics call description. The spoken narrative itself was quite straightforward" (Goble, 1992, p. 9). Audience participation was an important part of the performance. In his Iktomi books, Goble tries to achieve this sense of performance and

audience participation by having the trickster Iktomi address the reader and by giving visual cues in the form of different color print as to when readers (listeners) were to comment. Most often, however, writers use styles from familiar literary models to heighten tension, create visual images, and paint character. Barbara Esbensen (1992), author of *Star Maiden* (1988), says that literal translations of oral stories do not make for good reading because of the lack of careful sequencing that a well-shaped written version would have, as well as the uneven pacing of events and descriptions. Sometimes information that a reader needs in the beginning is not mentioned until later in the story, because the traditional audience did not need these explanations and the storyteller forgot to add them for the folklorist or anthropologist-collector until the story was under way. Finally, in an oral telling, the audience can interrupt for clarification.

Sexual and scatological content are the most frequently omitted elements of oral narratives in children's adaptations. Most of the trickster tales, whether from Africa, Europe, or North America, have many scatological and sexual episodes. Coyote is greedy for everything, including sex. So are Anansi, a West African trickster, and Reynard the Fox from medieval Europe. In one humorous episode, Coyote, disconsolate, has a conversation with his own droppings. Not surprisingly, these episodes are omitted from children's collections.

Violent episodes in stories have also been toned down. Many a story ends in far milder forms of punishment than had earlier versions. This move from more violent to less violent versions was evident already in the Grimms' work; they had the woodsman save Little Red Riding Hood and her grandmother, for instance, whereas Perrault's French version ends with her being eaten as a warning to young women against straying from the straight path and yielding to the sensual seductions of the wolf. Later in the nineteenth and early twentieth centuries both Perrault and the Grimms were considered too cruel, and any mention of Little Red Riding Hood's being swallowed was omitted (Zipes, 1983). Other stories underwent similar alterations.

Besides sex and violence, attitudes toward customs that were taken for granted in traditional literature have caused retellers to change or omit the stories. For instance, smoking tobacco was an integral part of ceremonial and religious customs among the Lakota (Sioux) and many other Native American tribes, but although he would like to do a story on the Peace Pipe, Paul Goble says he knows that a publisher is not likely to publish a book in which smoking is a central part of the story (1992). Wanda Gág (1936), who translated a number of Grimm fairy tales and folktales, mentions in her notes to "Clever Elsie" that she has altered the ending of the story because unless one knew the custom to which the story refers, her husband's wrapping her in a net with bells and sending her out of the village never to be seen again after she fell asleep in the rye, would seem incomprehensibly cruel.

Politics too have affected the availability of traditional literature as well as the way stories have been altered for children. The Grimms' original purpose in collecting and publishing German folk literature was primarily political; they were attempting to foster self-reflection among Germans, presenting what they considered to be the voice of the German people through folktales, mythology, poetry, and history. This purpose was heightened by Napoleon's recent occupation of Germany and the Grimms' desire to see Germany unified (Zipes, 1988). The politicization of Grimms' fairy tales, however, became most pronounced during the era between the end of World War I and the end of World War II. The Grimms were considered so quintessentially German that they were seen as the standard bearers for the nation during World War II, and their fairy tales were widely distributed (Bottigheimer, 1993). On the other hand, German-born storyteller Ruthilde Kronberg told researcher Kay Stone (1993), "As a child in Nazi Germany I used to get in trouble because I didn't do my homework. I read fairy tales instead. I think they saved my sanity because they taught me that the evil which was taking place around me would burn itself out. Which it did."

After the war the Grimms' tales came under attack by the American and English occupying forces, which prohibited their publication and removed them from German libraries and schools; valuable sets were sent to U.S. academic libraries (Bottigheimer, 1993). The stories were soon republished, however, and took further political turns as Germany was divided, with East Germany becoming a Communist state. In West Germany the new editions dropped some of the more violent or stereotyped stories, such as "The Juniper Tree" and "The Jew in the Thornbush." Some writers used parodies of the stories for social criticism. Others attacked the Grimms' fairy tales for their violence and sexist content. In East Germany, in spite of initial doubt about their authors' bourgeois origins, the tales were seen as belonging to the German folk and therefore worth preserving. The East Germans focused on stories that depicted class struggle—poor against rich—and, as the West Germans, toned down violence and brutality in the stories (Zipes, 1993).

The Grimms' fairy tales were not the only folk literature to be appropriated for political purposes. In the wake of the violence of the French Revolution, frightened English upper-class reformers railed against, and to some extent succeeded in suppressing, both fictional rags-to-riches stories and fairy tales with similar themes (Jackson, 1989). Throughout the communist world, folktales became elevated to a high status as the voice of the people. Those that were reprinted often emphasized the "right values," (e.g., clever and wise peasants outwitting oppressive overlords). In China, for instance, class struggle was sharpened by adding story details that heightened the wisdom of the peasants and made it evident that the rich were oppressive and unpatriotic. Stories were also rewritten to remove the magical and supernatural elements and to substitute the voice of the Communist Party for that of local gods, **demons**, sorcerers, and **shamans** (Dorson, 1965).

Women's changing role in society is also reflected by adaptations of fairy tales, especially in the last 30 years. Often conventional stories have been retold as parody or as social satire to highlight the fact that females are not helpless and can be instrumental in saving themselves from threat, as in James Thurber's "The Little Girl and the Wolf," and Michael Emberly's *Ruby* (1990) or even saving others, as in William Jay's *The Practical Princess* (1969), Babette Cole's *Princess Smartypants* (1987), and Robert Munsch's *The Paper Bag Princess* (1980). Because a great many traditional European stories cast women in the role of the villain or showed them as helpless victims, contemporary storytellers have sought out other variants of the stories in which women are not presented in such negative ways. Edith Phelps's *Maid of the North* (1981) is a collection of traditional tales with strong, positively portrayed female protagonists.

Other recent changes include presenting the stock villain as harmless and misunderstood, altering through humor the point of view of readers and making them rethink their prejudices and society's practices. The wolf has been recast in several recent stories. Roald Dahl's ambiguous poem "Red Riding Hood and the Wolf" makes Little Red not only self-reliant and tough but also predatory. In the *True Story of the Three Little Pigs* (1989) by Jon Scieszka the wolf tells us that he has been framed. Eugene Trivizas's *The Three Little Wolves and the Big Bad Pig* (1993) has a strong peace message. These adaptations are valuable means of looking critically at societal assumptions in traditional stories. As Temple, Martinez, Yokota, and Naylor suggest, however, in *Children's Books in Children's Hands* (2002), rather than suppressing stories whose values might no longer reflect society's values, students and teachers can openly discuss the implications of the stories, and teachers can also make sure that traditional stories that do not reinforce the same assumptions, for instance, of the passive female as prize for a prince, are also included.

◼ Why Use Traditional Literature with Children?

Traditional stories are so much part of our cultural heritage that they provide constant sources of allusions in literature, daily speech, advertisement, and even decision making. Knowing the sources of these allusions enriches our lives. Classic and contemporary literature and films often utilize the themes and structures of folk literature—for instance, the hero's journey—an ever popular theme. Traditional stories can also act as models of language usage through their storytelling devices: tight plotting with a clearly defined conflict, repetition, use of parallel sentence structures, figurative language, description, and so on. Story characters pass on cultural values in either a positive or a negative way, they provide an opportunity to learn about our own and others' historic customs and values, and they can be vehicles for critical thinking as children learn to question accepted stereotypes in some of the traditional stories. A feeling of hope and optimism engendered by many of the folktales with

happy endings is an important reason for using folktales with children, some of whose daily lives are not always hopeful. Children can better deal with the conflicts, pain, and sorrow of life not by being ignorant of them but by believing that they can be overcome. Psychotherapists such as Bruno Bettelheim (*The Uses of Enchantment,* 1975) and Sheldon Cashdan (*The Witch Must Die,* 1999) believe that fairy tales help children to resolve inner conflicts as they see story heroes overcome villains symbolizing their own unruly feelings. Most of all, traditional literature provides a vision of those things that unite us: our need and capacity for love, mirth, self-efficacy, wisdom, wonder, and making meaning out of the mysteries of our world (Temple et al., 2002).

Onawumi Jean Moss, is both a storyteller and Associate Dean of Students at Amherst College. Her stories bring alive life in 1940s Tennessee. Here she is performing at the National Storytelling Festival, Jonesboro, Tennessee, in 2002.

Photograph by Judith V Lechner, 2002. Used with permission by Onawumi Jean Moss.

2 Fables

Introduction

All cultures seem to find that teaching society's values is easier through stories, which people find appealing, than through straightforward lecturing, which people often resent or ignore. In some cultures, such as those of Native Americans, the stories take the form of pourquoi or "why" tales, in which animals (or other characters) develop their familiar characteristics as a result of mistakes that they have made (Bierhorst, 2002). Most European and Asian cultures, however, use fables, which are didactic tales that make the lesson to be learned explicit, sometimes literally spelling out the morals, as in Aesop's fables. The stories, which often use animal characters, are a memorable way of reinforcing moral and ethical precepts and of teaching practical lessons on how to get along in the world. They are also often used as political and social commentary, especially under repressive governments where tellers must learn to evade the heavy hand of the censor.

The two fable traditions that are most familiar to Americans—the ancient Greek Aesop's fables and the two strands of Indian fables, *The Panchatantra* and *The Jataka Tales*—are more connected than their geographical distance might suggest. Trade and migrations have resulted in exchange of stories, so what we think of as Aesop fables includes a fair number of stories that are traceable to *The Panchatantra* and to *The Jatakas* (Jacobs, 1894).

The same stories that are told as entertainment in one community might be made more explicitly into a fable by another community. For instance, some versions of tales about the West African trickster Anansi have distinct morals added at the end, while most

"The Frogs Desiring a King." Illustrated by Richard Heighway.

From: *The Fables of Aesop.* Joseph Jacobs. New York: Schocken, 1966. © by Macmillan Company, 1894.

versions have no spelled-out moral, leaving the audience to draw its own conclusions. In a close-knit community a storyteller might even choose a particular fable with a specific person in mind, using this device to chastise and correct without mentioning the individual by name, thus maintaining harmony within the community (Bruchac, 1996). Medieval preachers in Europe also used Aesop's fables along with the biblical parables in their sermons (Bottigheimer, 1996).

Aesop's Fables

The stories that we call Aesop's fables should more accurately be referred to as Aesopic fables, as they represent a conglomerate of brief animal tales from both oral and written sources. Aesop was said to have lived between 600 and 500 B.C.E. as a slave from the island of Samos, a Greek colony. Because his name means "dark" and has the same root as the word "Ethiopian" in Greek, he might have been African. Whether he truly ever lived or not, the legendary accounts of his life credit him with having used his sharp wits to tell fables, many of which not only taught lessons but were also veiled criticisms of the tyrannical leaders of his times. Told with great economy of words, Aesop's fables are characterized by tightly drawn sketches with two or three characters and a spelled-out moral. The characters of the fables represent human virtues and failings embodied most of the time in animal stereotypes. Thus fox acts as the perennial trickster, lion as regal and all powerful, and wolf as a brutish beast of prey.

The fables were recorded in 300 B.C.E. by Demetrius Phalerus, founder of the Library at Alexandria, and became widely available in medieval Europe through the first century Latin version of another slave, named Phaedrus (Jacobs, 1920). Though they were originally meant for adults as well as children, their brevity and spelled-out morals have made Aesop's fables popular teaching devices for centuries. They were used to teach grammar and rhetoric in Renaissance Europe, and John Locke endorsed them as educational material in the late 1600s (Lenaghan, 1967; Bottigheimer, 1996). They were also used as social commentary in England, according to Annabel Patterson in *Fables of Power* (1991), from the end of the fourteenth century through the beginning of the eighteenth century.

One of the first printed books in English was *Aesop's Fables,* published in 1484 by William Caxton.

In an era that was especially rife with conflict among the nobility in England (the era of Richard III and the War of the Roses, which culminated in the victory and ascendance of the Tudors), the fables began to be used as a commentary on power and its abuses (Patterson, 1991). The fables have traveled throughout the world with traders and conquerors. *Aesop's Fables* was one of the first books brought by the Spanish to the Americas, where the fables were adapted by the Aztecs (Bierhorst, 2002).

Although many of the stories have universal themes ("Don't count your chickens before they hatch" is meaningful in twentieth century America as it was in ancient India, where the story probably originated), it is interesting to note that the morals attached to them change with the mores of the times. The story of the tree and the reed, for instance, was told to the editor as a child in Hungary as a lesson in the value of being able to bend in arguments, while the identical tale, told here by Joseph Jacobs, who wrote at the turn of the twentieth century in England, is used to contrast the dangers of standing out too far from among the crowd and the value of obscurity.

Aesop's fables have often been told in verse form, one of the most famous versions being that of the seventeenth century French writer La Fontaine. They are continuously reinterpreted in illustrated and picture book editions, and their format continues to intrigue modern writers and illustrators such as Mem Fox, Robert Kraus, Leo Lionni, and Arnold Lobel, who have each written their own versions of fables.

The number of fables that are included in collections under the name of Aesop have varied from a handful to several hundred. In each era retellers select the stories that seem most relevant or most meaningful to their audience, so it is interesting to note which stories remain constant favorites throughout the centuries. "The Grasshopper and the Ant" is one of these. Its message, expressed sometimes harshly, other times more softly, has remained essentially the same. Here are five ways in which it has been expressed:

> And therefore there is one tyme for to doo some labour and werk/And one tyme for to have rest/he that werketh not ne doth no good/shall have ofte at his teeth gret cold and lacke at his nede. (*Aesop,* William Caxton, 1483)

"How spent you the summer?"

Quoth she [the ant], looking shame

at the borrowing dame [the grasshopper].

"Night and day to each comer

I sang if you please."

"You sang! I'm at ease;

For'tis plain at a glance,

Now, Ma'am, you must dance."

(*A Hundred Fables* by Jean de la Fontaine, reprinted by The Bodley Head; original French version, seventeenth century)

It is best to prepare for the days of necessity. (*The Fables of Aesop,* selected and told anew by Joseph Jacobs, London, Macmillan, 1894)

The idle get what they deserve. (*Fables of Aesop,* Julius Detmond, 1909)

There's a time for work and a time for play. (*The Aesop for Children,* Rand McNally, 1919/1984)

Finally, a completely different vision of this fable is expressed in Leo Lionni's *Frederick* (Pantheon, 1967), in which the mouse who lays stories by instead of food helps to keep his hungry companions' spirits up when the food they had carefully collected is finally gone. The mice say in appreciation, "Why Frederick, you're a poet," and Frederick bows and says "I know it."

Aesop's fables have been kept alive through such revisions, which suit different times and different purposes, as well as through numerous artistic interpretations. Some of these include the richly hand-painted miniatures of the *Medici Aesop* (reproduced, 1989), which was created to teach one of the Medici children in the 1400s; the meticulously executed woodcuts of Thomas Bewick, an illustrator who was frequently employed by John Newbery in the eighteenth century; the expressive line drawings of the contemporary African American artist Jacob Lawrence (1997); and the Web-based University of Massachusetts Aesop's Fables art project at www.umass.edu/aesop/ (accessed 4/6/02).

For a bibliography of a sampling of contemporary illustrated books of Aesop's fables, see "Picture Books Related to the Stories in the *Allyn & Bacon Anthology of Traditional Literature*" at www.ablongman.com/lechner.

All the Aesop fables reproduced here are from Joseph Jacobs's *The Fables of Aesop*. London: Macmillan, 1894. (A few of the expressions were changed to make the stories sound more colloquial to modern ears.)

The Grasshopper and the Ant

In *Proverbs* we are told: "Go to the ant, thou sluggard; consider her ways, and be wise: Which having no guide, overseer, or ruler, Provideth her meat in the summer, and gathereth her food in the harvest." (*The Holy Bible* [King James Version] Proverbs vi:6–8)

In a field one summer's day a Grasshopper was hopping about, chirping and singing to its heart's content. An Ant passed by, bearing along with great toil an ear of corn he was taking to the nest.

"Why not come and chat with me," said the Grasshopper, "instead of toiling and moiling in that way?"

"I am helping to lay up food for the winter," said the Ant, "and recommend you do the same."

"Why bother about winter?" said the Grasshopper; "we have got plenty of food at present." But the Ant went on its way and continued to toil. When the winter came the Grasshopper had no food and found itself dying of hunger, while it saw the ants distributing every day corn and grain from the stores they had collected in the summer. Then the Grasshopper knew:

It is best to prepare for the days of necessity. ■

The Bundle of Sticks

This story is also told of Genghis Khan in an Armenian collection, filmmaker Akira Kurasawa used it in *Ran*, a Japanese version of *King Lear*, and a similar *Jataka* tale (no. 74) is told of the trees of the forest resisting a great wind through their union while a single tree in a courtyard is easily uprooted.

An old man on the point of death summoned his sons around him to give them some parting advice. He ordered his servants to bring in a bundle of sticks, and said to his eldest son: "Break it." The son strained and strained, but with all his efforts was unable to break the bundle. The other sons also tried, but none of them was successful. "Untie the bundle," said the father, "and each of you take a stick." When they had done so, he called out to them: "Now, break," and each stick was easily broken. "You see my meaning," said their father.

Union gives strength. ∎

The Fox and the Crow

Note the different message of the similar *Jataka* tale (no. 294) "The Jackal and the Crow" in this anthology.

A Fox once saw a Crow fly off with a piece of cheese in its beak and settle on a branch of a tree. "That's for me, as I am a Fox," said Master Reynard, and he walked up to the foot of the tree. "Good-day, Mistress Crow," he cried. "How well you are looking to-day: how glossy your feathers; how bright your eye. I feel sure your voice must surpass that of other birds, just as your figure does; let me hear but one song from you that I may greet you as the Queen of Birds." The Crow lifted up her head and began to caw her best, but the moment she opened her mouth the piece of cheese fell to the ground, only to be snapped up by Master Fox. "That will do," said he. "That was all I wanted. In exchange for your cheese I will give you a piece of advice for the future."

Do not trust flatterers. ∎

The Frogs Desiring a King

Solon, the ancient Greek statesman and reformer, whose reforms paved the way for Athenian democracy, was reputed to have recited this story to the Athenians. A version of this story was also told in Madagascar, according to Joseph Jacobs.

The Frogs were living as happy as could be in a marshy swamp that just suited them; they went splashing about caring for nobody and nobody troubling them. But some of them thought that this was not right, that they should have a king and a proper constitution, so they determined to send up a petition to Jove to give them what they wanted. "Mighty Jove," they cried, "send unto us a king that will rule over us and keep us in order." Jove laughed at their croaking, and threw down into the swamp a huge Log, which came down, splash, to the swamp. The Frogs were frightened out of their lives by the commotion made in their midst, and all rushed to the bank to look at the horrible monster; but after a time, seeing that it did not move, one or two of the boldest of them ventured out towards the Log, and even dared to touch it. Still it did not move. Then the greatest hero of the Frogs jumped upon the Log and commenced dancing up and down upon. Thereupon all the Frogs came and did the same and for some time the Frogs went about their business every day without taking the slightest notice of their new King Log lying in their midst. But this did not suit them, so they sent another petition to Jove, and said to him, "We want a real king; one that will really rule over us." Now this made Jove angry, so he sent among them a big stork that soon set to work gobbling them all up. Then the Frogs repented when too late.

Better no rule than cruel rule. ∎

 ## The Lion and the Mouse

The themes of gratitude and of the worthiness of all creatures, great and small, appear also in *The Panchatantra* fable "The Elephant and the Mice" in this anthology. Joseph Jacobs, who believed in the dispersionist theory of folk literature, thought this story to have originated in India, as a *Jataka* tale. One might ask, however, whether it is not possible that similar stories arise independently of each other out of similar human needs and values.

Once when a Lion was asleep a little Mouse began running up and down upon him; this soon wakened the Lion, who placed his huge paw upon him, and opened his big jaws to swallow him. "Pardon, O King," cried the little Mouse: "forgive me this time, I shall never forget it: who knows, but what I may be able to do you a turn some of these days?" The Lion was so tickled at the idea of the Mouse being able to help him, that he lifted up his paw and let him go. Some time after the Lion was caught in a trap, and the hunters who desired to carry him alive to the King, tied him to a tree while they went in search of a wagon to carry him on. Just then the little Mouse happened to pass by, and seeing the sad plight in which the Lion was, went up to him and soon gnawed away the ropes that bound the King of the Beasts. "Was I not right? said the little Mouse.

Little friends may prove great friends. ∎

 ## The Wind and the Sun

This fable demonstrates the advantages and disadvantages of fables over proverbs. The familiar proverb "It is easier to catch flies with honey than with vinegar" is more pithy and easier to remember, but the small drama in this fable adds both an emotional and a visual dimension to the lesson.

The Wind and the Sun were disputing which was the stronger. Suddenly they saw a traveler coming down the road, and the Sun said: "I see a way to decide our dispute. Whichever of us can cause that traveler to take off his cloak shall be regarded as the stronger. You begin." So the Sun retired behind a cloud, and the

Wind began to blow as hard as he could upon the traveler. But the harder he blew the more closely did the traveler wrap his cloak round him, till at last the Wind had to give up in despair. Then the Sun came out and shone in all his glory upon the traveler, who soon found it too hot to walk with his cloak on.

Kindness effects more than severity. ∎

African Fables

Aesop's fables have been fixed in writing, and even more securely in print, for centuries. They are part of the world's literary heritage, as are the Indian fables, which have also been recorded for over 1500 years. African stories, by contrast, whether told for instruction or entertainment, have been orally transmitted until fairly recently and are part of the world's spoken arts heritage. As a result, what appears in print is, for the most part, but a pale reflection of the rich experience of the storytelling event. These storytelling experiences, which are far more than just narratives, make the lessons memorable.

There are many storytelling contexts in Africa, some formal, with a professional storyteller, others more like family gatherings. A typical informal community storytelling evening might begin with riddling tales as a warm-up, then a song which blends into a formula beginning such as a call and response between the storyteller and the audience: "Shall I tell you or shall I not?" "Yes, tell us," which is followed by the story and its formula ending (Berry, 1991). According to A. A. Roscoe, a folklorist who has worked in Malawi, oral literature is more than stories; it includes the songs that accompany the stories, praise poems, marriage songs, riddles, and proverbs. "Verse shades into prose, prose into verse; songs are poems, poems are songs; and almost everything can be danced" (Roscoe in Singano and Roscoe, 1980). Stories may be told for pure entertainment or for instruction.

Ben Amos, studying Nigerian storytelling in the 1960s, found family settings to be typical of the informal type of evening gatherings. The overall mood was relaxation after a day's work. Adults sat by rank, the head of the family sitting next to the family altar, and everyone could start a story or song, including the children (1972). The tradition of family storytelling continues today in Nigerian homes and is an important part of intergenerational communication, conflict resolution, relaxation, and the instruction of children through didactic stories among one ethnic group in southern Nigeria, the Igede (Ogede, 1999)

African didactic tales can be divided into two groups: straightforward instruction with spelled-out morals and open-ended dilemma tales (Abrahams, 1983). It is the context of the storytelling event that determines the type of tale to be told. The classic instructional tale is told by someone who is acknowledged to be a wiser person, such as a grandparent, parent, or uncle, to a younger audience in a family or community setting or by older women to younger women at a party or other occasion. The dilemma tale, on the other hand, is told to an audience of equals and is left open-ended for debate after the story ends. The issues raised are just as serious as those in the instructional tales, but the quality of the discussion is what matters the most. In some cases the final solution is given by the storyteller; in others the storyteller or participants decide which argument is best. The dilemmas may deal with such questions as who has contributed most in a certain situation, as in "The Girl and the Python," or which of two (sometimes terrible) alternatives is preferable. Although these types of stories are not unique to Africa, as shown by the biblical dilemma tale of King Solomon's judgment regarding a disputed baby, they are especially popular in Africa. William Bascom, a folklorist, compiled hundreds of them from throughout the continent, though he found more among some people, such as the people of Sierra Leone and the Nkundo of the Democratic Republic of the Congo (Zaire), than among others (1975).

As in the rest of the world, oral storytelling is no longer the primary mode of education for the community. School, print, and radio have largely taken over this function. Even 20–25 years ago children in traditional villages were far more likely to hear didactic tales than were students in big cities. In one study of Zulu high school students, rural teenagers remembered many more didactic tales (about 20% of all the stories), than did urban teenagers (6%) (du Toit, 1976). As the essays in Margaret Read MacDonald's *Traditional Storytelling Today: An International Sourcebook* (1999) indicate, however, it is impossible to generalize even about the status of storytelling in the home. Many of the writers who contributed to the *Sourcebook* discuss the important role storytelling in the home still has in West African countries, but others talk of the disappearance of the village storytelling event.

Whether in the home or in other locations, however, storytelling does continue. Stories are now told on the radio, by urban performers, often with modern adaptations, and by storytelling revival groups such as The Storytellers, a semiprofessional group who tell stories at cultural centers and in schools in Kenya (Alembi, 1999). Traditional stories have also been published in schoolbooks in many parts of Africa. Asenath Odaga's collection of Kenyan folktales,

Yesterday's Today: The Study of Oral Literature (1984), from which comes the story "All for Vanity," is a good example, as the author is both a writer and a folklorist. She provides the sources of her stories, has children think about the themes and motifs in the stories, and gives suggestions for students to do their own folklore collecting. Traditional stories are also still told by urban parents to their children, as Ghanaian-Australian storyteller Dorinda Hafner relates in her reminiscences of growing up in Ghana in *I Was Never Here and This Never Happened* (1996). She relates one incident when she came up with the impractical idea of piling one chair on top of another to reach a book on a high shelf, resulting in her little brother's tumbling down; her mother, instead of punishing her, told her a story about spider Anansi and his plan to collect all the common sense in the world.

For a bibliography of a sampling of picture and illustrated books of African fables, see "Picture Books Related to the Stories in the *Allyn & Bacon Anthology of Traditional Literature*" at www.ablongman.com/lechner.

All for Vanity

Africa: Kenya—Luo ethnic group

Reminiscent of the picture book version by Verna Aardema and Leo and Diane Dillon, *Why Mosquitoes Buzz in People's Ears* (1975), this cumulative tale provides a different ending from that in the picture book. Instead of the fly's being slapped as the mosquito is, as answer to whether people are still angry at it, it is Fly, the one who had started all the trouble, who delivers the last lecture. Odaga has also written a more

literary version of this tale, entitled "No Problem," in Mary Medlicott's *Tales from Africa,* and another version appears in Rogeria Barbose's *African Animal Tales.*

Source: "All for Vanity" from *Yesterday's Today: The Study of Oral Literature* by Asenath Bole Odaga. Kisumu, Kenya: Lake Publishers and Enterprises, 1984. Reprinted with permission by Asenath Bole Odaga. pp. 23–25.

One mid-morning, the fly tied a banana fibre rope around her waist and left her home to go out to the bush to collect some firewood. Near her home, she encountered the Rock Lizard, popularly known as Andhagaria, the son of the beautiful people. Andhagaria had just taken a bath and was lying on a rock warming himself.

"Mmmm, Andhagaria, the son of the beautiful ones," the Fly began, "I admire the beauty of your dark skin, for it glows, sparkles, and shines so! Oh, you are a marvel. It's incredible! You are truly good looking!" The Fly gave glowing compliments to Andhagaria for as you know, she is a creature with a good open heart. Hence she visits everybody and everything, in all sorts of places, indiscriminately!

Andhagaria didn't like such open admiration of his good looks. He was a vain stupid suspicious fellow, and felt that such praises might smudge or have a disastrous effect on the looks he so much cherished. So he rushed to escape from the Fly's probing eyes, but unfortunately, in his eagerness to get away, he found himself in the home of Apol, the Water Buck's [a type of antelope] cousin.

Now, Apol being the ostentatious fellow he was, felt indignant at Andhagaria's intrusion on his privacy. Although he objected unreservedly to Andhagaria, he still felt that due to the gravity of the matter, he had to register his objection to an audience as well. For this reason, he convened an urgent meeting of all the creatures of the wild. The move caused a real stir in the jungle. Each creature was anxious to find out the reason why Apol had convened such an urgent meeting.

On receiving the message of the meeting, Elephant hurriedly left and headed to the venue. By bad luck, he took neither enough caution nor his size into consideration whilst walking along the crowded road, leading to the venue of the impromptu meeting. Thus he stepped on the back of Tortoise, who in his great fury and pain, emitted fire through his bottom. The fire leapt and licked everything along its path and even burnt part of the Chief's house! Now, it happened that the Black Ant was airing his eggs on the roof of the Chief's house.

The Rain, on seeing that the Chief's house was burning, came down in a torrent, to put out the Fire in order to save the Chief's house! Unfortunately, however, it also washed away Black Ant's eggs and the water carried it all into the lake! By then all the creatures of the wild had gathered for the urgent meeting called by Apol the Water Buck's cousin.

Black Ant was furious. She demanded of the Rain saying, "Rain, why did you wash and scatter my eggs.

Please, you must explain why you came down at the wrong time?"

"Oh, I'm sorry, but what could I do?" replied the Rain, "when I saw the Chief's house on fire, surely I had to extinguish the fire."

"That sounds interesting," the Chief remarked. "House, why were you burning?" the Chief added, looking grave and authoritative.

"What could I do when Tortoise let out its fire which burnt all the vegetation and trees around me?" the House replied.

"Tortoise, my old friend, what happened? Why did you emit Fire from your body?" the Chief demanded. "You know how destructive and uncontrollable Fire is?"

Tortoise turned its head with difficulty as he was still feeling much pain from his back on which Elephant had stepped with its huge legs.

"I couldn't help it when Elephant stepped on my back. In fact, he's ruined me. My appearance is gone. I'll never be my old self again. My coat is cracked and broken all over," Tortoise lamented. The other creatures showed great sympathy for the Tortoise.

"This is treacherous," the Chief remarked with vehemence. "Elephant, why on earth didn't you look carefully before you stepped on the path? Your size doesn't give you exclusive right of way in the Jungle. I am the Chief, and I have given the right of way to every creature of the wild." All the other creatures nodded in agreement. The fellow had to take more care so as to safeguard the small ones.

"Oh, I'm indeed very sorry," Elephant said sadly, "but what could I do? I had to hurry to be here in time for Apol's meeting."

"Apol," the Chief of the Jungle called loudly, "Why did you convene an urgent meeting of all the creatures of the wild?"

"I had to, because Andhagaria invaded my privacy," Apol shouted, shaking with rage. "He just glided into my home where I live with my entire family. I had to demonstrate my full objection to the violation of an individual's right to privacy." Apol was still angered by what Andhagaria had done hours back in the morning.

The chief cocked his eyes and look hard at Andhagaria, and asked in a thunderous voice, "Andhagaria, please explain why you intruded into Apol's home without permission?"

"What could I do when Fly so openly extolled my beauty?" Andhagaria replied naughtily, looking around at the creatures of the wild as if to advertise his handsomeness. He began again after a little pause, "How could I tell what her motives were, or what she might do to me? Actually, I was both horrified and scared. Moreover, I've never before met a Fly with a rope around her waist. So I thought that I was probably seeing an apparition of a strange non-existent fly!" The other animals looked at Fly and began to laugh. All creatures of the wild laughed long and hilariously. The laughter was utterly deafening. It was like many thunders rolled into one.

When the great laughter died down, the Chief asked the Fly saying, "Fly, why did you so openly stop to admire Andhagaria's good looks?"

"Mmmmmmmmm," Fly exclaimed, "I, the Fly, the daughter of the small ones, who never live to see old age, what crime did I commit? I had no sinister motive, but merely stopped to admire the good looks of the beautiful ones! Was that serious enough to trigger off a chain of events?" The Fly looked mischievously at Apol and Andhagaria and went on, "Chief of the Jungle, great and mighty leader of us all, look at me. I'm small and insignificant. If the good-looking members of the wild display all their assets for the likes of me who are deprived of such gifts, then its only natural that I should look covetously at them! Please assist them to find an answer to their problem." The Fly then flew away! ■

The Goats Who Killed the Leopard

literal scapegoats

Africa: Eritrea

Like the fables of Aesop, this story is more social commentary than a lesson. The story has been traced to Arabic sources.

Once a leopard cub wandered away from his home into the grasslands where the elephant herds grazed. He was too young to know his danger. While the elephants grazed one of them stepped on the leopard cub by accident and killed him. Other leopards found the body of the cub soon after, and they rushed to his father to tell him of the tragedy.

"Your son is dead!" they told him. "We found him in the valley!"

The father leopard was overcome with grief.

"Ah, who has killed him? Tell me, so that I can avenge his death!"

"The elephants have killed him," the other leopards said.

"What? The elephants?" the father leopard said with surprise in his voice.

"Yes, the elephants," they repeated.

He thought for a minute.

"No, it is not the elephants. It is the goats who have killed him. Yes, the goats, it is they who have done this awful thing to me!"

So the father leopard went out in a fit of terrible rage and found a herd of goats grazing in the hills, and he slaughtered many of them in revenge.

And even now, when a man is wronged by someone stronger than himself, he often avenges himself upon someone who is weaker than himself. ■

Source: "The Goats Who Killed the Leopard" from *Fire on the Mountain and Other Ethiopian Stories* by Harold Courlander and Wolf Leslau. Copyright 1950 by Henry Holt and Company. Reprinted by permission of Henry Holt and Company. pp. 25–26.

Fire and Water, Truth and Falsehood

Ethiopia

This story is known widely throughout East Africa. The mountain setting is particularly appropriate for Ethiopia, which is mountainous with peaks reaching 8000 feet. Cattle grazing is an important part of the economy (Courlander and Leslau, 1950).

Truth, Falsehood, Fire, and Water lived together. They went out one day to hunt, and they found many cattle. Afterwards they decided to divide the cattle so that each of them received his share. But Falsehood wanted more for himself. So he secretly went to Water and said:

"You have the power to destroy Fire. If you do this, we can take his part of the cattle."

Water believed what Falsehood said, and he threw himself upon Fire and destroyed him.

Then Falsehood went to Truth.

"Fire is dead. Water has killed him, and he does not deserve to share with us. Let us take the cattle into the mountains for ourselves."

Source: "Fire and Water, Truth and Falsehood" from *The Fire on the Mountain and Other Ethiopian Stories* by Harold Courlander and Wolf Leslau. Copyright 1950 by Henry Holt and Company. Reprinted by permission of Henry Holt and Company. pp. 119–120.

So Truth and Falsehood drove the cattle into the mountains. Water saw them go, and he tried to pursue them, but he found he couldn't run uphill, but only down, and so they escaped.

When they arrived at a resting place in the mountains, Falsehood turned to Truth and said:

"Foolish one, I am strong and you are weak; I am the master and you are the servant. Therefore, all the cattle shall belong to me."

"No," Truth said, "I am not your servant. It is I who am strong, and therefore, I am the master." And he went forward and fought with Falsehood. They struggled back and forth across the mountain, without either one destroying the other.

So at last they went to Wind and asked him to judge which was right. He listened to their arguments, and then he said:

"It is this way: Truth is destined to struggle with Falsehood. Truth will win, but Falsehood will return, and again Truth must fight. As long as time, Truth must fight with Falsehood, because if he does not do so he is lost forever." ■

The Magic Tree

Africa: Malawi

Children are not the only ones who need to learn lessons from time to time, as this story, whose outcome is happier than that of "The Pied Piper of Hamelin," shows.

Source: "The Magic Tree" from *Tales of Old Malawi* by E. Singano and A. A. Popular Publications and Likuni Press, 1980. Reprinted with permission by Likuni Press. p. 63.

There was once a large village in the middle of a forest. Near to the village ran a wide deep river, and wild animals went to its banks in the heat of the day to drink. Even though it was such a dangerous place, the children of the village used to spend hours at the river each day, playing and bathing. Their parents never bothered to find out where they were, nor whether they were safe.

One day as the children were playing happily by the river, a violent storm arose. The wind blew wildly and rain fell in torrents, so heavily that the children could not see their path home. They were huddled together, crying miserably when suddenly the trunk of a huge tree nearby opened into a wide cavity. The children ran into it, and when the last one had entered, the tree closed around them. The children were frightened to be caught in this strange dark place. They shouted for help but they were not heard. Indeed they could not have been heard from the outside even if someone had been there. That evening, and every day following, food

was brought to the children by an unknown being, so they did not starve.

When the children failed to return home a search party was sent into the forest; but of course no trace of them was found. The storm was blamed for the disappearance. It was thought that they must have been drowned and swept away. The village wept.

Now, the chief called his people together to consult the ancestors about the disaster. A great sacrifice was offered, especially by the parents of the missing children. Then the chief had a dream. The ancestors told him that they had hidden them as a warning to parents who did not properly care for their children.

So the next day the young men of the village took their axes and cut open the tree. The children were safe. From that day on all the parents have been vigilant in keeping their children from danger. ∎

What Spider Learned from Frog

Africa: Ghana—Adengme ethnic group

Typically, the spider trickster Anansi of Ghana is seen as the epitome of greed and self-indulgence. His long-suffering wife believes in him, but he is as likely to trick her as he is his neighbors and "friends." When the story revolves around Anansi, it is a funny but also serious lesson on how not to be. In this story the moral is spelled out. Other times it must be deduced by the listener. In Eric Kimmel's stories about Anansi he has to learn a number of lessons about greediness and outsmarting others. The one closest in spirit to "What Spider Learned from Frog" is Kimmel, Eric. *Anansi Goes Fishing.* Illustrated by Janet Stevens. Holiday House, 1993.

Source: "What Spider Learned from Frog" from Berry, Jack. *West African Folktales.* Northwestern University Press, 1991. Reprinted with permission by Northwestern University Press. pp. 24–25.

A long time ago, Frog and Spider were the best of friends. They went everywhere together, and they did everything together. All the same, Spider used to treat Frog badly, even though he was his friend. For example, he would always eat most of the fish or meat in their food before serving the meal to Frog. Frog wasn't like that at all. When he shared a meal with Spider, he always gave him a fair share of the meat or any other especially good part.

One day, Frog decided he had enough of this sort of treatment, and he thought of a way to teach Spider a lesson. He told his wife to get a meal ready for Spider and himself, and he especially asked her not to put too much salt or pepper in the stew. By evening, Frog's wife had finished everything and had set the food on the table. As they were waiting for Spider, Frog pretended to think of something. He told his wife, "Look, I've forgotten my hunting knife. I left it at the farm, and I think I had better go back and get it. If Spider comes, welcome him and don't wait for me—serve the food immediately." When his wife went back to the kitchen, Frog jumped in the Stew and hid there.

Along came Spider shortly after, and he was given the message and was served the food. The first thing Spider did was to fish out all the meat from the stew and gobble it down greedily. Doing this he ate Frog, too, without even noticing.

When he had finished Spider got up to go, and he was just about to take leave of Frog's wife when he heard, "Greedeep! Greedeep!" in his stomach. He was frightened and began to run, but the faster he ran, the more the noise came from his stomach. "Greedeep! Greedeep!" This went on for forty days. It kept him awake at night, and he had no sleep and could eat no food. Spider could stand it no longer. He lay down and got ready for death. Then, suddenly, Frog jumped out of his mouth and said to Spider, "I have known for a long time about your greedy ways, and this should be a lesson you will never forget."

From this you should remember that when you are invited to share food, let the one who provides it serve it and divide it among the guests. ■

▨ African Dilemma Tales

The following two fables are dilemma tales. There is usually no right answer for these tales; the storyteller throws the debate open to the audience. At the end of the debate, the best solution carries the day. Even when correct answers are given by the storyteller, the discussion in the end is still the most important part of the experience. According to Bascom (1975), these stories provide training in debate and using reason to arrive at just decisions in community affairs. Both of the following stories have many variants throughout Africa and have been retold in children's books and at storytellings in the United States.

The Girl and the Python

Africa: Togo—Grushi ethnic group

The theme of a girl making an unwise decision, choosing a monster for a husband and later having to be rescued by her family (brothers), is a recurrent one in many parts of Africa, but the story is usually a cautionary tale for young women, not a dilemma tale. In this case the only hint that the young woman also has learned a lesson is that she never marries again.

The motif of four or five brothers each exhibiting his super abilities to save someone in the family recurs in many folktales throughout the world, including several in Africa:

- Courlander, Harold and George Herzog. "The Cowtail Switch" in *The Cowtail Switch*. Holt, Rinehart, and Winston, 1947.
- McDermott, Gerald. *Anansi The Spider: A Tale from the Ashanti*. Holt, Rinehart, and Winston, 1972.

Source: "The Girl and the Python" from *African Dilemma Tales* by William Bascom. The Hague: Mouton Publishers, 1975. p. 59. Reprinted with permission by Mouton de Gruyter a Division of Walter de Gruyter Gmbh & Co.

A chief's daughter fell in love with a python that had appeared in the form of a handsome man. During the night it resumed its python form, swallowed the girl, and carried her off to its home in a large lake. In the morning the chief ordered his people to follow, but they found no tracks. A man who could smell the faintest odor followed their trail to the lake. A man famous for his thirst drank the lake dry. A man known to work harder than anyone else dug out all the mud, revealing a hole so deep that its bottom could not be reached. A man whose arm could reach all over the country pulled out the python. It was killed, but when they cut open its stomach the girl was dead. A man who had medicine to raise the dead restored her to life. Now, which of the five men did best? Answer: they were all equally good. The girl never married again. ■

Mirror, Airplane, and Ivory Trumpet

Africa: Democratic Republic of the Congo—Nkundo ethnic group

Oral tales continue to change with the times, as this version of a traditional motif shows. An earlier variant involved a magic carpet.

A father gave a bicycle to each of his three sons, and they left home. They parted at a crossroads and later met there again. The first had found a mirror in which he could see everything; the second had found an airplane; the third had found an ivory trumpet that could revive the dead. The first saw that their sister was dead, they flew home in the airplane, and the third brother restored their sister to life. Their father wanted to reward them with an expensive ring, but there was only one ring. To whom will he give the ring? Which son did best? Answer: The three sons had done equally well, but it is good that the ring be given to the eldest son because he is his father's heir. ■

Source: "Mirror, Airplane, and Ivory Trumpet" from *African Dilemma Tales* by William Bascom. The Hague: Mouton Publishers, 1975. p. 50. Reprinted with permission by Mouton de Gruyter a Division of Walter de Gruyter.

Indian Fables

The Panchatantra

The Panchatantra, meaning five books, is the title given to a collection of fables of India, thought to have been first recorded around 300 B.C.E. The stories drew on a far older oral tradition. These oral stories were probably also the sources of many of the *Jataka Tales,* a set of Indian fables about the lives of the Buddha, but while the tone of *The Jataka Tales* was always moralistic, *The Panchatantra* were sophisticated and worldly, at times even cynical. The tales represented lessons for the right conduct of both everyday life—be resourceful, be wise in choosing and keeping friends, do not trust false friends—and courtly life—do not allow false advisers to create enmity between you and your true friends, know how to listen to wise counsel when dealing with an enemy, know how to distinguish between real danger and bluffing.

In one story about the fables an all-powerful king has three foolish sons who wish to learn nothing. In despair the king calls for advice and is told that if there is anyone who can teach his sons, it is Vishnusharman, a wise religious man. Vishnusharman tells the king that within six months the sons will become wise and educated if they will but memorize the stories he will teach them, for

Whoever always reads this work,
Whoever listens to it told

"The Banyan Deer." Illustrated by Ellsworth Young.
From: Jataka Tales: *Animal Stories*, Re-told by Ellen C. Babbitt. © 1940 Englewood Cliffs, N.J.: Prentice-Hall, Inc.

He will never face defeat, no
not even from the Lord of Gods, Himself.

—Chandra Rajan *The Panchatantra*.
New Delhi: Penguin Books India, 1993.

These framework stories might have influenced later famous framework stories such as *The Thousand and One Nights* as well as Chaucer's *The Canterbury Tales*. Legend has it that around 570 C.E. a Persian physician was sent to bring The Panchatantra back to Persia, where it was translated, and the wise counselor was renamed Bidpai. Around 750 C.E. the stories were translated from Persian into Arabic. It was the Arabic version that became most widely known during the Middle Ages and that was brought to Africa and Europe, where the collection was named Bidpai Tales. Some of the stories are similar to Aesop's fables. Note, for instance, the similarity between the story "The Mice That Set the Elephants Free" from *The Panchatantra* and "The Lion and the Mouse," an Aesop fable. Communication between the ancient Greeks and Indians would have made an interchange of stories possible. Like many of Aesop's fables, the stories are designed to teach lessons, but the lessons are expressed in verse and are interwoven in the story rather than being clearly spelled out at the end of each story (Ryder, 1925).

"The Blue Jackal" comes from the first of the five books of *The Panchatantra*, called "Loss of Friends." "The Mice That Set the Elephants Free" comes from the second book, called "The Winning of Friends." The last story, "How the Rabbit Fooled the Elephant," comes from the third book, "The Crows and Owls." The two Web Supplement stories, "The Jackal and the War Drum" and "Plan Ahead, Quick Thinker, and Wait and See," are also from the first book.

There are a few children's collections of Panchatantra fables and picture books of individual tales available in the United States.

For a bibliography of a sampling of picture and illustrated books of *Panchatantra* fables, see "Picture Books Related to the Stories in the *Allyn & Bacon Anthology of Traditional Literature*" at www.ablongman. com/lechner.

Book 1: Loss of Friends   The following stories are three of the many stories that Shrewd Jackal, King Lion's adviser, tells him. Over the course of Book One

Source: The Panchatantra by Arthur Ryder. Translated from ancient Sanskrit. Chicago: University of Chicago Press, 1925. This is an adaptation from Ryder's translation by J. Lechner. The primary change was the abbreviation and summarizing of the lengthy frame stories between the fables.

of *The Panchatantra,* Jackal tells many stories designed to teach about true and false friends. Jackal's aim is to find a way to separate King Lion from his good friend, Wise Bull. In this he succeeds. The ultimate lesson for a ruler is not to allow false advisers to come between him and a friend. The three young princes of the frame story could draw their own lessons from these stories as well. The frame story of King Lion and Shrewd Jackal, which is woven between each of the short fables in the first book of *The Panchatantra,* is also a brief *Jataka Tale* (no. 349) with the same cast of characters and moral.

The Blue Jackal

India

Marcia Brown's *Blue Jackal* (1977) a Caldecott honor–winning picture book as well as Mehlli Gobhai's *Blue Jackal* (1968) provide some visual details of the story's Indian setting. This story can also be found among the *Jatakas.*

There was once a jackal named Fierce-Howl who lived in a cave near a city. Being especially hungry one day, he came to the edge of the city to hunt for food. Soon the dogs in the neighborhood began to chase him. As he stumbled about looking for a way to escape, he stumbled into a fabric dyer's indigo vat. Somehow he managed to crawl back out and escape to the forest, but he was now an incredible indigo blue. When the other animals saw him, they in turn became terrified and fled shouting, "What is this creature with this rich, never-before-seen indigo-blue color? How tough and wild he must be! Let's run for our lives!"

When the Jackal heard the animals' terror, he called out, "Do not be afraid, animals. I have just come from Lord Indra, who realizing that the animals had no king, decided to anoint me, Fierce-Howl, and send me to you as your king. Rest here in the safety of the circle made by my unconquerable paws.

On hearing this, the Lion, Tiger, rabbits, other jackals and the rest of the animals bowed to him humbly and said "Lord Fierce-Howl, give us our duties that we may serve you well." So Fierce-Howl handed out jobs to everyone: Lion became prime minister, Tiger was lord of the bed chamber, the leopard was put in charge of the king's betel nuts, and the elephant was made doorkeeper. Everyone got a plum of a job except for the jackals. Fierce-Howl, like so many who rise to high positions, forgot his friends; he bossed the jackals around mercilessly, gave them beatings, and drove them away.

He was happy with his kingly duties and privileges, but when one evening he heard the howls of other jackals deep in the forest, he replied with a joyful howl of his own. Imagine the Tiger's, Leopard's, and Lion's amazement, when this blue creature began to sound like an ordinary jackal! Ashamed of their own foolishness and angry at Fierce-Howl for his pretending to be a great king, they pounced on him and tore him to pieces. ∎

By the end of *Book 1* Shrewd Jackal has led King Lion so far astray that King Lion decides to fight and kills his former friend Wise Bull. Only after the deed is done does he wake up to his folly and repent, while listening to Shrewd Jackal's brother, Honest Jackal, deliver the last lecture:

No wisdom lies in fighting,
Since it is the fools who fight,
The wise discover in wise books
What course is wise and right.
And wise books in the course that is
Not violent, delight.

Book 2: The Winning of Friends In this book the princes learn that through friendship and cooperation much can be accomplished, for:

The deer and turtle, mouse and crow
Had first-rate sense and learning; so,
Though money failed and means were few,
They quickly put their purpose through.

The Mice That Set the Elephants Free

India

This story is reminiscent of the Aesop fable "The Lion and the Mouse." It is possible that this story traveled with traders or with Alexander's army from Greece to India or vice versa, but it is also possible that similar stories arise independently in many parts of the world because they grow out of similar human experiences.

There was once a region that had been completely abandoned by its human inhabitants. After a while palaces, houses, and even temples fell into ruin but were still happily occupied by the oldest residents, the mice. Thousands of mice enjoyed happy and rich lives, with festivals, theatrical performances, wedding-feasts and many other entertainments. And so the time passed.

But this state of happiness was abruptly ended when an elephant king with his thousands of followers burst upon this scene. On their way to a lake, they marched through the mouse community, crushing them left and right.

The survivors held a convention. "We are being killed," they said "by these lumbering elephants! If they come this way again, we will be wiped out. We must find a solution to this crisis." They decided to send a delegation to the elephants. The delegation found the huge beasts at the lake and addressed them respectfully:

"O King, not far from here is our little community, where our ancestors have lived since ancient days. Now you gentlemen, while coming here to water, have destroyed us by the thousands. And, if you return the way you came, there will not be enough of us to ensure that our community will continue in the future. Surely a great people such as the elephants would not wish to destroy such small creatures as we are. Too, think about the fact that even such small creatures as we may prove to be of health to your highness some day.

Thinking this over, the elephant king decided that the mice were right, and granted them their request. One day animal trappers came to the forest and created a great trap for large animals. The elephant king and his herd were caught. When the trappers returned, they pulled the elephants out of the trap and tied them to large trees in the forest. When the elephant king and his herd were once again alone, tied to trees, they began to wonder how they could get themselves out of this predicament. Then the king thought of the mice. So he sent the mice a message by way of an elephant cow who had not become caught in the trap. When the mice learned of the elephants' distress, they gathered by the thousand, eager to return the favor shown them. Seeing the elephants all tied up they gnawed through the ropes and set their friends free. ∎

Book 3: Crows and Owls In this book the princes are taught about war, peace, and diplomacy. The first verse tells the princes:

Reconciled although he be,
Never trust an enemy.
For the cave of owls was burned,
When the crows with fire returned.

The King of the Crows lived in a banyan tree with his large family of crows. They had a great enemy, the King of the Owls, who out of pure malice continually hunted the crows, striking at night so that they could not see him. The King of the Crows called his many counselors together to ask for advice. Each suggested a different strategy. Some suggested peace, some suggested war, some suggested changing their base or making an alliance. The oldest and wisest of the crows said that all those were good ideas, but when the problem is too great, you might have to turn to trickery. The wise crow then told several stories. One of them was the following.

How the Rabbit Fooled the Elephant

India

Although the conflict in this story is the same as that in the story of "The Mice That Set the Elephants Free," note the difference in tone and in Rabbit's solution.

In a part of a forest lived King of the Elephants with his large following. One year there was a great drought and all the ponds in their part of the forest dried up. So the king sent out scouts to find a new pond.

Those who went east found a lake named Lake of the Moon. It was beautiful with swans, herons, ospreys and all kind of water creatures. It was surrounded by lovely shade trees and had plenty of water. When the scouts reported back to the king, the entire elephant herd decided to move immediately. As soon as the elephant herd arrived they plunged right in the lake, but in their haste and clumsiness they crushed thousands of rabbits who lived on the shore.

The remaining rabbits held an emergency council. "What are we to do now?" "How can we keep them from returning and squashing the rest of us?" One wise rabbit reassured them, "Don't worry, they won't come back," and with that he took off to find the King of the Ele-phants. Soon Rabbit came upon the King, who looked even larger and more glorious than he had imagined. Just to be safe from his feet, Rabbit climbed up on a large jagged rock near the King of the Elephants and ad-dressed him. "O, King, I hope all is well with you." "And who are you?" asked the king. "I come as an official mes-senger who serves the blessed Moon," replied Rabbit. "State your business," said the King of the Elephants.

Rabbit began, "O King, listen to the Moon's mes-sage. He says that you have greatly violated his sacred lake, which bears his name, by heedlessly entering it and thereby killing countless rabbits. Do you not know, that you have angered the Moon? I will show you, if you don't believe me." With that, Rabbit took Elephant King to the Lake of the Moon. By the time they arrived, it was nightfall, and the moon was up. Rabbit told the ele-phant to step in the lake. When Elephant King stepped in, however, the ripples in the lake made the moon shake. "See," said Rabbit, "the Moon shakes with anger. Leave forever, if you do not want to make the Moon permanently angry at you and your people." Ele-phant King promised and the rabbits were safe. ∎

The Crow King felt that he needed more advice, and the wise crow told several more stories about the weak prevailing against their stronger enemies by using their wits. The wise crow then devised a plan to defeat the owls. He had the King of the Crows tell his subjects to beat him up and pluck his wings on the pre-text that he had been disloyal to the king. He also ad-vised the king to leave him by the road and to take his subjects into hiding. Abandoned thus, the wise crow waited. Soon the owls found him and brought him to their king, who questioned the crow about his condition. The wise crow said that he had been punished for advising the crows to surrender to the owls. The King of the Owls asked for advice as to how to treat this half-dead crow. The owl king's advisers disagreed with each other. The first said, "Kill him, for you can never trust an enemy." The second said, "Treat him with compassion." The third advised taking him in and making him an honored member of their society so that he could help them fight the crows. The king listened to the third adviser. What he didn't know was that his new subject was gathering secret information about the owls' plans and was able to help his own people, the crows, defeat the owls.

The Jataka Tales

The Jataka tales are said to have been used by the Buddha, who lived around 500 B.C.E., as teaching devices to instruct his disciples. Many of these stories were probably in oral circulation long before the Buddha, however, and some appear in *The Panchatantra*, as well. Nor were the stories all necessarily known to the Buddha; some became associated with him by Buddhist teachers later on. The stories are old, however, as indicated by a third century B.C.E. bas relief sculpture that depicts some of the Jataka stories (Jones, 1979).

The Buddha taught that to escape the cycle of rebirths (**Samsara**) in which all sentient beings are trapped, according to both Hindu and Buddhist belief, one must accept and live four truths: earthly existence is pain; pain is caused by the desire for existence, which leads to the perpetuation of rebirths; when one stops craving existence, pain ceases; one must follow an Eightfold Path to be able to stop craving existence. When a soul reaches the highest level of wisdom, it is said to be Enlightened and can unite with the universal soul in a state of Nirvana, never to be reborn. Following the Eightfold Path is the way to achieve Enlightenment. The Eightfold Path consists of (1) Right View, (2) Right Intention, (3) Right Speech, (4) Right Conduct, (5) Right Means of Livelihood, (6) Right Effort, (7) Right Mindfulness, and (8) Right Meditation (Gonda, 1987). The first two steps of the Eightfold

Path are necessary to be able to start on the journey toward **Enlightenment**. They enable one to follow the other steps. Right View means having the right attitude. Right Intentions includes good will and loving-kindness, a selfless love toward all other beings. Following the precepts of the middle three steps, Right Speech, Right Action, and Right Livelihood, leads both to an ethical life, which should result in social harmony and reward in this or a future life (**Karma**), and to moral discipline, which is essential for being able to undertake the last two steps and ultimately for achieving Enlightenment. Some of the precepts associated with Right Speech include not lying, not saying slanderous things, and not talking hurtfully to others. Among the Right Actions is included the precept of abstaining from taking a life, which means not killing people, not hunting, and not slaughtering animals. Also among these precepts is abstaining from taking anything that is not given, in other words not stealing, not defrauding anyone, and not cheating anyone (Bodhi, 1994). It is the ethical nature of the precepts that is highlighted in the Jataka tales. Buddhist writings and teachings are complex and abstract, but the average Buddhist all over Southeast Asia learns the most basic Buddhist principles through the Jataka tales. Because of their concrete characters and settings, the stories are easily told orally and are accessible even to nonliterate people (Jones, 1979).

The Buddha was said to have reached Enlightenment, but instead of entering **Nirvana**, he chose to return as a teacher or **Bodhisatta** to help others reach Enlightenment through his teachings. Each Jataka tale is a story of one of his rebirths. Each tale consists of three parts: an introduction that portrays the Buddha among his disciples, teaching them about a specific principle, a story that illustrates the principle, and verses that encapsulate the principle (Jones, 1979).

The five hundred forty-seven tales that had been written down with commentary in the Pali language of Ceylon (Sri Lanka) in the fifth century C.E. were translated into English as *The Jataka, or Stories of the Buddha's Former Births* (E. B. Cowell, ed., London: Luzac, 1895). It is this translation that is the source of many of the picture book versions, such as Demi's *Buddha Stories* (1997).

Most children's versions of the Jatakas in the United States tell only the story but do not give the moral. Although sometimes the principle that is being conveyed is self-evident, as in the many stories of self-sacrifice for the sake of others, at other times the stories by themselves do not seem to convey a moral principle and simply resemble trickster tales. A case in point is the often retold story "The Monkey and the Crocodile" (tale no. 208), in which a crocodile with a craving for monkey heart lures a monkey down from his tree by promising to take him across the river to where the mangoes are better. Halfway across the river the crocodile tells the monkey that he will drown him and get his heart, to which the monkey replies that he has left his heart at home in his tree. The crocodile lets the monkey go back to get it, and the monkey escapes. Besides being a trickster story, this fable also illustrates the principle of abstaining from taking a life.

In each of the stories the Bodhisatta, as the Buddha is referred to before he entered Nirvana, the release from the cycle of rebirths, is represented by a highly respected human or animal, such as a king, an ascetic, a wise man, a merchant, an elephant, a lion, or a monkey. He might occasionally come back as a lower animal and still represent a virtue. In "The Monkey and the Crocodile" the monkey represents the Bodhisatta, and the crocodile represents his bad son, Devadatta, who is always seeking the destruction of the Bodhisatta and does not live by Buddhist principles (Jones, 1979).

Although most of the principles illustrated by the Jatakas are universal, many of the themes that recur in the Jatakas are uniquely Indian. The king renouncing his throne and family is one such theme. Another is complete self-sacrifice as an expression of selfless love. The story "Hare's Self Sacrifice," (tale no. 316) is one such story. Hare gives his life as the perfect gift rather than for the sake of saving others. There are several illustrated collections and picture book versions of Jataka tales.

For a bibliography of picture and illustrated books of Jataka fables, see "Picture Books Related to the Stories in the *Allyn & Bacon Anthology of Traditional Literature*" at www.ablongman.com/lechner.

The Banyan Deer

India: Jataka tale no. 385

The Banyan Deer in this story is the Buddha in one of his incarnations. It is the Banyan Deer who teaches the lessons of loving-kindness and compassion in this affecting story, which has been also rendered as a picture book by Margaret Hodges *The Golden Deer* (1992).

There was once a Deer the color of gold. His eyes were like round jewels, his horns were white as silver, his mouth was red like a flower, his hoofs were bright and hard. He had a large body and a fine tail.

Source: "The Banyan Deer" from *Jataka Tales: Animal Stories* by Ellen Babbitt. Prentice-Hall, 1940. pp. 58–62.

He lived in a forest and was king of a herd of five hundred Banyan Deer. Near by lived another herd of Deer, called the Monkey Deer. They, too, had a king.

The king of that country was fond of hunting the Deer and eating deer meat. He did not like to go alone so he called the people of his town to go with him, day after day.

The townspeople did not like this, for while they were gone no one did their work. So they decided to make a park and drive the Deer into it. Then the king could go into the park and hunt and they could go on with their daily work.

They made a park, planted grass in it and provided water for the Deer, built a fence all around it and drove the Deer into it.

Then they shut the gate and went to the king to tell him that in the park near by he could find all the Deer he wanted.

The king went at once to look at the Deer. First he saw there were two Deer kings, and granted them their lives. Then he looked at their great herds.

Some days the king would go to hunt the Deer, sometimes his cook would go. As soon as any of the Deer saw them they would shake with fear and run. But when they had been hit once or twice they would drop down dead.

The King of the Banyan Deer sent for the King of the Monkey Deer and said, "Friend, many of the Deer are being killed. Many are wounded besides those who are killed. After this suppose one from my herd goes up to be killed one day, and the next day let one from your herd go up. Fewer Deer will be lost this way."

The Monkey Deer agreed. Each day the Deer whose turn it was would go and lie down, placing its head on the block. The cook would come and carry off the one he found lying there.

One day the lot fell to a mother Deer who had a young baby. She went to her king and said, "O King of the Monkey Deer, let the turn pass me by until my baby is old enough to get along without me. Then I will go and put my head on the block."

But the king did not help her. He told her that if the lot had fallen to her she must die.

Then she went to the King of the Banyan Deer and asked him to save her.

"Go back to your herd. I will go in your place," said he.

The next day the cook found the King of the Banyan Deer lying with his head on the block. The cook went to the king, who came himself to find out about this.

"King of the Banyan Deer! did I not grant you your life? Why are you lying here?"

"O great King!" said the King of the Banyan Deer, "a mother came with her young baby and told me that the lot had fallen to her. I could not ask any one else to take her place, so I came myself."

"King of the Banyan Deer! I never saw such kindness and mercy. Rise up. I grant your life and hers. Nor will I hunt any more the Deer in either park or forest." ■

The Jackal and the Crow

India: Jataka tale no. 294

While the seemingly similar Aesop fable "The Fox and the Crow" is a worldly tale designed to warn against listening to the words of flatterers, this Jataka tale warns against using flattery to evade the truth. It is told to promote Right Speech.

Once upon a time, when Brahmadatta was king of Benares, the Bodhisatta became a tree spirit in a certain rose apple grove. A Crow perched upon a branch

Source: "The Jackal and the Crow" from: *Jataka Tales* by H. T. Francis and E. J. Thomas. New Delhi, India: Jaico Publishing House, 1956. pp. 133–134. Reprinted with permission by Jaico Publishing House.

and began to eat the fruit. Then came a Jackal, and looked up and spied the Crow. Thought he, "If I flatter this creature, perhaps I shall get some of the fruit to eat!" So in flattery he repeated the first stanza:

> Who is it sits in a rose apple tree—
> Sweet singer, whose voice trickles gently to me?
> Look a young peacock she coos with soft grace,
> And ever sits still in her place.

The Crow, in his praise, responded with the second:

> He that is noble in breeding and birth
> Can praise others' breeding, knows what they
>   are worth.

Like a young tiger thou seemest to be:
Come, eat what I give, Sir, to thee!

With these words she shook the branch and made some fruit drop. Then the spirit of the tree, beholding these two eating after flattering each other, repeated the third stanza:

Liars, foregather, I very well know.
Here, for example, a carrion Crow,
And corpse eating Jackal, with puerile clatter
Proceed one another to flatter!

After repeating this stanza, the tree spirit, assuming a fearful shape, scared them both away. ■

Fables from Other Traditions

The following fables are but a few of the many other fables of the world, some of which are elegant derivatives of Aesop-type fables, such as La Fontaine's French and Krylov's Russian fables; others are from an altogether different tradition.

For picture book versions of these stories, see Picture Books Related to the Stories in the *Allyn & Bacon Anthology of Traditional Literature* at www.ablongman. com/lechner.

The Grasshopper and the Ant

Europe: France

The French writer Jean de la Fontaine's sophisticated verses converted Aesopic and Jataka fables from their homey or religious originals to clever verses with an ironic tone. These verses are schoolchildren's fare not only in France but everywhere where children study French, including the United States. The following translation was done by former U.S. Poet Laureate Richard Wilbur.

Grasshopper, having sung her song
All summer long,
Was sadly unprovided-for
When the cold winds began to roar:

Not one least bite of grub or fly
Had she remembered to put by.
Therefore she hastened to descant
On famine, to her neighbor Ant,
Begging the loan of a few grains
Of wheat to ease her hunger-pains
Until the winter should be gone.
"You shall be paid," said she "upon
My honor as an animal,
Both interest and principal."
The Ant was not disposed to lend;
The liberal vice was not for her.
"What did you do all summer, friend?"
She asked the would-be borrower.
"So please your worship," answered she,
"I sang and sang both night and day."
"You sang? Indeed, that pleases me.
Then dance the winter-time away." ■

sassy!

Source: "The Grasshopper and the Ant" from *The Mind-Reader: New Poems* copyright © 1955 and renewed 1983 by Richard Wilbur. Reprinted by permission of Harcourt Brace and Company. HBJ, 1976, p. 36.

The Nail

Europe: Germany

This familiar proverb, fleshed out as a story, seems an appropriate one to reflect on as our world becomes more and more rushed.

A merchant had done good business at the fair; he had sold his wares and lined his money-bags with gold and silver. Then he wanted to travel homewards and be in his own house before nightfall. So he packed his trunk with the money on his horse and rode away.

At noon he rested in a town, and when he wanted to go farther the stable-boy brought out his horse and said, "A nail is wanting, sir, in the shoe of its left hind foot." "Let it be wanting," answered the merchant; "the

Source: "The Nail" from *Grimm's Household Tales* by Jacob and Wilhelm Grimm. Translated from the German by Margaret Hunt. London: George Bell and Sons, 1884. p. 303.

shoe will certainly stay on for the six miles I have still to go. I am in a hurry."

In the afternoon, when he once more alighted and had his horse fed, the stable-boy went into the room to him and said, "Sir, a shoe is missing from your horse's left hind foot. Shall I take him to the blacksmith?" "Let it still be wanting," answered the man; "the horse can very well hold out for the couple of miles which remain. I am in haste."

He rode forth, but before long the horse began to limp. It had not limped long before it began to stumble, and it had not stumbled long before it fell down and broke its leg. The merchant was forced to leave the horse where it was, and unbuckle the trunk, take it on his back, and go home on foot. And there he did not arrive until quite late at night. "And that unlucky nail," said he to himself, "has caused all this disaster."

Hasten slowly. ■

The Shoemaker and the Snake

Asia: Turkey

Gratitude seems to be a basic human trait, and reciprocity is a universal value. "The Suitor," a story from Malawi in the fairy tale section of this anthology, also involves a snake's refusal, out of gratitude, to execute a prisoner. "Padishah" was one title of the Sultan of Turkey.

Source: "The Shoemaker and the Snake" from *The Art of the Turkish Tale*, vol. 1 by Barbara K. Walker. Lubbock, TX: Texas Tech University Press, 1990. p. 178. Reprinted with permission by Barbara K. Walker, Curator of Archive of Turkish Oral Narrative.

Once there was a poor shoemaker. As he was walking along the street from his shop one day, he saw a man striking a snake, trying to kill it. The shoemaker said, "I shall give you five kuruş if you let that snake go without further harm." The man accepted this offer, and the shoemaker gave him the five kuruş. Thus the shoemaker saved the life of the snake.

Many years later, the padishah ordered a pair of shoes made by this same shoemaker. He gave the measurements and the description for the elegant shoes he wanted, and he said to the shoemaker, "If you do not make my shoes exactly as I want them, I shall have you strangled by the snake which is my executioner."

Try as he would, the poor shoemaker could not satisfy the padishah. As a result, he was thrown into the pit with the executioner snake. When the snake saw the man, it refused to touch him, for this was the same snake that had been saved by the shoemaker many years earlier.

In this way, a kind deed was rewarded. Indeed, a kind deed is never forgotten. ■

Heron and Hummingbird

North America: United States—Native American—Muskogee

pourquoi tale

Though more dignified than slow tortoise, the heron in this Native American version also proves the lesson that slow and steady wins the race. The version used here was recorded at the beginning of the twentieth century by John R. Swanton, who transcribed the stories as he heard them. I made minor changes to word order in some of the sentences to avoid awkward constructions that did not add stylistically to the story.

Heron and Humming Bird agreed to have a race. They said to each other "We will race for four days, and on the fourth day whichever of us first lands on the big dead tree standing on the bank of the river shall own all the water in the river." When the time came for the race, Heron started off, his great wings slowly pumping up and down, while Humming Bird darted forward swifter than the eye could see. Seeing flowers along the way he would zip over to them for a taste here or a sip there. While Humming Bird was going about tasting the flowers Heron overtook him. But Humming Bird had no problem catching up with and passing Heron. When he was a considerable distance ahead, he started tasting the flowers again. Flitting among the flowers, he suddenly noticed that Heron passed by once again, so Humming Bird took off once more and in no time overtook Heron. When night came Humming Bird was tired. Since he knew he was far ahead of Heron, he decided to go to sleep. Heron kept going and traveled all night. He passed sleeping Humming Bird, but when Humming Bird woke up he took off faster than ever and soon passed Heron again. They kept going, with Humming Bird staying easily ahead by day and sleeping each night. The third night he decided to sleep again. He slept all night but took off like an arrow in the morning. But when he got to where the dead tree stood, Heron had reached it first and was sitting on it. When Humming Bird got there Heron said to him, "We agreed that whoever got to the dead tree first should own all of the water. Now all of the water is mine. You must not drink water but only sip nectar from the flowers when you travel about." Ever since Humming Bird drinks only from the flowers. This is how it has always been told. ■

Source: "Heron and Hummingbird" from *Myths and Tales of the Southeastern Indians* by John R. Swanton. United States Government Printing Office, 1929 [Smithsonian Institution Bureau of American Ethnology Bulletin 88] p. 102.

Web Supplement Stories

Web supplement stories are located at **www.ablongman.com/lechner.**

Aesop's Fables

The Jay and the Peacock

This is one of those stories which bears further scrutiny. While one way of looking at it is that true worth goes beyond appearances, but the story also speaks to such issues as what constitutes worth as well as questions of group loyalty and of class distinctions.

From *The Fables of Aesop* by Joseph Jacobs. London: Macmillan, 1894.

The Milkmaid and Her Pail

Like the previous story, Jacobs thought this to have originated in India. *The Panchatantra* tale "The Brahmin's Dream" has a similar plot and the same moral. The moral, as told in the Aesop version, is part of everyday usage, even by people who do not know the story itself.

From *The Fables of Aesop* by Joseph Jacobs. London: Macmillan, 1894.

The Town Mouse and the Country Mouse

Rivalry between town and country (or big city versus small town) was as marked in ancient Rome when Horace, a champion of the agrarian life and a poet, recorded this story as it is today.

From *The Fables of Aesop* by Joseph Jacobs. London: Macmillan, 1894.

The Tree and the Reed

References to Aesop's fables often appear in literature. This story is referred to in Shakespeare's *Cymbeline* and is developed in Wordsworth's poem "The Oak and the Broom." A more direct alternate interpretation is that being flexible is conducive to survival.

From *The Fables of Aesop* by Joseph Jacobs. London: Macmillan, 1894.

Indian Fables—Panchantra

The Jackal and the War Drum

The first lesson the princes learn is that the unknown enemy holds far greater terror than the enemy one knows, and therefore, the best remedy is to face the unknown.

From: *The Panchantra* translated by Arthur Ryder. Chicago: University Press of Chicago, 1925.

Plan Ahead, Quick-Thinker, and Wait-and-See

This story, with a different moral, is also found among the *Jatakas Tales* (no. 114).

From: *The Panchantra* translated by Arthur Ryder. Chicago: University Press of Chicago, 1925.

Indian Tales—Jataka

The Merchant of Seri

Of the five-hundred-forty-seven *Jataka Tales* two thirds are about people rather than animals, and merchants representing the Bodhisatta appear thirty one times (Jones, 1979). This story is used to warn against "taking that which is not given," and promotes Right Action.

From: *Jataka Tales: Animal Stories* by Ellen C. Babbitt. Illustrated by Ellsworth Young. Prentice-Hall, 1940. pp. 13–17.

The Quarrel of the Quails

(Jataka tale no. 33) has a less optimistic ending than the analogous picture book version *The Ringdoves* by Gloria Kamen (1988), which was based on a story from *The Panchatantra*. The story seems to warn against harmful speech which creates disharmony, and promotes Right Speech.

From *Jataka Tales: Animal Stories* by Ellen C. Babbitt. Illustrated by Ellsworth Young. Prentice-Hall, 1940. pp. 30–33.

Fables from Other Traditions

My Own Self

Europe: England

Ruth Bottigheimer (1996) differentiates between fairy tales and tales about fairies. This didactic tale is one of the latter from England. Many an English nanny used tales like this as well as more scary ghost stories to frighten children into good behavior in the seventeenth through eighteenth centuries, a practice condemned by the late seventeenth-century English philosopher of education John Locke. The trick the boy uses suggested to Jacobs that this story may have been influenced by the story of Odysseus and the Cyclops.

From *More English Fairy Tales* by Joseph Jacobs. London: David Nutt, 1894. pp. 16–19.

The Old Man and His Grandson

Europe: Germany

No introduction seems required for this story, as any multigenerational family can identify with it. What seems surprising in this glimpse into the past is that the elderly were not always treated with as much respect as we imagine they were. Shel Silverstein's poem "The Little Boy and the Old Man" in *A Light in the Attic,* (1981) expresses a similar sense of loneliness and loss of respect as this story. The love and empathy children often feel toward their grandparents, as does the child here, is also reflected in many contemporary picture books such as Angela Johnson's *When I Am Old With You* (1990) and in Tomie de Paola's *Nana Upstairs & Nana Downstairs* (1973).

From: *Grimm's Household Tales* by Jacob and Wilhelm Grimm. Translated from the German by Margaret Hunt. London: George Bell and Sons, 1884. pp. 309–310.

Folktales

Introduction

What Are Folktales?

Folklorists have traditionally defined folktales as encompassing a wide variety of fictional narratives from anecdotes, nonsense tales, and formula tales (such as cumulative stories) to wonder tales, which are often referred to as fairy tales. Folktales express the wishes, hopes, fears, and desires of ordinary people and are usually thought of as orally transmitted. The stories did not all begin as oral tales, however, nor were they all first told by nonliterate people. The barrier between oral and written literature can be quite porous; oral tales are often adopted by writers but are *later* returned from the written to the oral repertoire. Romances of knights and their ladies were created by court poets of the Middle Ages and only later became part of oral literature—for example, "Sleeping Beauty." Stories of Reynard the Fox too started out as medieval literary satires of the nobility but were collected as oral tales of Reynard in many parts of Europe in the nineteenth and twentieth centuries. French, German, and Swedish folklorists include these tales in their collections. Renaissance stage comedies also became adopted as folkloric material and were collected by the Grimms from oral sources, as in the case of the story of Clever Elsie (Bolte and Polivka, 1963). Much of nineteenth century folktale collecting was characterized by the elusive search for authentic tales, unadulterated by written sources. Contemporary folklorists, however, such as Katharine Briggs, Linda Dégh, Richard Dorson, and Alan Dundes, accept the fact that the interplay between oral narratives and print is so pervasive that it is impossible to limit the study of folktales to "unspoiled"

versions of traditional stories. The story of the most famous and most influential folktale collection, the *Kinder-und Hausmärchen* (*Children's and Household Tales*), better known as Grimms' Fairy Tales, provides a good example of why it is difficult to identify "pure" traditional tales. When Jacob and Wilhelm Grimm began to collect German folktales, they espoused the ideal of preserving not only the stories but also the manner in which they were told by illiterate country folk. According to Jack Zipes (1988), a Grimm scholar, the Grimms hoped to show the greatness of the "true German spirit" at a time when German thinkers were looking for support for a unified German state and a stronger voice for the middle class. Though the Grimms were highly critical of earlier writers who had created sophisticated written versions of folktales, ignoring the oral style of the original tellers, their own work fell short of their ideals. After the 1812 first edition of their *Children's and Household Tales,* they began to reissue the stories with greater and greater alterations to appeal to a public who wished to use the books for teaching children the values of obedience, hard work, humility, cleanliness, and order (Zipes, 1988). The Grimms also began to "improve" on the stories by combining the best elements of several versions to arrive at an ideal that would have greater artistic appeal to a reading public. Thus with each new edition of the *Children's and Household Tales* the stories became farther and farther removed from their folk origins.

The Grimms did not even achieve their ideal of collecting the stories directly from German country folk. Many of their stories were told to them by their middle-class friends, several of whom were descendants

"The Clever Hedgehog." Illustrated by Norovsambuugiin Baatartsog.
From: *Mongolian Folktales,* by Hilary Roe Metternich. © Avery Press, 1996. Reprinted with permission by Avery Press, Inc.

of French Huguenots who had emigrated to Germany because of religious persecution. These middle-class young people enjoyed retelling the stories they had learned from their nursemaids or had read in books and related not only French folktales but also the literary fairy tales written by Charles Perrault, Madame de Villeneuve, and other seventeenth and eighteenth century French writers. The nursemaids in turn might have read the stories in the cheap little booklets called chapbooks that had been available to housekeepers, nurses, washerwomen, and other working-class people since the seventeenth century. In fact, even the Grimms' most productive informant, the wife of a tailor, was known to have been literate and was likely to have read stories as well as remembered them from oral sources (Zipes, 1988; Bottigheimer, 1996). Finally, the Grimms' collection became so widely known throughout Europe and the rest of the world that the stories entered the repertoire of nonliterate village storytellers and in turn affected the kinds of stories collectors were finding (Dégh, 1995).

Several factors account for the difficulty the Grimms and other nineteenth century folklorists encountered in collecting and retelling folktales in the authentic voice of the folk. Three of these were as follows:

1. The purposes of the collectors and retellers
2. The judgments of the collectors and retellers as to what constitutes a good story
3. The value the retellers placed on translating stories from what is effective in the oral format into what is effective in the written format

Purposes of the Collectors and Retellers Many collectors were seeking out the folktales of their own ethnic group or nation by choosing stories that fit their ideas of what represented their people. The Grimms belonged to this group, and other collectors throughout nineteenth century Europe and postcolonial twentieth century Africa followed their lead (Dorson, 1972; Okpewho, 1992).

Others collected the stories of "primitive" people to understand how human cultures have "evolved" (Dorson, 1972; Okpewho, 1992). Frequently, these collectors either had preconceived ideas of which stories represented a particular culture or were actually not told all the types of stories that members of the culture told each other (Okpewho, 1983; Berry, 1991). Bawdy stories were not told to colonial governors or to missionaries, while stories of tricksters such as the spiderman Anansi might have been collected out of proportion with their importance among the many story types told in West Africa because informants knew that European collectors liked them.

A third purpose of collecting and especially of retelling tales was to educate children. Morals were interwoven or added onto the stories, and the stories were altered to make them fit the morals. To make stories acceptable to parents, retellers omitted violent or sexual scenes from the more adult collections. The story of Sleeping Beauty as told by the Italian Giambatista Basile in his 1634–1636 collection of tales, *Pentameron,* has a (married) king rape Talia (Sleeping Beauty) in her sleep. Still sleeping, she gives birth to twins and is awakened when one of them accidentally suckles the finger she had pricked. The king, who actually loves her, returns, and the story ends happily (depending on whose point of view one takes) with Talia becoming the new queen. The jealous former queen proves to be ogrelike in her revenge, which backfires and ends in her own death. Perrault cleaned up the rape episode, having the princess wake and marry before she and the prince consummate the marriage, but Perrault kept the same violent ending except that the prince's mother takes the jealous wife's place. The story, which probably started out as a literary romance in the Middle Ages, entered the oral tradition after the Perrault version was published, and the Grimms seem to have known the story from both the written and oral versions. It was the Grimms who turned the tale into the charming and popular story that children have been enjoying since the nineteenth century (Zipes, 2001).

Wilhelm Grimm also rewrote the stories to create clearer moral messages with each new edition, according to Zipes (1988). Other retellers, such as Ludwig Bechstein in Germany, rewrote folktales to provide cheerful, wholesome, and whole family situations (Bottigheimer, 1996). In short, the folktales that were available to the reading public, especially to children, depended on the purposes of the collectors as well as of the retellers.

Judgments about What Constitutes a Good Story

The idea of what constituted a good folktale was based on the Grimms' *Children's and Household Tales,* which abounded in wonder tales. When collectors did not find exactly these types of tales, they often manufactured them (Dorson, 1977) or denigrated the culture's treasury of stories. This was the case in Africa, according to Okpewho (1992).

Many of the Grimms' heroes are brave, hardworking, and respectful. They frequently make use of magical objects and are aided by magical protection, but they are ultimately self-reliant and are willing to sacrifice their comforts to overcome great odds (Zipes, 1988). The wonder tale with its questing hero became the model for collectors in other countries, often making them ignore their own treasuries of stories. Some collectors even fabricated or imported stories from other cultures to pad their own collections with these "ideal" types of tales. Richard Dorson, in his introduction to *Folktales of England,* says that Joseph Jacobs became frustrated at the dearth of fairy tales to be found in England and "slipped across the border to lowland Scotland for selections, roamed the United States and Australia, and even adapted ballad stories into tales. He rewrote all his sources to please children" (Dorson, 1965, vii).

Translating Oral to Written Versions   Anyone who has tried to find new stories to retell for young audiences quickly becomes aware that the bulk of the stories in scholarly folklore collections were not meant for young children and do not make particularly interesting reading. Besides wishing to sanitize their stories, an important reason retellers such as the Grimms and Joseph Jacobs wrote stories in their own words was that there is a vast difference in what makes for an entertaining story in oral versus written forms. Isidore Okpewho (1992) and many others have noted that when early collectors recorded African stories, they took down only the bare bones of the plotline, ignoring the context and even more significantly the manner of the oral storytellers' performances. Yet in an oral storytelling the body language, eye contact, intonation, pauses, and pace of the storyteller are just as important as the content of the story. Contrasting written and oral artistry, Richard Dorson said,

> Novelist, essayist, biographer, and poet cater to private readers—except on occasions when a poet reads his pieces aloud, but even so he renders a fixed text, while the reciter, singer, or chanter continually varies his word. An author rewrites, edits, and polishes his composition before he sends it out to his readers. An oral performer does not worry about grammatical perfection, for his audience follows his

messages with a variety of signals. Pampered readers accustomed to fluency on the page are aghast to see how crooked and snarled are the sentences they have been listening to when congealed in type—whether delivered by an American president or a folk narrator. (Dorson, 1972, p. 11)

In evaluating folktales for use with children, it is important to look at the balance the author strikes between a polished literary style and one that has the immediacy of an oral tale. Skilled writers, such as Virginia Hamilton and Julius Lester, achieve this balance through dialog and judicious use of **dialect**—just enough to suggest it but not so much that it becomes hard to read—and through a variety of other culturally appropriate rhetorical devices. In the story "Wiley, His Mama, and the Hairy Man," Hamilton wanted the reader to "hear" the storyteller: " 'Wiley,' his mama tell him, 'the Hairy Man's got your papa and he's gone get you if you don't look out.' " (Hamilton, 1985, p. 90). Only the slightest elisions of sounds, as in "gone" for "going to" are used. One can almost hear Wiley's high-pitched voice as he promises his mama to follow her advice and taunts the Hairy Man, and Hamilton's description of the Hairy Man is made vivid through nouns and verbs rather than similes as in European fairy tales: "He had great big teeth, with spit all in his mouth and running down his chin." (Hamilton, 1985, p. 91).

The familiar formula opening "once upon a time" is typical of European fairy tales. Although folk tradition emphasizes action over description, fairy tales in written form are often descriptive and use figurative language to evoke images. "The Frog Prince" in the Grimms' *Children's and Household Tales*, as translated by Zipes in 1992, begins with an extended simile: "In olden times, when wishing still helped, there lived a king whose daughters were all beautiful, but the youngest was so beautiful that the sun itself, which had seen so many things, was always filled with amazement each time it cast its rays upon her face." (p. 2). The Grimms also often included rhymes, while the Russian collector Alexander Afanas'ev incorporated proverbs into his stories.

Retellers of West African stories use a call-and-response type formula beginning, repetition, onomato-poeia or ideophones, proverbs, songs, and formula endings to recreate the oral performance in writing (Berry, 1991; Owomoyela, 1997). Verna Aardema made generous use of ideophones in *Why Mosquitoes Buzz in People's Ears* (1975), as did Baba Wagué Diakité in *The Hatseller and the Monkeys* (1999). Diakité uses **ideophones,** onomatopoeic words for sounds we would expect in American stories, though the sound effects might be different, such as "kere té-té-té, kere té-té-té," instead of "zzzz" for snoring, but he also creates ideophones for movements that might cause almost no sound, such as "yolee, yolee, yolee—quietly, quietly, quietly" as the monkeys crept down from the treetop above the snoring hatseller's head.

Misapplication of stylistic devices can detract from the vitality of a story. Nineteenth century translators, for instance, often used European styles to describe "Indian princesses." Yet Native American stories are far more likely to use action and dialog than extended description, because it is the characters' actions that are memorable and that create the mood of a story. One is likely to experience joy, for example, when First Woman is stopped by the sight of strawberries in the Cherokee pourquoi tale *First Strawberries* (1993) by Joseph Bruchac, excitement when bat wins the ball game for the birds in the "The Birds and Animals Stickball Game" by Kathi Smith Littlejohn (Duncan, 1998, p. 66), and amusement at all of coyote's, hare's, Napi's, or Iktomi's outrageous actions in the many stories that feature these tricksters.

Where Did Folktales Originate?

In listening to or reading even a smattering of the world's folktales, one is struck by the similarities in the themes, plotlines, and casts of characters. Early nineteenth century researchers believed in a single source for the stories. They hypothesized it to be India and, starting with the Grimm brothers, looked for similarities among versions of stories as a way of tracing diffusions globally. The story of the turtle who wants to fly, for instance, which is found in the *Panchatantra*, can also be found in both Africa and Haiti. The likely path is the order given, since the *Panchatantra*, recorded around 200 B.C.E., was later translated into Persian and then Arabic (around 700 C.E.), and it was probably trade and travel between the Arab world and Africa that spread the story to Africa and from there to Haiti with the slaves. In other cases the direction of diffusion is not easily traceable. Richard Dorson mentions in *African Folklore* that for a long time he had espoused the idea that all African American folktales were of European origin until he came across an African version of the African American story "Rabbit Makes Fox His Riding Horse" (Dorson, 1972). Considering the widespread appearance of this tale in Africa (see, for instance, the Zulu "How Chakide Rode the Lion" among the trickster tales in this anthology), this story most likely originated in Africa. But stories did travel from the New World with repatriated Africans—freed slaves from the United States and the Caribbean—to Liberia and Sierra Leone in the nineteenth century (Hamilton, 1997).

The practice of comparing folktales became much more systematic when Antti Aarne, a Finnish folklorist, devised an index of tale types in 1910, which the American folklorist Stith Thompson revised in 1928 and again in 1961. The **tale type** index looks at recurring plots, characters, and themes. Cinderella, for instance, belongs to tale Type 510 A, which is a subdivision of the classification for stories of magic with supernatural helpers. With over 700 variants identified by Brigitta Rooth, a Swedish folklorist, Cinderella is one of the most widely traveled stories throughout Europe and Asia (Dundes, 1982). Folklorists also look at thematic elements within a story, such as Cinderella's slipper test of identity or Cinderella's promise to return home by a certain hour. These elements, called **motifs,** help to further identify recurring patterns and are important in comparing the distribution of the same tale type in different regions or comparing different tale types with some of the same motifs. Cinderella's glass slipper is found in European versions, but in Asian versions the slipper is not glass, and in some of the Middle Eastern versions she loses a bracelet, not a slipper. Cinderella's helpers and the place where she is first discovered vary with cultures too. The Chinese Cinderella, Yeh Shen, for instance, has a fish's bones for a magical helper and goes to the spring festival rather than a ball; the Appalachian Ashpet is helped by the witch woman on the other side of the mountain and meets the king's son at church; and an Iraqi Cinderella is helped by a red fish and goes to the pre-wedding party of a merchant's daughter where the mothers of bachelors inspect the eligible maidens. The Iraqi Cinderella also quotes proverbs and asks for Allah's blessings. Many of these are now available in picture book format, but the most influential of all is Disney's adaptation of Perrault's and the Grimms' versions.

Stith Thompson's six-volume *Motif Index* helps to identify these patterns. The motifs are much more likely to recur in cultures globally than are the stories in the tale type index (Aarne and Thompson, 1961). The same motifs can be found in stories with widely different themes, so it is important to look at the context of the story and the story as a whole before assuming that stories with similar motifs have the same meaning or origin. Transformations from beast to human or the reverse recur globally, yet the transformation can be a reward, a punishment, or release from a spell. In "The Boy Who Lived with the Bears," an Iroquois tale retold by Joseph Bruchac, becoming a bear is a positive outcome and an explanation for the origin of the Bear Clan. In the "Frog Prince" the kiss breaks the evil spell, and the frog becomes a human again.

Although worldwide diffusion of stories is rare, variants of story types tend to exist in regions, and the tale type index is invaluable in looking for variants of familiar European stories such as those from the Grimms or other folktale and fairy tale collections across Asia and Europe. The *Motif Index* is more useful outside Europe and Asia. As a number of folklorists have commented, a comprehensive tale type index for Africa and for the Americas has yet to be created. Two highly useful resources for teachers and librarians are the *Index to Fairy Tales* series, which was begun in the early twentieth century and covers all types of folktales, myths, and legends (the most recent edition was compiled by Joseph Sprug (1994) and Margaret Reed MacDonald's 800-page *The Storyteller's Sourcebook: A Subject, Title, and Motif Index to Folklore Collections for Children* (1982). Both these resources lead users to specific stories found in collections appropriate for children.

Why Do People Tell and Repeat Stories (Folktales)?

Unlike myths, which people tell to explain and reinforce beliefs of an existential nature, folktales are told to teach about everyday life, to reinforce a society's codes of behavior through positive and negative examples (e.g., kind and unkind sisters, rich and poor brothers, kind old man and selfish old man) to express deeply felt fears and desires, and simply to entertain. Tales of questing heroes overcoming the strong through wit, wisdom, courage, perseverance, and supernatural help and tales of unlikely or oppressed heroes winning the hand of the prince or princess through luck and because their heart is in the right place lift the spirit when life seems rough and unfair.

According to Jack Zipes, when you add up all the different heroes in the Grimms' fairy tales, the majority (113) are poor people and humble tradesmen, that is, sons and daughters of peasants, soldiers, millers, and tailors, rather than princes or princesses (although the two single largest categories were princes, 17, and princesses, 12). Zipes hypothesizes that the Grimms' choices might have satisfied their own need for justice and opportunity in a rigid class system in which the Grimms' own social and economic position depended on the whims of their noble patrons (Zipes, 1988).

Folktales have also been used as **allegories** to protest against tyrants, to identify social boundaries, and to frighten children into good behavior or to keep them safe. English nannies used stories of fairies, goblins, and bogeys to keep children from misbehaving, a practice that John Locke deplored, according to Bottigheimer (1996). In her humorous autobiographical stories of growing up in Ghana, storyteller Dorinda Hafner (1996) relates how her father told monster stories to frighten the children into staying in bed while he went out. Folklorist Robert Dentan (1999) describes a Malaysian ethnic minority's use of frightful stories of organ snatchers to keep children close to their family and village and to be cautious with strangers. (Organ snatching stories also circulate on the Internet in the United States and seem to have the same function: to keep young people wary in strange places).

Where stories are told and by whom also determine their purpose. When told within the family, they are a way of bonding among family members as well as teaching and entertainment. In a small, homogeneous community they might have the same functions and are also used to reinforce community values. West African stories, for instance, not only entertain, but also reinforce the value of cooperation, warn against greed, or demonstrate what happens when young girls listen to smooth-talking strange men, among other things. These stories, told as if to the whole community, are frequently directed at one particular person who has broken community mores, without naming the specific individual. Native American communal storytelling also has this function, according to Joseph Bruchac (1996).

Storytellers in cities, whether in Africa or the United States, tend to tell stories more for entertainment than for instruction and are more likely to draw on mass media sources: print, radio, or film and television. The latest medium of spreading stories, the Internet, abounds in anecdotes and jokes that highlight the frustrations of technologically advanced but alienating urban life. Today's folklorists, such as Jan Harold Brunvand, Linda Dégh, and Alan Dundes, are paying close attention to these new stories, many of which are old stories in new clothes. Dégh describes the use of traditional story themes and characters in disguise in advertising and television (Dégh, 1994).

What Are the Genres of Folktales?

There are several ways to categorize folktales—cumulative tales, fairy or wonder tales, noodlehead and other humorous tales, pouquoi tales, trickster tales—none of which is wholly satisfactory, as most tales exhibit characteristics of more than one category. Similarities in intent, similarities between characters, similarities between story structures, and similarities between plotlines are four ways in which people have tried to group folktales, but in most anthologies, this one included, these genres are mixed. The category of intent is further subdivided in three ways: didactic, explanatory, and entertainment tales. These, however, are overlapping categories; even a didactic tale must engage the listener to be effective, and explanatory tales are frequently meant to be didactic while purporting to offer explanations of nature phenomena. In this anthology the most distinctly didactic tales, the fables, whose primary function is to teach or to warn about human foibles, have been placed in a section of their own, but the **pourquoi tales**, also known as **why tales**, which may be meant both as explanations of familiar natural phenomena or customs and as teaching devices, are included in the folktales section.

Categories such as **animal tales**, fairy tales/wonder tales, trickster tales, and noodlehead tales have characters as the basis of their classification. These categories, however, also overlap. Fairy tales/wonder tales are tales of magic with human heroes, but often the heroes succeed because of magical animal helpers, as in the story "Puss in Boots." The protagonists of **trickster tales** use their wits to gain some advantage for themselves, to help others, or to get out of a tight spot. Like the best-known American trickster, Brer Rabbit, many tricksters are animals, as are many of their victims. Often the trickster's success is due to the victims' being noodleheads or numskulls, as in the story of the "Fox and the Crow," an Aesop fable. In **noodlehead tales** the protagonists seem to be impractical or take others' words literally but often turn out to be wiser than they appear, as in stories of the "Wise Men of Gotham," who act like fools to avoid an unwanted visit by King John (Leach, 1961).

Some humorous tales, such as **tall tales**, which are also called tales of lying, tell of the protagonist's unbelievable exploits and rely on the literary convention of exaggeration. **Jump tales**, which are humorously scary stories such as "The Golden Arm" or "Tailypo," rely on surprise. **Cumulative tales** are identified by their formulaic structures. The characters can be animals or people or both, as in "The Crow and the Sparrow" from India or the better-known "Gingerbread Boy."

Finally, folklore scholar Vladimir Propp (1968) identified two types of fairy tales; it was Propp who named these types of tales "**wonder tales**." One type, exemplified by "The Three Pigs," is the victim hero type; the other, exemplified by "Molly Whuppy" or "Jack and the Beanstalk," is the questing hero type. Propp's victim and questing hero categories, however, might not cover all the varieties of stories that people tend to label as fairy tales.

With no single satisfactory organization, the folktale categories chosen for this anthology follow the most frequently used groupings of stories in children's literature textbooks such as Huck et al (2001): cumulative tales, fairy tales, noodlehead and tall tales, trickster tales, and pourquoi or why tales. Included with the noodlehead and tall tales are the humorous supernatural tales. Animal tales, which often receive their own category, have been omitted as a separate category, but many tales in the other genres have animal protagonists.

▣ Cumulative Tales

Cumulative tales are **formula tales** in which the same event keeps repeating itself with more and more characters being added to the chain of events. In Aarne and Thompson's *The Type of the Folktale: A Classification and Bibliography* (1961), which gives a list of countries and sources where internationally recurring tales have been reported, cumulative tales have been assigned numbers 2000–2199. A glance at the descriptions and sources of the tales shows that they recur worldwide, and though the formula is the same, the plots vary: "The Gingerbread Man" and the songs "The Twelve Days of Christmas" and "There Was an Old Woman Who Swallowed a Fly" are three well-known examples of the cumulative formula. Because elements of the story are repeated and because they often include rhymes, these nonsensical tales are especially popular with young children. One of the first picture books published for children was a cumulative tale, *The House That Jack Built*, illustrated by Randolph Caldecott (1878). In some of the stories the chain of events builds up to a climax and ends with a surprise, as in "The Gingerbread Man"; in others the chain builds up and then unwinds until the original cause of the problem is resolved, as in "The Old Woman and the Pig," another popular cumulative tale. Both structures can be seen among the following stories.

There are also other type of formula tales, such as the endless tale, represented in this anthology by the Ethiopian story "The Storyteller" under "Noodleheads, Tall Tales, and Other Humorous Stories." In this story a king will reward any storyteller who can make him cry "enough!" The winner tells the endless story of an ant carrying away a mountain of wheat one grain at a time. Still another humorous formula is a chain involving contradictions (that's good, that's bad). Formula tales are amusing and help children build verbal and memory skills, especially if the children are invited to participate in the storytelling. Indeed, many of the cumulative tales in folklore collections were told to folklorists by children (Philip, 1992).

For picture book versions of the following stories, see Picture Books Related to the Stories in the *Allyn & Bacon Anthology of Traditional Literature"* on the Web Supplement at www.ablongman.com/lechner.

The Cat and the Mouse

Europe: England

Both this rhyming story and the better-known "The Old Woman and Her Pig" were collected by one of England's earliest folklorists, James Orchard Halliwell, in the 1840s. This is an international tale type (AT 2030). It is interesting to note that not only the chain structure but also the actual helpers are similar: Cat, mouse, dog, cow, and hay (often also stick, fire, and water) recur in cumulative tales from such widely different cultures as England, Hungary, and India. Folklorist Neil Philip (1992) points out that this sequence is found even in the Jewish Passover prayer book the *Haggadah* as a song at the end of the Passover meal. The final verse of the song runs as follows:

> Finally, came the Holy and Blessed One,
> and smote the Angel of Death,
> that slew the butcher, that slaughtered the ox,
> that drank the water, that quenched the fire,
> that burned the stick, that beat the dog,
> that bit the cat, that ate the kid,
> That Father bought for just two bits:
> One kid, a lonely kid.

—*The Passover Haggadah.* Translated by Saadyah Maximon. New York: Schulinger Brothers, 1960. pp. 63–64

Source: "The Cat and the Mouse" *Popular Rhymes & Nursery Tales of England* by James Orchard Halliwell. John Russell Smith, 1849. Reprinted by The Bodley Head, 1970. pp. 34–35.

The cat and mouse
Play'd in the malt house:

The cat bit the mouse's tail off. Pray, Puss, give me my tail. No, says the cat, I'll not give you your tail, till you go to the cow, and fetch me some milk:

> First she leapt, and then she ran,
> Till she came to the cow, and thus began,—

Pray, Cow, give me milk, that I may give cat milk, that cat may give me my own tail again. No, said the cow, I will give you no milk, till you go to the farmer and get me some hay.

> First she leapt, and then she ran,
> Till she came to the farmer, and thus began,—

Pray, Farmer, give me hay, that I may give cow hay, that cow may give me milk, that I may give cat milk, that cat may give me my own tail again. No, says the farmer, I'll give you no hay, till you go to the butcher and fetch me some meat.

> First she leapt, and then she ran,
> Till she came to the butcher, and thus began,—

Pray, Butcher, give me meat, that I may give farmer meat, that farmer may give me hay, that I may give cow hay, that cow may give me milk, that I may give cat milk, that cat may give me my own tail again. No, says the butcher, I'll give you no meat, till you go to the baker and fetch me some bread.

First she leapt, and then she ran
Till she came to the baker, and thus began,—

Pray, Baker, give me bread, that I may give butcher bread, that butcher may give me meat, that I may give farmer meat, that farmer may give me hay, that I may give cow hay, that cow may give me milk, that I may give cat milk, that cat may give me my own tail again.

Yes, says the baker, I'll give you some bread,
But if you eat my meal, I'll cut off your head.

Then the baker gave mouse bread, and mouse gave butcher bread, and butcher gave mouse meat, and mouse gave farmer meat, and farmer gave mouse hay, and mouse gave cow hay, and cow gave mouse milk, and mouse gave cat milk, and cat gave mouse her own tail again! ■

Talk

Talking objects and animals are not unusual in West African folktales. In "Gratitude," a noodlehead story in this anthology, objects as well as animals complain bitterly about their treatment by humans, and their complaints are not treated as anything unusual. Here, however, the divide between humans and other animals and inanimate objects is essential for the humor of the story, which, according to Courlander (1974) is meant to poke a bit of fun at established authority: the chief who judges all. A chief's stool is an elaborately carved seat, sometimes without arms, other times with a back and armrest, and is the functional equivalent of a king's throne. The surprise ending of this story makes it especially satisfying to tell rather than read aloud.

Once, not far from the city of Accra on the Gulf of Guinea, a country man went out to his garden to dig up some yams to take to market. While he was digging, one of the yams said to him:

"Well, at last you're here. You never weeded me, but now you come around with your digging stick. Go away and leave me alone!"

Source: "Talk" from *The Cow-Tail Switch and Other West African Stories* by Harold Courlander and George Herzog. © 1947, 1974 by Harold Courlander. Reprinted by permission of Henry Holt and Company, LLC. pp. 25–29.

The farmer turned around and looked at his cow in amazement. The cow was chewing her cud and looking at him.

"Did you say something?" he asked.

The cow kept on chewing and said nothing, but the man's dog spoke up.

"It wasn't the cow who spoke to you," the dog said. "It was the yam. The yam says leave him alone."

The man became angry, because his dog had never talked before, and he didn't like his tone besides. So took his knife and cut a branch from a palm tree to whip his dog. Just then the palm tree said:

"Put that branch down!"

The man was getting very upset about the way things were going, and he started to throw the palm branch away, but the palm branch said:

"Man, put me down softly!"

He put the branch down gently on a stone, and the stone said:

"Hey, take that thing off me!"

This was enough, and the frightened farmer started to run for his village. On the way he met a fisherman going the other way with a fish trap on his head.

"What's the hurry?" the fisherman asked.

"My yam said, 'Leave me alone!' Then my dog said 'Listen to what the yam says!' When I went to whip the dog with a palm branch the tree said, 'Put that branch down!' The palm branch said 'Do it softly!' Then the stone said, 'Take that thing off me!'

"Is that all?" the man with the fish trap asked. "Is that so frightening?"

"Well," the man's fish trap said, "did he take it off the stone?"

"Wah!" the fisherman shouted. He threw the fish trap on the ground and began to run with the farmer, and on the trail they met a weaver with a bundle of cloth on his head.

"Where are you going in such a rush?" he asked them.

"My yam said, 'Leave me alone!', the farmer said. The dog said 'Listen to what the yam says!' The tree said, 'Put that branch down!' The palm branch said 'Do it softly!' And the stone said, 'Take that thing off me!'

"And then," the fisherman continued, "the fish trap said, 'Did he take it off?' "

"That's nothing to get excited about," the weaver said, "No reason at all."

"Oh yes it is," his bundle of cloth said. "If it happened to you you'd run too!"

"Wah!" The weaver shouted. He threw his bundle on the trail and started running with the other men.

They came panting to the ford in the river and found a man bathing.

"Are you chasing a gazelle?" he asked them.

The first man said breathlessly:

"My yam talked at me, and it said, 'Leave me alone! And my dog said 'Listen to your yam!' And when I cut myself a branch the tree said, 'Put that branch down!' And the branch said 'Do it softly!' And the stone said, 'Take that thing off me!' "

The fisherman panted:

"And my trap said, 'Did he?' "

The weaver wheezed:

"And my bundle of cloth said, 'You'd run too!' "

"Is that why you're running?" the man in the river asked.

"Well, wouldn't you run if you were in their position?" the river said.

The man jumped out of the water and began to run with the others. They ran down the main street of the village to the house of the chief. The chief's servants brought his stool out, and he came and sat on it to listen to their complaints. The men began to recite their troubles.

"I went to my garden to dig yams," the farmer said, waving his arms. "Then everything began to talk! My yam said, 'Leave me alone!' My dog said 'Pay attention to your yam!' The tree said, 'Put that branch down!' The branch said 'Do it softly!' And the stone said, 'Take it off me!' "

"And my fish trap said, 'Well, did he take it off?' " the fisherman said.

"And my cloth said, 'You'd run too!' " the weaver said.

"And the river said the same," the bather said hoarsely, his eyes bulging.

The chief listened to them patiently, but he couldn't refrain from scowling.

"Now this is really a wild story," he said at last. "You'd better all go back to your work before I punish you for disturbing the peace."

So the men went away, and the chief shook his head and mumbled to himself, "Nonsense like that upsets the community."

"Fantastic, isn't it?" his stool said. "Imagine, a talking yam!" ■

The Young Gentleman and the Tiger

Asia: Korea

Similar cumulative tales in which various animals or objects are taken along and then work together to rid themselves of dangerous beings are told in many parts of the world, from England and Germany ("The Bremen Town Musicians") to India, China, and Korea. According to the collector and translator Zong In-Sob

(1982), this story reflects one of the Five Principles of Conduct of Confucianism: that of true friendship; the other four principles are loyalty to the King, respect for parents, harmony between husband and wife, and respect for elders.

Long, long ago a young gentleman went on a journey riding on a horse. Before he had gone very far a May-beetle came flying towards him. "Hullo, young gentleman!" it said when it reached him. "May I come with you?"

"Certainly," answered the young man. "Do come with me."

So the May-beetle alighted on the horse and they both rode on together. Then an egg came rolling along the road towards them, and it too said, "Hullo, young gentleman! May I come with you?" And once more the young gentleman answered, "Certainly. Do come with me." So the egg got on the horse.

The young gentleman, the May-beetle and the egg went on their journey on the horse. Then a crab came sidling along and asked, "Hullo, young gentleman! May I come with you?" And once more the young gentleman answered, "Certainly. Do come with me." So the crab got on the horse.

The young gentleman, the May-beetle, the egg, and the crab went on their journey on the horse. Then a rice-ladle came hopping along the road. "Hullo, young gentleman!" it cried. "May I come with you?" And the young gentleman answered, "Certainly. Do come with me." So the rice-ladle got on the horse.

The young gentleman, the May-beetle, the egg, the crab, and the rice-ladle went on their journey on the horse. Then an awl came hopping along the road, and said, "Hullo, young gentleman! May I come with you?" And the young gentleman answered, "Certainly. Do come with me." So the awl got on the horse.

The young gentleman, the May-beetle, the egg, the crab, the rice-ladle and the awl went on their journey on the horse. Then a mortar came tumbling along the road, and said, "Hullo, young gentleman! May I come with you?" And the young gentleman answered, "Certainly. Do come with me." So the mortar got on the horse.

The young gentleman, the May-beetle, the egg, the crab, the rice-ladle, the awl, and the mortar went on their journey on the horse. Then a rolled-up straw-mat came rolling along the road. "Hullo, young gentleman!" it said. "May I come with you?" And the young gentleman answered, "Certainly. Do come with me." So the straw-mat got on the horse.

The young gentleman, the May-beetle, the egg, the crab, the rice-ladle, the awl, the mortar, and the straw-mat went on their journey on the horse. Then a wooden pack-carrier came stalking along the road. "Hullo, young gentleman!" it cried. "May I come with you?" And the young gentleman answered, "Certainly. Do come with me." So the pack-carrier got on the horse.

The young gentleman, the May-beetle, the egg, the crab, the rice-ladle, the awl, the mortar, the straw-mat, and the pack-carrier went on their journey together, all riding on the horse. In the evening they came to a house in the mountains and knocked at the gate. No answer came from the house. So the young gentleman opened the gate himself and went in. In a room he found a young girl sobbing bitterly.

"What is the matter?" he asked. "Why are you sobbing?"

"There is a tiger in the mountain behind the house," she answered. "It has come down every night, and already it has eaten my father, my mother, my brother, and my sister. It will be my turn tonight. That is why I am crying."

So he said to soothe her, "Poor girl! Do not be alarmed. My friends and I can help you."

He called the May-beetle and told it to wait in the corner of the room and to blow out the candle when the tiger rushed in. He told the egg to go and bury itself in the ashes of the kitchen fire and burst out in the tiger's eyes when it came near. Then he posted the crab by the kitchen sink and told it to scratch out the tiger's eyes. He hid the rice-ladle behind the kettle, and told it to beat the tiger in the face. Then he put the awl under the floorboards by the door of the girl's room and told it to pierce the tiger's feet. He told the mortar to climb up on to the roof, and to throw itself down on the tiger

Source: "The Young Gentleman and the Tiger" from *Folk Tales from Korea*, 3rd ed., by Zong In-Sob. Elizabeth, NJ: Hollym International, 1982. Originally published by Routledge and Kegan Paul, 1952. Reprinted with permission by Routledge, Taylor and Francis, Garland Publishing. pp. 160–162.

to crush it. He sent the straw-mat and the pack-carrier to hide in the store-room, and told them to come out afterwards and carry the tiger away.

When he had sent them all to their posts the girl went to her room and lit a candle, while the young gentleman went and waited in the stable in the dark with his horse. Before long the tiger came down from the mountain and went into the house. It sprang into the girl's room and tried to seize her. At that moment the May-beetle blew out the candle with its wings. So the tiger said, "My dear girl, the light has gone out. I can't see where you are."

The girl answered, "You can't eat me in the dark. You had better go into the kitchen and blow the fire to get some light." So the tiger went to the kitchen and bent down to blow at the embers of the charcoal fire. Then the egg burst out and blew ashes in the tiger's eyes. "Oh, my eyes!" the tiger screeched in its pain,

and rushed over to the sink to bathe them in the water. Then the crab jumped out and gouged out the tiger's eyes with its claws. Blinded, the tiger rushed from the kitchen in a frenzy, and as it passed the kettle the rice-ladle jumped out and hit it violently in the face. Then it tried to get back to the girl's room, but when it stepped on the floor the awl pierced its foot. So it leapt out of the house on to the ground, and the heavy mortar jumped on to it from the roof, and crushed it to death. The straw-mat came and wrapped up the body, and the pack-carrier came and carried it off to the river and threw it into the water.

So the tiger was killed and the girl's life was saved. The young gentleman married her, and all his friends lived with them in the house.

—Told by Gim Du-Ri; Tang-Yong (1949). ◼

◼ Fairy Tales/Wonder Tales

Fairy tales are seldom about fairies, nor are they necessarily traditional tales. The term "wonder tale" more accurately reflects the stories' enchanted settings, adventurous plots, engaging heroes, figurative language, and capacity to evoke wonder in readers and listeners. Fairy tales have inspired writers as diverse as the anonymous ninth century Persian author of *The Thousand Tales* (the earliest known version of *The Thousand and One Nights,* or *The Arabian Nights*); Madame Leprince de Beaumont, the eighteenth century French aristocratic author of *Beauty and the Beast* (1756); Hans Christian Andersen, the nineteenth century son of a poor Danish cobbler and author of such memorable fairy tales as "The Little Mermaid," "The Steadfast Tin Soldier," and "Thumbelina"; and the contemporary American children's authors Robin McKinley (*Beauty,* 1978; *Rose Daughter,* 1996) and Gail Carson Levine (*Ella Enchanted,* 1997). After myths and Bible stories it is the wonder tales that have most frequently been represented in art, retold in poetry, set to ballet and opera, and made into movies. Psychoanalysts such as Freud, Jung, and Bettelheim have thought fairy tales' symbolic meanings to be

significant in the development of children's inner lives.

The typical fairy tale hero is young, often underestimated, and often deliberately kept from his or her rightful place in the world through jealousy or enchantment. The hero demonstrates merit not only through courage and perseverance but also through kindness, which is notably lacking in most of the other characters in the story. There are, of course, many exceptions. Heroes such as Jack in "Jack and the Beanstalk" and "Molly Whuppy" are more wily than kind. Some heroes show little initiative beyond performing a kind act toward an animal or acting respectful at the right time toward the right person. Though female protagonists most often exhibit these traits, such male protagonists can also be found. Even more surprising is the hero who acts more like an antihero. Ivan in "The Tale of Ivan Tsarevich, the Bird of Light, and the Grey Wolf" steals both the firebird and its cage, in spite of the wolf's warning not to do so, and cheats people who had treated him fairly in order to gain his ends. His chief merits are that he is brave and bold yet humble and respectful, and although he doesn't always follow advice well, he does

"Black Bull of Norroway." Illustrated by John Batten. This is a variant of "The Red Bull of Norroway."

From: *More English Fairy Tales,* by Joseph Jacobs. London: G. P. Putnam and Sons, 1922.

so when it really counts. As folklorists Iona Opie and Peter Opie put it, "The virtues which get rewarded are presence of mind, kindliness, willingness to take advice, and courage" (Opie and Opie, 1974, p. 16). Fairy tales are in many ways more worldly than idealistic and more a fantasy of wish fulfillment than a blueprint for right action. In most, however, after many hardships the good are rewarded and the wicked are punished. It is the essential optimism of fairy tales that makes them enduringly popular.

Fairy tales have recurrent themes as well as predictable plot structures. Russian folklorist Vladimir Propp, who broke down the plots of fairy tales into 31 steps or functions, identified two types of heroes: the questing heroes and the victim heroes. Questing heroes typically go out into the world to find something such as a treasure or a bride, or they go on a quest to rescue someone or to save their land from a threat such as a dragon. They are usually summoned, or they volunteer. Ivan in the "Tale of Ivan Tsarevich, the Bird of Light, and the Grey Wolf" is a typical questing hero. His father asks that someone retrieve the

Bird of Light, which had been stealing golden apples from his tree, and Ivan volunteers. It is easy to identify questing heroes, and both traditional and contemporary children's literature are replete with stories of heroes and their journeys. The hero's journey is likely to be an external one in traditional literature, the object of the quest being a literal prize. In modern fiction and fantasy the journey is often both an external and an internal one. The internal journey results in personal development and the attainment of wisdom.

Victim heroes start their journeys because of some harm that had been done to them. This might be an enchantment or a threat to their very existence. Hansel and Gretel were typical victim heroes. The various Cinderellas and kind sisters are also typical victim heroes. But what about stories such as "Beauty and the Beast" or its variants in this anthology, "The Red Bull of Norroway" from Scotland and the Appalachian "The Little Rusty Cookstove"? Technically, these are also victim hero stories, as in each one an interdiction or a promise is broken and must be kept, and the heroine is given to a monster. In "Beauty and the Beast" both an interdiction and a promise are broken: The father breaks off a forbidden flower, and Beauty fails to return on time to the Beast. In the other two variants a promise is given and must be kept. Soon, however, the victim becomes instrumental in saving an enchanted prince and, on losing him, goes on a quest to regain him. A mere kiss is not enough in these stories to break a spell. It is only through much greater effort and ingenuity on the part of the girls that the disenchantment is completed. In other words, they act more like questing heroes, and one might consider the stories hybrids.

Because of their poetic language and imagery, recurrent plot structures, and often universal themes, literary scholars have frequently turned their attention to fairy tales. Adapting Propp's structural analysis and classification of hero types, Steven S. Jones (1986) identified "Snow White" and its variants as "the persecuted heroine." He divided the story into two major sections, each with several episodes. In every variant the first section is constituted of three parts: (a) the initial threat to the protagonist due to jealousy (a mirror or the sun or another person warns the mother, stepmother, or sister that the heroine is becoming a beautiful young adult), (b) a hostile action against the protagonist (having her killed, lost in a remote place), and (c) an initial escape (the heroine is adopted by dwarves, giants, or thieves, etc.). The second section is divided into two parts: (a) renewal of threat as the jealous person discovers that the object of her jealousy is still alive, makes a second attempt with increased hostility, and succeeds against the life of the heroine and (b) a final escape in which the heroine is triumphant. Using psychoanalytic theory, Jones concludes that the heroine's triumph represents her successful initiation into adulthood. On awakening, Snow White is no longer a child but the bride of the prince and beyond the reach of her wicked step mother. Jones relates these stages to the lives of young girls as they move from childhood through puberty to adulthood, each stage representing a progression toward self-assertion and autonomy.

These analyses seem to apply best to European wonder tales. Among African wonder tales there seems to be less of an emphasis on the hero gaining as his prize a new kingdom of his own or on setting up her own household elsewhere. In African questing hero stories the heroes usually return to their own homes after having proved themselves, that is, having passed initiation tests, rather than becoming the rulers of new kingdoms. FEMK Senkoro, a scholar from Tanzania, reports that there is little psychological intergenerational tension in African hero tales; heroes return home to replicate the original family, as frequently the parents give the hero their blessing on his or her return and soon thereafter die (1996).

Other interpreters of fairy tales have focused on the historical and social conditions with which young people have had to contend as they moved from dependency to full autonomy. Marina Warner, a feminist scholar of folk literature, points out in *From the Beast to the Blond* (1995) that the frequent recurrence of the stepmother represents real family conditions of the past, when many children were raised by stepmothers because childbirth was often fatal. Warner also postulates that the word "stepmother" might have at times referred to mother-in-law and that many a young woman lived in her husband's home under the rule of his mother. The dire consequences in the stories to the stepmothers as a result of their cruel actions might have acted as symbolic warning to stepmothers and mothers-in-law.

When Antti Aarne devised the classification of stories into **tale types** according to plots and characters, he based his work on Finnish, German, and Scandinavian folktales, among which fairy tales are well represented. He classified fairy tales as Tales of Magic, and gave them the classification numbers 300–749. This classification was revised by Stith Thompson and was published in *Types of the Folktale,* 1928 and 1961. Folklorists use the classification system, identifying variants of internationally recurring tale types as **AT (Aarne-Thompson)** and a number from 1 to 2340. Cinderella, for instance, is classified as AT 510A. The system works best for the Eurasian continent and the northern half of Africa, but within that limitation it is valuable not only for folklorists but also for anyone who is interested in finding several versions of the same story from different cultures.

Stith Thompson's **Motif Index**, has greater worldwide applicability than does the Aarne-Thompson classification system, which looks at whole stories rather than elements or **motifs** of stories. One frequently recurring motif consists of transformations from animals into humans or the other way around, as in "The Tale of Ivan Tsarevich, the Bird of Light, and the Grey Wolf" from Russia and in "The Stepdaughter and the Black Serpent" from Turkey. Another frequently recurring motif is that of reviving a dead person or animal by reassembling its parts. This motif occurs in "Mshayandlela, Striker of the Road" from South Africa. Still other frequently seen motifs, often found together, are parents desperately wishing for a child, their getting a tiny child, and the child being swallowed by an ogre or giant as in the English Tom Thumb and the Japanese Issun Boshi (Little One Inch). It is interesting to compare the two, however, as Tom Thumb uses his wits to survive whereas Issun Boshi uses his valor.

Comparing stories that have the same tale type and stories with the same motifs helps readers gain a better understanding of the various ways in which characters have been presented and interpreted in different variants even within the same culture. Learning of differences among several variants of the "Tale of Ivan Tsarevich, the Bird of Light and the Grey Wolf," for instance, helped to solve for me the puzzling question of Ivan's strange behavior when he obtains the three prizes (bird, horse, and princess). In other variants the fact that he is learning to obey the animal helper's instructions is emphasized to a greater extent; his heroism in saving his brothers, who in turn kill him, is highlighted; and the enchanted nature of the animal helper, whom Ivan in turn helps to become human again, is also made clearer. Before I discovered these other variants from Scandinavia, Germany, Hungary, Greece, and Russia, Ivan's behavior was harder for me to understand.

Identifying motifs can also be done with children. Donna Norton in *Through the Eyes of a Child* (1998) models the classroom use of comparison tables of fairy tales from different cultures to help children identify universal themes and images that reveal people's wishes, desires, and fears. Such comparisons can also highlight differences in customs, foods, artifacts, and other details of the various cultures that tell these stories.

A final issue that must be considered regarding fairy tales is the way they are received. Concern has been raised over the last three centuries, during which fairy tales have moved from adult to children's domain about the kinds of values they present. In the eighteenth century it was primarily their fantasy element that was regarded as harmful because it led children away from rational thought. Today fairy tales are most often criticized for their violent elements and for their negative presentation of females as passive heroines. During the 1960s Germans began to reevaluate their own history and the effects the fairy tales might have had on children's values. Consequently, some tales were rewritten with less violent endings (Zipes, 1993).

Recently in the United States a conscious effort has been made to find fairy tales with strong women as role models for girls. Kathleen Ragan's *Fearless Girls, Wise Women, and Beloved Sisters: Heroines in Folktales from around the World* (1998) is a collection for adults that can be used to identify stories about strong women. Rosemary Minard's *Womenfolk and Fairy Tales* (1975) is an international collection of stories for children about brave, clever, and strong women, as is Alison Lurie's *Clever Gretchen and Other Forgotten Tales* (1980). Virginia Hamilton's *Her Stories: African American Folktales* (1995) includes a variety of folktales with African American women protagonists. Another approach has been to reevaluate the character of so-called passive female protagonists; feminist scholars have discovered that they in fact demonstrate much inner strength and resourcefulness (Stone, 1986).

In this anthology I have not included stories with wanton or unexplained violence and have included relatively few stories with helpless female protagonists. On the other hand, I did not edit out harsh endings or other details that one might not choose to use with children. It is up to the reader to select, interpret, and discuss with children some of the historical and symbolic reasons for these details. One might also discuss the effect of the distanced tone—"once upon a time"—of fairy tales on the reader's level of emotional involvement. An example of this effect could be demonstrated by comparing an oral retelling of "Hansel and Gretel" with Anthony Browne's picture book retelling of the tale in which the twentieth century setting makes the story of abandonment far more immediate and frightening.

The following stories were selected primarily for their variety in style and plot and for the diversity of their origins. Several variants of the same story type were also selected to afford readers the opportunity to compare the treatment of the same theme from different cultures. Three of the over 500 Cinderella variants (AT 510A) from around the world—"La Estrellita—Little Star" from the American Southwest, "Tattercoats" from England, and "Vasilisa the Beautiful" from Russia—are included in this collection. The two best-known variants, Perrault's "Cinderella or the Glass Slipper" and the Grimms' "Aschenputtel," are so readily available in collections and as individual picture books (e.g., by Marcia Brown and by Nonny Hogrogian) that they were not thought necessary to include. Though each of the five Cinderella variants features a victim hero, the girls show different levels of initiative, have different helpers, and perform different chores.

Another frequently recurring tale type in which a kind sister and an unkind sister (AT 480) receive their just rewards is represented here by five stories: "Kumba the Orphan Girl" (Gambia), "Mother Holle" (Germany), "Toads and Diamonds" (France), "The Twelve Months" (Czech Republic), and "The Two Stepsisters" (Turkey). "The Old Man Who Made Flowers Bloom" from Japan also belongs to this tale type. The three "Beauty and the Beast" variants (AT 425) are "The Red Bull of Norroway" (Scotland), "The Little Rusty Cook Stove in the Woods" (United States) and the "Stepdaughter and the Black Serpent" (Turkey).

Some story types have only a single representative among the fairy tales included in this anthology but exist in variants in many cultures. "The Suitor" from Malawi belongs to the grateful animals, ungrateful humans tale type (AT 160). This tale type is found in Europe as well, though it is far better represented in Africa. Other stories have motifs that recur several times among the fairy tales or other folktales in the anthology, including the Web Supplement, and in fairy tales and folktales elsewhere, such as the motif of resurrection from cut-up parts in "Mshayandlela—The Striker of the Road" and "The Tale of Ivan Tsarevich the Bird of Light, and the Grey Wolf"; a girl receiving a gift of three nuts that contain three irresistible items in "The Red Bull of Norroway" and "The Little Old Rusty Cook Stove"; or several companions, each using his special strength, succeeding in doing something extraordinary in "The Ship That Sailed on Land" and in "Mirror, Airplane, and Ivory Trumpet" (in Chapter 2 of this anthology). Whatever the tale type or motif, however, it is the kaleidoscopic combinations of plots, magical elements, and heroes with whom one can identify and the optimistic endings that keep these wonder tales alive.

For picture book versions of the following stories, see "Picture Books Related to the Stories in the *Allyn & Bacon Anthology of Traditional Literature*" on the Web Supplement at www.ablongman.com/lechner.

Kumba the Orphan Girl

Africa: Gambia—Wolof

The story of the kind and unkind sisters (AT 480) who through their behavior earn their just rewards seems so ubiquitous that it can evoke discussions of monogenesis (all stories having originated in one place) versus polygenesis (similar stories having developed in different cultures independently of each other). Compare, for instance, the following stories in this section to the story of Kumba: "Mother Holle" from Germany, "Toads and Diamonds" from France, "The Two Stepdaughters" from Turkey, and "The Twelve Months" from Czech and other Slavic traditions. The Caldecott Honor–winning picture book of the Louisiana variant, *The Talking Eggs* by Robert San Souci and Jerry Pinkney (1989), seems to be a blend of the African and French versions, but the African influence seems predominant. Each story maintains the basic plot: The hardworking, ill-treated daughter is sent to her death by her stepmother but instead meets a rich reward for her hard work, kindness, and respectful behavior, while the lazy daughter receives an awful "reward" for her laziness and meanness.

Kumba's behavior is explained by collector and translator Emil Magel (1984). Kumba the orphan girl represents the ideal Wolof young woman: hospitable, respectful, obedient, religious, courageous, and especially self-controlled and reticent. Her half-sister is the exact opposite. When Kumba the orphan meets unusual characters on her way to the Sea of Denyal, which represents death, she maintains control of her tongue and acts politely, but her half-sister shows no self-control.

Genevieve Calame-Griaule, a scholar of Dogon folklore from Mali, interprets a close variant of this story (1984). Her interpretation might shed further light on the symbolic meaning of this tale type, not only for West African cultures but for variants from other cultures as well. Calame-Griaule identifies the plot sequence as steps in a girl's initiation from child into mature woman. The initial sending away of the kind girl is the mother's (stepmother's) sending of the pubescent daughter to the initiation ceremony, which is held in a place away from the home. In the Dogon story the kind girl is sent to a lake to wash her father's bowl, and after passing all the tests of politeness, she meets the owner of the lake, who pulls her under the water and who then asks her to take care of her eggs. According to Calame-Griaule, this represents the initiation ceremony, which is the transformation from childhood to maturity—death of childhood and rebirth as a woman. The kind girl's treating the eggs correctly and the rich rewards she receives represent her being blessed with future fertility.

Source: "Kumba the Orphan Girl" from *Folktales of the Gambia: Wolof Fictional Narratives* by Emil A. Magel. Washington, DC: Three Continents Press, 1984. Reprinted with permission by Lynne Rienner Publisher. pp. 90–95.

In the following story the test seems to focus on controlling the old woman's beasts (one's own or men's animal nature?) and on creating something from nothing—food from what seem to be dry bones and a single grain of rice. On one level one might compare this to the skills women must develop: making the most of whatever resources they have. On another level one might again think of this creative act as the act of procreation.

There was a story . . .
Our legs are crossed . . .
It happened here . . .
It was so . . .

Once there was an old woman who had very many children. Her children were lions, hyenas, tigers, and all the other wild animals. She lived at the Sea of Denyal with her children.

In a village there were two girls who were both named Kumba. One of the girls' mothers was still alive while the other girl's mother was dead.

One day both Kumbas were tending their rice fields when two strange men approached them. When they reached the rice fields, they passed by Kumba the orphan to ask the other Kumba for some water, "Girl please give us some water to drink." But she replied very rudely, "Not from my hand and surely not from my mother's calabash. Use your own hands." "But we cannot use our hands," said one of the men. "Then go away," barked the girl. So the men left her and approached Kumba the orphan. They said, "Girl, please give us some water." She took her calabash and filled it with water. Then she politely handed it to the men. "Thank you," said the men, "and may a white chicken clap for you." They drank and drank until they were very full. Then they left.

When the stepmother arrived, her daughter told her what Kumba the orphan had done. The stepmother was very angry. She did not approve of Kumba the orphan using her calabash to give water to strange men. She yelled at the girl, "Now, since you were so daring, giving strange men water to drink, you must go to the Sea of Denyal and wash my calabash." Kumba the orphan picked up the calabash and began to cry and cry. She suddenly remembered all of the evil things that she had heard about the Sea of Denyal.

The next morning Kumba the orphan began to walk. She walked a long time until she reached the Sea of Denyal. There she saw an old woman who had one hand, one leg, and one ear. She greeted her and the woman said, "May a white chicken clap for you." She passed on, until she saw a tree that was braiding itself, branch to branch. She greeted it and it said to her, "May a white chicken clap for you." Further along her journey she saw two coconuts. They were trying to crack each other open by knocking into one another. She greeted them as she had greeted the others. She got down on her knees and said, "Salaam Alekum." They replied, "Alekum Salaam. May a white chicken clap for you." Even farther along the path, she saw a cloth laundering itself and then two cows attempting to carry each other. She greeted them and they replied in turn, "May a white chicken clap for you."

Soon she encountered an old woman. She genuflected and greeted her, "Salaam Alekum." The old woman replied, "My child, Alekum Salaam. What are you doing here?" The girl replied, "We were at our rice field when a man approached and asked for some water to drink. After I gave him water in our calabash, my mother sent me down here to wash it." "That woman, is she your real mother?" asked the woman. "No," replied the girl. "Then what is she to you?" "She is my step-mother. She is my father's second wife; she takes care of me since my mother is dead." "Alright," said the old woman. "Then hide your calabash in the tree and come and cook my meals for me." Kumba the orphan agreed.

She gave Kumba a piece of wood and a match stick. Then she brought a cooking pot and handed her a cup of water to pour into the pot. After the water was boiling, she gave her a year-old bone and told her to place it in the pot. Then she gave her a grain of rice to add to the mixture. It cooked and cooked until it was ready.

Later Kumba the orphan returned and opened the pot. To her surprise, it was full of rice and meat.

When the old woman returned she said, "Let us eat now. I have very bad children and since the sun is setting, they should soon be on their way home." They sat down and ate and ate until they were full. Then they drank until they were satisfied.

As it was getting late, the old woman told Kumba the orphan that it was time to go to bed. She advised

her, "Slightly stab my children with this pin through the mattress during the night. They will think that this bed is full of bugs. In that way they will rise up early in the morning and then you can safely return home." Soon after Kumba crawled under the bed, a hyena arrived and said, "Mother, I smell human meat. You must have been eating meat again." "I am the only one here, unless you wish to eat me," said the woman. "Of course I would not eat you, Mother," replied the hyena. Then the lion entered the compound. He said, "Mother, I too smell something." The mother replied, "It is nothing. Just go to bed. Soon the tiger returned and asked the same question. He got the same reply. "It is nothing. Now go to bed."

Soon they were all asleep in the same bed. Kumba the orphan was under it. She began to jab the lion with her pin. He yelled out, "Mother, there are too many bugs in bed." He got out of the bed and scratched himself. Then he got back into bed. Kumba then pricked the hyena with the pin. He cried and cried about the bugs in his bed. "Mother, these bed-bugs are terrible," he moaned. The tiger too complained about being bitten. He got out of bed and scratched himself, crying and complaining. All night long they kept getting out of bed and scratching and complaining. At hearing the first cock crow in the pre-dawn light, they all awoke. They gladly hurried out of their beds thinking that they were running away from the bugs.

When her children had gone far away, the old woman awoke Kumba. She told her to go and wash the calabash in the water. When the girl returned, the old woman gave her three eggs. As she handed them to her she said, "After you walk some distance, break this egg. But do not be scared. In this one egg there are many cows. There is an entire herd of cattle. After you go further on your journey, you should break this second egg. This one contains a flock of goats. Later, you should break the last egg. In it there are numerous servants." With that the old woman released the girl.

Kumba the orphan began to walk back to her village. After a long distance she cracked open one of the eggs. She saw a herd of cattle following her. She walked further and cracked the second egg. Out came a flock of goats. She walked further and then broke the last egg. Immediately numerous servants appeared. So they all walked in procession to the girl's village.

When they arrived at the village, all the people were very surprised. When her stepmother arrived she asked, "YOU, where did all this come from?" Kumba the orphan replied, "I brought it home from the Sea of Denyal." The stepmother was very jealous so she asked, "How did you get all these riches?" The girl explained, "When I went to the Sea of Denyal, I met an old woman whose children were lions and tigers and hyenas. She allowed me to stay there at her home for the night because it was too late to return to my own village. She gave me some wood and a match to light a fire. Then she handed me a cup of water, an old bone and a grain of rice. When the water was boiling in the pot, I added the bone and the grain of rice to cook. After it was cooked, I looked into the pot and saw that it was full of meat and rice. Then we ate. When it was time to go to sleep, the old woman gave me a sewing needle. She said that her children were lions, tigers, and hyenas. She ordered me to sleep under their bed and to prick them with the needle throughout the night. They complained about the bedbugs so they rose early in the morning and left the house. She then gave me three eggs and told me to break them on my way home. When I broke the eggs a herd of cattle, a flock of goats, and numerous servants began to follow me. That is how I got all these things from the Sea of Denyal."

Kumba's mother was so jealous that she beat her own daughter. Kumba cried and cried. He mother ordered her, "Now you too will go to the Sea of Denyal and bring home all those riches. You will do all those things that she did." So Kumba ran around the village telling everyone that she was going to the Sea of Denyal. "I am going to the Sea of Denyal. Do you see all the riches that Kumba the mother-less got from there? I bet that I will have *more* things since I have a living mother."

Kumba began her journey to the Sea of Denyal. She walked and walked until she reached the tree braiding itself. "My, what is this? Where have you ever seen a tree braiding itself?" she exclaimed. The tree replied, "You are very different from your companion that was here before. But go on, life is ahead of you." She walked on, until she came across the woman with one leg, one hand and one ear. "Now look at this strange sight," said the girl. "I know that if Kumba the orphan saw this she would have died." She yelled to

the woman, "Hey, One leg, one hand, one ear, how do you walk?" The old woman was too astonished to answer. Kumba then said, "Get out of my way. I must go to the water to wash and clean myself."

She walked closer to the water where she met the woman whose children were, lions, tigers, and hyenas. The old woman approached her and warned, "You, be careful. Your companion was here but she did not act this way." "I don't care about anybody here," screamed the girl. "That is the way I shall act," added Kumba rudely.

The old woman then asked, "Why do you not come and cook for me?" But the girl replied, "I am going to wash first before I cook for you." "Why do you not cook for me first? Do you not know that this sea belongs to me? That is why it is called the Sea of Denyal." "I don't care who owns this sea. I don't care about that," answered the girl. Then she went into the water and washed.

When she was finished, the old woman gave her a piece of firewood and a match to prepare the fire for cooking. "Is this all the wood you will give me?" questioned the girl. "How can I light a fire with only this one piece of wood?" When the fire was built the old lady gave Kumba a pot and a cup of water to put in it. When the water was boiling she gave her a year old bone and one grain of rice. "How can I cook a meal for you when you only give me this old bone and one grain of rice?" asked Kumba. The old woman said, "Just cook it, that is all." Kumba kept complaining like that till it was time for them to go to sleep.

The old woman handed Kumba a sewing needle and told her, "You must sleep under the bed because I have very bad children. If they discover you in their bed, they will kill you. When they go to sleep prick them through the mattress with the needle so that they will get up early and leave the house." The girl took the needle.

When the lion, tiger, and hyena arrived home they said, "It smells like human meat in here." Their mother replied, "It is only me that you smell. Now go to bed." After they were asleep Kumba stabbed the lion with the needle. He woke up and yelled, "Hey, these bugs are getting worse. They bite much harder than before." Their mother said, "Just endure it. It will soon be morning." Kumba then jabbed the hyena. He cried out,

"Mother, these bedbugs are terrible. I can't stand it."
"Just shut up. You are always complaining. Go back to
sleep," returned his mother. Kumba then stabbed the
tiger likewise, and he complained, "These bedbugs are
too much. I just can't sleep here." Before the first cock
crow all the woman's children were out of bed and running in the bush.

In the morning the old woman awoke Kumba and
greeted her, "How is the morning?" Kumba replied,
"Where are my eggs? You are supposed to give me
some eggs." The old woman gave Kumba her three
eggs. Then she told her, "After you walk a short distance you must break this egg. After a little further distance break this other egg. Then later you should break
the last egg." Without listening, Kumba grabbed the
eggs and began to run off towards her village. When
she was only a short distance away she broke all three
eggs at one time. Immediately there emerged numerous lions, tigers, and hyenas. As soon as they saw her

they attacked her, tore her up and ate her. The only
thing they left was her necklace. It lay on the ground.

A bird was flying by at that time and saw the necklace. It swooped down and picked it up. It then flew towards the village. There Kumba's mother was waiting
for her daughter to return with all the riches as Kumba
the orphan did. She sat in front of her compound
preparing her evening meal of steamed millet. The bird
soon arrived in the village and began to sing:

> THE GIRL WHO WENT TO THE SEA OF DENYAL,
> THIS IS HER NECKLACE!
> THE GIRL WHO WENT TO THE SEA OF DENYAL,
> THIS IS HER NECKLACE!

Then the bird dropped the necklace into the pot of millet. Kumba's mother picked up the necklace and immediately recognized that it belonged to her daughter.
At that moment she knew that her own Kumba had died
at the Sea of Denyal. ■

Mshayandlela—The Striker of the Road

Africa: South Africa—Zulu

This story is a blend of the victim hero and questing
hero types. The boy is only doing his job when
the cannibals, who represent a type of monster found
in folktales throughout Africa, attack. The fact that
the boy's chants have such power suggests that the
boy is more than a simple hero. He seems to have
knowledge that goes beyond earthly knowledge; not
only does he have control over his bull, he is also able
to restore the bull to life. The waters also part for him
and his herd, suggesting a mythic component to this
wonder tale. In the end, however, the hero's journey
returns him home, and his reward, bestowed on him
by his father, is the beginning of his own herd, an

important mark of wealth throughout east and south
Africa.

This translation by Brian du Toit from the Zulu
maintains much of the rhythm and poetic style of the
original oral tale. In particular, the repetition of the
name of the bull Mshayandlela in each line is a typical African oral poetic device. The boy's incantation is
emphasized by the word "say" rather than the more
colloquial "speak."

Once upon a time, a boy was herding. He was herding
a big herd. When he was herding, he would sit on top
of a big rock. One day, cannibals came. The cannibals
tried to climb and catch the boy but failed. They asked
saying, "Boy, how did you climb here?" The boy said, "I
climbed easily." When they said the boy must come
down, he refused. The cannibals then said, "Well, because we fail to climb, we shall take your cattle!"

Source: "Mshayandlela––The Striker of the Road" from *Content
and Context of Zulu Folk-Narratives* by Brian du Toit. Gainesville,
FL: University Presses of Florida, 1976. Reprinted with permission by University Press of Florida. pp. 35–38.

Cattle-raising scene based on cave paintings from Tassili, in the Sahara, painted around 5000 B.C.E.

Art by Janet D'Amato. Text and illustration copyright © 1971 by Janet D'Amato. From: *African Animals through African Eyes* by Janet and Alex D'Amato. New York: Simon & Schuster, 1971.

The cannibals rounded up the cattle and drove them away. The boy also came down from the rock and followed. After marching a short distance, the bull threatened them. This bull was big and its name Mshayandlela, "Striker of the Road." When the cannibals struck the cattle to make them move, the bull just stood and all the cattle stood. The cannibals said, "How are yours driven, boy?" The boy answered saying, "They go when I tell them to go." The cannibals said, "Say then, boy, and let them go before we eat you!" The boy then said:

Hamba Mshayandlela,
Amasela Mshayandlela,
Amebile Mshayandlela,
Zimthumbile Mshayandlela.

Go, Mshayandlela,
The thieves Mshayandlela,
Have stolen Mshayandlela,
They have captured him
Mshanyandlela.

The bull then turned and moved. All the cattle followed. They came to a ravine. Mshayandlela again stopped and refused to cross. The cannibals said, "Say, boy, before we eat you!" And again the boy said:

Hamba Mshayandlela,
Amasela Mshayandlela,
Amebile Mshayandlela,
Zimthumbile Mshayandlela.

Go, Mshayandlela,
The thieves Mshayandlela,
Have stolen Mshayandlela,
They have captured him
Mshanyandlela.

The bull then crossed over and the cattle crossed. Along the way, Mshayandlela kept on stopping because he did not know where they were heading. As soon as the boy sang, Mshayandlela would go. They went until they came to the kraal of the cannibals. When the cannibals tried to drive them into the cattle kraal, the bull refused. Then, the cannibals said, "Say, boy, before we eat you!" The boy said again. As soon as he said, the bull got into the kraal. The cannibals tried to stab the bull but it could not be stabbed. They said the boy must say again and the boy said, and the bull was stabbed. They skinned it until they finished. When they chopped it, it could not be chopped. The boy said and it was chopped. The meat was placed on top of the kraal.

The cannibals went to wash in the river before they ate the meat. They left the boy to watch it. At home remained the boy and a blind old woman. As soon as the cannibals left, the boy took Mshayandlela's hide and spread it on the ground in the cattle kraal. He collected all the meat and wrapped it in the hide. He struck the hide with a stick, singing, saying:

Vuka Mshayandlela,
Amasela Mshayandlela,
Amebile Mshayandlela,
Zimthumbile Mshayandlela.

Wake up, Mshayandlela
The thieves, Mshayandlela,
Have stolen Mshayandlela,
They have captured him
Mshayandlela.

The bull woke up. He then struck the cattle to go. They gave no trouble but just left. They came to a ravine that had much water. The water just split two ways and they crossed as Mshayandlela moved in front because he saw that the way led home. As soon as they crossed, the water came together.

When the cannibals arrived, they found the meat and the boy gone. The cannibals followed in haste. They saw him across the ravine. They shouted asking how the boy had crossed. The boy answered and said he crossed easily.

The boy then said do they want him to help them cross. The cannibals agreed. He plaited a long rope. He said all the cannibals must hold onto it. They held, and when they had held onto it and were in the water, the boy let go of the rope. All the cannibals drowned in the water.

The boy drove his cattle home. When he came home there was weeping because his parents thought he had died. He then told his parents all that had happened. The father then gave him the great bull, Mshayandlela, "Striker of the Road." ∎

The Suitor

Africa: Malawi

Although this international tale type (AT 160) of grateful animals, ungrateful human has been collected in Europe and appeared in the *Ocean of Stories* from twelfth century India, most of the stories listed in *Type of the Folktale* by Aarne and Thompson (1961) came from Africa. The fact that a good deed is rewarded with kindness by the animals but with betrayal by the human confirms the animals' view of humans. Commenting on human failings by presenting the perspectives of animals and even of inanimate objects seems to recur in other parts of Africa as well, as can be seen in "Talk," a cumulative story in which a yam complains about poor treatment by a farmer, and in "Gratitude," in which inanimate objects such as a dress and a mat refuse to come to a man's aid because people treat these things so carelessly. The story also includes an internationally found motif: an amazing cure effected by a "doctor" who is in fact being helped by an accomplice or by a magical item.

A long time ago a man fell in love with a daughter of a chief. Despite the willingness of the girl the chief forbade the marriage. The suitor was so frustrated that he decided to disappear into the bush.

Now, in the bush, he heard a call for help coming from a very deep hole. He lowered a rope into the hole and was very surprised when he pulled out a lion. Before the lion went on its way it said:

"There is still a man inside that hole but if you pull him out you will bring trouble upon yourself. I am grateful to you and one day I will repay your kindness."

However, the suitor heard louder screams, and lowered the rope into the hole again. This time he pulled out a python.

"Do not pull the man out of the hole," the python advised, "for human beings are naturally evil. I myself thank you, and will return your help when you are in need."

The outcast was left alone beside the hole, wondering about the advice he had been given.

Source: "The Suitor" from *Tales of Old Malawi* by E. Singano and A. A. Roscoe. Limbe, Malawi: Popular Publications and Likuni Press, 1980. Reprinted with permission by Likuni Press. pp. 67–68.

"It is impossible," he decided, "to leave a man to die when I have saved those beasts."

So for a third time he lowered the rope, and pulled until at last the man appeared. Both the suitor and the man he had saved went their separate ways.

After some time the suitor met the lion again.

"I wish to repay your kindness, my friend," said the lion.

"I will build a house for you."

And the lion brought poles, reeds and bundles of grass. He built a fine large house.

"Now I will fetch you a wife. Where is the girl you wish to marry?" asked the lion.

The suitor told of his love for the chief's daughter. The lion went to the village and, as the moon rose, saw the girl playing with her friends. He sprang, seized her, and took her away into the forest. And the couple, reunited, made a happy home together.

It was some years later that they were visited by the man who had been pulled from the hole. The man recognised the chief's daughter and hurried to the village with the news that he found the girl. A search party was sent into the forest, and the couple were arrested and returned to the village.

The suitor was imprisoned in a kraal, where he suffered alone for several days, until one night the python visited him.

"Why did you not heed our advice?" asked the python.

"Men can indeed be more cruel than beasts. However, I have a debt of gratitude to repay, and a plan that will help you. I will enter the belly of the chief, so he will become very sick. Only when you give medicine to him will he recover."

Thus the next day the chief fell seriously ill; many witchdoctors tried to cure him but none succeeded. The chief seemed to be dying when the suitor offered to give him medicine. Against the advice of his attendants the chief agreed to try the medicine. The python left the belly of the sick man, and he was well again.

Overjoyed to be cured the chief ordered the suitor's release.

"Let him marry my daughter and rule with her over part of my kingdom," he said. "And kill the man who so cruelly betrayed a friend who helped him." ■

Little One Inch

Asia: Japan

Issun Boshi, or Little One Inch, is a Japanese Tom Thumb (AT 700). Issun refers to a unit of measure that is close to an inch. Boshi means warrior. This little questing hero's story is one of the most popular in Japan. There is even a popular children's song about Issun Boshi's trip to Kyoto, the medieval capital of Japan (Seki, 1963). It is interesting to note that, as in this story, the antagonist in many Japanese folktales,

unlike those in European fairy tales, is not necessarily killed but chased away. Even in one of Japan's most popular fairy tales, "Momotaro" (Peach Boy), the wicked Oni, after being defeated, have their lives spared on condition that they'll never do any more wicked deeds, while in American retellings for children the wicked Oni are usually killed, as in Virginia Haviland's 1967 version in *Favorite Fairy Tales Told in Japan.*

Source: "Little One Inch" from *Folktales of Japan* edited by Keigo Seki. Translated by Robert J. Adams. © 1963 by the University of Chicago Press. Permission by University of Chicago Press. pp. 90–92.

Once long ago in a certain place there lived a man and his wife who loved one another very much. They had no children, but they wanted one so badly that they

"The One Inch Fellow." Illustrated by George Suyeoka.

From: *Favorite Fairy Tales Told in Japan* by Virginia Haviland. Copyright 1967 by Virginia Haviland (text). By permission of Little, Brown and Company, 1967. Illustration copyright © 1967 by George Suyeoka.

said that even a child as small as the end of a finger would be all right. One day they went to the shrine of Sumiyoshi-*sama* and prayed with all their might, "Sumiyoshi-*sama*, please give us a child, even if it is only as big as the end of a finger."

Now it happened that ten months after this, a charming little baby boy was born. The baby, however, was so tiny that it was only as large as the end of a finger, so they named him Issun Boshi, 'Little One Inch.' They raised him with loving care, but no matter how much time passed, he never grew any bigger at all. One day they decided to give him a sewing needle as a sword and send him away from home.

There was nothing else Little One Inch could do, so he took the rice bowl and chopsticks his mother gave him and set off. He used the rice bowl as a boat and the chopsticks as oars and started off for the capital city. After many, many days he finally arrived at the emperor's capitol. He walked about here and there, and after a while he stopped in front of a splendid big house. He went into the entrance hall of the house and called as loud as he could, "I beg indulgence, I beg indulgence!"

The people of the house thought it a strange-sounding voice and, wondering who it was, went to the entrance hall to see. There they saw the tiny little boy standing under the wooden clogs. "Little boy, was it you who called just now?"

"Yes it was; I am called Little One Inch. I have been sent away from home by my parents. Would you please take me into your house?" They thought him interesting, so they decided to take care of him. Little One Inch was small, but he was very clever. Whatever they asked him, he knew much more, and soon everyone was calling, "Little One Inch, Little One Inch," because they loved him so much. The daughter of the house, especially, came to be very fond of him.

One day she took Little One Inch with her and went to pray to the Goddess Kannon. On the way back, two *oni* met them. They were just about to seize the girl when Little One Inch drew the needle from its scabbard at his waist and brandishing it about, cried as loud as he could, "I don't know who you think I am. Well, I am Little One Inch who has accompanied the master's daughter on a pilgrimage to Kannon-*sama!*" In spite of this, one of the *oni* took Little One Inch and swallowed him whole. Since Little One Inch was so small, he could move about easily in the *oni's* stomach. The *oni* was so surprised that he coughed Little One Inch up and spit him out. When he did that the other *oni* grabbed him and was going to crush him, but Little One Inch saw his chance and jumped into the *oni's* eye. The *oni's* eye hurt so that both the *oni* ran away.

Little One Inch started home with the girl, who all this time had been standing to one side shaking with fright. Just as they set off, they saw a little hammer that had been dropped along the way. The girl picked it up, and Little One Inch asked what it was. The girl said, "This is a magic striking hammer. No matter what you want, you can strike with the hammer and you will get it."

"Then please strike me with it and see if you can make me grow taller, will you," asked Little One Inch. The girl waved the hammer and cried, "Grow taller, grow taller," and to their surprise Little One Inch's body began to grow and grow until soon he became a splendid young samurai. ■

The Old Man Who Made Flowers Bloom

Asia: Japan

In Japanese fairy tales it is not unusual for the hero to be an old man or old woman. In the popular story "The Tongue-Cut Sparrow," retold in a picture book of the same title by Momoko Ishii and illustrated by Suekichi Akaba (1987), the hero is also an old man, and in the story of *The Wise Old Woman,* retold by Yoshiko Uchida and illustrated by Martin Springett (1994), the protagonist is an older female. The good old man and bad old man theme is the most frequently recurring type of tale in Japan (Dorson in Seki, 1963). Some folklorists have included it with the kind and unkind sisters tale type (AT 480). The motif of the dire consequences of a bad or foolish person imitating the actions of a good or wise person fits the pattern not only of the kind and unkind sisters but also of many other folktales internationally. The transformations and the motif of help coming from a beloved's grave can be found in Africa and Europe as well, though the underlying themes are different: Consider Aschenputtel, the German Cinderella, who receives her dresses from the tree growing on her mother's grave. Creating beauty in nature might be particularly Japanese, but the motif of producing new life in the form of pumpkins by scattering the ashes of a beloved dog who had been killed occurs in a Chinese variant of this story, and the idea of new life springing from tears or blood also appears in European fairy tales.

Some of the details that give this story its Japanese flavor include the names Taro and Jiro, both popular Japanese names meaning first-born and second-born sons, respectively; the motif of being born from a peach, which appears in other stories such as "Momotaro"; the coins mentioned in the story, which were the most valuable denominations in Japan at one time; and the mild ending in which the bad old man is censured but no dire punishment is visited on him.

It is said that this once happened.

Long, long ago in a certain place there lived an old man and an old woman. The old man went to the mountains to cut firewood, and the old woman went to the river to wash clothes. While she was washing clothes, a huge peach came bobbing and floating, *ponpoko ponpoko,* down the river.

"Let another one come and I'll give it to Taro, let still another one come and I'll give it to Jiro," said the old woman. She picked up the peach, took it home with her, and put it in the big pounding mortar.

Soon the old man returned from the mountains. "Old woman, old woman, is there anything to eat?" he asked. "Yes, as I was washing clothes in the river, a huge peach came floating down the river. I put it in the mortar in the storeroom. You can get it and eat it," said the old woman.

"Ah, how delicious that should be. I'll have some of it," said the old man and went to get it. When he got to the storeroom, he was very surprised, more surprised than he had ever been before in his life. "Old woman, old woman, you said that this was a peach, but it is a young puppy," he cried with a look of amazement on his face.

Now it really was a puppy. The old woman said, "But I know that it was a peach that I brought from the river."

Source: "The Old Man Who Made Flowers Bloom" from *Folktales of Japan* edited by Keigo Seki. Translated by Robert J. Adams. © 1963 by the University of Chicago Press. Permission by University of Chicago Press. pp. 120–125.

"Well, no matter what, it is a puppy now," said the old man, and they both looked at it carefully and saw that it surely was a puppy. They kept it and cared for it very carefully, and it gradually grew bigger and bigger.

One day the dog spoke to the old man, "Grandfather, grandfather, please put a saddle on me."

"You are not strong enough to carry a saddle; I couldn't do that."

"It is all right; please put one on me."

The old man put a saddle on him, and then the dog said, "Grandfather, grandfather, please tie a straw bag on me."

"You are not strong enough; I couldn't tie a straw bag on you."

"It is all right; please tie one on me."

The old man tied a straw bag on the dog's back, and then the dog said, "Grandfather, grandfather, please tie a hoe on me."

"You are not strong enough; I couldn't tie a hoe on you."

"It's all right; please tie one on me."

Next the dog said, "Now follow me," and so the old man followed him. They went a long way into the mountains, and the dog said, "Old man, dig here." Then the old man took the hoe and the straw bag from the dog's back and began to dig. He dug for a while and soon had dug up a great number of *koban* and *oban* and *nibu* and *isshu* coins.

"Please put them in the straw bag and tie them on my back." said the dog.

The old man was overjoyed at the find but said, "You are not strong enough; I will carry them." But the dog said, "It is all right; please tie them on my back."

The old man tied the straw bag on the dog's back, and then the dog said, "Grandfather, grandfather, please ride on my back."

"You are not strong enough; I couldn't ride on your back," said the old man.

"It's all right; please get on," said the dog. The old man got on, and they galloped, *tontoko tontoko*, down the mountain. When they got home, he spread the contents of the bag out in the storeroom and began to count the *koban* and *oban* coins, when just then an old woman neighbor came over to borrow a hot coal to start her fire.

"Old man, old man," she said, "you are always saying that you have no money; where did you get such a lot of it?"

The old man told her everything that had happened, from the beginning to the end. The old woman said, "If he is such a good dog, please loan him to us for a day." The old man readily agreed and loaned her the dog.

When the dog was taken over to the neighbor's house, it again said, "Old man, old man, tie a straw bag on my back." Now the old man and the old woman were very greedy and said, "We borrowed you just so that we could tie a bag on your back." Then when the dog asked them to tie a hoe on his back and then get on and ride, the old man said, "We borrowed you in order to tie a hoe on you," and, "just so I could ride you."

So, with the old man riding, the dog set off for the mountains. They went for some way; the dog said, "Dig here." The old man took the hoe and began to dig, but he was very surprised to find that he could dig up nothing but huge snakes, frogs, centipedes, and all sorts of disgusting things like that. He became very angry and cried, "You worthless beast, why did you tell me to dig here?" Finally he killed the dog. He buried him beside that place and stuck a willow branch over the grave.

At home, the old man's wife was waiting for him to return, sure that he would be bringing the straw bag full of *oban* and *koban* coins, but when he came he looked very disgusted. "Old man, old man," she asked, "what is the matter?"

"You ask me what is the matter. Well, I'll tell you what's the matter. That dog was supposed to tell me where to dig—well he told me where to dig all right; right in the most disgusting spot!" When he told what had happened, the old woman, too, was very surprised.

Meanwhile the old man from whom they had borrowed the dog was saying, "I wonder what has happened to the dog we loaned our neighbor this morning; he hasn't returned it yet," and he went over to the neighboring old man's place to ask about it. There the old man angrily told him what had happened.

"Oh, what a pitiful thing to have done; you've killed my dog," he said. The next day he went to where the willow branch was stuck in the ground. When he got there, he saw that the little branch that had been stuck in the ground had grown up to be a big willow tree. The old man decided to cut down the willow tree and make a hand mill out of it as a memento of the dog.

When he and the old woman began to turn the hand mill, they were very surprised to find that in front of the old man *oban* coins came out and that in front of the old woman *koban* coins came out.

While they were turning the hand mill, the neighboring old woman again came over to borrow some coals to start her fire. "Where did you get all this money?" She asked.

"The willow which your old man stuck up where our dog was buried had grown into a large tree, so we took it and made a hand mill out of it. When we started grinding with it, all this money came out."

"Really! Well then, loan us the hand mill for a day, will you?"

"Please take it if you wish," they said.

The greedy old woman and the greedy old man borrowed the hand mill and began to turn it. When they did that, a terrible thing happened. In front of the old man, horse dung came out and in front of the woman cow dung came out. They became very angry. They took the hand mill and cut it up, then burned it in their fireplace.

The hand mill had not been returned, so the old man who had made it went to get it. The neighboring old man said, "That hand mill threw out horse dung in front of me and cow dung in front of my wife, and so we got angry and burned it up in the fireplace.

"What a terrible thing you have done. Anyway, do you still have the ashes?"

"I suppose they might be in a corner of the fireplace," said the neighboring old man, grudgingly.

The old man took the ashes and returned home with them. He climbed up in a tree and called out, "I am Japan's number-one ash-scattering old man!" Just then a splendid samurai passed by. He called, "Who are you up there?"

"I am Japan's number-one ash-scattering old man!"

"Then let's see you scatter some."

The old man scattered some of the ashes, and beautiful plum and cherry blossoms began to appear on the trees. The samurai praised him highly and gave him a great deal of money; then he went on his way.

As the old man and the old woman were counting the money, the neighboring old woman again came over to borrow some fire. "Where did all that money come from?" she asked.

"My old man took the ashes that he had gotten from your place and was scattering them from up in a tree, when just then a samurai came along. The old man scattered ashes for him, and he thought it was so pretty that he gave us all this money." The greedy old woman then asked to borrow the ashes and went home.

The greedy old woman told her husband to climb up in a tree and wait with the ashes until a samurai came by. He did so, and soon a samurai came by. He asked, "Who is that up there?"

"I am Japan's number-one ash-scattering old man."

"Then let's see you scatter some."

"Now I shall certainly be rewarded," thought the old man and began to scatter the ashes; but instead of beautiful flowers appearing, the ashes flew into the samurai's eyes, and he became very angry.

And so we must not try to imitate other people.

Katattemo kataraidemo sooroo. "No matter whether it is told or not, that is the way it happened." ■

The Mason Wins the Prize

Asia: China

The two women in the mason's life, his mother and his wife, both show great resolve in helping him; it is the wife's cleverness that saves her marriage in spite of the emperor's power to take her away from her husband. This version is similar to the Japanese tale "The Wife's Portrait," but it incorporates the Chinese Buddhist concept of the Western Heaven, which refers to the fact that Buddhism came from the west (India) as well as to the older belief that the land of the dead was to the west. The journey to the west is part of Chinese literary tradition with a seventh century monk's journey to bring back Buddhist sacred writings from India being the model for later stories (Scott, 1980). Perhaps this fairy tale reflects the influence of that tradition. The three precious things that the mason must obtain—a pearl from the mouth of a dragon, the shell of a tortoise spirit, and the golden-haired lion—are traditional in Chinese mythology and literature. One of the five beneficial dragons was the guardian of hidden treasures; the tortoise's shell is associated with the discovery of writing by the mythic first emperor Fu Xi; the lion is a guardian at doors with one paw on a ball or precious stone (Scott, 1980).

One day a magistrate sent for a mason to mend the roof on his house. The magistrate had a very beautiful daughter, who went out with her maid to watch the roof being mended.

The mason fell in love with her at sight and purposely cut his finger on a tile so that drops of blood fell upon her. When the young lady saw that the mason had wounded himself, she told her maid to fetch a piece of cloth and a needle to bind up his finger. The mason imagined that she had fallen in love with him. When he arrived home, he threw himself on his bed and fell ill, and every day became worse.

His mother, very worried by his condition, asked him what was the matter. The mason replied: "If you promise to do what I ask you, I will tell you; otherwise I must die." The mother promised, and the mason told her how he had seen the daughter of the magistrate and fallen so deeply in love that he wanted to marry her.

His mother said hesitatingly, "How can we arrange that? She is the daughter of an official and will never be willing to marry you." But the son had thought of a plan, which he explained to his mother. "You must take

Source: "The Mason Wins the Prize" from *Folktales of China* edited by Wolfram Eberhard. Copyright © 1965 by Wolfram Eberhard. Reprinted with permission by University of Chicago Press. pp. 34–37.

a wooden clapper and beat it in front of the magistrate's gate until someone comes. Tell them that you must see the magistrate himself, and then explain what I desire. You must go there every day until they can no longer bear the noise and will open the door."

His mother took a wooden clapper and went and banged at the door of the magistrate's house. This disturbed the servants so much that they begged her to go away. But she continued knocking until at last they asked her what she wanted. "I want to speak with your master," she said. Although they assured her they could arrange the matter themselves, she insisted on seeing the magistrate in person, until finally the servants, at their wits' end, had to let her in.

When the magistrate came and asked what she wanted, she related the story of her son's passion and illness, and begged him to allow her son to marry his daughter. The magistrate thought the matter over for a moment, and then replied, "That can be arranged, but first your son must bring me three precious things. The first is a pearl from the mouth of a dragon, the second the shell of a turtle spirit, and the third a golden-haired lion. If he succeeds, I will give him my daughter."

The old woman went home, and no sooner had she entered the house than her son was cured. He ran out to meet her, and asked, "Mother, have you seen the magistrate?" "Yes," she answered, "but there is no hope. He wants three precious things: a pearl from the mouth of a dragon, the shell of a turtle spirit, and a golden-haired lion. Only on these conditions will he give you his daughter." "That is easy," said the son. "I will go and get them now."

He started out toward the west, for he thought that such rarities were only to be found in the land of the Buddha in the western heaven. He had been journeying for several days when a dragon suddenly barred his path. He asked the dragon why he would not let him pass, and the dragon replied, "You are on the way to the land of the Buddha in the western heaven. If you promise to ask the Buddha a question on my behalf, I will let you go." "Just tell me what it is," said the young man, "and I will ask him." "You must ask the Buddha why the dragon at such and such a place, who has been morally perfecting himself for over one thousand years, may not ascend to heaven?" The mason noted his words, said good-bye, and continued on his way.

A few days later he was stopped by a turtle spirit, who refused to let him proceed. He begged the tortoise to let him go, since he was on his way to the western heaven. When the tortoise heard where he was going, he promised to release him if the mason asked a question for him. "Of course I will do that," said the mason, "if you will tell me what you want." "You must ask the Buddha why the tortoise at such and such a place, who has been morally perfecting himself for over one thousand years, cannot yet ascend to heaven?" The mason promised to do this, and the turtle set him free.

He went on for nearly a fortnight until he reached a temple, where he went in to rest. On the altar in front of the gods was a golden-haired lion. Since that was exactly what he was looking for, he went up and begged the animal to help him. The golden-haired lion nodded his head in answer, so the young man made an agreement with him to come on the day of his marriage and sit at his father-in-law's table. Then he continued on his way.

At last he arrived at the land of the Buddha in the western heaven and was granted an audience with the Buddha himself. He asked about the dragon and the tortoise, and the Buddha said, "The dragon cannot ascend to heaven because he has two pearls in his mouth, and all the other dragons have only one. If he spits out the superfluous one, he can ascend to heaven. The tortoise cannot ascend because his shell is too rough. If he can change it for another, he can come."

The mason was very pleased with these replies, because he had now found the three precious things he needed to marry the maiden. He thanked the Buddha and set off for home, stopping only to tell the tortoise and the dragon what the Buddha had said, and to receive from the former his shell and from the latter a pearl.

On his return, he at once delivered the two objects to the magistrate, and promised to produce the other on the wedding day. The magistrate could no longer withhold his consent and gave him his daughter. On the wedding day the golden-haired lion appeared, and all three presents stood on a table in the guest hall and were the wonder of the guests.

After the wedding the two loved each other dearly. The husband remained the whole day at home with his wife and could not be separated from her for even a quarter of an hour. One day the wife asked, "Why do you never work?" The husband answered, "Because I cannot bear to leave you." "Then," said the wife, "I will paint a picture of myself for you always to carry with you, and you can always look at me, just as if you were really seeing me."

From that time, when the husband went out he always took his wife's portrait with him. One day, when he had taken out the picture to look at it, there came a sudden gust of wind which tore it out of his hands. Farther and farther flew the picture, until finally it fell into the emperor's palace, where it was found by the emperor himself.

"Is there really such a beautiful woman?" asked the emperor. "You must seek her out, and I will make her my wife." The head eunuch searched high and low, until at last he discovered her name and where she lived, and brought her to the emperor. As she was leaving her husband, she consoled him, saying, "It is not so bad. We will meet again later. In three years come and see me with a large onion six feet long and a dress made of chicken feathers, and everything will be all right."

When the wife arrived at the palace, her face became as hard as stone and she refused to smile. When the emperor wanted to visit her, she told him she was ill. Finally his passion faded, and she was left alone in her house.

Time passes quickly. Three years went by in a flash. During this time her husband had sought everywhere for an onion six feet long, and day and night he sewed the dress of feathers. When both were ready, he put on the dress and went to the palace to see his wife, who burst out laughing when she saw him coming. The emperor noticed her beautiful smiling face and heard her happy laughter. Half pleased and half surprised, he asked, "I have not seen you laugh for three years; why do you laugh so much at this stupid man?" Then she answered, "If you were to put on a dress of chicken feathers and carry an onion more than six feet long, I would laugh at you too."

The emperor thought that that was simple and removed his fine robe and ordered the man to take off his feathered dress. As soon as they had exchanged their clothes, the wife called in the head eunuch and ordered him to kill the man with the feather dress. The emperor, in the feather dress, was too terrified to say a word and was beheaded by the eunuch. Then the mason became emperor, and husband and wife lived happily ever after. ■

The Two Stepdaughters

The two-volume collection from which this story comes is particularly interesting because the collector Barbara Walker heard these tales from storytellers within the last forty years. In other words, these stories are part of a living oral culture in spite of the fact that Turkey, like many other countries, has been very much influenced by print media and literary sources over the centuries. Persian and Arabic literatures have influenced Turkish culture, and Turkish children read Hans Christian Andersen, the Brothers Grimm, and La Fontaine (Walker, 1990). Nevertheless, oral stories still abound in the rural areas, and as this variant of the kind and unkind sisters tale (AT 480) attests, the stories have a uniquely Turkish flavor. Since many of the Turkish folktales have pious references, it is not surprising that one of the helpers offers to pray for the kind sister in return for her service to him. Note the opening formula and especially the typically Turkish closing formula. In comparing this story with the West African version in "Kumba the Orphan Girl" and the German "Mother Holle," it is interesting to note the differences between the tests the sisters must pass as well as the individuals whom they meet along the way.

Once there was and once there wasn't a woodcutter whose wife had died and left a young daughter to care for. Lonely, and troubled by the burden of rearing a girl by himself, he soon married again. Now, the new wife was a widow with a daughter of her own, and she brought her daughter with her. But the two stepdaughters were as different from one another as oranges are from pomegranates. His daughter was very kind and very beautiful, but hers was ugly, and, what's more, she was bad tempered.

The mother and her daughter were jealous of the beautiful one—oh, how jealous they were! And they

Source: "The Two Stepdaughters" from *The Art of the Turkish Tale,* vol. 1, by Barbara K. Walker. Lubbock, TX: Texas Tech University Press, 1990. Reprinted with permission by Barbara K. Walker, Curator, Archive of Turkish Oral Narrative. pp. 46–51.

were always at the father to take her away. At last he grew tired of their talking and agreed to please them. He took his daughter out into the forest and told her, "I'll be nearby cutting wood. Wait for me here."

But what he did was to get an empty pumpkin and tie it to a pine tree so that when the wind blew, the pumpkin knocked against the tree, making a *tum tum tum* noise. Then he went along home.

When her father did not return for her, the girl began to sing,

"My daddy who makes the *tum tum tum,*
Don't go away. Please let me come."

She sang and sang, and when there was no answer, finally she started home by herself. On the way, she met a baker with a great load of fresh bread. The baker said to her, "Where are you going?"

She answered, "I'm lost, and I'm trying to find my way home. And, uncle baker, I am so *hungry.* Could I please have a loaf of your fine, fresh bread?"

The baker said, "My girl, I have some work that you can do. Just come with me to my bakery and clean my workbench. If you do that work, I'll be happy to give you a loaf of bread."

Patiently, patiently, the girl cleaned that workbench until it shone from the scrubbing. "Very well, my girl," said the baker. "Here is your loaf of bread. May you eat it with a hearty appetite."

The girl ate the loaf of bread, and her hunger was satisfied. Then she went along the road, looking, looking. As she went, she met an old man with white hair and a long white beard.

"Where are you going?" The old man asked the girl.

"Oh, grandfather, I'm lost, and I'm trying to find my way home," she answered.

"My child," he said, "both my hair and my beard are just *filled* with lice. If you will take all the lice out for me, I shall pray for you that you find both good fortune and your way home."

"To find my way home would be enough, grandfather," said the girl. "Of course, I'll take the lice from your hair and your beard." And patiently, patiently, she found all the lice and killed every one of them. The old man prayed for her, and then she left him.

She went along the road, looking, looking, and suddenly she met a dog. The dog stopped his scratching and scratching, and he asked, "Where are you going, my girl?"

"Ah," said the girl, "I'm lost, and I'm trying to find my way home."

The dog said, "As you can see, my body is just *covered* with fleas. If you will pick all the fleas from my body, I shall give you a fine present. Besides, I'll show you your way home."

"To find my way home would be enough," said the girl. "Of course, I'll be glad to pick all the fleas from your body." And patiently, patiently, she found every flea and killed all of them.

"Now," said the dog, "here is a key. Take this key and go down the road until you come to a small hut. Unlock the door of the hut with this key. Inside the hut, you will find a yellow chest. Take the chest and, carrying it on your head, go farther along the road until you come to a bend in the road. Just around that bend, you will find your home."

The girl took the key and walked and walked until she found the hut. Unlocking the door, she went inside, and there indeed was a yellow chest. Carrying the yellow chest on her head, the girl walked along the road until she came to a bend in it, and just beyond the bend she saw her father's house. Now, the rooster saw her coming, and he called,

"*Üh-üh-üh-üh-üh-h-h!* The sister I love best

Is coming down the road with a big yellow chest!"

The girl's stepmother said, "How can she be coming, you foolish rooster? My husband left her deep in the forest! And where would she get a yellow chest?

But still the rooster crowed the news, and the woman went to look. There, indeed, came her stepdaughter, with a yellow chest balanced on her head. Her father was there, too, and he asked, "How did you find your way home, my dear? That was a long, long walk to come alone!"

"Well, my father, when I couldn't find you, I started walking, and I met a baker. He let me do some work for him; then he gave me a fresh loaf of bread and sent me on my way. As I went along, I met an old man with white hair and a long white beard. He had me clean the lice from his hair and beard; then he prayed for me and sent

me on my way. Next, I met a dog with fleas and fleas. He had me pick the fleas from his body; then he gave me a key and said, 'Along the road you will find a small hut. Unlock the door of the hut with this key and take the yellow chest you will find inside. Then go along that same road until you come to a bend in the road; just beyond the bend you will find your home.' I did as he said, and, indeed, there *was* a yellow chest. I brought it along with me, and as I came, I heard our rooster crowing."

Well, the father and the stepmother and the ugly stepdaughter said, all in one voice, "Open the chest!" When the girl opened it, they all saw that it was filled, just *filled,* with all sorts of jewels!

And oh, but the stepmother was jealous! "My own daughter should have a present like that, too," she said. "My husband, take *my* daughter out into the forest tomorrow and leave her where you left *your* daughter. She can then find the fortune that belongs to *her.*"

"Of course, my wife," said the father. And the next day, he took the ugly stepdaughter to the very spot where he had left his beautiful daughter the day before.

As soon as she was alone, the girl began walking down that same road. In a little while, she met a baker with a great load of fresh bread.

The baker asked, "Where are you going?"

She answered, "I'm lost, and I'm trying to find my way home. And I am *hungry.* Uncle, will you give me a loaf of bread?"

"My girl," he said, "first I have some work for you to do. You must clean my workbench. After that is finished, I'll give you a loaf of fine, fresh bread."

"Oh, am I supposed to clean your dirty workbench?" said the girl. "Well, I will not do it! You can *keep y*our loaf of bread." And she left without getting the bread.

Going on along the road, she met an old man with white hair and a long white beard. "Where are you going?" he asked the girl.

"Grandfather," said the girl, "I'm lost, and I'm trying to find my way home."

"My girl," he said, "if you will clean the lice from my hair and my beard, I shall pray for you."

"*Aman!* Am I supposed to clean the lice from your hair and your beard? No, I cannot do it. And you can just *keep* your prayer!" And she went on along her way.

Soon she came to a dog that was scratching and scratching himself. "Where are you going, my girl?" asked the dog.

The girl answered, "I'm lost, and I'm trying to find my way home."

The dog said, "As you can see, my body is just *covered* with fleas. If you will pick all the fleas from my body, I shall give you a fine present. Besides, I'll show you your way home."

"Oh!" Said the girl. "I cannot pick those dirty fleas from your body, and I *will* not! No, no! But I *will* take the present that you have for me."

"Very well," said the dog. "Take this key and go down the road until you come to a small hut. Unlock the door of the hut with this key, and go inside. There you will find a black chest. Take the chest and, carrying it on your head, go farther along the road until you come to a bend in the road. Just around that bend, you will find your home."

The girl took the key and walked and walked until she found the hut. Unlocking the door, she went inside, and there indeed was a black chest. Carrying the black chest on her head, the girl walked along the road until she came to a bend in the road, and just beyond the bend she saw her father's house. Now, the rooster saw her coming, and he called,

"*Üh-üh-üh-üh-üh-h-h!* The sister I detest

Is coming down the road with a big black chest!"

The girl's mother said, "Oh, you rooster! Why do you say such nasty things about my daughter?" But she went to look, and there indeed came her daughter, with a black chest balanced on her head. "Aha!" She said. "*My* daughter is much cleverer than *your* daughter. See how quickly she returned home!"

Her stepfather was there, and so was his own daughter. "Open the chest!" They said, both in one voice.

But the stepmother said crossly, "This is my own daughter's chest, her own fortune, and you have no business seeing what is in it. And she and her daughter took the black chest inside the house and closed the door and locked it. They pulled the curtains at the windows, too, so that no one else could see what treasure the girl had brought home. And then the stepmother and her daughter opened the chest.

Inside the chest, though, there were no sparkling jewels. Instead, there were the glittering eyes of snakes and snakes. Biting here and biting there, the snakes went about the business they knew best, and in less time than it takes to say so, both the stepmother and her ugly daughter were dead of their bites.

Hearing shouts and cries from inside the house, the father tried the door, but it was still locked. At last, he broke a window and went inside to see for himself. He could scarcely believe his eyes, for there lay his wife and his stepdaughter, lifeless, on the floor. And the chest was empty, for the snakes had scattered to all corners of the room.

He quickly unlocked the door and let his daughter in to see what he had seen. As soon as the door was opened, all the snakes slithered across the doorstep and out into the open air and away from there.

Well, the stepmother and her bad-tempered daughter had the fortunes they deserved. And the father and his beautiful daughter were left in health and happiness.

Three apples fell from the sky: one for the teller of this tale, one for the listener, and one for whoever will pass the tale along. ■

The Stepdaughter and the Black Serpent

Asia: Turkey

The elaborate and humorous opening to this story announces that it is a wonder tale. This is a recurrent tale type (AT 433) in which a bride is sought for a prince who is a serpent and kills all his would-be nurses and teachers. It is related to "Beauty and the Beast" (AT 425A), since the heroine must marry a beast, but it is also perhaps typically Turkish in that the heroine is more active in "taming" her beast than Beauty ever was. According to collector Barbara Walker, active heroines are not uncommon among Turkish folktales. In this story the stepdaughter, like Cinderella, is helped by the spirit of her dead mother, but she must still act courageously to carry out her mother's advice. Stories of girls who must tame and wed a snake prince come from all over Europe, but the largest number were reported from Greece and Turkey.

Folklorists Barbara and Warren Walker collected folktales throughout Turkey from the 1960s through the 1980s. Because rural custom prevents women and men from interacting in public, Barbara Walker could not accompany her husband to collect stories in rural Turkey, where the stories were often told in coffeehouses, a male domain. The rural women, however, came to her; and in Ankara, the capital, she was able to collect stories from rural people, many of them women, who came to the city to take jobs as laundresses, seamstresses, cooks, gardeners, and babysitters. A great many stories such as this one are told by women (Walker, 2000).

Once there was and once there wasn't, when Allah's creatures were many and it was a sin to talk too much—well, in those times there was a padishah (sultan) who ruled over a great kingdom. But, alas, this ruler had no son.

"Someday," he thought, "I am going to die, and my kingdom will be broken up. The winds will sigh through my abandoned palace." He made vows, offered sacrifices, watched entire nights in prayer. But the heavens remained mute. Then one day the padishah could restrain himself no longer. "O Allah all-powerful, if indeed You exist, prove Your existence; give me a son, if it be only a serpent."

Now, this was the hour when the gates of heaven were open, and the wish reached the divine ear. In nine months, nine days, and nine hours the padishah's wife

Source: "The Stepdaughter and the Black Serpent" from *The Art of the Turkish Tale*, vol. 1, by Barbara K. Walker. Lubbock, TX: Texas Tech University Press, 1990. Reprinted with permission by Barbara K. Walker, Curator, Archive of Turkish Oral Narrative. pp. 183–188.

bore a son, a black serpent. Nurses were called to care for him, but he bit everyone who approached him, and he thus killed one after another all the nurses who tried to rear him. Terror reigned in the country because the padishah's servants sought unceasingly the wives and daughters of the peasants to serve as nurses of the monster.

But there was a poor young girl, beautiful and wise, who lived in a cottage with her stepmother. The stepmother hated her and had long wished to be rid of her. When the padishah's soldiers passed through her village, even though all the other women of the village had hidden in the forest, the stepmother opened her door and pointed out her stepdaughter. "Come, my girl," she said. "It is an honor to serve as nurse to the prince. Go, now, and follow the soldiers."

The poor girl left without a word, but she knew that the road she would walk led straight to death. As they went, they passed by a small graveyard. "Oh, soldiers," begged the girl, "we are passing by the cemetery where my mother is buried, at the foot of those tall cypress trees. Please let me kneel at her grave."

The soldiers stopped, and the young girl threw herself down on her mother's grave. "Oh, Mother I have come to you," she cried. "In whom else can I confide my grief? Do you hear me, Mother? Do you hear me? My stepmother is sending me as nurse to the serpent prince!"

And her mother answered her from the depths of the earth: "Oh, my daughter, do not fear the black serpent. As soon as you arrive at the palace, ask for a golden box, held by two handles, and having the cover pierced by seven holes. Through these seven holes pour the milk of seven cows and present it to the black serpent. He will come and plunge himself into the creamy milk. Immediately close the lid and put the box into a diamond cradle. If other dangers threaten you, come again to me."

The young girl took comfort from her mother's words. She kissed the grave, and then she returned to the soldiers. They hastened to the palace, where the stepdaughter, following her mother's directions, tempted the black serpent with the milk. He entered the golden box and she placed it, tightly sealed, in a diamond cradle. The serpent prince grew and grew. When he was hungry, he found a new golden box full of milk, and, satisfied, slept again. Soon peace returned to the country, and the girl was taken back to her stepmother's cottage.

But the prince had grown large. In seven months he was the size of a seven-year-old. One day he said to his mother, who sat by him daily, "Mother, Mother, ask the padishah my father to find me teachers and books so that I may learn to read and write."

The padishah's wife went to find her husband. "My lord, our prince the black serpent wants to learn to read. He wishes teachers and books. What do you say?"

"My wife, there is no lack—Allah be praised!—of scholars in this kingdom." And the very next day a *hoca* [hodja, a teacher and preacher who is learned in the Koran] of ample turban and white beard was summoned to the palace. But scarcely had the black serpent left the box when he threw himself upon the old man and killed him with a crushing bite. One after another, scholars came to teach the prince, and one after another they met the same fate. Soon there was not a scholar left in the court, and the palace soldiers were sent out in search of the most humble village teachers. They came at last to the cottage where the young girl lived out her hard life with her stepmother.

The stepmother opened the door at once. "Ah, don't you know you have found here what you have been seeking? She who nursed the serpent is surely able to teach him to read." And she thrust the young girl toward the soldiers.

"You are right," said an officer. "No one at the palace had thought of that. Come, my girl, and teach our prince to read."

Again, as they went, they passed by the small graveyard. "Oh, please, sirs," she begged. "May I stop for a moment to kneel at my mother's grave?"

The soldiers, pitying the young girl, stopped their march, and the girl ran and threw herself down on her mother's grave. "Oh, Mother," she cried, "I have come to you again. To whom else can I confide my grief? This time my stepmother has sent me to teach the serpent prince to read."

From beneath the earth came the mother's voice: "My dear daughter, the serpent prince will do you no harm. Cut from my tomb a branch of the rosebush and a branch of holly. If he will not obey, or if he does

not read to suit you, strike him four times with the branch of the rosebush and once with the branch of holly. At the end of forty days, he will read. Go, my daughter, and if other dangers threaten you, come again to me."

The young girl did as her mother had directed. When the black serpent came out of his box, he recognized his nurse, but as he was raising his head, hissing, the stepdaughter struck him four times with the branch from the rosebush and once with the branch of holly. Then the serpent stopped before the open book and read on the first page the first letter of the alphabet: "Aaaaaa."

"Aaaaaa," heard the padishah, listening at the door.

"Aaaaaa," repeated his wife.

"Aaaaaa," repeated all their servants.

"Aaaaaa," repeated the soldiers of the guard.

"Aaaaaa," repeated the entire city. "Our prince is learning to read. Again this time we are saved."

The black serpent took good advantage of his lessons, and the young girl was again returned to her stepmother's cottage. "Back again, you worthless creature?" said the stepmother as her only greeting, and the same life began for the girl, full of abuse and misery.

Meanwhile, the serpent grew from day to day, and he sent a message to his father the padishah. "My father, I wish now to take a wife."

"My son, young girls are not lacking in my kingdom. Choose whomever you please."

And indeed this was done. There was brought to the young prince the first girl who pleased him. But in the morning they found her dead and drained of blood. Another met the same fate. In forty nights he caused forty brides to perish.

Again the guards of the palace went in quest, knocking at all the doors, ransacking all the villages. It was necessary, said the serpent prince, to have a bride each night. At last they arrived at the cottage where the young girl lived.

"Ah, my good sirs!" said the stepmother as soon as she saw the soldiers. "You know well that what you seek can be found here. She who has nursed and taught the black serpent is surely able to become his wife. Come, my girl; be on your way." And the woman was satisfied that at last she had rid herself of the young girl.

Again, as they went, they passed by the small graveyard. "Oh, please, sirs," she begged. "May I stop for a moment to kneel at my mother's tomb?" And the soldiers, knowing well the fate to which the girl was going, halted their march.

The young girl ran and threw herself down on her mother's grave. "My mother," she cried, "I am here again. This time they are taking me as a wife to the black serpent, whom I nursed and taught, and I shall die just as did the other girls whom he has killed all the other nights."

But from the depths of the tomb came her mother's voice:

"My daughter, do not fear. This time you will become a queen. Before entering the chamber of the black serpent, put on, one after the other, forty hedgehog skins. When the serpent approaches you, he will prick himself on the quills. 'Remove those skins,' he will say. 'Oh, my prince, remove your own skin yourself,' you must answer. When he has cast his own skin, you shed one skin yourself. When he has cast his fortieth skin, order him to throw them all into the fire, and do the same with yours. Then you will become a queen."

The young girl kissed her mother's grave and left with the soldiers for the palace. The servants there wanted to dress her beautifully for her wedding with the serpent prince, but she refused all the jewels and all the ornaments. "I wish only," she said, "forty hedgehog skins."

When she had dressed, they led her to the bridal chamber. The black serpent threw himself upon her, but he stopped short. "Bride, take off that skin full of quills."

"Prince, take off your own skin and I shall remove mine."

And for each snake skin which fell, the girl in her turn removed one hedgehog skin. Finally came the fortieth skin.

"Now gather up your skins and throw them into the fire." she said. The fire leaped up and a great light filled the room. The black serpent had been transformed into a young prince as handsome as the fourteenth of the moon. Then the girl threw into the flames the forty hedgehog skins and she became more beautiful than the moon itself.

When the young couple went out of the bridal chamber, the padishah nearly fainted with joy. And as he was very old, he at once gave his throne to his son and to his son's wife. The realm from that time on dwelt in peace.

Only the stepmother of the young queen did not get her just reward. In spite, she threw herself into the densest underbrush of the forest, and all that could be seen was a yellow serpent gliding among the dead leaves. ∎

 # Mother Holle

Europe: Germany

In spite of the cultural and geographic differences between Gambia and Germany, there are remarkable similarities between "Kumba the Orphan Girl" and

Source: "Mother Holle" from *Grimm's Household Tales* by Jacob and Wilhelm Grimm. Translated from the German by Margaret Hunt. London: George Bell and Sons, 1884. pp. 104–107.

"Mother Holle," not only in basic kind and unkind sisters plot (AT 480) but also in symbolism. In both stories the protagonists are girls sent to or into water, implying that they are sent to their deaths. Instead, they return. In both "Kumba the Orphan Girl and "Mother Holle" the woman at the end of their journey represents more than a powerful old woman; she seems to be a force of nature. In "Kumba the Orphan Girl" she is the mother of all the wild beasts. In "Mother Holle" her featherbed is the source of snow on earth. Respect for elders is emphasized in all of the kind and unkind sisters tales (see also the Turkish tale "The Two Stepsisters," and the Czech tale "The Twelve Months," and the French tale "Toads and Diamond" on the Web supplement. "Mother Holle" is one of the most frequently retold stories in German fairy tale collections for children.

There have been numerous illustrated editions of the Grimms' fairy tales for children since the original *Kinder-und Hausmärchen* first appeared in 1812; the first one designed for popular appeal was the English *Grimms' Popular Stories* translated by Edgar Taylor and illustrated by George Cruikshank in 1823.

There was once a widow who had two daughters—one of whom was pretty and industrious, whilst the other was ugly and idle. But she was much fonder of the ugly and idle one, because she was her own daughter; and the other, who was a step-daughter, was obliged to do all the work, and be the Cinderella of the house. Every day the poor girl had to sit by a well, in the highway, and spin and spin till her fingers bled.

Now it happened that one day the shuttle was marked with her blood, so she dipped it in the well, to wash the mark off: but it dropped out of her hand and fell to the bottom. She began to weep, and ran to her step-mother and told her of the mishap. But she scolded her sharply, and ordered mercilessly, "Since you have let the shuttle fall in, you must fetch it out again."

So the girl went back to the well, and did not know what to do, and in her heart's sorrow, she jumped into the well to get the shuttle. She lost her senses, and when she awoke and came to herself again, she was in a lovely meadow where the sun was shining and many thousands of flowers were growing. Along this meadow she went, and at last came to a baker's oven full of bread, and the bread cried out, "Oh, take me out! take me out! or I shall burn; I have been baked a long time!" So she went up to it, and took out all the loaves one after another with the bread-shovel. After that she went on till she came to a tree covered with apples, which called out to her, "Oh, shake me! shake

me! we apples are all ripe!" So she shook the tree till the apples fell like rain, and went on shaking till they were all down, and when she had gathered them into a heap, she went on her way.

At last she came to a little house, out of which an old woman peeped, but she had such large teeth that the girl was frightened, and was about to run away.

But the old woman called out to her, "What are you afraid of, dear child? Stay with me; if you will do all the work in the house properly, you shall be the better for it. Only you must take care to make my bed well, and to shake it thoroughly till the feathers fly—for then there is snow on the earth. I am Mother Holle."

As the old woman spoke so kindly to her, the girl took courage and agreed to enter her service. She attended to everything to the satisfaction of her mistress, and always shook her bed so vigorously that the feathers flew about like snow-flakes. So she had a pleasant life with her, with never an angry word, and boiled or roast meat every day.

She stayed some time with Mother Holle, and then she became sad. At first she did not know what was the matter with her, but found at length that it was homesickness. Although she was many thousand times better off here than at home, still she had a longing to be there. At last she said to the old woman, "I have a longing for home, and however well off I am down here, I cannot stay any longer. I must go up again to my own people." Mother Holle said, "I am pleased that you long for your home again, and as you have served me so truly, I myself will take you up again." Thereupon she took her by the hand, and led her to a large door. The door was opened, and just as the maiden was standing beneath the doorway, a heavy shower of golden rain fell, and all the gold stuck to her, so that she was completely covered over with it.

"You shall have that because you are so industrious," said Mother Holle, and at the same time she gave her back the shuttle which she had let fall into the well. Thereupon the door closed, and the maiden found herself up above upon the earth, not far from her mother's house.

And as she went into the yard the cock was standing by the well, and cried—

"Cock-a-doodle-doo!
Your golden girl's come back to you!"

So she went in to her mother, and as she arrived thus covered with gold, she was well received, both by her and her sister.

The girl told all that had happened to her, and as soon as the mother heard how she had come by so much wealth, she was very anxious to obtain the same good luck for the ugly and lazy daughter. She had to seat herself by the well and spin, and in order that her shuttle might be stained with blood, she stuck her hand into a thorn bush and pricked her finger. Then she threw her shuttle into the well, and jumped in after it.

She came, like the other, to the beautiful meadow and walked along the very same path. When she got to the oven the bread again cried, "Oh, take me out! take me out! Or I shall burn, I have been baked a long time!" But the lazy thing answered, "As if I had any wish to make myself dirty?" and on she went. Soon she came to the apple tree, which cried, "Oh, shake me! shake me! we apples are all ripe!" But she answered, "I like that! one of you might fall on my head," and so went on.

When she came to Mother Holle's house she was not afraid, for she had already heard of her big teeth, and she hired herself to her immediately.

The first day she forced herself to work diligently, and obeyed Mother Holle when she told her to do anything, for she was thinking of all the gold that she would give her. But on the second day she began to be lazy, and on the third day still more so, and then she would not get up in the morning at all. Neither did she make Mother Holle's bed as she ought, and did not shake it so as to make the feathers fly up. Mother Holle was soon tired of this, and gave her notice to leave. The lazy girl was willing enough to go, and thought that now the golden rain would come. Mother Holle led her to the great door, but while she was standing beneath it, instead of the gold a big kettleful of pitch was emptied over her. "That is the reward of your service," said Mother Holle, and shut the door.

So the lazy girl went home, but she was quite covered with pitch, and the cock by the well, as soon as he saw her, cried out—

"Cock-a-doodle-doo!
Your pitchy girl's come back to you!"

And the pitch stuck fast to her, and could not be got off as long as she lived. ■

The Red Bull of Norroway

Europe: Scotland

This simple variant of "Beauty and the Beast" (AT 425A) includes the essential theme of a young girl agreeing to marry a beast and discovering that he is a beautiful human being after all. In this version, as in the Greek myth of Eros and Psyche, the discovery comes before she makes a supreme effort to be reunited with him. Other motifs in this story, such as the three sisters bragging about the man they would marry and the heroine bribing the hero's false bride in order to regain

his love, appear in other stories as well, including the more humorous "The Little Rusty Cook-stove" from the Appalachians, included in this anthology.

As in many fairy tales, the virtuous sister is also the beautiful one; the mean, selfish, or treacherous sisters are ugly. Some people, especially in the past, have literally believed that inner beauty is reflected in external appearances; now most see these descriptions as symbolic. James Orchard Halliwell, who included "The Red Bull of Norroway" in one of the earliest English collections of folktales in 1849, said that this story was mentioned in a sixteenth century Scottish book, *The Complaynt of Scotland*

Source: "The Red Bull of Norroway" from *Popular Rhymes & Nursery Tales of England* by James O. Halliwell. London: John Russell Smith, 1849; The Bodley Head, 1970. pp. 49–52.

To wilder measures next the turn;
The black black bull of Norroway!
Sudden the tapers cease to burn,
The minstrels cease to play!

Once upon a time there lived a king who had three daughters; the two eldest were proud and ugly, but the youngest was the gentlest and most beautiful creature ever seen, and the pride not only of her father and mother, but of all in the land. As it fell out, the three princesses were talking one night of whom they would marry. "I will have no one lower than a king," said the eldest princess; the second would take a prince, or a great duke even. "Pho, pho," said the youngest laughing, "you are both so proud; now, I would be content with the Red Bull o' Norroway." Well, they thought no more of the matter till the next morning, when, as they sat at breakfast, they heard the most dreadful bellowing at the door, and what should it be but the red bull come for his bride. You may be sure they were all terribly frightened at this, for the red bull was one of the most horrible creatures ever seen in the world. And the king and queen did not know how to save their daughter. At last they determined to send him off with the old henwife. So they put her on his back, and away he went with her till he came to a great black forest, when, throwing her down, he returned, roaring louder and more frightfully than ever. They then sent, one by one, all the servants, then the two eldest princesses; but not one of them met with any better treatment than the old henwife, and at last they were forced to send their youngest and favourite child.

On traveled the lady and the bull through many dreadful forests and lonely wastes, till they came at last to a noble castle, where a large company was assembled. The lord of the castle pressed them to stay, though much he wondered at the lovely princess and her strange companion. When they went in among the company, the princess espied a pin sticking in the bull's hide, which she pull out, and, to the surprise of all, there appeared not a frightful wild beast, but one of the most beautiful princes ever beheld. You may believe how delighted the princess was to see him fall at her feet, and thank her for breaking his cruel enchantment. There were great rejoicings in the castle at this; but, alas! at that moment he suddenly disappeared, and though

every place was sought, he was nowhere to be found. The princess, however, determined to seek through all the world for him, and many weary ways she went, but nothing could she hear of her lover. Travelling once through a dark wood, she lost her way, and as night was coming on, she thought she must now certainly die of cold and hunger; but seeing a light through the trees, she went on till she came to a little hut, where an old woman lived, who took her in, and gave her both food and shelter. In the morning, the old wifie gave her three nuts, that she was not to break till her heart was "like to break, and owre again like to break"; so, showing her the way, she bade God speed her, and the princess once more to set out on her wearisome journey.

She had not gone far till a company of lords and ladies rode past her, all talking merrily of the fine doings they expected at the Duke o' Norroway's wedding. Then she came up to a number of people carrying all sorts of fine things, and they, too, were going to the duke's wedding. At last she came to a castle, where nothing was to be seen but cooks and bakers, some running one way, and some another, and all so busy that they did not know what to do first. Whilst she was looking at all this, she heard a noise of hunters behind her, and someone cried out, "Make way for the Duke o' Norroway!" and who should ride past but the prince and a beautiful lady! You may be sure her heart was now "like to break, and owre again like to break," at this sad sight; so she broke one of the nuts, and out came a wee wifie carding. The princess then went into the castle, and asked to see the lady, who no sooner saw the wee wifie so hard at work, than she offered the princess anything in her castle for it. "I will give it to you," said she, "only on condition that you put off for one day your marriage to the Duke o' Norroway, and that I may go into his room alone tonight." So anxious was the lady for the nut, that she consented. And when dark night was come, and the duke fast asleep, the princess was put alone into his chamber. Sitting down by his bedside, she began singing:

Far hae I sought ye, near am I brought to ye,
Dear Duke o' Norroway, will ye no turn and speak
to me?

Though she sang this over and over again, the duke never awakened, and in the morning the princess had to leave him, without his knowing she had ever been there. She then broke the second nut, and out came a wee wifie spinning, which so delighted the lady, that she readily agreed to put off her marriage another day for it; but to the princess came no better speed the second night than the first, and, almost in despair, she broke the last nut, which contained a wee wifie reeling; and on the same condition as before the lady got possession of it. When the duke was dressing in the morning, his man asked him what the strange singing and moaning that had been heard in his room for two nights meant. "I heard nothing," said the duke; "it could only have been your fancy." "Take no sleeping draught tonight, and be sure to lay aside your pillow of heaviness," said the man, "and you will also hear what for two nights has kept me awake." The duke did so, and

the princess coming in, sat down sighing at his bedside, thinking this the last time she might ever see him. The duke started up when he heard the voice of his dearly loved princess; and with many endearing expressions of surprise and joy, explained to her that he had long been in the power of an enchantress, whose spells over him were now happily ended by their once again meeting. The princess, happy to be the instrument of his second deliverance, consented to marry him, and the enchantress, who fled, the country, afraid of the duke's anger, has never since been heard of. All was hurry and preparation in the castle and the marriage which now took place at once ended the adventures of the Red Bull o' Norroway and the wanderings of the king's daughter. ■

Tattercoats

Europe: England

Iona Opie and Peter Opie wrote of the many variants of "Cinderella," (AT 510A) of which "Tattercoats" is one, that "however much kings or princes are enamored of Cinderella while she is in her beauteous enchanted state, she cannot be won until—as in many another fairy tale—she has been recognized by her suitor in her mundane, degraded state" (1974, p. 121). This probably is the great appeal of the story: One does not have to be dazzling to be worthy, and one's true love will recognize one's worth in any disguise. In "Tattercoats," some of the elements of the more familiar Cinderella story are missing: There is no stepmother or sister, and her protector is a young gooseherd rather than a friendly animal sent by the spirit of her mother. More important, she is recognized for her true beauty by the prince before she receives her fine clothes.

Source: "Tattercoats" from *More English Fairy Tales* by Joseph Jacobs. David Nutt, 1894. pp. 61–65.

In a great Palace by the sea there once dwelt a very rich old lord, who had neither wife nor children living, only one little granddaughter, whose face he had never seen in all her life. He hated her bitterly, because at her birth his favorite daughter died; and when the old nurse brought him the baby, he swore, that it might live or die as it liked, but he would never look on its face as long as it lived.

So he turned his back, and sat by his window looking out over the sea, and weeping great tears for his lost daughter, till his white hair and beard grew down over his shoulders and twined round his chair and crept into the chinks of the floor, and his tears, dropping on to the window-ledge, wore a channel through the stone, and ran away in a little river to the great sea. And, meanwhile, his granddaughter grew up with no one to care for her, or clothe her; only the old nurse, when no one was by, would sometimes give her a dish of scraps from the kitchen, or a torn petticoat from the rag bag; while the other servants of the Palace would drive her from the house with blows and mocking words, calling her "Tattercoats," and pointing at her bare feet and shoulders, till she ran away crying, to hide among the bushes.

And so she grew up, with little to eat or wear, spending her days in the fields and lanes, with only the gooseherd for a companion, who would play to her so merrily on his little pipe, when she was hungry, or cold, or tired, that she forgot all her troubles, and fell to dancing, with his flock of noisy geese for partners.

But, one day, people told each other that the King was traveling through the land, and in the town nearby was to give a great ball, to all the lords and ladies of the country, when the Prince, his only son, was to choose a wife.

One of the royal invitations was brought to the Palace by the sea, and the servants carried it up to the old lord who still sat by his window, wrapped in his long white hair and weeping into the little river that was fed by his tears.

But when he heard the King's command, he dried his eyes and bade them bring shears to cut him loose, for his hair had bound him a fast prisoner and he could not move. And then he sent them for rich clothes, and jewels, which he put on; and he ordered them to saddle the white horse, with gold and silk, that he might ride to meet the King.

Meanwhile Tattercoats had heard of the great doings in the town, and she sat by the kitchen door weeping because she could not go to see them. And when the old nurse heard her crying she went to the Lord of the Palace, and begged him to take his granddaughter with him to the King's ball.

But he only frowned and told her to be silent, while the servants laughed and said: "Tattercoats is happy in her rags, playing with the gooseherd, let her be—it is all she is fit for."

A second, and then a third time, the old nurse begged him to let the girl go with him, but she was answered only by black looks and fierce words, till she was driven from the room by the jeering servants, with blows and mocking words.

Weeping over her ill success, the old nurse went to look for Tattercoats; but the girl had been turned from the door by the cook, and had run away to tell her friend the gooseherd, how unhappy she was because she could not go to the King's ball.

But when the gooseherd had listened to her story, he bade her cheer up, and proposed that they should go together into the town to see the King, and all the fine things; and when she looked sorrowfully down at her rags and bare feet, he played a note or two upon his pipe, so gay and merry, that she forgot all about her tears and her troubles, and before she well knew, the herdboy had taken her by the hand, and she, and he, and the geese before them, were dancing down the road towards the town.

Before they had gone very far, a handsome young man, splendidly dressed, rode up and stopped to ask the way to the castle where the King was staying; and when he found that they were going thither, he got off his horse and walked beside them along the road.

The herdboy pulled out his pipe and played a low sweet tune, and the stranger looked again and again at Tattercoats' lovely face till he fell deeply in love with her, and begged her to marry him.

But she only laughed, and shook her golden head.

"You would be finely put to shame if you had a goose girl for your wife!" said she; "go and ask one of the great ladies you will see tonight at the King's ball, and do not flout poor Tattercoats."

But the more she refused him the sweeter the pipe played, and the deeper the young man fell in love; till at last he begged her, as a proof of his sincerity, to come that night at twelve to the King's ball, just as she was, with the herdboy and his geese, and in her torn petticoat and bare feet, and he would dance with her before the King and the lords and ladies, and present her to them all, as his dear and honored bride.

So when night came, and the hall in the castle was full of light and music, and the lords and ladies were dancing before the King, just as the clock struck twelve, Tattercoats and the herdboy, followed by his flock of noisy geese, entered at the great doors, and walked straight up the ballroom, while on either side the ladies whispered, the lords laughed, and the King seated at the far end stared in amazement.

But as they came in front of the throne, Tattercoats' lover rose from beside the King, and came to meet her. Taking her by the hand, he kissed her thrice before them all, and turned to the King.

"Father!" he said, for it was the Prince himself, "I have made my choice, and here is my bride, the loveliest girl in all the land, and the sweetest as well!"

Before he had finished speaking, the herdboy put his pipe to his lips and played a few low notes that sounded like a bird singing far off in the woods; and as he played, Tattercoats's rags were changed to shining robes sewn with glittering jewels, a golden crown lay upon her golden hair, and the flock of geese behind her, became a crowd of dainty pages, bearing her long train.

And as the King rose to greet her as his daughter, the trumpets sounded loudly in honor of the new Princess, and the people outside in the street said to each other:

"Ah! now the Prince has chosen for his wife the loveliest girl in all the land!"

But the gooseherd was never seen again, and no one knew what became of him; while the old lord went home once more to his Palace by the sea, for he could not stay at Court, when he had sworn never to look on his granddaughter's face.

So there he still sits by his window, if you could only see him, as you some day may, weeping more bitterly than ever, as he looks out over the sea. ■

The Ship That Sailed on Land

Europe: France

"The Extraordinary Companions" is an international tale type (AT 513B) with counterparts worldwide in such widely varied regions and countries as Africa, China, Finland, Portugal, the Polynesian Islands, Russia, and the United States (in both a French Louisianan and a Native American variant). In some of the variants, as in the "Five (or Seven) Chinese Brothers," the protagonist is about to be executed or is about to die but the helpers, often brothers or sons, use their special powers to prevent this calamity. In most variants, however, as in this story, the helpers aid the suitor to win the bride he loves. A survey of this tale's variants in Margaret Read MacDonald's *Storytelling Source Book* (1982) shows that as in the "Ship That Sailed on Land," the helpers bring extraordinary physical skills and attributes to the aid of the suitor: eating and drinking prodigious amounts, seeing for miles, hearing a fly land, and so on. In many of the variants, as in this story, the young hero does things right: He acts kindly to an animal helper or to an old man, while

Source: "The Ship That Sailed on Land" from *French Legends, Tales and Fairy Stories* by Barbara Leonie Picard. [Oxford Myths and Legends] Oxford University Press, 1955, 1992. By permission of the author. pp. 159–167.

frequently his brothers do not. The story is usually told as a fairy tale, but in its African variants, it may also be presented as a dilemma tale, the audience being asked to decide which of the helpers, usually brothers, deserves the most credit. "The Girl and the Python" in Chapter 2 of this anthology is such a story. In some variants, such as a Mongolian version, it is also a story about how the seven stars of the Big Dipper ended up in the sky, each star having been a brother with special powers who helped the Khan defeat his enemies. (MacDonald, 1982).

There was once a king who ruled over a large kingdom. He had all the pleasant things which money can buy, and he had, moreover, a daughter who was the most beautiful maiden in all his land. But in spite of his power and his riches, and in spite of his affection for his daughter, he was surly and discontented, and he grumbled night and day because amongst all his treasures he had not a ship which could sail on the land as well as over the water.

At last he issued a proclamation that he would give the hand of his daughter and half his riches to the man who could bring him such a ship. His messengers went all about his kingdom reading the proclamation in every market square and on every village green, but no one of all those who heard it had any idea where such a ship was to be found.

Now, on the edge of a forest there lived three brothers, the sons of a woodcutter, who earned a bare living by cutting wood for other people's fires. When they heard the proclamation they all three said, "It would be a fine thing to marry the Princess and have half the riches of the King." And the eldest brother took up his axe, a loaf, a goat's milk cheese, and a jug of wine. "I am going to try my hand at making this ship," he said, and went off alone into the forest.

In the forest he chose out a tall oak tree and set to work to fell it, and so hard did he work that before long it lay on the ground before him. Well pleased with the result of his labours, he sat down to rest himself and eat his bread and cheese and drink his wine in the shade. While he ate, a magpie flew on to a tree branch near by, and there it hopped from branch to branch, chattering and clacking, "Save a little for me! Save a little for me!"

The eldest brother looked up. "Go away, you noisy creature. I have no food to waste on you." And he went on eating.

The magpie came nearer. "What will you be making, woodcutter, out of that fine tree?"

"What is that to you?" replied the eldest brother, annoyed. He laughed mockingly. "If you must have an answer, I shall be making spoons."

"Spoons!" said the magpie. "Spoons! Spoons!" And it flew away clacking, "Spoons! Spoons! Spoons!"

When he had rested, the eldest brother took up his axe and set to work again, but each piece of wood he cut from the tree he had felled became at once a spoon. He hacked away with all his might, but the harder he worked, the faster came the spoons, until he was standing in a heap of wooden spoons right up to his knees. Large ladles to stir a pot of soup, little ladles for salt, spoons for cooking, spoons for eating with, everywhere were spoons; until at last he flung down his axe in despair and went home.

"How did you fare?" asked his brothers.

"I think, after all, that I would not care to marry the Princess," said the eldest brother, and he would say no more.

"It would please me well enough," said the second brother. And the next day he took his axe and a loaf and a goat's milk cheese and a jug of wine and went into the forest. It happened to him as to his brother, and when he had chosen and felled his tree and was sitting down to eat his bread and cheese and drink his wine, the magpie came with a great chattering, "Save a little for me! Save a little for me!"

"Away with you, you feathered thief. I have no food to spare for you."

"What will you be making, woodcutter, out of that fine tree?"

"What is that to you?" replied the second brother, annoyed. He sneered. "If you must have an answer, I shall be making spindles."

"Spindles! Spindles!" said the magpie. And it flew away clacking, "Spindles! Spindles!"

When the second brother set to work again, every piece of wood he cut turned into a spindle, until he stood knee deep in spindles, large, small, and middling sized; and then, in despair, he flung down his axe and went home. "I think, after all" he said to his brothers, "I would not care to marry the Princess." But more he would not say.

The next day the youngest brother took his axe and a loaf and a goat's milk cheese and a jug of wine and went out to the forest. And it happened to him as to his brothers, and when he had chosen and felled his tree, and was sitting eating his bread and cheese and drinking his wine, the magpie came chattering, "Save a little for me! Save a little for me!"

The youngest brother looked up and smiled. "You are welcome to share with me," he said. And he scattered crumbs and bits of cheese on the ground for the magpie, who quickly pecked them up. "What will you be making, woodcutter, out of that fine tree?"

"I should like, if I have skill enough, to make a ship which will sail on the land as well as over the water, so that I may take it to the King and win his daughter and half his riches."

"A ship which will sail on the land! A ship which will sail on the land!" said the magpie. And it flew away clacking, "A ship which will sail on the land! A ship which will sail on the land!"

When the youngest brother set to work again, every piece of wood he cut became part of a ship: keel, ribs, stem, and stern, as they fell to the ground they sprang into place of themselves; so that in a very short while the tree had become a ship, complete with mast and sail, decorated with carving all about her sides and with a figurehead at her prow.

The young woodcutter jumped into the ship, gave a word of command, and away the ship went, sailing merrily over meadow and moorland, hill and dale, towards the palace of the King.

On the way the woodcutter saw a man sitting by the wayside. He had a great mouth as wide as an oven door, full of huge teeth, and he was gnawing at a dry bone as hungrily as any stray dog. "Why do you do that, my friend?" asked the woodcutter.

"I am hungry," replied the man. "But I have spent all my money on food, and can buy no more."

"I am going to the palace of the King," said the woodcutter. "There should be food enough in a King's palace. Come along with me, and perhaps I can help you to something to eat."

The man threw away his bone and jumped into the ship, and off they went together, the hungry man and the young woodcutter.

A little way on they came to a stream. A man knelt beside it drinking the water as fast as he could. While they watched him the water grew lower and lower until the stream was dry, and all in a matter of moments. "Why do you do that, my friend?" asked the woodcutter.

"I am thirsty," replied the man, "and I cannot afford wine, for times have been bad with me."

"In the palace of the King there should be wine enough. Come with me, and I may be able to help you."

The man jumped into the ship, and away they went together, the hungry man, the thirsty man, and the young woodcutter.

A little farther on, they came up upon a strange sight: a young man with shoulders as broad as you have ever seen, walking along carrying half a forest on his back. "Why are you doing that, my friend?" the woodcutter called out.

The young man grinned. "I am tired of my stepmother's nagging. She always complains that I never bring home enough wood for the fire. So today I thought that I would take her half the forest."

"That should content her," said the woodcutter.

The young man laughed. "You do not know my stepmother," he said.

"If you would be quit of your stepmother," said the woodcutter, "come with me. For I am going to the palace of the King, and I doubt if she would think to look for you there."

The young man threw down the trees he carried, all save one oak, and jumped into the ship. And away they went together, the hungry man, the thirsty man, the strong man, and the young woodcutter.

A little way along they saw an even stranger sight. A man with a pair of bellows as large as a house was standing in the middle of a hayfield blowing away hard with his bellows up into the sky. "Why are you doing that, my friend?" asked the woodcutter.

"I am blowing away the rain clouds, so that my master's hay harvest may not be spoilt. And a tedious task it is to be sure, and small thanks does he give me for it."

"Then come with me to the palace of the King, and maybe I can find other work for you," said the woodcutter.

The man jumped into the ship with his bellows, and away they went together, the hungry man, the thirsty man, the strong man, the man with the bellows, and the young woodcutter.

At last they came to the palace, and there the woodcutter offered the ship to the King; and when the King saw that the ship could indeed sail upon the land as well as over the water, he was, you may be sure, very pleased. But he looked at the woodcutter and thought to himself, " A woodcutter is hardly a fitting bridegroom for my only daughter," and he searched in his mind for some way of evading his promise.

"No doubt you are thinking that now you have brought me the ship you have won the Princess for your wife," he said to the woodcutter. "And so you have. But there is still a little matter to be settled. In my larders are ten roasted oxen, ready for eating. We want no cold meats for the wedding-feast, but until they are cleared from the spits, we can roast no more. If you and your men can eat them, all ten, by tonight, then we can talk of the marriage."

"That is easily done, your majesty." And the woodcutter nodded to the hungry man, who had been waiting for just such a chance, and he was away to the kitchen in a moment, and back again, long before sundown, licking his lips. "That was the first good meal I have had in my life," he said. "Many thanks, your majesty."

The king frowned. "After eating comes drinking," he said to the woodcutter. "In my cellars are ten barrels of wine. It is a little sour, and therefore unfitted for a wedding, but until the barrels are emptied, new wine cannot be poured in."

"They will be easily emptied, your majesty," interrupted the young woodcutter, and he nodded to the thirsty man, who had been listening to the King's words eagerly. Away he ran to the cellar, and was with them again in an hour or two, wiping his mouth with the back of his hand. "At last my thirst is almost quenched—for the time being, at any rate. And I remembered to drink your majesty's health."

But by now the King was really angry, and he called out his soldiers. First the foot soldiers came running, swords in hand, a truly fearsome sight. But the strong man stepped forward. "Just leave them to me," he said

to the woodcutter. And holding his oak tree by the trunk, he swept the soldiers away with the leafy branches as easily as a housewife sweeps dust off a floor with a broom.

Then the cavalry came charging, horses neighing and swords flashing, enough to terrify the bravest heart. "This is my task," said the man with the bellows to the young woodcutter. And he puffed with his bellows and away the cavalry was blown, men, horses, swords, and all.

"Stop, stop!" called the King. "I give you my daughter, and you shall marry her tomorrow."

So the young woodcutter married the Princess and had half the King's riches beside: and he did not forget his four companions. And you may be sure that the hungry man was never hungry again, nor the thirsty man thirsty; while the strong man never needed to go home to live with his stepmother, and the man with the bellows found better ways of spending his time than by blowing away the rain clouds from any master's fields. ■

 # Vasilisa the Fair

Europe: Russia

Vasilisa is a more typical Cinderella type of story (AT 510A) than "Tattercoats" is. As in most Cinderella versions it is the dead mother's love that protects her young daughter through her trials. The fairy godmother in the French version by Charles Perrault is also a "mother." The German "Aschenputtel" and the Scottish and Appalachian "Rashin Coatie" both identify the mother's spirit as active in the life of the heroine. Baba Yaga, the cannibalistic witch, is a **stock character** in Russian folklore. She recurs in many stories as threatening and dangerous but at the same time

as a protector of the weak, especially children. Baba Yaga might have been a pre-Christian goddess who had been relegated to witch status after Russia adopted the Eastern Orthodox faith. The fact that Vasilisa wins the heart of the prince through her outstanding weaving and needlework reflects Russian traditional values.

Vasilisa is also a stock character in Russian folklore. She appears in many fairy tales, sometimes as wise, sometimes as brave, sometimes as the bride of Prince Ivan, who is another stock character. J. Patrick Lewis brings all the stock characters together, including the evil magician Koschey, in *The Frog Princess,* in which Vasilisa is the enchanted frog bride of Prince Ivan. He breaks Koschey's spell with the aid of Baba

Source: "Vasilisa the Fair" from *Russian Folk-Tales* by Alexandr Nikolaevich Afanas'ev. Translated by Leonard A. Magnus. London: Kegan Paul, Trench, Trübner & Co., 1915. pp. 109–118.

Yaga. The illustrations by Russian-American artist Gennady Spirin evoke the opulence of the Imperial Russian court.

Once upon a time there was a merchant who had been married for twelve years and had only one daughter, Vasilísa the Fair. When her mother died the girl was eight years old. On her death-bed the mother called the maiden to her, took a doll out of her quilt, and said, "Vasilísushka, hear my last words. I am dying, and I will leave you my mother's blessing and this doll. Keep this doll always by you, but show it to nobody, and no misfortune can befall you. Give it food and ask it for advice. After it has eaten, it will tell you how to avoid any evil that threatens you." Then the wife kissed her daughter and died.

After the wife's death the merchant mourned as proper, and then he thought of a second wife. He was a handsome man and found many brides, but he liked one widow more than any one. She was no longer young, and had two daughters of about the same age as Vasilísa. So she was an experienced housewife and mother. The merchant married her, but he had made a mistake, for she was not a good mother to his own daughter.

Vasilísa was the fairest in the entire village, and the stepmother and the sisters envied her for it. And they used to torture her by piling all the work they could on her, that she might grow thin and ugly, and might be tanned by the wind and the sun. And the child lived a hard life. Vasilísa, however, did all her work without complaining, and always grew more beautiful and plumper, while the stepmother and her daughters, out of sheer spite, grew thinner and uglier. Yet there they sat all day long with their hands folded, just like fine ladies. How could this be?

It was the doll that had helped Vasilísa. Without her the maiden could never have done her tasks. Vasilísa often ate nothing herself, and kept the tastiest morsels for the doll, and when at night they had all gone to bed, she used to lock herself up in her celleret below, give the doll food to eat, and say, "Dollet, eat and listen to my misery. I am living in my father's house, and my lot is hard. My evil stepmother is torturing me out of the white world. Teach me what I must do in order to bear this life."

Then the doll gave her good advice, consoled her, and did all her morning's work for her. Vasilísa was told to go walking and plucking flowers. All her flower-beds were done in time, all the coal brought in, and the water-jugs carried in, and the hearthstone was hot. Further, the doll taught her herb-lore. So, thanks to her doll, she had a merry life, and the years went by.

Vasilísa grew up, and all the lads in the village sought her. But the stepmother's daughters nobody would look at, and the stepmother grew more evil than ever and answered all her suitors, "I will not give my youngest daughter before I give the elders." So she sent all the bargainers away, and to show how pleased she was, rained blows on Vasilísa.

One day the merchant had to go away on business for a long time; so the stepmother in the meantime went over to a new house near a dense, slumbrous forest. In the forest there was a meadow, and on the meadow there was a hut, and in the hut Bába Yagá lived, who would not let anybody in, and ate up men as though they were poultry. Whilst she was moving, the stepmother sent her hated stepdaughter into the wood, but she always came back perfectly safe, for the doll showed the way by which she could avoid Bába Yagá's hut.

So one day the harvest season came and the stepmother gave all three maidens their task for the evening: one was to make lace and the other was to sew a stocking, and Vasilísa was to spin. Each was to do a certain amount. The mother put all the fires out in the entire house, and left only one candle burning where the maidens were at work and herself went to sleep. The maidens worked on. The candle burned down, and one of the stepmother's daughters took the snuffers in order to cut down the wick. But the stepmother had told her to put the light out as though by accident.

"What is to be done now?" they said. "There is no fire in the house and our work is not finished. We must get a light from the Bába Yagá."

"I can see by the needles," said the one who was making lace.

"I also am not going," said the second, "for my knitting needles give me light enough. You must go and get some fire. Go to the Bába Yagá!" And they turned Vasilísa out of the room.

And Vasilísa went to her room, put meat and drink before her doll, and said, "Dolly dear, eat it and listen to my complaint. They are sending me to Bába Yagá for fire, and the Bába Yagá will eat me up."

Then the Dollet ate, and her eyes glittered like two lamps, and she said, "Fear nothing. Vasilísushka. Do what they say, only take me with you. As long as I am with you the Bába Yagá can do you no harm." Vasilísa put the doll into her pocket, crossed herself, and went tremblingly into the darksome forest.

Suddenly a knight on horseback galloped past her all in white. His cloak was white, his horse and the reins were white, and it became light. She went further, and suddenly another horseman passed by, who was all in red, and his horse was red, and his clothes were red, and the sun rose. Vasilísa went on through the night and the next day. Next evening she came to the meadow where Bába Yagá's hut stood. The fence round the hut consisted of human bones, and on the stakes skulls glared out of their empty eyes. And, instead of the doorways and the gate, there were feet, and in the stead of the bolts there were hands, and instead of the lock there was a mouth with sharp teeth. And Vasilísa was stone-cold with fright.

Suddenly another horseman pranced by on his way. He was all in black, on a jet-black horse, with a jet-black cloak. He sprang to the door and vanished as though the earth had swallowed him, and it was night. But the darkness did not last long, for the eyes in all the skeletons on the fence glistened, and it became as light as day all over the green.

Vasilísa trembled with fear, but remained standing, for she did not know how she could escape. Suddenly a terrible noise was heard in the forest, and the tree-boughs creaked and the dry leaves crackled. And out of the wood Bába Yagá drove in a mortar pushing it with the pestle, and sweeping her traces away with a broom. At the door she stopped, sniffed all the way round, and cried out, "Fie, fie, I smell the blood of a Russian! Who is there?"

Vasilísa, shuddering with dread, stepped up to her, bowed low to the ground, and said, "Grandmother, I am here. My stepmother's daughters sent me to you to ask for fire."

"Very well," said Bába Yagá, "I know them. Stay with me, work for me, and I will give you fire. Otherwise I shall eat you up."

Then she went to the door, and she cried out, "Ho! my strong bolts, draw back, my strong door, spring open!" And the door sprang open, and Bába Yagá went in whistling and whirring, and Vasilísa followed her.

Then the door closed, and Bába Yagá stretched herself in the room and said to Vasilísa, "Give me whatever there is in the oven. I am hungry."

So Vasilísa lit a splinter from the skulls on the hedge and fetched Bába Yagá food out of the oven, and there was food enough there for ten men. Out of a cellar she fetched beer, meat, and wine. Bába Yagá ate and drank it all up. But all there was left for Vasilísa was a little of some kind of soup, and a crust of bread, and a snippet of pork.

Bába Yagá lay down to sleep and said, "In the morning, to-morrow, when I go away you must clean the courtyard, brush out the room, get dinner ready, do the washing, go to the field, get a quarter of oats, sift it all out, and see that it is all done before I come home. Otherwise I will eat you up."

And, as soon as ever she had given all the orders, she began snoring.

Vasilísa put the rest of the dinner in front of the doll and said, "Dollet, eat it up and listen to my woe. Heavy are the tasks which the Bába Yagá has given me, and she threatens to eat me up if I don't carry them all out. Help me!"

"Have no fear, Vasilísa, thou fair maiden. Eat, pray, and lie down to sleep, for the morning is wiser than the evening."

Very early next day Vasilísa woke up. Bába Yagá was already up and was looking out of the window. The glimmer in the eyes of the skulls had dimmed, and the white horseman raced by and it dawned. Bába Yagá went into the courtyard, and whistled, and the mortar, the pestle, and the broom appeared at once. The red horseman came by and the sun rose. Bába Yagá sat in the mortar and traveled by, thrusting the mortar with the pestle, while with the broom she removed every trace of her steps.

Vasilísa, left all by herself, looked over the house of the Bába Yagá, wondered at the horde of goods, and began to consider what she should start with. But all the work was already done, and the doll had sifted out the very last of the ears of oats.

"Oh, my saviour!" said Vasilísa. "You have helped me in my great need."

"You now have only to get dinner ready," the doll answered, and clambered back into Vasilísa's pocket. "With God's help get it ready, and stay here quietly waiting."

In the evening Vasilísa laid the cloth and waited for Bába Yagá. Twilight came, and the black horseman galloped by, and it became dark at once, but the eyes in the skulls glowed. The trees shuddered, the leaves crackled, Bába Yagá drove in, and Vasilísa met her.

"Is it all done?" Bába Yagá asked.

"Yes, grandmother, look!" said Vasilísa.

Bába Yagá looked round everywhere, and was rather angry that she had nothing to find fault with and said, "Very well." Then she cried out "Ye my faithful servants, friends of my heart! Store up my oats." Then three pairs of hands appeared, seized the oats and carried them off.

Bába Yagá had her supper, and, before she went to sleep, once more commanded Vasilísa, "To-morrow do the same as you did to-day, but also take the hay which is lying on my field and clean it from every trace of soil, every single ear. Somebody has, out of spite, mixed earth with it."

And, as soon as she had said it, she turned round to the wall and was snoring.

Vasilísa at once fetched her doll, who ate, and said as she had the day before, "Pray and lie down to sleep for the morning is wiser than the evening. Everything shall be done, Vasilísushka."

Next morning Bába Yagá got up and stood at the window, and then went into the courtyard and whistled. The mortar, the broom, and the pestle appeared at once, and the red horseman came by, and the sun rose. Bába Yagá sat in the mortar and went off, sweeping away her traces as before.

Vasilísa got everything ready with the help of her doll. Then the old woman came back, looked over everything, and said "Ho, my faithful servants, friends of my heart! Make me some poppy-oil." Then three

pairs of hands came, laid hold of the poppies and carried them off.

Bába Yagá sat down to supper, and Vasilísa sat silently in front of her. "Why do you not speak; why do you stay there as if you were dumb?" Bába Yagá asked.

"I did not venture to say anything, but if I might, I should like to ask some questions."

"Ask, but not every question turns out well, if you know too much, you'll grow old too soon."

"Still, I should like to ask you of some things I saw. On my way to you I met a white horseman, in a white cloak, on a white horse. Who was he?"

"The bright day."

"Then a red horseman, on a red horse, in a red cloak, overtook me. Who was he?"

"The red sun."

"What is the meaning of the black horseman who overtook me as I reached your door, grandmother?"

"That was the dark night. Those are my faithful servants."

Vasilísa then thought of the three pairs of hands and said nothing.

"Why don't you ask any further?" Bába Yagá asked.

"I know enough, for you said yourself 'if you know too much, you'll grow old too soon.' "

"It is well you asked only about things you saw in the courtyard, and not about things without it, for I do not like gossips, and I eat up everybody who is too curious. But now I shall ask you, how did you manage to do all the work I gave you?"

"By my mother's blessing!"

"Ah, then off with you as fast as you can, blessed daughter, for no one blessed may stay with me!"

So she turned Vasilísa toward the door and kicked her outside. Then she took a skull with burning eyes from the fence, put it on a staff, gave it to her and said "Now you have fire to give to your stepmother's daughters, for that was why they sent you here."

Then Vasilísa ran home as fast as she could by the light of the skull, and the flash in it went out with the dawn.

By the evening of the next day she reached the house, and was about to throw the skull away, when she heard a hollow voice coming out of the skull saying, "Do not throw me away. Bring me up to your step-mother's house." And she looked at her stepmother's house and saw that there was no light in any window, and decided to enter with the skull. The sisters welcomed her and they told her that ever since she had gone away they had no fire as they were able to make none, and all they borrowed from the neighbors went out as soon as it came into the room.

"Possibly *your* fire may burn!" said the step-mother.

So they took the skull into the room, and the burning eyes looked at the stepmother and the daughters and singed their eyes out. Wherever they went, they could not escape it, for the eyes followed them everywhere, and in the morning they were all burned to cinders. Vasilísa alone was left alive.

Then Vasilísa buried the skull in the earth, locked the house up, and went into the town. And she asked a poor old woman to take her home with her and to give her food until her father came back. She said to the old woman, "Grandmother, sitting here idle makes me feel dull. Will you buy me some of the very best flax, I should like to spin."

So the old woman went and bought good flax. Vasilísa set herself to work, and the work went merrily along, and the skein was as smooth and fine as hair, and when she had a great deal of yarn, no one would undertake the weaving, so she turned to her doll, who said, "Bring me some old comb from somewhere, some old spindle, some old shuttle, and some horse's mane, and I will do it for you."

Vasilísa went to bed, and the doll in that night made a splendid spinning stool, and by the end of winter all the linen had been woven, and it was so fine that it could be drawn like a thread through the eye of a needle. In the spring they bleached the linen, and Vasilísa said to the old mistress, "Go and sell the cloth, and keep the money for yourself."

The old woman saw the cloth and admired it, and said, "Oh, my child! nobody except the Tsar could ever wear such fine linen. I will take it to Court."

The old woman went to the Tsar's palace, and kept walking up and down in front of it.

The Tsar saw her and said, "Oh, old woman, what do you want?"

"Almighty Tsar, I am bringing you some wonderful goods, which I will show to nobody except you."

The Tsar ordered the old woman to be given audience, and as soon as ever he had seen the linen he admired it very much. "What do you want for it?" he asked her.

"It is priceless, Bátyushka," she said. "I will give it to you as a present."

And the Tsar thought it over and sent her away with rich rewards.

Now the Tsar wanted to have shirts made out of this same linen, but he could not find any seamstress to undertake the work. He thought for long, and at last he sent for the old woman again, and said, "If you can spin this linen and weave it, perhaps you can make a shirt out of it?"

"I cannot weave and spin the linen," said the old woman; "only a maiden can who is staying with me."

"Well, she may do the work."

So the woman went home and told Vasilísa everything.

"I knew that I should have to do the work!" said Vasilísa. And she locked herself up in her little room, set to work, and never put her hands again on her lap until she had sewn a dozen shirts.

The old woman brought the Tsar the shirts, and Vasilísa washed and combed herself, dressed herself, and sat down at the window, and waited. Then a servant of the Tsar came and said, "The Tsar wishes to see the artist who has sewn him the shirts, and he wants to reward her with his own hands."

Vasilísa the Fair went to the Tsar. When he saw her, he fell deeply in love with her. "No, fairest damsel; I will never part from you. You must be my wife." So the Tsar took Vasilísa, with her white hands, put her next to him, and bade the bells ring for the wedding.

Vasilísa's father came back home, rejoiced at her good luck, and stayed with his daughter. Vasilísa also took the old woman to live with her, and the doll remained ever in her pocket. ∎

The Little Old Rusty Cook Stove in the Woods

North America: United States—Appalachian

Aunt Lizbeth Fields told this story and many others in the collection *The Cloud Walking Country* in the early 1930s (Campbell, 1958). She included biographical details and made this traditional European story, a variant of "Beauty and the Beast" (AT 425A), uniquely Appalachian. The detail about how people reacted to cookstoves when they first replaced open hearth cooking (around the end of the nineteenth century in the Appalachian region) is an enjoyable addition. The heroine's active search for her groom in this variant is similar to the heroine's quest in the Scottish "Red Bull of Norroway," included in this anthology. The ending, with its sexual innuendo, is just subtle enough to make this the kind of story that audiences of different ages understand differently. Don Davis, a popular contemporary storyteller from North Carolina, says of his own experience with stories when he was a child that storytelling was not restricted to children but was the evening entertainment for all ages. Children strayed in and out during storytelling on the front porch and were packed off to bed only when the stories turned too ribald.

An old woman my granny knowed told me about the first cook stove she ever saw back here in the mountain country. She said she was used to eating things cooked on a fireplace hearth, and stove victuals riled her stomach—and I've heard other folks say that too. Then this here old woman told me a tale about a little old rusty cook stove in the woods; and, cook stoves being a new things to me when I was a girl, it pleasured me a heap to hear such a tale.

A king's daughter wandered off in the woods like she had been told not to, and she got lost. She was

scared mighty bad, and she hollered loud as she could. Then she heard somebody else holler. Whoever it was kept on hollering, and she tried to find out where the hollering came from. After a time she stumbled over a little old rusty cook stove in the woods. Seemed like the hollering came from inside the little old rusty cook stove.

When she listened again, a low voice came from inside the little old rusty cook stove and it was a king's son witched into being shut up inside the little old rusty cook stove. It said it would help her find her way back to the castle where she lived if she would get him out of the fix he was in and then marry him. She said she would.

He said for her to bring some kind of tool and poke a hole in the stove and let him out. She said she would. Then he found somebody to show her the way back to her castle—how he could I don't know and him shut up in that little old rusty cook stove. Anyhow, she got back to her castle, and she told the king what happened in the woods and how she had to go back and poke a hole in the little old rusty cook stove and let the king's son come out, and that she had promised to marry him.

The king said his daughter wouldn't do any such a thing; it was too big a risk. So he sent the miller's daughter to the woods to do what the king's daughter had promised. The miller's daughter poked and poked at the little old rusty cook stove in the woods but she couldn't even scrape off any of the rust. The king's son inside the little old rusty cook stove made her say things that gave away who she was, and he sent her back home.

Then the king sent a fisherman's daughter. Same thing. Then the king could see that he would have to let his daughter keep her promise. She went back to the woods and poked at the little old rusty cook stove. In a few minutes time she had made a peep hole. She peeped in and she saw a good-looking young man. She went back to work poking harder and pretty soon made a hole big enough for him to crawl out of.

He let her go back to her castle to tell the king goodbye, providing she wouldn't say no more than three words. She got to talking and said a heap more than three words. When she got back to the woods, the little old rusty cook stove and the good-looking king's son weren't there no more. She looked and looked till it got dark in the woods. She was scared witless, and she climbed up a high tree to be safe.

Up in the tree, she could see a light a far piece off through the woods. She climbed down out of the tree and ran fast as she could to where the light was. It was a little old house full of toad-frogs having a play-party.

She knocked on the door and the biggest toad-frog of all opened it. He listened to her tell, and then he stopped the play-party and asked the other toad-frogs what to do to help her out. They thought about the matter, and they agreed the best way to help her out would be to give her two needles and a plow wheel and three nuts—what kind of nuts it doesn't tell. She thanked them kindly, and they gave her instructions how to travel and what direction to take. They said she would have to use the needles to climb a glass mountain. I never did hear tell if they told her what she would use the plow wheel and the three nuts for. Anyhow, she got across the glass mountain and came to the castle where the stove man lived.

She hired herself out to be a cook. After supper she cracked one of the nuts in her pocket, aiming to pick out the kernel and eat it. The nut kernel was a pretty blue dress all soft and silky. The girl that was the bride of the stove man wanted the dress, and the king's daughter said she could have it if she would let her sleep that night in the room with the stove man. The bride promised, but she put magic herbs in some wine, and he slept so sound it was no satisfaction for the king's daughter to be there in the room with him.

The next night another fine dress, white as milk and soft as fur, came out of another nut kernel. The bride made the same trade for that dress, but she made the stove man drink wine with magic herbs again, and he never did know who stayed in the room with him all night.

Another night a golden dress came out of the nut kernel. The bride wanted it the worst of all. She made the same bargain, but that night the stove man wouldn't drink no wine. He said it made his head ache and gave him a misery in his stomach the next morning after. That night he didn't sleep sound, and he heard the king's daughter talking to herself about how she helped him out of the little old rusty cook stove in the woods. He got wide and awake and he loved her to her satisfaction, and he got rid of the girl that had fooled him. He married the king's daughter. And I always wondered what they done with that little old rusty cook stove. When I was a little girl, I used to wish I could have it to play with in my playhouse in the edge of the woods by a big old hollow tree. ■

La Estrellita—Little Star

North America: United States—Hispanic

Paulette Atencio (1991) recalls that this was one of her favorite stories as a child in northern New Mexico. She thinks of it as the Spanish version of "Cinderella." What makes this story interesting is its colonial Southwestern setting and the fact that it is a combination of the kind and unkind sisters (AT 480) and Cinderella (AT 510A) tale types. The motif of star and horns on the kind and unkind sisters' foreheads is paralleled by an Iranian variant, which has been interpreted as possibly having been derived from an ancient fertility ritual to the moon goddess (Dundes, 1982).

Source: "La Estrellita—Little Star" from *Cuentos from My Childhood: Legends and Folktales of Northern New Mexico* by Paulette Atencio. Translated by Ruben Cobos. Santa Fe, NM: Museum of New Mexico Press, 1991. pp. 38–42.

The harmonious ending of the New Mexican Hispanic variant told by Atencio makes it especially appealing.

Many years ago, there lived a kind and humble man. He was a hard worker and his life had been blessed with happiness. He had a beautiful wife and a daughter who loved him dearly. One day, the wife became sick and, within a few weeks, died. The poor man was left alone to raise his young daughter. She was very kind and showed due respect for her elders. Years passed by and the young girl realized how lonely her father was. She prayed that someday he would find a kind lady whom he could marry.

There was a widow, raising two daughters, who lived nearby. She pretended to be kind and generous to her young neighbor. She combed the little girl's hair and even made a pretty dress with a matching bow for her. The little girl pleaded with her father to marry this wonderful lady. It made all the sense in the world to her. Both adults were alone and in need of companionship. Together, they could all become a family again.

After several months, the two were married. Things were fine for a few weeks, but with three more mouths to feed, the father was forced to leave home to work as a sheepherder. He had not been gone more than two days when the stepmother began to show her true nature. She slept all day and refused to do any work. The stepsisters were worse. The kind young girl did not understand. She blamed herself and decided that if she did everything for them, they, in turn, would be happy and wouldn't be so mean to her. Unfortunately, this was not the case. The harder she worked, the more demands they placed on her.

One day, they received a letter from the young girl's father with some money for all of them. Part of the money was intended to purchase a sheep. Immediately, they bought the sheep and slaughtered it. The stepmother ordered the young girl to go wash the *tripitas* (intestines) in the river. The *tripitas* would be used to prepare *chonguitos* (Mexican sausage). The stepmother yelled, "Don't lose even one of them. I want them as clean as possible! If you mess up, you'll land up in the chicken coop with nothing but grain to eat." The stepsisters laughed. The kind young girl packed a piece of bread and jar of water and went to the river to begin working. She was almost finished when she dropped one of the intestines into the river. She panicked and ran along the river in hope of recovering the intestine. She was crying so hard that she couldn't see where she was going. Suddenly, amidst a great cloud of smoke, *la viejita de la buena suerte* (the little old lady of good luck) appeared. In a soft voice, she spoke to the young girl. "Please don't cry." "Oh!" said the young girl. "You don't know what my stepmother will do to me if I go home with one less intestine." At that moment, the old lady handed her the lost intestine. The young girl hadn't felt such happiness in a long time. "How can I repay you?" asked the young girl. The old lady smiled and asked her for some food. The young girl gave her the piece of bread and some of the water she had brought to the river. Before the young girl left, the old lady touched her forehead and said goodbye.

When the girl walked into the kitchen, her stepmother began to scream. She demanded to know how she had gotten the beautiful little star on her forehead. The girl had no idea what the stepmother was talking about. Suddenly, the stepmother tried to remove the star. Instead of coming off, the little star shone brighter and made the young girl more beautiful. From that day on, she was known as *Estrellita* (Little Star).

The stepmother eventually discovered what actually happened down by the river. Instead of being angry, she decided to send her own daughters, in hopes that they might have the same luck. They grudgingly complied and took some fresh *tripitas* down to the river. When they got there, they pretended to lose some of the *tripitas*. They also pretended to cry, muttering under their breath, "That old lady better hurry! We don't have all day!" Just then, the old lady appeared and returned the *tripitas*. Instead of thanking the old lady, the ugly daughters replied, "It's about time!" The old lady asked for food but received nothing from them. They both insisted that she touch their foreheads. The old lady did so, and off went the girls. They walked back with an air of confidence, sure that all had gone well.

When they arrived home, their mother became hysterical. *Estrellita* sat there in shock. The two daughters believed that their newfound beauty was causing all the commotion. They found a mirror with which to admire themselves and soon let out piercing screams! Instead of beautiful stars imprinted on their foreheads, one had a horn and the other had a donkey's ear! Their step-mother tried in vain to remove the ugly horn and ear, but it only caused them to grow longer.

Meanwhile, a very young and handsome man had been elected as Governor of the state. He invited every-one to attend the Governor's Ball. The stepmother and her daughters were excited and spent days getting ready. Finally, the evening arrived and the stepmother and her daughters left in great haste. *Estrellita* did not have a dress or shoes to wear, but she decided to follow them to the ball. She stood outside, looking through the win-dow. Everyone was dancing to the wonderful music. Peo-ple were so light on their feet that they seemed to float in the beautiful rhythm. Oh, what great joy the music brings to the people of this land, she thought. Suddenly, the music stopped. Everyone was talking, pointing in her direction. "What is shining so brightly? It is blinding us," the voices said. *Estrellita* realized the attention was fo-cused on her star, and she ran all the way home.

Her stepmother and stepsisters were furious. The dance had come to an end soon after. The Governor

heard of the beautiful *Estrellita*. He and several other men went to her house. When they arrived, they found her crying in her room. One of the men encouraged her to come out. As soon as she stood up and took a cou-ple of steps forward, there was a flash. With every step *Estrellita* took, her appearance changed. The tattered clothes turned into a gorgeous gown with matching shoes. The little star on her forehead shone like a diamond. She had never felt more beautiful. The young Governor could not believe his eyes. He loved her from the first moment he saw her! He knew that soon they would marry. The stepmother and her daughters fell on their knees, begging for forgiveness. *Estrellita*, filled with so much love, patience, and understanding, placed her hand on the forehead of each sister. At that moment, something magical happened! The horn and the donkey ear disappeared from their foreheads and the sisters were transformed into gentle and kind ladies. *Estrellita* sent for her father. He arrived just in time to walk his beautiful *Estrellita* down the aisle. ■

[handwritten margin note: forgiveness—different ending]

Noodlehead Tales, Tall Tales, and Other Humorous Tales

Definition of Humor

If you have to explain a joke, it is no longer funny. As E. B. White said, "Humor can be dissected, as a frog can, but the thing dies in the process and the innards are discouraging to any but the pure scientific mind" (cited in Cart, 1995, p. 5). Nevertheless, philosophers, literary scholars, psychologists, sociologists, and the medical profession from Plato to the present have studied how and why humor works, and why humor is so important to human beings (Cart, 1995). The fact that there is such a wide range of humorous folklore, from songs, jokes, anecdotes, and riddles to noodle-head, trickster, and tall tales, attests to humor's im-portance to all ages and cultures.

Paul Lewis, in his *Comic Effects: Interdisciplinary Ap-proaches to Humor in Literature,* characterizes humor as "a complex and diverse phenomenon, richly expressive of individual and group values" (1989, p. 32). He dis-

tinguishes among *laughter,* a physiological response; comedy, a genre of literature; and *humor,* which is so elusive that a simple definition is not possible.

According to Lewis, humor consists of the per-ception of incongruity (i.e., the pairing of events or images that are not usually seen as paired) and its resolution, especially if accompanied by surprise. Whether a joke is perceived as humorous depends on psychological and social factors relating to the teller and the listener as well as to the listener's values. An example is the response to an ethnically disparaging joke. Depending on whether a joke is about one's own ethnic group and whether it is told by an insider ver-sus an outsider, one might be amused, hurt, scornful, angered, or even frightened if the teller has power over the listener. One might also be offended by such a joke if it violates one's principles (Lewis, 1989).

There are, according to Avner Ziv, a humor re-searcher, over one hundred theories of humor. The theory that humor is a result of perceived incongruity and its resolution is more widely accepted today than

"Juan Bobo." Illustrated by Don Bell.

From: *The Emerald Lizard: Fifteen Latin American Tales to Tell in English and Spanish* by Pleasant DeSpain. Little Rock, Arkansas: August House. Illustration copyright © 1999 by Don Bell. Reprinted with permission of Don Bell.

many of the others (Lewis, 1989). But humor is just one of three possible responses to incongruity. The other two are problem solving and fear. Lewis explains how the three responses to the incongruous differ. The folktale "Teeny Tiny" is mildly frightening as the incongruity builds when the unidentified voice continues to demand, "Give me back my bone." The incongruity is resolved humorously when the Teeny Tiny Woman in one brave move ends the suspense by saying, "Take it." At a more frightening level, Joseph Bruchac's heroine Molly, in *Skeleton Man,* a modern horror-fantasy based on a traditional Iroquoian supernatural figure, uses her courage and a great deal of problem solving to escape from the cannibalistic Skeleton Man, who poses as a kindly uncle. Molly resolves this frightful incongruity, and the reader

experiences relief (though not humor). In situations and stories in which there is no resolution to the incongruous, the result is fear.

Functions of Humor

One of the oldest theories of the function of humor is that it provides the teller or listener with a sense of superiority. The philosopher Thomas Hobbes, like Plato and Aristotle, believed in the superiority theory: "[laughter] arises from a sudden conception of some eminency in ourselves, by comparison with the infirmity of others or with our own [former infirmities]" (cited in Cart, 1995, p. 6). The attraction of noodlehead stories can easily be interpreted using this theory, as can such contemporary children's literature as Peggy Parrish's Amelia Bedelia, stories, in which we laugh at another who lacks common sense or at our [younger] selves when we took common expressions literally.

A function of humor identified by Freud is that it serves as a vehicle for expressing forbidden impulses and wishes. Socially unacceptable topics are also expressed through jokes, but whether they will be perceived as humorous or not depends on the values of both the teller and the listener. If the two do not match, the joke may be found offensive rather than humorous (Lewis, 1989). From children's bathroom jokes to bawdy tales about sexual adventures the world of comedy is filled with such humor.

Research into children's humor by Martha Wolfenstein (1978) reveals the important role it plays in helping children (and adults) gain a sense of control, even if fleetingly, of their world. Wolfenstein, who studied young children's humor development, found that children told jokes as a way of coping with situations that were too difficult to express directly, as, for instance, the frustration of feeling powerless in the face of adult authority and size. One function of jokes and humorous stories children told was to minimize the power of the adults by making their story giants ridiculously large and powerful as well as foolish. Wolfenstein makes the point that although in their make-believe play and fantasy stories, children are the heroes who "alter reality in wished-for directions," in their joking, children minimize the importance of their unattainable wishes and feelings of powerlessness

(p. 52). One can see in humorous folktales a need for adults to similarly minimize their own feelings of powerlessness. The German "Hans-in-Luck" might be on the one hand a warning against being impractical, but it might also be saying that wealth, such as Hans might have attained, is only a burden. The characterization of giants and trolls as huge and fearsome but inept and easily fooled in folktales from England ("Jack and the Beanstalk," "Molly Whuppy"), Norway ("The Three Billy Goats Gruff" and other troll stories), and France ("Puss in Boots") serves to diminish the power of powerful figures. The frightful is made manageable through humor.

Humor is also used to rebel against authority or to expose the moral inadequacy of authority through pretense at misunderstanding orders and through parody (Wolfenstein, 1978). The trickster Till Eulenspiegel deliberately misunderstands the orders of mean bosses in order to both resist and parody overbearing and pompous masters. In one story, for instance, when Till asks what he should bake the first night he is left to work on his own as a baker's apprentice, the baker replies, sarcastically, "owls and long-tailed monkeys." Till takes him at his word and uses up all the baker's flour for owls and long-tailed monkeys instead of breakfast breads. Furious, the baker throws him out after making him pay for the flour. Till shows up the baker a second time when he sells these unusual cookies to the novelty-hungry people of the town.

Finally, humor can be used to present a world view that says that people cannot hope to understand and predict the ways of this world: It is not the deserving but the lucky who win. Lazy Jack, for instance, who represents a foolish (childlike) character, succeeds in spite of himself when he loses everything he earns but gains a princess.

Types of Humor

Nonsense   According to poet X. J. Kennedy (1991), nonsense stories and verse have a logic of their own. In what he calls "strict nonsense," the storyteller or verse writer creates a secondary world in which details fit. Kennedy gives Lewis Carroll's *Through the Looking Glass* as the perfect example of a story that sets aside the laws of nature but follows the logic imposed by the rules of chess and the idea of living in a world in which everything is reversed (as in a looking glass). In the Japanese folktale "An Exaggeration" in this anthology, one can visualize a secondary world on top of the man's head, once the nonsense premise of a tree growing out of someone's skull is accepted.

In what Kennedy calls "loose nonsense," only one element of the story or verse needs to be nonsensical; the author works around this one element. In the Mother Goose rhyme "The Three Wise Men of Gotham," only the fact that "The three wise men of Gotham, went to sea in a bowl" is nonsensical, while the result, "if the bowl had been stronger, my song had been longer," is a natural consequence, funny in its swift ending.

Noodlehead Tales   Noodlehead stories seem to exist universally and rely on a group's shared concepts of what constitutes common sense. Three frequent assumptions about common sense are that there are some learned and highly intellectual people who lack simple common sense, that ordinary people have a good grasp of the knowledge they need to get along in everyday life, and that the people or things that do not fit either of the above molds are disturbing (Geertz, 1983). The numskull or noodlehead does not fit either mold because he or she is of the common folk yet lacks common sense. This incongruity accounts for much of these tales' humor.

But what is common sense? Clifford Geertz asserts that although people act as if common sense is knowledge that anyone in their right mind should have (e.g., "you should know enough to come in out of the rain"), it is often knowledge that only those within a culture share (1983). An outsider, a child, or a noodlehead does not have the knowledge the rest of a society takes for granted. The Puerto Rican Juan Bobo, for instance, dresses the family pig in his mother's clothes and high heels so the pig can go to church.

Some of the characteristics of the noodlehead include not doing the obvious, being impractical so that anyone can predict that their actions will lead to certain failure, taking figurative language literally, and acting shamelessly and unapologetically (Geertz, 1983). Noodleheads, however, also often turn out to be far cleverer than initially thought. The entire town of Gotham, England, was said to have deliberately gained a reputation for foolishness to avoid having a highway built through their town (or having to entertain King John).

Tall Tales   Tall tales, with their hyperboles, especially in contrast to their carefully drawn realistic details, play on the incongruity between the reader's life experiences and the storyteller's grand assertions. This form of humor seems to be far more prevalent in pioneer societies, such as the United States, than in long-settled ones (Ziv, 1988). Facing the challenges of nature as they moved into the western frontier, Americans matched its "natural extravagance with the contrived extravagance of the oral yarns" (Cart, 1995, p. 106). Early tall tale characters such as Davy Crockett and Mike Fink were humans whose stature and prowess continued to grow after their deaths. Eventually, many of them assumed the animal characteristics of their greatest adversaries: Davy Crockett was said to have introduced himself by saying, "I'm that same Davy Crockett; fresh from the backwoods, half horse, half-alligator, a little touched with the snapping turtle" (cited in Cart, 1995, p. 109).

The early American tall tale heroes were exaggerations of regional heroes; later they were composites, representing an entire industry—Pecos Bill, cowboys; Paul Bunyan, loggers; Joe Magarac, steel workers. Today people find these composite characters, born from the pens of advertising pamphleteers and newspaper men, more humorous and better meeting modern expectations of a good story than the folkloric prototypes, which were not polished and gained their humor in the oral telling (Cart, 1995). Esther Shephard's polished version of the "fakelore" (as folklorist Richard Dorson dubbed it) of Paul Bunyan is typical of the style of literary writers in contrast with the style of the tall tales that were passed on orally and then recorded in local newspapers and in *Davy Crockett's Almanack.*

Tales of the Supernatural and Horror   Tales of horror are often "perched on the thin line between humor and fear.... Fear marshals our concentration and humor celebrates the release from tension" (Lewis, 1989, p. 114). Although many tales of the supernatural belong among serious legends and frequently act as morality tales, others are told as entertainment, playing on people's subconscious fears. Stories that combine the incongruity of the supernatural with a surprise ending release tension and frequently achieve a humorous effect. The jump tale is one type of scary story that functions this way. "Teeny Tiny" works for younger children; the "Golden Arm" is more appropriate for older children.

Trickster Tales   Tricksters are closely related to noodleheads in folklore. Often the same stock character is by turns clever and foolish, sometimes both within the same story. Brer Rabbit, Anansi, and Coyote (and Bugs Bunny) usually trick others, but sometimes they outsmart themselves. Nasreddin Hoca, a humorous figure in Turkish folklore, is just as often foolish as he is clever. His dual nature may add up to one thing: teaching wisdom through humor. Tricksters function as teachers of social values. They can also be a vehicle for social rebellion, in which case they are seen as **culture heroes**. Stories of Nasreddin Hoca in which he tricks the foreign tyrant Tamerlane function in this way.

There are other types of humorous literature besides those described above. Some, such as **satire** and **parody**, however, tend to fall outside the range of folk literature, while others, such as **burlesques**, fall outside the range of material used with children.

The humorous folktales that follow represent a small fraction of the wide range of stories that people around the world tell. Although folklorists report that fairy tales and other oral tales are in decline around the world, humorous anecdotes that are passed on orally are as popular as ever. Because trickster figures appear prominently in the stories of so many cultures, a separate section is devoted to them. Other sections of this anthology also include humorous stories. For instance, many fables are not only didactic, but also humorous. Both folk wisdom and research have shown that people learn better when humor is employed than from a direct lecture, perhaps because a lighthearted approach that removes tension facilitates the learning process (Lewis, 1989). It might also be that the pleasure of hearing a humorous story makes people pay closer attention to the content of the message.

For picture book versions of the following stories, see "Picture Books Related to the Stories in the *Allyn & Bacon Anthology of Traditional Literature*" on the Web Supplement at www.ablongman.com/lechner.

Goha and the King

Africa: Egypt, as told by Samia I. Spencer

Stories about Goha (often spelled "Djuha" in the Roman alphabet) are told throughout Arabic-speaking countries. There is a large and varied body of stories that have been attached to this beloved character over the last thousand years. The first known record of the Goha comes from a tenth century book, *The Eccentricities of Djuha.* Goha, however, is truly part of the oral tradition. According to folklorist Inea Bushnaq (1986), even people who know no other stories can tell one about the Goha. He is considered a wise fool: His actions seem foolish, sometimes even crooked, but there is always something to learn. Different aspects of Goha are emphasized by different tellers or in different places. In Egypt, according to Spencer, his lack of common sense is emphasized, whereas in many of the stories collected by Bushnaq, Goha's wisdom and his ability to highlight other peoples' greed and folly are the focus. In a Syrian story retold by Bushnaq (1986), for instance, Goha borrows a large copper kettle from his neighbor, and when he returns it, the neighbor is delighted to find a small kettle inside the large one. Goha tells him that the large one had just given birth to it. Later Goha borrows the kettle again and fails to return it. On being questioned about the kettle, Goha tells the neighbor that it had died. When the neighbor angrily demands how a copper kettle can die, Goha replies, "If a kettle can give birth, it can also die." Goha might have been the prototype for the Turkish Nasreddin Hoca (Hodja). In any case, the stories told about these two stock characters, including the one about the kettle, are often identical.

The following Goha story, which has a close Syrian variant, was retold by Dr. Samia Spencer who grew up in Egypt and is Castanoli Professor of French at Auburn University. Dr. Spencer has not only written down the story but also provided both an introduction to the storytelling context of Goha tales in Egypt and an interpretation of the meanings of "Goha and the King" within that culture. As in so many of the other stories, one might laugh at Goha's lack of common sense, but one is buoyed by his sunny spirit and ability to be thankful for what is good rather than being brought down by what is bad.

Children growing up in Egypt relish hearing stories about Goha, and adults delight in telling them. The tales are innumerable. They are told over and over again, but no one ever tires of hearing about the misadventures of poor Goha. Even when the element of surprise is gone after the first time a story is heard, people still savor it because at each telling, the personality, gestures, and body language of the storyteller gives a different flavor to the same tale. A trusting, gullible, kind-hearted, well-meaning, but simple-minded, ordinary man, Goha just cannot stay out of trouble despite his many qualities and good intentions, because of his lack of judgment and common sense. In other words, qualities of the heart alone are not sufficient in life, people must also use the power of their minds.

To this day, some of Goha's more notable actions remain part of everyday language, often quoted as proverbs, when a person does something that is not very smart. For example, if someone goes about doing a simple task in a complicated manner, s/he is told: "Where is your ear, Goha?" (*Fein wednak, ya Goha?*)—pointing to their lack of common sense. The phrase refers to an incident—perhaps the ending of a longer story now forgotten—when Goha is asked to show his ear. To respond to the command, Goha raises his left arm over his head, and with his left hand touches the tip of his right ear!

Even when he tries to outsmart others, Goha falls victim to his own trap. For example, one day

Goha was harassed by a bunch of children. In order to get rid of them, he points them to another direction from where he was heading, and tells them that a wedding ceremony is taking place there; they could join the party and have fun. The children believe him and run in the direction of the party. A few moments later, seeing the joy of the children running toward the wedding, Goha himself changes his own route, and runs toward the wedding party—believing the tale he had just made up!

The amusing story of Goha's encounter with the king is full of messages, and reveals an enormous amount of information about the culture in which the story is told. It goes as follows.

One day, Goha decides to make a gift to the king. After deep and hard thinking about the present to offer, he settles in favor of a basket of turnips. On his way to market, he meets a friend, and they start to talk. When the friend finds out what Goha has in mind, he advises against the turnips—not fit for a king. Instead, he recommends taking a basket of fruits, perhaps figs—somewhat more appropriate for a monarch. Trusting the advice of his friend, Goha buys a basket of figs, heads toward the palace, and asks to meet the king. After proper greetings, Goha presents the gift to the king. Taking a look at the basket of fruit, and offended by an insignificant donation unworthy of his position, the king orders his guards to place Goha against a wall and throw the figs one by one at his face. While the guards execute the order, they are intrigued by Goha's reaction. Each time a fig hits his face, he declares: "Thanks be to God!" (*Al hammed' lil l'ah!"*). Finally, one of the guards asks Goha why he thanks God each time his face is hit by a fig. Goha simply answers: "I thank God for buying figs instead of turnips!" ∎

Many details could be noted in this story and many lessons learned from it, both from what is said and what is not said. For example:

- While it is appropriate for individuals of different stations in life to interact with each other, one should never forget where one stands in relation to others, and one should behave with them accordingly. Goha makes a fool of himself not because he wanted to give a gift to the king, but because his gift was not commensurate with the position of the king. Goha behaved as if the king were an ordinary person like himself and made his choice on the basis of what an ordinary man might appreciate, neglecting to properly evaluate what a man as important and as powerful as the king might think, or how he might react. While a common man might appreciate a basket of fresh vegetables, a king does not. One of the morals of the story is that a gift reflects both the gift giver and the gift recipient. A giver in a lower position should not pull down the recipient; instead, she or he should bring himself up to the level of the recipient.

- People in this culture are generous. They make gifts, even to those holding power, without asking for favors or expecting something in return. Goha did not want anything from the king; he was simply being his generous self. The friend was not surprised that Goha intended to offer a present to the king, nor did he recommend against the visit. No evil thought crossed his mind at the idea of a gift to the king: he did not assume that Goha was trying to ingratiate himself with the king.

- Rulers are close to the people and attentive to their needs. When Goha, a common man, asks to meet the king, he is given an audience. Yet kings behave and are expected to behave like kings, not like ordinary citizens. They expect to be treated with the respect and deference due to their station in life. For example, children who listen to the story in this culture would not think that the king was cruel or ungrateful or that he should have accepted the gift, pretended that he liked it, and thanked Goha for it.

- When friends meet, they do not just nod and acknowledge each other with a passing greeting. They stop and talk.

- It pays to listen to others. Goha's fate was easier to bear, thanks to the advice of his friend. Unfortunately, although the friend was somewhat more intelligent than Goha in assuming that turnips were not fit for a king, he still did not fully realize the distance between the ordinary person and the king.

Gratitude

"Gratitude," with its spelled out moral and didactic tone, might have been placed with the fables. It could just as well have been placed with the trickster tales. Since for every trickster there must be a dupe, however, one can also see this as a story about a numskull who deserved to be fooled. This story has international counterparts; the tale type is named for "The Brahmin and the Tiger" from India (AT 155), in which an ungrateful tiger wants to eat the Brahmin who had let him out of captivity. The motif of talking objects and animals complaining about their treatment by humans shows up in other West African stories, most notably in "Talk" from the Ashanti of Ghana, retold by Harold Courlander and George Herzog in *The Cowtail Switch* (1947), or in its picture book version, Angela Shelf Medearis's *Too Much Talk* (1995). In *The Hunterman and the Crocodile* (1997), a modern picture book adaptation of "Gratitude," West African–born artist Baba Wagué Diakité emphasizes the theme of living in harmony with nature rather than the earlier theme of gratitude. As in "Gratitude," the animals and objects refuse to come to a hunter's aid because he had not treated them right in the past, but in Diakité's version, the hunter learns to respect nature and his place in it.

A hunter went out in the bush. He met an antelope. He killed the antelope. Boaji (the civet) passed by. Boaji said: "Give me some of that meat. I am hungry. I beg you for it. I'll do you a favor some other time." The hunter gave Boaji some of the antelope's meat. Boaji ran off.

The next day the hunter went out in the bush again. He came to a place where the bush was overgrown and it was hard to see where one was going. There, in the middle of the bush, he met a crocodile. The hunter said: "How did you get here? Don't you be-

Source: "Gratitude" from *African Genesis* by Leo Frobenius and Douglas C. Fox. New York: Benjamin Blom, 1937, pp. 163–170. Reprinted with kind permission from Ayer Company Publishing, Inc. North Stratford, NH 03590.

long in the water?" The crocodile said: "Last night I went out hunting, and now I am far from the river. I cannot find my way back. I beg you, show me the way to the river. If you do, I'll give you five loads of fish." The hunter said: "I'll do that gladly." The hunter tied a thong around the crocodile's foot and led him to the Niger. At the water's edge the crocodile said: "Now undo the thong, and I'll go into the water and fetch you five loads of fish." The hunter freed the crocodile, the crocodile went into the water and the hunter waited on the bank.

The crocodile came out of the water with a great big fish and laid it high on the bank. The crocodile slipped back into the water. The crocodile returned with a second load of fish and laid it lower on the bank. The hunter climbed down and carried it higher. The crocodile returned with a third load which he left at the water's edge. The hunter carried the third load up the river bank. The crocodile brought a fourth load and laid it in the shallows. The hunter came down, picked the fish out of the shallows and carried it high up the bank. The crocodile returned with a fifth load of fish which it laid on edge of the deep water. The hunter came down from the bank, waded through the shallows and came to the edge of the deep water. As he was about to pick up the fish the crocodile snapped at his foot, caught it fast and dragged the hunter under the water.

The crocodile brought the hunter to his brother crocodiles who lay on a sandbank in midstream. The crocodile called all his friends and said: "We have caught a hunter. We are going to eat him. Come, all of you." The crocodiles came from every side and swarmed around the hunter. The hunter said: "Is that fair? This crocodile lost his way in the bush. I brought him back to the river. And now he wants to eat me." The crocodiles said: "We will ask four other people what they think about it."

Down the river floated an Asubi (colored, oval mat woven by the Benue in the Kutigi region). The Asubi was old and torn. The hunter cried: "Asubi, help me!" The Asubi said: "What is the matter?" The hunter said:

"This crocodile here was lost in the bush, and I brought him back to the river. I saved his life, and now he wants to take mine. Is that fair?" The Asubi said: "You are a man. I know men. When a mat is young and useful, they keep it clean, do not step on it with their feet, roll it up when they have used it and lay it carefully to one side. But when a mat is old they forget what it used to be like. They throw it away. They throw it into the river. The crocodile will do well if he treats you as men have treated me." The Asubi drifted on. The crocodile said: "Did you hear what the Asubi said?"

A dress, old, torn and worn, came floating down the stream. Someone had thrown it away. The hunter cried: "Dress, help me!" The old dress said: "What is the matter?" The hunter said: "I brought this crocodile here, who had lost his way, back to the river. And now he wants to eat me. I saved his life and now he wants to rob me of mine. Is that fair?" The dress said: "You are a man. I know men. So long as a dress is young and beautiful they wear it everywhere, accept its beauty for their own and say, 'Aren't we lovely?' But it is the dress which is lovely. And the people know that they lie for they fold the dress carefully, smooth out the wrinkles and wrap it up. But as soon as the dress is old they forget what it used to be before. They throw it in the river. The crocodile will do well if he treats you as men have treated me." The old dress drifted on downstream.

The crocodile said: "Did you hear what the old dress said?"

An old mare came down to the river to drink. The mare was old and thin. Her masters had turned her out because she was no longer of any use to them. The hunter cried: "O mare, help me!" The old mare said: "What is the matter?" The hunter said: "I brought this crocodile here, who had lost his way, back to the river. Now he wants to eat me. I saved his life and now he wants to rob me of mine. Is that fair?" The old mare said: "You are a man. I know men. When a mare is young they build a stall for her. They send out boys to cut her the best grass. They give her the best grain and when she is in foal they give her double of everything. But when a mare is old and cannot foal, when she is weak and ill, they drive her out into the bush and say, 'Take care of yourself as best you can.' Just look at me. The crocodile will do well if he treats you as men have treated me."

The mare trotted off. The crocodiles said to the hunter: "You heard what the old mare said?"

Boaji came down to the bank of the Niger to drink. It was the Boaji whom the hunter had helped the day before. The hunter cried: "Boaji, help me!" Boaji said: "What is the matter?" The hunter said: "I brought this crocodile here, who had lost his way in the bush, back to the river. And now he wants to eat me. I save his life and now he wants to rob me of mine. Is that fair?" Boaji said: "That is difficult to decide. First I must know everything. I do not want to hear only your side of the story but the crocodile's side too—that is, if the crocodile is willing to accept my decision." The crocodile said: "I will tell you." Boaji said: "How did the hunter bring you here?" The crocodile said: "He tied a thong around my foot and dragged me after him." Boaji said: "Did it hurt?" The crocodile said: "Yes, it hurt." The hunter said: "That is not possible." Boaji said: "I cannot decide that until I have seen it. Come ashore here and show me what you did." The crocodile and the hunter went to the shore. Boaji said to the hunter: "Now tie the thong around his foot, just as you did before, so that I can judge whether it hurt him or not." The hunter bound the thong around the crocodile's foot. Boaji said: "Was it like that?" The crocodile said: "Yes, it was like that. And after a while it begins to hurt." Boaji said: "I cannot judge that yet. The hunter had better lead you back into the bush. I will come with you." The hunter picked up the thong and led the crocodile into the bush. Finally they came to the place where he and the crocodile had met. The hunter said: "It was here." Boaji said: "Was it here?" The crocodile said: "Yes, it was here. From here on the hunter dragged me behind him to the river." Boaji said: "And you were not satisfied." The crocodile said: "No, I was not satisfied." Boaji said: "Good. You punished the hunter for his bad treatment of you by grabbing his foot and dragging him to the sandbank. So now the matter is in order. In order to avoid further quarrels of this kind the hunter must unbind the thong and leave you here in the bush. That is my decision."

Boaji and the hunter went off. The crocodile stayed in the bush. The crocodile could not find the way back to the river. The crocodile hungered and thirsted. The hunter thanked Boaji.

There comes a time for every man when he is treated as he has treated others. ■

How the Animals Kept the Lions Away

Africa: Algeria

Animal tales come in several varieties in Arabic folk-lore. There are the didactic tales that range from the stories that teach Islamic principles to the fables of Bidpai, an Arabic translation of the Indian Pan-chatantra tales, and the tales of Luqman, a Koranic sage, whose stories are similar to and in some cases identical with Aesop fables. Many of the other animal tales are wisdom tales as in a Syrian story of the Mouse King, who, thinking that the Cat King has been reformed by his pilgrimage (Haj) to Mecca, tries to convince the other mice to welcome the Cat King as befitting a Hajji, (pilgrim), only to discover that the Cat King may pray like a Hajji, but he pounces like a cat (Bushnaq, 1986, p. 216). The most popular type of animal tale, however, is the trickster tale, in which the common sense and shrewdness of the defenseless overcome the brute strength of the powerful (Bush-naq, 1986). There is, for instance, the Moroccan tale "Two Close Calls," in which a goat who runs into a lion avoids being eaten by pretending that he is an angel from heaven sent to summon seven lions. The goat tells the lion that he is not one of those fated to go with him that day. The lion, happy to be spared, runs away (Bushnaq, 1986, p. 238). Though the following story begins like "The Bremen Town Musi-cians," with worn-out animals left behind by their owners, the characters are stock Algerian (Berber) folk characters, with the lion playing his typical powerful but gullible role (Bushnaq, 1986).

Once when a tribe of Beduins moved their camp to a new site, they left behind them a lame rooster, a bro-ken-backed donkey, a sick ram, and a desert greyhound suffering from mange. The animals swore brotherhood

and determined to live together. They wandered until they came to an unfrequented oasis, where they de-cided to settle.

One day when the rooster was flying to the top of a tree, he noticed something important: the opening to a grain silo full of barley. The food was wholesome, and he began to visit the place daily. Soon his feath-ers became glossy as polished silk, and his comb began to glow like the fire inside a ruby. The donkey, observing the improvements, asked his friend, "How is it that your cap has grown so bright?" The rooster feigned surprise and tried to change the subject. But with the perseverance of his race, the donkey contin-ued to pester the fowl until at last it said, "very well, I shall show you the reason why my cap has grown so bright, but it must remain a secret between us." The donkey promised to be discreet and the rooster led him to the grain silo.

At the sight of the barley the donkey flung himself into the grain and fed until he could eat no more. Brim-ming with well-being, he danced back to the others and said, "I feel the urge to sing come upon me. With your permission I shall bray awhile!" The animals objected. "What if a lion should hear you?" they said. "He will surely come and devour us all!" But despite, his friends, the donkey could not contain his high spirits. He cantered off by himself and began to bray long and noisily.

Now, a lion did hear the sound and came streak-ing across the wilderness on his silent feet until he was within one spring of the donkey. Almost too late the donkey became aware of the danger. "Sire," he said, "I see that my fate has been written, but I beg you to do me the favor not to devour me without my friends. It would be more honorable, considering that the animals of this oasis have sworn an oath of brotherhood to live together and die together, if you made an end to us all without exception." The lion conceded the merit of this plea and allowed the donkey to guide him to his friends.

Source: "How the Animals Kept the Lions Away" from *Arab Folk-Tales* translated and edited by Inea Bushnaq, copyright © 1986 by Inea Bushnaq. New York: Pantheon, pp. 242–244. Used by permission of Pantheon Books, a division of Random House, Inc.

When the other animals saw the donkey leading a lion toward them, they put their heads together and said, "How can we defend ourselves against a lion!" And they made their plans. When the lion came near they all said with one voice, "Greetings and welcome, uncle lion!" Then the ram butted him in his side and knocked the breath out of his lungs, and rooster flew up and pecked at his eyes, and the dog buried his teeth in the lion's throat. The lion died, of course. His flesh was given to the dog to eat, but the animals kept his skin and tanned it.

After that the four friends were able to live in peace for a time. However, soon the donkey was announcing, "I sense that I must bray again!" "Be still, O ill-omened animal!" said the others. But the donkey could not suppress his feelings, and his unmelodious voice rang repeated in the air.

A second lion prowling that quarter of the desert was attracted to the braying. With water running in his mouth, he hurried to the oasis. Again the donkey invited the lion to kill all of the animals, and the lion gladly complied. This time too the rooster, the ram, and the dog put their heads together when they saw the lion approaching and made a plan.

But what they said to the visitor was, "Welcome, may you be a thousand times welcome!" Then the rooster hinted to the ram, "Our guest should be made comfortable and have a carpet to sit on!" The ram trotted into their dwelling and brought out the tanned lion skin. "Be ashamed, O ram!" chided the rooster when he saw him. "Our guest is of a noble tribe. His presence among us is an honor. Do you want to disgrace us by offering him that old, worn-out mat?" Meekly the ram carried the lion skin back into the house and brought it out a second time. This time the dog expressed impatience. "Surely we have a softer carpet than that, O ram! Besides, this one is quite faded." Obediently the ram took the lion skin inside and returned with it a third time. Now the donkey chimed in, "For one of such eminence as the lion, nothing but the finest can serve the occasion! Choose more carefully from among our store!" The ram withdrew into the house, but the lion did not linger further. He jumped to his feet and without bidding his hosts a formal farewell, ran away as fast as he was able.

Although the donkey continued to bray from time to time, no lion was seen near the animals' oasis again. ■

The Storyteller

Africa: Ethiopia

The Storyteller's story-within-a-story is a formula tale of the endless tales type (AT 2300). Children enjoy the silliness of the lack of conventional story structure, though most adults, including the insatiable king to whom it is being told, do not. Folklorist Wolf Leslau heard "The Storyteller" in the city of Gondar

Source: "The Storyteller" from *The Fire on the Mountain and Other Ethiopian Stories* by Harold Courlander and Wolf Leslau. Copyright © 1950 by Henry Holt and Company. Reprinted by permission of Henry Holt and Company, Inc. pp. 58–66.

from a Falasha storyteller. The Falasha, a Jewish group, make up only a small percent of the country's population, most of whom are either Christian or Muslim, but the theme is known throughout Ethiopia, according to Courlander and Leslau (1950). Telling a story to gain riches, a kingdom, a bride, or even one's own life is a recurrent theme in many cultures: Jack, in an Appalachian tale, tells a whopper that wins him the king's daughter; Odysseus relates his adventures to gain a king's aid in returning home; and Scheherazade regales her husband, Sultan

Schahryar, with a thousand and one stories to save herself and other women from his daily execution of wives.

Once there was a king in the land of Shoa who loved nothing so much as listening to stories. Every moment of his spare time was spent in listening to the tales told by the storytellers of the country, but a time came when there were no stories left that he hadn't heard. His hunger for stories came to be known in the neighboring kingdoms, and wandering singers and storytellers came to Shoa to be rewarded for whatever new tales they could bring. But the more tales the king heard the fewer were left that he had not heard. And so, finally, in desperation he let it be known throughout the land that whatever story-teller could make him cry, "Enough! No more!" would receive a great piece of land and the title of Ras, or prince.

Many men, inspired by the thought of such wealth and honors, came to tell him stories, but always he sat and listened eagerly without ever protesting that he had had too much.

But one day a farmer came and offered to tell stories until the king was so full of them that he would cry out in protest. The king smiled.

"The best storytellers in Ethiopia have come and gone without telling me enough," he said. "And now you come in your simple innocence to win the land and the title of Ras. Well, begin, you may try."

And so the farmer settled himself comfortably on a rug and began:

"Once there was a peasant who sowed wheat," he said. "He mowed it when it was grown, threshed it, and put all the precious grain in his granary. It was a rich harvest, one of the best he had ever had.

"But, and this is the irony of the tale, in the granary there was a tiny flaw, a hole big enough to pass a straw through. And when the grain was all stored an ant came and went through the hole and found the wheat. He carried a single grain of it to his anthill to eat."

"Ah-ha!" the king said, showing interest. For this story was one that he hadn't heard.

"The next day," the farmer continued, "another ant came through the hole and found the wheat, and he, too, carried away a grain of it."

"Ah-ha!" the king said.

"The next day another ant came and carried away a grain," the farmer said.

"Ah-ha!"

"The next day still another ant came and carried away a grain."

"Yes, yes, I understand, let us get on with the story," the king said.

"The next day another ant came, and carried away another grain. And the next day another ant came and carried away another grain."

"Let us not dally with the details," the king said. "The story is the thing."

"The next day another ant came," the farmer continued.

"Please," the king said, "please!"

"But there are so many ants in the story," the farmer said. "And the next day another ant came for a grain of wheat, and . . . "

"No, no, it must not be!" the king said.

"Ah, but it is the crux of the story," the farmer replied. "And the next day another ant came and took away a grain . . . "

"But I understand all this," the kind protested. "Let us pass over it and get on with the plot."

"And the next day another came and took his grain. And the next day . . . "

"Stop, I want no more of it!" the king shouted.

"The story must be told in the proper way," the farmer said. "Besides, the granary is still nearly full of wheat, and it must be emptied. That is the story. And the next day . . . "

"No, no, enough, enough!" the king shouted.

"And the next day another ant . . . "

"Enough, enough, you may have the land and the title of Ras!" the king shouted, jumping up and fleeing from the room.

So the farmer became a prince and owned a great parcel of land.

This is what people mean when they say: "One grain at a time brings good fortune." ■

"The Talking Skull." Illustrated by Geoffrey Whittam.

From: *Tortoise the Trickster and Other Folktales from Cameroon* by Loreto Todd. New York: Schocken Books, 1979.

The Talking Skull

Africa: Nigeria—Nupe

Both the plot and the lesson in this story were preserved and passed on by Africans in America during slavery. There is a cycle of John and Old Master stories in which John, a clever slave, usually outsmarts Old Master John but sometimes gets in trouble himself. In the American versions of this story John hears a skull talking in the woods or in a graveyard. When he goes to Old Master to tell him about it, the results are the same as in the version below (Bascomb, 1992). In some versions, he gets a whipping, an outcome that would have been realistic (Dundes, 1973). The warning was clear to possible informers: "do not carry tales about us to master" (Roberts, 1989). In this Nupe story, the warning might be more simply "Don't talk too much," an attitude that several different West African peoples seem to share, as can be seen in *Why Mosquitoes Buzz in People's Ears* retold by Verna

Source: "The Talking Skull" from *African Genesis* by Leo Frobenius and Douglas C. Fox. New York: Benjamin Blom, 1937, pp. 161–162. Reprinted with kind permission from Ayer Company Publishing, Inc. North Stratford, NH 03590.

Aardema (1973), *Too Much Talk* retold by Angela Shelf Medearis (1995), and "Kumba the Orphan Girl" retold by Emil Magel and included in this anthology.

A hunter goes into the bush. He finds an old human skull. The hunter says: "What brought you here?" The skull answers: "Talking brought me here." The hunter runs off. He runs to the king. He tells the king: "I found a dry human skull in the bush. It asks you how its father and mother are."

The king says: "Never since my mother bore me have I heard that a dead skull can speak." The king summons the Alkali, the Saba and the Degi and asks them if they have ever heard the like. None of the wise men has heard the like and they decide to send guards out with the hunter into the bush to find out if his story is true and, if so, to learn the reason for it. The guards accompany the hunter into the bush with the order to kill him on the spot should he have lied. The guards and the hunter come to the skull. The hunter addresses the skull: "Skull, speak." The skull is silent. The hunter asks as before: "What brought you here?" The skull does not answer. The whole day long the hunter begs the skull to speak, but it does not answer. In the evening the guards tell the hunter to make the skull speak and when he cannot they kill him in accordance with the king's command. When the guards are gone the skull opens its jaws and asks the dead hunter's head: "What brought you here?" The dead hunter's head replies: "Talking brought me here!" ■

An Exaggeration

Asia: Japan

The specifics of this nonsense story might be unique, but its spirit can be recognized in Edward Lear's limericks, in Lewis Carroll's *Alice's Adventures in Wonderland* verses, in Mother Goose rhymes, and even in the artist M. C. Escher's endless stairwells and inside-out buildings. This tale type (AT 2335) belongs with others that rely on contradictions for their humor, as in the rhyme "One dark night in the middle of the day, two dead boys came out to play. . . ." A spirit of playfulness is essential for the appreciation of nonsense tales, which might be why their appeal is so great for the youngest children, for whom incongruity seems to be enough, without the need most of us eventually develop for resolution, according to humor scholar Paul Lewis (1989).

Source: "An Exaggeration" from *Ancient Tales in Modern Japan: An Anthology of Japanese Folk Tales.* Selected and edited by Fanny Hagin Mayer. Bloomington, IN: Indiana University Press, 1984. p. 218. Reprinted by permission.

A certain man happened to swallow an orange seed and it sprouted in his stomach. It grew and grew until it came out of his head. When the fruit appeared and ripened on the tree, children came clamoring to pick the fruit.

They were such a nuisance that the man declared, "It's all because of that tree that there is such a fuss." He pulled up the tree.

That left a big hole in his head into which the rain fell and finally formed a pool. When that happened, the children came again, this time to fish. Their lines caught in the man's ears and eyes.

The man declared, "I can beat this by dying." He leaped into the pond and drowned. ■

—*Story was collected by Iwakura Ichiro at Kikaijima, Kagoshima.*

The Golden Fan and the Silver Fan

Asia: Japan

The story of the poor man who goes to the shrine of a local deity to beg for an end to his poverty recurs in several Japanese folktales, as does the use of some kind of magical object to make a nose grow or recede (Mayer, 1984). In medieval Japan, people referred to the country as "the land of the gods" because there were so many gods attached to local shrines in natural settings. The description of Gonemon's petitioning the deity for a better life in "The Golden Fan and the Silver Fan" is typical of medieval Shinto religious practice. People would spend a week at a shrine or temple petitioning the deity. They expected an answer to their petition through a dream. If no answer came, they could, like Gonemon, repeat the week of petitioning two more times. Having the deity appear in the guise of an old man is also typical. Though Buddhism was the more formal and philosophical religion of Japan, people also continued Shintoist practices. Legends even tell of how the local gods accepted Buddhism and its teachings; the two practices, Shintoism and Buddhism, are not considered mutually exclusive. Shrines continue to be important throughout Japan and are found even in urban places such as the roofs of department stores (Tyler, 1987).

Once upon a time there was a man called Gonemon who was always poor, and he wore such tattered clothes that people called him Ragged Gonemon.

The man finally could no longer endure his poverty and went to the shrine of Kangamo Myōjin to begin a petition lasting three times seven or twenty-one days. He prayed earnestly, "Please make me a rich man."

On the twenty-first day, the final day of the petition, the deity appeared in the form of a white-haired old man. He said, "Since you have offered your prayers faithfully, I will make you rich." He held out a gold fan and a silver fan and said, "If you fan with the gold fan, you can make the nose of anyone you wish long, and with the silver fan you can make it short again. You can use these fans any way you want, but you must never use them improperly." He gave careful instructions.

Gonemon was delighted. He waited for a good chance to use the fans. Then he heard that the chōja's [a newly rich man] only daughter was going to look at cherry blossoms. Gonemon went there ahead of the girl and stood behind a cherry tree. He fanned the girl's nose two or three times with his gold fan. The girl's nose lengthened two or three feet in plain sight of everybody.

No doctor they hired could cure the girl's nose. She could only weep for shame. The chōja and his wife and everybody wondered how such a strange illness should befall their precious girl. They were overcome with grief.

The family finally decided to take as son-in-law anyone who could cure their girl. They had a notice to this effect written on a tall sign and set up in front of their house. After three days had passed, Gonemon walked by the chōja's house, calling, "Massage treatment for noses! Massage treatment for noses!"

He was called in hurriedly. He made the girl eat grains of rice with flour on them, saying that it was medicine. In the meantime he fanned the girl's face a little from a distance with his silver fan. Her nose began to get shorter a little at a time. After a day or two, it looked like it always had. The chōja then recalled his promise and reluctantly made the filthy man his son-in-law. From that time Gonemon wore good clothes and ate good things all the time. He lived a life of ease without any effort.

One day Gonemon remembered the fans that were by then in the cupboard and covered with dust. He had only used them on someone else until then, but he wondered what would happen if he tried them on himself. He sprawled out on his back and began to fan his nose with the gold fan. It felt good as it lengthened out, so good that he dozed off as he fanned it.

His nose lengthened until it reached the sky and pierced the clouds. It happened that they all were all in the midst of toasting mochi at Thunder's house. They saw a strange looking soft round horn come pushing up through the ashes. The people were uneasy about it. They heated one of their metal chopsticks red hot and poked it through that thing that looked like a horn. Gonemon below could not endure the pain.

He screamed, "It's hot! It's hot!" and hurriedly fanned with his silver fan, but the tip of his nose was held fast by the metal chopstick. As his nose shrank, Gonemon's body was drawn up higher and higher. Finally he reached a place below the floor of Thunder's house. He could go no farther up or down.

He is probably still hanging there in the sky. He will have to stay there until Thunder decides to pull the chopstick out. ■

—Story was collected by Dobashi Riki at Nishiyatsushiro-gun, Yamanashi.

Source: "The Golden Fan and the Silver Fan" from *Ancient Tales in Modern Japan: An Anthology of Japanese Folk Tales.* Selected and edited by Fanny Hagin Mayer. Bloomington, IN: Indiana University Press, 1984. pp. 136–137. Reprinted by permission.

The Silence Match

Asia: Japan

Because "The Silence Match" strongly parallels the Scottish ballad "Get Up and Bar the Door" (AT 1351), this anthology includes both. Silly contests of will and wits between husbands and wives seem to recur from one end of the world to the other. This story is a little different from its European counterparts, as the object of the contest is not to avoid some trivial chore, such as washing dishes, but to win an extra treat (mochi). Exaggeration in which there is a contest seems to be a popular story motif in Japan (*Yanagita Kunio Guide, to Japanese Folktale*, 1986). There are contests of strength, lies, boasts, and laziness. Mochi, a popular food, is rice cake made of fresh rice that has been pounded until sticky and smooth and is either round or square shaped. The cake can be filled with sweet bean jam and eaten right away or allowed to harden to keep for a long time and then eaten in broth or steamed and wrapped in seaweed. For New Year's celebration, people cut the big squares into small squares, decorate them, and place them around the house for good luck. Every region has its own prized recipes. In the old days, a person was supposed to eat as many mochi as his years, but health-conscious Japanese no longer do that (personal communication, Hamae Okamoto, 2002).

Once upon a time a couple was living near Hiroshima in Akinokuni. They liked mochi very much and they received 15 pieces of it from somebody one day. They each ate seven pieces for supper and agreed that the one who did not speak for the longest would have the piece left over. They put it into the cupboard and went to bed silently with the light on.

A robber with a long sword at his side broke into the house that night. He went up to the set of drawers where the clothes were put away. The couple lay quaking but silent under their bedding. They were scared, but they were thinking about that piece of mochi. The robber took out all their clothes and all their money. Then he went towards the cupboard.

The wife, looking on from under the covers, forgot and cried, "Father, that man is going to take our mochi." The husband threw off the covers and got up. He took the piece of mochi from the cupboard and knelt as he held it up to the robber. He pointed to it and said, "Please leave at least this much."

The silence was broken and the robber burst out laughing. ■

—Story was collected by Ishii Kendo in Hiroshima at Hiroshima

Source: "The Silence Match" from *Ancient Tales in Modern Japan: An Anthology of Japanese Folk Tales.* Selected and edited by Fanny Hagin Mayer. Bloomington, IN: Indiana University Press, 1984. p. 236. Reprinted by permission.

The Tiger and the Persimmon

Asia: Korea

Tigers, the largest and most dangerous of animals in Korea, were common in the mountains and were worshiped as the "God of the Mountain" or "Sacred Spirit of the Mountain" (Zong, 1982). In Korean folktales, however, they are also frequently portrayed as brutal but foolish, much as the big bad wolf is in

European folktales from the "Three Little Pigs" to "Little Red Riding Hood."

One night a tiger came down to a village. It crept stealthily into the garden of a house and listened at the window. It heard a child crying. Then came the voice of its mother scolding it. "Stop crying this very minute! The tiger is here!" But the child took no notice and went on crying. So the tiger said to himself, "The child is not the least bit afraid of me. He must be a real hero."

Source: "The Tiger and the Persimmon" from *Folk Tales from Korea*, 3d ed. Zong In-Sob. Elizabeth, NJ: Hollym International, 1982. Originally published by Routledge and Kegan Paul, 1952. With permission by Routledge, Taylor and Francis, Garland Publishing. p. 184.

Then the mother said, "Here is a dried persimmon." And the child stopped crying immediately. Now the tiger was really frightened and said to himself, "This persimmon must be a terrible creature." And it gave up its plan of carrying off the child.

So the tiger went to the outhouse to get an ox instead. There was a thief in there, and he mistook the tiger for an ox and got on its back. The tiger was terrified, and ran off as fast as it could go. "This must be the terrible persimmon attacking me!" it thought. The thief still rode on its back and whipped it up so that he might get away before the villagers saw him stealing an ox.

When it grew light the thief saw he was riding on a tiger and leapt off. The tiger just raced on to the mountains without looking back. ■

Get Up and Bar the Door

Francis Child, an American folklorist, identified several versions of this humorous contest between husband and wife (AT 1351). He examined written sources from the seventeenth through the nineteenth centuries and included Arabic, French, German, Italian, and Turkish versions. Child would not have known of the Japanese version, "The Silence Match," included in this anthology, since it was translated into English after Child did his collecting. The consequences of the husband and wife's obstinacy range from the couple being robbed to the husband almost being hanged. In each version one or the other of the couple speaks up just in the nick of time to avert complete disaster and ends up having to close the door or wash the dishes or some other trivial chore. There is a Philippine variant that is a humorous pourquoi story explaining why women do the dishes. The following

Source: "Get Up and Bar the Door" from *The English and Scottish Popular Ballads*, vol. 5. Francis J. Child. New York: Cooper Square, 1962. p. 98. Reprinted from the 1894 edition.

version takes place in early November, as Martinmas is celebrated on November 11 in Scotland. The ballad form and Scottish dialect make this a memorable version.

It fell about Martinmas time,   [St. Martin's day,
around November 11]

And a gay time it was then,
When our goodwife got puddings to make,
And she's boild them in the pan.

The wind sae cauld [so cold] blew south and north,
And blew into the floor;
Quoth our goodman to our goodwife,
"Gae [go] out and bar the door."

"My hand is in my hussyfskap,   [housewifeship,
housewifely work]
Goodman as ye may see;
An it should nae [not] be barrd this hundred year,
It's no be barrd for me."

They made a paction [pact] tween them twa,
They made it firm and sure,
That the first word whaeer should speak,
Should rise and bar the door.

Then by there came two gentlemen,
At twelve o clock at night,
And they could neither see house nor hall,
Nor coal nor candle-light.

"Now whether this is a rich man's house,
Or whether is it a poor?"
But neer a word wad ane [would one] o them
        speak,
For barring of the door.

And first they ate the white puddings,
And then they ate the black;
Tho muckle [much] thought the goodwife to hersel,
Yet neer a word she spake.

Then said the one unto the other,
"Here, man, tak [take] ye my knife;
Do ye tak aff the auld man's beard,
And I'll kiss the goodwife."
"But there's nae water in the house,
And what shall we do than?"
"What ails ye at the pudding-broo [broth],
That boils into the pan?"

O up then started our goodman,
An angry man was he:
"Will ye kiss my wife before my een [eyes],
And scad me wi pudding-bree?"

Then up and started our goodwife,
Gied three skips on the floor:
"Goodman, you've spoken the foremost word,
Get up and bar the door." ∎

The Golden Arm

Europe: England

In a footnote to this story, Henderson commented on the way the storytellers he had observed narrated the story to their young audiences. The suspense of the dialog would be increased until, at the end, the narrator shrieked the words "Thou hast it!" and extinguished the candle that lit the room. Henderson wrote, "No one desires to know what became of the avaricious husband." Told in the above manner, this story could be quite frightening, but with the lights left on, the final shriek simply ends the mounting tension, resulting in relief if not outright humor. Versions of both "The Golden Arm" and "Teeny Tiny" were collected in Alabama by students of folklorists Jack and Olivia Solomon between 1958 and 1977 and were

printed in *Ghosts and Goosebumps: Ghost Stories, Tall Tales, and Superstitions from Alabama,* (University of Georgia Press, 1994). Both stories are treated as jump tales in the style of "Raw Head Bloody Bones." In jump tales the tension mounts as the ghost or Bloody Bones approaches closer, and closer, with the storyteller finally grabbing at a listener. For instance, in the Alabamian version of "The Golden Arm" the woman's ghost approaches her sleeping husband and says,

I'm on the first step, I want my golden arm,
I'm on the second step, I want my golden arm,
I'm on the porch, I want my golden arm . . .
I'm at you bed, I want my golden arm.

The storyteller jumps at the listener and shouts "I got you" (Solomon and Solomon, 1994, p. 61).

Source: "The Golden Arm" from *Notes on the Folk-lore of the Northern Counties of England and the Borders* by William Henderson. London: Longmans, Green, 1866. pp. 338–339.

There was once a man who travelled the land all over in search of a wife. He saw young and old, rich and poor, pretty and plain, and could not meet with one to his mind. At last he found a woman young fair, and rich, who possessed the supreme, the crowning glory, of having a right arm of solid gold. He married her at once, and thought no man so fortunate as he was. They lived happily together, but, though he wished people to think otherwise, he was fonder of the golden arm than of all his wife's gifts besides.

At last she died. The husband appeared inconsolable. He put on the blackest black, and pulled the longest face at the funeral: but for all that he got up in the middle of the night, dug up the body, and cut off the golden arm. He hurried home to secrete his recovered treasure, and thought no one would know.

The following night he put the golden arm under his pillow, and was just falling asleep, when the ghost of his dead wife glided into the room. Stalking up to the bedside it drew the curtain, and looked at him reproachfully. Pretending not to be afraid, he spoke to the ghost, and said, "What hast thou done with thy cheeks so red?" "All withered and wasted away," replied the ghost in a hollow tone.

"What hast thou done with thy red rosy lips?"— "All withered and wasted away."

"What hast thou done with thy golden hair?"—"All withered and wasted away."

"What hast thou done with thy *Golden Arm*?"— "Thou hast it!" ■

Teeny Tiny

In the nineteenth century, following the Grimms' lead, folklorists throughout Europe were searching for folktales and fairy tales. Russian, Scandinavian, and Eastern European folklorists found treasure troves of fairy tales in their countries. English folklorists were disappointed to find few oral sources of fairy tales. The countryside, however, was rich in legends and folktales about the supernatural. Katharine Briggs has listed a rich variety of supernatural characters, which included bogeys, goblins, hobs, hobgoblins, pixies, Robin Goodfellows, tam-o-shanters, and will-o-the-wisps, to name just a few. In this jump tale the fact that the voice is never identified helps to build suspense.

> Note (from the original printing): This simple tale seldom fails to rivet the attention of children, especially if well told. The last two words should be said

Source: "Teeny Tiny" from *Popular Rhymes & Nursery Tales of England* by James O. Halliwell. London: The Bodley Head, 1970. pp. 27–28. Reprint of 1849 edition.

loudly with a start. It was obtained from oral tradition, and has not, I believe, been printed.

Once upon a time there was a teeny-tiny woman lived in a teeny-tiny house in a teeny-tiny village. Now, one day this teeny-tiny woman put on her teeny-tiny bonnet, and went out of her teeny-tiny house to take a teeny-tiny walk. And when this teeny-tiny woman had gone a teeny-tiny way, she came to a teeny-tiny gate; so the teeny-tiny woman opened the teeny-tiny gate, and went into the teeny-tiny churchyard. And when this teeny-tiny woman had got into the teeny-tiny churchyard, she saw a teeny-tiny bone on a teeny-tiny grave, and the teeny-tiny woman said to her teeny-tiny self, "This teeny-tiny bone will make me some teeny-tiny soup for my teeny-tiny supper." So the teeny-tiny woman put the teeny-tiny bone into her teeny-tiny pocket, and went home to her teeny-tiny house.

Now when the teeny-tiny woman got home to her teeny-tiny house, she was a teeny-tiny tired; so she went up her teeny-tiny stairs to her teeny-tiny bed, and she put teeny-tiny bone into a teeny-tiny cupboard. And when this teeny-tiny woman had been to sleep a teeny-tiny time, she was awakened by a teeny-tiny voice from the teeny-tiny cupboard, which said, "Give me my bone!" And this teeny-tiny woman was a teeny-tiny frightened, so she hid her teeny-tiny head under the teeny-tiny clothes, and went to sleep again. And when she had been to sleep again a teeny-tiny time, the teeny-tiny voice again cried out from the teeny-tiny cupboard a teeny-tiny louder, "Give me my bone!" This made the teeny-tiny woman a teeny-tiny more frightened, so she hid her teeny-tiny head a teeny-tiny further under the teeny-tiny clothes. And when the teeny-tiny woman had been to sleep again a teeny-tiny time, the teeny-tiny voice from the teeny-tiny cupboard said again a teeny-tiny louder, "Give me my bone!" And this teeny-tiny woman was a teeny-tiny bit more frightened, but she put her teeny-tiny head out of the teeny-tiny clothes, and said, in her loudest teeny-tiny voice, "Take it!" ■

 # Paul Bunyan

North America: United States

Overcoming the impossible or surviving to tell about an extraordinary experience is the material on which tall tales are built. The story might be built around a small core of facts, but it is the exaggerations, told in a deadpan style in which each polished detail suggests scrupulous accuracy, that marks the tall tale as uniquely American (Pavonetti and Combs, 1999). The United States needed larger-than-life American heroes once the Revolution was won and the nation began to explore and eventually settle the vast wilderness west of the Alleghenies. The grand exaggerations surrounding the heroes' lives, however, could no longer be taken seriously. Instead, the outlandish tales added a new genre to our national repertoire of oral and written literature: the tall tale (Dorson, 1977).

The story of Paul Bunyan, as told here, is not a true folktale, though elements of the story seem to have existed among loggers in Canada and Minnesota before the story was fleshed out in 1914 in its familiar form by a logging company publicist, W. B. Laughead, and further publicized in the 1920s by James Stevens, a newspaper writer. Esther Shephard's book version in 1924 was one of the earliest major successes

for children and, along with a spate of other Paul Bunyan books for children, helped to spread his story through the 1920s and 1930s (Leach, 1958; Dorson, 1976). Shephard's use of hyperbole, detail, and picturesque language reflects the traditional tall tale style of storytelling that was found in nineteenth century newspapers, almanacs, and books and thus perpetuated not only the story but also the style of writing tall tales for children.

Though not an authentic folktale character, Paul Bunyan has become an American icon, one of the few who, along with his pet, Babe the Blue Ox, is widely known throughout the United States, though few people seem to know his actual accomplishments (Dorson, 1976). The many contemporary picture books, such as those by Steven Kellogg, *Paul Bunyan: A Tall Tale,* in which the illustrations match Esther Shephard's humorous description, continue to ensure Ol' Paul's popularity.

That first fall I was workin' for Paul was when he got the big hotcake griddle. Always in the woods in them days the boys was mighty fond of hotcakes—just like men are pretty generally anywheres, I guess—and if there was anything could be said for Paul was that he tried to treat his men right. And so, naturally, he wanted

Source: "The Camp on the Big Onion" from *Paul Bunyan* by Esther Shephard. New York: Harcourt, Brace & World, 1924, 1952. With permission by Harcourt, Inc. pp. 16–22.

'em to have hotcakes if there was any way he could fix it, and then besides, the way he ate 'em afterwards, he was more'n a little fond of 'em himself.

Well, in camp before that they hadn't never had hotcakes, because they didn't have no griddle big enough to cook 'em on, and no stove they could of put the griddle on if they'd of had it anyway, and so what they had for breakfast before that and what they was havin' when I went to work for Paul was just sourdough biscuits. And even so the cook used to have to get up twenty-six hours before daylight to get the biscuits cooked in time because all he had to cook 'em on was one of them there drumhead stoves they used to have and he couldn't only cook but sixty-four drippin' pans full at a time.

But that year Paul made up his mind he was goin' to have hotcakes for the men and he was goin' to have a griddle big enough to cook 'em on. And so he went down to the plow-works in Moline, Illinois, and contracted for 'em to make him one to suit him. The steel that went into this griddle of Paul's was what would have gone into two hundred and sixty breakin' plows, and when it was done finally, it measured two hundred and thirty-five foot across.

And then the men at the plow-works, of course, didn't have no way to ship it up to Paul and they was out there in the yard at the works figgurin' on how they could build some sidetracks and put several flatcars alongside each other and try to ship it up on them, when Paul happened to come along to see if his griddle wasn't finished yet.

"Never mind that," he says to the men when he seen 'em out there. "Never mind tryin' to build any extra tracks. We couldn't never get enough cars anyway, I don't believe. I'll just raise 'er up on edge and hitch my Blue Ox to 'er and she'll roll right along."

And so after they'd got out of the way he raised 'er up, and hitched on, and started right out for home.

And when he come to within four or five miles of the camp, like he'd calculated it out beforehand, I guess, he just unhitched the Blue Ox and let the griddle spin on by itself. And here she come, rollin' right along. And when she got to just the right place, where he'd figgured to place her, she begun to spin round and round like spin-the-plate at a play-party and dug a nice

big hole in the fire to go in under it, and settled right down and was all ready to go.

Paul had the bull-cooks pile in an acre or two of brush for a good fire, and him and Ole the Blacksmith rigged up a tank for the cook to make his batter in and a flume with a stop-cock in it, so's he could run it out onto the griddle and then shut it off whenever he had enough. Paul got flunkies with slabs of bacon strapped to their feet to skate around on the griddle to keep it greased, and a chicken wire fence all around for 'em to climb up on when the batter come in too thick. We rigged up a kind of block and tackle arrangement to haul the hotcake off with when it was done—that's on the first griddle. Afterwards, like the camp in North Dakota, Paul, of course, always had donkey engines.

There was four hundred bull-cooks bringin' in the spruce-boughs for the bunks in the big bunkhouse at that first camp I was in; it had eighty tiers of bunks, most of 'em muzzle loaders but the two bottom layers, they was sidewinders. And the men used to go to bed in balloons at night and come down in parachutes in the mornin'.

A pretty sight it used to be to watch 'em comin' down.

"R-o-oo-ool out! Daylight in the swamp!" one of the cookees would yell, and then in minute or two they'd all be rollin' out of their blankets, and the parachutes would open and they'd all come sailin' down. It sure was a pretty sight—about as fine a show as I ever laid eyes on.

Sometimes in the mornin' I used stop at the door of the bunkhouse, on my way from the barn, to watch 'em. For Bill and I generally used to be on our way in to breakfast about that time, and Bill'd sometimes take the time to stop for a minute or so.

"I like to see 'em," he'd say to me. "Angus, that's a mighty fine show. They come faster now than they used to when it was just for sourdough biscuits. But we'll have to hustle along and get our hotcakes. We got to get back to the Ox."

That spring on the Big Onion we had an awful lot of trouble with the garlic that growed there where Garlic Crick joins Big Onion River—a kind of V-shaped tract in there along the loggin' road, that was just full of it. The cook tried to use it all up seasonin' the soup but the Frenchies wouldn't stand for it in their pea soup after the first week, and even with that he only got the top layer off and then there was four more layers growin' under that one. It beats all how thick that wild garlic can grow when it gets a good start. Everybody that even went by that place was seasoned so strong there wasn't nobody else could live with him, and worst of it, he couldn't stand to live with himself even. And we pretty near just had to break up camp, but then Paul heard that the Italian garlic crop was goin' to fail that year and so we grubbed up the whole piece, every last layer of it, and shipped it all to Italy and that way we got rid of it at last; just in time when a good many of us was goin' on the drive anyway, though. ■

Bye Bye

The Caribbean: Haiti

If only tortoise had used common sense, his trip would have been relatively short from Haiti to New York—much shorter than this story's migration from India to Haiti via Africa. The story in all its essentials was recorded in India in *The Panchatantra* around 200 B.C.E. It can be found as an African story as well as an African American one in Virginia Hamilton's *The People Could Fly*. The lesson is always the same, sometimes spelled out, but the specifics of this one are contemporary, reflecting the emigrants' mixed emotions: curiosity and anxiety about the place of their destination and a bit of pride in having some knowledge of the language of their new country. Perhaps this story has a slightly poignant twist, since not all people who wish to emigrate can. The tone in which the story was told to Ms. Wolkstein, however, was merry, as the Creole-speaking storyteller Michelle and the other villagers who had gathered that evening on the porch of Dr. Jeanne Philippe, a country doctor and one of Ms. Wolkstein's Haitian friends, proceeded to try out their own English on her (Wolkstein, 1978).

Source: "Bye Bye" from *The Magic Orange Tree and Other Haitian Folktales* by Diane Wolkstein. New York: Knopf, 1978. pp. 190–191. Reprinted with the permission of Diane Wolkstein.

All the birds were flying from Haiti to New York. But Turtle could not go, for he had no wings.

Pigeon felt sorry for Turtle and said, "Turtle, I'll take you with me. This is what we'll do. I'll hold in my mouth one end of a piece of wood and you hold on to the other end. But you must not let go. No matter what happens, do not let go or you'll fall into the water."

Pigeon took one end of a piece of wood and Turtle the other end. Up into the air Pigeon flew and Turtle with him, across the land and toward the sea.

As they came near the ocean, Turtle and Pigeon saw on the shore a group of animals who had gathered together to wave goodbye to the birds who were leaving. They were waving steadily until they noticed Turtle and Pigeon. Turtle? They stopped waving and a great hubbub broke out.

"Look!" they cried to each other. "Turtle is going to New York. Even Turtle is going to New York!"

And Turtle was so pleased to hear everyone talking about him that he called out the one English word he knew:

"Bye-bye!"

Oh-oh. Turtle had opened his mouth, and in opening his mouth to speak, he let go of the piece of wood, and fell into the sea.

For that reason there are many Pigeons in New York, but Turtle is still in Haiti. ■

Juan Bobo

Originally, Juan Bobo might have derived from a literary figure in Spanish picaresque novels of the seventeenth century, in which a traveling rogue meets different types of people and plays practical jokes on them to parody their trades and manners. The Juan Bobo stories came to the Americas, however, as oral tales (Lastra, 1999). They can be found in many Central American and South American countries, but they are particularly beloved in Puerto Rico. Below, Belpré has combined two of the stories about Juan Bobo.

"Bobo" means "fool", but Juan Bobo is not just a fool. He is also a culture hero for Puerto Ricans, who have had to deal first with Spanish-aristocratic domination and then with U.S. cultural domination after the Spanish-American War (Lastra, 1999). In the first story, Juan Bobo seems to play the impractical fool, a typical numskull who comes up with an outlandish solution to a simple problem. Yet even this typical noodlehead tale can be taken as a satire of those who would put on airs, like the pig in fancy clothes (as Corsaro points out in her review of Pitre's *Juan Bobo and the Pig* in *Booklist*, October 15, 1993). In the second story Juan is more overtly the culture hero as he manages, in spite of his initial foolishness, to squeeze both money and a delicious meal out of the rich man.

In other stories Juan Bobo shows his lack of common sense by taking things literally. He brings suit against some flies, and when the judge tells him that he should just kill any fly he finds, he immediately kills one on top of the judge's head, thus landing in jail. This story, however, illustrates another interpretation of the character of Juan Bobo. He is the outsider who

does not know social custom, the peasant who is not conversant with the legal intricacies of a government that holds power over him. This aspect of the Juan Bobo character is even more evident in a story for children, "Do Not Sneeze, Do Not Scratch, Do Not Eat" in Carmen T. Bernier-Grand's easy reader *Juan Bobo: Four Folktales from Puerto Rico*. In still other stories Juan Bobo inverts the social hierarchy when he cheats his landlord out of all his possessions. He has even been called a Puerto Rican superhero who takes on the powerful and beats them at their game (Lastra, 1999). In most children's versions, however, he is a simple, impractical, and lovable noodlehead.

Once upon a time there was a boy who lived with his mother up in the highlands. There was no other boy like him in the entire land. He was both cunning and silly in a way all of his own. His name was Juan, but everyone called him Juan Bobo. Juan's mother had a pig and a duck. The pig was her pet and the duck an investment which she intended to sell at the right time.

One morning, after breakfast, she said: "Juan, the year has been good to us. I am going to church and give thanks for all our gifts. Mind the house, feed the duck and take good care of the pig."

"Don't worry, Mamá. I'll take care of everything," Juan assured her.

When she was ready to leave he walked to the edge of the road with her. She stopped near the pigsty, patted the pig, and said: "*Adiós.*" Juan watched her go down the hill and disappear behind the tall trees. Then he went back to the house. He swept, he scrubbed and he dusted. He mixed the feeding for the duck and put it into a gourd. Just then a shrill squeal filled the air. "The pig," cried Juan, and ran out to see what was the matter. He found the pig pacing the sty and squealing as she had never done before.

"What is the matter?" he said. He remembered how quiet she had been when his mother had patted

Source: "Juan Bobo" from *The Tiger and the Rabbit and Other Tales* by Pura Belpré. Illustrated by Tomie dePaola. New York: Lippincott, 1965. pp. 49–54. Reprinted with permission from Centro de Estudios Puertoriquenos, Hunter College, CUNY.

her a few minutes before. "Aha, I know. You want to follow her," he said, glad he had solved the problem. So he brought her to the house and went to his mother's room. He opened the trunk and took out a skirt, a shirt, a pair of loop earrings and a small mantilla. He dressed her in all these things and brought her to the edge of the road. "Go," he said, "you will find Mamá at the church." He gave her a gentle push to start her on the way, and then hurried to the house to finish his chores.

Off went the pig, down the steep hill and into the road. Suddenly her snout began to twitch. She dashed across the road and entered the woods. She grunted with delight. A few more trots and she came face to face with a muddy water hole. She plunged in and began to splash to her heart's content.

At noon Juan's mother returned from church. She noticed the empty sty, but thought Juan had removed the pig to the shade. But when Juan saw her alone, he said: "Where is the pig, Mamá?"

"What do you mean?" said his mother.

"Didn't she come back with you?"

"What did you do with the pig?" said his mother, a tone of alarm in her voice.

"Well, she began to squeal very loud. I thought she wanted to follow you. So I dressed her in some of your clothes and sent her to church."

"Oh, Juan," cried his mother. "Now we have lost the pig."

"Don't worry, Mamá. We still have the duck," said Juan trying to console her.

"That duck must go before something else happens to it. Tomorrow you must go to town and sell it. And be sure you get a good price for it."

"Sí, Sí, Mamá. I'll take care of everything," Juan promised.

The following morning Juan left with the duck under his arms. He was not the only one on the road. Vegetable, charcoal and fruit vendors, some on foot, others on donkeys, were hurrying to the market. Eager to sell the duck, Juan began to call: "A duck for sale. A duck for sale." Now and then someone would stop and ask to examine the duck. But, after much consideration, they would return it. "Its meat won't be sweet enough," he would say. Juan kept up his calling. But, no matter how much he called, or how often he was

stopped, the remark was always the same: "Its meat won't be sweet enough." And Juan who had never tasted duck meat in any form or fashion, wondered what they were talking about.

By and by he came to a sugar cane mill. He was tired of calling, he was hot and very thirsty, he thought of the cool guarapo—the sweet drink made from the fermented sugar cane juice. One glass of that drink was just what he needed to quench his thirst. He decided to go in and ask for a drink. He tied the duck to a shrub near a wide earthen jug, and hurried to the shed where the men were working.

Refreshed and rested he came back to pick up the duck. But, where was it? Part of the string was still hanging from the bush, but the duck was nowhere in sight.

He looked through the tall grass about the place. He ran to the road and searched along the bushes, but found nothing. He ran back to the sugar mill and circled the tall piles of dried sugar cane stubs, with no success. As he stood there wondering where to search next, he heard a feeble, "quack, quack," coming from the earthen jug. He looked into it, and there, waddling in thick molasses, was the duck.

Juan began to laugh. He laughed and he laughed. Now he could sell his duck, he was sure of it. He pulled it out and sped to town as fast as he could. Once there he began to call: "A duck for sale. A duck for sale. Meat as sweet as molasses. Meat as sweet as molasses."

His calls awoke Don Alfonso, who was taking a siesta on his cool balcony. He looked down the street and recognized the vendor. "Juan, bring your duck up here," he called.

Juan hurried up the stairway. The duck feathers glistened as if they had been lacquered. Don Alfonso was impressed. "Why, I have never seen a duck like this before. I'll give you fifty pesetas for it, Juan."

"Not enough," said Juan. "This is not an ordinary duck. Its meat is sweet as molasses."

Don Alfonso thought for a while. It was not always easy to deal with Juan Bobo. If you weren't careful he would get the best of you. "A hundred pesetas, not a centavo more," he offered. He counted the money and gave it to Juan.

"*Gracias,*" Juan said and turned to go.

"Wait, I have a favor to ask of you. Will you go and tell my friends to come to my house for dinner? This duck will make a fine treat."

"That will cost you more money," said Juan.

Don Alfonso left the balcony. Juan thought he had gone to get more pesetas, but he had gone for a paper.

"Here are the names and addresses. Go, I will pay you twenty pesetas for the errand."

Juan looked at the list. "Twenty-five pesetas. Your friends live all over the town," said Juan.

"Very well," Don Alfonso shook his head and sighed.

Juan ran down the steps two at a time. He went from house to house delivering the message. When he returned, the table was set for dinner. He sat in a corner to rest his legs.

By and by the guests began to arrive. They were all businessmen. Don Alfonso noticed Juan sitting in the corner. Why don't you go home?" he whispered.

"I am waiting to be paid for the errand," he whispered back.

"Here is the money. Go home," said Don Alfonso sternly.

The cook brought the duck to the table.

"Now, my friends, let us sit down and enjoy this treat. The meat is as sweet as molasses." He took the knife to carve the duck. Just then he noticed Juan still sitting in the corner. His face got as red as a beet. He was angry.

"Why haven't you gone?" he cried.

"I would like my mother to taste the sweet meat," said Juan.

Don Alfonso carved a leg, wrapped it in a napkin, and handed it to Juan.

Juan took it and sat down again.

"But, why don't you go now?" asked Don Alfonso.

"A duck has two legs. If I bring just one to my mother she will wonder where the other one had gone," explained Juan.

Don Alfonso opened his mouth to speak, but no words came out of it. Like one hypnotized, he carved the other leg, wrapped it in a napkin, and handed it to Juan.

"*Gracias,* Don Alfonso," said Juan and ran down the steps.

Don Alfonso sat down and mopped his forehead. "To think that they call that one Juan Bobo," he said.

The guests burst out laughing. And while they were eating the remains of the duck, Juan Bobo was hurrying home with a fine meal for his mother, and enough pesetas in his pockets to make up for the lost pig. ■

The Dance of the Animals

The Caribbean: Puerto Rico

"Puerto Ricans are great friends of dancing. The origin of their dances has been traced to the great Indian Areytos and the . . . rhythms of the Congo and other regions of Africa. . . . However, we don't want to

Source: "The Dance of the Animals" from *The Tiger and the Rabbit and Other Tales* by Pura Belpré. Illustrated by Tomie dePaola. New York: Lippincott, 1965. pp. 97–103. Reprinted with permission from Centro de Estudios Puertoriquenos, Hunter College, CUNY.

imply that all dances are Afro-Indian since we also have Spanish and Arabian influences," said Nazario de Figueroa (cited in Lastra, 1999). According to Lastra the folklore of Puerto Rico reflects the country's multicultural and multiethnic makeup: Native American, African, Spanish, and modern urban. The dances Belpré mentions in the following story—tangos, jotas, waltzes, mazurkas, and traditional dances as well as the drums and guitars—underscore this blend of influences. Before the advent of television, dances, storytelling, and the singing of decimas, which are sonnet-like poems, at people's homes were popular, informal affairs where people came and went throughout the evening (Lastra, 1999). The trick, used in the following story, of getting one's adversary to throw one to safety while hiding in a pile of leaves recurs in folktales from other Latin American countries.

Once upon a time, a Lion and a Lioness lived together near a great forest and had for neighbors such couples as Señor Horse and Señora Mare, Señor and Señora Donkey, Señor Bull and Señora Cow, Señor and Señora Dog, and Señor and Señora Goat.

Times were bad for them, and soon the day came when they faced each other with nothing in the house to mix for a meal.

"We must do something," said the Lioness. "If times keep up like this, we shall certainly perish, a thing which should not happen, for are we not the strongest beasts in the forest? Has it not been said that the biggest fish shall eat the smaller?"

"True enough," answered the Lion. "Something must be done." And he set to thinking for a while.

"I have it," said he, after a while, "and a splendid idea it is, even if I have to say it myself! Listen."

"Which meat do we like the best?"

"Goat's meat," answered Señora Lioness.

"Right," said the Lion.

"It is the finest, the juiciest, and certainly the tastiest."

"Ah, Señora mía, you shall see," explained the Lion.

"But how are we to get such fresh and delicious meat?" asked the Lioness. "To hear you talk, one would think we are kings."

"I will tell you," said Señor Lion, "listen carefully. We shall give a ball, a grand ball, and to it we shall invite our friends. You who are so well liked will invite our neighbors, and they will not refuse. Outside the back door we will build a fire. When the dance begins and everyone is on the floor, I will push the goat and cast him into the fire. The rest depends on me. How do you like my plan?"

Señora Lioness thought for a while, shaking her head slowly at first as if the plan did not meet with her approval. Then, suddenly realizing what it all meant, she exclaimed, "Oh, most generous idea! Meat at last."

"You will have to hurry if my plans are to be carried out," said Señor Lion.

Señora Lioness went out to invite the neighbors, while Señor Lion stayed home to prepare the house for the big affair.

"*Hola!* Señora Mare," exclaimed Señora Lioness, as she came upon her in the forest.

"*Hola!* Señora Lioness! What are you doing around these parts, my good friend?"

"I came to invite you to a dance at our house. You and Señor Horse have such fine long legs and such strong hoofs. We need you for our orchestra. Could you not come and play the drum?"

"Oh, most certainly," answered Señora mare. "Only yesterday was I saying that we needed a little recreation. Yes, we will come and play the drum!"

"*Gracias,*" said Señora Lioness and went her way.

Pretty soon she found Señora Donkey.

"Ah, *amiga mía,*" said she, greeting her friend. "I was just going to your house. We are giving a ball and would like to have you and Señor Donkey come. Señor Horse and Señora Mare are coming to play the drum. Won't you and Señor Donkey come and play the trombone?"

"Why, yes, Señora Lioness, we will be there without fail."

"*Gracias! Gracias!*" said Señora Lioness. "You see your voices are so rich that without their resonance our ball would be a failure . . . "

On went Señora Lioness, faster and faster as she felt the pangs of hunger in her empty stomach. She had not had goat's meat in such a long time. She crossed lane after lane inviting here and there and giving each invitation with such graciousness that those invited felt that the dance would not be a success unless they accepted.

When she reached Señora Dog's house she found them sitting under the shade of a great tree.

"*Hola amigos!*" cried she, a little breathless, for she had walked quite a distance now and her throat was beginning to feel dry after so much talking.

"There is a great ball at my house tonight. You must both come," said Señora Lioness.

"I will go," said the dog, "but Señora Dog stays home.'

"I will go, too," said Señora Dog quickly.

"No, no," shrieked Señor Dog.

"Sí, sí," yelled Señora Dog.

"Oh, my friends," said Señora Lioness, hurriedly, "I must leave you to decide the matter yourselves. I must call at Señor Goat's house."

"Wait, Señora Lioness! Señor Goat is my best friend. I will take you there," said Señor Dog.

Once at Señor Goat's house, Señor Dog drew him aside and suggested that he should go alone to the dance.

It was done as he said. So Señora Dog and Señora Goat missed Señora Lioness's ball.

Señora Lioness left with a sad heart, for Señor Goat would not render enough meat for two.

Why did she have to invite the dog first? Why didn't she ignore him just this once? What would Señor Lion say when he heard that only Señor Goat was coming? Señor Goat, so thin and lanky!

She soon reached home. Señor Lion had straightened things, and outside the door a large bonfire flared. On a tripod hung a large earthenware pot. Señora Lioness heard the water sizzle and reach the boiling point. She hurried in.

"Well, you are here at last," cried the Lion! "Are they all coming?"

"Yes, all—that is, except—"

She never finished the sentence, for so excited was Señor Lion that he danced around the house for joy and then went out to tend the fire.

Señora Lioness had hardly finished placing a garland of coffee flowers on her neck when the first guests arrived.

"*Buenos días,*" said she, greeting Señor and Señora Donkey.

The newcomers looked spotlessly clean, and in order to play freely they had refrained from wearing ornaments.

"What a beautiful garland!" exclaimed Señor Donkey. "And how becoming!"

"*Gracias,* my friend," answered Señora Lioness.

Another pair came along. This time it was Señor and Señora Cat.

"Oh!" exclaimed Señora Lioness, a note of admiration in her voice, "What an adorable necklace!"

Señora Cat had woven honeysuckle and pinned a bunch around her neck on a blue ribbon. She looked like a flower herself, her beautiful eyes dancing for pure joy. Her white fur stood out as if it had been freshly brushed. As she moved about, the delicate scent of honeysuckle spread, perfuming the air.

When Señor Bull and Señora Cow appeared, they were as pretty as a picture. From the river they came, yet dry and shining! They had threaded gray and red chaplets around their horns. The tan of their hides had a lustrous shine and the gray and red of the berries stood out against the black of their large soft eyes.

Last came Señor Dog and Señor Goat.

"And the Señoras?" inquired Señor Lion. "Aren't they coming?"

"No," said Señor Goat.

"Oh no!" said Señor Dog.

"My dear," whispered Señor Lion to Señora Lioness, "we shall have to eat them both, since Señora Goat did not come."

"Like Señor and Señora Donkey, Señor Goat and Señor Dog wore no ornaments; but their guilt in leaving their respective wives home showed in their faces.

Motioning to the orchestra to begin, Señor and Señora Lioness opened the dance. The couples whirled, stamped, and bellowed. What tangos and jotas! Waltzes mingled with mazurkas and traditional dances. And the orchestra! Never had there been one like it! Señora Ant played the guitar. The drum was placed in such a convenient place that Señor Horse had no difficulty in striking it with his hoofs, as he danced around.

What a resonance! Señor Dog barked and howled. Señor and Señora Cat miaowed, while the constant stamping of Señor Donkey and the bombarding brays of Señora Mare filled the place. On and on the couples danced until the floor creaked under the weight of their bodies.

Suddenly on one of the turns of a dance Señor Goat and Señor Dog, who for lack of partners were dancing together, spied the bonfire outside the door.

"*Amigo,*" said the goat, "I do not like the look of that fire. Let us go, for this bonfire is meant for us and so is the pot of boiling water hanging over it. No doubt, Señor Lion means to eat us up."

Through the dancing couples they pulled and pushed, skipping all the time until they reached the farther door. Once out, they ran as fast as their legs could carry them, looking back now and then to see if they were being followed.

Meanwhile, at the ball, things went on as before. Suddenly Señor Lion missed Señor Dog and Señor Goat. As quickly as he could, without causing suspicion, he left the house.

The afternoon was cool and the air was heavy with the scent of the acacia trees in full bloom. The wind began to blow and with it a sprinkle of rain, which came slowly at first and then in great torrents. On and on ran Señor Lion and, coming out at the turn of the road, he spied Señor Dog and Señor Goat, running ahead of him. Faster and faster ran the Lion, yet faster went Señor Dog and Señor Goat.

They soon reached the river. It was swollen with the sudden downpour. The Dog was not afraid and swam across, but the goat did not know what to do. Looking back he saw Señor Lion coming closer and closer.

"Oh, for a good place of safety!" he said.

As he turned around, he spied a large bunch of hay. He quickly got under it and rolled himself until only his tail stuck out. Presently Señor Lion reached the shore.

"Where have they gone?" exclaimed he. He heard a sharp call. He looked across the river and there he saw Señor Dog happily jumping and mocking him. Señor Lion snarled and showed his fangs. If he could only swim across, he thought, he could show this impudent dog what he could do. But he could not and, what was more humiliating, Señor Dog knew it, too.

"You are so clever and quick," called the Dog from across the river. "Why don't you swim? Surely the current will help you."

Señor Lion was furious. Swim indeed!

He looked around. The place was full of stones. He picked up one and hurled it at the dog across the river. Señor Dog saw it coming and jumped out of reach.

"Oh, my friend," he called, "see that bundle of straw near you? Why don't you try and throw a stalk of that at me?"

"One stalk, indeed," roared Señor Lion, fully realizing that Señor Dog was making fun of his strength. "I will throw you the pack."

So saying he leaned forward and tried to pull at the pack, which besides being slippery because of the rain, was quite heavy with the weight of the Goat inside of it. No sooner had he pulled at it than he slipped and fell on his back.

At this Señor Dog leaped up and barked for joy. "Try again, my friend," he called at Señor Lion.

Señor Lion stood up and went at the straw pack again. He pulled and pulled and, finally raising it, he hurled it across the river. No sooner did it land on the ground than Señor Goat jumped out of his hiding place and accompanied by Señor Dog began to cut capers in the air.

"Señor Lion," he called, "thanks for ferrying me over. If I did lose my tail, my life indeed, I saved!"

Señor Lion's rage had no limit and, looking down at his paws, he discovered that he had a large amount of fur entangled in his claws. Then he laughed and answered:

"So you have, my friend, but by your stump you'll tell your tale."

And it is true, because even to this day, goats have only a stump for a tail. ∎

▨ Trickster Tales

Of all the characters populating the world's folk literature, it is the trickster who provides the most fun for listeners and readers, as well as the greatest challenges to their sense of ethics. Tricksters can be mythical and imbued with creative powers, as are the Native American tricksters, or simply human, as are the German Till Eulenspiegel, the Turkish Nasreddin Hoca, the Arabic Goha, the Latin American Pedro de Urdemalas, and the African American John (also referred to as High John the Conqueror). The trickster, how-

"How Till Owlyglass Caused an Innkeeper to be Terrified of a Dead, Frozen Wolf." Illustrated by Fritz Wegner.

From: *The Wicked Tricks of Till Owlyglass* Text 1989 Michael Rosen. Illustrations © 1989 Fritz Wegner. Reproduced by permission of Walker Books Ltd., London.

ever, is always an ambiguous figure. Sometimes he is the bringer of good things, such as light or stories, or he is the speaker for the underdog. At other times the trickster's actions are reprehensible. He may be killed, but he will come back over and over again for one more clever or foolish trick to entertain, to shock, and to instruct.

There are many instances in which female characters also act like tricksters, using their wit and wisdom to overcome their exploiters or to save their loved ones from danger; Gretel from "Hansel and Gretel" comes to mind. But females are seldom recurrent **stock characters** in the way male tricksters are, and females seem less ambiguous, less likely to create trouble and excitement for its own sake (Jurich, 1998).

The following description by Richard Erdoes and Alfonso Ortiz (1998) refers to Native American tricksters: "always hungry for another meal swiped from someone else's kitchen, always ready to lure someone else's wife into bed, always trying to get something for nothing, shifting shapes (and even sex), getting caught in the act, ever scheming, never remorseful." African tricksters too are notorious for their defiance of conventions, particularly of communal values regarding sharing and work, always ready to take advantage of others and, as Roger Abrahams puts it, ready to stir things up for the "sheer joy of taking on the challenge" (1985, p. 3). "If there is any advice for real-life behavior in the stories, it is to remind us to be on guard constantly for others' tricks and to remind us to admire those who are able to win the contest by their wits" (Abrahams, 1985, p. 20). The trickster encompasses the ambiguities of Everyman—sometimes divine-like, striving for greatness, at other times base and foolish, but always inventive and resilient, trying to survive in a messy world. If it is difficult to define the trickster, perhaps it is because he is slippery and always in a state of becoming, but good or bad, he endears himself through his wit, his defiance of convention, and most of all, his indomitable spirit.

In spite of these universals, it is important to pay attention to how specifically a trickster works in his own society (Pelton, 1980). Across Native North America, the trickster figure is both culture hero and fool. He is called by different names by the different tribes: Coyote by the Nez Percé and other Idaho, Oregon, and Northern California tribes; Yehl [Raven] by Pacific Northwest tribes; Veeho by the Cheyenne; Iktomi [Spider] by the Lakota (Sioux); Napi by the Siksika (Blackfoot); Nanaboozoo by the Ojibway; Nixant by the Gros Ventres; and Masau'u by the Hopi. The trickster participates in the act of creation (Bright, 1993) by bringing light, fire, and the healing arts; he teaches humans right from wrong; and he also introduces death into the world. As William Bright, in his *The Coyote Reader,* says, the trickster, through his creative acts, brings reality with all its messiness to what might have been an ideal world (1993). The Native American trickster can be an impulsive, generous bungler, as is Nanaboozhoo (Johnston, 1995); he can be fun-loving but also cruel as is Napi (Bullchild, 1985), he can be clever, greedy, scatological, and often a fool, as is Coyote (Bright, 1993); and he can be envious and mischievous as is Rabbit in the Cherokee tales (Ross, 1994).

Africa's many trickster figures also differ in their assumed animal forms and have much in common, not only in their basic natures but also in some of their specific adventures. Hare (or tortoise) makes leopard his riding horse in West Africa, while in South Africa, it is Chakide (a weasel-like creature) who manages to get a ride on the back of lion. Hare is also important in East Africa, for instance, in Kenya. A more lovable trickster, Cunie Rabbit or Dwarf Antelope, outsmarts leopard in Sierra Leone and Zaire. Owomoyela says this of the Yoruba trickster, the tortoise Ajapa: "[The Yoruba admire] his resourcefulness and his resilience while they disapprove of his duplicity and disdain for reciprocity" (1997, pp. xii–xiv), and frequently refer to him as " 'Master of Sundry Wiles' for his seemingly inexhaustible supply of mischievous tricks to secure some advantage to himself with little or no expenditure of physical effort" (pp. xi). The African trickster can take on mythic proportions, bringing good things to the world, as when Anansi contends with the Sky

God for ownership of stories. At other times, the trickster is cruel, even a criminal.

When hare, tortoise, and spider were transported to the Americas by African slaves, they not only changed their names to Brer Rabbit, Brer Terrapin, and Annancy or Aunt Nancy but also adapted to the new world in other ways. No longer serving unique tribes, they came to serve African American communities whose cultural heritage was more pan-African than tribal (Roberts, 1989). The function of the trickster also changed, as numerous scholars, from Zora Neal Hurston (1935) to John Roberts, have observed. Whereas the stories about tricksters' selfish tricks frequently served as negative examples in Africa, stories about their American counterparts helped to ensure the psychological and cultural survival of the slaves. The trickster's opponent is more commonly a stronger, meaner character than is the case in African trickster tales. Brer (Brother) Rabbit is usually, though not always, pitted against Brer Bear, Brer Fox, Brer Alligator, and Brer Wolf. Brer Rabbit can stir up trouble just for the fun of it, for instance, when he introduces Brer Alligator to Trouble, but more often he is defending himself against becoming the dinner of Brer Fox or Brer Wolf. While calling each other politely Brer or Sis, it is clear that the animals are no more friends than were master and slaves in the plantation system. The trickster served as a role model for survival (Roberts, 1989).

Rex Nettleford, a folklorist, writes about Annancy, the Jamaican trickster, "This picaresque character misses no chance for chicanery . . . as though he lives in a world that offers him no other chance for survival. . . . [T]o cope with an unstraight and crooked world one needs unstraight and crooked paths" (cited by Van Sertima, 1989, p. 107). Van Sertima points out, however, that even while using the trickster stories to maintain resistance in the face of oppression and hardship, the storytellers disassociated themselves from the censurable actions of Annancy by closing each story with the disclaimer "Jack Mandora me no choose none" as "a plea to the doorman of Heaven's gate to absolve them of responsibility for Annancy's wickedness" (Van Sertima, 1989, p. 108).

Some African stories on both sides of the Atlantic seem almost identical, as in the case of the talking skull stories, in which a skull, when asked how it got there, tells the listener "by talking too much." But in these cases, the stories were generally used somewhat differently. In the African versions, the story might be simply a warning against loose talk in general, whereas in the American versions, the story's function was to warn John, a stock trickster-slave character, against talking too freely to the slave owners, that is, from jeopardizing his own people (Roberts, 1989).

In Latin American stories, the three traditions (Native, European, and African) are at times distinct and at other times blended (Delacre, 1996, Gonzalez, 1997; Bierhorst, 2002). This is evident in the choices of popular trickster characters in different parts of Latin America. According to Gonzalez (1997), Anansi's and Brer Rabbit's cousin, Tio Conejo (Uncle Rabbit), appears in those countries (outside of the Caribbean) where there were large plantations and African slaves. There are also Venezuelan and Nicaraguan stories about these characters. Elsewhere, the popular trickster is the fox of European origins. In Mexico, coyote and hare stories are widely told both by Native and Latino people.

In Asia, there seem to be several kinds of tricksters, of which one kind is the usual animal trickster. The animals are given human motives, but their characters also reflect people's perceptions of the animals that are important to them. In Mongolia, for instance, the deer is seen as sly and untrustworthy, the hedgehog tricky and dishonest, the camel as honorable and stalwart, and the horse as magical (Khorloo, 1996). As in other parts of the world, some animals trick each other out of food, engage in fantastic lying contests, and cause each other to look foolish or to get into trouble. Stories similar to those about Brer Rabbit in the United States and Reynard the Fox in Europe are told about foxes and otters in Japan.

Another kind of trickster one encounters in Asian folktales is the shape shifter. In Japan, three such shape shifters are the tengu, the raccoon dog (a badger-like creature), and the fox. According to Royall Tyler (1987), all of these shape shifters specialize in fooling humans and even each other, through illusion. The tengu, who are depicted in art as long-nosed and winged mountain ascetics, specialized in deceiving

Buddhist monks in medieval Japan. In more recent stories, they are likely to deceive anyone. Foxes often take on human shapes, especially that of a beautiful woman with whom her husband lives happily until he discovers her true nature. Chinese lore reflects similar beliefs about foxes (Scott, 1980). Animal tricksters such as the raccoon dog (badger) and the fox do not get away with their tricks and often come to a sad end in Japanese tales. Tengu, however, seem immortal. Tony Johnston's picture book *The Badger and the Magic Fan* is based on the exploits of these characters.

A third kind of trickster in Asian literature is the clever man or woman who uses his or her wits to get themselves or a loved one out of trouble. They are much like clever peasants or soldiers in European folktales. In a number of these stories, it is the wife who shows ingenuity when her husband is at a loss for a solution to their problems. As with European clever women, however, these wives are not named or do not have a recurrent set of exploits attached to them.

One trickster who crosses the continents of Europe and Asia is the figure of the Hoca or Hodja of Turkey. A Hoca is any member of the community who is learned in the Koran and therefore can give sermons or act as teacher and judge. The most famous is Nasreddin Hoca, who not only takes on the role of wise teacher and witty commentator on life, but who, in some accounts, was also said to have been the champion of oppressed Turks during the invasion of Turkey by Tamerlane in the fifteenth century. Stories of the Hoca can be found throughout the former Ottoman Empire, from the Balkans to Turkey, and as far east as India, where comic book versions of the Hoca's adventures are being sold today. The Goha is an Arabic trickster figure whose exploits are very similar to the Hoca's and whose stories also span two continents: Asia and Africa.

Two of Europe's best known tricksters, Reynard the Fox originally from France and Till Eulenspiegel of Germany, Belgium, and the Netherlands (spellings vary), have folkloric forbears but became fully developed characters through written literature. Over the centuries, however, they have slipped back into folklore. Modern French collectors of folklore have found legends about Seigneur Reynard in the region of Ile de France and in Lorraine (Massignon, 1968), and the name Reynard has become synonymous with "fox" in many parts of Europe.

Whereas Reynard is a representative of a rapacious aristocracy, as suggested in his depiction as the lord of a castle to which he retreats whenever besieged by his enemies (Owen, 1994), Till Eulenspiegel is a representative of the wily Renaissance peasant trying to find a livelihood in town (Oppenheimer, 1991); Till can be nasty and harsh, but usually the target of his tricks is a master craftsman who has treated him meanly or exploitatively because of Till's lower station in life. Till also likes to trick pompous, greedy, or hypocritical priests, innkeepers, doctors, and scholars. Many of the stories told about Till are crude, but they are, even after 500 years, still funny. Though the specific stories about him might not be common knowledge today, German children still hear people refer to him. Germans today think of him as someone who was able to come out on top in any circumstance and who thumbed his nose at the pompous and the powerful.

A third European trickster, the peasant boy who is braver and cleverer than the rich landlords, noblemen, and kings, appears in a wide variety of stories from humorous to heroic. He is known as Jack in

England and Ireland and is famous for robbing giants and outsmarting the devil. As a nineteenth century runaway apprentice and homeless boy in Manchester, England, told a social investigator, "the best man in the story is always Jack" (Philip, 1992, p. 20). Most of the Jack tales, however, have been found not in England but in the United States, in the Appalachians, where the stories not only were kept alive by descendants of English and Scottish immigrants but also were adapted to the New World.

There are tricksters other than those included here. What I hope to do in this chapter is to introduce the character of the trickster in some of his or her many incarnations and kaleidoscopic personalities. After children have been introduced to these characters and to the folk who have told their stories, they will be able to recognize tricksters in other guises, such as in television cartoons, literary works, and real life. After all, one of our national icons is that "wascally wabbit," Bugs Bunny.

activity idea

For picture book versions of the following stories, see "Picture Book Related to the Stories in the *Allyn & Bacon Anthology of Traditional Literature*" on the Web Supplement at www.ablongman.com/lechner.

The Fantastic Lying Contest

Africa: Ghana—Ashanti

The original home of Anansi the spider is among the Ashanti [Asante] tribe of Ghana. His popularity is such that he is now known by other names in neighboring West African countries and is well-known in the Caribbean where his name is often spelled as Annancy. In *I Was Never Here and This Never Happened*

Source: "The Fantastic Lying Contest" excerpted from *I Was Never Here and This Never Happened* © Dorinda Hafner, 1996. Used by permission of Ten Speed Press, Berkeley, California. pp. 114–116.

(1996), Dorinda Hafner's lively memoir of growing up in Ghana, the author recalls "the mixture of joy and horror" of her childhood in post-independence Ghana, when different parties fought for control of the government and the country was in anarchy. In the traditional stories too, she says, there is much turmoil, but "it's usually solved with cleverness, not force" (p. 114). Lying contests and tall tales are popular from Mongolia to the United States, but here the lying contest has the added function of saving Anansi's hide one more time. There are story collections, plays, and musicals about the exploits of Ananse or Anansi in Africa.

One day, the fly, the ant, and the mosquito went hunting together.

They came upon Mr. Ananse, the spider, in the forest, and decided to gang up on him. But Ananse was stronger than he looked and after mighty struggle, they had to stop for a rest.

"Why are you trying to kill me?" Ananse asked them.

"Because we are hungry," they replied. "After all, everybody needs to eat."

"Well, I need to eat too," he said. "Why shouldn't I eat you?"

"You aren't strong enough to overpower us," they answered, in one voice.

"Ah, but nor are you three strong enough to overpower me," he pointed out. "So let's make a bargain. Each of us will tell the others a most extraordinary fantastic story. If I say I don't believe any of your three stories, you may eat me. And if you don't believe my story, I will eat you."

This sounded fair enough. The ant went first. "Before I was born," said the ant, "my father inherited a new piece of land. But the very first day he went out to clear, it, he cut his foot with a bush knife and couldn't work it. So I jumped out of my mother's womb, cleared the land, cultivated the ground, planted it, harvested my crop, and sold it at the market. When I was born a few days later, my father was already a rich man."

The three friends looked at Ananse expectantly, waiting for him to call this a lie so they could eat him. But instead he said, "Ah, how interesting. Clearly this story has a ring of truth about it."

Then the mosquito told his story. "One day when I was only four years old," he began, "I was sitting in the forest, peacefully gnawing on an elephant I had killed, when a leopard crept up to me. He opened his jaws to swallow me, but I just reached my hand down his throat, grabbed the inside of his tail, and gave it a good yank to turn him inside out. Well, it seems this leopard had just eaten a sheep, because suddenly the sheep was on the outside and the leopard inside *him*. The

sheep thanked me quite profusely, and went off to graze somewhere else.

Again, the hunting partners waited for Ananse to denounce this story as a lie, because they were quite eager to make a meal of him, but instead he said, "What a fascinating story. How I love to hear fantastic things!"

So then the fly took his turn. "Just the other day," he said, "I came upon an antelope. I aimed my gun at him and fired, then ran up and caught him, threw him to the ground, skinned him, and dressed the meat. Just then the bullet from my gun came along, so I caught it and put it back in my pocket. I carried the antelope meat up into the tallest tree around, built a fire, cooked up the entire antelope, and ate it all. But when it was time to climb down, I had eaten so much and my stomach was so swollen that I was too heavy to climb. So I went back to the village, and got a rope, which I brought back to the tree I was in. Then I tied the rope around my waist and carefully let myself down to the ground."

The three waited patiently for Ananse to say, "You are lying," but instead he cried, "Ah, what a miraculous true story!"

Finally, it was Ananse's turn to tell a tale. "Last year," he said, "I planted a coconut tree. One month later, it had grown very tall, and was bearing fruit. I was hungry, so I harvested three ripe coconuts. When I opened the first one, a fly flew out. I opened the second, and an ant crawled out. And when I opened the third one, out flew a mosquito. Now clearly, since I had planted the coconut tree, the ant, the fly, and the mosquito belonged to me. But when I tried to eat them, they ran away. I have been searching for them ever since so that I could eat them, as it's only fair—and now, at last I've found you."

The three hunters were silent. If they said, as Ananse had to their stories "How true, how true", then he would be within his rights to claim them as his property, and he would eat them. But if they said that he had lied, then by the rules of the contest he would also be allowed to eat them. They couldn't make up their minds what to say, so they turned tail and ran away as fast as they could.

And ever since then, Ananse has eaten every mosquito, fly, and ant he catches, because he outwitted them in the lying contest. ■

How Chakide Rode the Lion

Africa: South Africa—Zulu

Chakide is more a mythical dwarf who is cunning and possesses magical powers than a purely human-like animal trickster. According to folklorist Brian DuToit, Chakide (or Chakijana, his full name) looks like a weasel but is not limited to acting like a weasel. He had a miraculous birth, calling out from his mother's womb (a frequently recurring motif in Africa), and he is cunning and has magical powers. Although he isn't always a trickster, he often performs that role (Du Toit, 1976). This is a Zulu folktale, but Chakide also exists among the Xhosa and the Tsonga further north. Like his counterparts in many regions of Africa as well as in the Caribbean and the United States, where Brer Rabbit manages to pull off this trick, Chakide fools a much more powerful character into letting him ride him.

Once upon a time, the animals were staying together—their King being the lion. Chakijana alleged to the other animals that although the lion was feared by all, he could ride him like a horse. During this allegation the lion was away to get food. The animals were surprised to hear such an allegation against their King. Chakide left the animals, requesting that the animals should not tell the lion.

After his departure, the King arrived and all the animals rushed to tell him. The lion, as a result, became very angry and promised that day that he would not sleep before having eaten Chakide's meat. He searched for Chakide until he found him. Then he said, "Yes, you, Chakijana, told your friends that I am your horse?" "No, oh King, I did not say so. Let us repair to them and question the lot. How could I refer to you as such when there are many nonentities belonging to your August person. I never even refer to them as such." "Let us go and inquire," said the lion. On the way, Chakijana said he was suffering from a headache and was unable to walk. The lion offered to carry him on his back. As the were proceeding, the lion found a *sjambok** and Chakijana asked, "Please, oh King, let me take the sjambok to drive away the flies." They again found riding breeches and a cap, whereupon Chakijana said, "King, the sun has made me suffer on the head and feet." The lion handed the goods to Chakijana who dressed himself completely. When they were about to emerge where the animals were grazing, Chakijana started to strike the lion with the sjambok and he ran with speed past the animals. He was heard saying, "Do you realize now that this is a proper horse?" Chakijana passed riding his horse. When he came to a thick bush, Chakijana jumped and left saying, "Goodbye, oh fool!" ∎

Source: "How Chakide Rode the Lion" from *Content and Context of Zulu Folk-Narratives*, Brian M. DuToit. Gainesville, FL: University of Florida, 1976. Reprinted with the permission of the University Presses of Florida. pp. 46–47.

*This is a cowhide whip in which the handle and whip are frequently made from one piece of hide. The best known is the hippo-hide sjambok, which starts at about three quarters of an inch thickness and tapers off to less than one quarter of an inch. These whips are usually about 36 inches long.

The Peas Thief

Africa: Kenya—Giriama Ethnic Group

Asenath Odaga author of many children's books in Kenya, is also a collector of folktales. She encourages schoolchildren to be active folktale collectors as well. In the anthology from which this story is taken, she gives definitions, sources, suggestions for further collecting, and thought-provoking questions for children to consider regarding recurrent themes and symbols in the stories. Odaga is particularly concerned with folktale collecting from throughout Kenya, as the majority of earlier folktale collections represented just one or two Kenyan ethnic groups. She identifies both the place where the story was collected and the person who told it. Odaga collected this story, a popular trickster tale in East Africa, at Kaloleni, Kilfi District, Coast Province of Kenya; it was told to her by Paul John Kambi (Odaga, 1984). In it, a universally popular trick is used to catch the peas thief. "Tar baby" stories have been told from India to the Southwestern United States, but the most famous, Brer Rabbit, in the United States, might well be a relative of Hare in this story. Hare's escape is also a familiar motif.

Once upon a time, there was a farmer who had planted some peas in his field. When the peas were almost ready for harvesting, the farmer used to go to visit the field everyday. But on every visit, he noticed that some of the peas had been eaten. So he decided to lay a trap to catch whoever it was that was stealing and

Source: "The Peas Thief" from *Yesterday's Today: The Study of Oral Literature,* by Asenath Bole Odaga. Kisumu, Kenya: Lake Publishers & Enterprises, 1984. Reprinted with permission by Asenath Bole Odaga. p. 22.

eating his peas. He made a figure of a man with wax and placed it right in the middle of the *shamba*.

The following day, the Hare who was the culprit went as usual to the garden. He saw the figure and approached it asking, "Are you a human being?" but the figure didn't reply. The Hare asked again a second time and once more, there was no answer, so he gave it a hard blow with its right hand which got stuck, then he punched it hard with his left hand. This also got stuck, then he kicked it with both his right and left legs and these too got stuck on the wax.

"Leave me alone, you dumb fool," the Hare shouted, but the human figure made of wax just stayed quiet and made no movement!

"I'll hit and knock you down with my head," he shouted and true to his words, he butted the figure with his head which also got stuck. Now, the Hare was unable to move even a little, but remained suspended in a most uncomfortable position.

When the farmer came, he removed him from the wax figure of a man and shoved it in a basket, and was going to sew the basket up with a sisal string. But the Hare cried saying, "Yes, by all means, sew up the basket, but please use banana fibre." The Hare looked so helpless that the farmer granted him his request without giving it too much thought. He looked for a banana fibre and used it to sew the basket. He continued to work. Soon the sun dried the banana fibre which fell off, leaving the Hare free to escape! ∎

The Rat and the Ox

Asia: China

Emperor Huang-ti, also known as the Yellow Emperor, was the third of the five "Mythic Emperors" of China, according to one grouping of mythic predecessors established a thousand years later during the

Source: "The Rat and the Ox" from *Folktales of China* edited by Wolfram Eberhard. © 1965 by Wolfram Eberhard. Reprinted with permission by University of Chicago Press. pp. 74–75.

Han dynasty (206 B.C.E.–263 C.E.). Huang-Ti was the legendary predecessor of the founder of China's Shang Dynasty (approximately 1600–1027 B.C.E.), the first dynasty for which there is ample archeological evidence. The first mythic emperors were credited with bringing the beginnings of civilization to humankind: agriculture, domestication of animals, cookery, music, writing. The Yellow Emperor was said to have introduced the idea of government, coinage, wooden houses, boats, the bow and arrow, and the calendar with its sixty-year cycle. The Yellow Emperor's wife was given credit for introducing silkworm breeding and the weaving of silk (Scott, 1980; *Britannica 2002* CD-ROM).

Archeological evidence shows that the calendar had been established in China by the fourteenth century B.C.E., that is, the era of the Shang Dynasty, and was systematized during the Han Dynasty, 206 B.C.E.–221 C.E. (Girardot, 1987).

The traditional Chinese calendar is a solar/**lunar calendar** with twelve 29- or 30-day months. Each month begins with the moon in its dark phase. To keep the years even, so that the New Year always falls in winter (usually late January or early February) and the winter solstice always falls during the eleventh month, a leap year month is added from time to time (*Britannica 2002* CD-ROM).

The years within the sixty-year cycle have names. Each year's name has two components: the ten celestial branches, with names that have not been translated into English, and the twelve terrestrial branches with the familiar names of the twelve animals: rat, ox, tiger, hare, dragon, serpent, horse, goat, monkey, rooster, dog, and boar.

The most popular of the animals is the playful monkey, who can do all kinds of transformations and whose somersaults carry him great distances on his legendary trip to the West in search of the secret of life. The tiger is a powerful protector; the marking on its forehead is the Chinese character for "king." The dragon is the most auspicious of the animals in the calendar. There are five kinds of beneficial dragons in Chinese folklore, including one that brings rain and one that guards the imperial throne and protects humankind (Scott, 1980).

With so many powerful animals in the calendar, it is not surprising that stories would arise about how it was that rat came first. In this version, rat knows what successful politicians know: that people are more likely to be impressed by appearances than by substance or else that people are ever hungry for novelty while they take enduring worth for granted. Variants of the contest among the animals for first place in the zodiac are told in East Asia wherever the influence of Chinese culture had spread, from Mongolia to Singapore.

There was once a deity living among men—I forget exactly at what time—who wanted to find twelve animals for the zodiac in order to name the years.

He had already placed the dragon, the snake, the tiger, and the hare when the rat and the ox began to quarrel about which was the bigger. Naturally, the body and the appearance of the ox was much larger; when it heard the claims of the rat, it shook its horns and shouted, "Everyone knows that I, the ox, am big and immeasurably strong. How can a rat that only weighs a few pounds dare to compete with me? I call it ridiculous."

The sly and cunning rat merely laughed coldly at the boasts of the ox, and said, "Everyone is so conceited about his own size and capabilities. There is no standard. We must bend to the judgment of the majority. It is true that I am only a poor little rat, but I will measure myself with you today."

Fearing that the battle of words between the ox and the rat would develop into a serious conflict, the deity quickly interrupted. "Naturally a rat is not as big as an ox. But since he won't believe it, we must trust to the decision of the crowd. That is the just way to decide. I suggest that you think the matter over and then go out and hear the people's verdict." The ox agreed at once to the suggestion of the deity, since he thought that his victory was assured.

The rat, however, pretended to be in despair and sunk in gloom. He said, "I must be a little bigger before I can appear before the people."

Seeing the rat so disheartened, the ox thought that, whatever happened, the rat would still be smaller than he, and he agreed to its doubling its size. He himself did not bother, because he was already one hundred times bigger than the rat.

When the rat had grown, they went out into the town. "Look! Never before have I seen such a big rat. It is incredibly big." From the moment they left the house until their return, they heard on all sides exclamations of wonder at the size of the rat; but no one looked at the ox, because people see oxen every day, whereas they had never before seen such a large rat.

The stupid ox had fallen into the rat's trap, but it did not realize that it had been tricked—it merely thought the people had no eyes. Since it had lost, it had no dignity left, and had to resign the first place to the rat. From that time the rat became the first animal in the zodiac. ∎

The Clever Little Hedgehog

Asia: Mongolia

Whether hunting in the forests of Africa or huddled on the windswept treeless steppes of Mongolia, listeners appreciate a good lying contest. In this story, hedgehog is the winner, outfoxing even fox. This is to be expected in a Mongolian tale, as according to the Mongolian folklorist Pureviin Khorloo (1996), hedgehogs are considered dishonest because they never look people in the eye but point their snouts toward the ground. They are bad luck indoors, but a hedgehog skin with its spine pointing outward, when placed above the door, will keep away bad spirits and snakes.

The artist Norovsambuugiin Baatartsog, whose illustrations appear in *Mongolian Folktales,* practices a modern version of the ancient art of cutting shapes out of cloth to create intricate pictures. Mr. Baatartsog's papercut artworks are famous throughout Mongolia, where he is a professor of art at the Institute of Design in Ulaanbaatar.

Once upon a time, a Wolf, a Fox, and a Hedgehog lived together on the rolling steppes of Mongolia. One day, a long caravan of camels bearing all manner of goods from faraway lands passed near their home. When the dust raised by the caravan had settled, the three friends discovered a little plum that had fallen from one of the many sacks.

The animals had heard about plums, but none had ever seen one, let alone tasted one. They began to discuss which of them should have the privilege of eating this exotic fruit: there was only enough for one.

Source: "The Clever Little Hedgehog" from *Mongolian Folktales,* by Hilary Roe Metternich. Illustrated by Norovsambuugiin Baatartsog. Boulder, CO: Avery Press, 1996. Reprinted with permission by Avery Press, Inc. pp. 43–45.

After a long debate, the friends finally agreed to a contest. It was the Wolf who had the idea:

"I know!" he cried. "I think the one who gets drunk on *airak**** the quickest should have the pleasure of eating this plum!"

Thinking, of course, that he would win, the Wolf continued:

"As for me, I get drunk after just one sip of *airak!*"

The Fox was next to speak, and knowing that he was much smarter than the Wolf, he said: "That's nothing! I get drunk just by smelling *airak!*"

The last to speak was the Hedgehog, whom the others looked down upon because he was so small. He told his friends:

"Well, it's very sad for me, but I get drunk just hearing about *airak!*"

And with that, the Hedgehog swayed as if he were drunk.

The other animals had to admit that this clearly made the Hedgehog the winner. But before the Hedgehog could open his mouth to eat his prize, the envious Fox shouted:

"Wait! I have another idea. We need a second contest, I think that the one of us who runs the fastest should get to eat the plum!"

They all agreed to this second match, and prepared themselves for the race. The Hedgehog, who knew he stood no chance of winning because of his short legs, had already thought of a trick.

As the Wolf and the Fox took off in a cloud of dust, the Hedgehog caught hold of the fluffy tail of the Fox, and held on tight.

**Airak is a Mongolian drink made from fermented mare's milk.

Just before the speedy Fox crossed the finish line, he stopped and looked back to check where the others were. At that moment, the little Hedgehog dropped off his tail, scurried under his belly, and from the winning side of the finish line called out:

"Well, hello there Mr. Fox! Hello Mr. Wolf! I see you've finally arrived! What took you so long?"

This is how the Hedgehog also won the second contest.

As the Wolf and the Fox looked on enviously, the clever little Hedgehog gobbled up the plum.

And a plum never tasted better. ∎

Three Tales of the Mouse-Deer (Tale 3)

Asia: Indonesia—Borneo

Among the people of Indonesia, Kanchil, or Mouse-Deer, is a tiny deer that is loved for its swiftness and cleverness. The mouse-deer is local to Indonesian rain forests, but its exploits are performed by tricksters internationally. I first heard the motif of an animal crossing a river on the backs of a lineup of crocodiles or alligators from a storyteller in Georgia, who was retelling a Cherokee tale.

One day a mouse-deer was running through the forest when he fell into a deep pit that was covered over with leaves. He struggled mightily to climb up the muddy sides of the pit, only to fall back again to the bottom. He leaped into the air until he was exhausted. In despair, he crouched in a corner, trying to think what he could do.

Just then an elephant came by and peered into the pit. "Why, what are you doing down there?" he asked in surprise.

The mouse-deer said quickly, "Oh, I got word that the sky will soon fall, and that all the creatures in the forest will be crushed to death. So I climbed down here to save myself."

"The sky's going to fall?" the elephant repeated in alarm.

The mouse-deer nodded. "And all of you will be crushed to death."

"When will it happen?" the elephant asked.

"Very soon now."

"Let me come down there with you," the elephant begged. "I don't want to be killed."

The mouse-deer appeared to think this over. "There's scarcely room for you—and me," he said finally. "But I feel sorry for you. Come on down."

The elephant thanked him heartily and crashed clumsily into the pit, while the mouse-deer cowered in a corner. When the elephant was safely down, the nimble mouse-deer sprang onto his back and was so close to the top of the pit that with one leap he was over the edge and on his way.

Finally the kanchil came to a river, but he discovered that it was too deep and broad for him to cross because he could neither wade nor swim. He thought hard, for he *must* get across the river.

Standing on the riverbank, he had an idea. He called loudly for all the crocodiles to come together. The oldest crocodile said, "Why?"

"Because the king has sent me as his messenger. He said that all the crocodiles in the river must be counted."

The oldest crocodile told the others and they began to come together in one spot. They came by twos and threes and fours, by tens and dozens.

Source: "Three Tales of the Mouse-Deer" from *Indonesian Legends & Folk Tales,* told by Adele De Leeuw. Thomas Nelson & Sons, 1961. Copyright © 1961 by Adele De Leeuw. Reprinted by permission of McIntosh & Otis, Inc. pp. 77–80.

When they were all assembled the mouse-deer said importantly, "Now line up in a row from bank to bank, so that I can count you."

The crocodiles meekly ranged themselves in a row that extended from one bank of the river to the other, and the little mouse-deer leaped on the first crocodile's back. "One!" he shouted. He jumped on the back of the second crocodile. "Two!" he cried. And so he went, from one to the other, counting as he jumped . . . until he came safely to the other side of the river.

"What foolish creatures you are," he teased, "to believe everything you hear, and to do as anyone says!"

They were angry, but the oldest crocodile was more than angry. He was determined to have revenge on the tricky little mouse-deer. So he bided his time and when, at last, the mouse-deer came down to the river's edge to get a drink, the oldest crocodile was waiting for him and grabbed one of the kanchil's legs in his mouth.

The mouse-deer thought swiftly. He picked up a branch from the bank and said, "That's not my leg you have—that's a stick of wood. My foot is here!"

The crocodile let go of the mouse-deer's leg and grabbed the piece of wood, and the clever mouse-deer bounded away like a streak of lightning, while the crocodile gazed stupidly at the piece of wood in his mouth.

He was cross at being fooled. "I'll lie in wait for him," he vowed, "and make him sorry he tricked me." He lay in the water, half-submerged and very quiet, so that he would look like a water soaked log. He knew that the mouse-deer would have to come down to the river again to drink.

And after a while the mouse-deer came. He stood on the edge of the river and looked toward the crocodile. He would never be able to drink while the crocodile was there. So he said loudly, "That may be a log . . . and then again, it may be a crocodile."

The oldest crocodile remained motionless.

"Of course," the kanchil said, just as loudly, "if it's a crocodile it will float downstream."

The crocodile was determined not to give himself away, so he scarcely breathed. He was very, very still.

"But," the mouse-deer called, "if it's a log, it will float upstream."

At that the crocodile began to swim against the current, and the mouse-deer burst into laughter.

"Stupid one!" he cried. "I've fooled you again! Now I can have my drink in peace." ■

 # The Hoca and the Dessert

Asia: Turkey

"Hoca" (pronounced ho-dja) means "[Muslim] preacher." According to folklorist Barbara Walker, a hoca, who in the villages in the past might have been the only person who could read, was both the

Source: "The Hoca and the Dessert" from *The Art of the Turkish Tale,* vol. 2, by Barbara K. Walker. Lubbock, TX: Texas Tech University Press, 1993. Reprinted with permission by Barbara K. Walker, Curator of Archive of Turkish Oral Narrative. p. 246.

schoolteacher (for boys only) and the one who delivered the Friday noon sermon. Dr. Walker found that stories and anecdotes about the hoca are as common in Turkey as preacher and traveling salesmen stories are in the United States. Though a hoca is respected, some of the stories do not present him in a positive light, perhaps indicative of people's ambivalent feelings toward those who had knowledge they lacked (the ability to read). The hoca in this story meets another Turkish stock story character: a Bektashi, a member of a Muslim dervish order similar to the religious orders among Christian monks.

The hoca in "The Hoca and the Dessert" is anonymous, a generic hoca. The best-known and loved hoca throughout Turkey and the former Ottoman empire, however, is Nasreddin Hoca, who was said to have been a thirteenth century teacher and preacher from central Anatolia (now Turkey) and who was legendary for his wit and wisdom. He was reputed to have outwitted even the dreaded conqueror Tamerlane (Walker, 1993). According to Talat Sait Halman, "he is Aesop, the Shakespearean clown, Till Eulenspiegel, Mark Twain, and Will Rogers all rolled into one. His humor incorporates subtle irony and black comedy, whimsical observations about human foibles and outrageous pranks, self-satire and bantering with God, twists of practical logic, and the outlandishly absurd" (Halman in Walker, 1990, p. xii). A narrator who begins a story with the words "'One day the Hoca,'... is certain to draw an appreciative audience who are well aware that the subject of this fikra [anecdote] is no ordinary hoca but Nasreddin Hoca himself" (Walker, 1993, p. xxvi). Though not simply a trickster, Nasreddin Hoca often acts as one, whether to teach a lesson, get out of a predicament, or outwit a powerful adversary. Stories about Nasreddin Hoca are told as far east as China by Turkic-speaking Muslim minorities and as far west in Europe as Serbia and Croatia, which had been part of the Ottoman Empire before World War I. Frequently depicted in pictures as riding backwards on a donkey in the traditional scholar's broad-brimmed turban with its conical top, Nasreddin Hoca's image is known today internationally, as an international art contest on the Web in which people were asked to draw Nasreddin Hoca indicates. Stories about the hoca or hodja can also be found on the Web.

One evening a hoca and a Bektashi [a member of a mystical Muslim order] were invited to dinner at the home of a friend. After the main part of the meal was finished, the host brought the dessert and placed it in the middle of the dining tray.

Looking closely at the dessert, the hoca said to his host and the Bektashi, "My friends, that dessert seems rather small for three people. If we divide it into three equal portions, none of us will have more than a taste. I have a suggestion. Let's not eat it tonight but save it until tomorrow. Then the one who has had the most interesting dream tonight will be given the whole dessert to eat."

The other two agreed to this suggestion, and the dessert was placed on a shelf. The three men talked together hour after hour. And then since it was so late, the host rolled out sleeping mats for his guests for the night. At last they all retired.

In the middle of the night, however, the hoca awakened and felt somewhat hungry. He went quietly to the shelf, found the dessert, and ate the whole dishful himself.

When they arose in the morning and were seated at breakfast, the host said, "Let us now tell our dreams to see who will get the dessert from last night's dinner. Hoca, you tell your dream first."

"No," said the hoca, "I'd rather tell mine last. You and the Bektashi tell your dreams first."

The Bektashi said, "I dreamed last night that I was somehow down under the surface of the earth. I kept going down and down and down into the underworld until at last I reached the seventh level below the surface. There I saw such and such." And the Bektashi told them all about what he had seen there.

The host then told his dream. "Last night I dreamed that I could fly. I flew higher and higher and higher into the air until I had reached the seventh level of heaven. There I saw such and such." He then proceeded to tell his friends what he had felt and what he had seen up there.

Now it was the hoca's turn to tell his dream. He said, "It's curious, but last night in my dream I saw my Bektashi friend seven levels below the earth and my host seven levels above the earth. You were both so very far away from this world that I supposed neither of you would ever return. I therefore got up and ate that dessert myself." ∎

How Till Owlyglass Caused an Innkeeper to Be Terrified by a Dead, Frozen Wolf

Europe: Germany

"Till Owlyglass" is the literal translation of the German "Till Eulenspiegel," a legendary character who was said to have lived in the mid-1300s. Only references to him, without actual stories, survive from that era. The first full-blown account of his exploits is found in an early printed book of 1515 from Strasbourg (now French but at that time a German city) by a writer who identified himself only as "N." Though, as was the custom in the late Middle Ages, the author pretended to lack learning in his introduction to the book, he was probably well versed in Latin and Renaissance literature. Critics have been able to identify several of his literary sources, and he peppers his stories with Latinisms, which suggest that the author is joking when he claims to know no Latin (Oppenheimer, 1991). His immortal character Till, however, thumbs his nose at authority, opposes whatever is mean-spirited, and ridicules pomposity, whether among the clergy, the rising middle class, as represented by artisans and storekeepers, or the "learned" doctors and scholars of the time. When treated meanly, he usually gets back his own, often by following the words of authority literally.

Till is typically depicted as wearing a jester's outfit and carrying his symbols, an owl and a mirror that reflects people's follies onto themselves. Though few Germans can recount any of the specific adventures of Till, almost everyone knows about him. Statues have been erected to him in Germany, Holland, and Belgium, and at least one musical piece, "Till Eulenspiegel's Merry Pranks" by German composer Richard Strauss, keep his name and reputation alive.

In his retelling of Till Eulenspiegel's adventures for children, Michael Rosen uses the frame device of two rambunctious English-speaking children whose parents have taken them to Germany. The children are kept occupied with tales of Till's adventures, which match their own unruly exploits. Rosen retells 29 of the 95 stories from the 1515 edition of *Till Eulenspiegel, His Adventures*. He reorganized the stories so that those that fit together—for instance, the time Till beats the scholars at the University of Prague at riddles and the time he proves to the scholars that he can teach a donkey to read—are told in the same chapter. Though reorganized, this is a lively and faithful retelling of the tales. The illustrations add both to the merriment and to the depiction of the late medieval, early Renaissance German setting.

Till was on his way to Prague and it was winter. There was no time Till hated more than cold winter nights. In the summer he could sleep out in the open, or find a barn and sleep in the hay. But in winter he had to tramp along the road all day, his feet getting frozen, hoping to find an inn where he could sit and warm himself by a big roaring fire. Of course, if he did find an inn, he could sit there and tell people all the funny things that had happened to him. And perhaps he could try out a trick or two on them.

One evening, after a long cold walk through the snow and wind, he came to an inn in the town of Eisleben. The innkeeper was another boastful man, who kept saying how brave he was. Till went in and sat down by the fire.

Not long after, three more travelers came in out of the dark cold night.

"What time do you call this?" the innkeeper said. "Where have you lot been that keeps you out so late? Or have you been hanging about on the road or something?"

The travelers said, "Keep your temper, innkeeper. A wolf was lying in wait for us by the side of the road through the forest and we had to deal with him. In the

Source: Extract from *The Wicked Tricks of Till Owlyglass*. Text © 1989 Michael Rosen. Illustration © 1989 Fritz Wegner. Reproduced by permission of Walker Books, Ltd., London. pp. 88–94.

end we were able to fight him off, but that's why we're a bit late."

When the innkeeper heard this, he burst out laughing. "You were held up by one single little wolf? I tell you, if I met *two* wolves while I was out I would deal with them single-handed and finish them off. And there wouldn't be much left of them, I can tell you. And there you were, three of you, and you were scared of one single silly little wolf." The innkeeper went on and on laughing at the three travelers.

All the time Till sat by the fire listening. In the end it was time for bed, and Till slipped into the room where the three of them were sitting talking.

"We'll have to think of some way of dealing with this awful man," one of them was saying, "so that he doesn't bother us any more."

So Till said, "Look friends, I think our innkeeper is all talk. Listen to me and I don't think he'll ever boast about wolves again."

Of course the travelers were really pleased to listen. They promised they'd give Till some money if he could do what he said, and more than that, they'd pay his bill.

"This is what you've got to do," said Till. "Tomorrow you must leave the inn, go about your business and then when you've finished, just come back again, as normal. I'll be here as well and you'll see, I'll make him shut his mouth about this wolf affair.

The travelers agreed, and the next day, off they went, paying their bill and Till's as well.

As they went, the innkeeper called after them, "Mind how you go, chaps. Make sure no big beastly wolf scares you on your way," and he fell about laughing.

And the travelers said, "Thanks very much, innkeeper. Mind you, if the wolves eat us then we won't be coming here again, will we?"

Till left the same day. He hunted down a wolf, killed it and covered it with snow and ice until it was frozen hard. Then he made his way back to the inn, hiding the dead wolf in a big sack. The travelers were already back at the inn, and the innkeeper was still going on about the wolf. "Three men and one wolf, what brave chaps you are. I tell you, if I met two wolves, I would grab one by the throat till it died and at the same time cut the other one to pieces." And so he went on until bedtime.

Till kept quiet all the while. Then, just as before, he crept up to the travelers' room and said, "Gentlemen, don't put your light out yet, all right?"

When the innkeeper was safely in bed and the whole inn was quiet, Till crept out of his own room. He took the dead, frozen wolf out of the sack and carried it into the kitchen. He propped it upright, stuck two children's shoes into its mouth then nipped back into the travelers' room.

A few minutes later Till called out loudly for the innkeeper, "Innkeeper! Innkeeper! Hey, Innkeeper!"

The innkeeper, half-asleep, called out, "What do you want?"

"Send the maid to fetch us a drink or we'll die of thirst," Till shouted.

"The innkeeper wasn't happy about it. "For goodness' sake, you lot, drinking day and night, you'll drive me mad!" But he sent for the maid all the same, to fetch them all a drink.

Then maid got up, went down the kitchen, and there was the wolf! Terrified, she saw the shoes in its mouth and thought it had eaten the children, and now it would eat her. She rushed out of the inn, and hid behind a barrel in the yard.

A few minutes later Till called out again, "Innkeeper! Innkeeper! Where's our drink? What's keeping you?"

Now the innkeeper called the man-servant, not knowing what had happened to the maid. And when the servant went downstairs to the kitchen he saw the wolf and thought it had eaten the maid and the children, so he dashed off in a panic and hid in the cellar.

Now Till turned to the travelers and said, "Hang on, lads, it's the innkeeper's turn next and we're in for a really good laugh." Then he called out, "Innkeeper! Innkeeper! Where's that drink, in heaven's name? We're dying of thirst here. If the maid and the man-servant can't fetch it, fetch it yourself, will you?"

The innkeeper was furious. "You people make me sick with your constant drinking. Drink, drink, drink—it's all work for me, you know!"

But even so, up he got and went downstairs. And there was the wolf with the children's shoes in its jaw. He rushed upstairs straight into the travelers' room.

"Come quick! Quick!" he cried. "Help me, help! Downstairs in the kitchen there's a terrible beast! It's eaten the children, the maid and the man-servant! What am I going to do?"

So Till and the travelers crept downstairs with the innkeeper. When they went into the kitchen, Till walked over to the wolf and gave it a kick, so that it fell over with a bang. Then he called the maid from the yard and the man-servant from the cellar, and he turned to the innkeeper and said, "Look at it! The wolf is dead. And there's you, screaming you head off. What a scared little fellow you are. Do you think a dead wolf's going to

bite you? But hang on—wasn't it you last night who was so brave that one wolf wouldn't be enough for you to have a fight with? Weren't you the man who said you needed two wolves to prove yourself?"

When the innkeeper heard this from Till, he crept back to his room. He felt so ashamed that he had been scared of a dead, frozen wolf.

But the travelers loved it. They laughed and they laughed and gave Till a purse full of money and took him with them on the way to Prague. ■

Reynard and the Wolf

Europe: France

The wily fox who often falls victim to his own schemes was a favorite stock character in France in the Middle Ages. Reynard and his companions and victims, such as Isengrin, the brutish and dull-witted wolf, Tibert, the cat, Bruin, the bear, King Noble, the lion, and Chanticleer, the vain rooster later immortalized by Chaucer, probably arrived in France through the fables of Aesop. Most of their stories, however, were created by twelfth and thirteenth century poets, some of whom might have been monks. Most of the characters represented the royal court, members of the nobility, and the higher clergy. Some of the characters, however, represented the people these upper classes oppressed, such as the ordinary peasants and the lower clergy. No one in these stories comes off well, as the poets poked fun at the hypocrisies, power plays, brutish behavior, and vanities of the upper as well as the lower classes. Reynard, an unabashed trickster whose victims include both friend and foe, is a master at escaping punishment by a wide variety of ruses. When all else fails, he feigns repentance and retires to the woods as a "holy" hermit. As a Christ-

ian, King Noble is always moved to give Reynard one more chance, and if religious appeal doesn't work, the insinuation of a hidden treasure, the hiding place of which only Reynard knows, helps him escape from the gallows.

Religion infuses all the stories, if only as a trapping for worldly adventures. In one story, Reynard thoughtlessly jumps into a well bucket and sinks, then escapes by fooling Isengrin. Reynard gets Isengrin to jump into the second bucket by telling him that the buckets are the scales whereby his merits are being weighed so that he can go to Paradise. When Isengrin wonders why Reynard is rising as he is going down, Reynard tells him that it is because he is going to Paradise, while Isengrin is heading for Hell.

One can obtain impressions of medieval French life through Reynard's adventures. According to D. Owen (1994) who translated a verse form of the story, "The setting for Reynard's adventures is no fantasy realm, but takes us down the highways and more often byways of rural France offering glimpses of real townships and villages . . . penetrating into farmsteads, monastery enclosures, and even a parish church or two" (p. xiii). This translation of a French fable from a Latin version by Walter the Englishman expresses sentiments which echo those of many cultures with regard to their tricksters. They might love them and

Source: "Reynard and the Wolf" from *The Romance of Reynard the Fox.* Translated with an Introduction and Notes by D. D. R. Owen. Oxford: Oxford University Press, 1994. Reprinted with permission by Oxford University Press. pp. 253–255.

have endless fun listening to their stories, but they also condemn their behavior and like to see them punished (though always hoping for another reprieve). Intended primarily for oral delivery, the rhyming couplet form of this beast epic is typical of the way these stories were written (Owen, 1994).

This fable is from the French *Isopet* translated from the Latin version by Walter the Englishman, who may have been Henry II's chaplain.

The Constable Sir Isengrin,
The story tells, was idling in
His house, whose larder was replete
With ample stocks of fish and meat,
Bread, wine, and other tasty food
To meet his stomach's every mood.
The hungry Reynard made his way
By forest tracks in search of prey
Until he reached that corner where
His old companion had his lair.
Doffing his cap, he bared his head.
"How are you, my good friend?" he said.
"I really hope there's nothing wrong,
As I've not seen you for so long.
You've not been ill in bed, I trust?"
Half-rising then, Isengrin just
Replied as follows to Reynard:
"Dear friend of mine, as God's my guard,
My health is very good indeed;
And I have everything I need,
For all I could desire is here.
—God grant you too may live many a year!—
And yet I must tread warily:
You've come to play some trick on me;
But you'll not catch me unaware!"
Says Reynard: "You're quite wrong, I swear.
My only purpose was to find
Something on which I might have dined.
So give me some scrap you'd not miss,
Then may your father's soul find bliss
And, friend, God's blessings on you fall!"
—"Oh, I've no decent food at all
For such a thief as you to scoff
And fill your maw; so just be off!"
Hearing that, Reynard turns away
Without ado, and makes his way

To find a certain peasant, who
Hated the wolf, as he well knew.
"Spare me, Cowman," he said, "and then
You'll have the wolf your enemy
Here at your mercy, thanks to me.
I'll get him for you so that he's
Yours to deal with just as you please.
I shall go first, followed by you;
And then I'll point him out close to."
They both set off without delay.
Isengrin by his fireside lay,
Resting upon his mattress there,
Of their approach quite unaware.
The peasant takes him by surprise
Without a word, there where he lies;
And with drawn sword he is not slow
To launch at him a deadly blow.
With that wound he can live no more!
Reynard at once made for his store
Of food, and gorged with such a will
That in the end he had his fill.
Thus he pursued his crafty ways,
And hale and hearty spent his days.
Yet tricksters' fortune cannot last:
Their reign on earth is quickly past.
While on that course Reynard was set,
He chanced to fall into a net.
Trapped and despairing of relief,
Too late he gave vent to his grief:
"Alas, why did I trick my friend
And bring him to his sorry end?
Though he wronged others in his time,
I have committed a grave crime
In wronging him deceitfully,
So rightly pay the penalty."

THE MORAL

Let him who seeks folk to ensnare
And do them harm himself beware
Lest he in his own trap be caught,
Then cry: "Ah, woe is me! I ought
Not to work others' injury!
It's right the harm should come to me
And that I, once my trap is set,
Should fall myself into the net." ■

—(*Ysopet et Avionnet,* ed. Pauphilet, pp. 510–512)

Jack and the Varmints

Richard Chase has done for Appalachian stories, especially the Jack tales, what Joseph Jacobs did for English tales. He has collected many from one particular family that is well known for their storytelling tradition and retells them for children in a lively and readable style. He has combined features of several different oral versions to provide satisfying written tales.

Jack tales reflect their European origin: "Jack and the Varmints" is a variant of "The Brave Little Tailor" (AT 1640), a Grimm tale; "Jack and the Robbers" is a variant of "The Bremen town Musicians"; and "Old Fire Dragaman" is told in a similar version in Hungary. But Jack's home is clearly the Appalachian mountains. He tears around in the mountains, goes down to the gap, minds the water mill, and has familiar conversations with the king who lives in a big farmhouse. Don Davis, a storyteller from North Carolina, and Caldecott Medal winner Gail Haley, who also lives in North Carolina, have created audio tapes and picture book versions of the best-known Jack tales.

Jack was a-goin' about over the country one time, happened he passed by a place where a man had been rivin' boards, saw a little thin piece and picked it up, started in to whittlin' on it. Jack was so lazy he never noticed much what he was doin' till he'd done made him a little paddle. He didn't know what he'd do with it, just carried it along. Directly he came to a muddy place in the road where a lot of little blue butterflies had lit down to drink. So Jack slipped up right close to 'em and came down with that paddle right in the middle of 'em—*splap!* Then he counted to see how many he'd killed.

Went on down the road, came to a blacksmith shop. He got the blacksmith to take some brads and make him a sign in big letters on his belt; buckled that around him and went on.

Source: "Jack and the Varmints" from *The Jack Tales* by Richard Chase. © 1943, © renewed 1971 by Richard Chase. Reprinted with permission by Houghton-Mifflin. pp. 58–66.

Pretty soon here came the King on his horse, says, "Hello, Jack."

"Howdy do, King."

"What's all that writin' you got around ye, Jack? Turn around so's I can read it."

The old King read it off:

"*STRONG—MAN—JACK—KILLED—SEVEN—AT—A—WHACK.*"

"You mean you've done killed seven in one lick, Jack? You must be gettin' to be an awful stout feller. I reckon you could do pretty nigh anything, couldn't ye?"

"Well," says Jack, "I don't know. I've pulled a few tricks."

King says, "Well, now, Jack, if you're up to that advertizement you got on your belt there, you're the very man I'm a-lookin' for. There's a big wild hog been tearin' around in my settlement, killin' lots of sheep. If you help us get shet of that hog, I'll pay ye a thousand dollars. All my men are scared of it."

"Well," says Jack, "I'll try."

So the King took Jack over on the mountain where that wild hog was a-usin'. Time he got up in the holler a ways, he turned his horse around, says, "You go on up in the mountain and find it, Jack. I got important business back home."

And the King gave his horse a lick and made it go back in a hurry.

Jack he knowed that if the King was so scared of that hog, it must be awful dangerous. Decided he'd just not get mixed up with such a varmint. Said he'd wait a little while and then he'd slip out and get away 'fore that old hog smelled him. Well, directly Jack got to plunderin' around in there tryin' to get out, heard that hog a-breakin' bresh up the mountain, and then he saw it comin'. So Jack lit out through the woods—him and the hog . . .

Whippety cut!
Whippety cut!
Whippety cut!

and the wild hog right in behind him.

Jack looked behind and saw it was gettin' closer; they say Jack commenced jumpin' fifteen feet ever' step, but the old hog kept right on a-gainin'. Jack came out in a field, looked down it a ways and saw a waste-house standin' there with no roof on it. Jack made for that house, ran in the door, and scrambled up the wall. That old hog was so close it grabbed hold on Jack's coat-tail, but Jack was a-goin' so fast it jerked his coattail plumb off. Jack got up on top of the wall, looked down at the hog standin' there with his forefeet up on the logs a-lookin' up after him. Then Jack jumped down and ran around outside, pushed the door to and propped it right quick with some timbers. Saw the hog couldn't get out, so then he pulled back to the King's house.

"Hello, Jack. Did ye do any good?"

"Why, no, King. I couldn't find no wild hog up there. Hunted al over that mountain, didn't see nothin'."

"Why Jack, that old hog just *makes* for ever'body goes up there. You must 'a seen it."

"Well, there wasn't nothin' but a little old boar shoat, came bristlin' up to me, kept follerin' me around. I ran it off a time or two, but it kept on taggin' after me. The blame thing got playful after a while, jump up and jerked a piece out of my coattail. That made me a little mad, so I took it by the tail and ear and throwed it in a old waste-house up there, barred it in. I don't reckon that was what you wanted. You can go up and see if ye want to."

When the King rode up there and saw it was that wild hog, he like to beat his horse to death gettin' back. Blowed his horn and fifty or sixty men came runnin' up. They took a lot of Winchester rifles and went on up that old house; but they were so scared they wouldn't go close enough to get a shoot at it. So fin'ly Jack he went on down there, poked around with a rifle and shot two or three times. That old hog went to tearin' around and when it fell it had tore that house plumb down.

So the King's men skinned it out. Hit made two wagonloads of meat.

The King paid Jack the thousand dollars, and Jack started to pull out for home.

The King called him, says, "I got another job for ye, Jack. They say there's a unicorn usin' back here on an-other mountain, doin' a sight of damage to people's livestock. Hit's a lot more dangerous than that hog, but a brave feller like you oughtn't to have no trouble killin' it. I'll pay ye another thousand dollars, too."

Well, Jack tried to back out of it, but he saw he couldn't, so the King took him up there where they said the unicorn was, turned his horse around and just burnt the wind.

Jack watched the King out of sight, says, "Thousand dollars'll do me a right long while. I don't want to get mixed up with no unicorn. I'll get out of here and go back another way. I'm not a-goin' to fool around here and get killed."

But Jack hadn't gone very far 'fore he heard that varmint breakin' bresh and a-comin' straight down the mountain. So Jack started runnin' around in amongst the trees as hard as he could tear. Looked around directly and saw that old unicorn so close to him it was just about to make a lunch and stick that horn right through the middle of his back. Jack reached out and grabbed hold on a white oak tree, swung around behind it. The unicorn swerved at him, hit that oak tree, and stove its horn plumb through it. Horn came out the other side, and like to stuck Jack. Time he saw that, he snatched some nails out'n his overhall pocket, grabbed him a rock right quick and wedged the horn in tight. Then he got him a switch and swarped the unicorn a few times to see could it break loose; saw it couldn't, so he pulled on back down to the King's house.

"What luck did ye have this time, Jack?"

"Why, King, I didn't see no unicorn."

"Now, that's a curious thing to me, Jack. Nobody else ever went in there but what that old unicorn came right for 'em. What did ye see, Jack?"

"Nothin' much, just some kind of a little old year-lin' bull, didn't have but one horn. Came down there actin' big, a-bawlin' and pawin' the ground. Got to follerin' me around pretty close and sort of gougin' at me with that horn, till fin'ly hit kind of aggravated me. So I took it by the tail and neck, stove its horn through a tree. I reckon it's still fastened up there where I left it at. We can all go on up and see it if ye want to."

So Jack took the King and his men with all them rifles up where the unicorn was. They wouldn't none of'em get close enough to get a good aim, so Jack went on up to it, cut him a little branch and switched it two or three times, says, "See, men? There's not a bit of harm in him."

The men fin'ly shot it, and when it fell, they say it tore that oak tree plumb up by the roots.

Then they skinned it and brought back the hide.

The King paid Jack another thousand dollars, says, "Now, Jack, they've just brought in word here that a lion has come over the mountains somewhere in Tennessee, been makin' raids on a settlement over the other end of this county, killin' ever'thing it comes across: cattle, and horses, and they say it's done killed several men tried to go after it. I told'em about you, Jack, and they made me a promise to send ye."

"Well, King, that sounds like the dangerest of all."

"I'll pay ye another thousand dollars, Jack."

"I don't know as I favor workin' any more right now, King. They'll be worried about me if I don't get back in home 'fore dark. Besides, my daddy's cuttin' tobacco and he needs me bad."

"Come on now, Jack. I'll pay ye two thousand dollars."

"Well, I don't know. I'll have to study on it awhile."

"Here's a thousand dollars down, right now, Jack, and I'll pay ye the other thousand when ye get it killed. I'd sure like to get shet of that lion."

"I reckon I'll do it then," says Jack—"try to."

So the King took Jack up behind him on his horse and they rode over where they said the lion was last seen.

The King says, "Now Jack, that lion's right up in yonder somewhere. I'll not venture any further."

Jack slipped off the horse.

The King turned him around, says, "When hit smells ye, Jack, you'll sure hear from it!" And then the King left there a-gallopin'.

Well, Jack felt of that three thousand dollars he had down in his overhall pocket, said he'd try to get out of there for good and go on back home. But 'fore he'd hardly took a step or two, that old lion smelled him and commenced roarin' up there in the woods, roared so hard it jarred the mountain. Then Jack saw it comin'— tearin' down trees, breakin' logs in two, bustin' rocks wide open—and Jack didn't waste no time tryin' to run. He made for the tree nearest to him and skinned up it like a squirrel. He didn't stop neither, till he was clean to the top.

The old lion growled around down there, smelled up the tree a time or two, and then it went in to gnawin' on the treetrunk. Jack looked, and it was a sight in the world how the bark and the splinters flew. It near shook Jack out the tree.

But it seemed like the lion got tired when he had the tree about half gnawed through; he quit, laid up against the foot of the tree and went sound asleep.

Jack waited awhile till his heart quit beatin' so fast, and then he 'lowed he might have a chance to slip down and get away from there 'fore the old lion woke up. So he started slidin' down the tree. He was keepin' such close watch on the lion's eyes to see would he wake up or not, Jack never noticed when he set his foot on a brickly snag. Put all his weight on that rotten limb, and hit broke, and Jack went scootin' down, landed right straddle the old lion's back.

Well, that lion started in roarin' and jumpin' around, but Jack he just held on. Then the old lion got to runnin' and he was so scared he didn't know he was headed right for town. Got on the public highway and kept right on till next thing Jack knowed they were sailin' all around the courthouse. All the people were runnin' in the stores and climbin' trees gettin' out the way, and everybody shoutin' and hollerin', and the King's men came and started in tryin' to shoot the lion without hittin' Jack, till fin'ly one of'em drawed a bead on the old lion's head and tumbled him up.

Jack picked himself up out the dirt, commenced breshin' it off. Ever'body came over directly to see that lion, when they saw it was sure 'nough dead.

The king came along right soon and Jack says to him, says, "Look-a-here, King. I'm mad."

"Why, how come, Jack?"

"These men have done killed your lion."

"My lion? What ye mean, Jack?"

"Why, I'd 'a not had it killed for three thousand dollars, King. After I'd caught it and 'gun to get it gentled up, now, bedads, your men have done shot it. I was just a-ridin' it down here to get it broke in for you a ridey-horse."

So the old King went over to where his men were and raised a rumpus with 'em, says, "Why, I'd 'a felt big ridin' that lion around. Now you men will just have to raise Jack three thousand dollars for killin' our lion."

So Jack went on home after that; had a whole pile of money down in his old ragged overall pocket.

And the last time I went down there Jack was still rich, and I don't think he's worked any yet. ■

Brer Tiger and the Big Wind

North America: United States—African American

Brer Rabbit is probably the best-known American trickster. His ability to outwit the strong and powerful gave strength to the African slaves in America who first began telling these stories (Van Sertima, 1989). Brer Rabbit revels in outsmarting bullies such as Brer Wolf, but he is not always simply the champion of the underdog. Sometimes, as in the story of the Tar Baby, he is too full of conceit and is taken down a peg. Sometimes, like hare, his African counterpart, he just wants to stir up trouble for its own sake (Van Sertima, 1989). When all is said, however, it is Brer Rabbit's joyous triumphs that endear him, for who can help but rejoice when he lands in the briar patch and shouts, "Hot lettuce pie! This is where I want to be. . . . Here is where my mama and papa had me born and raised. Safe at last!" (Hamilton, 1985, p. 19).

Besides being entertaining and psychologically liberating, Brer Rabbit tales, like many other trickster tales, have been used to instruct others in what is and what is not acceptable behavior and to warn others to avoid untrustworthy people or situations or to be cautious about what they say and to whom. Brer Rabbit gets around. He turns up as Compère Lapin in Louisiana, as Bruh Rabbit in the sea islands of South Carolina, and as Rabbit on Trinidad and other West Indian islands. Most of his stories can easily be traced to Africa, but others show European influences or are international stories with counterparts throughout the world. In one story, for instance, Brer Wolf gets caught after Brer Rabbit empties a man's cart of fish, and in another story, Brer Rabbit, who lands on the bottom of a well after thoughtlessly jumping in the bucket to cool off, manages to exchange places with Brer Fox by pretending that he

is fishing for suckers. Both these stories were told of Reynard the Fox by twelfth century French monks (Owen, 1994). There is also a Japanese version of another popular story about Brer Rabbit in which he eats the butter that was to be shared by him and his "friends." Each storytelling community makes the story its own by infusing it with its own values, customs, and storytelling styles. The following story has a strong message about economic equity. It is also a story that begs for audience participation. The earliest and still best-known collection of Brer Rabbit stories is Joel Chandler Harris's *Tales of Uncle Remus series.* These were important but are hard to read today. There are several contemporary picture books and story collections today, but the first well-told modern retelling was the following one by William Faulkner.

In olden days, the creatures used to plow in the fields and plant their crops the same as menfolks. When the rains came, the crops were good. But one year no rain came, and there was a famine in the land. The sun boiled down like a red ball of fire. All the creeks and ditches and springs dried up. All the fruit on the trees shriveled, and there was no food and no drinking water for the creatures. It was a terrible time.

But there was one place where there was plenty of food and a spring that never ran dry. It was called the Clayton Field. And in the field stood a big pear tree, just a-hanging down with juicy pears, enough for everybody.

So the poor hungry creatures went over to the field to get something to eat and something to drink. But a great big Bengal tiger lived under the pear tree, and when the creatures came nigh, he rose up and said, "Wumpf! Wumpf! I'll eat you up. I'll eat you up if you come here!" All the creatures backed off and crawled to the edge of the woods and sat there with misery in their eyes, looking at the field. They were so starved and so parched that their ribs showed through their hides and their tongues hung out of their mouths.

Source: "Brer Tiger and the Big Wind" from *The Days When Animals Talked: Black American Folktales and How They Came to Be* by William J. Faulkner. Illustrated by Troy Howell. Chicago: Follett, 1977. Reprinted with permission by Africa World Press. pp. 89–94.

Now, just about that time, along came Brer Rabbit, just a-hopping and a-skipping, as if he'd never been hungry or thirsty in his life.

"Say, what's the matter with you creatures?" asked Brer Rabbit.

"We're hungry and thirsty and can't find any food or water—that's what's the matter with us," answered the creatures. "And we can't get into the Clayton Field because Brer Tiger said he'd eat us up if we ever came over there."

"That's not right," said Brer Rabbit. "It's not right for one animal to have it all and the rest to have nothing. Come here. Come close. I'm going to tell you something." And Brer Rabbit jumped up on a stump so that all could see him as they crowded around. When Brer Rabbit had finished whispering his plan, he said, "Now, you-all be at your posts in the morning; everyone be there before sunup."

The first animal to get to his post was Brer Bear. Before daybreak, he came toting a big club on his shoulder and took his place alongside an old hollow log. The next creature to arrive was Brer Alligator Cooter, a snapping turtle, who crawled in the hollow log. Then Brer Turkey Buzzard and Brer Eagle and all the big fowls of the air came a-sailing in and roosted in the tops of the tall trees. Next to arrive were the tree-climbing animals, like Brer Raccoon and his family and Sis Possum and all her little ones. They climbed into the low trees. Then followed the littler creatures, like Brer Squirrel, Brer Muskrat, Brer Otter, and all kinds of birds. They all took their posts and waited for Brer Rabbit.

Pretty soon, when the sun was about a half hour high, along came Brer Rabbit down the big road with a long grass rope wrapped around his shoulder. And he was just a-singing. "Oh, Lord, oh, Lord, there's a great big wind that's a-coming through the woods, and it's going to blow *all* of the people off the earth!" And while he was singing his song, a powerful noise broke out in the woods.

There was Brer Bear a-beating on the hollow log with all his might, bic-a-bam, bic-a-bam, bic-a-bam, bam, bam! Inside the log Brer Cooter was a-jumping, bic-a-boom, bic-a-boom, bic-a-boom, boom, boom. Brer Turkey Buzzard, Brer Eagle, and Brer Chicken Hawk were a-flapping their wings and a-shaking the big trees,

and the trees were a-bending, and the leaves were a-flying. Brer Raccoon and Sis Possum were stirring up a fuss in the low trees, while the littler creatures were a-shaking all the bushes. And on the ground and amongst the leaves the teeny-weeny creatures were a-scrambling around. All in all it sounded like a cyclone was a-coming through the woods!

All this racket so early in the morning woke Brer Tiger out of a deep sleep, and he rushed to the big road to see what was going on. "What's going on out there, huh?" he growled. "What's going on out there?"

All of the creatures were too scared to say anything to Brer Tiger. They just looked at him and hollered for Brer Rabbit to "Tie me! Please, sir, tie me!"

Now, all this time Brer Rabbit just kept a-hollering, "There's a *great* big cyclone a-coming through the woods that's going to *blow* all the people off the earth!" And the animals just kept making their noise and a-hollering, "Tie me, Brer Rabbit. Tie me."

When Brer Rabbit came around by Brer Tiger, Brer Tiger roared out, "Brer Rabbit, I want you to tie me. I don't want the big wind to blow *me* off the earth!"

"I don't have time to tie you, Brer Tiger. I've got to go down the road to tie those other folks to keep the wind from blowing *them* off the earth. Because it sure looks to me like a *great big hurricane* is a-coming through these woods."

Brer Tiger looked toward the woods, where Brer Bear was a-beating and Brer Cooter was a-jumping and the birds were a-flapping and the trees were a-bending and the leaves were a-flying and the bushes were a-shaking and the wind was a-blowing, and it seemed to him as if Judgment Day had come.

Old Brer Tiger was so scared he couldn't move. And then he said to Brer Rabbit, "Look-a-here, I've got my head up against this pine tree. It won't take but a minute to tie me to it. Please tie me, Brer Rabbit. Tie me, because I don't want the wind to blow me off the face of the earth."

Brer Rabbit shook his head. "Brer Tiger, I don't have time to bother with you. I have to go tie those other folks; I told you."

"I don't care about those other folks," said Brer Tiger. "I want you to tie *me* so the wind won't blow *me* off the earth. Look, Brer Rabbit, I've got my head here against this tree. Please, sir, tie me."

"All right, Brer Tiger. Just hold still a minute, and I'll take out time to save your striped hide," said Brer Rabbit.

Now while all this talking was going on, the noise kept getting louder and louder. Somewhere back yonder it sounded like thunder was a-rolling! Brer Bear was still a-beating on the log, bic-a-bam, bic-a-bam, bic-a-bam, bam, bam! Brer Cooter was still a-jumping in the log, bic-a-boom, bic-a-boom, bic-a-boom, boom, boom! And the birds were a-flapping and the trees were a-bending and the leaves were a-flying and the bushes were a-shaking and the creatures were a-crying—and Brer Rabbit was a-tying!

He wrapped the rope around Brer Tiger's neck, and he pulled it right; he wrapped it around Brer Tiger's feet, and he pulled it tight. Then Brer Tiger tried to pitch and rear, and he asked Brer Rabbit to tie him a little tighter, "because I don't want the big wind to blow me off the earth." So Brer Rabbit wrapped him around and around so tight that even the biggest cyclone in the world couldn't blow him away. And then Brer Rabbit backed off and looked at Brer Tiger.

When he saw that Brer Tiger couldn't move, Brer Rabbit called out, "Hush your fuss, children. Stop all of your crying. Come down here. I want to show you something. Look, there's our great Brer Tiger. He had all the pears and all the drinking water and all of everything, enough for everybody. But he wouldn't give a bite of food or a drop of water to anybody, no matter how much they needed it. So now, Brer Tiger, you just stay there until those ropes drop off you. And you, children, gather up your crocus sacks and water buckets. Get all the pears and drinking water you want, because the Good Lord doesn't love a stingy man. He put the food and water here for all His creatures to enjoy."

After the animals had filled their sacks and buckets, they all joined in a song of thanks to the Lord for their leader, Brer Rabbit, who had shown them how to work together to defeat their enemy, Brer Tiger. ■

The Moon in the Pond

North America: United States—African American

"The Moon in the Pond" is one of the Brer Rabbit tales that belongs to an international tale type (AT 34). In the Mexican and other variants, however, the fools (coyote or wolf) dive for the "cheese" in the water. This variant brings in Brer Rabbit and his usual friends and adversaries. The earliest and the most comprehensive collection of African American stories was Joel Chandler Harris's collection of Uncle Remus stories in eight volumes, starting with *Tales of Uncle Remus* in 1880. Harris, a journalist, used the frame story of Uncle Remus, a nostalgic former slave,

telling the tales to a white boy on the plantation. This frame worked well for Harris's column in *The Atlanta Constitution*, where he first introduced stories of Brer Rabbit in 1876, and for many years these were the only retellings available to children. Disney's film adaptation in *Song of the South* popularized the tales starting in the 1940s but preserved the stereotypes associated with Uncle Remus as a "happy" slave. Because of its frame and because the stories were recorded in a dialect that was hard to read and was no more recognizable to black readers than to white, the stories fell out of favor. Augusta Baker, children's librarian and storyteller in the New York Public Library, recalled, in her introduction to Julius Lester's retelling of *The Tales of Uncle Remus,* (1987), how frustrated she had been that there were no truly satisfactory books of African American folktales until

Source: "The Moon in the Pond" from *The Tales of Uncle Remus: The Adventures of Brer Rabbit* by Julius Lester, illustrated by Jerry Pinkney. Copyright © 1987 by Julius Lester. Used by permission of Dial books for Young Readers, a division of Penguin Putnam, Inc. pp. 96–99.

Lester's *The Knee-High Man* (1972) was placed on her desk. "Here were black folktales told perfectly. Lester had used the voice and the language of black people" (p. ix). Finally, Baker said, that the stories she had loved as a child had been retold in a way that was accessible to today's children. By the time Lester's *The Tales of Uncle Remus* appeared, an accessible collection of African American animal tales, which were collected and adapted for children by William J. Faulkner, had been published in *The Days When the Animals Talked* (1977). Lester's version, however, preserved both the character of Uncle Remus and the tales Harris had collected. Lester preserves the character of Uncle Remus to give a voice to the storyteller while changing Uncle Remus to a transmitter of cultural heritage, teacher, and entertainer not to one child but to a whole community. His voice is "the voice of a people, the black people of Kansas City, Kansas; Pine Bluff, Arkansas; Nashville, Tennessee; and the state of Mississippi." (p. xvii). Lester emphasizes in his introduction that the stories are set down only as a guide and will continue to live only if they are told and retold by others who love them, respect their origins, and tell them in their own voices. He calls his version a "modified contemporary southern Black English, a combination of standard English and Black English where sound is as important as meaning" (p. x). Since this collection and its two successive volumes have come out, Virginia Hamilton has also brought out several anthologies of African American tales which include stories about Brer Rabbit. Three of these are *Her Stories* (1995), *The People Could Fly* (1985), and *A Ring of Tricksters* (1997).

Brer Rabbit went to see Brer Turtle one evening. Brer Turtle could tell by his sweet smile that he had some trick in mind, and if anybody was born to be a partner in trickery, Brer Turtle was the man. He was a man among men!

"I got an idea, Brer Turtle."

"Tell me something I don't know."

Brer Rabbit grinned. "I'm going to tell Brer Fox, Brer Wolf, and Brer Bear that I'm having a fishing party down at the pond tomorrow night. I need you to back me up no matter what I say. You understand?"

Brer Turtle said he sho' did. "And if I ain't there tomorrow night, then you know the grasshopper flew away with me," and he laughed.

Brer Rabbit and Brer Turtle shook hands and Brer Rabbit went home and went to bed. Brer Turtle knew that if he was going to be at the pond by tomorrow night he best get started now.

Next day Brer Rabbit sent word to all the animals about the fishing frolic. Brer Fox invited Miz Meadows and Miz Motts as his guests.

That night Brer Bear brought a hook and line. Brer Wolf brought a hook and line too. Brer Fox brought a dip net, and Brer Turtle brought the bait. Miz Meadows and Miz Motts brought themselves dressed up all pretty.

Brer Bear said he was going to fish for mudcats. Brer Wolf said he was going to fish for horneyheads. Brer Fox wanted to catch some perch for the ladies. Brer Turtle said he'd fish for minnows, and Brer Rabbit looked at Brer Turtle and said he was going to fish for suckers.

They got their fishing poles and what-all ready and Brer Rabbit went to edge of the pond to cast first. He drew back his arm to throw his fishing line in the water and suddenly stopped. He stared. The pole dropped from his hand. He leaned forward. He stared. He scratched his head and stared some more. "I don't believe it," he said finally, in a hushed voice.

Miz Meadows thought he might have seen a snake and she hollered out, "Brer Rabbit, what in the name of goodness is the matter?"

Brer Rabbit didn't say nothing, and scratched his head some more. Then he turned around and said, "Ladies and gentlemen, we might as well pack up our gear and go on down to the fish store and buy some fish. Ain't gon' be no fishing at the pond this night."

Brer Turtle said, "That's the truth! That's sho' nuf' the truth."

"Now, ladies don't be scared. All us brave gentlemen here will take care of y'all. Accidents do happen, but I don't have any idea how this one took place."

"What's the matter?" Miz Meadows asked, exasperated now.

"Why, look for yourselves. The Moon done fell in the water."

Brer Fox looked in and said, "Well, well, well!"

Brer Bear looked in. "Mighty bad, mighty bad!"

Miz Meadows stared at it and squalled out, "Ain't that too much?"

Brer Rabbit shrugged his shoulders. "You can say what you want. But unless we get that Moon out of the water, ain't gon' be no fishing party tonight. You can ask Brer Turtle. He know more about water than anybody here. He'll tell you."

"That's the truth," piped up Brer Turtle.

"How we gon' get the Moon out?" Miz Motts asked Brer Turtle.

"We best leave that to Brer Rabbit."

Brer Rabbit stared up in the sky like he was thinking hard. After a while he said, "Well, if we could borrow Brer Mud Turtle's seine net, we could drag the Moon out."

"Brer Mud Turtle's my first cousin," Brer Turtle said. "I calls him Unk Mud, we so close. He wouldn't mind your borrowing his net."

Brer Rabbit went to borrow the net. When he was gone, Brer Turtle said his grandparents had told him that whoever took the Moon out of the water would find a great pot of money underneath. Brer Fox, Brer Wolf, and Brer Bear got real interested. They said they wouldn't be gentleman if they let Brer Rabbit do all the work of getting the Moon out of the pond after he done all the work to get the seine net.

When Brer Rabbit got back, they told him they'd take the net and get the Moon out. Brer Turtle winked at Brer Rabbit, and after an appropriate number of protests, Brer Rabbit turned the net over to them.

Brer Fox grabbed hold of one end, Brer Wolf grabbed the other, and Brer Bear came along behind to unsnag the net if it got caught on any logs or debris.

They made one haul—no Moon. They hauled again—no Moon. They went farther out in the pond. The water was getting in their ears. Brer Fox and Brer Wolf and Brer Bear shook their heads to get it out and while they were shaking their heads they got to where the bottom of the pond dropped away, and that's just what they did—dropped off the edge of the shelf right into the deep water. Have mercy! They kicked and sputtered, went under and came up coughing and snorting and went under and came up again.

Finally they dragged themselves out, dripping water like waterfalls.

Brer Rabbit looked at them. "I guess you gentlemen best go home and get into some dry clothes. Next time we'll have better luck. I heard that the Moon will always bite at a hook if you use fools for bait."

Brer Fox, Brer Bear, and Brer Wolf sloshed away, and Brer Rabbit and Brer Turtle went home with Miz Meadows and Miz Motts. ∎

The Signifying Monkey

North America: United States—African American

When slavery was ended, new genres and heroes joined and often replaced the once popular animal tales (Roberts, 1989). The manner and place of telling stories also changed. With migration from the rural South to the urban North, new oral forms developed. The story "The Signifying Monkey" is an example of the often noted fact that although we live in an age of print, oral literature is still alive. A predecessor of rap, the **toast**, of which this story is an example, is a narrative in verse that was first developed in the 1920s and continued to be a popular form of entertainment and one-upmanship until the 1960s or 1970s among young African American men. Telling and creating toasts with friends was a favorite adolescent pastime of Tony Bolden, a poet and professor of English. Bolden created the following version of "The Signifying Monkey" to introduce his own young son to this story, which is usually told in the tough language of

Source: "The Signifying Monkey" © 1999 by Tony Bolden. Reprinted with permission by Tony Bolden, Assistant Professor, University of Alabama.

the city streets. To "signify" in this context means to make yourself known and to let others know that you have something to say. Bolden gives a more extensive overview of the toast and its place in African American culture in his doctoral dissertation, *All Blues: A Study in African American Resistance Poetry* Louisiana State University (1998).

Way down in de jungle deep,
The bad ole lion stepped on de Signifyin
   Monkey's Feet
De Monkey said to the de Lion, "Look, Mistah
   Lion, cain't chou see?
Why, you standin on ma achin feet!"
De Lion said, "I ain't heard three words you said.
And if you say three mo I'll be stand on ya
   head."
De liddle Monkey lived in a ole oak tree.
He used to be just as happy as can be,
Teasin de Lion every day of de week.
But every night, when de Monkey came down,
Dat Lion would beat him up all throughout de
   jungle town.
De liddle Monkey got wise, started usin his wits.
He said, "I'm gon trick dis Lion, jes a liddle bit."
So he ran up to de Lion de very next day.
He said, "Ooo, Mistah Lion,
Dere's a big, bad animal comin yo way.
He talked about ya family in a heck of a way.
He talked about ya family till ma hair turned gray.
He called ya mama a dummy; he said ya daddy
   was, too.
He said I'll be doggone if you doan look like one,
   too.
He said ya auntee and ya uncle was both a
   buncha fools
He said he knew for certain dey nevah spent a
   day in school."
He said, "Now, you know, Mistah Lion,"
He said, "You know dat ain't right.
So whenevah you see de elephant, be ready to
   fight.
And he's somebody dat you happen to know,
Cause he's dat great big gray one
Dat just came back from de circus show."
Well, de Lion jumped up in a heck of a rage,

Like a young somebody fulla gage.
He let out a roar, tail cocked back like a forty-
   four.
He went through de jungle knockin down trees,
Kickin giraffes down to de knees.
He walked up to de elephant, who was talkin to
   de swans.
He said, "All right, you big, bad ole animal.
It's gonna be yo reputation or mine."
De elephant looked at him
Outta de corna of his eye and said, in a *real
   deep voice,*
"You bettah go pick on somebody yo own size."
But de Lion made a fancy pass.
De elephant side-stepped and cold cocked him
   fas.
He broke his jaw and smashed in his face
And knocked his whole body clean outta place.
He slammed de Lion up against de tree
And dere was nothin but Lion parts as far as de
   eye can see.
He picked him up, and rolled him in de sand
and jes beat him all up like a natural man.
Well, dat Lion dragged hisself back into de jungle
   mo dead dan alive.
Liddle did he know dat he had to listen to mo'
Of dat liddle Monkey's signifyin jive.
He said, "What's de mattah Mistah Lion.
You doan look so well.
Seems to me like somebody jes rung yo bell.
Now you comin round here witcha nose all
   snotty.
If ya didn't know what de game was all about, ya
   shoulda axed somebody.
I tole my wife befoe you lef, I shoulda beatchou
   up all by maself.
Every night, I'm up in de tree, wid my children,
   tryna read a liddle bit.
And den here you come roarin and shoutin dat
   ole "I'M DE KING" bit.
Shut up, Mistah Lion.
And don'tcha roar. Cause if you do, I'm gonna
   talk about you some mo.
And don'tchou look up here wid dat ole sucka-
   paw case,
Cause I'll jump right down de fork a dis tree

And laugh right in yo big ole ugly face."

De Monkey got happy and started to jump up and
down.

His feet missed de limb and his body hit de
ground.

Like a streak a lightnin in a bolt a white heat,

Dat Lion was on toppa dat Monkey wid all fo
feet.

De liddle Monkey cried wid tears in his eyes.

He said, "Look, Mistah Lion, I apologize."

He said, "Please, Mistah Lion, doan take my life.

I have thirteen kids and a very sickly wife."

He said, "Look, Mistah Lion, you haven't fought
dat well,

Why, everybody saw you jump on me, after I
slipped and fell.

Why, if ya fought like honest men should,

I'd whup you up all over dese woods."

Dis was de boldest challenge de Lion had evah
had.

So he rared back, ready to fight.

But dat liddle Monkey jumped clean outta sight,

Landed in a banana tree and started to grin.

He said, "Ooo, Mistah Lion, I jes tricked you
again.

De things I tole you befo will nevah part,

But what I'm gonna do now is break yo good fa
nothin heart.

Now I'm gonna sit up here, and eat dis here
banana,

And talk about you like de Star Spangled
Bannah,

And if you evah mess wid me again,

I'm gonna send you back to my elephant friend."

And dat's why de Monkey is de smartest animal
in de jungle. ∎

Rabbit Escapes from the Wolves

North America: United States—Cherokee

Storyteller Gayle Ross is a descendent of John Ross, leader of the Cherokee during the time of the Trail of Tears. Ross draws on stories she learned from other storytellers in Oklahoma. These are also the stories that are still told in the Cherokees' traditional home in Tennessee and North Carolina. Ross also draws on James Mooney, a nineteenth century collector. In many of the Cherokee stories, rabbit is the trickster who provides the fun and the lessons on how not to act. He causes mischief, often because he is jealous of another animal's skills or beauty, and his actions result in permanent changes for the animals, from otter discovering that he loves playing in the water to deer's teeth becoming

small and blunt. Rabbit also suffers consequences, such as losing his long tail. In this story one can hardly blame him for using his wit to his own advantage. Gayle Ross's telling of this and other Cherokee stories have appeared in picture books and on audio tape.

A long time ago, when the people and the animals still spoke the same language, Rabbit lay sleeping in the forest. He was having a very good dream. In his dream, Rabbit was at a dance and all the people had asked him to lead the songs. He was having a fine time, showing off his voice and watching all the pretty girls dance. In his dream, the dancers were crowding closer and closer until one of them actually stepped on his foot!

Rabbit's eyes flew open and he found that he was surrounded by wolves, laughing and poking him. "Wake up, Rabbit!" said a wolf. "We are going to eat you!"

Source: "Rabbit Escapes from the Wolves" from *How Rabbit Tricked Otter and Other Cherokee Trickster Stories* told by Gayle Ross. Illustrated by Murv Jacob. Text copyright © 1994 by Gayle Ross. Used by permission HarperCollins Publishers, Inc. pp. 24–28.

Rabbit thought very quickly. "Oh, it's that way, is it?" said Rabbit. "I wasn't sleeping. My eyes were closed because I was thinking about a new dance I know. If you were not in such a hurry to eat I could teach it to you."

Well, everybody knows that wolves love to sing, but Rabbit knew they also love to dance. Sure enough, the wolves let Rabbit up and formed a circle around him while he got ready to sing. Rabbit made a great show of clearing his throat and preening his fur. At last, he began patting his feet and humming. Then he started to dance around in a circle. Finally, he began to sing:

> "*Tlage'situn' gali'sgi'sida'ha*
> *Ha'nia' lil! lil! Ha'nia lil! lil!*
> On the edge of the field I dance about—
> *Ha'nia lil! lil! Ha'nia lil! lil!*"

The wolves began to dance in a circle around Rabbit, following his steps. Rabbit called, "When I sing 'edge of the field,' I will dance in that direction!" Rabbit began the song again, and this time his dance steps took him toward the field. "Now," said Rabbit, "this time when I sing *lil! lil!* you must all close your eyes and stomp your feet hard!"

The wolves thought this was a fine dance, so Rabbit began another round singing the same song. When he sang "edge of the field," he danced that way; and when he sang *lil! lil!* the wolves closed their eyes and stomped their feet. Rabbit sang louder and louder. He kept on dancing closer and closer to the field. At last, on the fourth round of songs, when the wolves were stomping as hard as they could and thinking only of the dance, Rabbit made one long jump and was off through the long grass.

Rabbit scurried through the grass, twisting and turning, as fast as he could. The wolves were after him at once, however, and they are very swift runners. Rabbit was almost out of breath when he spied a hollow tree trunk. He dove through a hole at the roots and climbed up the inside of the trunk.

When the wolves reached the tree, they began arguing about the best way to get Rabbit out of that trunk. Finally, one of them put his head through the hole and peered up a Rabbit. But Rabbit spit right into his eye, and the wolf had to pull his head out. Now, spitting on someone is one way to put a powerful curse on them, and the wolves were becoming frightened! When no other wolf wanted to put his head in the hole, they all went away and left Rabbit hiding in the trunk. When he was sure it was safe, Rabbit climbed out and went on about his business. ■

 # Napi and the Mice

North America: United States—Siksika (Blackfoot)

Like so many other Native American tricksters, Napi is both sacred and profane, both a creator and a troublemaker. Percy Bullchild was in his sixties when, dissatisfied with the way non–Native Americans had presented and interpreted the Blackfoot legends and

Source: "Napi and the Mice" from *The Sun Came Down* by Percy Bullchild. Copyright © 1985 by Percy Bullchild. Reprinted by permission of HarperCollins Publishers, Inc. pp. 205–209, including illustration p. 207.

histories and concerned that the younger generation was losing knowledge of their heritage, he felt compelled to research and tell the Blackfoot stories as they were passed down to his generation. He credits his own grandmother, who died in 1927 at close to age 100, with many of the stories. He has learned from numerous other people since then, however, not only from his own tribe but also from Native Americans throughout the continent.

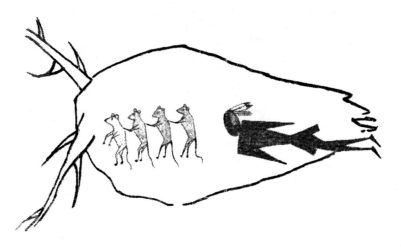

"Napi and the Mice." Illustrated by Percy Bullchild.

From: *The Sun Came Down* by Percy Bullchild. Harper & Row. Reprinted by permission of HarperCollins Publishers, Inc. Illustration © 1985 by Percy Bullchild.

Napi, like his better known counterpart, Coyote, is often referred to as "Old Man," and like Coyote, he is divine yet also base. Many have struggled with the dual nature of the trickster. George Bird Grinnell, a nineteenth century collector who lived for a while with the Blackfoot, felt that two characters, the Sun, who was the creator of the universe and giver of light, and Napi, who was a mixture of wisdom and foolishness and who was often selfish, childish, and weak, were accidentally fused into one because both were referred to as "Old Man" (Erdoes and Ortiz, 1998). Bullchild (1985), however, explains Napi's dual nature as follows: When Creator Sun decided to leave the earth forever, he felt that he must leave a part of himself behind to help guide his human creations. He saw that without this guidance human beings were becoming wicked. So he created Napi from his own spirit, giving him the shape of a handsome and strong middle-aged man with a proud and distinguished look, the fringes of his shirt and leggings made of red woodpecker feathers, a tobacco pouch attached to his side, and a stick-like cane in his hand. People would take him for a chief. He traveled from place to place, teaching people how to live right. Napi, Old Man, could transform himself into any shape, just as Coyote could. A teacher and healer, he could use his

magic even to bring the dead back to life at times. As he traveled throughout North America, he began to forget his original purpose and began to use the magic Creator Sun had given him for his own glory, creating more and more mischief as time went on, until he forgot the teachings of righteousness that he was to spread among the children of Creator Sun and Mother Earth. Instead, he became a foolish and selfish figure whom even the people no longer respected. Paul Goble, who has created picture books of both Blackfoot and Lakota (Sioux) stories, has several books about Napi's Lakota counterpart, Iktomi. Iktomi's outfit is depicted in much the way Bullchild describes Napi above.

Napi is not always mean and selfish; sometimes he is just childlike in his playfulness and impulsiveness. In this, he resembles Iktomi, his Lakota (Sioux) cousin. He also resembles the impulsive Ojibway creator and trickster Nanaboozhoo or Nanabush, as described by Basil Johnston in *The Manitous* (1995). Paul Goble has created several picture books about Iktomi, including one about Iktomi finding a buffalo skull, meeting the singing mice and getting stuck inside the skull. According to Goble (1990), this is a frequently recurring theme among Native American tribes throughout the Great Plains. An underlying meaning for Plains Indians is that the buffalo is not to be treated in the irreverent manner in which Iktomi treats it.

Napi had left the camp of people and was going back to the good old nature that he had lived with all the time. It may be a little hard to get by at times, but you sure didn't get left out. Napi came to what is now known as the Province of Alberta as he was going along, trying to get far from the people, at least for this time.

Napi never worried about where he was going to sleep or eat until the time comes. Napi laid down to sleep any place, as long as he had his old standby, the thick tanned buffalo robe. If it's to eat, that was something else, food wasn't always an easy thing for him to obtain.

Napi had traveled all that day. It was getting a little late as he made his way down into one of the rivers throughout the country. Along any waterway, it's always almost inaccessible because of the thickets, trees, and bushes. But there were always small openings where there wasn't any kind of foliage except thick, high grass. It was one of these fairly large open places among the trees and bushes that he happened upon. Darkness was coming on fast. Without going any farther, Napi threw his robe down on the ground and there he was going to spend the night. As the darkness came, Napi covered himself good and closed his eyes to go to sleep. He was so leg worried that he just couldn't get to sleep right away like he wanted to. At last that drowsiness came to him. It must've been fairly late now. As he was falling asleep, something awoke him, a faint sound like singing. Napi thought he was just hearing things just because of his tiredness. Not paying much attention to what he heard, Napi only moved about in his bed for a more comfortable position and tried to doze off again.

That was singing, and it got louder this time as it awoke Napi for the second time. Sitting up in his bed, Napi listened carefully for that singing. There were many small voices singing and talking at the same time, whoever they were and whatever they were doing, there were many of them and they weren't very far away from here. Napi sat very still, trying to get the direction of the noise and what it was about.

Napi's curiosity was aroused. Slowly he got up from his bed listening for the sound. He went towards it, every once in a while stopping to listen for the direction of that small sound of singing. This was a small open park and wherever the sound was coming from, it shouldn't be too far. Napi crawled along towards that singing, he could hear them very plain now as he was going directly towards it and getting closer to it. He didn't want to walk right up to them or he would've scared them off, whatever they were.

Crawling along ever so slow, Napi was very careful not to make any kind of noise that might scare them off. It was very dark as he groped towards the sound of the singing. Crawling a little farther along, just ahead of him, along the edge of the bushes, Napi spotted something white. This something white was an old sun-bleached elk skull that had laid there a long time. It was from within this elk skull the singing was coming from. Crawling ever so slowly and coming to the elk skull without even as much as cracking a dry grass, Napi peeked in through one of the eyes of this elk skull. This was really something, what he seen. It was a bunch of mice inside of the elk skull dancing and singing. The mice all stood around in a circle with their little paws held up about even with their little cheeks. They were jumping up and down on their little feet as they went around in a circle and sang as they went around. Those that were sitting down were against the wall of elk skull, they too were singing to the rhythm of the dancers. Every one of the mice was having the time of their lives and like always, Napi wanted to join them.

"*Kyi-neh-ski-nah-yah ahwa-bi-new-si, kyi-neh-ski-nah-yah ahwa-bi-new-si, kyi-neh-ski-nah-yah ahwa-bi-new-si.* Mice fluttering your eyes as you a dancing." The mice sang on into the night. Over and over they sang this with a little interval to catch their wind, then back to singing and dancing they went.

Napi went sneaking back towards where he came from. Picking up his robe, he slung it over his shoulder and walked slowly towards the old bleached elk skull where the mice dance was taking place. As he neared the skull, his old, old familiar wail was heard by the mice. "*Aye, aye, aye, niss-gah-nuk ohn-ni nah-goo-kah-wahn-ists ah-hey.* Aye, aye, aye, little brothers, what you are doing, let me do too." Over and over he cried this same cry as he slowly walked towards the old bleached elk skull where the mice dance was taking place.

His voice, being louder than those of the mice, was heard above their pattering little feet and their singing. All quit singing and dancing as they heard the crying coming towards their skull dancing area. One of the older mice peeked out from the skull and seen Napi coming, telling the rest of them, "It's only our big brother Napi, he's crying to join our dance." Without any further argument, all of the mice agreed to let Napi join them in their little dance. The leader of the these mice telling Napi that it was too small a place for Napi's size, all he could do was to get his head in through the neck part of the skull and that had to be done by the mice's magic. He could sway his head back and forth to the time of their singing and dancing. This was all right with Napi. One of the elders of this mice family used his magic to get Napi's head through the small openings of the neck part of this old bleached elk skull.

"You are not one of us," said the leader of the mice, "we have a restriction for those that aren't one of us. We dance for four nights, this is only the first night. At daybreak, we disperse until night falls again. We continue this way until after four nights, then we go our separate ways. Through all of these nights, you must not fall asleep or bad things shall happen to you. We will have to leave your head in here until after the last night, then we will let your head out of here. Don't fall asleep while we are dancing at night. Beware."

Napi was always ready to agree to all of this, he wanted to have a good time for once, he wanted to learn the mice dance. The mice once more began their dance, while Napi kept his head in motion back and forth and to the sides to the rhythm of the mice music. Napi was having the time of his life that night.

Just breaking day, the mice all left. Napi fell asleep with his head inside of the elk skull. All day he slept like a dead thing. If it weren't for the mice returning for their continued dancing that night, Napi would have slept on. He woke up as the mice were coming in and all of them with their happy voices, talking excitedly.

The mice dance went on as Napi done his part of swaying his head this way and that way to the time of the music. All night the dance went on with nothing happening except all were having a good time. At daybreak once again, the mice disappeared out into the bushes for the day and Napi's head was alone once more for the day. This time he didn't get much sleep, he was getting very tired from laying one way, on his stomach mostly.

Nightfall brought the mice back again for their fournight dance. This was their third night of dancing. Through the night the mice danced as Napi's head bobbed about in time with the music, his way of taking part in this mice dance. Once more, daylight came and the mice dispersed for the coming day as Napi's head was left all alone again in this old bleached elk skull. He just couldn't sleep too much this day. He was awful tired laying on his stomach, he had been on it for three nights now, which was a very long time for anyone.

Trying to fall asleep, Napi's day just wasn't long enough. He just couldn't sleep and when he did start to go to sleep, it was night and the mice all returned for their last night of dancing. It started out all right with Napi, he was wide awake when the dance began again. His head was again bobbing about to the rhythm of the mice singing and dancing. Every once in a while Napi's head would fall forward as he would doze off, he was really fighting his sleepiness. It was well towards morning, Napi had almost made it to daylight, when he just couldn't get his head back up. He fell asleep as the mice danced on.

The noise didn't waken Napi back up, he was fast asleep. The restriction the mice mentioned to Napi had to be carried out, it was a mouse custom. While Napi was fast asleep, the mice chewed Napi's hair all off of his head, Napi was just plumb bald as he slept on into the day. The other part of their restriction was to leave Napi's head in the elk skull if he fell asleep, and he did. Waking up, he didn't notice his hair all chewed off, that he was just plumb bald, but he did notice that he couldn't get his head out of this old bleached elk skull. And to make things worse, he couldn't see where to go, the bone of the skull was in the way of his eyes. Napi couldn't break the skull off either, or he would hurt himself. He found out the restrictions of the mice for falling asleep while the mice were dancing.

Napi got up with the elk head over his head, feeling his way, this way and that way. The elk skull was top heavy, which made Napi stagger this way and that way. He went along as he felt the ground with the feet and hands. He fought his way through the undergrowth and trees, he really didn't know which way to turn. Stumbling and staggering along, trying to find his way out to the open land where he could get along better without his eyesight. Not knowing where he was going, Napi was still groping about through the brush, when all of a sudden the bottom seemed to drop away, and down into the river he fell. Not knowing which direction to swim, the weight of the elk skull would submerge him every once in a while as he tried to swim to where he thought the shore was. Instead, he was going out towards the middle of this river and it got deeper. There he was, floating down river bobbing out of sight with the elk skull still over his head.

Napi didn't know how long he had been in this river, floating down with the current. He had swallowed a lot of water, he was still going under the water at times, he was fighting for dear life to stay afloat. The darn old bleached elk skull made it that much worse, its weight took Napi under water as he floated along. Napi was hollering out every chance he got, but this elk skull muffled all of his hollerings, no one to hear him.

Far down this river was a large camp. The men of the camp had just returned from a hunt. The women were all down along the banks of this river, washing the fresh entrails off and readying them to eat. One of these women spotted the elk skull as it came floating towards them. She let out an excited scream, saying at the same time, "There comes an elk swimming down the river!" All of the women dropped what they were doing and turned to the middle of river where the elk skull was floating. The elk skull got closer and closer. The women still thought it to be an elk swimming down river. As this elk skull was almost even with them, the women noticed it wasn't an elk swimming, it was a human being with an elk skull over its head.

The women lost no time to get a rawhide rope long enough to reach out to where this thing was float-

ing, they could see the arms frantically grasping for something to hang on to. Now they could hear a muffled sound from within the elk skull, calling for help. One of the stronger women threw the rawhide rope out to the man that seemed to be in trouble. The first try was a lucky one. It had to be, otherwise someone would've had to swim out after the elk skull. He made a few wild grabs for whatever it was that he felt. One of his tries was good, his hands got ahold of this thing, some one yanked on the rope. Napi knew that help was at hand. To the shore he was pulled, he was close to drowning again, his stomach was full of water.

Getting him pulled ashore, the women couldn't figure out how this man got his head in this elk skull. The women helped him further, after trying to pull the old bleached elk skull off of his head without success, the women got ahold of a stone hammer and broke the elk skull off as easy as they could from Napi's head. As the skull broke free from Napi's head and the women seen the naked head—it was just kind of shining—they all ran off screaming. All got scared of this hairless person, no one had ever seen a hairless person before this. Slowly reaching up to his head, as he stood there not knowing what the women were all running from, his hands touched his head and he almost broke into a run too. He felt nothing but naked skin on his head. This was a bit embarrassing to Napi, he didn't know how to act or what to do.

Being a good actor, Napi went into one of his acts. He acted like a man out of his head, crazy, running here and there and hollering as he went. The women all took off in many directions from this dangerous character. All scattered, it was a good time for Napi to disappear from sight, into the trees he ran, screaming and hollering as he went, still acting like a wildman.

Running far away from the camp, Napi slowed down and became himself again. Reaching up and getting a better feeling of his head, Napi knew he was just plumb bald and he would have to stay out of sight for a long time to regrow his hair. And that's what he did, never forgiving those mice. And to this day he never did trust mice with anything. ∎

A Satisfying Meal

North America: United States—Hopi

Coyotes were traditionally found in the western part of the North American continent, from Alaska to Mexico. Though their range now extends as far east as Alabama, the stories told about Coyote the trickster are from the animal's original areas. In the stories, Coyote and the other animals are referred to as the First People, the people who existed before the arrival of the humans. The First People were larger, more mythic, and more powerful than the animals we see today. According to William Bright (1993), a researcher of Coyote tales throughout North America, Coyote is viewed differently by different people. Among the people of the northern and northwestern United States, such as the Nez Percé and the Klamath Indians, he is seen as a creator. For them Coyote is instrumental in bringing about many of the animals' present-day features or bringing them to a specific habitat, creating humans, bringing fire, and bringing death into the world. Farther south, as among the Hopi, he is seen as a human-like trickster. His tricky actions, which usually succeed, do not result in mythic changes. Instead, he temporarily satisfies his insatiable appetite. In Mexico he is seen more as a bungler. His tricks usually backfire. A traveler, always on the move, always outside of the normal bonds of society, he has few friends and is deceitful even toward his usual companions, such as fox.

Coyote and Fox are not very fond of each other, because they are always competing for the same kind of food. So whenever he has a chance to play a trick on Fox, Coyote will do it.

Source: "A Satisfying Meal (Hopi)" from *American Indian Trickster Tales* by Richard Erdoes and Alfonso Ortiz. Copyright © 1998 by Richard Erdoes & The Estate of Alphonso Ortiz, text. Copyright © 1998 by Richard Erdoes, line drawings. Used by permission of Viking Penguin, a division of Penguin Putnam. pp. 36–38.

One day Fox managed to catch a prairie dog. He killed it. He said: "This is a fine, fat prairie dog. It will make a tasty meal."

Fox got some wood and made a fire. When the wood had been reduced to glowing embers, Fox pushed the prairie dog under the hot ashes to roast it. "It will take a while until the meat is done," Fox said to himself. "I think I'll have a little nap in the meantime." So he went to sleep.

Not far away, Coyote came walking along, scrounging for something to eat, sniffing around. The wind brought to him a scent of roasted meat. Coyote's nose quivered with delight. "Ah," he said, "I am smelling something good."

Following his nose, Coyote came to the spot where Fox was sleeping. He dug out the prairie dog from under the still-glowing embers. He ate it up in no time at all. He said: "this meat is very tender, cooked just the way I like it." He left only the bare bones. He took a little of the fat and smeared it around Fox's mouth. Then Coyote went off laughing.

Fox woke up. He noticed that his mouth was greasy. He said: "I must have eaten the prairie dog. Funny, I don't remember it." He dug underneath the ashes and pulled out what was left—the prairie dog's bones. "I was right," he said, "I did eat the meat, even though I don't remember it."

Fox sat down on a rock. He was thinking. He said to himself: "If I had eaten that prairie dog, I should feel sated. Instead I am hungry, very hungry. Therefore I did not eat that meat." He jumped up: "Now I know what happened. That evil trickster, that no good Coyote, has stolen my meat. I will find him and kill him!"

Fox followed Coyote's tracks. Coyote saw him coming. Coyote said to himself: "Fox is faster that I am. I cannot get rid of him by running away." So Coyote stood up and leaned against an overhanging cliff. Fox came running. "Watch out, Coyote, you miserable trickster," he cried. "I've come to kill you!"

"Fool," Coyote cried. "Halfwit! Don't you see I'm holding up this overhanging cliff, which is about to crush us both to death? Here, you lean against the cliff and hold it up while I go for a tree trunk to wedge against this rock wall, so that we both can get out from under it without being crushed. Lean against it real hard or it will flatten you. I'll be right back!" Fox leaned against the cliff real hard. He waited and waited, but Coyote did not come back. "This evil Coyote has tricked me again," said Fox, as he jumped away from the rock wall, still looking up to see whether it would fall down on him. "Yes, Coyote has made a fool out of me."

Once more, Fox followed Coyote's tracks. He found him sitting on a tree stump near a stream. Again Coyote did not try to flee. Fox came running, foaming at the mouth: "Watch out, Coyote, this time I'll make an end of you, once and for all. I'll tear your throat out!"

It was sunset. The red setting sun was reflected in the stream's water. "Nitwit!" Coyote shouted, pointing at the sun's reflection. "Idiot, look at this hunk of fine red meat in the water. Instead of bothering me, you should try to get it before the current sweeps it away. Here, I'll hold on to your tail to pull you up after you've grabbed the meat!"

Fox fell for it. As he jumped into the water, Coyote quickly tied a heavy rock to Fox's tail. Fox drowned. "Finally I'm rid of this pest," said Coyote. But of course he was wrong. No matter how often Coyote and Fox kill each other, they always come to life again. ∎

Toad and Donkey

The Caribbean: Jamaica

Although in Africa this story tends to involve tortoise and hare, in Jamaica the hopping toad, indigenous to the island, is given the role of trickster. Not for him "slow and steady wins the race." When the odds are great, it is wit that wins and mindless acceptance of surface appearances that loses. This international tale type (AT 275A) can also be found as a race between hare and hedgehog in Europe. In "Toad and Donkey," the donkey, convinced of his own superiority, does not even look closely enough at his adversary to notice the trick played on him.

Walter Jekyll's early twentieth century collection of Jamaican songs and tales (1907) has proven to be an important resource to modern Jamaican dramatists and storytellers such as Louise Bennett (1966), helping them recall the stories they used to hear and tell as children. Jekyll's inclusion of songs that are an integral part of Jamaican storytelling is especially valuable. In this story, the song imitates the sounds of donkey and toad, the toad's last notes to be sung deep in the throat. The Jamaican dialect of the turn of the twentieth century, as recorded by Jekyll, has been preserved in this retelling. A few words have been changed to make it easier to read the story. An example is using "to" instead of "fe."

Although there are many different types of stories in Jamaican folklore, all the stories have acquired the name "Annancy Stories," hence the title of the book from which "Toad and Donkey" was selected. Most picture books of Jamaican stories are about Annancy himself, many of them directly related to West African variants.

Source: "Toad and Donkey" from *Jamaican Song and Story: Annancy Stories, Digging Sings, Ring Tunes, and Dancing Tunes* collected and edited by Walter Jekyll. London: David Nutt, 1907. pp. 39–43.

One day a King had a race and Toad and Donkey were to be the racers. An' Toad tell Donkey that him will win the race, an' Donkey mad when he hear him say so. And the race was twenty mile.

An' Donkey say, "How can you race me? I have long tail an' long ear' an' a very long foot too, an' you a little bit a Toad. Let me measure foot an' see which one longer."

An' Toad say to Donkey, "You no mind that, man, but I will win the race."

An' Donkey get very vex about it.

An' Donkey say to the King, "I ready now to start the race."

An' the King made a law that Donkey is to bawl at every mile that the king might know where he is.

Now that little smart fellah Toad says to the King that he hasn't fix up his business yet, an' will he grant him a little time.

An' the King grant him a day, an' say to the two of them, "Come again tomorrow."

An' Donkey didn't agree, for he know that Toad is a very trickified thing.

But the King wouldn' hear, an' say, "No, tomorrow."

Now Toad have twenty children. An' while Donkey is sleeping, Toad take the twenty children along with him to the race ground, an' at every milepost Toad leave one of his children an' tell them that they must listen for Mr. Donkey when he is coming. "An' when you hear that fellah Mr. Donkey bawl, you must bawl too." An' Toad hide one of his children behind every milepost until him end the twenty mile.

So the race begin.

Donkey was so glad in him heart that he was going to beat Toad that he say to himself, "Tche! That little bit a fellah Toad can't manage me, so I have plenty of time to eat some grass."

So him stand by the way, eat grass and poke him head through the fence where he see some potato-slip, an' try a taste of Gungo peas. An' he take more than an hour to catch up the first mile-post, an as him get there him bawl:

Ha! Ha! Ha! Me more than Toad.

An' there comes the first child call out:

Jin-ko-ro-ro, Jin-kok-kok-kok.

An' Donkey quite surprise, an' say, "Tche! How him manage to be before me?"

An he think, "Me delay too long with that grass, I must be quicker next mile."

An' him set off with a better speed an' only stop a minute for a drink of water. An' him get to the next post him bawl:

Ha! Ha! Ha! Me more than Toad.

An' there come the second child call out:

Jin-ko-ro-ro, Jin-kok-kok-kok.

An Donkey say: "Lah! Toad travel for true. Never mind, we will chance it again."

So him start, an' when him reach the third mile post him bawl:

Ha! Ha! Ha! Me more than Toad.

An' the third child behind the post say:

Jin-ko-ro-ro, Jin-kok-kok-kok.

Jackass get vex when he hear Toad answer him, an' he go to mash Toad, an' Toad being a little man hide himself in a grass.

Then Donkey say, "Hey! fellah gone ahead; see if I can catch up the next mile-post before him." An' he take him tail an' touch it like a horsewhip an' begin to gallop.

An' him get to the fourth mile-post an' bawl!

Ha! Ha! Ha! Me more than Toad.

An' there comes the fourth child answer him:

Jin-ko-ro-ro, Jin-kok-kok-kok.

When him hear, him stand up same place an' trimble, an' say, "My goodness King! What me a go do? Are you going to make me gallop so I knock all me hoof upon the hard dirt because I must win the race?"

An' he gallop so fast than he ever do before, until when he get to the fifth mile-post he was really tired an' out of breath.

But he just have enough to bawl:

Ha! Ha! Ha! Me more than Toad.

When he hear:

Jin-ko-ro-ro, Jin-kok-kok-kok.

This time he really mad, an' race on harder than ever. But always the same story. Each mile-post he catch

him bawl: "Ha! Ha! Ha! me more than Toad." An' always come answer: "Jinkororo, Jinkokkokkok."

An' Donkey begin to get sad in his mind for he see that he lost the race. So through Toad smartness Donkey can never be racer again.

*Jack Mantora me no choose any.** ■

*Typical Jamaican formula ending—equivalent to "don't blame me".

The King of Leaves

Central America: Nicaragua

This story is typical of the way many strands can come together in the Americas to create new stories. According to M. A. Jagendorf and R. S. Boggs (1960), the motif of using a pair of shoes to trick someone shows up in African American stories as well as in stories told by people of French origin in Missouri. Jack uses the same trick to make off with a man's ox in the Appalachians. The trick is also used in stories told in Belgium, Finland, India, Italy, Lapland, and Norway.

Tio Conejo (Uncle Rabbit) is a popular trickster character in Nicaragua and other Central American countries. He might well be related to Hare from Africa or to Brer Rabbit from the United States. In at least two Nicaraguan stories he is kept from drinking at the common well as punishment, a

motif that also appears in the Ewe (African) tale "Why Hare Runs Away" (Abrahams, 1985). Tio Conejo as well as other animals use the leaf trick to disguise themselves in several Latin American countries.

Tío Conejo—Uncle Rabbit, or Br'er Rabbit, as we call him—has a very bad reputation in Nicaragua. He is famous for being a clever rascal and a shameless rogue. And because he is always making trouble for everybody, the people are tired of him. But he always says he doesn't care what people think or say about him, and he never changes his bad habits.

One day the king of the land said, "We must do something about that troublemaker." The king and his advisers talked it over for a long time, and finally the king said, "Tío Conejo has given us trouble for many years. We must get rid of him. Go out, all of you, and catch him and bring him back to me, dead or alive!"

They all went out, giving suggestions to one another on the best way to catch Tío Conejo. Finally some

Source: "The King of Leaves" from *The King of the Mountains: A Treasury of Latin American Folk Stories* by M. A. Jagendorf and R. S. Boggs. Copyright © 1960 by M. A. Jagendorf and R. S. Boggs. Renewed copyright 1988 by André Jagendorf, Merna Alpert & R. S. Boggs. Used by permission of Vanguard Press, a Division of Random House, Inc. pp. 218–221.

said, "Let us go to the water hole, where all the animals come to drink and hide. Rabbit will get thirsty and come there. Then we'll catch him and take him back to the king. Or maybe if he sees us and is thirsty and can't get any water, he'll go away to another land." They did not know that Rabbit was right behind the bushes, listening to them talk.

"I will drink all the water I want, and I'll not go away to another land," he said, laughing to himself.

He went to another village and passed by a shoe shop. The shoemaker had beside him a fine pair of shoes for the princess.

"*Buenos días*, Señor; good morning, sir," Rabbit said cheerily to the shoemaker. "It's a hot day."

"It is a very hot day," replied the shoemaker.

"You should sit inside, where it's cool and the sun the won't burn you. At least you should have a drink of cold water. It will do you good."

"That's a good idea," said the shoemaker. "I am thirsty. I'll go into the house and have a drink of cool water from my clay jar."

As soon as he had gone into the house, Tío Conejo took the pretty shoes and away he went—lippety-lop. He came to a highway and followed it—lippety-lop, lippety-lop, lippety-lop.

Far down the road he saw a man coming toward him. The man was walking with his head bent forward and a big gourd on his back.

"Hah! That man is carrying a heavy gourd full of sweet honey. Now, that is something I like," said Rabbit, and he quickly dropped one of the shoes he was carrying in the middle of the road and hid behind some bushes.

As rabbit had thought, the man was a honey merchant, and on his back was a big gourd full of sweet, golden honey, which he was carrying to market to sell.

He saw the shoe in the road and stopped. "What a pretty shoe!" he said. "But where is the other one?"

He looked around everywhere, but he could not find the other shoe. "Well," he said, "one shoe is not worth taking. One must have two to make a pair." So he left the shoe in the road and walked on.

Tío Conejo knew what he was doing. He ran ahead as fast as he could, and when he came a turn in the road he threw the other shoe down and again hid in the bushes.

Soon the honey man came along and saw the other shoe.

"Ah! There is the other shoe. I'll run back and pick up the first shoe and then I'll have the pair. I'll just put this heavy gourd of honey right here beside the road, behind this bush, where no one will see it, so I won't have to carry it all the way back."

He ran back down the road. As soon as he was gone Tío Conejo jumped out, picked up the gourd, and scampered off with it through the woods. He didn't stop until he came to an open place covered with dead leaves.

There he sat down and ate and ate honey until he was so full he could not swallow another bit. Then he poured the rest of the honey over himself, over his head and long ears, all over his furry body, and over his soft feet and bushy tail. Then he lay down and rolled over and over, until dead leaves had stuck to all parts of his body. Never in this world has anyone ever seen an animal like that. He looked like a great pile of leaves on the move.

Back to the village he went, lippety-lop, lippety-lop. Everybody stared at him. No one had ever seen anything like that before. Many were afraid to come neat him.

He went to the water hole where the king's men were waiting to catch him, but no one recognized him. No one came near him. He put his mouth into the water and drank and drank until he was full and could not drink another drop.

"Who are you?" they asked him.

"I'm the King of the Leaves," he answered, and then walked away slowly.

This was exactly the way Tío Conejo had said it would be. He came up boldly, drank all the water he wanted, and did not leave the village! ■

Coyote Rings the Wrong Bell

North America: Mexico

Hare is a popular trickster in Mexico, where he is often in conflict with another trickster, Coyote. In Mexican folktales, Coyote tends to be the one who is fooled. In fact, he is so gullible, it's hard to recognize him as that clever, let alone mythic, creator/trickster one meets in tales from the Pacific Northwest to New Mexico.

Mexican culture, more than any other in North America, is a synthesis of pre-Columbian Native American culture, especially Aztec, and European culture brought over by the Spanish Conquistadores, Franciscan monks, and subsequent Spanish immigrants. The blending of the cultures is most evident in the majority Mestizos' (people of Indian and Spanish ancestry) synthesis of Aztec and Christian beliefs and customs. The Virgin of Guadalupe, whose image can be seen throughout Mexico is thought to be an example of synthesis: the Virgin Mary and an Aztec mother goddess, Tonantzin (Dorson, 1970). The colorful festivals and ceremonies for which Mexico is famous are also a blend of Spanish Catholic and Aztec pageantry, which was encouraged by the early Franciscan monks.

It was not only the religion, legends, and festivals that became a mixture of the two cultures. The stories too, especially the animal stories, were blended. The Spaniards brought their animal tales, including Aesop's fables; the Native Americans had their animal stories. In the stories Coyote often meets animals that were brought over by the Spanish, such as sheep and burros.

But Coyote is still Coyote, the Native American trickster who in many tales agrees to switch places with the hare because he is greedy for food or women. In a story that is popular throughout Mexico Hare gets caught by a farm woman using the tar baby trick, but he doesn't get boiled for supper. Instead, he persuades Coyote to switch places with him by convincing Coyote that the boiling water is being prepared for cooking chickens in honor of Hare. Hare manages to prevent Coyote, who has survived the boiling water treatment, from taking revenge by distracting him several more times with promises of food. One of the promises is that schoolchildren, whose "school" is a wasp's nest, would bring him food (Paredes, 1970). This motif closely parallels the one in the following story.

In Mexico there are many tales about animals, but most of them are about Hare and Coyote. These two always argue and try to outwit each other; they are rivals in hunting and in everything else. Since Coyote is much the stronger, Hare has to match his wits against Coyote's strength.

Now, one day Hare finished a fine meal and lay down under a tree for his siesta. Sometimes he gazed up at the blue sky, and sometimes he just closed his eyes. Finally he was fast asleep. Coyote came along, very quietly, looking for Hare. He was hungry. When he saw Hare sleeping, he approached very slowly and silently, and when he was near, he took a great jump and *plppp!* he landed squarely on top of Hare with all four paws.

Hare awoke with a frightened start and saw at once that he was in deep trouble. But he was not afraid.

"Now I have you, Hare!" said Coyote. "You must have had a fine dinner, for you feel nice and fat. Mmm, what a meal you will make!"

Hare was thinking fast.

"Yes, I did have a fine meal, and I don't mind if you eat me, for my flesh is old and dry and I don't have

Source: "Coyote Rings the Wrong Bell" from *The King of the Mountains: A Treasury of Latin American Folk Stories* by M. A. Jagendorf and R. S. Boggs. Copyright © 1960 by M. A. Jagendorf and R. S. Boggs. Renewed copyright 1988 by André Jagendorf, Merna Alpert & R. S. Boggs. Used permission of Vanguard Press, a Division of Random House, Inc. pp. 187–190.

much longer to live anyway. But just be patient and wait a bit. Perhaps I can give you something to eat that is much more tender and softer than I am."

"I wouldn't mind having something more tender, but I don't see anything better to eat around here. So it will have to be you, Brother Hare. Ho, ho, ho!"

Hare did not laugh.

"I know," he said, breathing hard, for Coyote was sitting right on top of him and he was heavy. "I know you see only me right now, because all the tender little hares are in school, but that is just a little way from here. They are all there, soft and juicy, and just the right age."

Coyote licked his lips.

"I know," he said, "that these little hares are very soft and juicy. Where is that school, Brother Hare?"

"Just a little way down the hill. They are waiting for me to ring the bell for them to come out and play. But I can't ring it for a long time, not until the sun reaches the tops of the trees up on the hill. Then I can ring the bell. It's right up here in this tree." And he pointed to the tree under which they were lying and in which there was a big brown hornets' nest.

"Will the little hares come out if you ring the bell?" asked Coyote.

"They will, indeed, but I have to wait a long time. It's too early now. They must stay there a long time yet."

"Would they come out if you rang the bell now?"

"They would, but I won't ring it now. I must wait for the right time."

"Brother Hare, I'm not hungry, and I won't eat you. See, I am letting you get up. Why don't you go for a little walk, to stretch and get the stiffness out of your joints? I'll stay and ring the bell for you at the right time."

Coyote got off Hare, and Hare stretched himself slowly.

"I don't mind running off if you will promise that you will stay and ring the bell. But don't forget; you must not ring it until the sun reaches the tops of the trees on the hill."

"I won't forget. But you must tell me how to ring the bell."

"It's very easy, Brother Coyote. All you do is shake the tree very hard. Then they will hear it at the schoolhouse. But shake it violently, so they will be sure to hear it."

"You can be sure I'll shake the tree hard enough, Brother Hare. Now, run along!"

Hare was off in a flash. When he was at a safe distance, he shouted, "Be sure to wait for the sun to reach the trees, Brother Coyote."

"I won't forget, Hare. Now, be on your way!"

Hare ran off, while Coyote watched. No sooner was Hare out of sight than Coyote rushed up to the tree and began shaking it with all his might. He shook it and shook it; but no bell rang. Finally he threw all his weight violently against the tree and *klppp!* down fell the hornets' nest and landed squarely on his back. Suddenly the air was filled with hornets as they flew out in fury from their nest, stinging Coyote all over his body, from the point of his nose to the tip of his tail. You couldn't see his fur anywhere for the hornets.

He ran as fast as he could, howling, but the hornets were after him all the way, stinging him at every step, to teach him a lesson for knocking down their nest.

And so Coyote had sharp stings instead of juicy little hares. ∎

Pourquoi or Why Tales

Pourquoi or "why" tales are a blend of myths, legends, and fables. There is a fine line between serious etiological stories with mythic power, which are told as explanations of the way something came about, and lighthearted, humorous explanations of observed phenomena and customs that might or might not ever have been taken seriously. Many of these latter type of stories seem to be explanations of why some phenomenon came about, such as why the possum's tail is bare or why turtle's back is cracked, but are actually allegories of human behavior and provide a light tone for teaching what is acceptable behavior to children.

Whether a pourquoi tale is more mythic or more fable-like might be determined by its tone as much as by its content. The explanations for why Turtle's back is cracked in three different cultures demonstrates this difference. The first two explanations are from two different Nigerian ethnic groups, the Yoruba, as told by Oyekan Owomoyela in *Yoruba Trickster Tales* (1997), and the Igbo, as summarized by Isidore Okpewho in *Myth in Africa* (1983), while the third is a Cherokee explanation, as told by Gayle Ross in *Why Turtle's Back Is Cracked* (1995). In the Yoruba story Tortoise's back is cracked because, acting as trickster, he got in trouble when he tried to implicate his rival the dog in the murder of a princess and was thrown down a cliff as punishment. In the Igbo version the animals had, during a famine, agreed to eat their mothers. All complied except the squirrel brothers, who put their mother in heaven. She in turn let down a rope for them to climb to heaven whenever they were hungry. When Tortoise tried to trick her into feeding him and the other animals, he fell to earth and cracked his shell. The Cherokee explanation, like the Yoruba story, focuses on Tortoise's human-like misbehavior and, like the Yoruba story, is humorous. Tortoise not only brags immoderately but also brags about accomplishments that are not his own when he eats corn chowder with a spoon made of a wolf's ear, the sign of a great hunter. The primary purpose of the Yoruba and Cherokee stories is to teach a lesson on correct human behavior rather than to explain why the tortoise's back is cracked. The settings are real-world setting—a king's court in the Yoruba story, the U.S. Southeastern woods in the Cherokee story. The Igbo tale, however, suggests a mythic time and a more serious tone and message. The problem—famine—is familiar, but the solution to which all the animals but the squirrel brothers succumb is taboo in all cultures. The mythic nature of the story is further developed by having the squirrels place their mother in heaven and reaching her and the bounty of heaven through ritual chants.

Pourquoi tales are told in many parts of the world, but they are especially popular with Native Americans as a way of passing on cultural values and of reminding individual children of something they might have done wrong, such as bragging or acting hastily and in anger. According to folklorist John Bierhorst, even when a story is a Native American adaptation of a European fable, as many in Latin American countries are, the explicit morals are dropped and the story is transformed into a pourquoi tale (2002). Several of the pourquoi tales included here, such as "The Origin of Strawberries" and "How Possum Lost His Tail," are being told today by Native American storytellers Joseph Bruchac, Gayle Ross, Kathi Smith Littlejohn, and Freeman Owle. The other pourquoi tales were collected in Africa and the Caribbean throughout the twentieth century. These easily told stories seem popular with children and, because they don't take long to tell, can be fitted into a busy day or told as part of an evening's entertainment. Because this type of story is usually short and has both a fanciful component and a lesson, it may lend itself to creative writing or oral performance with children.

For picture book versions of the following stories, see "Picture Books Related to the Stories in the *Allyn & Bacon Anthology of Traditional Literature*" on the Web Supplement at www.ablongman.com/lechner.

How Crab Got His Shell

Africa: Ghana

Guessing someone's correct name, according to Berry (1991), is often used to incite a dispute in West Africa. A secret name that has to be learned and remembered is a recurrent theme in African stories; in one story type animals must find out from an old woman a tree's secret name to be able to enjoy its fruits. Secret names feature in other cultures too. Rumpelstiltskin immediately comes to mind, but a more closely analogous story is a Puerto Rican one told by Pura Belpré about an orphan boy raised by a witch who won't feed him enough until he is able to guess her secret name. In that story too the animals help the child. Ashley Brian (1989) created a picture book for young children that uses some of the elements found in "How Crab Got His Shell": a long name, a secret name, the help of animals in learning the name of grandmother, and the protagonist (a little boy in Brian's book) having to remember the name all the way home.

There was once a poor orphan girl who had been left in the care of her wicked old grandmother. The old woman was very cruel to the child. This mean woman would send her to fetch water in a sieve and things like that. She even refused to give the child enough food until the child had called her by her proper name, but the child didn't know her grandmother's name, and the grandmother wouldn't tell her. It was a hard life for the poor girl, and she would often go to the river and sit there weeping for her dead parents and her unhappy life.

One day she was sitting by the river, sobbing quietly, when a crab came out of its hole and asked her why she was crying. The girl told the crab her story, how her cruel grandmother would only give her enough food if she could call her by her proper name, and how she didn't know her grandmother's name, and didn't know how to find out because her grandmother wouldn't tell her. The crab said, "That is easy; I'll help you. Your grandmother's name is Sarjmoti-Amoa-Oplem-Dadja." The girl said, "Thank you, Crab," and set off.

On the way home the girl kept repeating the name to herself so she wouldn't forget. But halfway home she heard a bird singing a most beautiful song. She stopped to listen. She enjoyed the bird's song very much, but when she set off for home again and tried to say her grandmother's name, she found she had forgotten it.

So she went back to the river and found the crab and asked it to tell her the name again. This time, the crab refused to tell her. It explained why, saying, "I've been thinking about this, and I'm not going to say that name again because your grandmother will know who told it to you. She is a wicked old woman and will come after me." The girl pleaded with the crab, who was feeling really sorry for her, so he finally gave in and told her the name again: Sarjmoti-Amoa-Oplem-Dadja.

All the way home, the girl repeated that name—Sarjmoti-Amoa-Oplem-Dadja, Sarjmoti-Amoa-Oplem-Dadja. Over and over again she said it. She got home safely and started to prepare food for the evening meal. As she prepared the food she said to herself, "Sarjmoti-Amoa-Oplem-Dadja." The old lady came home. As the poor child began to serve the food, her grandmother asked, "And what is my name?" The girl appeared not to know, so the grandmother took all the food, and just as she was going to eat it, her granddaughter called her by her name, "Sarjmoti-Amoa-Oplem-Dadja."

"Who told you my name?" demanded the wicked old woman. The girl said, "I got it at the river," but she didn't mention the crab. The old lady grabbed a calabash and went straight to the river.

She went all along the riverbank asking everyone she saw, "Did you tell that girl my name?" Everyone she asked told her, "No, I didn't!" Then she came to Crab.

He was very much frightened and confessed that he had told the girl the name. Then he turned and tried to run away. Furious, the old lady chased Crab, waving the calabash. She reached out and clapped the calabash down on the crab, and he ran off with it into the forest.

That is how the crab got the shell it has today. ∎

Source: "How Crab Got His Shell" from *West African Folktales*, collected and translated by Jack Berry. Edited with an introduction by Richard Spears. Copyright © 1991 by Northwestern University Press. pp. 106–107. Reprinted by permission.

Why Bats Fly by Night and Birds by Day

Brian Du Toit, the collector of this tale, distinguishes among three types of Zulu folk narratives: explanatory tales, teaching tales, and entertainment tales. This story belongs more in the explanatory tales category than in either of the other two. Although it does not deal with larger existential issues such as the origins of the world or of the human condition, it does not directly teach correct behavior as many of the Native American pourquoi tales do. Rather, it explains an observed nature phenomenon in mythic terms. Du Toit explains that when bats are described in the last line of the story as hanging upside down to avoid the sun, the Zulu word used for "avoid" is the same one that is used for ritual avoidance of people one is not supposed to be in contact with, as is (or was traditionally) the case between sons-in-law and mothers-in-law. The context in which the story is told, however, is informal: Grandmothers and any other nonspecialized storytellers are allowed to tell tales like this. The story is rendered as close to the oral narrative style of the Zulu storyteller from whom it was collected as du Toit could manage in English, to preserve the Zulu idioms and the tone of the account.

Source: "Why Bats Fly by Night and Birds by Day" from *Content and Context of Zulu Folk-Narratives* by Brian du Toit. Gainesville, FL: University Presses of Florida, 1976. Reprinted with permission of the University Press of Florida. pp. 20–21.

In ancient times, birds and bats were great friends. At one time the chief of the bats fell ill and an herb to cure him was sought. The bats sent messengers to the birds to ask for help, requesting them to help with the knowledge of herbs they believed the birds had. The birds simply laughed at them, refusing to help and telling the bats to go ask the rats since they were more ratlike than birdlike. The bats, being desperate, went to consult the rats who wouldn't help either saying that there never was a flying rat.

The bat chief became more ill than before, and it became clear that death was imminent. The bats went to ask the sun for help believing that the sun should have vast knowledge of herbs since it shone everywhere. But the sun said it was unable to help because it lacked the required knowledge.

The bat messengers came back without the required information and found that the chief was already dead.

From that day onward the bats would not fly by day as they bore the birds an everlasting grudge over their refusal to come to their rescue in their hour of need.

Because of the sun's bad deed of refusing to show them where they could find the right herb, the bats decided to fly in the night out of the sun's sight. Because the bats hated the sun they chose to sleep with their heads down, thus avoiding the sun. ■

Why Hens Scratch the Ground

Like the story "Why Bats Fly by Night and Birds by Day," this is more an explanatory story than a teach-

ing story, but one can easily draw a lesson based on the interactions between hawk and the hens. The slight awkwardness of the written English version reflects the almost literal translation of the original Zulu oral version. Even when told in the same language, the oral versions of stories must be adapted for print to make up for the body language and vocal inflections of the teller as well as the "core reservoir of clichés, fixed symbols and frames of reference" that tellers and listeners share (du Toit, 1976, p. 26). Du Toit chose to word this story as closely to the original as possible to preserve its Zulu character. Readers, however, should retell it, rather than read it aloud, for full effect. This type of story is (was) usually told in the home by grandmothers and great-grandmothers as recently as the early 1970s, in urban settings as well as in rural ones. Earlier in the twentieth century, children would congregate in the late afternoon in the grandmother's house to hear stories. As in many other cultures, there was a rule against telling stories in the daytime. The simple explanation for this is that storytelling distracts from the daily work that needs to be done. The evening was a good time to relax and tell stories. Children, however, were told that if they listened to stories in the daytime, they would grow horns (du Toit, 1976).

Once upon a time, there was a hawk who owned an axe that he used to earn a living. He used it every day. He would go into the mealie field and keep walking up and down with the axe.

One day the hens asked him to lend them the axe. He let them have it. The hens didn't know that they were getting themselves in a jam. The hawk requested them to keep an eye on the axe and make sure they didn't lose it.

The hens were very happy and delighted and took it to the mealie fields. They cut lots of mealies and settled down to eat. None of them cared or still felt concerned about the axe—bent on making the best of the feast.

It wasn't long before the hawk came back from his journey. The hens became apprehensive when they saw the hawk circling above their heads. He flew down, settled among them and asked for his axe; he wanted to use it as he was at the time feeling hungry, too.

The hens searched and searched, but the axe was nowhere to be seen. The hawk waited until his patience wore out and he spurned them saying, "I do not want the axe anymore. From this day onwards I am going to live on your young ones!"

The hens cried, pleading with the hawk to bear with them, but the hawk was exasperated beyond reason. He flew away and left them. The hens searched through night and through day for the axe but they couldn't find it.

As they searched, they optimistically hoped the hawk would forgive them and withdraw his threat if they found the axe.

It wasn't long before the hawk was seen stealing chickens. The hens began to spend their days in misery. In the meantime, the hens carried on their search, scratching the ground in search of the lost axe.

Up to this date, the hens still scratch the soil searching for the axe. We believe that the old hens left word among the generations that succeeded them that the only way of obtaining the hawk's forgiveness was to find his axe. ■

Source: "Why Hens Scratch the Ground" from *Content and Context of Zulu Folk-Narratives* by Brian du Toit. Gainesville, FL: University Presses of Florida, 1976. Reprinted with permission of the University Press of Florida. pp. 25–26.

The Ear of Corn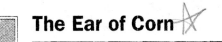

Europe: Germany

This religious pourquoi tale (AT 779) speaks to the importance of revering God's gifts. The fact that the story involves "corn," the British English name for "wheat" is relevant, as the sacred nature of bread is reflected in religious practices in Judeo-Christian religions, from the unleavened bread, or Matzoh, of Passover to the wafer of the Communion. Throwing away bread is therefore considered sacrilegious in many European countries. Though a folktale, this story reflects the idea of the Garden of Eden and the fall of humans or the idea of the Golden Age and humankind's descent from it as presented by the ancient Greek Hesiod.

In former times, when God himself still walked the earth, the fruitfulness of the soil was much greater than it is now; then, the ears of corn did not bear fifty or sixty, but four or five hundred-fold. Then the corn grew from the bottom to the very top of the stalk, and according to

Source: "The Ear of Corn" from *Grimm's Household Tales* by Jacob and Wilhelm Grimm. Translated from the German by Margaret Hunt. London: George Bell and Sons, 1884. p. 341.

the length of the stalk was the length of the ear. Men, however, are so made that when they are too well off they no longer value the blessings which come from God, but grow indifferent and careless. One day a woman was passing by a corn-field when her little child, who was running beside her, fell into a puddle, and dirtied her frock. On this the mother tore up a handful of the beautiful ears of corn, and cleaned the frock with them.

When the Lord, who just then came by, saw that, he was angry, and said, "Henceforth shall the stalks of corn bear no more ears; men are no longer worthy of heavenly gifts." The bystanders who heard this, were terrified, and fell on their knees and prayed that he would still leave something on the stalks, even if the people were undeserving of it, for the sake of the innocent birds which would otherwise have to starve. The Lord, who foresaw their suffering, had pity on them, and granted the request. So the ears were left as they now grow. ■

The Birds and Animals Stickball Game

North America: United States—Cherokee

The Cherokee migrated to what is now the North Carolina, Tennessee, northern Alabama, and northern Georgia area from the Great Lakes region. Archeological evidence shows that they have been in the region at least since 500 C.E., but their history in the Southeast might be a great deal longer. They were among the "Five Civilized Tribes" because they adapted to European-American culture: Sequoia developed a Cherokee writing system and published a newspaper, and the Cherokee became land owners. Nevertheless, they were forcibly removed from the Southeast after gold was discovered in Georgia. After most of the Cherokee people's forcible removal from

Source: "The Birds and Animals Stickball Game" from *Living Stories of the Cherokee* edited by Barbara R. Duncan. Copyright © 1998 by the University of North Carolina Press. Used by permission of the publisher. pp. 66–68.

the eastern states to Oklahoma in 1838, the stories continued both in Oklahoma and in the East, where some of the Cherokee managed to return or to remain by hiding in the woods.

Cherokee stories were collected and recorded by James Mooney in the late nineteenth century, at which time it was thought that the stories were going to disappear because of the U.S. government's policy of assimilating all Indians into mainstream culture. The language was nearly eradicated, but the culture and stories survived, and the stories continued to be told within families and the community. Recently, Cherokee storytellers have begun to share the stories with the general public (Duncan, 1998).

Kathi Smith Littlejohn, who belongs to the Eastern Band of Cherokee Indians in North Carolina, is Director of Health and Human Services for the tribe as well as a storyteller. She tells most of her stories at schools, where she also teaches children storytelling in the hopes that they will pass them on.

Duncan has recorded the stories of contemporary storytellers such as Kathy Littlejohn and Freeman Owle with line breaks to maintain the oral rhythmic style in which the stories are told. They are meant to be read aloud for full effect. The most important points come at the beginning of the sentence and are flush with the left margin. Less important points are indented. Kathi Littlejohn's humor and warmth are reflective of both her personal style (one fellow storyteller says that angels sit on her shoulders when she tells stories) and the Cherokee storytelling style, with its humor and many puns in the Cherokee language (Duncan, 1998).

Lacrosse, the game referred to as stickball in the story, originated with Native Americans and was popular among the Southeastern Indians (Cherokee, Chickasaw, Choctaw, Muskogee, Seminole, and others). Ritual dances by men and women that preceded the game emphasized its sacred nature, according to James Mooney (Philip, 2001). The story of a ball game between the birds and the animals is also widespread among Southeast Indians. Freeman Owle tells a slightly different version. The lesson one might draw from his telling, however, is quite different. In Owle's version, the mouse is rejected by the bear, the leader of the animals' team, so he tells the eagle that he would like to play on their side. Instead of rejecting him, the birds make wings for him, and he becomes a great flier (a bat) and wins the game for the birds, thus showing that everyone has skills and abilities and no one's contribution should be despised.

Storyteller: Kathi Smith Littlejohn

At one time,
   many years ago,
   human beings and animals
   could talk the same language
It was a very magic time.
And more than that,
   the animals and the birds
   could talk the same language, too.
They all had good times together,
   but occasionally they would argue.

Occasionally they would start to fight,
   and sometimes they would even hurt one another.
One day the birds argued with the animals
   that they were number one.
They were stronger, they were better, they were better looking.
They argued back and forth,
   and finally it almost broke into a war.
So they decided that they would do what the Cherokee men did:
   they would settle this by playing a game of stickball,
   and they set up the game.
Animals and birds came from miles around to bet on the game.
They were real excited.
This was going to be the battle to end all the arguments
   who was going to be number one forever.
And the game started.
First the birds scored,
   and then the animals scored,
   then the birds would score,
   then the animals would score,
   and finally it was tied up.
Eleven-eleven.
Whoever would score the next point would win the game,
   because the games end at twelve.
The birds got the ball, and they were streaking toward the goal,
   and they dropped it.
Oh, no.
The animals got the ball,
   and they threw it from one to another,
   and they finally threw it to their secret weapon,
   Mr. Skunk.
Mr. Skunk put that ball in his mouth,
   and he started waddling down the field,
   and everybody backed off.
Nobody wanted to tackle Mr. Skunk. "Go for it, go for it, get the ball, he's gonna score."
Finally Mr. Buzzard, brave Mr. Buzzard, swooped down.
He grabbed the skunk so hard
   he ripped a white streak right down his back
   that he still has today.
And the skunk sprayed him.
Oh, shoo, did he spray him.

He sprayed him so bad, and he stunk so much
  that even today he flies all by himself,
  all alone,
  because he still stinks bad.
Oh, and Mr. Owl said,
—"No, I can do it, I can do it."
And he swooped down and he tried to get the ball and
he got sprayed.
He got sprayed so bad it knocked rings around his eyes,
  and he still has those today.
Finally Mr. Bluejay said, "Watch me."
He swooped down all around the skunk's head,
  and the hummingbird swooped in real small
  and got the ball out of his mouth
  while the bluejay distracted him.

They went on and they scored the winning point.
The birds were so happy.
And Mr. Bluejay took all the credit—
  he knew that he was the one
  that won the game.
So he went and he put a big sign hanging around all the
trees
  that said the birds are number one.
And if you go out in the woods today,
  and you find a bluejay's nest,
  you look:
  and he'll have a piece of stringing hanging down
  right in the bottom of it
  as a signal to all the animals below
  that the birds are number one. ∎

How the Possum Lost His Tail

North America: United States—Cherokee

Freeman Owle, who taught school in North Carolina, researches Cherokee history and culture and tells traditional stories to a wide range of audiences. Owle learned these stories the traditional way, as a child from his family during winter storytelling sessions by the fire, parching corn. After college Owle returned to Cherokee, North Carolina, to teach and continue the art of storytelling. He began by telling stories to his students in school and expanded from there. Included among his stories are popularly told pourquoi tales such as this one; ghost stories, which were very popular with his students; legends from mythic times; and historical accounts from Cherokee history. He included the experience of the Trail of Tears of 1838. Owle tells stories to Indians (the Cherokee prefer that term to "Native American") and to the general public. One of his purposes is to educate the general public

about Cherokee culture, dispelling misconceptions about Indians. (Duncan, 1998). The story "How Possum Lost His Tail" is a popular Cherokee story that has also been told by Kathi Smith Littlejohn, another Cherokee storyteller. The story's charm is enhanced by the fact that it is a living story and "explains" a familiar animal's behavior. The lesson it teaches is universal. Duncan's poetic line breaks reflect the oral rhythm of the teller, the lines that are flush left representing the most emphasized points and the indented lines the less important ones.

Storyteller: Freeman Owle

Many stories were told.
Many stories were teaching stories.
The old story of possum was told
  to keep children from bragging and boasting.
The possum was a beautiful creature, but he didn't
know that.
And one day he was walking out beside the waters

Source: "How the Possum Lost His Tail" from *Living Stories of the Cherokee* edited by Barbara R. Duncan. Copyright © 1998 by the University of North Carolina Press. Used by permission of the publisher. pp. 212–215.

and looked into the very, very still waters and saw a reflection of himself
> and realized that his tail was big and fluffy and beau-
>> tiful and many, many colors.

So he began to admire himself,
> and he walked by that water all day long
> until the wind began to blow.

And then he walked away
> and began to boast and brag to the other animals in
>> the forest.

And early every morning he was out
> in the center of the forest
> and waking all the animals up
> to see how beautiful his tail was that day.

Many, many days passed,
> and they began to get tired of it—
> of his boasting and bragging—
> because they knew he was beautiful.

And the fox and the cricket got so tired of it
> that they made a plan to put an end to it.

They had a contest set up in the squaregrounds of the Cherokee the next day
> and invited Mr. Possum to come down and participate,
> because it was a contest to see who had the most
>> beautiful tail.

And sure, he would do that, he knew he would win, and that would be fine.

But they coaxed him into going with them that night
> to comb and brush his tail.

And when he went into the cave of the fox,
> they began to brush his tail and groom it,
> and he began to get a little sleepy.

And as he began to get sleepy,
> they brushed a little faster,
> and soon Mr. Possum was fast asleep.

The cricket, being the creature that he is, began to chew,
> and he chewed *every* hair off the possum's tail.

Well, it was not a very pretty tail at that time,
> and they tied it up with a piece of deerskin
> and tied a beautiful bow on the end of it.

And early next morning when the possum awakened, he said,
> "What did you do to my tail?"

being very upset.

And they said, "Oh, we combed and brushed it so beautifully
> that we felt like we had to wrap it up
> so it would not get messed up."

And so he was in agreement to that,
> and he bounced on off to the squaregrounds.

And the animals began to go across the stage.

And you had the skunk
> with his beautiful black tail
> with a white streak down the middle.

And of course he didn't smell very good,
> but all the people were pleased,
> at a distance.

And the other animals crossed the stage,
> the squirrel,
> and the red fox
> with his big, beautiful orange tail with the black spot
on the end.

The possum couldn't wait any longer,
> and he began to get antsy.

So he jumped on the stage
> and he said,
> "It's my time, we need to get this thing settled."

So he said,
> "Take this thing off my tail."

And when they took it off,
> all the animals, and all the people in the audience
> began to roll and laugh and giggle.

And he looks back at his tail,
> and he sees what they're laughing about.

He has the most ugly,
> rat-looking tail
> that he's ever seen in his life.

And first he begins to snarl and spit
> and become very angry.

But after a little while they laugh again
> and he can't stand it anymore,
> and he rolls over on his back and he plays dead.

The old possum boasted too much.

And if you go out today
> and you find him in your trash cans,
> you will see that he begins to snarl like he's going to
>> tear you to pieces.

And if you poke him with a little stick,
  he'll remember
    that he boasted too much.
And he'll roll over on his back
    with all four feet sticking into the air.
And you can pick him up by the tail
    and carry him back into the forest.

So the teaching of the Cherokee possum story is:
You should let *other* people
  tell you that you're beautiful.
Don't go around telling everyone else
  that you are.
Okay? ■

First Man and First Woman

North America: United States—Cherokee

Kathi Smith Littlejohn tells traditional stories in schools both to Cherokee children and to children outside of western North Carolina, where the Eastern Band of Cherokee Indians live. During the nineteenth century, at a time when people thought that Native American culture was disappearing, collector James Mooney published a comprehensive volume of traditional Cherokee stories. That collection is the source for most modern picture book versions of Cherokee tales. Cherokee tales, however, are not just living fossils. Barbara Duncan's *Living Stories of the Cherokee,* from which the following story is reprinted, focuses on those traditional folktales and myths that Cherokee storytellers tell today. Duncan's purpose in creating this collection was not to "save" the stories from extinction but to show that they are alive and strong today. To capture the sound of oral performance, Duncan has followed the rhythmic pattern of the storytellers' style on the printed page, giving further evidence of the living nature of the narratives. She also provides variants of several of the stories, including Freeman Owle's "The Origins of Strawberries" (see

the next story in this anthology), which is another version of "First Man and First Woman."

Storyteller: Kathi Smith Littlejohn

Now,
  how many of you have ever had a fight
  with your brother or sister,
  your best friend or teacher?
Oh no, no, now you better not tell me you had a fight
with your teacher.
Oh my goodness.
Did—
  before you know it—
  you were yelling ugly mean things
  that you really didn't mean to say,
  mainly about what they looked like and smelled like,
  they were kind of stupid,
  and you hated them,
  and you really didn't,
  but when we get angry
  we say these things without thinking first, don't we.
Well, a long time ago,
  that's exactly what happened between first man and first woman.
And they were so much in love,
  and they loved one another,

Source: "First Man and First Woman" from *Living Stories of the Cherokee* edited by Barbara R. Duncan. Copyright © 1998 by the University of North Carolina Press. Used by permission of the publisher. pp. 55–58.

and they loved their animal friends.

What happened that day

nobody can even remember,

but all of a sudden first woman said,

"You are the slowest man on the face of the earth.

I asked you two days ago to help me with this,

and now look what happened."

"Well, you call me slow, you're as slow as an old turtle."

"I asked you if you'd do this."

"And not only that, but you're fat."

"Fat, well you're ugly."

Oh, the ugly things they said about one another,

and oh, he got so mad,

and they were yelling and screaming.

First woman burst into tears,

and she ran out the door.

He ran after her,

and he hollered,

"You go on and don't you ever come back."

Oh, and he was still so angry,

and he stomped around

and he thought,

"She called me fat! Fat? How dare she?

She ought to look at herself before she—

Oh, don't you ever come back and tell me that."

Then it got later and later,

and he got a little more worried about her.

So he went to edge of the clearing and kinda called her name,

and no answer.

And he thought,

"That's all right.

You stay out there all night.

See if I care."

And he walked back in and slammed the door,

and it got real late, and real dark.

There were no lights then,

and he was really worried, and he thought,

"Gosh, what if something really has happened to her?

Oh no, oh I can't wait to see her and tell her I'm sorry.

I told her she was ugly. She's not ugly.

Oh, I'm so sorry."

And at first light, the next day,

he started out to try and find where she was,

and he began to see little signs,

and he found a broken leaf or a broken branch,

and he could see the bent grass where she ran.

So pretty soon,

he started noticing there was a little flower,

just about the space of a woman's foot if she were running,

and it was in a straight line.

He'd never seen these flowers before,

and he followed the little white flowers

that led him straight to where she was.

She had lain down and gone to sleep.

She stayed right there so he could find her.

He woke her up and said,

"Oh, my baby, I'm so sorry."

And she went,

"Oh, smooch smooch honey darlin'."

Oh, mushy mushy.

And they promised they wouldn't fight any more,

they put their arms around each other,

and started walking back home, lovey-dovey.

And as they stepped over each of the white flowers,

they bloomed out into a strawberry.

And the strawberries are supposed to remind us now

not to ever fight with the people that we care about.

They're just a reminder

about the first man and first woman's fight,

and how we got strawberries in the world.

That's how the Cherokee people got the first strawberries.

And the legend goes on to tell us

that we should keep them in our home at all times:

maybe a picture,

maybe jelly,

it may be strawberry jam.

To remind us not to argue

as first man and first woman did. ■

The Origin of Strawberries

The same story, told slightly differently, takes on a different meaning. Although here it is primarily a teaching story that tells how we should act toward one another, with the origins of strawberries providing a lovely image to make the lesson sweeter, the version Kathi Smith Littlejohn tells in "First Man First Woman"—the previous story—provides a vision of mythic times and the way the first husband and wife had to learn to get along. Davey Arch, a third storyteller recorded by Duncan, also emphasizes the role of the strawberry as the first gift of a man to his wife to gain or regain her affection. All three stories highlight the Cherokee value placed on harmony and balance (Duncan, 1998). Comparing the two versions in this anthology, one can also see two different styles of storytelling.

Storyteller: Freeman Owle

One of the ones that I like to tell people here—
    and through my storytelling
      I've tried to sort of analyze what the stories really
        meant
      when they were presented to the children back in the
        old times.
And I found specifically that stories
    like the story of the creation of strawberries
    have special meanings, and I'll try to convey that.
They say once there was a man who,
    in this matrilineal society,
      his wife had told him to go out and kill a deer that
        day.

Source: "The Origin of Strawberries" from *Living Stories of the Cherokee* edited by Barbara R. Duncan. Copyright © 1998 by the University of North Carolina Press. Used by permission of the publisher. pp. 226–228.

And he went out with good intentions of bringing back a deer,
    because her family was coming that evening to have
      dinner with them,
    and the grandmother, her mother, was a very important person in that society.
So he went out that day and he was looking for a deer,
    preferably the best one he could find.
And he happened to come across a fellow who had fallen into a ravine,
    and his leg was broken,
    and so he went down in the ravine and helped him out,
    and carried him back to his village,
    and by the time he made it back to the village,
    it was very late in the day.
So he went back to the forest real quickly and started to hunt.
And by that time all the deer had gone in and he couldn't find one.
So he came back to his village where his wife was living.
And she saw him coming on the hillside.
And he didn't have a deer.
So she got very angry,
    and she began to throw things,
    and she ran away out of the village and left
    and went back to her own village, her mother's village.
And he came back
    and was praying to the Great Spirit
    and was telling him that he would like for the Great Spirit to slow her down,
    so he could tell her what happened that day
    and the reason for him not bringing the deer back.
She was moving very quickly, and the Great Spirit said that he would.

So he began to put beautiful flowers in her path.
And this didn't slow her down at all,
   she just kept right on running as fast as she could go.
And so he began to put fruit trees in her path,
   and she would go around them
   and was not even interested in the fruit.
So the Great Spirit said that he would have to put something in the path
   that smelled delicious,
   that looked beautiful to the eye,
   and tasted very, very good.
So he put this little plant right down near her feet,
   because she was angry and looking down.
And she saw these beautiful little white flowers,
   and then began to see a red fruit on the ground.
Then eventually she smelled it, and it was wonderful.
And then she began to pick some of them and taste them,

and they were so good that she sat down in the middle of the patch.
And the young man caught up with her
   while she was eating the strawberries,
   and he apologized to her
   and told her what had happened.
So she realized that she had left in anger
   and went back to the village.
I think this is a teaching to the children
   that we shouldn't in the heat of anger
   jump up and run away
   and make real drastic decisions or actions at that
    point.
And so each and every story had a real reason for it.
The Cherokees did not have schools,
   so they had to tell stories to teach their children. ∎

Why the Chicken Can't Fly

North America: United States—African American

The following story was told by Dr. David Banks and recorded by Judith Lechner on July 2, 1999, in Auburn, Alabama. Though raised in Tuskegee in the 1960s, David Banks spent his summers at his aunt and uncle's farm in Thomasville, Alabama in a place so far back in the woods that the telephone and power lines ended at the house. There was no television; the single light bulb and the radio were all that the electricity powered. As Banks puts it, he was fortunate in having experienced this era of subsistence farming, with lots of animals and his family growing their own fruits and vegetables. The rhythm of the day began with men chopping wood for the wood stove and the boys going to the spring to fetch buckets of water; they had to make two trips on Wednesdays, one for filling up the wash tub and one for

cooking. They all worked hard during the day, but the evening was family time. Everyone gathered on the porch, where an oil-soaked piece of cotton was burned to keep off the bugs, and the adults told stories while the children listened. Each adult tried to out-tell the other. First the uncle would tell a story, then his mother, then his aunt, and if friends came along, they started all over, and the friends told new stories. The story "Why Chickens Can't Fly" was David Banks's favorite. Though Dr. Banks does not claim to be a professional storyteller, he tells stories to his family; and when the Auburn University Gospel choir, which he directs, travels, he tells stories to the children at the churches. His own choir members crowd up with the children on the floor until they are reminded to let the children sit up front. The following written version represents a direct transcription of the oral version, complete with David Banks's introduction.

I guess you'd call this a behavioral modification story that's told to children to keep them from being hard-headed. And it's a farm story. Children always ask a lot of questions, especially on a farm because they see so many things: animals and nature and humans and their interactions. Children are always asking why this or why that. Back in the days when storytelling was popular, adults used to tell stories to satisfy this inquisitive nature as well as to take advantage of the time to teach them and raise them.

This particular story is based on the question of why chickens can't fly. It is a farm story and it was told to me like this:

Out on the farm you have all kinds of animals: cows, chickens, pigs, dogs, cats. And then you have a lot of wild animals like birds and things, possums, raccoons and what have you. And then you also have insects. Chicken was in the pen and one day he looked up and saw wasp flying around, making his rounds, looking for water, looking for food, seeing what was going on. The chicken looked up at the wasp and asked him to come teach him how to fly. The wasp said, "Sure I'll teach you how to fly." So he flew on down and told the chicken,

"Now the first thing you have to do is, you got to get you a running start." Chicken said "I know, I know, I know!" Chicken ran, ran into the fence, and boom. Feathers everywhere. So the wasp said, "Wait a minute, if you had waited, I would have told you to build up enough speed." The chicken said "I know, I know, I know!" So the chicken took off running, built up enough speed, and did the same thing again. Ran into the fence. Feathers flying everywhere. The wasp said, "Just hold on for a minute! I will tell you what to do. You take off running, build up speed, spread your wings, and —" The chicken said, "I know, I know, I know!" He ran, built up speed, spread his wings, and bam, he ran into the fence again. The wasp said, "Look, if you just take your time and listen, I will tell you how to fly. You take off running, build you up some speed, spread your wings, and then you start to flap —" Chicken said, "I know, I know, I know." Chicken took of again. He ran, he built up speed, and he spread his wings, but instead of flapping both his wings together, he flapped them one at a time. He started wobbling and again he ran into the fence. The wasp just looked at the chicken and shook his head and flew off. And that is why chickens can't fly. ■

Cat and Dog and the Return of the Dead

The Caribbean: Haiti

Diane Wolkstein, a New York City storyteller, went to Haiti to research and collect the stories in *The Magic Orange Tree.* Wolkstein had the opportunity to hear stories from both ordinary folks, villagers living about 15 miles south of the capital, Port-au-Prince, and from one of the rarely seen master storytellers (*maîtres conte*), who carry on the tradition, popular during the eighteenth century, when *maîtres conte* used to travel

Source: "Cat and Dog and the Return of the Dead" from *The Magic Orange Tree and Other Haitian Folktales* by Diane Wolkstein. Drawings by Elsa Henriquez. New York: Knopf, 1978. Reprinted with permission by Diane Wolkstein. pp. 66–68.

from plantation to plantation, performing during festivals and at wakes (Wolkstein, 1978). In the 1970s, when Ms. Wolkstein collected these tales, storytelling was still a popular pastime, and young children would mouth the words of the adult storytellers as they absorbed the stories for future retelling. In her collection, Wolkstein gives background notes about the Haitian tellers and the customs related to each of the stories. She explains, for instance, both Haitian attitudes toward the dead and their view of God. People are careful not to offend their deceased because the dead might haunt them if they had not shown proper honor to them during their funeral. Someone who feels that he or she is being haunted consults a *hungan* or *mambo*—someone who can communicate with the dead—to find out what the problem is and how it can be remedied (Wolkstein, 1978). According to Wolkstein, people are more comfortable with Papa God, who is seen as kind and forgiving and is given humanlike characteristics. This pourquoi tale is humorous in tone yet has a mythic dimension in its explanation of an existential fact of life. The story was told to Wolkstein by Antoine Exavier, who lived and worked in Diquini, ten miles from Port-au-Prince. Wolkstein emphasizes his laughter and enjoyment of this and another story about Papa God, further suggesting that this story is closer to being a folktale than a myth—that is, it is seen more as entertainment and a lighthearted explanation of the way things are than as a sacred story.

One evening Cat and Dog were sitting together by the fire discussing the problems of the village. The hours passed, and Dog turned the conversation to his own concerns.

"If only there were more people," Dog said. "Then I would have much more to eat."

"More people!" Cat exclaimed. "There is not enough food for everyone now. What would happen if more people came?"

"If more people came, there would be more food eaten, and more bones for me!" Dog answered. At the thought of it, his eyes glowed. "Bones . . . " he repeated, smiling. Then he leaped into the air. "That's it. That's how to get more people. I shall go to Papa God and ask him to bring back the dead to fill up the earth."

"Fill up the earth! Dog, there are already people living wherever you can see. Where will they go?"

"Well," Dog considered. "If everyone is forever mourning the dead, they ought to be able to make room for those they miss so much. Yes. My idea is a very good one. I shall visit Papa God tomorrow."

The next morning, Cat was first in line at the butcher's. He bought eight large bones and started on

his way to Papa God's house. En route he dropped the bones in places Dog would be certain to notice.

Cat knocked on Papa God's door. No answer. He put his ear to the door. zzzz . . . zzzz. . . .

"Papa God! Papa God!" he called.

When at last Papa God came to the door, Cat bowed politely three times and explained, "Papa God, I have come to warn you of some recent foolish talk on earth. Dog has been thinking of inviting the dead back. But the truth is, there are already so many people there is not much left to eat, nor much space to live. I know you like your peace and quiet (especially in the mornings), and if the dead return, there will be so much expansion that they'll soon be building houses near you. And certain people can be quite noisy, especially the dead, since they've been quiet for so long."

"Well, well," Papa God said, "sit down and have some coffee."

While Cat sipped his coffee, Papa God thought about how much he enjoyed sleeping late in the mornings. Cat finished his coffee, bowed again politely, and set off for home.

Not until evening did Dog arrive. He had eaten all eight bones and looked twice as fat as in the morning. Papa God was sitting on the porch. Dog tried to bow, but he was so stuffed he could only nod his head.

"Papa God," Dog began, "since you made me without teaching me a trade, it is through the kindness of the people on earth that I eat. I have come to ask you to allow the dead to return to earth so there will be more food and more—"

"More!" Papa God echoed. "MORE! I have never seen such a fat dog as you. Go back home and be glad there is someone who is feeding you so well."

It was only then that Dog realized who might have left all those bones on the way to Papa God's house. It was too late. Dog bowed as best he could to Papa God and went home.

Since that time, the dead have never returned to the earth, nor has Dog ever confided in Cat again. ∎

Why Fowl Catch Cockroach

What is lost when translated?

No one likes a shirker or to be made a fool of, and few people are fond of cockroaches, so one can hardly grieve at the rooster's (Fowl's) solution to his problem. Collected at the beginning of the twentieth century, this story reflects a dialect that is no longer heard in the Caribbean islands. The story reproduced here is the way Johnson published it in 1921, with only slight editing, substituting th's for d's and adding one or two words for clarity. "Cunneyman" probably means "cunning man." A contemporary telling by storyteller Ramona Bass, reprinted in *Talk That Talk: An Anthology of African American Storytelling* (1989), has roach singing:

> Cock-a-tee hee! Cock-a tee hee!
>
> Rooster sow and hoe the row.
>
> Roach him reap a heap of crop.
>
> Rooster him dumb, Roach him smart!
>
> Cock-a-tee hee! Cock-a-tee hee? Cock-a-tee hee!

Bass's version maintains the Caribbean flavor of the story by using "him" for "he" but eliminates such features of the earlier dialect as changing tenses throughout the story and using plural verb endings for third person singular. By using her own words, Bass has infused this tale with new vitality. For stories to stay alive, they must be told by each new generation in their own way. Trying to use a dialect that is not one's own results in a stilted and disrespectful rendition.

This cockroach is a big one. They come near big as you' hand. There you find them in the roofs. They make

Source: "Why Fowl Catch Cockroach" from "Folk-lore from Antigua, British West Indies" by John H. Johnson. *Journal of American Folk-lore 34*(131), 1921. pp. 66–67.

a noise like this: "Crum, crum, crum, crum, crum, crum!"

Cockroach and Fowl bought land to cultivate. Each day the fowl would go to the field to work the land. Cockroach would not go. So the fowl would leave an' go to the field. Then Cockroach get out the bed an' start to play. This cockroach fool Fowl. Fowl say, "You must come to work the field."

"Me ain't go out. I's too sick." This what the cockroach tell Fowl. An' he would not get out a bed. Soon Fowl gone, he jump out an' play. He playin' and singin' also,—

> "Cockroach a cunnyman, a cunnyman, a cunnyman,
>
> Cockroach a cunnyman, a cunnyman, a cunnyman."

He keep foolin' this fowl. An' he would not go out. Fowl get suspicious. He get one a the neighbor to watch for him.

This mornin' he goin' to the field. Cockroach say he won't go. Say, "I's too sick. Can't go out. Me is sick." And he didn't go. Fowl try to persuade him. He wouldn't go. Fowl gone to the field, cockroach jump from the bed. He is happy. Play an' sing,—

> "Cockroach a cunnyman, a cunnyman, a cunnyman,
>
> Cockroach a cunnyman, a cunnyman, a cunnyman."

An' the neighbor see him goin' so. This neighbor went an' tol' Fowl what Cockroach do. This fowl mad now. Come back and grab the cockroach. That fowl jus' claw that cockroach up and swallow him that quick. That is why fowl will cotch the cockroach. Finish. ∎

Why the Fox Has a Huge Mouth

South America: Peru

Though not clearly traceable to Inca sources, this story, collected in Peru, has a Native South American flavor. The importance of the flute to the story, the name of the bird, and the fact that a lesson is taught but the outcome is also used as an explanation for the fox's mouth all suggest the story's Native South American rather than Spanish origin (Bierhorst, 2002).

One day many years ago, at a time when his mouth was still small and dainty, as in fact it used to be, the fox was out walking and happened to notice a huaychao singing at a hilltop. Fascinated by the bird's flute-like bill, he said politely, "What a lovely flute, friend Huaychao, and how well you play it! Could you let me try it? I'll give it back in a moment, I promise."

Source: "Why the Fox Has a Huge Mouth" from *Black Rainbow: Legends of the Incas and Myths of Ancient Peru*, edited and translated by John Bierhorst. New York: Farrar, Straus & Giroux, 1976. Reprinted by permission of John Bierhorst. pp. 111–112.

The bird refused. But the fox was so insistent that at last the huaychao lent him its bill, advising him to sew up his except for a tiny opening so that the "flute" would fit just right.

Then the fox began to play. He played on and on without stopping. After a while the huaychao asked for its bill back, but still the fox kept on. The bird reminded him, "You promised. Besides, I only use it from time to time; you're playing it constantly." But the fox paid no attention and kept right on.

Awakened by the sound of the flute, skunks came out of their burrows and climbed up the hill in a bustling throng. When they saw the fox playing, they began to dance. At the sight of the dancing skunks, the fox burst out laughing. As he laughed, his lips became unstitched. His mouth tore open and kept on tearing until he was grinning from ear to ear. Before the fox could regain his composure, the huaychao had picked up its bill and flown away.

To this day the fox has a huge mouth—as punishment for breaking his promise. ∎

Web Supplement Stories

Web supplement stories are located at **www.ablongman.com/lechner.**

Cumulative Tales

The Pancake

Europe: Norway

Many variants of the "The Fleeing Pancake" (tale type 2025) occur throughout Europe and in North America: "Johnny Cake" (British), "The Wonderful Cake" (Irish), "The Wee Bannock" (Scottish), "The Bun" (Russian), and, best known in the United States, "The Gingerbread Man" (southern United States)

(Hearne, 2000). The folk versions portray an exuberant and boastful runaway pancake, cookie, bun, or dumpling and end with the escaping food's surprise demise through the trickery of a fox or a pig. There are numerous picture book versions that retell the story in the spirit of warning against bragging and overconfidence.

From: *Tales from the Field: Popular Tales from the Norse* by Sir George Dasent. New York: Putnam, 1895. pp. 121–125.

The Carrot

Eastern Europe: Hungary

This cumulative tale is popular with children throughout Eastern Europe; its best-known version in the United States, which usually features a turnip, comes from Russia. The version in the Web Supplement is a retelling by the editor, based on recollection from hearing it as a child in Hungary. The Hungarian word *répa* means "turnip," but carrots are called yellow *répa,* and parsnips are called white *répa.* Never having seen a turnip, as a young child I assumed that this root vegetable was a carrot. The animals also change among versions; for instance, the Russian folklorist Alexander Afanas'ev has four fleas at the end.

From: Retold by Judith Lechner from her recollection of the way the story was told in Hungary.

▣ Fairy Tales/Wonder Tales

The Faithful Prince

Asia: India—Punjab

India has a long tradition of collecting wonder tales. One of the early collections is the twelfth century *Ocean of Stories,* which includes a Sanskrit variant of "The Princess and the Pea." *The Arabian Nights,* with such colorful tales of adventure as "Sinbad the Sailor" and "Aladdin's Lamp," includes many stories that have been traced to India.

Prince Bahrâmgor is the classic questing hero. He goes on an adventure at first to catch the golden deer but later to gain a greater prize: his lost bride. The story includes typical Indo-European fairy tale numbers: The prince travels for seven days and seven nights on the back of the deer; he examines one hundred rooms; he walks seven miles in each direction; and he obtains three magical objects to find his lost bride. The magical objects, especially the cap of invisibility, are also classic.

This fairy tale was a folk variant of a popular literary tale about King Bahrâmgor, a Persian king who reigned from 420 to 438 C.E. Legends grew up around the king, who was said to have jumped in a lake after a wild ass that he was chasing during a hunt. Neither he nor the ass was ever seen again (Steel, 1894). Perhaps that helped to create the scenario for the prince's disappearance into Demonland on the back of a golden deer.

Demons in Hindu mythology are not evil; they are just more chaotic than the gods and can have a tendency toward evil. They can also be generous and devout. So the demons in this story are not unusual. The names of the demons are interesting; according to Steel, they are the names of legendary historic as well as well-known fantasy characters. Steel traces the name of the main demon, Jasdrûl, to the Hindu hero Rama's father (Dasaratha). Steel states that the second demon's name, Nânak Chand, is easily traceable to Nânak Shâh, the sixteenth century founder of the **Sikh** religion, the predominant religion of the Punjab in India.

From: *Tales of the Punjab: Folklore of India* by Flora Annie Steel. New York: Macmillan, 1894. pp. 23–34.

Princess Pepperina

Asia: India—Punjab

The Punjab is a state in northern India. When Flora Annie Steel collected these stories, at the end of the nineteenth century, most of India was under British rule. Her husband, as magistrate, would hold court in the villages under a shade tree, and Mrs. Steel would lay down a carpet farther away, where the idlers, mostly young boys, would gather around her. Little by little she was able to elicit stories from the largely illiterate folk, and sooner or later one person whose ability to relate stories was recognized by the others was pushed forward. He would tell the stories with colorful imagery and hyperbole: If a princess is slender, she weighs "only five flowers;" if two demons usually guard her, they multiply into ten thousand demons, according the introduction to *Tales of the Punjab.*

What was unique about Flora Annie Steel was her patience in listening to story after story, many told in fragments by several tellers, and piecing them together to complete the stories while preserving the language of the tellers' nonliterary style rather than using the literary style of *The Arabian Nights* to which her British audience was accustomed. The beautiful images of a single emerald pepper tree in a barren garden, a princess born from an emerald egg, and a

Jinni whose heart breaks at the loss of his princess suggest that oral storytelling styles might have been affected by the literary style of *The Arabian Nights*.

The reference in this story to the bulbul bird also suggests a literary influence. The bulbul bird, which is a nightingale-like little brown bird with a beautiful voice, inspired ancient Persian poetry. **Jinn**, too, frequently appear in *The Arabian Nights*. In pre-Islamic Indian and Arab cultures Jinn were considered powerful and malevolent nature demons who inhabited deserted places, but Islam recognizes both good and evil Jinn of varying degrees of power, according to *Funk & Wagnall's Standard Dictionary of Folklore, Mythology, and Legend* (Leach, 1972). Created from fire, they must obey God's laws in the same way that humans must. Good Jinni, like the one in this story, have accepted the teachings of Mohammed. (Muttaqun Online, http://muttaqun.com/ an Islamic education site. Accessed Feb. 15, 2002.).

From: *Tales of the Punjab: Folklore of India* by Flora Annie Steel. New York: Macmillan, 1894 pp. 159–166.

The Goose Girl

Europe: Germany

The German Goose Girl with her flowing blond hair has a Palestinian counterpart whose hair is "black as the carob" and whose beauty is so widely famed that a faraway prince wishes to marry her. As in this story, the wedding party travels a long distance, and it is during the trip to the groom's palace that a treacherous servant takes the heroine's place. Both stories abound with vivid images and rhyming chants and spells. Numerous stories of this tale type (AT 533) have also been found in other cultures from the Appalachians to Armenia. The image of the talking horse's head that reveals the truth about the Goose Girl is particularly memorable and does not appear in all the versions. The ultimate punishment of the usurping servant girls in these stories seems excessively cruel and violent, but such dire punishments are typical of fairy tales in which an ambitious maid or witch or a jealous mother-in-law causes the princess's or queen's loss of her rightful place. Similar punishments for impersonating royalty were historic fact during the Middle Ages (Mueller, 1986).

According to psychiatrist Sheldon Cashdan (1999), clear-cut punishment, with no chance of the wicked person's return, is psychologically important for children's feeling of control as they struggle with fears of their own "wicked" selves. The distanced tone and setting of "Once upon a time" also helps children see the violence as symbolic, rather than real. Research on children's ability to distinguish between fantasy and reality has shown, however, that there is a significant change between the ages of six and nine, so this story would be more appropriate for third through fifth graders than for younger children (Applebee, 1978).

From: *Grimm's Household Tales* by Jacob and Wilhelm Grimm. Translated from the German by Margaret Hunt. London: George Bell and Sons, 1884. pp. 10–16.

The Princess on the Glass Hill

Europe: Norway

The plot of a princess on a glass hill or in a high tower whom only the hero reaches with the help of a magic horse (AT 530) is widespread in Scandinavia, Russia, and other European countries. In this version, Boots, a Norwegian stock character, is the hero. Boots is always a youngest son and usually starts out seeming to be a fool or at least the protected son who is ignorant of the ways of the world, but in the end, he always succeeds.

Peter Christian Asbjørnsen and Jørgen Moe were the great collectors of Norwegian folktales in the nineteenth century. Aware that speaking styles change, Asbjørnsen gave specific directions to his editors to update the language in the stories when new editions appear (Pellowski, 1990). The Grimms, who pioneered folktale collecting in Europe, introduced the use of a colloquial tone in retelling fairy tales. Frequently, however, translators substituted a formal style, especially during the Victorian era. Sir George W. Dasent tried to capture the dialect of the Norwegian original as written by Asbjørnsen and Moe, but, like all translators, he was faced with the challenge of finding English words and expressions that convey the equivalent colloquial tone. He seems to have solved this problem by using some Scottish expressions.

From: *Popular Tales from the Norse,* 3rd ed., by Sir George W. Dasent. Detroit: Grand River Books, 1971. (Reprint of 1904 edition.)

Toads and Diamonds

Europe: France

At the end of this version of the kind and unkind sisters tale type (AT 480) the narrator comments that the prince considered the diamonds and pearls that appeared every time the kind girl spoke of greater worth than any dowry. This might be seen as a rather cynical comment, but it can also be seen as symbolic of the value of kind and beautiful speech. Charles Perrault, who included this story in his *Histoires ou Contes du Temps Passé* with the title "The Fairies," gives two morals at the end of the story, and the second one spells out this symbolic meaning. The first one was probably aimed at the worldly adults who, in the calculating milieu of the late seventeenth century French court life, would have appreciated the prince's comments about the monetary value of the diamonds and pearls. This era was also the era of salons hosted by upper-class women, which served as intellectual gathering places where witty conversation was developed to a high art. Through this story, Perrault might have been commenting on what he thought were overly outspoken women, or people whose speech was more witty than kind.

This version can be compared with the Louisiana variant in Robert San Souci and Jerry Pinkney's picture book *The Talking Eggs,* as well as with other versions in this anthology ("Kumba the Orphan Girl," "Mother Holle," "The Two Stepdaughters," and the "Twelve Months," and to some extent "La Estrellita").

From: *The Blue Fairy Book* by Andrew Lang. London: Longman, Green, and Co., 1889.

The Twelve Months

Europe: Czech Republic

The idea of violets and strawberries in winter has lost some of its magic with hothouse horticulture and cold storage shipping, but only 40 years ago in Central Europe, particularly during the scarcities of the post–World War II days, this story was just as enchanting to a child as the wonder of diamonds and pearls springing from the mouth of a girl in "Toads and Diamonds," another variant of the kind and unkind sisters tale type (AT 480). In this variant the water element is missing, unless one counts snow as frozen water, but death is definitely a threat, just as it is in "Mother Holle," "Kumba the Orphan Girl," and "The Two Stepsisters." The variant with the magical Month Brothers is known in Greece as well, but the image of the Month Brothers is part of the Czech literary heritage.

From: *The Shoemaker's Apron: A Second Book of Czechoslovak Folk Tales* by Parker Fillmore. New York: Harcourt, Brace and Co. 1920. pp. 3–21.

The Tale of Ivan Tsarevich, the Bird of Light, and the Grey Wolf

Europe: Russia

Until the eighteenth century, oral storytelling was not relegated to the lower classes in Russia but was the primary mode of narrative entertainment for all classes, from the Czar on down. Regardless of social class, storytelling was a highly developed art. A Russian proverb says, "The song is beautiful through its harmony, and the tale through its narrative style" (Jakobson, 1945, p. 644). Russian tales incorporate proverbs, riddles, incantations, and fanciful ornamentation. They have elaborate formulaic beginnings and endings, which unfortunately are left off in the following translation. According to Jakobson, the love of storytelling did not die during the Soviet era, and storytellers could be found in factories and other industrial settings, as well as in remote villages.

The Russian name Ivan is the equivalent of John in English and, like Jack in English tales, Ivan represents everyman. Although in this story Ivan is the son of a Czar, he is the youngest son, a role that might be seen as a symbolic representation of the powerless. Prince Ivan is a recurrent hero whose stories intertwine with those of two other stock characters in Russian folklore: Baba Yaga the witch and Vasilisa, a beautiful, clever, and brave girl.

Prince Ivan fits the Russian folklorist Vladimir Propp's model of a questing hero. He sets out on his adventure in search of a perceived lack, a Bird of

Light that his father must have. During his quest, his actions are bold but not always morally exemplary. He succeeds, however, through his perseverance and humility, which are rewarded by forgiveness and further help from a protecting animal. There are many variants of this tale type (AT 550), including Appalachian, Arabic, Greek, Hungarian, Mexican, Scottish, and Swahili. The Russian version, however, is probably best known. In some variants Ivan takes more of a heroic role by saving his brothers, who later turn on him. The wolf, which in some variants is a fox, turns out to be an enchanted human whose spell is broken when Ivan, at the wolf's request, cuts off his head. The wolf's actions in this story, however, seem more like the actions of shamans in Siberian and probably pre-Christian Russian mythology. He communicates with two other shamanistic animals, the ravens, and he restores Ivan to life through the use of the "Waters of Life and Death."

The Bird of Light is often referred to as the Firebird. Stravinsky, the Russian composer, created a ballet by this name. In this story, another stock character, the magician Koschey, keeps a princess prisoner. The Firebird leads Ivan to Koschey's enchanted garden, and it is through Ivan's bravery that the princess is rescued. Jane Yolen has written a picture book of the ballet version of the story, *The Firebird,* illustrated by Vladimir Vagin (HarperCollins, 2002). Two other picture books of the ballet include Margaret Greaves, *The Firebird* (Dial, 1986) and Rachel Isadora, *The Firebird* (Putnam, 1994).

From *Russian Folk-Tales* by Alexandr Nikolaevich Afanas'ev. Translated by Leonard A. Magnus, edited by Judith V. Lechner © 2003. London: Kegan Paul, Trench, Trübner & Co., 1915. pp. 78–90.

▣ Noodlehead Tales, Tall Tales, etc.

Lazy Jack

Europe: England

Jack, the hero who can outsmart giants, can be also a noodlehead. He exhibits his lack of common sense by taking everything that his mother says literally and by being impractical when solving problems. Yet he ends up lucky. Perhaps when hard work could gain very little for the ordinary peasant, the element of luck was essential for keeping hope alive for a better life. Equally, the title suggests that it is a story parents might tell themselves when they despair that their youngsters will ever amount to anything. After all, "Lazy" Jack did not turn out to be lazy.

The adventures of Jack have crossed the Atlantic and have been retold in the Appalachians for generations. Not all the versions are as upbeat and lighthearted as those made familiar by Richard Chase, who collected them in the 1940s, and by Don Davis, a contemporary storyteller who grew up on Jack tales in North Carolina and tells Jack tales at storytelling events and on audio recordings. Jack can be a mean trickster, greedy, and truly lazy, as contemporary storyteller Olivia Sexton-Carter presents him in her feminist version, "Lazy Jack" (Fine, 1999). In short, Jack is Everyman with all his good and bad qualities.

From *Popular Nursery Tales of England.* by James O. Halliwell. London: The Bodley Head, 1970. pp. 37–38. Reprint of 1849 edition.

Bastianelo and the Three Fools

Europe: Italy

Being able to laugh at one's forebodings helps one cope with life (Wolfenstein, 1978; Ziv, 1988). The bride in this story and her counterparts in the English "Three Sillies" as well as the German "Clever Elsie" (AT 1450) demonstrate the paralyzing effect of an imagination run wild. Because the stories are so exaggerated, however, listeners laugh at both the characters' foolishness and their own as they recognize analogous situations in their own lives. American variants of both "The Three Sillies" and of "Clever Elsie" were told in New York and in Ohio and were published as "Borrowing Trouble" in Botkin's *A Treasury of American Folklore* (1944). The Italian variants are close to the English, but some of the fools whom the young man meets seem more culturally specific to Italy: In a Sicilian version a child gets his fist stuck in a hole because he won't drop the peach pits with which he is playing a game called nocciole.

The following story is a combination of two Italian variants. Most of the plot and wording are from Crane's Bastianelo (p. 279) from Venice. In that variant, however, the young man is already married, and one of the set of fools he meets are a husband and wife; the wife is holding a man's trousers open so that her husband can jump into them. I have substituted the old woman who tries to make her pig help her from the Sicilian variant, "The Peasant of Larcàra," also from Crane (p. 282). I did this because the ending of the second variant was so amusing and because it is different from the more familiar English "Three Sillies." I have also shortened Bastianelo somewhat, leaving out some of the description.

From: *Italian Popular Tales* by T. F. Crane. Houghton Mifflin, 1885; "Bastianelo" (Venice), pp. 279–282, and "The Peasant of Larcàra" (Sicily), p. 282, were combined and adapted by J. V. Lechner.

Hans-in-Luck

Europe: Germany

Hans as numskull represents the outsider who lacks the common sense everyone else seems to take for granted. Others (the grown-ups) know the value of money and material goods; children have to learn, sometimes the hard way, as Shel Silverstein's poem "Smart" reminds us or as any teenager who has bought a lemon of a car knows. Hans's example serves as a lesson that, because of its humor, is easy to remember: Watch out for yourself because no one else will when you are out in the world. As lacking in common sense as Hans seems, however, he has one treasure that no one can take away from him: his sunny disposition, which allows him to see the positive in any situation. Perhaps this is what makes him a lucky fellow after all. This seems to be Don Davis's interpretation in "Jack Seeks His Fortune" included on the audiotape *Jack's First Job* (1993).

From: *Grimm's Household Tales*. Translated by Margaret Hunt. London: George Bell & Sons, 1984.

Wiley and the Hairy Man

North America: United States—African American

Set in the American South, this story's main elements, such as the hairy ogre-like creature that tries to chop down a tree while his victim is in the tree, the ogre's fear of dogs, and the use of conjure, have African

roots (Bascomb, 1992). According to storyteller and writer Judy Sierra (1996), the African counterpart of the Hairy Man is named Amazimu or Irimu and has matted hair. The American Hairy Man, Sierra says, is a combination of the African Amazimu and the European image of the devil. Wiley is up against a formidable enemy. The humor comes from both Wiley's ability to outwit the Hairy Man and the relief at the end, when Wiley's mother fools the Hair Man one last time.

Wiley's use of hound dogs that take off after a pig (shoat), his mother's knowledge of conjure, and Wiley's house with its loft and fireplace set at the edge of a swamp give the story a Southern flavor. One can almost see the Spanish moss hanging from the cypresses and live oaks.

This version of the story was collected in Alabama by Donnell Van der Voort, a writer for the Federal Writers' Project of the Works Progress Administration during the Great Depression. The Federal Writers' Project was one way in which the government helped unemployed writers as well as the arts, while at the same time helping to preserve the folklore of our nation. Some writers collected folktales and folk songs; others collected slave narratives, pioneer experiences, mining lore, and rural life stories. All of these narratives, songs, and lore have been preserved in the Library of Congress, and many are available on the American Memory Project (www.memory.loc.gov).

From *Manuscript of the Federal Writers' Project of the Works Progress Administration for the State of Alabama,* by Donnell Van de Voort. Reprinted in *A Treasury of American Folklore,* edited by B. A. Botkin.

▣ Trickster Tales

The Clever Peasant Girl

Europe: Italian

Cultures from India to Italy tell stories about intelligent and witty women who are able to assert themselves and prove that their judgment is superior to their husband's or even the king's. She is called Clever Manka in Russia and Catherine in another Italian version retold by Italo Calvino. Typically, she outwits the prince by solving his riddles, performs impossible tasks by using her brains instead of brawn, and outsmarts her foolish husband one more time in a way that's sure to rebuild his fragile ego and win his heart. This tale type (AT 875) has been found in Chile, Armenia, and Syria and in the Appalachians as well.

From *Italian Popular Tales* by T. F. Crane. Boston: Houghton Mifflin, 1885.

The Three Aunts

Europe: Scandinavia

This is one of the recurrent female trickster-type stories that is told throughout Europe (AT 501). I grew up with a Hungarian version, and Italo Calvino retells an Italian version. The plot is much like that of Rumpelstiltskin, but the hapless girl is saved by three wise women who use their guile not only to solve her present predicament but also to prevent her being further exploited.

From *Popular Tales from the Norse* by Sir George Webbe Dasent. New York: Putnam's 1904. pp. 193–198.

Pourquoi or Why Tales

How Turtle Got His Tail

North America: United States—Okanogan

Told by Mourning Dove/Humashima

A great deal of folklore research has gone into the concept of diffusion of tales. The folklorist Stith Thompson researched European tale types in Native American folktales in the first half of the twentieth century. Although most Native American folktales, including those Humashima told, are unique to this continent, the 400 years of contact between Europeans and the indigenous people of North America inevitably resulted in cross-cultural influences. The first Spanish conquistadores brought along a copy of Aesop's fables, which the Aztecs adapted to suit their values and local animals. This story, too, seems to have undergone a transformation from Aesop's "The Hare and the Tortoise." Instead of a spelled-out moral, we learn about a nature phenomenon. The Okanogan people live in the Northwest, near the Columbia River. Like Humashima, who lived at the beginning of the twentieth century and was a Christian, many Okanogans would have had contact with European culture through missionaries.

From: *Coyote Stories* by Mourning Dove. Caldwell, ID: The Caxton Printers, Ltd., 1933. Reprinted with permission by Caxton Press. pp. 81–83.

Myths

Introduction

Definitions

Myths and religious stories help people make sense of their world. They concern the large issues of the origins and endings of the universe and all things in it, life and death, good and evil, and the place and duty of humans with regard to the divine and to one another. Using the language of poetry—symbolism, metaphor, and allegory—myths express the things that humans sense but cannot fully comprehend (Doty, 1986; King 1986/7). The term **Mythology** refers to the complex network of myths that together constitute the stories that explicate the belief system of a people.

When told as part of a living belief system, myths and religious stories are considered not fictional but vital, true accounts. Within a cultural or religious system the stories may be viewed as literally true or as allegorical. These stories are culturally significant and culturally specific, in spite of the numerous examples of universally recurring themes and motifs. Local environmental factors affect the focus of the myths: The Norse gods battle ice giants, and Hawaii's goddess, the feared Pele, punishes her sister by burning down her beautiful forests, just as volcanic eruptions do from time to time.

Culturally specific beliefs and social systems also affect the myths. The creator might live in a village in the sky-world that is much like a village on earth, as is the case in the Iroquois creation myth, or the gods might engage in activities that are like those of earth people, from playing flutes and drums to stealing cattle, as Hermes does in Greek mythology. Sacred numbers differ among cultures: 3 among African, Asian,

"The Elephant-Headed God and Other Hindu Tales." Illustrated by Margaret Jones.

From: *The Elephant-Headed God* by Debjani Chatterjee. Cambridge, England: Lutterworth, 1989. Reprinted by permission of Lutterworth Press. Illustrations Copyright © 1989 by Margaret Jones.

and European cultures, for example, and 4 among Native Americans.

There are four major definitions of myths in the fourth edition of the *American Heritage Dictionary* (2000), which reflect the four ways in which the term is commonly used. In this chapter only the first definition, which corresponds to the description above, will be used. The second definition refers to important secular beliefs held in common by a people: "A popular belief or story that has become associated with a person, institution, or occurrence, especially one considered to illustrate a cultural ideal." An example of this definition is our national belief, formulated in the *Declaration of Independence,* that "all men are created equal," that they have "unalienable rights to life, liberty, and the pursuit of happiness," and that governments derive their "just powers from the consent of the governed."

The third and fourth definitions are those most frequently encountered in the news media and in popular parlance: "A fiction or half-truth, especially one that forms part of an ideology" and "A fictitious story, person, or thing." Though this view of myths too has ancient roots—Plato in rejecting the literal stories about the Greek gods referred to myths as false stories—this is not the definition that scholars of religion, folklore, or literature employ. Discussions of myths in this anthology, therefore, follow the scholarly convention of viewing myths from the perspective that they are or were stories of truth for the people who told them.

Functions of Myths

Since the time of Plato and Aristotle people have tried to understand the meaning and function of myths. Some scholars have emphasized the myths' social and political functions for the community; others have focused on their spiritual and psychological functions for the individual.

The following are some representative ideas on the social and political functions of myths:

- Myths provide a concrete medium for expressing abstract ideas and values (Doty, 1986, p. 128).
- Myths provide an accounting of origins, whether of the universe, of specific natural phenomena, of humankind, or of human institutions (Eliade, 1963).

- Myths provide needed knowledge to allow people to be in touch with the original sacred time for renewal. Reenactments of the stories and other ceremonies during new year festivals and initiation, fertility, and healing rites renew the world and assure its continuance for many cultures (Eliade, 1963).
- Myths provide models for human behavior, helping humans to survive in their natural environment and in society. Society's values are expressed through religious conceptions and are made concrete through stories that are projected into a mythic realm outside of the everyday world as models for society. The stories act as social cement (Doty, 1986, pp. 28–29, 32, 43, 46, based on Durkheim, Malinowski, and Kluckhohn).
- Myths provide explanations for rituals and sacred places (e.g., the story of White Buffalo Woman tells the Sioux the meaning of the sacred pipe).
- Religion, aided by myths, helps to express and create the unity of a society (Doty, 1986, p. 45, based on Goode).
- Myths provide the meaning people ascribe to the facts and events historians record (Ricoeur, 1986/87).
- Myths tell of not only what was but what will always be (Doty, 1986).
- Myths tell about a people's roots (Doty, 1986).
- Myths give legitimacy to existing political and social structures (e.g., boundaries, class strata, and leaders) (Doty, 1986). The Roman emperors, for instance, used the image of Jupiter's power as a god of thunder to represent Rome's might (Powell, 1998).
- In times of turmoil myths reinforce ideals that seem to be missing, weakening, or changing in society (Doty, 1986).

Some spiritual and psychological functions of myths for the individual are described in the following statements:

- Myths awaken a sense of awe in and gratitude for the mystery of being (Doty, 1986, p. 52, based on Campbell).
- Myths identify the place of humans within the universe and help them answer the questions

"who am I," "who are my people?" (Doty, 1986, pp. 25, 33).

- Myths lead us out of our individual isolation to a shared vision of the universe (Doty, 1986).
- Myths help humans to understand the relationship between observed nature and cultural institutions. For instance, the story of the love between the Heavenly Weaver (the star Vega) and the Cowherd (a star in Aquila) in a Chinese, Japanese, and Korean myth models constancy and loyalty between husband and wife as well the virtues of filial piety.
- Myths shake us out of our habitual way of thinking through their language and the way they represent reality. One instance of this is the dimming of opposites; in many myths the earth and sky were not separate in mythic time. Another instance is showing the inverse effect of what is expected: A seemingly tragic outcome turns out to be the greatest good for mankind.
- Myths provide models for human activity (Bolle, 1986/7)

As myths are retold at different times and under different circumstances, they serve different functions. The same culture also tells different myths at different times in response to changing cultural needs or political realities (Levy, 1998). The Iroquois have recorded three sets of myths, for instance. The earliest describe the structure of the universe, the creation of life on earth including the "three sisters" of agriculture (beans, corn, and squash), the establishment of ceremonies (the use of tobacco to send thanks and requests), and the establishment of institutions (the origins of the clan system). Responding to changes in political circumstances, later myths involve the establishment of the Iroquois Confederacy formed out of the five original tribes—the Cayuga, Mohawk, Oneida, Onondaga, and Seneca—by Deganawidah and Hayentwentha/Haiwatha. Finally, the most recent set of culturally significant myths, the Kai'wi:yo (the good message), tells of the revelations of the nineteenth century Seneca prophet Handsome Lake that established the present-day Longhouse religion through a synthesis of early and later traditions (Converse, 1908; Parker, 1923, 1989; Fenton, 1962, 1998).

Recurrent Themes in Myths

Although it is important to place each myth in its cultural context to understand the very different world views of the people who tell them, there are many themes that mythographers (researchers of myths) have found to recur across cultures. The following are recurrent themes that readers will encounter while reading the myths of different cultures:

Supernatural Creators Most cultures look back to their origins as established by one or several creators. The Creator(s) may continue to be active in the lives of people (God in Christianity, Islam, Judaism) or may have withdrawn after having created the world and left the development of the world as we know it to other supernatural beings. In Ojibway mythology the Great Manitou created the world, but Nanaboozoo completed it, getting rid of ancient monsters and recreating the earth after a great flood. (Kawbawgam, 1994; Johnston, 1995).

Origins of the World A vision of the creation of order out of chaos is central to many of the world's mythologies, such as the Mesopotamian, Greek, and Norse. In other traditions, such as many of the Native American myths, a prototype of the world exists in the sky, below the ground, or on the earth before the world itself is created, as in the Iroquois myth "The Woman Who Fell from the Sky" in which a woman looks through a hole in the sky left by the uprooting of the world tree and falls down to where birds and animals await her and create a landing place (earth) for her. These are **cosmogonic** myths.

Origins of Nature Phenomena These range from explanations for the heavenly bodies to specific landmarks, such as Devil's Tower in Wyoming. Myths reflect the perceived violence of natural upheavals such as volcanic activity and the formation of rivers and lakes. They also give explanations for phenomena such as the distance of the sky from the earth.

Origins of Animals and People These stories recur in all mythologies, though in some, such as the Judeo-Christian story of creation, we are simply told that

God created the animals and are given only a little more detail about how He created man and then woman. In other mythologies the creation of specific animals and plants is described, and food crops are given special emphasis, as in Native American myths of the creation of corn. The creation of humans is frequently portrayed as a special problem, as, for instance, among the Aztecs and the Maya, where the Creators have to try several times before they create humans capable of thought and proper speech with which to praise the Creators.

Origins of the Human Condition These issues include the origins of death, why people have to work, the different roles of the sexes, the reason for different languages, social or ethnic differences among people, and how people obtained useful tools.

Issues to Consider

One of the questions to ask about myths is whether they are vital to a culture, shaping the culture directly. In other words, are they a part of a living religion or world view, or have they become secondary, almost unconscious themes that continue to turn up in literature and the visual arts as well as in attitudes toward nature and humankind's place in it, toward the relationship between men and women, toward health and disease, and so on? When Sophocles, Aeschylus, and Euripides wrote their tragedies and Aristophanes his comedies during the fifth-century B.C.E., educated Greeks no longer believed literally in the myths, yet the gods still played active roles in their plays. Also, long after witches were no longer part of European mythologies, farmers continued to believe that animals sickened because of witchcraft performed by an ill-wishing neighbor.

In this anthology we will make a distinction between classic myths, which are no longer part of a religious tradition, though they continue to have cultural value, and living myths, which continue to be viewed as vital and sacred by various contemporary cultures. One implication of this distinction is that while we can study, tell, appropriate, and adapt the classic myths, we must be more careful to accord respect to literature that is part of a living religion.

A story related by storyteller Anne A. Simpkinson illustrates the difference between collecting and retelling myths as ordinary stories and sharing in the lived experience of a religion. Simpkinson quotes Laurens van der Post, a South African who joined a group of San in the Kalahari Desert to learn about their stories. Though San people gladly shared other information with van der Post, the stories were not forthcoming until one day he joined them in a thanksgiving ceremony after a successful antelope hunt. Van der Post describes how the preparations, dance, the weather (approaching thunderstorm), and even the howls and cries of the animals converged to create a moment of intense religious experience for him: "Never had I heard human voices go so far back in time, so deeply down in the pit of being. This, I thought, was the cry of longing, anguish, and desire of the first man on earth. . . . I can only say that I myself have never felt more dedicated and nearer God than at that moment, and stood there almost in tears as one with revelation in a temple." It was only after van der Post shared in the Sans' religious experience that they could trust him with their stories (Simpkinson, 1997, pp. 25–26).

Another distinction between myths is whether they are part of a literary tradition, as the Bible, the Hindu and Buddhist religious stories, and the Greek myths are, or whether the stories are primarily part of the oral tradition, for which written accounts by anthropologists are pale reflections of their vitality. Even myths with a highly developed literary tradition, if they are also part of a living religion, are different in effect when told orally. The retelling of a Bible story during a religious service in a church or synagogue can present a different religious experience from reading the same stories in one's own home. Interpretations also change over time even if a body of myths is set down in writing.

When myths are passed on orally, many versions may exist, and retellings can change to fit changes in the society. South American myths are good examples of a body of stories with multiple versions describing the same event, for instance, the obtaining of fire or the world flood that came out of a tree and brought seed crops to all humans. Even within a single ethnic group there are varying accounts of the obtaining of fire and of the flood.

No one myth expresses a culture. Taken together, a culture's mythology gives an indication of that culture's belief system, but we have to be cautious about making generalizations about an entire culture's beliefs on the basis of examples of their myths. We might not have all of the myths that were considered important at the time of their telling, and our ability to interpret or respect another people's myths is limited by our own perspectives. Additionally, as was noted above, every culture keeps changing, and several variants of a myth are likely to exist (Doty, 1986, p. 51).

The explanatory power of myths is always an issue. One way in which the contradictions between myths and empirical science have been resolved is to recognize that myth and science are two different ways of knowing. W. Richard Comstock, an anthropologist who studies the social functions of myths within their societies, said this of the relationship between science and myth: "Myth, properly understood, is not an early attempt to do what modern science can now do better, any more than a poem is an early attempt to express what a geometrical theorem and proof can state more clearly and convincingly" (cited in Doty, 1986, p. 61). Doty goes on to say, "Myths convey the sorts of psychological and adaptational learning that enable us to live harmoniously within natural and cultural frameworks, that enable us to express and to be enriched by meanings and significances, by the realms of morally pregnant realities" (Doty, 1986, p. 62). When certain myths are no longer functional for a society, they are usually changed, discarded, or superceded.

Why We Study Myths

Familiarity with myths provides understanding of others and of ourselves, both within our own diverse society and globally. Many religions and their accompanying myths are represented in the United States. By studying diverse myths, we become aware of the values that have shaped us—those that we share with many other people and those that make us unique.

Myths are rich sources of metaphors for our lives. Many Bible stories need no elaboration. Their mere mention resonates with listeners: "The Prodigal Son" tells us of God's love for his children and his welcoming back those who stray from the path; Jacob's wrestling with the Angel is a metaphor for humankind's submission to the will of God; the story of Jonah and the whale tells us that we cannot avoid our duty; Naomi and Ruth show us loyalty and love between daughters and mothers-in-law; and the many stories of martyrdom continue to support people's resolve to keep their faith even when pressured to abandon it. Even myths that are no longer part of a living tradition provide rich sources of metaphors. The story of Orpheus the musician in Greek mythology, who nearly succeeded in bringing back his beloved Eurydice from the dead, has inspired poets, artists, and composers over the centuries with its theme of the spiritually uplifting nature of music and the poignancy of our mortal limits. Because myths use cadenced language and the poetic devices of symbols, metaphors, and similes, they provide literary pleasure for the listener or reader.

Finally, myths, particularly Greek and Norse ones, are a part of our lives through the names of planets, constellations, chemicals and other scientific concepts, the days of the week and months of the year, as well as the literature we read, which frequently alludes to or even rewrites myths for modern needs. As the literature that students read becomes more diverse, knowing some of the myths to which writers from cultures other than one's own refer enriches the reader's experience.

There are numerous collections of myths of specific cultures and a number of international collections. Most easily found are the Greek and Roman myths, with Norse and Native American myths a distant second. Today there are also more collections of myths from previously underrepresented cultures. In selecting collections of myths, it is important to look at when the myths were retold. Although earlier collections of Native American myths were at times thorough and accurate, the retellings, especially for children, often trivialized the stories, misrepresented their meanings, or told them in a style that made them sound awkward and more like a European fairy tale than a Native American myth. When selecting collections of myths, one should look for representation of a variety of cultures (not necessarily in a single volume), for a respectful tone, and for adequate cultural context and source notes, as well as for a lively, readable style. One should use the same criteria when judging the text and illustrations of picture book versions of myths (Hearne, 1993a, 1993b).

For picture book versions of the following stories, see "Picture Books Related to the Stories in the *Allyn & Bacon Anthology of Traditional Literature*" at www.ablongman.com/lechner.

▨ Divine Beings and Their Realms

The Birth of Ganesha, the Elephant Headed God

Asia: India

Ganesha, the elephant-headed god, the "Remover of Obstacles," and god of wisdom, is one of the most popular gods among the Hindu pantheon. Although, according to Hindu belief all gods are only manifestations of the one God, people find it easier to envision the supreme, all-pervading soul [**Brahman**] through personified gods and images, and Hindus maintain temples and shrines to specific gods (Sen, 1961; Ions, 1983).

It is Ganesha's good humor and kindness, according to Debjani Chatterjee (1992), that make him so popular. Because he is the god who removes obstacles, people seek Ganesha's favor before any important undertaking such as a journey, business enterprise, or writing a book or even a letter—which is especially fitting, since he is also the god of scribes (Ions, 1983). Kiran Bharthapudi, a graduate student at University of Illinois, recalls having been taken to Ganesha's temple at age 3, as children typically are, so that he could trace his first letter in the raw rice strewn before Ganesha's shrine. He thus started his education under the eyes of the god of wisdom.

Source: "The Birth of Ganesha, the Elephant Headed God," retold by Kiran Bharthapudi. Copyright © 2001 by Kiran Bharthapudi. Used by permission of the author.

Ganesha is the oldest son of Shiva the Destroyer, one of the three main aspects of God along with Brahma the Creator and Vishnu the Preserver. Shiva embodies the reconciliation of opposites. He is the force of life when the rhythm of his dancing keeps the world's rhythm going and the force of destruction when his dance becomes a dance of death. He is generous and loving as well as fearful and terrifying. His bull, Nandi, is a symbol of fertility, and Shiva's third eye, with which he can incinerate whatever he looks on, is the tool of destruction. It is with his third eye that Shiva the Destroyer annihilates the world at the end of each cycle of creation (O'Flaherty, 1975).

According to the Hindu worldview, the universe exists as part of a continuous cycle of creation, slow deterioration through four great ages, and destruction. The first of the great ages is the golden age, when duty stands on four legs and harmony prevails, and the last is the age of Kali (our present age), in which duty barely stands on one leg, and crime, oppression, famine, war, and natural calamities dominate until Shiva destroys the universe. The Preserver Vishnu, however, continues on, asleep, floating on the ocean for thousands of years, until a lotus blossom grows from his navel and Brahma the Creator emerges from the blossom to start the cycle again.

Shiva's wife, Parvati, who in the stories about Ganesha appears in her benevolent, motherly phase, is also Shiva's destroyer female half, Kali. The concept of opposites reconciled within the same person is basic to Hindu philosophy and is clearly shown in the stories about Shiva and the other gods. All good does not reside in the gods, and all evil does not belong to the demons. A demon can attain merit through meditation and ascetic practices as well as through propitiation of the gods. A god can have flaws, such as Shiva's quick temper in this story. The gods tend toward the light, order, and good, however, while the demons tend toward the underworld's darkness, chaos, and evil (Ions, 1983). Ultimately, however, all individual souls (**atman**) are part of the Universal Soul (Brahman), or one God.

Gasajura, an elephant demon, was a great king and devotee of Lord Shiva. One reason for this was that he wished to attain immortality, and to do this he had to obtain Lord Shiva's Atma Linga (Shiva's Soul) and keep it in his heart. To gain Lord Shiva's favor, he withdrew into the forest where he performed rigorous acts of penance (tapasya) and engaged in deep meditation, withstanding the scorching heat of summer, the harsh chills of winter, and the relentless rains of the monsoon. Lord Shiva, who is renown for his kindness and generosity, especially toward those who engage in rigorous penance and meditation, appeared before Gasajura and granted him what he had asked for, the supreme soul, Shiva's Atma Linga. But to do this Shiva had to leave his wife Parvati, his home Kailasa, and everything else that was dear to him, to live in the heart of Gasajura.

Parvati, who loved her husband greatly, began to miss him and to worry as his absence lengthened from weeks to months and from months to years. Parvati went before Lord Vishnu, the supreme god, and begged him to bring back Lord Shiva to her. Vishnu, Brahma, Nandi and all the other gods then disguised themselves as a dance troop and went down to earth, to the kingdom of Gasajura, in an effort to bring back Lord Shiva.

Gasajura, who loved music and dance was delighted to learn that a highly talented dance troop had arrived in his kingdom. Summoning them to his court,

he ordered them to perform for him and promised them that he would grant them whatever they asked for if their performance moved his heart.

Vishnu's and the other gods' performance surpassed anything Gasajura could envision and completely enchanted the demon king. Greatly moved, Gasajura ordered the performers to ask for anything they liked. Reverting to their godly forms, they asked Gasajura to return Lord Shiva.

Though a demon, Gasajura was honorable. True to his word, he ripped open his chest, released Lord Shiva, and died.

News of Lord Shiva's release immediately reached Parvati, who felt jubilant in anticipation of her husband's return. After months of neglecting her appearance as she grieved for Lord Shiva, Parvati now prepared for his return by carefully planning how she would adorn herself to welcome him in her full beauty.

Parvati began by applying turmeric all over her body. Next she planned to take a bath. First, however, she took some of the turmeric in her hand and with it she fashioned a small boy, infused it with life, and blessing him as her son, set him to guard Kailasa.

When Lord Shiva arrived at Kailasa, he was met at the gate by a boy he'd never seen before who would not allow the wild looking stranger with his matted hair, snake belt, and necklace made of skulls (Shiva's symbols of asceticism and of life and death) to enter. Shiva tried to persuade him to let him enter his home, but the boy was adamant about carrying out his mother's orders. Kind and generous as Shiva usually was, when his anger was aroused he was terrifying. His third eye of destruction flashed, and the boy's head was reduced to ashes without another thought.

When Parvati saw what Shiva had done she was distraught, and when Shiva finally calmed down and realized what he had done, he wanted to revive the child. But the head could not be restored. Shiva had with him however, the head of Gasajura, the elephant demon, which he had kept in memory of the honorable demon, and so he attached the head to the boy's body. Thus was created Ganesha, the Elephant Headed God, whose kindness, wisdom, and merry love of life make him the favorite of children. ■

Minerva (Athena)

Europe: Greece

Zeus, "lord of the sky" and father of both gods and men, attained his position by killing Cronus, his father, who in turn had killed Uranus, his own father. Uranus, the original Sky, whose union with Gaia, the Earth, brought forth the world, did not want his children to live, and only through a revolt by his children could the beginnings of the present order of the world be established. The cosmic order was completed by Zeus, but though he was the all-powerful figure of life and of law and justice, he feared a revolt against himself similar to the one he had conducted against his own father. When Athena's mother, Metis, became pregnant by him, Zeus swallowed Metis (her name meant "cleverness"), thinking to stop the birth. Athena, however, was born from Zeus's forehead in a flash of blinding headache.

Though the Greeks had a patriarchal society with strict limitations set on women, Athena, a female deity, was the one who taught humans the knowledge of a wide range of crafts and arts, from weaving to carpentry. She protected heroes in battle or on impossible quests, but she stood for reason, not brute power. Powell (1998) contrasts her character with those of several of the male gods: "Athena represents reason's control over elemental force. Poseidon sired the horse Arion, but Athena built the first chariot, which controls the horse. Poseidon rouses the waves, but Athena built the ship that rides on them. Hermes protects the flocks in distant mountains, but Athena taught how to spin the wool from which cloth is made" (p. 192). Though Athena often helped mortals, she, like the other gods, did not tolerate immoderate pride (hubris), as Arachne in the following story was to learn. Stories such as this were myths of warning. Arachne is also an etiological tale, suggesting the origins of spiders.

Source: "Minerva (Athena)" from *The Outline of Mythology: The Age of Fable, The Age of Chivalry, Legends of Charlemagne* by Thomas Bulfinch. New York: Review of Reviews Company, 1913. pp. 107–110.

As the only source for this story today is from the writings of Ovid, the first century Roman writer who tended to write satirically about the Greek gods, it is not clear to what degree Minerva's rather petty-seeming vindictiveness represented the Greek view and to what extent it is Ovid's ironic perspective. Because Bulfinch uses Ovid as his source, he also uses the Latin rather than Greek names for the gods. Thus Athena is Minerva, Zeus is Jove or Jupiter, Poseidon is Neptune, and so on.

Minerva [Athena], the goddess of wisdom, was the daughter of Jupiter [Zeus]. She was said to have leaped forth from his brain, mature, and in complete armor. She presided over the useful and ornamental arts, both those of men—such as agriculture and navigation—and those of women—spinning, weaving, and needlework. She was also a warlike divinity; but it was defensive war only that she patronized, and she had no sympathy with Mars's savage love of violence and bloodshed. Athens was her chosen seat, her own city, awarded to her as the prize of a contest with Neptune [Poseidon], who also aspired to it. The tale ran that in the reign of Cecrops, the first king of Athens, the two deities contended for the possession of the city. The gods decreed that it should be awarded to that one who produced the gift most useful to mortals. Neptune gave the horse; Minerva produced the olive. The gods gave Judgement that the olive was the more useful of the two, and awarded the city to the goddess; and it was named after her, Athens, her name in Greek being Athene.

There was another contest, in which a mortal dared to come in competition with Minerva. That mortal was Arachne, a maiden who had attained such skill in the arts of weaving and embroidery that the nymphs themselves would leave their groves and fountains to come and gaze upon her work. It was not only beautiful when it was done, but beautiful also in the doing. To watch her, as she took the wool in its rude state and formed it into rolls, or separated it with her fingers and carded it till it looked as light and soft as a cloud, or twirled the spindle with skillful touch, or wove the web, or, after it was woven, adorned it with her needle, one would have said that Minerva herself had taught her. But this she denied, and could not bear to be thought a pupil even of a goddess. "Let Minerva try her skill with mine," said she, "If beaten I will pay the penalty." Minerva heard this was and displeased. She assumed the form of an old woman and went and gave Arachne some friendly advice. "I have had much experience," said she, "and I hope you will not despise my counsel. Challenge your fellow mortals as you will, but do not compete with a goddess. On the contrary, I advise you to ask her forgiveness for what you have said, and as she is merciful perhaps she will pardon you." Arachne stopped in her spinning and looked at the old dame with anger in her countenance. "Keep your counsel," said she, "for your daughters or handmaids; for my part I know what I say, and I stand to it. I am not afraid of the goddess; let her try her skill, if she dare venture." "She comes," said Minerva; and dropping her disguise stood confessed. The nymphs bowed low in homage, and all the bystanders paid reverence. Arachne alone was unterrified. She blushed, indeed; a sudden color dyed her cheek, and then she grew pale. But she stood to her resolve, and with a foolish conceit of her own skill rushed on her fate. Minerva forbore no longer nor interposed any further advice. They proceeded to the contest. Each took her station and attached the web to the beam. Then the slender shuttle was passed in and out among the threads. The reed with its fine teeth struck up the woof into its place and compacted the web. Both worked with speed; their skillful hands moved rapidly, and the excitement of the contest made the labor light. Wool of Tyrian dye was contrasted with that of other colors, shaded off into one another so adroitly that the joining deceived the eye. Like the bow, whose long arch tinges the heavens, formed by sunbeams reflected from the shower, in which, where the colors meet they seem as one, but at a little distance from the point of contact are wholly different.

Minerva wrought on her web the scene of her contest with Neptune. Twelve of the heavenly powers were represented. Jupiter, with August gravity, sitting in the midst. Neptune, the ruler of the sea, held his trident, and appeared to have just smitten the earth, from which a horse had leaped forth. Minerva depicted herself with helmed head, her Aegis covering her breast. Such was the central circle; in the four corners were represented incidents illustrating the displeasure of the gods at such presumptuous mortals as had dared to contend with them. These were meant as warnings to her rival to give up the contest before it was too late.

Arachne filled her web with subjects designedly chosen to exhibit the failings and errors of the gods. One scene represented Leda caressing the swan, under which form Jupiter had disguised himself; and another, Danaë, in the brazen tower in which her father had imprisoned her, but where the god effected his entrances in the form of a golden shower. Still another depicted Europa deceived by Jupiter under the disguise of a bull. Encouraged by the tameness of the animal Europa ventured to mount his back, whereupon Jupiter advanced into the sea and swam with her to Crete. You would have thought it was a real bull, so naturally was it wrought, and so natural the water in which it swam. She seemed to look with longing eyes back upon the shore she was leaving, and to call to her companions for help. She appeared to shudder with terror at the sight of the heaving waves, and to draw back her feet from the water.

Arachne filled her canvas with similar subjects, wonderfully done, but strongly marking her presumption and impiety. Minerva could not forbear to admire, yet felt indignant at the insult. She struck the web with shuttle and rent it in pieces; she then touched the forehead of Arachne and made her feel her guilt and shame. She could not endure it and went and hanged herself. Minerva pitied her as she saw her suspended by a rope. "Live," she said, "guilty woman! and that you may preserve the memory of this lesson, continue to hang, both you and your descendants, to all future times." She sprinkled her with the juices of aconite, and immediately her hair came off, and her nose and ears likewise. Her form shrank up, and her head grew smaller yet; her fingers cleaved to her side and served for legs. All the rest of her is body, out of which she spins her thread, often hanging suspended by it, in the same attitude as when Minerva touched her and transformed her into a spider. ■

Thrym Steals Mjollnir

Europe: Norse—Scandinavian

The world the Norse gods, known as the Aesir, inhabit is continuously threatened by the very things Northern Europeans feared: darkness and ice. With his hammer, which, like many of the other implements and weapons of the Norse gods, had a name (Mjollnir), red-bearded Thor kept at bay the forces of chaos, represented by the frost and rime giants. Although wise Odin was called the head or father of the gods by the thirteenth century Christian scholar Snorri Sturlason of Iceland in his *Prose Edda,* for ordinary people it was Thor who was the chief protector of both gods and men, and it was to him that they built temples throughout Scandinavia, Iceland, and the Viking strongholds of Ireland and Normandy.

In this story, retold at a time when the old gods were no longer venerated, Thor is presented in a humorous light, more like a brawny but not-too-bright human than a god. The loss of his hammer, however, is still shown as a great calamity for the gods. Thor's hammer, Mjollnir, which he obtained as a gift from a dwarf through the trickery of Loki, has several possible symbolic meanings. Although most frequently seen as a battle weapon representing the power of lightning, it is also shown to have a creative aspect. In this story it is used to bless a marriage, and in a story about Thor's trip to **Jotunheim**, the land of the giants, it restores Thor's goats to life (Turville-Petre, 1964). The hammer's symbolism of life and fertility was retained until recent times in the rural Swedish marriage custom of hiding a hammer in the bride's bed (Lindow, 1994). The hammer may also be seen to symbolize the difference between raw nature (the giants) and the world of culture (gods and men). As a tool, it not only destroys, but also creates (Lindow, 1994).

This story also introduces two other characters from the world of the Norse myths: Freya and Loki.

Source: "Thrym Steals Mjollnir" from *Norse Mythology: Legends of Gods and Heroes* by Munch, Peter Andreas. Translated from the Norwegian by Sigurd Bernhard Hustvedt. New York: American-Scandinavian Foundation, 1926. Reprinted with permission by American-Scandinavian Foundation. pp. 76–79.

Seen as a northern Venus, Freya was one of the goddesses of fertility, whose cult lasted well beyond those of the other pagan gods into Snorri's own Christian era (Davidson, 1964). As half-god and half-giant, Loki plays an ambiguous role among the gods occasionally using his tricks to help the gods but more often to harm and finally to destroy them. In the final battle between the gods and the giants Thor's hammer destroys the evil that surrounds the world, the Midgard Serpent, one of Loki's offspring, but the gods themselves are also destroyed. Unlike the Greek gods, the Norse gods were not immortal. Hope, however, does not die. In their cyclical worldview the Norse people envisioned the birth of a new and better world.

At length it so happened that Thor found an opportunity to steal into Jotunheim and glut his hatred of the Giants. He had lain down to sleep, and when he awoke he missed his hammer. Enraged beyond bounds, he at once sought the advice of Loki, who promised to go out in search of the hammer provided Freyja would lend him her bird plumage. Freyja being willing, Loki flew off to Jotunheim and came into the presence of Thrym, king of the Thursar, who was sitting on a mound braiding gold cords for his dogs and clipping the manes of his horses. "What news among the Æsir? What news among the Elves? And what brings you to Jotunheim alone?" asked Thrym. "There is something wrong somewhere," Loki answered; "you do not happen to have hidden Thor's hammer, do you?" "Yes," retorted Thrym, "I have hidden it eight miles deep in the earth, and no man will get it before he brings me Freyja to wife." Loki brought the bad news back to Asgard. He then went with Thor to ask Freyja if she would consent to become the wife of Thrym; highly incensed, she gave them a curt "No" for answer. The Æsir accordingly met in conclave to determine what steps were to be taken; no one was able to suggest anything to the purpose until Heimdal proposed that they should dress Thor to take the place of Freyja, decking him out to that end with the Necklace of the Brisings and other appropriate ornaments. Thor pronounced the plan far beneath his dignity but at last gave in; so they dressed him in bridal linen, adorned him with the Necklace of the Brisings, hung jingling keys at his belt, put a kerchief on his head, and wrapped him in the long garments of a woman. Loki, in the habit of a handmaiden, followed in his train. Hitching Thor's goats to the cart, the two drove off at a pace that split mountains asunder and struck the earth into flames. As they drew near the domain of the Thursar king, Thrym bade the Giants rise to their feet and deck the benches for the coming of the bride. "In my possession are cows with gold horns, black bulls, heaps of treasure, and mounds of jewels," said Thrym; "Freyja is now my sole desire." When evening had come, food was borne in before the two guests. Thor by himself ate a whole ox, eight salmon, and all of the delicacies prepared for the women, and washed it all down with three crocks of mead. "Did any one ever see a bride take bigger and harder bites or drink more mead? asked Thrym. "For eight days on end," answered Loki, "Freyja has not tasted a morsel, so great has been her longing after Jotunheim." Thrym now bowed his head beneath the kerchief to kiss the bride; but she shot such piercing glances upon him that he started back. "Why does Freyja look so grim? Her eyes dart fire." "Eight nights on end," answered Loki, "Freyja has not slept a wink, so great has been her longing after Jotunheim." Just at that moment the hideous old grandmother came in and asked for a bridal gift. Thrym gave commands that Mjollnir should be borne in and laid on the bride's lap so that the wedding might go forward. When Thor once more beheld his hammer, his heart laughed within him. First he slew Thrym, then his old beldame, and thereafter he crashed into atoms all the kindred of the Giants. Thus Thor got his hammer back after all. ■

The Death of Balder

Europe: Norse—Scandinavian

As hard as Thor fought against the frost giants, he could not preserve the gods (**Aesir**) from doom forever. The concept of a cyclical universe that moves from a time of innocence and purity to increased malevolence and ultimate destruction, only to begin the cycle again, has counterparts in many of the world's religions, most notably Hinduism (Schnurbein, 2000). The death of Balder, whose name, according to Germanic scholar Frank Hugus, might have meant "shining," "noble," "high one," or "lord," and whom Snorri Sturlason called "the Good," was the beginning of the end for the gods and their world.

What Balder represented has been a point discussed among scholars since the eighteenth century

Source: "The Death of Balder" from *Norse Mythology: Legends of Gods and Heroes* by Munch, Peter Andreas. Translated from the Norwegian by Sigurd Bernhard Hustvedt. New York: American-Scandinavian Foundation, 1926. Reprinted with permission by American-Scandinavian Foundation. pp. 80–86.

(Lindow, 1991). Unlike Thor, whose widespread worship was clearly commemorated in temples, place names, personal names, iron and silver hammers, and wood carvings, few places in Scandinavia bear memories of Balder, and few poems or references to Balder have been found after over a hundred years of scholarship. Balder's death might have meant the end of summer and light and the beginning of a long, hard, and dark winter. Such an interpretation would make this a seasonal myth, similar to the Greek story of Demeter and Persephone. One difference between this story and the story of Persephone, however, is that whereas Persephone returns every year as spring comes, Balder remains in the underworld until the end of this world and will return only after Ragnarok, the final battle between the gods (Aesir) and giants (Jotun). Scholars have suggested that Balder, like Tamuz and Dionysus in the Middle East and Greece, was a fertility god who had to be sacrificed for new vegetation to grow. Balder's resurrection and return after the end of the world might show Christian influence (Turville-Petre, 1964). Other scholars consider the murder of Balder and the subsequent vengeance that the gods wreak on Loki to be a reflection of the kinds of family feuds that were prevalent in Iceland, where the two main sources of this version of the story have been found (Lindow, 1997). Whatever the precise symbolic meaning of the story, the idea of something pure and good being snuffed out by two innocent instruments, a weak mistletoe and a blind brother, retains its tragic grandeur.

Amid confusion and struggle of various kinds, life thus ran its course among the Æsir. Yet Balder still remained to them, the god of innocence and purity; while he survived, evil and violence could not gain supremacy in the universe. There came a time, however, when he began to be visited by disquieting dreams, which filled all the gods with foreboding. The Æsir and the goddesses held a general assembly to inquire into the meaning of these portents. Odin himself rode forth on Sleipnir into the very depths of Niflheim to take counsel with a departed sibyl or prophetess. He arrived at the high hall of Hell; and to the east of the door, where lay the grave of the sibyl, he took his station and chanted his incantations to waken the dead. The sibyl, compelled to rise from her grave, asked who had come to disturb her rest. "The snow covered me," she said, "the rain beat upon me and the moist dews fell over me; I had long been dead." Odin answered "I am named Vegtam, the son of Valtam; tell me now for whom Hel has adorned her hall." "For Balder the mead is brewed, and the Æsir are sore afflicted." "Who then shall bring death upon Balder?" "Hod shall bring death to Balder," was her response. "Who shall avenge his death upon Hod?" asked Odin. "Rind shall bear a son (Vali) in the West-Halls," she replied; "he shall neither wash his hands nor comb his hair until he has brought Balder's slayer to the funeral pyre; one night old, he shall kill him." "Speak, be not yet silent," said Odin; "still more would I fain learn: who are the maidens that are weeping sorely and throwing their neckerchiefs into the air?" "Now I know that you are not Vegtam, as you have said, but Odin," answered the prophetess. "And you are neither sibyl nor wise woman; you are the mother of three Thursar." "Ride home again, Odin,"

said the prophetess, "and return to me when Loki has regained his freedom and the Twilight of the Gods is near at hand."

Frigg now bound all things by an oath that they would do Balder no harm—fire and water, iron and all manner of metals, rocks, earth, trees, maladies, beasts and birds, poisons and serpents. Now the Æsir, deeming themselves secure, even found amusement at their assemblies in having Balder stand forward while the others shot missiles at him, aimed blows at him, or threw stones at him; whatever they might do, he suffered no wound. Loki, meanwhile, was not pleased. Assuming the shape of a woman, he paid a visit to Frigg at Fensalir. Frigg asked the woman what Æsir were occupied with at their assembly. "They are all shooting at Balder without working him the least injury," she said. "Neither weapons nor trees will do him any harm, for I have bound all things by an oath." "Is it really true that all things have sworn to spare Balder?" the woman asked. "All things, except only a tiny sprig growing west of Valhalla, called Mistletoe (*mistilteinn*); I deemed it too young a thing to be bound by an oath." Now Loki went away, tore up the mistletoe, and carried it off to the assembly. Hod, because of his blindness, was standing at the outer edge of the circle. Loki asked him why he too was not shooting at Balder. "I cannot see where he is standing; and besides, I have no weapon," answered Hod. "Nevertheless, you ought to follow the example of the others," said Loki, "and thus pay equal honor to Balder. Take this wand and shoot at him; I will show you where he is standing." Hod grasped the mistletoe, took position according to Loki's bidding, and let fly at Balder; the bolt sped directly through his body, and he sank down dead. Thus came about the greatest mischance that ever befell gods or men. When the Æsir saw Balder fall to the ground, they were speechless with fear, and none moved a finger to lift him up; they looked at one another, and all alike were filled with wrath at the man who had brought that deed to pass; yet they were powerless to avenge the murder, since the spot on which they stood had been solemnly set aside as a sanctuary. For a time they were unable to utter a word for weeping; Odin above all felt the full force of the blow, for he saw most clearly what a loss had befallen the Æsir through Balder's death. When the gods had in part regained their composure, Frigg asked who among the

Æsir would undertake to gain her favor by riding the Hell-Ways to seek speech with Balder and to learn from Hel what recompense she would demand for permitting Balder's release and return to Asgard. Hermod the Bold, Odin's son, declared himself willing; having got the loan of Sleipnir for the journey, he mounted and took the road with the utmost speed.

The Æsir took Balder's body and bore it down to the sea. There lay his great ship, Ringhorni, drawn up on land; with the intention of using it for Balder's funeral pyre, they strove to launch it but were unable to move it from the spot. They were therefore compelled to send a messenger to Jotunheim to summon the Giantess Hyrrokkin, and she came riding to them mounted on a wolf, which she guided by vipers in lieu of reins. She dismounted, and Odin assigned four Berserks to the task of holding her steed; they could not restrain the wolf, however, before they had thrown it to the ground. The Giantess stepped to the prow of the boat, and at the first effort shoved it off so fast that the rollers burst into flame and the whole earth trembled. Thor, his wrath getting the better of him, wanted to crush her head, but all the other gods interceded on her behalf. Now the body of Balder was carried out onto the ship, and when his wife Nanna saw what was happening, her heart broke for sorrow; so her body also was laid on the pyre. The fire was then kindled and Thor came forward and consecrated the pyre with Mjollnir; just at that moment a Dwarf named Lit ran in front of him, and Thor spurned the Dwarf into the fire, where he too was burned. Beings of many kinds came to see the burning. First of all was Odin, and with him Frigg, the Valkyries, and Odin's ravens. Frey drove a cart drawn by the boar Gullinbusti, otherwise called Slidrugtanni. Heimdal rode his horse Goldtop, and Freyja drove her cats. Throngs of Rime-Thursar and Cliff-Ettins presented themselves likewise. Odin laid on the pile the ring Draupnir. Balder's horse also was led fully caparisoned onto the blazing ship.

In the meantime Hermod was on his way to Hell. Nine nights he rode through dark and deep valleys and saw nothing until he came to the river Gjoll and rode out onto the Bridge of Gjoll, which is paved with gleaming gold. A maiden named Modgud, who keeps watch over the bridge, asked his name and kindred. Then she told him that not many days before five companies of dead men had ridden across the bridge; "and yet," she said, "it thunders as loudly beneath your paces alone as beneath the feet of all of them together. Nor have you the visage of a dead man; why are you riding alone on the way to Hell?" "I am riding to Hell," answered Hermod, "in search of Balder. Have you seen him pass along the Way of Hell?" She told him that Balder had already traversed the Bridge of Gjoll: "The Way of Hell lies downward and northward." Hermod rode on until he arrived at Hell-Gate. There he dismounted, tightened his saddle-girths, mounted once more, and struck spurs to his horse; the horse jumped so high above the gate that he did not so much as touch it with his hoof. Hermod rode straight to the hall, dismounted, and stepped inside; there he saw his brother Balder sitting in the high seat. He remained in the hall during the night; in the morning he asked Hel to permit Balder to ride away with him, telling her at the same time how great was the grief of the Æsir. Hel answered that she meant to assure herself beforehand whether Balder was really so much beloved as he was reputed to be. "If all things on earth," she said, "be they quick or dead, will weep for him, then he shall return to the Æsir; but if there is one thing that will not weep, he shall remain with me." Then Hermod arose, and Balder followed him out through the door and bade him give Odin the ring Draupnir in memory of him. Nanna gave into his charge a kerchief for Frigg and other gifts besides, and for Fulla a finger ring. Thereupon Hermod rode forth on his journey until he came back to Asgard, where he imparted to the gods all that he had seen and heard.

The Æsir now sent messengers throughout the whole world to ask all things to weep for Balder's release from Hell; all things did weep, men, beasts, earth, trees, and all manner of metals, and they can still be seen weeping whenever they pass from frost to heat. But when the messengers, their errand done, were returning home again, they discovered among the rocks a Giantess named Thokk; her too they asked to weep Balder out of the bounds of Hell but she replied:

> Thokk shall weep
> Dry tears
> On Balder's pyre.
> Nor in life nor in death
> Did Karl's son bring me joy;
> Hel hold what she hath!

Balder's homecoming thus came to naught. The Giantess was none other than Loki, who by such means finished his evil deed. Retribution, however, soon fell upon him. Upon Hod as well as Balder's death was to be avenged; and according to the sibyl's decree to Odin, vengeance was to come at the hands of Vali, the son of Odin and Rind. The particulars of his doom are not recorded in the *Eddas*. ■

Origin and Creation Myths

How the World Was Created from a Drop of Milk

Africa: Mali—Fulani

Though this myth has a formula tale structure (a chain of events linked by the last item mentioned in each line), the mythic rather than playful nature of the story is evident from both the theme and the ending, in which God's omnipotence is proclaimed. The Fulani, a formerly pastoral people, were the only people who were cattle raisers in West Africa, where they live today. They have migrated east from their original home in Senegal in search of water and pastures. They are spread out from Senegal on the Atlantic coast to the Central African Republic, and many no longer raise cattle but are either farmers or urban dwellers. The Fulani have been Muslims since the sixteenth century and have at times led Islamic theocracies (Encarta Africana, 2000). The fact that life began, for the pre-Islamic Fulani, in a drop of milk seems natural to their close reliance on cattle, but we can also see the drop of milk as a universal symbol of motherhood.

The elements mentioned in the myth represent the four elements (earth, fire, water, and air) of many traditional cultures, including that of Europe before the scientific age, with a fifth, iron, added. The rest of the sequence seems to be based on relationships of power and humility. As Beier (1966) says in his introduction to his collection of African myths, "truth and fact are not necessarily the same" (p. x).

At the beginning there was a huge drop of milk.
Then Doondari came and he created the stone.
Then the stone created iron;
And iron created fire;
And fire created water;
And water created air.
Then Doondari descended the second time. And he
    took the five elements
And he shaped them into man.
But man was proud.
Then Doondari created blindness and blindness
    defeated man.
But when blindness became too proud,
Doondari created sleep, and sleep defeated blindness;
But when sleep became too proud,
Doondari created worry, and worry defeated sleep;
But when worry became too proud,
Doondari created death, and death defeated worry.
But when death became too proud,
Doondari descended for the third time,
and he came as Gueno, the eternal one,
And Gueno defeated death. ■

Source: "How the World Was Created from a Drop of Milk" from *The Origin of Life & Death* by Ulli Beier. Heinemann, 1966. pp. 1–2.

Why the Sun Rises When the Rooster Crows

The myth of how one sun came to be in the sky has many variants. Some scholars believe that during the Shang Dynasty (ca. 1600–1027 B.C.E.) people postulated the existence of ten suns, one for each day of a ten-day week. The myth continued to be told during the later Chou (or Zhou) Dynasty (1027–256 B.C.E.) at a time when scholars such as Confucius thought it self-evident that there was only one sun in the sky: "Heaven does not have two suns, the people do not have two kings" (cited in Christie, 1985, p. 61). Myths of origins, including the myth of ten suns, were recorded in literary works during the Han Dynasty (202 B.C.E.–221 C.E.). It was said that the ten suns lived in a mulberry tree by a lake in the east. Each sun crossed the sky in a horse-drawn (or dragon-drawn) chariot on a different day, coming to rest at night in a tree by a lake in the West. Each morning the suns were bathed by their mother in the waters of the lake and, perched in the lower branches of the mulberry tree, awaited their turn to cross the sky.

If all ten suns ended up in the sky at the same time, it was seen as a portent—a sign that all was not well in the world of humans. It was said that such a phenomenon occurred when an emperor, through some kind of wrong action, upset the harmony of the world. In the classic Han version of this myth it was the fourth mythical emperor of pre-dynastic China, Emperor Yao, who might have done so by appointing someone other than his son to be next emperor (Christie, 1985). The fact that his archer shot down nine of the ten suns, however, suggests a new beginning, with a new world order that restores the har-

mony of the universe. The idea that harmony in the universe must be maintained through correct actions on the part of humans had been a key concept in all of the Chinese philosophies and religions since ancient times, according to Chinese religion scholar N. J. Girardot (1987).

"Yi, the Archer, shoots down nine suns." Illustrated by Song-Nan Zhang.

Taken from *Five Heavenly Emperors* © 1994 by Song Nan Zhang, published by Tundra Books. Reprinted with permission.

The Hani version presented here is more folkloric in tone than the classic Han version, as the archer is a giant rather than a mythical archer, and it is a common domestic animal, the rooster, that finally gets the last sun to come out from hiding.

In very ancient days the Hani people were not a happy people. They were plagued by the glare and heat of nine giant suns that were always shining and burning, and they did not know how to get rid of them.

They had endless meetings, with oceans of words, but still they had no idea how to rid themselves of the glare and heat of nine suns. Their lives were miserable. Nothing grew in the earth; they were hungry.

Each day they met and discussed different ideas on how to get rid of so many suns. One day one of the elders said, "The best thing would be to make a giant winnowing basket and shield the suns in the sky with it.

"Good, but how will we tie the winnowing basket to the sky?" And so, like many of their plans, the idea was not carried out.

The glare and the heat became worse.

One day another of the elders cried, "Let us stay in caves under the earth where the heat will not reach us."

"Then who will plant and reap? We will starve to death!"

Plan after plan was proposed, but not a single one could be used.

Finally one of the oldest among the elders said, "Why not beg Urpupolo, the great bushy giant, to help us? He is the strongest man in our land, and his weapons are the deadliest in all the world. Let us go to him and beg him to shoot the suns with his powerful arrows."

"Yes, only Urpupolo can help us. We must ask him!" came the cry from all sides.

So a man was chosen to go to Urpupolo, who lived in a deep dark cave. There he sat silently. He was a giant in size, with wild hair all over his head, bushy as a mound of hay. His eyebrows were coal black and hung over his gleaming eyes, and his waist was as thick as a great tree trunk

The messenger stood before him and spoke. "Urpupolo, great giant of our land, I have come to you to ask you to help us, unless you want to see all the Hani people die."

"Who is threatening you?" grumbled Urpupolo in a deep voice.

"Great giant Urpupolo," continued the man, "nine suns sit in the sky trying to destroy us with their fierce glare and heat. We cannot plant, and many of us are going blind. Only you can help us. Destroy eight of the suns with your powerful arrows. One sun will be enough for us. We will then have a happy life."

"That is easy and I will help you."

He lifted his huge body off the ground and picked up his big bow and arrow. Then he took a few giant steps and stood in the middle of the land. The nine suns were over him in the sky, shining fiercely. He put one of the arrows on his bow, took careful aim at a sun and . . . twang! it fell with a thundering hissing noise into the black water.

Urpupolo shot seven more arrows and each hit its mark. Sun after sun fell, and each one sank deep, deep into the endless dark water.

The ninth sun, seeing how all his brothers were destroyed, was seized with fear and fled behind a giant mountain so swiftly that Urpupolo did not see him.

Now the whole world was dark and cold, but Urpupolo found his way home to his cave. But the Hani people did not like the darkness. They liked light—not burning, but warm, good light. Soon they were as unhappy as they had been before. It was dark and cold . . . no plants, no growth!

"The sun must come out from behind the mountain," the elders cried, and so did all the Hani people.

They shouted in the direction of the mountain, begging the sun to come out. But the ninth sun felt safe behind the big mountain and stayed there.

Again meetings were held. Everyone, old and young, argued about how the sun could be coaxed from behind the mountain.

"We must use sweet and begging voices!"

"But we all did beg with our sweetest voices."

"It must be a voice sweeter than ours," one of the elders said.

"Why not ask a bird?"

This seemed like a good idea and many birds were named. In the end they agreed on the golden oriole.

The golden oriole was proud of her voice and happy she was chosen. She flew high in the air in front of the mountain, singing proudly, in the most enchanting tones for the sun to come out, for the birds wanted the sun as much as the Hani people did. But with all the pleading songs, the sun would not come from behind the mountain. Maybe Urpupolo was still there with his arrows!

The Hani people were in despair.

"Let us try another bird," someone suggested, and the choices fell on the skylark.

The skylark was proud of his voice and happy to be chosen. He was sure he could bring back the sun.

The bird flew high, high up in the blue air and began his sweet song, begging the sun to come out. He sang a long time, but it was of no use. No sun came out from behind the mountain.

The Hani people were in hopeless misery.

"We must try again; we must not give up. There must be some bird who can coax the sun out."

"Let us try the thrush!" He has a sweet pleading voice. Perhaps he will succeed," another cried. The others agreed.

So they asked the thrush. He was a proud bird who thought he had the finest of all voices.

"Just let the sun hear me," he cried, "and he will surely come out." He raised his voice and warbled and trilled with all his might. But though he tried again and again, the sun would not come out.

The Hani people were in black distress.

"We must get the sun to shine on us and our land. We must, or we will all die!"

Everyone was thinking and thinking. Then one of the younger men spoke, "We have asked birds of high degree to plead for the sun to come from behind the mountain. Let us try some bird not so famous. Maybe he can plead better."

"We will try any bird! Name him!" came from all.

"Let us give the beautiful rooster a chance. He is strong and manly and brave. His voice may not be very beautiful, but it is sincere and fearless.

Everyone agreed this was not such a bad choice, so a delegation was sent to the rooster.

The rooster listened to the delegation. He was no braggart, but he had courage. Yet he hesitated.

"I don't think I can help you. The best I can do is cry 'cock-a-doodle-doo.' "

"Try it! Try it!" was the cry. "Maybe the sun will listen to you."

The next morning the rooster came early. He had begged the other birds to help him. Everybody wanted the sun to shine, so they all promised.

The rooster's feathers glistened even in the dark. The winds blew around his large red comb, and he knew the importance of his task. An endless number of birds gathered near him. He stretched his neck toward the mountain and cried out with all his strength, "Cock-a-doodle-doo. . . . Cock-a-doodle-doo!"

The sun heard the strange cry. It was not sweet, but it was strong, sincere, and frank. The sun peeked out a little.

For the second time the rooster stood on his hard toes, stretched his neck high, spread his wings wide, and sang out, "Cock-a-doodle-doo; Cock-a-doodle-doo."

The sun heard it and his fear and anger began to wane. He peeped out a little more, but did not come out yet.

Once again the rooster stood high, wings spread wide, and cried pleadingly, "Cock-a-doodle-doo" three times. All the birds sang with him. It was truly a heavenly chorus.

The sun heard it and his anger and fear melted away. Slowly he came out from behind the mountain. And, as he came out, there came light and warmth that had not been there for a long time.

Everyone was happy now—the Hani people, the birds, the beasts, the sea, and the earth.

From that time on, the sun always comes out when the rooster crows three times and the birds join cock-a-doodle-doo with their songs. ∎

The Great Deeds of King Yü

Asia: Chinese—Han

Throughout Chinese history the emperor was the most important connection between the world of Heaven (Tien) and that of humans. Since the Shang Dynasty, (ca. 1600 B.C.E.–1027 B.C.E.) he was said to have the "Mandate of Heaven" as long as he ruled wisely and in the interest of the people. This concept of meritorious rule was particularly emphasized by Confucius, while the idea that the Emperor's role was to communicate with Heaven and to interpret the will of Heaven was emphasized by Taoist philosophy.

Chinese mythology speaks of five mythic emperors who helped to establish the world of civilized humans. The fourth of the mythic emperors, Yao, was depicted as the ideal of virtue, righteousness, and unselfish devotion in the earliest written sources of China from the Chou and Han dynasties (Girardot, 1987). It was under him that Yü the Great performed his feat of conquering the uncontrollable floods that were plaguing the Empire. Yao had first set his minister Kun to the task of controlling these floods. Kun labored for seven years, but in spite of the many dams he built and his other efforts, he failed to govern the waters. Kun was executed, but from his body sprang his son Yü the Great. Instead of fighting nature, Yü found natural underground channels that helped to control the floods and made it possible for humans to conduct agriculture and to live in a more orderly world. It was also under Emperor Yao that another disaster, that of the ten suns destroying the land, was averted by his Lord Archer.

Source: "The Great Deeds of King Yü" from *The Magic Boat and Other Chinese Folk Stories.* M. A. Jagendorf and Virginia Weng. Copyright ©1980 by M. A. Jagendorf and Virginia Weng. Used by permission of Vanguard Press, a division of Random House, Inc. pp. 11–14.

Taoist teaching pointed to Yü's way (tao) as a model for dealing with human nature as well. Rulers should find human beings' natural channels, that is, their inclinations, rather than using coercion (Girardot, 1987). Thematically, both the story of the ten suns and the story of the deluge can be seen as the restoration of harmony in the universe after an excess of one kind or another (fire: Yang, water: Yin). It is the balance of opposites (Yang and Yin) that makes for a balanced universe (Girardot, 1987).

Yü the Great was said to have been the ancestor of the founder of the Hsia dynasty, (pre-1600 B.C.E.), the oldest dynasty for which there is at least some archeological evidence (Scott, 1980).

In the endless years that have no beginning and no end, there lived in China a great king named Yü. Many tales are told of his great exploits, but none was greater than how he directed the flow of waters from the sky and how he built gray mountains and tall peaks.

King Yü was truly a king of the people. With his great strength he worked day and night to serve them. He had calloused hands and wore straw shoes on his feet. His face was deeply tanned by the rays of the sun and was as dark as a black *kuo* [wok].

One day he looked around his beloved land and noted that the hot sun always rose in the east of the Heaven.

The king said to ministers, "I must make the waters flow to the east, where the burning sun always rises, for the heat is so great there that no man can live, nor any crops grow. I must direct the floods in that direction so that they will not drown anyone or cause any harm to plants." He set to work at once.

Seeing that there were floods, he decided to move some boulders to stop them. First he pushed the giant rocks, which lay in heaps, apart. He piled them in baskets, which he carried on the ends of his shoulder pole. In three days and three nights he moved ninety loads from T'ai Shan, the highest mountain in Shantung. The ninety loads made nine great piles, which stopped the floods in the south. They stand high and mighty against the blue sky and form nine sections of a new mountain range. The Chinese call these the Long White Mountains.

Then the king spoke to his people: "Now I must make separate, deep river beds through which the waters will flow easily."

He spoke magic words and there came up first one of the giant dragons of the land. He was blue in color and his scales glowed in the sun. His four feet were each as big as a giant tree, ending in sharp claws. A straggling green beard hung from his chin and he had a long coiling tail. He breathed mists and clouds as he twisted and turned his giant body in all directions. Great geysers of water rushed from his nostrils.

Following the dragon was a giant snake so long you could not see his end. His tongue, thick and narrow, darted and moved in his open mouth.

Spoke King Yü to the mist-breathing dragon, "Dig a ditch beside these mountains for the waters to flow to the east." Then he turned to the snake and said, "You, too, must make a deep bed on the other side through which the waters will flow in the right direction." Then he left them to do their work.

The dragon began to at once. He dug his claws in, right and left, flinging earth and stones in all directions. He moved is body this way and that way and soon he made a deep bed through which the waters would flow easily.

The giant snake was lazy. He just rolled around, this way and that way, making only a shallow depression in the earth.

"That is good enough," hissed the giant Snake, "I am tired of working."

"My ditch is deeper," roared Dragon, "it is better than yours."

"Mine is good enough," hissed Snake. "Besides, I finished first." And then, hissing with all his might so he could be heard far away, he zished, "I am finished, King Yü. I am finished."

"I am also finished, Great King Yü," Dragon bellowed so that the boulders shook and trembled.

Far away in his house, sitting on a stone boulder he had rolled in, King Yü heard them hissing and roaring.

"Good," he shouted, "I will come to see what you two have done."

He came to the mountain and saw the deep ditch Dragon had dug with his giant claws.

"You have made a good place for the river," King Yü said, "and I will reward you for your fine work. I will put you into the Heaven, where you will direct the rains to the earth for the growth of grain and trees and flowers and plants."

So King Yü put the dragon into the sky and there he has been ever since, sending life-giving water to the earth for the benefit of man and land.

Then King Yü turned to see what the snake had done and saw the shallow wide depression he had made by merely rolling from side to side a few times.

"Shame on you, Snake, for making such a shallow bed for a river! For this I order you to stay for the rest of time in the deep ocean where the ever-beating waves will pound you without stopping. That will be your punishment for making such a poor water bed."

And so it happened; the snake was put into the ocean and the dragon into the sky.

Then King Yü ordered the water to flow through the river beds made by the dragon and the snake. He was pleased at the sight.

"Perhaps it would be good to have two giant peaks beyond the Long White Mountains," he said. He took off his straw shoes and emptied the sand and dust in them on the ground. The two piles grew into two tall yellow peaks beyond the Long White Mountains, and there they have been ever since.

This is just one of the tales they tell of King Yü, the hero, who lived in ancient China. There are many more. ■

Why the Sun Forsook the Tundra

Asia: Russian Federation—Koryak

The arctic and subarctic regions of the world circle the globe, encompassing the northern parts of European countries such as Norway, Sweden, and Finland; the European and Asian parts of the Russian Federation; and Alaska, Canada, and Greenland in the Western Hemisphere. This area was once thought of as a frozen wasteland where people lived isolated from one another, but more recently, anthropologists and archeologists have come to recognize the long existence of cultural and material exchange among peoples along the Arctic from the Saami or Lapps in Europe to the Eskimos of the New World (Eskimos and Aleutians of Alaska and Inuits of Canada and Greenland). From a global, circumpolar perspective the arctic and subarctic regions acted as "highways rather than barriers to the flow of plants and animals, peoples and cultures" (Fitzhugh, 1997).

The Koryak peoples, along with several other ethnic groups of northeastern Siberia and the Eskimos and Aleutians of Western Alaska, belong to the Paleoarctic language group and share myths and beliefs that emphasize the importance of Raven and other animals. The Koryaks consider the wolf a relative. Siberian as well as North American native peoples relied on **shamans,** spiritual leaders who, after arduous training and trials, achieved the ability to get in touch with the spirit world to gain help for their people. The spirit of powerful animal helpers such as the bear was invoked and propitiated through sacrificial offerings to ensure success in fishing and hunting or to help with curing the sick (Hultkrantz, 1987).

Fishing and hunting were equally important on both sides of the North Pacific and reindeer, known as caribou in North America, were important as part of the diet. On the Siberian side, but not on the Ameri-

can side, of the Bering Strait, which, when frozen, provided a bridge between the continents before 11,000 B.C.E., reindeer herding also became important. Inland Koryaks as well as some other Siberian ethnic groups continue to herd reindeer and are nomadic, while coastal Koryaks are settled in villages and hunt sea mammals and fish. Reindeer used to be the staple diet away from the coast and provided both clothing and the covering for the yaranga, a wigwam-like tent made of skins stretched over poles. Reindeer were also useful in trade across the Arctic; herders would exchanged reindeer skins for walrus and seal fat from the coastal people and for pipes, bracelets, knives, and other products with people farther south (Riordan, 1990).

Today the Koryak, like the other Siberian peoples, are few in number and have to deal with issues such as environmental degradation and pollution due to mineral exploration and industrial development that had been imposed on them by Soviet state policies and that continue in the Russian Federation as business interests affect the native peoples' traditional way of life. Not only the traditional beliefs in the efficacy of shamans but also the Koryaks' and other Siberians' languages were suppressed by Russian and Soviet policy in the twentieth century. In the new Russia, though, there may be some revival of both as a result of more liberal policies of encouraging indigenous cultures (Riordan, 1990; Fitzhugh, 1997).

One day long ago, the Sun sent his sister the Moon down to earth to gather some berries. She glided gracefully through the sky, landed lightly on a bed of moss and walked over the tundra. She had not gone far when she met Mistress Crow and at once they made friends. Together, the Moon and the Crow collected berries until their baskets were full.

Since the task was uncommon to the Moon, she soon felt tired; so she lay down on a stretch of grass and was shortly fast asleep. As she slumbered, her

Source: "Why the Sun Forsook the Tundra" from *The Sun Maiden and the Crescent Moon: Siberian Folk Tales,* published by Interlink Books, an imprint of Interlink Publishing Group, Inc., 46 Crosby Street, Northampton, MA 01060. Text copyright © by James Riordan 1989. Reprinted by permission. pp. 41–47.

companion gazed at her pale and delicate countenance and was amazed at her beauty.

"What a lovely bride she would make for my brother," breathed Mistress Crow.

As dusk was falling, the Moon awoke and the two friends made their way for shelter to the Crow's yaranga. And there the Crow's brother was immediately captivated by the pale incandescent Moon.

"See how lovely the Moon Maiden is," whispered his sister. "She would make you a worthy wife. Listen, I have a plan: when she goes berrying in the tundra tomorrow, you accompany her dressed as me."

Young Master Crow rose early next morning, put on his sister's brown dress and wakened Mistress Moon. They partook of some reindeer meat, drank tea and set off to look for berries.

But while Moon was about her task, she again felt tired and soon lay down to take a rest. When at last she awoke, there was no sign of her companion. Instead she found a handsome hunting knife by her side. Concealing it in the folds of her dress, Mistress Moon decided it was time to return to her brother the Sun. With her basket of berries and hunting knife, she therefore flew up to the sky. But as she flew through the air, she felt the knife slip from her and fall towards the earth. How surprised she was to see it turn into the crow brother of her first companion!

Master Crow steadied himself and flew up in pursuit of the fleeing Moon.

"You cannot fly with me to the Sun," called the Moon. "You will be scorched and will shrivel to nothing."

Master Crow declared his love.

"I cannot leave you, O my beloved Moon," he moaned. "I'll fly with you just as long as my strength lasts; and then I shall fall to the cruel rocks below. I cannot live without you."

Poor Mistress Moon took pity on the Crow and returned to earth with him. They began to live together and it was not long before a child was born.

In the meantime, the Sun was waiting impatiently for his sister; all the Sun's children, the little sunbeams, were singing mournful songs of the young maiden who had lost her way on earth. But there was no sign of Mistress Moon. At last, the Sun descended to earth himself and lit up the entire tundra with his rays—all the mountain caverns, the deep ravines and the fast-flowing rivers—until all was as clear as crystal. It was not long before one of the Sun's rays fell upon his sister the Moon, sitting within the Crow's yaranga.

At once the Sun flew there, peeped behind its felt curtain and discovered his long-lost sister.

"Why did you stay so long on earth, my sister?" he asked.

"I know I have wronged you, my brother," answered the Moon. "But I could not leave my husband and my earth-child."

At that the Sun grew angry and set upon the Crow.

"Moon is my only sister; her place is in the sky. She must return to me at once."

"But Moon is also my wife," objected the Crow. "And she has my child."

The Sun and the Crow argued long about who was to have the Moon. And finally it was decided to settle the question in a contest: each would nominate a sewing-woman and the one who [whose nominee] could sew a suit of clothes faster would be the victor.

The Crow summoned Mistress Ermine, while the Sun called Mistress Mouse. Each received a reindeer skin and was ordered to sew a fur robe from it. In no time at all, Mistress Ermine had made a most delightful robe, while Mistress Mouse had hardly begun.

Next Crow chose Mistress Marmot, and the Sun chose Mistress Gopher. And they began to sew fur trousers. In no time at all, Mistress Marmot had finished a handsome pair of fur trousers, while Mistress Gopher had not done half the job.

Then the Crow summoned Mistress Otter, and the Sun called Mistress Fox. They were to sew fur stockings. Once again, the Crow's choice won. Then it was the turn of Mistress Bear against Mistress Wolf; in no time at all the nimble Mistress Bear had made a splendid pair of fur boots, leaving Mistress Wolf far behind. The Crow had won again. After that, he summoned Mistress Goat, while the Sun called Mistress Lynx to sew a pair of mittens. Once again the contest began and the Goat made a fine pair of mittens in record time, long before the Lynx had completed just one.

Seeing that he was losing the contest, the Sun sent his rays to fetch the beautiful Ice Maiden to the Crow's yaranga. Caught in the rays of the Sun, Ice

Maiden's countenance gleamed and sparkled brilliantly, blinding the Crow with her beauty.

"Give me back my sister," said the Sun, "and you shall have the lovely Ice Maiden for your wife."

The Crow was sorely tempted, but he replied:

"No, I shall not. No maiden can compare with the lovely Moon."

Then the Sun sent his rays after the Snow Maiden and had her brought to him. As she entered the yaranga enveloped in the bright rays of the Sun, the Snow Maiden sparkled with many fires and the yaranga at once shone brightly.

The Crow's greed got the better of him at last.

"Take your sister and leave me these two lovely maidens!" he said finally. Together with the Moon and her child, the Sun returned to the heavens, leaving Master Crow in the company of the lovely Ice Maiden and the lovely Snow Maiden. But they no longer dazzled and gleamed without the brilliant rays of the Sun.

And the Sun, cross with the Crow for parting so easily with his beautiful sister, departed for lands far away to the south. And ever since, the long long winter has been cold and dark throughout the tundra. ∎

Demeter (Ceres)

Europe: Greece

Persephone, a beautiful young maiden, is carried off by Hades, the Lord of the Dead, and is married to him. In effect she has died and will remain underground for part of the year until the annual turn of the seasons brings her rebirth. Traditionally, the story has been interpreted as an allegory in which Demeter (*Meter* means "mother") represents the fertility of Mother Earth and Persephone represents the grain of seed that is sown in the ground and lies dormant (as if dead), only to return as new growth in the spring.

The first known version of this story was a poem known as a Homeric Hymn to Demeter, probably originally composed orally between the seventh and sixth centuries B.C.E. as part of a religious rite invoking the goddess. One of the most important religious cults of ancient Greece, the Eleusinian Mysteries, was devoted to the worship of this goddess, whose promise of regeneration was so necessary for the continuation of agriculture. Though the story lost its specific religious meaning after the advent of

Source: "Demeter (Ceres)" from *Mythology* by Edith Hamilton. Copyright © 1942 by Edith Hamilton; Copyright © renewed by Dorian Fielding Reid and Doris Fielding Reid. By permission of Little, Brown and Company (Inc.). pp. 57–63.

Christianity in Greece, it has continued to resonate with readers and poets, including John Milton and Thomas Hood. Percy Bysshe Shelley wrote:

> Sacred Goddess, Mother Earth
> Thou from whose immortal bosom
> Gods, and men, and beasts, have birth,
> Leaf and blade, and bud and blossom,
> Breathe thine influence most divine
> On thine own child, Proserpine.

Rita Dove, Poet Laureate of the United States in 1993–1994, devoted a collection of poems, *Mother Love*, to the varied feelings of mother and daughter as a young girl matures and leaves home.

[Hamilton's intro] This story is told only in a very early poem, one of the earliest of the Homeric Hymns, dating from the eighth or the beginning of the seventh century [B.C.E.]. The original has the marks of early Greek poetry, great simplicity and directness and delight in the beautiful world.

Demeter had an only daughter Persephone (in Latin Proserpine), the maiden of the spring. She lost her and in her terrible grief she withheld her gifts from the earth, which turned into a frozen desert. The green and flowering land was icebound and lifeless because Persephone had disappeared.

The lord of the dark underworld, the king of the multitudinous dead, carried her off when, enticed by the wondrous bloom of the narcissus, she strayed too far from her companions. In his chariot drawn by coal-black steeds he rose up through a chasm in the earth, and grasping the maiden by the wrist set her beside him. He bore her away, weeping, down to the underworld. The high hills echoed her cry and the depths of the sea, and her mother heard it. She sped like a bird over sea and land seeking her daughter. But no one would tell her the truth, "no man nor god, nor any sure messenger from the birds." Nine days Demeter wandered, and all that time she would not taste of ambrosia or put sweet nectar to her lips. At last she came to the Sun and he told her all the story: Persephone was down in the world beneath the earth, among the shadowy dead.

Then a still greater grief entered Demeter's heart. She left Olympus; she dwelt on earth, but so disguised that none knew her, and, indeed, the gods are not easily discerned by mortal men. In her desolate wanderings she came to Eleusis and sat by the wayside near a well. She seemed an aged woman, such as in great houses care for the children or guard the storerooms. Four lovely maidens, sisters, coming to draw water from the well, saw her and asked her pityingly what she did there. She answered that she had fled from pirates who had meant to sell her as a slave, and that she knew no one in this strange land to go to for help. They told her that any house in the town would welcome her, but that they would like best to bring her to their own if she would wait there while they went to ask their mother. The goddess bent her head in assent, and the girls, filling their shining pitchers with water, hurried home. Their mother, Metaneira, bade them return at once and invite the stranger to come, and speeding back they found the glorious goddess still sitting there, deeply veiled and covered to her slender feet by her dark robe. She followed them, and as she crossed the threshold to the hall where the mother sat holding her young son, a divine radiance filled the doorway and awe fell upon Metaneira.

She bade Demeter be seated and herself offered her honey-sweet wine, but the goddess would not taste it. She asked instead for barley-water flavored with mint,

the cooling draught of the reaper at harvest time and also the sacred cup given the worshipers at Eleusis. Thus refreshed she took the child and held him to her fragrant bosom and his mother's heart was glad. So Demeter nursed Demophoön, the son that Metaneira had borne to wise Celeus. And the child grew like a young god, for daily Demeter anointed him with ambrosia and at night she would place him in the red heart of the fire. Her purpose was to give him immortal youth.

Something, however, made the mother uneasy, so that one night she kept watch and screamed in terror when she saw the child laid in the fire. The goddess was angered; she seized the boy and cast him on the ground. She had meant to set him free from old age and from death, but that was not to be. Still, he had lain upon her knees and slept in her arms and therefore he should have honor throughout his life.

Then she showed herself the goddess manifest. Beauty breathed about her and a lovely fragrance; light shone from her so that the great house was filled with brightness. She was Demeter, she told the awestruck women. They must build her a great temple near the town and so win back the favor of her heart.

Thus she left them, and Metaneira fell speechless to the earth and all there trembled with fear. In the morning they told Celeus what had happened and he called the people together and revealed to them the command of the goddess. They worked willingly to build her a temple, and when it was finished Demeter came to it and sat there—apart from the gods in Olympus, alone, wasting away with longing for her daughter.

That year was most dreadful and cruel for mankind over all the earth. Nothing grew; no seed would spring up; in vain the oxen drew the plowshare through the furrows. It seemed the whole race of men would die of famine. At last Zeus saw that he must take the matter in hand. He sent the gods to Demeter, one after another, to try to turn her from her anger, but she listened to none of them. Never would she let the earth bear fruit until she had seen her daughter. Then Zeus realized that his brother must give way. He told Hermes to go down to the underworld and to bid the lord of it to let his bride go back to Demeter.

Hermes found the two sitting side by side, Persephone shrinking away, reluctant because she longed for her mother. At Hermes' words she sprang up joyfully, eager to go. Her husband knew that he must obey the word of Zeus and send her up to earth away from him, but he prayed her as she left him to have kind thoughts of him and not be so sorrowful that she was the wife of one who was great among the immortals. And he made her eat a pomegranate seed, knowing in his heart that if she did so she must return to him.

He got ready his golden car and Hermes took the reins and drove the black horses straight to the temple where Demeter was. She ran out to meet her daughter as swiftly as a Maenad runs down the mountainside. Persephone sprang into her arms and was held fast there. All day they talked of what had happened to them both, and Demeter grieved when she heard of the pomegranate seed, fearing that she could not keep her daughter with her.

Then Zeus sent another messenger to her, a great personage, none other than his revered mother Rhea, the oldest of the gods. Swiftly she hastened down from the heights of Olympus to the barren, leafless earth, and standing at the door of the temple she spoke to Demeter.

> Come, my daughter, for Zeus, far-seeing, loud-
>   thundering, bids you.
> Come once again to the halls of the gods where
>   you shall have honor,
> Where you will have your desire, your daughter,
>   to comfort your sorrow
> As each year is accomplished and bitter winter is
>   ended.

> For a third part only the kingdom of darkness will
>   hold her.
> For the rest you will keep her, you and the happy
>   immortals.
> Peace now. Give men life which comes alone
>   from your giving.

Demeter did not refuse, poor comfort though it was that she must lose Persephone for four months every year and see her young loveliness go down to the world of the dead. But she was kind; the "Good Goddess," men always called her. She was sorry for the desolation she had brought about. She made the fields once more rich with abundant fruit and the whole world bright with flowers and green leaves. Also she went to the princes of Eleusis who had built her temple and she chose one, Triptolemus, to be her ambassador to men, instructing them how to sow the corn. She taught him and Celeus and the others her sacred rites, "mysteries which no one may utter, for deep awe checks the tongue. Blessed is he who has seen them; his lot will be good in the world to come."

> Queen of fragrant Eleusis,
> Giver of earth's good gifts,
> Give me your grace, O Demeter.
> You, too, Persephone, fairest,
> Maiden all lovely, I offer
> Song for your favor. ∎

The Council Tree
Hah-nu-nah, the Turtle
The Two Brothers

North America: United States—Iroquois/Haudenosaunee

The Iroquois, a confederation of five tribes—Cayuga, Mohawk, Oneida, Onondaga, and Seneca (later joined by the Tuscarora)—shared a vision of creation with other Native Americans from the Great Lakes to the southeastern region of the United States: The cosmos was multilayered and hierarchical. The highest

"Evil Minded Pours Ashes on Corn." Illustration by Jesse J. Cornplanter.

Copyright 1938 by Jesse J. Cornplanter and Namee Price Hendricks. Copyright renewed © 1966 by Mrs. Jesse Cornplanter. Reprinted by Permission of HarperCollins Publishers, Inc.

layer, above the sky dome, was the abode of the people who lived before the earth was created. The people in the Sky-world (sometimes referred to as a floating island) were more powerful versions of the people (Iroquoian) who occupy our world. Sky-chief was a powerful being in the Sky-world.

According to folklorist and historian William Fenton (1962), 25 versions of the Iroquoian story of creation have been collected, but all of them have the same basic elements, which include the Sky-world; the uprooting of the light-giving tree; the Woman who falls from the sky; Earth-diver (usually muskrat) who brings back mud to build the island for the woman to land on; the twins, Good-mind and Evil-mind, who fight for the creation of the world; Good-mind liberating the animals that Evil-mind hid; Good-mind

Source: "The Council Tree" and "Hah-nu-nah, the Turtle" are from *Myths and Legends of the New York State Iroquois* by Harriet M. Converse and Arthur Caswell Parker. Albany, NY: New York State Museum, 1908. Museum Bulletin 125. pp. 32–33; "The Two Brothers" is reprinted with permission from *Iroquois Stories: Heroes and Heroines, Monsters and Magic* © 1985 by Joseph Bruchac. Published by The Crossing Press, Freedom, California. pp. 19–22.

bringing corn to earth; Good-mind's final battle with Evil-mind and the latter's banishment; and Good-mind and Sky-woman returning to the Sky-world after promising to return at the end of the world (Fenton, 1962). Sky-woman's descent and the attempts of the animals to create a safe landing for her are a popular motif in Iroquoian art (Fenton, 1998). That part of the story is retold here in "The Council Tree and Hah-nu-nah, the Turtle," by Helen Converse, a nineteenth century advocate of the rights of the Iroquois, who was officially adopted by the Seneca Nation in 1884 and by the Onondaga in 1891. The story of Good-mind and Evil-mind and the creation of plants and animals is from the contemporary Abenaki storyteller and writer Joseph Bruchac's personal retelling, which he based on written and oral versions of the stories.

In other versions of the creation myth, Sky-woman, the grandmother of Good-mind and Evil-mind, takes the part of Evil-mind and rejects Good-mind. Good-mind must seek out his father (the East Wind) and must prove himself worthy before returning for his final battle and triumph over Evil-mind.

Arthur Parker, a Seneca folklorist and storyteller, wrote footnotes to Helen Converse's retelling that provided cultural context for the stories. About Sky-chief, who in some versions is referred to as Great Spirit and to whom Converse refers as Great Ruler, Parker said that it was only after the coming of the missionaries that the concept of a supreme ruler became emphasized. Rather, he was seen as a powerful being, not as creator and ruler of all. The dichotomy of good and evil too, according to Parker, are relatively new dimensions attached to the twins Good-mind and Evil-mind, who earlier in Iroquois history represented creation and destruction, not moral forces. Other names for Good-mind are "The Creator," "Sky-Holder," and "Sapling." As Sapling he represents first man, an earthly culture hero (Parker, 1908, p. 32).

The Council Tree

The earth was the thought of The Great Ruler who is also known as "He Who Created Us," "He Who Governs," and "Good Mind." He lived on a floating island of eternal peace in space. In its abundance there were no burdens to weary; in its fruitfulness all needs were endlessly provided. To its perpetual calm death never came, and to its tranquility, no desire, no sorrow nor pain.

In the far away days of this floating island there grew one stately tree that branched beyond the range of vision. Perpetually laden with fruit and blossoms, the air was fragrant with its perfume, and the people gathered to its shade where councils were held.

One day The Great Ruler said to his people: "We will make a new place where another people may grow. Under our council tree is a great cloud sea which calls for our help. It is lonesome. It knows no rest and calls for light. We will talk to it. The roots of our council tree point to it and will show the way."

Having commanded that the tree be uprooted, The Great Ruler peered into the depths where the roots had guided, and summoning Ata-en-sic [Sky-Woman], who was with child, bade her look down. Ata-en-sic saw nothing, but The Great Ruler knew that the sea voice was calling, and bidding her carry its life, wrapped around her a great ray of light and sent her down to the cloud sea. ■

Hah-nu-nah, the Turtle

Dazzled by the descending light enveloping Ata-en-sic, there was great consternation among the animals and birds inhabiting the cloud sea, and they counseled in alarm.

"If it falls it may destroy us," they cried.

"Where can it rest?" asked the Duck.

"Only the *oeh-da* [earth] can hold it," said the Beaver, "the oeh-da which lies at the bottom of our waters, and I will bring it."

The Beaver went down but never returned. Then the Duck ventured, but soon its dead body floated to the surface.

Many of the divers had tried and failed when the Muskrat, knowing the way, volunteered to obtain it and soon returned bearing a small portion in his paw. "But it is heavy," said he, "and will grow fast. Who will bear it?"

The Turtle was willing, and the *oeh-da* was placed on his hard shell.

Having received a resting place for the light, the water birds, guided by its glow, flew upward, and receiving the woman on their widespread wings, bore her down to the Turtle's back.

And Hah-nu-nah, the Turtle, became the Earth Bearer. When he stirs, the seas rise in great waves, and when restless and violent, earthquakes yawn and devour. ■

The Two Brothers

It was not long after
she had fallen from the Sky-World
and the earth had been made
as a place for her to stand
that the Sky-Woman gave birth
to a beautiful daughter.
Together they lived
in peace upon this world
which rested upon the turtle's back
until the daughter became a woman.
One day she came to her mother and said,
"Mother, while I slept in the meadow, I felt
a wind sweep over me and I heard someone
whisper sweet words into my ear."

Then it was that the Sky-Woman knew
the West Wind had taken
her daughter as his wife.

Soon the daughter of the Sky-Woman
grew heavy with child
and from her stomach
the voices of two children
could be heard.
One of the voices was angry and quarrelsome.
"My brother," it said, "let us tear our way out.
I think I see light through our mother's side."

The other voice was loving and gentle.
"No, my brother," said the other voice.
"We must not do that, for it would cause her death."

Before long the time came
for the brothers to be born.
The good-minded brother was the first
and entered this life in the normal way.
But the brother of evil mind
tore his way through their mother's side
and she died when he was born.

The Sky-Woman was saddened
at her daughter's death.
She looked at the children
who stood before her.
"My grandsons," she said,
"your mother has gone
before us to that good place
where all who live good lives
shall dwell some day.
Let us bury her now
and something good may happen."

Then the brother
who was good of mind
helped to bury his mother's body,
while the other brother, the Evil Mind
paid no attention
and either slept or cried for food.

Soon green shoots rose
from their mother's grave.
From her fingers came the bean plants,
from her feet came the potatoes.
From her stomach came the squashes

and from her breasts, the corn.
Last of all, from her forehead,
grew the medicine plant, tobacco.

Then the Good Mind listened
to his grandmother's words
teaching him, telling him how
to shape the earth and bring good things
to be used by the humans who were to come.

When she finished, she departed,
back into the Sky-World,
where she still looks down
on us through the nights
as the moon, our grandmother.

Then the Good Mind touched the earth
and from it grew the tall elm tree
which gives its bark for the lodges of the people.

But the Evil Mind struck the earth
and the briars and bushes with thorns sprang up.

Then the Good Mind touched the earth
and from it flowed the springs of pure water.

But the Evil Mind struck the earth,
kicking in dirt to muddy the springs.

Then the Good Mind touched the earth,
making the rivers and running streams
to carry people from place to place,
with currents flowing in each direction.

But the Evil Mind made rapids and falls
and twisted the streams, throwing in great rocks
so that travel would not be an easy thing.

Then the Good Mind made animals and birds
and creatures friendly to human beings,
to be his companions and provide him with food.

But the Evil Mind made evil creatures:
The Flying Heads and the monster bears,
great horned serpents, Stone Giants and beings
who would trouble the lives and dreams of the people.

So it was that in the two brothers
all that was good and all that was evil
came to this world and the long contest
between the Good and the Evil Minds began.

And even today, this world we walk in
is made of both good and evil things.
But if we choose the Good Mind's path,

remembering right is greater than wrong,
we will find our reward at journey's end. ■

 # The Hunting of the Great Bear

North America: United States—Iroquois/Haudenosaunee

In his introduction to *Seneca Myths & Folk Tales* Arthur Parker, a Seneca anthropologist and folktale collector from the turn of the twentieth century, explains that Monster Bear, "Niǎ''gwai'he'gōwā, is the most feared of magic beasts and the most frequent among them to enter into the fortunes of men." (Parker, 1923, p. 17). The bear in this story, however, according to Parker, is not the bear we are familiar with today but a monster bear from before "the creation of our kind of man-beings." Except for one vulnerable part he cannot be killed, and his bones form powerful magic medicine. The Bear is associated with magical and spiritual power and is both feared and honored throughout Native North America as well as Siberia in Asia. The version of the story told by Joseph Bruchac is close to Parker's version but sounds more colloquial to modern audiences. Bruchac, a writer and storyteller, reads versions of the stories recorded in the nineteenth and early twentieth centuries and listens to multiple tellings of the same story by contemporary Native storytellers. He does not record the story but lets it become part of him until he can retell it in his own words (Bruchac, 1986). Bruchac emphasizes the importance of giving credit to the teller from whom one learns a story and of learning as much as possible about the meaning of a story before retelling it (Bruchac, 1996).

There were four hunters who were brothers. No hunters were as good as they at following a trail. They never gave up once they began to track their quarry.

Source: "The Hunting of the Great Bear" from *Iroquois Stories: Heroes and Heroines, Monsters and Magic* © 1985 by Joseph Bruchac. Published by The Crossing Press, Freedom, California. pp. 189–195. Reprinted with permission.

One day, in the moon when the cold nights return, an urgent message came to the village of the four hunters. A great bear, one so large and powerful that many thought it must be some kind of monster, had appeared. The people of the village whose hunting grounds the monster had invaded were afraid. The children no longer went out to play in the woods. The long-houses of the village were guarded each night by men who stood by the entrances. Each morning, when the people went outside, they found the huge tracks of the bear in the midst of their village. They knew that soon it would become even more bold.

Picking up their spears and calling to their small dog, the four hunters set forth for that village, which was not far away. As they came closer they noticed how quiet the woods were. There were no signs of rabbits or deer and even the birds were silent. On a great pine tree they found the scars where the great bear had reared up on hind legs and made deep scratches to mark it territory. The tallest of the brothers tried to touch the highest of the scratch marks with the tip of his spear.

"It is as the people feared," the first brother said. "This one we are to hunt is Nyah-gwaheh, a monster bear."

"But what about the magic that the Nyah-gwaheh has?" said the second brother.

The first brother shook his head. "That magic will do it no good if we find its track."

"That's so," said the third brother. "I have always heard that from the old people. Those creatures can only chase a hunter who has not yet found its trail. When you find the track of the Nyah-gwaheh and begin to chase it, then it must run from you."

"Brothers," said the fourth hunter who was the fattest and laziest, "did we bring along enough food to eat? It may take a long time to catch this big bear. I'm feeling hungry."

Before long, the four hunters and their small dog reached the village. It was a sad sight to see. There was no fire burning in the center of the village and the doors of all the longhouses were closed. Grim men stood on guard with clubs and spears and there was no game hung from the racks or skins stretched for tanning. The people looked hungry.

The elder sachem of the village came out and the tallest of the four hunters spoke to him.

"Uncle," the hunter said, "we have come to help you get rid of the monster."

Then the fattest and laziest of the four brothers spoke. "Uncle," he said, "is there some food we can eat? Can we find a place to rest before we start chasing this big bear. I'm tired."

The first hunter shook his head and smiled. "My brother is only joking, Uncle," he said. "We are going now to pick up the monster bear's trail."

"I am not sure you can do that, Nephews," the elder sachem said. "Though we find tracks closer and closer to the doors of our lodges each morning, whenever we try to follow those tracks they disappear."

The second hunter knelt down and patted the head of their small dog. "Uncle," he said, "that is because they do not have a dog such as ours." He pointed to the two black circles above the eyes of the small dog. "Four-Eyes can see any tracks, even those many days old."

"May Creator's protection be with you," said the elder sachem.

"Do not worry, Uncle," said the third hunter. "Once we are on a trail we never stop following it until we've finished our hunt."

"That's why I think we should have something to eat first," said the fourth hunter, but his brothers did not listen. They nodded to the elder sachem and began to leave. Sighing, the fattest and laziest of the brothers lifted up his long spear and trudged after them.

They walked, following their little dog. It kept lifting up its head, as if to look around with its four eyes. The trail was not easy to find.

"Brothers," the fattest and laziest hunter complained, "don't you think we should rest. We've been walking a *long* time." But his brothers paid no attention to him. Though they could see no tracks, they could feel the presence of the Nyah-gwaheh. They knew that if they did not soon find its trail, it would make its way behind them. Then they would be the hunted ones.

The fattest and laziest brother took out his pemmican pouch. At least he could eat while they walked along. He opened the pouch and shook out the food he had prepared so carefully by pounding together strips of meat and berries with maple sugar and then drying them in the sun. But instead of pemmican, pale squirming things fell out into his hands. The magic of the Nyah-gwaheh had changed the food into worms.

"Brothers," the fattest and laziest of the hunters shouted, "let's hurry up and catch that big bear! Look what it did to my pemmican. Now I'm getting angry."

Meanwhile, like a pale giant shadow, the Nyah-gwaheh was moving through the trees close to the hunters. It's mouth was open as it watched them and its huge teeth shone, its eyes flashed red. Soon it would be behind them and on their trail.

Just then, though, the little dog lifted its head and yelped. "Eh-heh!" the first brother called.

"Four-Eyes has found the trail," shouted the second brother.

"We have the track of the Nyah-gwaheh," said the third brother.

"Big Bear," the fattest and laziest one yelled, "we are after you, now!"

Fear filled the heart of the great bear for the first time and it began to run. As it broke from the cover of the pines, the four hunters saw it, a gigantic white shape, so pale as to appear almost naked. With loud hunting cries, they began to run after it. The great bear's strides were long and it ran more swiftly than a deer. The four hunters and their little dog were swift also though and they did not fall behind. The trail led through the swamps and the thickets. It was easy to read, for the bear pushed everything aside as it ran, even knocking down big trees. On and on they ran, over hills and through valleys. They came to the slope of a mountain and followed the trail higher and higher, every now and then catching a glimpse of their quarry over the next rise.

Now though the lazy hunter was getting tired of running. He pretended to fall and twist his ankle.

"Brothers," he called, "I have sprained my ankle. You must carry me."

So his three brothers did as he asked, two of them carrying him by turns while the third hunter carried his spear. They ran more slowly now because of their heavy load, but they were not falling any further behind. The day had turned into night, yet they could still see the white shape of the great bear ahead of them. They were at the top of the mountain now and the ground beneath them was very dark as they ran across it. The bear was tiring, but so were they. It was not easy to carry their fat and lazy brother. The little dog, Four-Eyes, was close behind the great bear, nipping at its tail as it ran.

"Brothers," said the fattest and laziest one, "put me down now. I think my leg has gotten better."

The brothers did as he asked. Fresh and rested, the fattest and laziest one grabbed his spear and dashed ahead of the others. Just as the great bear turned to bite at the little dog, the fattest and laziest hunter leveled his spear and thrust it into the heart of the Nyah-Gwaheh. The monster bear fell dead.

By the time the other brothers caught up, the fattest and laziest hunter had already built a fire and was cutting up the big bear.

"Come on brothers," he said. "Let's eat. All this running has made me hungry!"

So they cooked the meat of the great bear and its fat sizzled as it dripped from their fire. They ate until even the fattest and laziest one was satisfied and leaned back in contentment. Just then, though, the first hunter looked down at his feet.

"Brothers," he exclaimed, "look below us!"

The four hunters looked down. Below them were thousands of small sparkling lights in the darkness which, they realized, was all around them.

"We aren't on a mountain top at all," said the third brother. "We are up in the sky."

And it was so. The great bear had indeed been magical. Its feet had taken it high above the earth as it tried to escape the four hunters. However, their determination not to give up the chase had carried them up that strange trail.

Just then the little dog yipped twice.

"The great bear!" said the second hunter. "Look!"

The hunters looked. There, where they had piled the bones of their feast the Great Bear was coming back to life and rising to its feet. As they watched, it began to run again, the small dog close on its heels.

"Follow me," shouted the first brother. Grabbing up their spears the four hunters again began to chase the great bear across the skies.

So it was, the old people say, and so it still is. Each autumn the hunters chase the great bear across the skies and kill it. Then, as they cut it up for their meal, the blood falls down from the heavens and colors the leaves of the maple trees scarlet. They cook the bear and the fat dripping from their fires turns the grass white.

If you look carefully into the skies as the seasons change, you can read that story. The great bear is the square shape some call the bowl of the Big Dipper. The hunters and their small dog (which you can just barely see) are close behind, the dipper's handle. When autumn comes and that constellation has turned upside down, the old people say, "Ah, the lazy hunter has killed the bear." But as the moons pass and the sky moves once more towards spring, the bear slowly rises back on its feet and the chase begins again. ∎

▨ Origins of the Animals, Humans, and the Human Condition

Will the day never come for ceasing unending labor and warfare, or a night to stop the destruction? or will the immortals forever keep piling fresh bitter causes of quarrels and hatreds upon us?

—Hesiod *Works and Days* (171–173), circa 700 B.C.E., translated from ancient Greek by Barry B. Powell

What a piece of work is a man! how noble in reason! how infinite in faculty! in form and moving how express and admirable! in action how like an angel! in apprehension how like a god! the beauty of the world! the paragon of animals!

—William Shakespeare, *Hamlet*, Act 2, scene ii (1601)

Chameleon carved of wood and painted with bright designs by the Bobo Tribe [of Burkina Faso].

Text and Illustration Copyright © 1971 by Janet D'Amato. From: *African Animals Through African Eyes* by Janet and Alex D'Amato. New York: Simon & Schuster, 1971. Redrawn from exhibits and photographs by Janet D'Amato. Chameleon and lizard are recurrent characters throughout Africa and are often charged with delivering God's decree relating to whether humans will live forever, as in the story "Death" from Kenya.

Death

Africa: Kenya—Luo

There are over 700 variants throughout Africa of the theme that immortality was within the grasp of humankind but for a problem with the messenger. In some versions the messenger garbles the message; in others the messenger maliciously gives the wrong message or an enemy of humankind interferes at the last moment; and in one version the question of whether death is permanent is left by the storyteller for the audience to answer (Beier, 1966). Beier published a version by the Margi people of the Central African Republic in which Death had already entered the world but people sent Chameleon to God to find out what they could do about it. God told Chameleon that if the people threw porridge over the corpse, it would come back to life, but since Chameleon was slow in returning with the message and since Death was on a rampage, the people sent a second messenger, Lizard, with the question. This time, angered by humankind's impatience, God told Lizard that people should bury the dead. Fast Lizard returned with this second message before Chameleon could deliver the first; thus through human impatience, immortality is lost. There are many other explanations for the origin of death in Africa, including the biblical motif of the forbidden fruit, the disobedience of man, and the jealousy of woman, or, as in many of the Native American stories of choosing death, man is allowed a choice but makes a bad decision. Finally, in one version man accepts death in return for being given children (Beier, 1966).

Yesterday's Today is a junior high school reader with some probing questions for the students. Oral culture is being promoted through the schools. At the time that Odaga published her book, Kenya had only recently gained independence from Great Britain, and

Source: "Death" from *Yesterday's Today: The Study of Oral Literature,* by Asenath Bole Odaga. Kisumu, Kenya: Lake Publishers & Enterprises, 1984. Reprinted with permission by Asenath Bole Odaga. pp. 16–17.

this book was probably one of many ways in which Kenyan children were encouraged to explore their culture and to deal with cultural diversity within Kenya where the Agikuyu are the dominant ethnic group but where many other ethnic groups must also coexist. The author, in her questioning, for instance, encourages students to discuss the symbolic value of Chameleon and Lizard within their own culture and compare it with their presentation in this story from the Luo ethnic group.

This thing happened long time ago when people first appeared on the earth. One day the people were told that if they didn't want to die they should send a Chameleon with a fat piece of meat to take to the Moon who would pass it to God. They were also told to give the Lizard a hoe to take to the Moon. Then, if Chameleon reached the Moon with the fat piece of meat before Lizard with the hoe, the people would not die, but would live for ever.

That day, the people never slept a wink. They stayed awake throughout the night and early the next morning they sent Chameleon far ahead of Lizard. However, on the way, the temptation to taste the succulent appetizing piece of meat proved too great, so Chameleon stopped to taste a little of the meat. The Lizard came hurrying and passed him on the way while he was still enjoying the fat meat. The meat proved to be tender and juicy and Chameleon ended up eating a big chunk of it. The remaining piece that was to be taken to the Moon became dirty, covered with soil. Once Chameleon realized that he was late, he lowered the meat down from his back and began to hurry, dragging it along. As Chameleon hurried along, all the other animals stared at him, sniggered and hid away. But of course most of them had been envious of Chameleon for the important errand on which he had been sent. So they were happy to see that he had failed.

By the time Chameleon reached the Moon, with the dirty piece of meat, Lizard had already handed the hoe over to the Moon and man thus lost a golden opportunity to acquire immortality. The Moon chased away the Chameleon and threw the dirty piece of meat after him. The hoe which Lizard carried was to be used by the Luo to dig graves and bury their dead. Death had been born.

Since the time that Chameleon messed up the Moon's gift meat, the type of death from which an individual would die is fixed right on the day of his or her birth! And initially death didn't come secretly to human beings. Death just sent word to whoever he wanted to take away to get ready on a particular day. But since no one liked to die, people used to give Death a hard time. He always had to chase one person for days, before he overpowered and caught him. People used all sorts of tricks to evade Death, so he decided to come secretly and catch them unaware. That's why human beings never know the date they will die. ■

 # Prometheus

Europe: Greece

In this account, Padraic Colum (1937) combines three stories about the beginnings and development of humankind. The accounts of the Ages or Races of Man

Source: "Prometheus" from *Orpheus Myths of the World* by Padraic Colum. New York, Macmillan, 1937. Reprinted with permission by The Estate of Padraic Colum. pp. 64–67.

and of Prometheus' gift of fire are described in the earliest existing sources of Greek myths, which are Hesiod's poems called *Works and Days* and *Theogony* (ca. 700 B.C.E.). The story of a flood as punishment for human wickedness (or as a population control measure) spread from the Near East. Its most familiar form in the West is through the story of Noah. These stories had probably been told by ancient Greeks for centuries, but the first existing written accounts are from Ovid and from Apollodorus, a Roman and a Greek poet from the first and second centuries C.E. (Powell, 1998).

The idea of four succeeding ages of humankind (Gold, Silver, Bronze, and Iron), with each more debased than the one preceding it, existed earlier than Hesiod in Near Eastern writings and probably in Greek oral tradition. Hesiod inserted a fifth age: the Heroic Age. G. S. Kirk (1970), a scholar of classical mythology, subdivides Hesiod's Iron Age, creating six paired ages: Gold/Silver; Heroic/Bronze, and two stages of Iron. According to Kirk, Hesiod envisioned Iron Age 1 as the present stage and Iron Age 2 as a future stage that will be even worse in that all our present ills and faults will be further magnified so that babies will be born old and offspring will not take care of their elderly parents. People in the worst of each pair of stages exhibited *hubris,* an antisocial arrogance and lack of reverence for the gods.

Hesiod's pessimistic view of human nature as ever worsening might have been in part due to the turmoil that characterized his own era, a time of change from a simple agrarian society to an urban, monetary society with landholdings concentrated in the hands of a few and others losing their land and sinking in the social order, often into slavery (Powell, 1998). The idea of humankind in decline recurs frequently in Western thought.

There are several accounts of how humans were made. One account credits Prometheus (Forethought) with having created humans from wind or water and mud, a conception that was probably influenced by Mesopotamian creation myths. After having created humans, Prometheus took special care to help them rise from bestial ignorance by teaching them all the human arts, including house building and medicine. For his most important gift, fire, Prometheus was punished by Zeus. Prometheus' gifts, sacrifice, and punishment are vividly described by the Greek playwright Aeschylus in *Prometheus Bound.*

Colum (1937) implies in his account of the great flood that the destruction of humans was a whim of Zeus (similar to the Mesopotamian version), but this is a bit of poetic license as Ovid and Apollodorus describe Zeus' decision to have been prompted by the widespread wickedness on earth, exemplified by king Lyceum, who practiced human sacrifice and cannibalism (Powell, 1998). Deukalion (Prometheus' son) and Pyrrha (Epimetheus' daughter), sole survivors of the flood, repopulate the world by throwing stones behind them, from which new people grow. Prometheus' fashioning of people from wind, water, and mud and Deukalion and Pyrrha's repopulating the world by sowing stones represent two different conceptions of the creation of humankind: the artisan model and the agrarian model (Powell, 1998). Most collections of Greek myths include the story of Prometheus, a central myth in Western culture.

The Gods upon Olympus more than once made a race of men. The first was the Golden Race. Very close to the Gods was the Golden Race; the men of that race lived justly, although there were no laws to compel them. In the time of the Golden Race the Earth knew only one season; that season was everlasting spring. The men and women of the Golden Race lived as through a span of life that was far beyond that of the men and women of our day, and when they died it was as though sleep had become everlasting with them. They had all good things, and they had them without labour, for the Earth without any forcing bestowed fruits and crops upon them. They had peace all through their lives, and after they had passed away their spirits remained above the Earth, inspiring the men of the race who came after them to do great and gracious things and to act justly and kindly to one another.

After the Golden Race had passed away, the Gods made for the Earth a second race—the Silver Race. Less noble in spirit and in body was the Silver Race, and the seasons that visited them were less gracious. In the time of the Silver Race the Gods made the seasons—summer and spring, autumn and winter. The men of the Silver Race knew parching heat; they knew the bitter winds of winter, and snow, and rain, and hail. It was the men of the Silver Race who first built houses for shelter. They lived through a span of life that was longer than our span, but it was not long enough to give them wisdom. Children were brought up at the mothers' sides for a hundred years, playing at childish things. And when they came to years beyond a hundred they quarelled with one another, and wronged one another; moreover, they did not know enough to give reverence to the immortal Gods. Then, by the will of Zeus, the Silver Race passed away as the Golden Race had passed away. Their spirits stay in the Underworld, and they are called by men the blessed spirits of the Underworld.

And then there was made the Third Race—the Race of Bronze. They were a race great of stature, terrible, and strong. Their armour was of bronze, their swords were of bronze, their implements were of bronze, and of bronze too, they made their houses. No great span of life was theirs, for with the weapons that they took in their terrible hands they slew one another. And so they passed away; they went down under the Earth and they left no name that men might know them by.

Then the Gods created a fourth race—our own—a Race of Iron. We have not the justice that was amongst the men of the Golden Race; we have not the simpleness that was amongst the men of the Silver Race; we have not the stature nor the great strength that the men of the Bronze Race possessed. We are of iron that we may endure. It is our doom that we must never cease from labour and that we must very quickly grow old.

But miserable as we are today, there was time when the lot of men was more miserable. With poor implements they had to labour on hard ground. There was less justice and kindliness in those days than there is now.

Once it came into the mind of Zeus to destroy this fourth race and to leave the Earth to the nymphs and the satyrs. He would destroy it by a great flood. But Prometheus, the Titan who had given aid to Zeus— Prometheus who was named the Forethinker—would not consent to the race of men being destroyed utterly, and he considered a way of saving some of them. To a man and a woman, Deukalion and Pyrrha, just and gentle people, he brought word of the plan of Zeus, and he showed them how to make a ship that would bear through what was about to be sent upon the Earth.

Then Zeus shut up in their caves all the winds except the wind that brings rain and clouds. He bade this wind, the South Wind, sweep over the Earth, flooding it with rain. He called upon Poseidon and bade him let the sea pour in on the land. And Poseidon commanded the rivers to put forth all their strength, and sweep dykes away, and overflow their banks.

The clouds and the sea and the rivers poured upon the Earth. The flood rose higher and higher, and in places where pretty lambs had gambolled the ugly sea-calves now played; men in their boats drew fishes out of the tops of elm trees, and the water-nymphs were amazed to come on men's cities under the waves.

Soon even the men and women who had boats were overwhelmed by the rise of the water—all perished then except Deukalion and Pyrrha, his wife; them the waves had not overwhelmed—they were in a ship that Prometheus had shown them how to build. The flood went down at last, and Deukalion and Pyrrha climbed up to a high and a dry ground. Zeus saw that two of the race of men had been left alive. But he saw that these two were just and kindly and had a right reverence for the Gods. He spared them, and he saw their children again peopling the Earth.

Prometheus, who had saved them, looked upon the men and women of the Earth with compassion. Their labour was hard, and they wrought much to gain little. They were chilled at night in their houses, and the winds that blew in the daytime made the old men and women bend double like a wheel. Prometheus thought to himself that if men and women had the element that only the Gods knew of—the element of fire—they could make for themselves implements for labour, and they could build houses that would keep out the chilling winds, and they could warm themselves at the blaze.

But the Gods had not willed that men should have fire, and to go against the will of the Gods would be impious. Prometheus went against the will of the Gods. He stole fire from the altar of Zeus, and he hid it in a hollow fennel stalk, and so he brought it to men.

Men, possessing fire, were then able to hammer iron into tools; they were able to cut down forests with axes, and sow grain where the forests had been. They were able to make houses that the storms could not overthrow, and they were able to warm themselves at the hearth-fires. They had rest from their labour at times. They built cities; they became beings who no longer had their heads and backs bent, but were able to raise their faces even to the Gods.

Zeus spared the men who now had the sacred element of fire. But Prometheus he did not spare. He knew that Prometheus had stolen the fire even from his own altar. And he thought on how he might punish the great Titan for his impiety.

He brought up from the Underworld, from Tartaros, the Giants Kottos, Briareos, and Gyes. He commanded them to lay hands on Prometheus and to fasten him with fetters to the highest, blackest crag upon Caucasus. And Kottos, Briareos, and Gyes seized upon the Titian, and carried him to Caucasus, and fettered him with fetters of bronze to the highest, blackest crag—with fetters of bronze that may not be broken. They left the Titan stretched there, fettered, under the sky, with the cold winds blowing upon him and with the sun streaming down upon him. And, that his punishment might exceed all other punishments, Zeus sent a vulture to prey upon him—a vulture that tears at his liver each day.

And yet Prometheus does not cry out that he has repented of what he has done for man; although the winds blow upon him, and the sun streams upon him, and the vulture tears at his liver, Prometheus will not cry out his repentance to Heaven. And Zeus may not utterly destroy him. For Prometheus the Forethinker knows a secret that Zeus would fain have him disclose. He knows that, as Zeus overthrew his father and made himself ruler in his stead, so, too, another will overthrow Zeus. One day Zeus will have to have the fetters broken from around the limbs of his victim, and will have to bring from the rock and the vulture, and even into the Council of the Olympians, the unyielding Titan, Prometheus. ■

Orpheus

The myth of Orpheus, the musician who can move even the gods to tears and can soften the heart of unbending Death, has beguiled Western imagination since ancient times. Virgil, the Roman poet (first century B.C.E.), is one of the early sources of the much older Greek myth. The Renaissance revival of interest in classical culture resulted in the invention of the opera as an art form during the Baroque era (the 1600s) and the first opera was entitled *Eurydice* by the Italian Jacopo Peri. Operas about Orpheus continued to be created for centuries. The Brazilian film *Black Orpheus* gives the story a new, modern setting and emphasizes the theme of the immortality of music.

The story of Orpheus, who had knowledge of the afterlife, also inspired a religion, the Orphic Mysteries.

Source: "Orpheus" from *Orpheus Myths of the World* by Padraic Colum. New York, Macmillan, 1937. Reprinted with permission by The Estate of Padraic Colum. pp. 80–83.

Founded in sixth century B.C.E. Greece, it was based on the idea that humans have a divine spirit entrapped in earthly flesh, and it called for a strict moral code. Unlike the religions based on sacrifices to the Olympic gods, Orphism offered hope for justice and for an afterlife; the soul was regarded as immortal and the afterlife as a time during which the soul was purified before rebirth on earth. As to why Orpheus loses Eurydice, different retellings of the story suggest different explanations. Padraic Colum's view (1937) that it was thoughtlessness rather than lack of faith that caused the disaster reflects Virgil's interpretation. Others emphasize Orpheus' lack of faith in the promise of Hades; he looked back because he did not believe that Eurydice was following him.

The motif of losing the chance to reclaim a loved one from death can be seen in other cultures as well. In a Cherokee myth the Sun's daughter dies and is nearly brought back from the land of the dead but is permanently lost when her rescuers prematurely open the box in which they carry her; her soul flits out and becomes the cardinal bird. Both myths suggest that death is final. This is a difficult story to present to young children, and most retellings are for middle school age and up.

Many were the minstrels who, in the early days of the world, went amongst men, telling them stories of the Gods, of their wars and their births, and of the beginning of things. Of all these minstrels none was so famous as Orpheus; none could tell truer things about the Gods; he himself was half divine, and there were some who said that he was in truth Apollo's son.

But a great grief came to Orpheus, a grief that stopped his singing and his playing upon the lyre. His young wife, Eurydice, was taken from him. One day, walking in the garden, she was bitten on the heel by a serpent; straightaway she went down to the World of the Dead.

Then everything in this world was dark and bitter for the minstrel of the Gods; sleep would not come to him, and for him food had no taste. Then Orpheus said, "I will do that which no mortal has ever done before; I will do that which even the Immortals might shrink from doing; I will go down into the World of the Dead, and I will bring back to the living and to the light my bride, Eurydice."

Then Orpheus went on his way to the cavern which goes down, down to the World of the Dead—the Cavern Tainaron. The trees showed him the way. As he went on, Orpheus played upon his lyre and sang; the trees heard his song and were moved by his grief, and with their arms and their heads they showed him the way to the deep, deep cavern named Tainaron.

Down, down, down by the winding path Orpheus went. He came at last to the great gate that opens upon the World of the Dead. And the silent guards who keep watch there for the Rulers of the Dead were astonished when they saw a living being coming towards them, and they would not let Orpheus approach the gate.

The minstrel took the lyre in his hands and played upon it. As he played, the silent watchers gathered around him leaving the gate unguarded. And as he played the Rulers of the Dead came forth, Hades and

Persephone, and listened to the words of the living man.

"The cause of my coming through the dark and fearful ways," sang Orpheus, "is to strive to gain a fairer fate for Eurydice, my bride. All that is above must come down to you at last, O Rulers of the most lasting World. But before her time has Eurydice been brought here. I have desired strength to endure her loss, but I cannot endure it. And I have come before you, Hades and Persephone, brought here by love."

When Orpheus said the name of love, Persephone, the queen of the dead, bowed her young head, and bearded Hades, the king, bowed his head also. Persephone remembered how Demeter, her mother, had sought her all through the world, and she remembered the touch of her mother's tears upon her face. And Hades remembered how his love for Persephone had led him to carry her away from the valley where she had been gathering flowers. He and Persephone stood aside, and Orpheus went through the gate and came amongst the dead.

Still upon his lyre he played. Tantalos—who for his crime had been condemned to stand up to his neck in water and yet never be able to assuage his thirst—Tantalos heard, and for a while did not strive to put his lips towards the water that ever flowed away from him; Sisyphus—who had been condemned to roll up a hill a stone that ever rolled back—Sisyphus heard the music that Orpheus played, and for a while he sat still upon his stone. Ixion, bound to a wheel, stopped its turning for a while; the vultures abandoned their torment of Tityos; the daughters of Danaos ceased to fill their jars; even those dread ones the Erinyes, who bring to the dead the memories of all their crimes and all their faults, had their cheeks wet with tears.

In the throng of the newly-come dead Orpheus saw Eurydice. She looked upon her husband, but she had not the power to come near him. But slowly she came when Hades, the king, called her. Then with joy Orpheus took her hands.

It would be granted them—no mortal ever gained such privilege before—to leave, both together, the World of the Dead, and to abide for another space in the World of the Living. One condition there would be—that on their way up neither Orpheus nor Eurydice should look back.

They went through the gate and came out amongst the watchers that are around the portals. These showed them the path that went up to the World of the Living. That way they went, Orpheus and Eurydice, he going before her.

Up and through the darkened ways they went, Orpheus knowing that Eurydice was behind him, but never looking back upon her. As he went his heart was filled with things to tell her—how the trees were blossoming in the garden she had left; how the water was sparkling in the fountain; how the doors of the house stood open; how they, sitting together, would watch the sunlight on the laurel bushes. All these things were in his heart to tell her who came behind him, silent and unseen.

And now they were nearing the place where the cavern opened on the world of the living. Orpheus looked up towards the light from the sky. Out of the opening of the cavern he went; he saw a white-winged bird fly by. He turned around and cried, "O Eurydice, look upon the world I have won you back to!"

He turned to say this to her. He saw her with her long dark hair and pale face. He held out his arms to clasp her. But in that instant she slipped back into the gloom of the cavern. And all he heard spoken was a single word, "Farewell!" Long, long had it taken Eurydice to climb so far, but in the moment of his turning around she had fallen back to her place amongst the dead. For Orpheus had looked back.

Back through the cavern Orpheus went again. Again he came before the watchers of the gate. But now he was not looked at nor listened to; hopeless, he had to return to the World of the Living.

The birds were his friends now, and the trees and the stones. The birds flew around him and mourned with him; the trees and stones often followed him, moved by the music of his lyre. But a savage band slew Orpheus and threw his severed head and his lyre into the River Hebrus. It is said by the poets that while they floated in midstream the lyre gave out some mournful notes, and the head of Orpheus answered the notes with song.

And now that he was no longer to be counted with the living, Orpheus went down to the World of the Dead, going down straightway. The silent watchers let him pass; he went amongst the dead, and he saw his Eurydice in the throng. Again they were together, Orpheus and Eurydice, and them the Erinyes could not torment with memories of crimes or faults. ∎

The Spirit Chief Names the Animal People

North America: United States/Canada—Okanogan

Humishuma, known also as Mourning Dove, was an Okanogan writer in the early twentieth century. The Okanogan people are from the region around the Columbia River in both Washington State and British Columbia. In her introduction to her Coyote Stories, Humishuma recalls how in the 1890s she and the other children, as well as their busy mothers, would

Source: "The Spirit Chief Names the Animal People" from *Coyote Stories* by Mourning Dove. Caldwell, ID: The Caxton Printers, Ltd., 1933. Reprinted with permission by Caxton Press. pp. 17–26.

look forward to the arrival of the traveling storytellers. The children were thoroughly entertained by the wide range of stories, from histories to why tales to myths, and would not realize that they were also being instructed. The traveling storytellers were men, but the women also told stories in their own homes.

The stories were called "chip-chap-tiqulk," the word used for the Animal People, who were here before any of today's animals and humans; they were the **First People** during mythic time. Coyote's Okanogan name is Sinkalip, and he was the most important of the Animal People. This is how Humishuma

describes him: "Coyote was the most important because, after he was put to work by the Spirit Chief, he
did more than any of the others to make the world a
good place in which to live. There were times, however, when Coyote was not busy for the Spirit Chief.
Then he amused himself by getting into mischief and
stirring up trouble. Frequently he got into trouble himself, and then everybody had a good laugh—everybody but Mole. She was Coyote's wife." (Mourning
Dove, 1933, p. 7). Humishuma encapsulates Coyote's
dual nature. As the Creator's helper he creates the
world as we know it by fighting monsters, stealing fire
for the people, and choosing death for humankind so
that the world may not become unlivable through
overcrowding. But then he forgets his mission and acts
greedy, foolish, even cruel, stirring up trouble wherever he wanders. Throughout the West, but especially
in the Pacific Northwest, Coyote is both a mythic
giant and an ordinary human trickster.

In this story Humishuma also introduces the sacred nature of a religious practice, the use of the **sweat
lodge**. Its construction is prescribed and its spiritual
use continues today among most of the Native American tribes, including those of Central America.

The following story, in which Coyote tries to grab
the best name but misses, has its Iroquoian counterpart from New York State in the Seneca story "How
the Crow Got His Black Clothes" in a collection for
children by Hay-en-doh-nees (Leo Cooper) (1995).

Told by Mourning Dove/Humishuma

Hah-ah' Eel-me'-whem, the great Spirit Chief, called
the Animal People together. They came from all parts
of the world. Then the Spirit Chief told them there was
to be a change, that a new kind of people was coming
to live on the earth.

"All of you *Chip-chap-tiqulk*—Animal People—must
have names," the Spirit Chief said. "Some of you have
names now, some of you haven't. But tomorrow all will
have names that shall be kept by you and your descendants forever. In the morning, as the first light of
day shows in the sky, come to my lodge and choose
your names. The first to come may choose any name
that he or she wants. The next person may take any
other name. That is the way it will go until all the names
are taken. And to each person I will give work to do."

That talk made the Animal People very excited.
Each wanted a proud name and the power to rule some
tribe or some part of the world, and everyone determined to get up early and hurry to the Spirit Chief's
lodge.

Sin-ka-lip'—Coyote—boasted that no one would
be ahead of him. He walked among the people and told
them, that he would be the first. Coyote did not like
his name; he wanted another. Nobody respected his
name, Imitator, but it fitted him. He was called *Sin-
ka-lip'* because he liked to imitate people. He thought
that he could do anything that other persons did,
and he pretended to know everything. He would ask a
question, and when the answer was given he would
say:

"I knew that before. I did not have to be told."

Such smart talk did not make friends for Coyote.
Nor did he make friends by the foolish things he did and
the rude tricks he played on people.

"I shall have my choice of the three biggest
names," he boasted. "Those names are: *Kee-lau-naw*,
the Mountain Person—Grizzly Bear, who will rule the
four-footed people; *Milka-noups*—Eagle, who will rule
the birds, and *En-tee-tee-ueh*, the Good Swimmer—
Salmon. Salmon will be the chief of all the fish that the
New People will use for food."

Coyote's twin brother, Fox, who at the next sun
took the name *Why-ay'-looh*—Soft Fur, laughed. "Do
not be so sure, *Sin-ka-lip'*," said Fox. "Maybe you will
have to keep the name you have. People despise that
name. No one wants it."

"I am tired of that name," Coyote said in an angry
voice. "Let someone else carry it. Let some old person
take it—someone who cannot win in war. I am going to
be a great warrior. My smart brother, I will make you
beg of me when I am called Grizzly Bear, Eagle, or
Salmon."

"Your strong words mean nothing," scoffed Fox.
"Better go to your *sewhool-luh* (tepee) and get some
sleep, or you will not wake up in time to choose any
name."

Coyote stalked off to his tepee. He told himself
that he would not sleep any that night; he would stay
wide awake. He entered the lodge, and his three sons
called as if in one voice:

"*Le-ee'-oo!*" ("Father!")

They were hungry, but Coyote had brought them nothing to eat. Their mother, who after the naming day was known as *Pul'-laqu-whu*—Mole, the Mound Digger—sat on her foot at one side of the doorway. Mole was a good woman, always loyal to her husband in spite of his mean ways, his mischief-making, and his foolishness. She never was jealous, never talked back, never replied to his words of abuse. She looked up and said:

"Have you no food for the children? They are starving. I can find no roots to dig."

"*Eh-ha!*" Coyote grunted. "I am no common person to be addressed in that manner. I am going to be a great chief tomorrow. Did you know that? I will have a new name. I will be Grizzly Bear. Then I can devour my enemies with ease. And I shall need you no longer. You are growing too old and homely to be the wife of a great warrior and chief."

Mole said nothing. She turned to her corner of the lodge and collected a few old bones, which she put into a *klek'-chin* (cooking basket). With two sticks she lifted hot stones from the fire and dropped them into the basket. Soon the water boiled, and there was weak soup for the hungry children.

"Gather plenty of wood for the fire," Coyote ordered. "I am going to sit up all night."

Mole obeyed. Then she and the children went to bed.

Coyote sat watching the fire. Half of the night passed. He got sleepy. His eyes grew heavy. So he picked up two little sticks and braced his eyelids apart. "Now I can stay awake," he thought, but before long he was fast asleep, although his eyes were wide open.

The sun was high in the sky when Coyote awoke. But for Mole he would not have wakened then. Mole called him. She called him after she returned with her name from the Spirit Chief's lodge. Mole loved her husband. She did not want him to have a big name and be a powerful chief. For then, she feared, he would leave her. That was why she did not arouse him at daybreak. Of this she said nothing.

Only half-awake and thinking it was early morning, Coyote jumped at the sound of Mole's voice and ran to the lodge of the Spirit Chief. None of the other *Chip-chap-tiqulk* were there. Coyote laughed. Blinking his sleepy eyes, he walked into the lodge. "I am going to be *Kee-lau-naw*," he announced in a strong voice. "That shall be my name."

"The name Grizzly Bear was taken at dawn," the Spirit Chief answered.

"Then I shall be *Milka-noups*," said Coyote, and his voice was not so loud.

"Eagle flew away at sunup," the other replied.

"Well, then I shall be called *En-tee-tee-ueh*," Coyote said in a voice that was not loud at all.

"The name Salmon also has been taken," explained the Spirit Chief. "All the names except your own have been taken. No one wished to steal your name."

Poor Coyote's knees grew weak. He sank down beside the fire that blazed in the great tepee, and the heart of *Hah-ah' Eel-me'-whem* was touched.

"*Sin-ka-lip'*," said that Person, "you must keep your name. It is a good name for you. You slept long because I wanted you to be the last one here. I have important work for you, much for you to do before the New People come. You are to be chief of all the tribes."

"Many bad creatures inhabit the earth. They bother and kill people, and the tribes cannot increase as I wish. These *En-alt-na Skil-ten*—People-Devouring Monsters—cannot keep on like that. They must be stopped. It is for you to conquer them. For doing that, for all the good things you do, you will be honored and praised by the people that are here now and that come afterward. But, for the foolish and mean things that you do, you will be laughed at and despised. That you cannot help. It is your way."

"To make your work easier, I give you *squas-tenk'*. It is your own special magic power. No one else ever shall have it. When you are in danger, whenever you need help, call to your power. It will do much for you, and with it you can change yourself into any form, into anything you wish.

"To your twin brother, *Why-ay'-looh*, and to others I have given *shoo'-mesh*. It is strong power. With that power Fox can restore your life should you be killed. Your bones may be scattered but, if there is one hair of your body left, Fox can make you live again. Others of the people can do the same with their *shoo'-mesh*. Now, go, *Sink-ka-lip'*! Do well the work laid for your trail!"

Well, Coyote was a chief after all, and he felt good again. After that day his eyes were different. They grew slant from being propped open that night while he sat by his fire. The New People, the Indians, got the slightly slant eyes from Coyote.

After Coyote had gone, the Spirit Chief thought it would be nice for the Animal People and the coming New People to have the benefit of the spiritual sweat-house. But all of the Animal People had names, and there was no one to take the name of the Sweat-House—*Quil'-sten,* the Warmer. So the wife of the Spirit Chief took the name. She wanted the people to have the sweat-house, for she pitied them. She wanted them to have a place to go to purify themselves, a place where they could pray for strength and good luck and strong medicine-power, and where they could fight sickness and get relief from their troubles.

The ribs, the frame poles, of the sweat-house represent the wife of *Hah-ah' Eel-me'-whem.* As she is a spirit, she cannot be seen, but she always is near. Songs to her are sung by the present generation. She hears them. She hears what her people say, and in her heart there is love and pity. ■

The Theft of Fire

North America: United States—Hitchiti

Fire, as a symbol of the sun, was the most sacred element in the southeastern United States, where the Hitchiti, a tribe related to the Creeks or Muskogee, lived before the Indian removals during the early nineteenth century from the Southeast to Oklahoma (Brown and Owens, 1985; Philip, 2001). Each year at the first harvest, according to Creek (Muskogee) poet and writer Louis Littlecoon Oliver (1990), all fires were extinguished and then relit using prescribed rituals. All other fires had to be lit from the sacred fire. A Master of Fire was named, and he was responsible for building and lighting the fire correctly. He drew a sacred circle around the fire, and if anyone accidentally stepped over the line, the fire had to be extinguished and relit. The stories of the Creeks, Hitchiti, and several other southeastern tribes were collected in Oklahoma between 1908 and 1914 by John R. Swanton (1929).

In this version the Southeastern Indians' trickster figure, Rabbit, steals fire for all the people. Previously, it had been held by the First People, whose extraordinary power becomes apparent when they make it rain

Source: "The Theft of Fire" from *Myths and Tales of the Southeastern Indians* by John R. Swanton. Washington, DC: United States Government Printing Office, 1929 [Smithsonian Institution Bureau of American Ethnology Bulletin 88]. pp. 102–103.

to put out the fire Rabbit had stolen. In other versions of the story throughout North America, culture heroes specific to the region accomplish the same feat. Often it isn't fire but light that has to be stolen.

Rabbit ran away with the fire and scattered it. At that time people were forbidden to build a fire except at the Big Harvest Ceremonial dance. Rabbit knew there was to be a dance and thought, "Why shouldn't we have fire whenever we need it? I will run away with some fire." He considered the matter and decided how he would do it. He had his head rubbed with pine tar so as to make his hair stand up. Then he set out. When he arrived at the dance ground a great number of people were already gathered there. While Rabbit was sitting about and the people were dancing, they said that he must lead the next dance. Rabbit got up and danced ahead of them in a circle around the fire. As he danced the people followed him and Rabbit started singing. When everyone was dancing very hard, Rabbit circled closer to the fire and bent his head as if he were going to take hold of the fire. The people said, "When he is leading Rabbit always acts that way." He kept on bending toward the fire as he continued to circle just outside the sacred line. Presently he poked his head into the fire and ran off with his head ablaze, while the people shouted, "Hulloa, catch him, throw him down!"

They shouted at Rabbit as he ran away, and they chased him, but he disappeared. Then the guardians of the fire made it rain and it continued to rain for a long time. On the fourth day they said the rain must have put the fire out. So it stopped raining and the sun shone and the weather was fine. But Rabbit had built a fire in a hollow tree and stayed there while it rained, and when the sun shone he came out and set new fires. Rain came again and put the fires all out, but the fires could not be stopped entirely. Then everyone began to take fire and they ran off with it. Rain kept on putting the fires out at intervals but each time it stopped raining all the people distributed the fire again. When the rain ended fire was established for good. This is the way it is told. Therefore, they say that Rabbit distributed fire to all people. ■

The Origin of the Caduveo

Native South American and North American myths seldom follow similar patterns or include the same supernatural beings. The trickster creator who interferes with or completes the work of the chief Creator, however, appears on both continents. Like Coyote in North America, Caracara, a kind of hawk, is responsible for the human condition as we know it; death, hard work, the kinds of trees and other plants that we encounter today replaced the ideal world that the kind Creator Onoenrgodi had in mind.

The Caduveo, from whom this myth was collected in 1950, are among the formerly nomadic peoples of the Gran Chaco region of the western plains of Brazil, near the Paraguayan border. In a variant of this myth Caracara justifies his insisting that people work hard by saying, "It isn't good [that old clothing should be automatically renewed by the creator]: that way a lazy man won't work, and neither will his wife have anything to do. When a piece of clothing is old and worn-out, [the creator should] keep it like that so that the people will have the spirit to work and buy new clothes" (Wilbert and Simoneau, 1989, pp. 37–38). Of course not all people work hard; the storyteller said he had seen people riding the railway line who had no spirit to work and consequently had no clothes, but because of Caracara's advice most people do work hard. The storyteller thus found relevance in the myth for contemporary life. The recency of the following variant of the myth is apparent by the attempt it makes to account for the political status of the Caduveo relative to other peoples in historic times.

The ancestor went to steal fish from the Creator's stream. After he had gone five times to steal, Onoenrgodi [the creator] went to count his fish and noticed that some were missing. He also found footprints but did not know who had made them. Onoenrgodi asked: "What Indians have stolen my fish?" Since he did not know, he said to a white heron: "My brother, watch my fish for me." When the sun went down the heron fell asleep. In the morning he said to Onoenrgodi: "I went to sleep too early and did not see anything." Onoenrgodi then let the chaja bird watch. The sun went down, and the chaja continued to call, but when Venus went down, the chaja slept. The next morning he said to Onoenrgodi: "I fell asleep too soon and did not see anything."

Onoenrgodi then called upon the *carão* ibis: "My brother, watch my fish carefully for me." "I'll watch all night." "That's good, my brother." Carão did not sleep;

Source: "The Origin of the Caduveo" in *Folk Literature of the Caduveo Indians,* edited by Johannes Wilbert and Karin Simoneau. Los Angeles: UCLA Latin American Center Publications, 1989. pp. 23–24. Reprinted with permission from The Regents of the University of California.

he called throughout the night. As dawn was approaching the ancestor became hungry and went to steal fish. Carão followed him to the great hole, Rgobegi. In the morning when Onoenrgodi came, Carão said to him: "I saw Indians who are living in the hole steal fish." The following day the god put on his moccasins and called his two dogs; they followed the tracks and found the hole. The ancestor beat the dogs. Onoenrgodi said: "My poor dogs, who beat them?" But he saw nothing. The hole was covered with a big clay pot. When he removed the pot he saw many human faces in the hole. He pulled out all the people. The first one was a Paraguayan. Then came the Portuguese, Guana, Tereno, Sarapana, and all the other Indians.

Onoenrgodi divided up the earth among all these people. To the Paraguayans and the Portuguese he gave houses, cattle, and arms. The Tereno got maize, manioc, and the like, and the other Indians were given bows, arrows, and the hunt. The effort made Onoenrgodi tired. Then the caracara bird came and said: "Master, you haven't thought of the Caduveo at all." Onoenrgodi replied: "That's true; I didn't think of 'my people' at all, but perhaps there are still some left." He returned to the large hole and looked into it. Two men and two women were still there. The men were called Otigitrgedi and Ecenua; the women, Takonrgedi and Nuanorgodo. Onoenrgodi pulled them out of the hole. There were only those four; that is why there are so few Caduveo. Onoenrgodi went to Caracara and said: "There are only four Caduveo and there's no land left for them, but when they die I'll let them revive again." Caracara answered: "No, why should they revive? Let them fight with other Indians instead and steal their land, women, and children." That is why the dead do not come back to life, and that is why the Caduveo steal and have the right to make other tribes their slaves.

But the Caduveo were hungry, and they cried. Onoenrgodi said to Caracara: "I'll prepare some food for them." Caracara replied: "Why? They should hunt and gather honey."

According to another legend Onoenrgodi let cotton cloth grow on trees, but on the advice of Caracara he tore it up and threw it on the shrubs. That is how the cotton plant started. The god said: "When they have no more clothes left I'll make them new ones." But Caracara said again: "No, don't. They have cotton and can spin and weave; they can make snares and dress with animal furs." Those poor people! There were only four of them and they had to work so hard. The god wanted to make everything all right for the Caduveo but Caracara would not allow him to do so. The god feared Caracara.

[Onoenrgodi feared Caracara because the latter wanted to eat him while he was asleep. Caracara (hawk) really eats human flesh. Onoenrgodi preferred to make friends with him and they became companions, but he still feared Caracara.] ■

Informant: Akárge
Source: Friç 1912, pp. 397–399.

The Obtaining of Fire

South America: Brazil—Gé Indian

The obtaining of fire is a universal theme with a wide range of explanations found among different cultures.

Source: "The Obtaining of Fire" in *Folk Literature of the Gé Indians*, edited by Johannes Wilbert and Karin Simoneau. Los Angeles: UCLA Latin American Center Publications, 1978. pp. 160–163. Reprinted with permission from The Regents of the University of California.

The Gé account has some features that uniquely reflect their society. According to John Bierhorst (1988), the Gé of Central Brazil live in strictly ordered villages with carefully prescribed rules for social interaction, especially among in-laws. Politeness is paramount. Thus a story in which a man abandons his brother-in-law or mistreats a guest describes behaviors that contradict the standards of the society and are likely, according to Bierhorst, to serve as a source of amusement by revealing tensions that are normally not acknowledged. Pud and Pudleré, mentioned only at the beginning of the story as the original owners of fire, are Sun and Moon, who recur as personified creators, companions, and adversaries in a great many of the Gé myths. Sun and Moon have many adventures on the earth and set up Gé society but eventually ascend to the sky and leave their children, the Gé (Wilbert and Simoneau, 1978). The characterization of the Jaguar as both benevolent (husband) and dangerous (wife) to the hero recurs widely in South America, although the roles of the husband and wife are often reversed.

In the beginning there were just Pud and Pudleré. Pudleré had fire, and so did Pud. But they didn't give their children the fire. So when they left the village to hunt, the children couldn't cook the meat of the animals they had killed. They just baked it in the sun. They put the meat in the sun to dry, and thus it was raw when they ate it. When Pud went up to the sky there wasn't anything more to eat. He left the children hungry, without manioc or corn. They didn't have these foods. The children of Pud and Pudleré had only *puba* wood [an inedible wood] to eat and raw meat when they killed animals.

Things went on in this way until a young man married and had a son like mine (the son of the narrator was ten years old). There was a macaw nest high on the vertical side of a rock, and his brother-in-law said to him: "Let's go and get that macaw. I'll put up a tree trunk and you climb up and get it." He put the trunk in place for the young man, who then climbed up. The brother-in-law overturned the pole. The young man had to stay up on the rock, and he cried and cried while his brother-in-law went back to the village. When the brother-in-law got back, his wife asked: "Where is my brother?" He said: "I don't know. I think he stayed in a hole high up on a rock."

The young man on the rock was crying and shouting: "Let me down!" The macaws were very fearful of him, but after two days went by they got used to him. Their droppings were falling on him and his head was full of vermin. He was very hungry, and he became weak from lack of food. His sister was looking for him but couldn't find him. A jaguar coming along the edge of the rock passed by the hole where the young man

was sitting, and he stuck his head out to look at the animal. The jaguar saw the man's shadow, jumped at it, and caught it. He was holding it, but the man pulled his head back into the hole. Then he stuck his head out again, and again the animal jumped on the shadow but didn't catch anything. When the head came out again, the jaguar looked up and saw the young man sitting up there. The jaguar said: "Come on, nephew, get down!" The man said: "No, I won't; you'll eat me." But the jaguar said: "No, I won't eat you. I'm your uncle." The [young] man said: "No, no, I can't come down, or you'll eat me." The jaguar said: "You can jump down; I'll catch you. You won't fall!" The man jumped, and the jaguar caught him and took him away. "Let's go to my house. Now I'm your uncle, and you are my nephew. Let's go now, because you are hungry. I'll feed you and I'll get rid of all the vermin on your head."

The jaguar took the young man with him. When they arrived at the jaguar's house, the man saw the jaguar's fire. (In those days only Pud and Pudleré had fire; when they left their children, they didn't leave fire.) The jaguar took the man into his house. On the table there was a lot of monkey and deer meat. The first thing the jaguar did was to wash and clean the man's head. Then he gave the man meat and *beiju*. They ate together.

The jaguar spoke to his wife, who was pregnant and had a big stomach. Her husband was giving her advice: "Look, our nephew is here. Don't do anything to scare him! I'm going hunting again." After he left to go hunting, his wife began to scare the young man. When she showed him her claws and teeth, he began to cry with fear. But she said: "Don't cry; I'm just playing with you. I'm not going to eat you!" Then the man left and went to look for the jaguar in the woods shouting, "Oh, *ketí!*" [uncle]. The jaguar answered and soon came back to where the man was. He asked: "What is it?" The man said: "Your wife frightened me!" The jaguar said: "Let's go, then, let's go. I'm going to tell her off. I won't go hunting."

When they got back to the house, the jaguar said to his wife: "Didn't I tell you not to scare our nephew? If you do it again, I'm going to make a little bow for him, and he'll shoot you in the paw if you show your claw." When it was morning, he said: "Now, young man, stay here, but don't be afraid. I'm going out to hunt." After he left, he heard the man shouting again: "Ailálá!" Then the husband (the jaguar) returned. The man had left the house and was crying in fear. The jaguar found him in the middle of the road, saying: "She's going to eat me! She showed her teeth and her claws again!" Then the jaguar told the man: "If she frightens you again I'm going to make a little bow for you." He made the bow and gave it to the man. He also made arrows. Then he said: "Here are the bow and arrows. If she frightens you again, you must shoot her!"

In the morning he said to his wife: "Don't keep scaring our nephew. I have already told you how to treat him." After thus warning her, he again left to go hunting. But soon he heard a shout of fear (the narrator imitated the man's shout). The man picked up his bow and ran into the woods after the jaguar. The female jaguar stayed at home. The male jaguar returned and saw the man sitting on the road. The young man said: "She almost ate me!" The jaguar, becoming impatient, said: "Go back there. I want to go hunting, and I'm not going home again! If she scares you, shoot her, as I told you before. Look, I'll show you how. Stay near this road, which goes to the village. If you shoot her, you can run there, because I'm going to the woods to hunt!"

So the man returned to the jaguar's house, and the latter's wife asked: "Where is my husband?" The man said: "I don't know. I turned around and came back, so I didn't see where he went." As the man sat there with his little bow and his arrows, the female came close to him and sat down. She said: "Look here, nephew!" She opened her claws and bared her teeth, and the young man cried. He put the end of the arrow on the bowstring. She was sitting beside him. When she showed her claws again, he shot her in the paw and ran. The female, bellowing loudly, ran after him, but she couldn't run very well with her paw wounded.

She yelled at him: "Oh, you devil, I could have made a meal out of you!"

The man ran along the road until he got to the village. When he arrived, he told the people about the fire the jaguars had: "Over there, there is a jaguar's fire." The old Indians said: "You know now where the fire is. Let's go, let's go to bring it home." All the Indians went along. They spread out as they walked until they came near the jaguar's house. They chose someone to carry the fire away with them. An old Indian said: "We need a good runner; you, come here! You go ahead of us and get the fire. Go into the house, and the rest of us will stay here in the middle of the road, waiting for you." The chosen one slowly approached the house. The female was lying down with her big stomach, crying because of her sore paw. Her husband, who had arrived earlier, asked her; "Where is my nephew?" "He wounded me in the paw and left." The jaguar said to his wife: "I told you not to bother our nephew!" Again he left the house, saying to his wife: "Well, I'm going to be out late."

By that time the Indians were already very close to the house, and after the jaguar left they came a little closer. Then the fast runner entered the house and picked up a firebrand. He put it over his shoulder and ran away with it. He carried it, another carried it, another got tired, and then another took it, then another tried, and another took it, until finally the fire reached the village. As the fire was carried into the village, each householder broke off an ember and took it home to make a fire. Thus they no longer had to eat raw meat. They have fire now because of the jaguar. If it wasn't for him, we would still be eating raw meat. ■

Source: Schultz 1950, pp. 72–74. (Craho)

The Theft of Fire

Maui, half god and half man, is a trickster and culture hero throughout the Polynesian Islands, from New Zealand to Hawaii. His parents' names and the number of his siblings vary from place to place, but he is celebrated, by the same name, with only slight variations, wherever the ancient Polynesian explorers sailed and settled. More man than god, in Hawaii he was said to be the ancestor of King Kamehameha, who united the Hawaiian islands. He was always mischievous and up to so many tricks that his brothers (or uncles) were often glad to get away from him, as they did one early morning when they thought they would have a quiet morning of fishing without him, only to discover that Maui had stowed away. Before they knew it, Maui had spread out the ocean, and they found themselves in the open far from their familiar bay. Maui set to work fishing with his magic fishhook made of his grandfather's jawbone and soon caught the gable of the palace that belonged to the son of the sea god. His brothers helped him haul up the catch, which turned out to be an entire island complete with mountains, rivers, fields, and birds. While Maui was appeasing the sea god's son, the brothers began to fight over the riches and ended up hacking deep gashes in the land. The island is New Zealand's South Island with its deep gorges and mountain precipices. Later they also hauled up the rest of New Zealand: North Island and Stewart Island (Reed, 1974).

Maui continued his island fishing ways throughout the South Pacific, his route perhaps representing the island discoveries of the ancient Polynesians. When Maui hauled up the Hawaiian islands, one of which was named after him, the islands, like fish, kept getting away until Hina (variously represented as his sister or wife in different countries of Oceania) tied them together (Reed, 1974).

Maui is much like trickster culture heroes elsewhere, such as Raven, Coyote, Nanaboozoo, and Great Hare among different Native North American tribes and Prometheus in ancient Greece. He made life on the earth more comfortable and civilized for humans through his interventions and inventions: He slowed down the sun in Hawaii so that the days became long enough for people to finish their daily work; he invented more effective hunting spears, fishing hooks, fish nets, and eel traps (he learned about barbed hunting spears from his mother); he developed a de-

sign that became part of the sunrise and sunset; and he brought fire to the world, as he did in the following story from Tonga (an island kingdom approximately 3000 miles southwest of Hawaii) (Reed, 1974). The role of grandparents seems important in the stories of Maui. Grandfather furnishes Maui with fire in this story. In the Hawaiian story of how Maui slowed down the sun, it was his grandmother who supplied him with a magic club and told him what to do. In traditional societies the role of grandparents in passing on technical and cultural knowledge was invaluable.

Amongst his many other feats of strength and dexterity, Maui can claim to be the Prometheus of the Pacific. There are many versions of how he conferred the gift of fire on mankind. In Tonga the demi-god is regarded as the son of the youngest of four Maui brothers who lived in the underworld. Maui-atalanga, the father, was of an adventurous disposition and grew tired of the gloomy life of the netherworld.

"Come," he said to Maui-kijikiji, his son, "we will leave this place and make a home in the world of light."

His brothers overheard him and made a great outcry. "You cannot leave us," they said. "If you go, who will attend our plantations? Let Maui-kijikiji go. We'll gladly spare him, for he's nothing but a mischief maker. We'll be glad to see the last of him."

"Calm down," Maui-atalanga said. "I promise to return from time to time and keep the plantation weeded and in good order. As for my son, I'll leave him up there. He won't trouble you any more."

It was a convincing argument, for his brothers were heartily sick of their precocious nephew.

The two Mauis, father and son, reveled in the freedom of the world under the great inverted bowl of the sky, and took up their abode at Vavau. From time to time Maui-atalanga quietly disappeared to fulfill his promise of working in the plantations of the underworld. Maui-kijikiji was mystified by these disappearances. He was young when his father took him to Vavau, and had no recollection of life with his uncles.

A mystery was meat and drink to young Maui. He kept a close watch. The next time his father left home he followed him stealthily and saw him disappear into a hole in the ground. Groping his way through tunnels of darkness, he was surprised to find himself in a land

Source: "The Theft of Fire" from *Myths and Legends of Polynesia* by Alexander W. Reed. Illustrated by Roger Hart. Wellington, New Zealand: A. H. & A. W. Reed, 1974. Reprinted with permission by Reed Publishing. pp. 55–59.

strangely like the one he had left, where colours were muted and there was no sound except wind in the stunted trees. He climbed into a nonu tree and saw his father bending over a digging implement. Presently he plucked a fruit from the tree, sank his teeth into it, and threw what was left at his father. Maui-atalanga looked round, but could see no one. He bent to his work again. Feeling the impact of another fragment of fruit, he picked it up and compared it with the first one. The teeth marks corresponded.

"Where are you, you rascal?" he called.

"Here, father," the young man replied.

"Oh dear," Maui-atalanga exclaimed. "I never thought you'd find the way here. But seeing you are here, I might as well make use of you. See that patch of weeds? I want you to pull them out, but whatever you do, don't look behind you."

"Why not?"

"Never mind why not. Do as you're told."

His father's warning served to stimulate Maui-kijik-iji's curiosity. He kept glancing over his shoulder, with disastrous results. Each time he did so a fresh crop of weeds sprang up. It happened so often that in exasperation Maui-atalanga sent him away to light a fire.

"Fire?" exclaimed Maui-kijikiji. "What is fire?"

"Never mind what it is. Go to your grandfather Maui-motua and ask him to give you some."

Maui-kijikiji went to the old man's home and was given a burning branch. He was fascinated by the red and yellow fire and the black smoke. He swung it round his head, and dropped it into a pool of water to see what would happen.

"Sorry, grandfather," he said. "The fire went out."

"Be more careful this time," the old man grumbled. "I've only got two burning logs left."

As soon as he was out of sight Maui-kijikiji rolled the log along the ground, clapping his hands as tufts of grass caught alight. Before long the burning log was a blackened smoking billet of wood.

"Sorry, grandfather," Maui-kijikiji said again as he returned for yet another gift of fire. "Let me have that one," pointing to a huge casuarina log that was blazing in the open fireplace.

Grandfather Maui-motua held his sides to stop his belly shaking with laughter. "If you can carry that away with you, young Maui, you're welcome to it."

To his surprise his grandson lifted it with one hand and walked away with it. This time he carried it carefully, nursing the flame, and held it out to his father.

"It's a peculiar thing," he said wonderingly. "It looks as though it's alive but it's really dead. I don't understand it. The fire must be the part that comes and goes. When it's gone it never comes back."

"Put it down, Maui. Why have you taken so long?"

"There was a reason for that, Father. The fire kept going out. I had to go back for more."

"I see," his father said impatiently. "Now I'll show you how to use fire."

He impaled a plucked bird on a pointed stick and roasted it in the flames.

"Wonderful," his son exclaimed as he sank his teeth into the succulent flesh, with the fat running down his chin. "We must take fire back with us to Vavau. I've never tasted food like this before."

"We'll do nothing of the sort," his father said sharply. "Fire is something that belongs to this world, not to the one where we live. You've no idea how much harm might come from it. It's all right when tamed, but when it gets out of control, it could set the whole island on fire. We'll return home before you get into further mischief. You lead the way."

"No, you go first."

Maui-atalanga looked at him suspiciously. "Why? Oh well, I'll lead the way, but mind you behave yourself."

As soon as his father's back was turned Maui-kijikiji snatched a small branch that had burst into flame and hid it under his garment.

They climbed upwards through the dark tunnel.

"What's that light flickering on the walls?" Maui-atalanga exclaimed.

"It's the light from the underworld, father."

Presently the light from the overworld began to penetrate the gloom.

"Something's burning!" Maui-atalanga said. "What are you doing, Maui?"

"You're imagining things," the young man said, laughing. "Perhaps it's the smell of the food we ate down below."

Maui-atalanga was still suspicious. He hid in a clump of bushes. As his son went past he saw a wisp of smoke coming from under his loin-cloth. What he had feared had come to pass. Fire had come to the world of men, fire that would change their way of life, fire that would keep men and women warm at night, fire that would cook their food, fire that could escape from the cooking-sheds and set the whole world alight. He called on the gods to send rain. The clouds disgorged their contents on the island.

Maui-kijikiji threw the burning brand into the trees. "Flee!" he shouted at it. "Flee to the shelter of the trees, to the coconut tree, the breadfruit tree, the hibiscus—go to every tree you can find."

And the fire went—lying latent in the timber, to be brought to life at the touch of the fire drill and the rubbing stick. ∎

Web Supplement Stories

Web supplement stories are located at www.ablongman.com/lechner.

Divine Beings and Their Realms

Isis and Osiris

Africa: Egypt

The ancient Egyptian pantheon was envisioned as an elaborate hierarchy. Most important among the gods was Ra, the god of the sun, later named Amen-Ra. The other important gods representing the forces of nature were Khnemu, the spirit of the life-giving Nile; Nut, the sky god and in some versions the mother of Ra; Geb, the earth god; Isis, the principle of life and reproduction; and her husband Osiris, god of the dead and the rebirth of new life (crops). Osiris acted as judge in the afterlife, and it was said that he would one day return from the land of the dead, or Duat, to be the eternal Pharaoh. Seth, the brother of Isis and Osiris, represented evil in some eras but was associated with the pharaohs under Ramses II through Ramses IV, 1279–1150 B.C.E. (Green, 1968).

While Osiris is depicted as culture giver for the Egyptians and the rest of the Mediterranean world, Isis is depicted as the queen and mother in charge at home. She persuaded men of the virtues of marriage and taught women spinning. She raised the royal baby Horus, who is depicted with a hawk's head. One of the dominant images of Isis was that of the mother nursing the baby god, wearing a blue robe. The crescent moon and the star of the sea were her symbols. By the Greco-Roman era, from the first century B.C.E.

through the early years of the Common Era, she had become the most powerful and most widely worshiped goddess in Egypt and was honored by the Greeks and Romans as well. She was a fertility goddess in some places, was thought to have great magical powers, was invoked to aid the sick, and was seen as protector of seafarers and of the dead (*Encyclopedia Britannica 2000,* CD-ROM). The cult of Isis was spread through the Roman empire; a temple to Isis has been found as far north and east as today's Hungary. Her symbols of the star, the crescent moon, and the blue robe later became associated with the Virgin Mary and can be seen in church sculptures in Italy and in folktales such as "La Estrellita" ("Little Star"), a New Mexican Cinderella tale that is included in this anthology (Powell, 1998).

Astarte, who appears in the story "Isis and Osiris," was a foreign deity from Mesopotamia who was introduced as a result of conquests in Syria under Tutmose III in the fifteenth century B.C.E. and subsequent pharaohs for several hundred years (Green, 1968). The similarity between the Greek goddess Demeter's attempt to make Demophon immortal (one incident in her search for her daughter Persephone) and Isis's attempt to make Diktys immortal is an indication of the international nature of some of the myths. For a comparison see "Demeter" in this anthology.

The pharaoh, at the apex of the human world, was also the connection to the divine world. Although some of the surviving texts from tombs and temples suggest that the pharaohs were not really thought of as gods throughout the entire history of ancient Egypt, pharaohs went to great pains to establish their divinity, and the priests gave them elaborate instructions and maps for joining Ra, the sun and lord of the gods. The reign of Akhenaton (about 1350 B.C.E.), who decreed that there was only one god, the god of the sun, represented a brief departure from the ancient Egyptian belief, professed through 3000 years, that each god had his or her own function in governing the lives of humans (Green, 1968). Each reigning pharaoh identified with Horus, and each pharaoh's dead father represented Osiris (Powell, 1998).

The story of Isis and Osiris comes down to modern times through the writings of Plutarch, a first century C.E. Roman writer, but its details have also been pieced together from hieroglyphic inscriptions and from wall paintings in the pyramids, tombs, and temples of the early pharaohs (Green, 1968).

From: *Tales of Ancient Egypt* (1968) by Roger Lancelyn Green published by Bodley Head. Used by permission of Random House Group Limited. pp. 21–36.

Origin and Creation Myths

Echo and Narcissus

Europe: Greece

The Greeks and Romans were among the early monogamous societies. The men, however, seemed to revel in stories of Zeus' (Jupiter's) adulterous escapades with goddesses as well as humans and enjoyed tales of the jealousies of his wife, Hera (Juno).

As a myth of warning, this story cautions against excesses of several kinds: meddling, talking too much, and too much self-love. Edith Hamilton, whose *Mythology* (1942) is widely read in high schools and colleges, points out, however, that the myth of the narcissus flower, as well as other Greek myths in which a youth dies and is reborn as a beautiful flower (Adonis: anemone, Hyacinthus: Hyacinth) might have been an allegorical reference to human sacrifice. This was common practice in animistic societies, which believed that the earth's spirit must be replenished by

blood in order to bring forth new life. By the time of Homer (700 B.C.E.) the practice of human sacrifice had ended (Powell, 1998), but myths continued to be told long after the original meanings of the stories were lost to memory. In its present version, as told by Ovid, the beautiful image of the origins of the echo and the narcissus, as well as the universal themes of the sorrows of unrequited love and the dangers of excessive self-love, has appealed to numerous poets throughout the centuries and remains appealing to young people today.

From: *Outline of Mythology: The Age of Fable, The Age of Chivalry, Legends of Charlemagne* by Thomas Bulfinch. New York: Review of Reviews Company, 1913. pp. 101–103.

The Creation or Age of Beginning

North America: United States—Navajo/Diné

The emergence myth of the Diné [Dee-nay], as the Navajo call themselves, represents an agricultural vision of origins, with the first sacred beings emerging from the earth. The origin myth names the four sacred colors and the four sacred directions: east (white), south (blue), west (yellow), and north (black), and it establishes the customs and the traditional home of the Diné, which encompasses southwestern Colorado, northwestern New Mexico, and northeastern Arizona.

The first beings, also referred to as **First People**, were not like those that inhabit the earth today but were spirits. First Man and First Woman were sacred beings and did not stay on earth once Changing Woman, the daughter of Earth and Sky, perhaps symbolic of the changing earth, created the humans and animals that populate today's world. It was Changing Woman who taught the ancestors of the Navajos their most important prayer chants and the Blessingway ceremony. It was also Changing Woman, referred to in this version as White Shell Girl, who taught the Navajos most of the rules of living in harmony and balance with nature, with each other, and within themselves (Wyman, 1970).

There are several versions of the Navajo emergence myth, and depending on the tradition followed, the present world may be the fourth or the fifth world.

The first creative forces responsible for the multitudinous life on earth may also differ, with a being named Begochidi representing the creative force in some versions, while here it is First Man and First Woman and the union of the sexes that represents the creative force. Coyote's dual nature as creative force and as spoiler is represented by two coyotes, Coyote-Who-Was-Formed-in-an-Egg and coyote who was called "First Angry" (Levy, 1998).

The version Aileen O'Bryan recorded was told by Sandoval [Hostiin Tlo'tsi hee], who had heard it from his grandmother (O'Bryan, 1953). He also gave accounts of the myths to other collectors. O'Bryan recorded the myth verbatim, and as a result there were a number of repetitions that I have eliminated. Also, in the interest of keeping the myth shorter, two of the incidents were abbreviated: First Man and First Woman's seeking each other by sighting each other's fires across the distance and the elaborate description of the quarrel between the men and the women and their attempts to live apart, which highlights the fact that males and females need and complement each other for a balanced world. Joseph Bruchac retells the Navajo emergence myth in a more accessible format for children in *Keepers of the Earth: Native American Stories* and *Environmental Activities for Children* (Caduto and Bruchac, 1989). This version provides a more direct account of the emergence into the fourth (not fifth) world, it does not emphasize the sexual tension between males and females among the First People, and the creative force is represented by Begochidi instead of Coyote.

After the people emerged the world still had to be organized. Changing Woman taught the people how to build and how to live, but many land features still had to be created.

From: *The Diné: Origin Myths of the Navaho Indian* by Aileen O'Bryan. Smithsonian Institution Bureau of American Ethnology. Bulletin no. 163. U.S. Government Printing Office, 1956. pp. 1–13.

Ga-do-wa as, His Star Belt, the Milky Way

North America: United States—Iroquois/Haudenosaunee

The Iroquois, according to Arthur Parker (1908), believe that when a person dies, his or her soul takes a path along the "great sky road" (i.e., the Milky Way) and that each soul is guided by its own star. Good souls take a different path from evil souls. Some Great Plains tribes such as the Lakota Sioux too believe that the Milky Way is the path of dead souls (Leeming and Page, 1997). Paula Giese, critic and author of "Native American Indian Resources" (1996), suggested that one meaning of the story of *The Rough Face Girl* by Rafe Martin, in which the Cinderella-like youngest daughter was alone in being able to see the Invisible Chief, was that she had actually found the heavenly path, meaning that she died, when she married the Invisible Chief whose bow was the Milky Way. Giese's point was that this story is an amalgam of the Native American myth and the European "Cinderella" folktale and should not be taken as a variant of the familiar folktale with its happy ending. Stith Thompson, coauthor of the Aarne-Thompson *Types of the Folktale* (Aarne, 1961), and specialist in Native American folktales, considered the Cinderella type (AT 510A) found among Native Americans to be European influenced. It is likely that Native Americans, having heard Cinderella variants from French, English, and Spanish immigrants, developed them into new stories with new meanings for the tellers. Not all the versions involve the Milky Way. In the Southwest, for instance, a Cinderella-type story, "The Turkey Girl," seems to be an etiological tale about why turkeys now live apart from humans and a warning to keep one's promises.

From: *Myths and Legends of the New York State Iroquois* by Harriet M. Converse and Arthur Caswell Parker. Albany, NY: New York State Museum, 1908. Museum Bulletin 125. pp. 56–57.

▣ Origins of Animals, Humans, etc.

Cupid and Psyche

Europe: Greco-Roman

Though probably part of an older Greek oral tradition, the popular European story of a beautiful girl marrying a "beast," discovering his inner beauty, losing him for lack of trust or by thoughtlessness, and regaining him through a long and arduous quest had its first written appearance in the Latin novel *The Golden*

Ass, written by Apuleius, a Hellenistic philosopher who lived in North Africa during the second century C.E. The story was intended as an allegory of the longing of the Soul (Psyche) to unite with Desire (Cupid/Eros) and the hardships that must be overcome to attain this union, which we call true love. To underscores the allegorical nature of the story, Apuleius names Venus' servants Convention, Worry, and Gloom, and it is they who cause Psyche to almost give up at each obstacle (Powell, 1998). But it is not necessary to use these devices of allegory for the story to have as much meaning for modern audiences as it did for those of ancient Greece or Rome.

From: *Old Greek Folk Stories Told Anew* by Josephine P. Peabody. London: George Harrap, 1910. pp. 89–103.

Icarus and Daedalus

Europe: Greece

Daedalus' feat of human flight is now taken for granted, but the human desire to achieve greater and greater heights still seems boundless. Like another mythical character from ancient Greece, the winged horse Pegasus, Daedalus' name has over the centuries come to be associated with human imagination and invention. *Daedalus* is the title of the journal of the American Academy of Arts and Sciences, the name of novelist James Joyce's hero in his autobiographical novel *A Portrait of the Artist as a Young Man,* the name of a publisher, and the name of many a creative project and business on the Internet. As for Icarus, his lesson was typically Greek: When man forgets to follow the golden mean, disaster is sure to follow, a lesson that needed frequent reiteration for the Greeks, according to classical scholar Barry Powell (1998), and one that has not lost its value for our times.

Minoan Crete, the setting of this story, was a complex island civilization. It preceded that of the Greeks on the mainland and it seems to have been destroyed by a combination of earthquakes around 1500 B.C.E. and incursions of the Mycenaean Greeks from the mainland a hundred years later (*Britannica 2002* CD-ROM). Peabody's characterization of Daedalus as a great inventor and architect who is wise enough to know the limitations of humankind and its inventions is in keeping with the myth. The motivation driving Icarus, the joy of freedom and flight, seems to be part of the story as the Roman Ovid and the Greek Apollodorus told it. Both ancient poets also emphasized the headlong rashness of youth. Contemporary retellers such as Olivia Coolidge in *Greek Myths* (1949), however, have emphasized Icarus' desire to be like the gods, which would make this an act of hubris, that is, boundless pride, against which the Greeks were also strongly warned.

From: *Old Greek Folk Stories Told Anew* by Josephine P. Peabody. London: George Harrap, 1910. pp. 36–39.

Coyote Fights Some Monsters

North America: United States/Canada—Okanogan

Coyote, like other powerful people among Native Americans, is able to draw on his personal mystic power, often referred to as "**medicine.**" Throughout North America traditional Native Americans use smoke, usually from tobacco, as one way to commune with the higher spirits, which is why Coyote keeps asking the monsters to allow him to smoke his pipe. In this story Coyote is a culture hero rather than a selfish trickster. He travels far from his home in the Pacific Northwest as he helps the Creator to make the world a livable place by fighting all the larger-than-life animals and by bringing about their familiar, domestic counterparts. There are numerous myths about how Coyote created various landmarks such as Multnomah Falls and the course of the Columbia River.

From: *Coyote Stories* by Mourning Dove. Caldwell, ID: The Caxton Printers, Ltd., 1933. Reprinted with permission by Caxton Press. pp. 41–48.

Legends, Hero Tales, and Epics

▣ Introduction

Definitions

In the world of folklore, legends occupy a place halfway between the sacred matters of myths and the human affairs of folktales. Like myths, legends are narratives that are told and received as truth, but they are set in historic rather than mythic times and focus on the lives of humans and extraordinary events relating to humans. Legends usually contain a kernel of historic truth around which stories, meaningful to the community, have accumulated. An archeologist used the legend of the Trojan Wars to find the actual site of Troy. Although legends have been used as history, they have also had a long tradition of being considered unreliable. Discarding legends would be a mistake, however, both because of their value as the only record available to historians at times and because their meaning often endures long after the facts have lost their importance. (Morris, 1973; Cavendish, 1982).

Whereas the public telling of folktales is frequently the province of skilled storytellers, legends—with the exception of the epic poems about a culture's heroes—are usually told by any member of the community (Dorson, 1971a). Legends tell a people who they are or how they wish to be seen. They tell of a culture's heroes; of unusual occurrences, from religious revelations to fearful or even humorous but memorable events; of the origins of place names; why certain plants or animals appear the way they do; and the like. Some legends, such as the stories about King Arthur and his knights and the story of Saint George and the dragon, may travel across boundaries, but they are told because they have acquired meaning locally.

"Sir Gawaine Finds the Beautiful Lady." Illustrated by Howard Pyle.

From: *The Story of King Arthur and his Knights* by Howard Pyle. New York: Charles Scribner's Sons, 1903.

Arthur might have started out as an early medieval Celtic war leader resisting the Saxon takeover of Britain, but by the time the French nobility had adopted his legends 600 years later, he had become transformed into a courtly king who fitted the ideals of French chivalry. Similarly, the legend of St. George and the dragon is based on a martyred Roman Christian soldier from 300 C.E. who died near Lydia in

229

Palestine. It is St. George the dragon slayer and protector of the princess Una of legend, however, who came to symbolize the Christian soldier, defender of the Church (the princess) against evil (the dragon) throughout Europe (Cavendish, 1982).

Although these and other legends, such as the ancient Greek Homeric epics *The Iliad* and *The Odyssey,* have become part of the repertoire of international literature, they have the most meaning to their original people. The legend of Robin Hood, for instance, is popular in the United States, having been brought across the ocean as ballads from England in colonial times (Leach, 1955) and having been popularized for children by Howard Pyle in his *The Merry Adventures of Robin Hood,* but the story lives more vividly in England. Schoolchildren in Nottingham look for records related to the character of Robin Hood in the city archives, and several graves have been identified as belonging to Little John (Joan Nist, personal communication, 2001). Searches for King Arthur's birthplace, castle, and last battle are equally intense in the British Isles, claims being made in such geographically disparate places as Cornwall in the south and the border of Scotland in the north (Alexander, 1996). Visitors flock by the thousands to these sites every year.

Legends, though told as true histories, frequently incorporate folktale elements that recur in stories from a wide range of cultures. One such element is the hero's inauspicious or even endangered birth, which causes him to be hidden until the right time comes (e.g., Arthur of Britain, Finn MacCoul and Cuchulain of Ireland, Krishna of India, Theseus of Greece, and Sundiata of Mali). Other typical folkloric elements that are woven into legends are events occurring in threes, enchantments, and battles with monsters such as dragons.

Although most legends were local and were transmitted orally until folklorists in the eighteenth, nineteenth, and twentieth centuries began to collect them, some became raised to national importance as epic poetry. These were recited at the courts of kings and noblemen by bards with special training rather than by ordinary people. Homer describes a blind **bard**, Demodokos, in *The Odyssey* who relates the story of Odysseus' exploits at Troy to King Alkínoös and his court and who is probably Homer the poet

himself. **Griots** in Africa have similar functions. They sing long memorized epics that they pass on from one generation of highly trained griots to the next. The bards of Ireland, Wales, and the Germanic countries and the **troubadours** of France also recited long epics made memorable through rhythm, rhyme and alliteration. Many of the famous epics have been recorded, but others, such as the *Sundiata Epic,* have no authentic written version because the official version is the secret knowledge of the griots (Jansen, 2001).

The eighteenth and nineteenth centuries saw the rise of nationalism and a corresponding rise in the search for "lost" national epics similar to *Beowulf* of England, *El Cid* of Spain, *The Iliad* and *The Odyssey* of ancient Greece, *The Mahabharata* and *The Ramayana* of India, *Roland and Oliver* of France, and the *Shahname* of Iran. In 1835, for instance, Elias Lönnrot, convinced that the folktales and songs about Finland's ancient heroes were part of a lost epic, created a national epic for Finland, *The Kalevala* ("The Land of Heroes"). *The Kalevala* in turn inspired Henry Wordsworth Longfellow to compose "The Song of Haiwatha," based on legends of the founding of the Iroquois Federation (Deutsch, 1949). James MacPherson, an eighteenth century Scottish poet, created a Celtic revival among artists and poets when he fraudulently claimed to have discovered two epics about the poet-warrior Ossian from third century Ireland. He composed the poems himself.

Why People Tell Legends

Even when people are aware that the historic accuracy of legends is questionable, the tales often endure because they convey something important about the community's values, perception of who they are or wish to be, or concerns for their safety and well-being. Different types of legends are told for different reasons.

Legends about a culture's heroes reflect that culture's ideals with the hero acting as a role model. Although it is safe to say that some heroic characteristics, such as courage and perseverance, are universal, others are emphasized to a greater or lesser extent in different cultures. Odysseus represents the Athenian ideal of moderation and the use of intelligence and pragmatism to solve problems. He is different from his culture's earlier ideal of the hero, as embodied by the popular Hercules, who was physically strong and daring but given to excesses of gluttony, impulsiveness, and passion (Powell, 1998). Odysseus is frequently referred to as wily; although it is obvious that he is strong and skilled, he survives by using his head more than his muscles. One can admire Odysseus' intelligence, courage, wisdom, and perseverance, but one would be hard put to admire his honesty or fairness. By contrast, in the medieval romances King Arthur represents a courtly ideal that is different from that of the ancient Greeks. He and his knights defend the weak and champion justice, fight equals and follow rules of combat that include giving their opponent an opportunity to ask for mercy, and obey complicated rules of courtship and courtesy toward the ladies. Most epics are about male heroes, but women warriors did exist in many cultures, as Marianna Mayer's Women Warriors (1999) indicates.

The word *legend*, which means literally "to be read," was first applied to stories about the lives of the Christian saints. The saints, especially the martyrs, demonstrate the courage and perseverance of the traditional heroes. In fact, it is probably among the saints that we will find some of the strongest legendary female heroes in Western cultures. The lives of saints were recorded and embellished to present role models for ordinary people (Cavendish, 1982). Some, such as Saint Catherine of Alexandria, were "pious fictions," and the Vatican eliminated their feast days from the calendar in 1969, but most were historic figures about whom were told both accurate and fictional tales. St. Patrick, for instance, brought Christianity to Ireland around 430 and was the first to build churches in rural areas instead of focusing on large urban centers as had earlier bishops (Cahill, 1994), but he did not drive the snakes out of Ireland. Frequently, the saints' lives were refashioned by their biographers to fit a biblical precedent. For instance, Helena, the mother of the first Christian Roman Emperor, Constantine, is portrayed as extraordinarily philanthropic, the biblical model of the charitable matron. In 326 C.E. she was reputed to have discovered the cross on which Christ had been crucified, thus creating a symbolic tie between Helena and the Virgin Mary, with Constantine as the allegorical new Christ who resurrected the

dying Roman Empire as the new Christian empire (Cavendish, 1982; Coon, 1997).

Legends of holy people, saints, and martyrs exist in other religions as well. Hindu holy people model the ascetic life, which renounces the pleasures and concerns of this world in order for the soul to achieve *moksha* or *nirvana* (liberation from the cycle of rebirth). The Buddha was one of the most famous Hindu holy men. He began as Prince Siddhartha, who renounced his life of privilege when he discovered how people suffer in the world. After years in the wilderness, seeking answers to the question of human suffering, he reached enlightenment and eventually started Buddhism (Sen, 1961).

A Sufi Islamic legend with a similar theme is told. King Ibrahim, who lived a life of luxury, once heard a man walking on the roof of his palace, and when he was told the man was looking for his camel up there, Ibrahim chided him for foolishly looking in such a place. The man's response was that he was far less foolish than King Ibrahim, whose search for God was made impossible by his luxurious lifestyle. After receiving several more mysterious warnings, the king renounced his kingdom and, taking up the beggar's bowl, followed a holy teacher and performed miracles himself (Cavendish, 1982).

In the Jewish tradition the wisdom and teachings of famous rabbis became legendary. Similar to stories of Christian saints, there are also legends about rabbis who worked miracles and to whose graves people made pilgrimages, leaving petitions. Medieval legends even talk of some rabbis who were able to create a human-like servant made of clay, a golem, to serve the general good, not for personal use. Activated by a parchment with special letters inscribed on it placed under its tongue (or inscribed on its forehead) and deactivated by removing the parchment (or erasing the first letter of the word), a golem could carry out many tasks. As time went on, the legend changed. Sometime in the seventeenth or eighteenth century stories began to accumulate around a famous rabbi, Rabbi Loew of Prague, who had lived in the sixteenth century. Though there is no evidence that he ever experimented with creating a golem, legend attached its creation to him. At around the same time a new concept was added to the legend. The golem was beginning to be seen as dangerous by outgrowing its master and becoming uncontrollable. We are reminded of Mary Shelley's *Frankenstein* and his monster. The last piece of the legend as it is told today, that of the Golem of Prague as protector of the Jews at a time of great danger, was not added until the beginning of the twentieth century, perhaps in response to the fears of pogroms (violent attacks on Jewish villages) that were occurring in the Ukraine and Russia at that time (Kieval, 1997). The development of the legend of the golem is an example of the way legends meet people's needs and change with altered political or social conditions. Several picture book retellings of the golem legend have been created, including two Caldecott honored books by Beverly McDermott (1976) and David Wisniewski (1996).

Legends often tell of the founding of a nation or the settling of an ethnic group's homeland. Some examples from various cultures are the long wanderings and hardships, as in Exodus; the sign indicating that the people had reached their destined place, as in the legend of the Aztecs finding their home in Tenochtitlan on the spot where an eagle, perched on a cactus growing in stony ground, is swallowing a snake; and the taking of the homeland by peaceful or warlike means, as in the legends of the Celtic ancestors of today's Irish people. The founding-of-the-nation legend helps to reinforce the group's identity and helps the group to persist in the face of threats to its existence, whether through assimilation or destruction by other groups. Some founding legends are alive today. Each year during the Passover meal the story of Exodus is retold in Jewish homes. The emblem in the center of the Mexican flag shows the eagle perched on a cactus, swallowing a rattlesnake. Legends of this kind and the related legends of famous battles won (or lost) can have both powerful positive and negative effects, as can be seen from many historical examples in which legends have been used to justify wars and territorial takeovers but also to give people courage to resist oppression.

Legends do not necessarily have the same meaning for every member of a community, as James Fernandez demonstrated in his research of several villages in a mountainous region of Spain during the 1960s. La Torre, a village known for its scenic location in the mountains, prided itself on its hospitality to travelers. The villagers tell a legend from the Middle Ages about an *hidalgo* (knight) who refused shelter one stormy winter night to an Old Man who had begged for it in the Savior's name. When out hunting some time later, the *hidalgo* became lost in the freezing mountains, and he in turn was denied admittance to any of the houses in a village he had managed to reach. Knowing that he was freezing to death, he called on the Savior, and at once the Old Man appeared. When the *hidalgo* saw that the man's palms were nail-pierced, he fainted but woke later to find himself in a church near his village, beneath the statue of the Savior. On that day he removed his coat of arms from the lintel of his Great House and chiseled a sign there instead that read: "He will give shelter to the poor/Whoever lives in this house/ Neither occupying nor inheriting it/He who refuses to give it" (Fernandez, 1986, p. 141). The sign is still there.

Fernandez found that the miners of the village, who tended to be socialists in the 1960s, either mocked the legend or thought of it as demonstrating the miserly ways of the gentry and identified the poor with the Savior. The cattle farmers, who tended to be conservative, saw the legend as showing the need for *noblesse oblige* and piety. Fernandez used the varied ways in which this community responded to the legend to warn against using legends to stereotype national or even regional character. Legends tell about people's values and perceptions of themselves, but these values cannot be readily deduced just by reading the text. Legends are living stories whose relationship to the person repeating them is as important as their contents.

One more example vividly demonstrates the importance of a story's context. King Arthur is probably one of the best-loved legendary heroes in Britain and has been adapted to fit the needs of each new era. Though nominally identified as a sixth century Celtic king, starting in the thirteenth century, the Norman rulers of England made political use of his legend. Having conquered England in 1066, they wished to extend their rule over all of Britain (England, Wales, Scotland) as well as Brittany in today's France. They based their claim on Geoffrey of Monmouth's 1138 *History of Britain,* in which Arthur was described as ruler of all Britain and conqueror of Gaul (today's

France) (MacColl, 1999). A great round table was manufactured between 1250 and 1280 for one of the Norman kings (either Henry III or Edward I); for centuries it was venerated as Arthur's very own Round Table. (Carbon dating in 1976 destroyed this cherished belief.)

Three hundred years later another newly conquering king, the Tudor Henry VII, named his first son Arthur in an attempt to convey royal legitimacy to his family line. Arthur died young, but Henry VII's second son, Henry VIII, used the legend by commissioning a painting of King Arthur and the Round Table, with Arthur bearing a strong resemblance to himself (Alexander, 1996). The use of the legend for political or inspirational purposes has continued to this day: Churchill during World War II was hailed as a new Arthur, and in 1963, within days of President Kennedy's assassination, First Lady Jackie Kennedy told biographer Theodore H. White that her husband's favorite musical was *Camelot* and, quoting a line from the musical, created the image of the three years of the Kennedy presidency as "a magic moment in American history, when gallant men danced with beautiful women, when great deeds were done and when the White House became the center of the universe." (A. Ferguson in *Time,* Aug. 13, 2001, p. 34). Finally, as recently as the 1997 general elections in Britain, the Scottish Conservatives drew a sword from a stone to symbolize the reaffirmation of the union between Scotland and England (MacColl, 1999). This last use of Arthur is ironic; some legends, written around 1100 (six hundred years after Arthur's death) by monks in northern Wales and Scotland, describe a very different Arthur—a lowland tyrant who ruled over the Welsh and Scots—capturing an alternative view of Arthur (Morris, 1973 p. 122).

Legends of local communities are usually of greatest interest to local people, whose motives for telling the legend range from recognizing something about their own identity to entertaining tourists (Fernandez, 1986). In England and the United States, legends, rather than folktales and fairy tales, seem to be the dominant form of extended oral narrative (Dorson, 1965; Dorson, 1971b). New England and Southern communities have their stories of haunted houses, the West is rich with stories of lost mines, and in most

really?

locations there are stories of tricksters (con-men or folks who outwitted the law), local heroes, healers, and the origins of place names.

Folklorist Richard Dorson (1971a, 1971b) suggests that much can be learned about American history through the study of legends. He mentions, for instance, a sighting by a group of colonists of a spectral ship that flew up into the clouds during a thunderstorm in 1648 in New Haven harbor. The colonists' minister explained that this was God's way of setting the people's minds at ease about their families and friends whose ship had not reached the New World. The legend had both a religious component—God communicating directly to His people through nature—and a psychological component—many immigrants must have been lost at sea, and their loved ones must have grieved.

A nineteenth century African American legend of a group of newly arrived African slaves tells of their flying back to Africa while still chained together (or walking back at the bottom of the ocean). *In the Time of the Drums* is a Coretta Scott King Award–winning picture book retelling of the legend by Kim L. Siegelson and illustrated by Brian Pinkney (1999).

Stories of buried treasure and hidden or lost mines have a long history in the New World. One of the earliest was the legend of El Dorado, which sent Sir Walter Raleigh and numerous others on daring expeditions to the Americas. Contemporary tourist pamphlets and local newspapers often retell legends of buried treasures or lost mines, and the theme recurs in young adult books by such popular Newbery Award–winning authors as Sid Fleischman in *Bo and Mzzz Mad* (2001), Walter Dean Myers in *Mouse Rap* (1990), and Louis Sachar in *Holes* (1998).

An American ideal hero from earlier times, Daniel Boone, represented the frontiersman who braved the wilderness alone, fought bears bare-handed much like Hercules, and "made the vast continent habitable" by fighting the Indians. Changing times call for new heroes. The fact that Martin Luther King, Jr., has become a national hero is indicative of new ideals of democracy and inclusiveness that have become part of the way we wish to see ourselves as a nation. That we don't all act accordingly does not mean that as a nation we do not hold these values.

Yikes! Problematic

Contemporary **urban legends** continue to reflect some of our earlier concerns and interests as well as new ones. Like legends in general, these narratives are told as if true and are passed on through the mass media, by electronic mail, or via Web sites. They present sufficient detail to seem plausible but tend to happen to people who are not clearly identified except by a vague reference as a **"friend of a friend,"** referred to by folklorists as FOAF. The time frame is usually unclear, although the incident seems to have happened "just the other day." Some of the common themes include unusual crimes, medical cures or calamities, stories that highlight our distrust of strangers by either using or ridiculing racial stereotypes, stories about business frauds, and occasionally stories of unusually kind acts. Many of these legends are gruesome, reflecting contemporary society's fears. Even the humorous stories, such as the many "college-student bloopers" jokes, reflect our current concerns—for instance, our anxiety as a society, about the "deterioration of our educational standards." Many of the stories, however, have a long history. Jan Harold Brunvand, a folklorist, describes in his book *The Choking Doberman* (1984) how contemporary legends such as "The Vanishing Hitchhiker" and "The Hook" evolved over time.

One humorous urban legend that has made the rounds on the Internet for years is the story of the Neiman Marcus cookies. The story demonstrates the nature of today's legends and the way they are passed on. Like any true urban legend, this one seems so plausible. One version of the story was about a colleague of a colleague of mine (a friend of a friend) who attended a conference in Dallas, Texas, and went to Neiman Marcus for coffee and cookies. The cookies were so delicious that he asked for the recipe, and when he was told that Neiman Marcus does not give out recipes, he offered to buy it. Having been told it would cost two fifty, he told them to put it on his credit card. It was not until a month later, when he got his credit card bill, that the man discovered that he had been charged two hundred and fifty dollars, not two dollars and fifty cents. When the department store refused to return his money, he vowed to get vengeance by sending the cookie recipe around the world via e-mail.

According to a December 23, 1996, article, "This Computer Cookie Story Crumbles" by Chris Yurko in the *Daily Hampshire Gazette,* there have been variants of this story for several decades. In its earlier version the corporate culprit was Mrs. Fields' Cookies. Many different cookies have been identified. Whatever the source, the corporation, or the cookie, this trivial-seeming story continues to live because it deals with our feelings of helplessness at the hands of large corporations while at the same time providing a psychological boost through the element of revenge via a contemporary technology, the Internet. Studying a people's legends, whether traditional or contemporary, helps one gain some insights into the group's values and concerns.

The legends section of this anthology is divided into three parts: "Hero Tales and Epics"; "Legends about People, Places, Animals, and Plants"; and "Legends of the Supernatural." "Hero Tales and Epics" is the largest part, and it includes some internationally known epics that have intrigued readers, writers, and researchers for centuries. The other two parts are more local but important to the cultures that tell them. Although many famous epics and wonderful local legends have been left out for lack of space, the purpose of this anthology is to introduce a few representative examples from the world's rich supply of legends. There are relatively few collections of such legends for children compared with folktales, but the number of picture books and illustrated collections that include legends of various cultures is increasing. For those who wish to learn more about the central legends of cultures worldwide in order to be able to introduce them to children, Richard Cavendish's *Legends of the World* (Schocken, 1982) is an excellent resource. Cavendish retells the legends of cultures from every region of the world and provides explanations of cultural contexts for each region and for each story. Many of the legends can be read to or by children themselves. A site for modern urban legends, not recommended for children but of interest to adults, is http://www.snopes.com. This site includes every kind of urban legend from the humorous to the gross, but it is useful because the accuracy of urban legends and other rumors is investigated.

For picture book versions of the following stories, see "Picture Books Related to the Stories in the *Allyn & Bacon Anthology of Traditional Literature*" on the Web Supplement at www.ablongman.com/lechner.

Hero Tales and Epics

Sundiata—The Lion's Awakening

The story of Sundiata (pronounced "Sunjata"), the Lion King of Mali, has been recited since the thirteenth century by griots, oral poets of West Africa, who were and to some extent still are the preservers of history. Sundiata was the legendary king who made the Kingdom of Mali so great that within a hundred years its university at Timbuktu became renowned throughout North Africa and the Middle East because of its wealth of knowledge and manuscripts. Its king, Mansa Musa (1307–1332), astounded the Arab world with the riches he brought on his pilgrimage to Mecca, and on his return he established Egyptian scholars in Timbuktu.

In the past each king and today government leaders have their own griots. In the following excerpt Doua, the griot of Sundiata's father, is court adviser, and Doua's son, Balla Fasséké, becomes Sundiata's griot and closest companion. The epic of Sundiata has many versions, but the official version is the secret knowledge of the Kiete tribe's griots, the Diabate, whose history is as old as the legend of Sundiata itself (Niane, 1965/1986).

Although the position of the griot is hereditary, it involves long training. An epic such as Sundiata must be memorized exactly. When performed at the seven-yearly ceremony for the restoration of a ceremonial house that commemorates the life of Sundiata, the words of the griots as they recite the epic provide the power to complete the restoration, the raising of the new roof, allowing society to become once more complete. The epic is not just a story, it is the defining story for Mali society (Jansen, 2001).

There are few griots today who, like their ancestors, can devote their lives to preserving history. In the modern world printed records have taken away this role. Though griots are still needed for ceremonies, many give concerts, make recordings, and work at other jobs to make a living (Niane, 1965/1986; Jansen, 2001).

Sundiata was referred to by many names; Maghan after his father and Mari Djata were his given names, but he usually went by Sogolon Djata after his mother, whose name was Sogolon Kedjou, and Sundiata seems to be a contraction of "Sogolon Djata." His father, a just and beloved king whose ancestry the griots traced to a close associate of the Prophet Muhammad, received a prophecy that his son by an ugly stranger would become Mali's Alexander the Great. When Sogolon, an extremely homely woman, the spirit of a great buffalo, was brought by two hunters to court, Sundiata's father made her his second wife. Unfortunately, his first wife, Sassouma Bérété, whose son was already eight years old, was extremely jealous, though when Sundiata was born ugly and weak, she became hopeful and lost no time in taunting Sogolon with her son's weakness. Sundiata was unable to stand up for the first seven years of his life but, crawling from compound to compound, stole food from everyone's pot to sate his enormous appetite, thus earning another name: "the thief." After his father died, the lot of Sundiata, his mother, and his sisters became even harsher. The excerpt begins at the moment when the hero emerges from his inauspicious beginnings and starts the first phase of his life as a hero.

Source: "Sundiata—The Lion's Awakening" from *Sundiata: An Epic of Old Mali* by Djibril Tamsir Niane. © Longman Group Limited, 1965. Reprinted by permission Pearson Education Limited. pp. 18–26.

The following key of names, arranged according to the order in which the name appears in the story, should help readers keep characters straight:

Naré Maghan—the King, Sundiata's father.
Sogolon or Sogolon Kedjou—Sundiata's mother.
Mari Djata or Sogolon Djata or Djata—Sundiata, the hero.
[Sogolon] Kolonkan and [Sogolon] Djamarou—Sundiata's sisters
Doua—King Naré Maghan's griot.
Sassouma Bérété—King Naré Maghan's first wife.
Dankaran Touman—King Naré Maghan's and Sassouma Bérété son, and Sundiata's older half-brother.
Balla Fasséké—Sundiata's griot, older friend, and teacher, son of Doua the former griot.
Manding Bory—Sundiata's age mate and best friend, sometimes referred to as brother
Soumosso Konkomba—head of the witches whom Sassouma Bérété sends to kill Sundiata.

A short while after this interview between [king] Naré Maghan and his son the king died. Sogolon's son was no more than seven years old. The council of elders met in the king's palace. It was no use Doua's defending the king's will which reserved the throne for Mari Djata, for the council took no account of Naré Maghan's wish. With the help of Sassouma Bérété's intrigues, Dankaran Touman was proclaimed king and a regency council was formed in which the queen mother was all-powerful. A short time after, Doua died.

As men have short memories, Sogolon's son was spoken of with nothing but irony and scorn. People had seen one-eyed kings, one-armed kings, and lame kings, but a stiff-legged king had never been heard tell of. No matter how great the destiny promised for Mari Djata might be, the throne could not be given to someone who had no power in his legs; if the jinn loved him, let them begin by giving him use of his legs. Such were the remarks that Sogolon heard every day. The queen mother, Sassouma Bérété, was the source of all this gossip.

Having become all-powerful, Sassouma Bérété persecuted Sogolon because the late Naré Maghan had preferred her. She banished Sogolon and her son to a back yard of the palace. Mari Djata's mother now occupied an old hut which had served as a lumber-room of Sassouma's.

The wicked queen mother allowed free passage to all those inquisitive people who wanted to see the child that still crawled at the age of seven. Nearly all the inhabitants of Niani filed into the palace and the poor Sogolon wept to see herself thus given over to public ridicule. Mari Djata took on a ferocious look in front of the crowd of sightseers. Sogolon found a little consolation only in the love of her eldest daughter, Kolonkan. She was four and she could walk. She seemed to understand all her mother's miseries and already she helped her with the housework. Sometimes, when Sogolon was attending to the chores, it was she who stayed beside her sister Djamarou, who was quite small as yet.

Sogolon Kedjou and her children lived on the queen mother's left-overs, but she kept a little garden in the open ground behind the village. It was there that she passed her brightest moments looking after her onions and gnougous. One day she happened to be short of condiments and went to the queen mother to beg a little baobab leaf.

"Look you," said the malicious Sassouma, "I have a calabash full. Help yourself, you poor woman. As for me, my son knew how to walk at seven and it was he who went and picked these baobab leaves. Take them then, since your son is unequal to mine." Then she laughed derisively with that fierce laughter which cuts through your flesh and penetrates right to the bone.

Sogolon Kedjou was dumbfounded. She had never imagined that hate could be so strong in a human being. With a lump in her throat she left Sassouma's. Outside her hut Mari Djata, sitting on his useless legs, was blandly eating out of a calabash. Unable to contain herself any longer, Sogolon burst into sobs and seizing a piece of wood, hit her son.

"Oh son of misfortune, will you never walk? Through your fault I have just suffered the greatest affront of my life! What have I done, God, for you to punish me this way?"

Mari Djata seized the piece of wood and, looking at his mother, said, "Mother, what's the matter?"

"Shut up, nothing can ever wash me clean of this insult."

"But what then?"

"Sassouma has just humiliated me over a matter of baobab leaf. At your age her own son could walk and used to bring his mother baobab leaves."

"Cheer up, Mother, cheer up."

"No. It's too much. I can't."

"Very well then, I am going to walk today," said Mari Djata. "Go and tell my father's smiths to make me the heaviest possible iron rod. Mother, do you want just the leaves of the baobab or would you rather I brought you the whole tree?"

"Ah, my son, to wipe out this insult I want the tree and its roots at my feet outside my hut."

Balla Fasséké, who was present, ran to the master smith, Farakourou, to order an iron rod.

Sogolon had sat down in front of her hut. She was weeping softly and holding her head between her two hands. Mari Djata went calmly back to his calabash of rice and began eating again as if nothing had happened. From time to time he looked up discreetly at his mother who was murmuring in a low voice, "I want the whole tree, in front of my hut, the whole tree."

All of a sudden a voice burst into laughter behind the hut. It was the wicked Sassouma telling one of her serving women about the scene of humiliation and she was laughing loudly so that Sogolon could hear. Sogolon fled into the hut and hid her face under the blankets so as not to have before her eyes this heedless boy, who was more preoccupied with eating than with anything else. With her head buried in the bed clothes Sogolon wept and her body shook violently. Her daughter, Sogolon Djamarou, had come and sat down beside her and she said, "Mother, Mother, don't cry. Why are you crying?"

Mari Djata had finished eating and, dragging himself along on his legs, he came and sat under the wall of the hut for the sun was scorching. What was he thinking about? He alone knew.

The royal forges were situated outside the walls and over a hundred smiths worked there. The bows, spear, arrow, and shields of Niani's warriors came from there. When Balla Fasséké came to order the iron rod, Farakourou said to him, "The great day has arrived then?"

"Yes. Today is a day like any other, but it will see what no other day has seen."

The master of the forges, Farakourou, was the son of the old Nounfaïri, and he was a soothsayer like his father. In his workshops there was an enormous iron bar wrought by his father Nounfaïri. Everybody wondered what this bar was destined to be used for. Farakourou called six of his apprentices and told them to carry the iron bar to Sogolon's house.

When the smiths put the gigantic iron bar down in front of the hut the noise was so frightening that Sogolon, who was lying down, jumped up with a start. Then Balla Fasséké, son of Gnankouman Doua, spoke.

"Here is the great day, Mari Djata. I am speaking to you Maghan, son of Sogolon. The waters of the Niger can efface the stain from the body, but they cannot wipe out an insult. Arise, young lion, roar, and may the bush know that from henceforth it has a master."

The apprentice smiths were still there, Sogolon had come out and everyone was watching Mari Djata. He crept on all-fours and came to the iron bar. Supporting himself on his knees and one hand, with the other hand he picked up the iron bar without any effort and stood it up vertically. Now he was resting on nothing but his knees and held the bar with both his hands. A deathly silence had gripped all those present. Sogolon Djata [Mari Djata] closed his eyes, held tight, the muscles in his arms tensed. With a violent jerk he threw his weight on to it and his knees left the ground. Sogolon Kedjou was all eyes and watched her son's legs which were trembling as though from an electric shock. Djata was sweating and the sweat ran from his brow. In a great effort he straightened up and was on his feet at one go—but the great bar of iron was twisted and had taken the form of a bow!

Then Balla Fasséké sang out the "Hymn to the Bow," striking up with his powerful voice:

"Take your bow, Simbon,
Take your bow and let us go.
Take your bow, Sogolon Djata."

When Sogolon saw her son standing she stood dumb for a moment, then suddenly she sang these words of thanks to God who had given her son the use of his legs:

"Oh day, what a beautiful day,
Oh day, day of joy;
Allah Almighty, you never created a finer day.
So my son is going to walk!"

Standing in the position of a soldier at ease, Sogolon Djata, supported by his enormous rod, was sweating great beads of sweat. Balla Fasséké's song had alerted the whole palace and people came running from all over to see what had happened, and each stood bewildered before Sogolon's son. The queen mother had rushed there and when she saw Mari Djata standing up she trembled from head to foot. After recovering his breath Sogolon's son dropped the bar and the crowd stood to one side. His first steps were those of a giant. Balla Fasséké fell into step and pointing his finger at Djata, he cried:

"Room, room, make room!
The lion has walked;
Hide antelopes
Get out of his way."

Behind Niani there was a young baobab tree and it was there that the children of the town came to pick leaves for their mothers. With all his might the son of Sogolon tore up the tree and put it on his shoulders and went back to his mother. He threw the tree in front of the hut and said, "Mother here are some baobab leaves for you. From henceforth it will be outside your hut that the women of Niani will come to stock up."

Sogolon Djata walked. From that day forward the queen mother had no more peace of mind. But what can one do against destiny? Nothing. Man, under the influence of certain illusions, thinks he can alter the course which God has mapped out, but everything he does falls into a higher order which he barely understands. That is why Sassouma's efforts were vain against Sogolon's son, everything she did lay in the child's destiny. Scorned the day before and the object of public ridicule, now Sogolon's son was as popular as he had been despised. The multitude loves and fears strength. All Niani talked of nothing but Djata; the mothers urged their sons to become hunting companions to Djata and to share his games, as if they wanted their offspring to profit from the nascent glory of the buffalo-woman's son. The words of Doua on the name-giving day came back to men's minds and Sogolon was now surrounded with much respect; in conversation people were fond of contrasting Sogolon's modesty with the pride and malice of Sassouma Bérété. It was because the former had been an exemplary wife and mother that

God had granted strength to her son's legs for, it was said, the more a wife loves and respects her husband and the more she suffers for her child, the more valorous will the child be one day. Each is the child of his mother; the child is worth no more than the mother is worth. It was not astonishing that the king Dankaran Touman was so colourless, for his mother had never shown the slightest respect to her husband and never, in the presence of the late king, did she show that humility which every wife should show before her husband. People recalled her scenes of jealousy and the spiteful remarks she circulated about her co-wife and her child. And people would conclude gravely, "Nobody knows God's mystery. The snake has no legs yet it is as swift as any other animal that has four."

Sogolon Djata's popularity grew from day to day and he was surrounded by a gang of children of the same age as himself. These were Fran Kamara, son of the king of Tabon; Kamandjan, son of the king of Sibi; and other princes whose fathers had sent them to the court of Niani. The son of Namandjé, Manding Bory, was already joining in their games. Balla Fasséké followed Sogolon Djata all the time. He was past twenty and it was he who gave the child education and instruction according to the Mandingo rules of conduct. Whether in town or at the hunt, he missed no opportunity of instructing his pupil. Many young boys of Niani came to join in the games of the royal child.

He liked hunting best of all. Farakourou, master of the forges, had made Djata a fine bow, and he proved himself to be a good shot with the bow. He made frequent hunting trips with his troops, and in the evening all Niani would be in the square to be present at the entry of the young hunters. The crowd would sing the "Hymn to the Bow" which Balla Fasséké had composed, and Sogolon Djata was quite young when he received the title of Simbon, or master hunter, which is only confirmed on great hunters who have proved themselves.

Every evening Sogolon Kedjou would gather Djata and his companions outside her hut. She would tell them stories about the beasts of the bush, the dumb brothers of man. Sogolon Djata learnt to distinguish between the animals; he knew why the buffalo was his mother's wraith and also why the lion was the protector of his father's family. He also listened to the history of the kings which Balla Fasséké told him; enraptured by the story of Alexander the Great, the mighty king of gold and silver, whose sun shone over quite half the world. Sogolon initiated her son into certain secrets and revealed to him the names of the medicinal plants which every hunter should know. Thus, between his mother and his griot, the child got to know all that needed to be known.

Sogolon's son was now ten. The name Sogolon Djata in the rapid Mandingo language became Sundiata or Sondjata. He was a lad full of strength; his arms had the strength of ten and his biceps inspired fear in his companions. He had already that authoritative way of speaking which belongs to those who are destined to command. His brother, Manding Bory, became his best friend, and whenever Djata was seen, Manding Bory appeared too. They were like a man and his shadow. Fran Kamara and Kamandjan were the closest friends of the young princes, while Balla Fasséké followed them all like a guardian angel.

But Sundiata's popularity was so great that the queen mother became apprehensive for her son's throne. Dankaran Touman was the most retiring of men. At the age of eighteen he was still under the influence of his mother and a handful of old schemers. It was Sassouma Bérété who really reigned in his name. The queen mother wanted to put an end to this popularity by killing Sundiata and it was thus that one night she received the nine great witches of Mali. They were all old women. The eldest, and the most dangerous too, was called Soumosso Konkomba. When the nine old hags had seated themselves in a semi-circle around her bed the queen mother said:

"You who rule supreme at night, nocturnal powers, oh you who hold the secret of life, you who can put an end to one life, can you help me?"

"The night is potent," said Soumosso Konkomba, "Oh queen, tell us what is to be done, on whom must we turn the fatal blade?"

"I want to kill Sundiata," said Sassouma. "His destiny runs counter to my son's and he must be killed while there is still time. If you succeed, I promise you the finest rewards. First of all I bestow on each of you a cow and her calf and from tomorrow go to the royal granaries and each of you will receive a hundred measures of rice and a hundred measures of hay on my authority.

"Mother of the king," rejoined Soumosso Konkomba, "life hangs by nothing but a very fine thread, but all is interwoven here below. Life has a cause, and death as well. The one comes from the other. Your hate has a cause and your action must have a cause. Mother of the king, everything holds together, our action will have no effect unless we are ourselves implicated, but Mari Djata [Sundiata] has done us no wrong. It is, then, difficult for us to compass his death."

"But you are also concerned," replied the queen mother, "for the son of Sogolon will be a scourge to us all."

"The snake seldom bites the foot that does not walk," said one of the witches.

"Yes, but there are snakes that attack everybody. Allow Sundiata to grow up and we will all repent of it. Tomorrow go to Sogolon's vegetable patch and make a show of picking a few gnougou leaves. Mari Djata stands guard there and you will see how vicious the boy is. He won't have any respect for your age, he'll give you a good thrashing."

"That's a clever idea," said one of the old hags.

"But the cause of our discomfiture will be ourselves, for having touched something which did not belong to us."

"We could repeat the offence," said another, "and then if he beats us again we would be able to reproach him with being unkind, heartless. In that case we would be concerned, I think."

"The idea is ingenious," said Soumosso Konkomba. "Tomorrow we shall go to Sogolon's vegetable patch."

"Now there's a happy thought," concluded the queen mother, laughing for joy. "Go to the vegetable patch tomorrow and you will see that Sogolon's son is mean. Beforehand, present yourselves at the royal granaries where you will receive the grain I promised you; the cows and calves are already yours."

The old hags bowed and disappeared into the black night. The queen mother was now alone and gloated over her anticipated victory. But her daughter, Nana Triban, woke up.

"Mother, who were you talking to? I thought I heard voices."

"Sleep, my daughter, it is nothing. You didn't hear anything."

In the morning, as usual, Sundiata got his companions together in front of his mother's hut and said, "What animal are we going to hunt today?"

Kamandjan said, "I wouldn't mind if we attacked some elephants right now."

"Yes, I am of this opinion too," said Fran Kamara. "That will allow us to go far into the bush."

And the young band left after Sogolon had filled the hunting bags with eatables. Sundiata and his companions came back late to the village, but first Djata wanted to take a look at his mother's vegetable patch as was his custom. It was dusk. There he found the nine witches stealing gnougou leaves. They made a show of running away like thieves caught red-handed.

"Stop, stop, poor old women," said Sundiata, "what is the matter with you to run away like this. This garden belongs to all."

Straight away his companions and he filled the gourds of the old hags with leaves, aubergines and onions.

"Each time that you run short of condiments come to stock up here without fear."

"You disarm us," said one of the old crones, and another added, "And you confound us with your bounty."

"Listen, Djata," said Soumosso Konkomba, "we had come here to test you. We have no need of condiments but your generosity disarms us. We were sent here by the queen mother to provoke you and draw the anger of the nocturnal powers upon you. But nothing can be done against a heart full of kindness. And to think that we have already drawn a hundred measures of rice and a hundred measures of millet—and the queen promises us each a cow and her calf in addition. Forgive us, son of Sogolon."

"I bear you no ill-will," said Djata. "Here, I am returning from the hunt with my companions and we have killed ten elephants, so I will give you an elephant each and there you have some meat!"

"Thank you, son of Sogolon."

"Thank you, child of Justice."

"Henceforth," concluded Soumosso Konkomba, "we will watch over you." And the nine witches disappeared into the night. Sundiata and his companions continued on their way to Niani and got back after dark.

"You were really frightened; those nine witches really scared you, eh?" said Sogolon Kolonkan, Djata's young sister.

"How do you know?" retorted Sundiata, astonished.

"I saw them at night hatching their scheme, but I knew there was no danger for you." Kolonkan was well versed in the art of witchcraft and watched over her brother without his suspecting it. ■

Gilgamesh

Asia: Mesopotamia

The Gilgamesh epic might be the oldest written hero story available to modern readers. The first accounts of the historic Gilgamesh, king of the Sumerian city of Uruk, were recorded on clay tablets in **cuneiform writing** around 2500 B.C.E., two hundred years after

Source: "Gilgamesh" from *Gilgamesh & Other Babylonian Tales* by Jennifer Westwood. New York: Coward-McCann, 1968. Reprinted with the permission of the author. pp. 37–44.

his death. Credited with having built the walls and ziggurat of the city of Uruk, Gilgamesh, a Sumerian king, became a hero throughout the region; consequently, his story was recorded in many languages and versions over the next 1500 years. Sumerian, Babylonian, and Assyrian accounts have been found, and even over such great length of time and across languages the epic has remained remarkably similar. The most complete version has been found on 12 clay tablets from around 800–700 B.C.E. Ironically, whereas fires are devastating to books and scrolls, their heat makes clay tablets even more durable.

Because cuneiform writing was deciphered relatively recently (around 135 years ago) and because the fragments of the clay tablets are still being found and reassembled, no complete version of the epic exists. Many of the tablets, however, are largely complete, including Tablet XI, which tells the story of Utnapishtim, the Mesopotamian version of Noah, who was said to be the only human given immortality by the gods.

The story begins with praise of Gilgamesh but also with complaints by the people of Uruk that he is too energetic and that he demands too much of the young men and women of Uruk. From the existing texts it is hard to tell in exactly what way he is too demanding, but the following version by Westwood seems plausible. To temper his energy, the goddess Aruru creates a man from clay who grows up in the wilderness and who is then tamed and brought to town. This is how Enkidu, the wild man and match of Gilgamesh is described:

> His whole body was shaggy with hair
> he had a full head of hair like a woman
> his locks billowed in profusion like Ashnan [the
>   goddess of grain].
> He knew neither people nor settled living,
> but wore a garment like Sumukan [the god of
>   wild animals]
> He ate grasses with the gazelles,
> and jostled at the watering hole with the animals;
> as with animals, his thirst was slaked with
>   (mere) water."
>
> —(M. G. Kovacs, *The Epic of Gilgamesh*, 1989, p. 6)

It is tempting to see this state of nature as positive compared with Gilgamesh's hedonistic city life, but the authors of the epic were contrasting civilized living with what they saw as the ignorance of primitive humans in the beginning of the world (Sandars, 1960). Still, it is sad for the modern reader to see Enkidu lose his ability to talk with the animals.

On one of the adventures Enkidu and Gilgamesh so offend the gods by mercilessly killing the giant of the Cedar Forest, Humbaba, despite his prayers for mercy, and by killing the "Bull of Heaven" that they condemn Enkidu to death. Dying, Enkidu complains about having become civilized only to be abandoned to death after such a short life as a hero's friend and protector. Distraught over his friend's death and the knowledge of his own mortality, Gilgamesh searches out his ancestor, Utnapishtim, to learn how he could become immortal. At the end of his quest Gilgamesh learns that he will not be able to live forever. Utnapishtim does tell him where he may find a thorny plant that can keep him young for the rest of his life, but on his way home he loses even the plant to a snake, which eats it and thus becomes "rejuvenated" every time it sheds its skin. Returning home to Uruk, Gilgamesh completes its wall and embeds the very epic we are reading in the wall, thus becoming immortal after all. The poetically expressed anguish of Gilgamesh over the death of his beloved friend Enkidu was written over 4500 years ago, but the emotions are as fresh as today. Three themes emerge from this version of the story: What is the purpose of human life, how are nature and civilization to be balanced, and how can we live when we know our end is death?

This anthology includes one episode from the epic. The following story from Westwood's novel-length retelling for middle school age children tells of Gilgamesh and Enkidu's first meeting. Westwood followed the storyline closely and, while rendering the original verse form in prose, maintained the poetic tone of the epic.

Listen to the tale of Gilgamesh, of Gilgamesh the golden, King of Kings, who carved his name where great men's names were carved; and where no names were, there he built an altar to the gods.

He was the King in Uruk, where he raised great walls and ramparts, and the temple of Eanna for the father of the gods, Anu, Lord of all the Firmament, and for Ishtar, Queen of War and Love. There was no city on the face of earth more splendid than Uruk; there was no king more brave and strong than Gilgamesh, its lord. But he was two parts god and one part man, his human form unable to contain the restless vigour of divinity. So he became a tyrant and he took the young men of the city from their homes to labour on the temples and the walls, performing tasks that were beyond their strength. Sons lost fathers, fathers lost their sons— but worse than this in all the people's eyes was that he forced young maidens and new brides to be his own wives, leaving those they loved and those who loved them stricken with despair. The old men grumbled in their houses every day:

"Such is the shepherd of his flock, such is our king! No ravening wolf that slaughters the young lambs is crueller than he is, for he leaves no son to his old father and no bride to her new-wedded husband. Is there none who can restrain this tyrant, and relieve the sorrow that is weighing on our hearts, through the fault of Gilgamesh the King?"

The Making of Enkidu

The gods heard lamentations rising up out of the city, and they went before the throne of Anu, god of Uruk.

"Lord," they said, "in Uruk sons lose fathers, fathers sons, husbands lose wives upon their marriage-day, all through the fault of Gilgamesh the King."

The goddess of creation, Aruru, was standing by, and they all turned on her: "*You* made him, Aruru, now you must make a match for him, his equal, strength for strength. Let them strive together, wild heart with wild heart, and in their striving let the city rest."

The goddess formed an image in her mind. She washed her hands and, pinching off some clay, she shaped it to the pattern she had made and cast it on the plains, where it became a man like none those lands had ever seen. His name was Enkidu. He had Ninurta's strength, but his hair hung down his back as thick as grain, and long as any woman's. He was huge, and had a shaggy hide like Samuqan the cattle god. He roamed the plains and drank at water-holes with wild gazelle, neither he nor they knowing that he was of human-kind.

But a trapper met him one day, face to face, down at a water-hole; a second day, and then a third they met. The trapper's face was frozen with cold fear. He took his game and went to his house. His fear locked up his heart; he could not speak, but seeing him look strange, his father said: "What has befallen you, my son?"

"Father," said the trapper, "a wild man roams the plains and drinks at water-holes with the gazelle. He eats grass like the beasts and sucks their milk. He sets them free from all my traps, fills in the pits. I am afraid to hunt. What shall I do?"

His father said: "Go now to Gilgamesh, the King in Uruk, and tell *him* your tale. Then he will send a temple-woman here, for if she sits at evening by the wells the wild man, seeing her, will draw to her, attracted by her beauty; he will know that he is one of her kind. Then the beasts will run from him, as from all other men, and he will leave the plains."

The trapper went, and told the King his tale.

"Lord," said the trapper, "a wild man roams the plains and drinks at water-holes with the gazelle. He eats grass like the beasts and sucks their milk. He sets them free from all my traps, fills in the pits. I am afraid to hunt. What shall I do?"

"Take back a temple-woman to the plains, for if she sits at evening by the wells the wild man, seeing her, will draw to her, attracted by her beauty; he will know that he is one of her kind. Then the beasts will run from him, as from all other men, and he will leave the plains."

The trapper took a temple-woman back. They journeyed to the wells and there sat down to wait for Enkidu. He did not come the first day, nor the next, but on the third he came with the gazelle down from the plains, at evening, at the setting of the sun. When he saw the temple-woman, she seemed fairer than the beasts; when she spoke, her voice seemed sweeter than the birds'. The wild man stayed for six days by the wells and from the woman learned the speech of men, but when he would have gone back to his herd, the wild beasts ran from him, as they would run from any man. He grieved and was perplexed, for now he could not run as fast as they. He went back to the wells and there sat down at the woman's feet, to learn what he must do.

In Uruk, Gilgamesh awoke from sleep and, rising, went to seek his mother out in her temple. When he came there, he bowed down and said: "My mother, I have dreamed a dream. A star fell out of heaven at my feet. I tried to lift it, but I was too weak. I tried to move it but could not prevail. All the land had gathered round the star, the men thronged round it and some kissed its feet. I put my forehead to it, raised it up. I lifted it and carried it to you, and you put it on a par with me, your son."

Ninsun, the wise one, answered Gilgamesh: "The star of heaven which fell down at your feet, which I myself put on a par with you, is the wild man of the plains and like a star in his great strength. He is the friend who, wild heart for wild heart, will equal you and be your second self, to guard your back in battle and in peace sit by your side; to laugh when you laugh and to share your grief. He will not forsake you."

That same night, Gilgamesh dreamed again and, waking, went to Ninsun in her temple.

"Mother, I have dreamed another dream. In Uruk lay an axe, and the people thronged about it in the street. I laid it at your feet and you yourself put it on a par with me, your son."

Ninsun, the wise one, answered Gilgamesh: "The axe you saw is the wild man of the plains. His strength is like an axe. He is the friend who, wild heart for wild heart, will equal you and be your second self, to guard your back in battle and in peace sit by your side; to laugh when you laugh and to share your grief. He will not forsake you."

"May I be granted such a friend," said Gilgamesh.

Meanwhile, the woman talked to Enkidu.

"*You* are no beast to crop the grass," she said, "or drink at water-holes with the gazelle. You are no wild man now. Come, Enkidu, come with me into Uruk, where the king is Gilgamesh the Tyrant, whose vast strength is such that nowhere can he find his match. Now, therefore, he prevails over his people like some great wild ox, not caring for their pain."

Enkidu grew eager at her words. He longed to find a friend—could this be he? Could this be one to share his secret thoughts?

He told the woman: "Take me to Uruk, where Gilgamesh walks restless in his strength. I will challenge him and cry: 'I am the one born on the plains, the strongest of all men, come here to change the proud ways of the tyrant Gilgamesh!' "

"You have no cause to boast," the woman said, "for though you may be strongest of all *men,* yet he is two parts god, and stronger still. Never does he rest by night or day. But I will show you him, if you will come to Uruk, where each day is holiday and people walk the streets in gay attire, as bright as butterflies; where all

the air is filled with scents of spices and perfumes; where wines abound to make your heart rejoice; where all would be as joyous as the sun, if Gilgamesh the King would mend his ways."

The woman halved her robe and clothed the man. She led him like a mother, by the hand down to the sheep-folds, where the shepherds were. They gathered round to see him, brought him bread; he stared at it, because he did not know how he was to eat it. They brought wine, but he was used to drink milk from the beasts and when he tried to lap like any dog, the shepherds laughed and made a mock of him. When they had taught him both to eat and drink, he rubbed his hairy body down with oil and then put on a garment. Now, indeed, he seemed to them the comeliest of men. He was the shepherds' watchman; since he had come they slept at night, while he caught the wolves and lions that fell upon their flocks.

But one day, by the sheep-folds where he sat, he lifted up his eyes and saw a man come running from the city, and he said: "Woman, go bring him to me. Ask him why he comes here."

She called out: "Why do you come here?"

"For help," the man replied. "There is to be a wedding at the meeting-house, and Gilgamesh will surely come and carry off the bride to be his wife. Will you not stop him, Enkidu?"

The wild man shook, his face went white with anger at the stranger's words. He set out with the woman and they hastened to Uruk. They entered into the city and, when they reached the market-place, the people gathered round. Some said: "He looks like Gilgamesh!"

"No, he is much shorter, though heavier of bone, I think."

"They *say* he roamed the plains and ate the grass like any beast!"

The people made him welcome: "A mighty man has come to us. He has arisen like a god to be a match for Gilgamesh!"

And when the King came through the town to the meeting-house of Uruk, his way was barred by Enkidu, who stood there in the street and would not move aside for him. He blocked the doorway with his foot to prevent the King from going in. The two began to fight. They grappled with each other, both snorting like two mighty bulls. They broke the doorpost, and the wall was shaken by their blows. They wrestled in the doorway, in the street, and in the market-place, till Gilgamesh, because he was part-god, threw Enkidu. He threw him to the ground and, standing there, he looked at him. Then his anger was abated and he turned to go away. After he had turned, the fallen Enkidu called out to him: "Your mother, Ninsun, bore a son exalted over all! Enlil himself decreed for you your kingship over Uruk. There is none like you, for your strength is more than that of man."

"It is a god's," said Gilgamesh. "I could not so have thrown you had it been otherwise, and yet I found it hard to do. Truly, you are my equal! Will you be my companion, the friend to know my secret thoughts?"

"I will," said Enkidu, and they sealed a pact of friendship which would endure between them in happiness and sorrow, while both their lives should last. ■

The March to Lanka [from *The Ramayana*]

Asia: India

Lord Vishnu, the preserver aspect of God, was said to have come to earth in different human incarnations or **avatars** whenever the balance between good and evil became too heavily tilted toward evil and **demons** began to dominate the world. Two of Vishnu's most celebrated incarnations, Krishna, King of Dwarka, and Rama, King of Kosola, are retold in India's great epics, *The Mahabharata,* written between 300 B.C.E and 300 C.E., and *The Ramayana,* written in 200 B.C.E.–200 C.E. (Sen, 1961; O'Flaherty, 1975). *The Ramayana* epic, though a literary work, has many different oral versions, and most people learn the story orally. The adventures of the just King Rama; Sita, his faithful bride; Lakshmana, his loyal brother; Hanuman, the monkey general; and Ravana, the ten-headed demon king of the Rakshasas (demons), whose capital was the island of Sri Lanka, are performed through song, story, and drama in every Hindu community in India, as well as in the countries of Burma, Cambodia, Thailand, and Indonesia (on the island of Bali), during the

yearly festivals of Diwali and Dussehra (Khorana, 1999, p. 149).

Whereas in *The Mahabharata* Vishnu as Lord Krishna teaches religious philosophy, especially the meaning of duty (**dharma**) through selfless action and devotion to God (bhakti), in *The Ramayana* as Prince Rama he models the ideal hero. He represents the culture's values, which were much like those of the courtly heroes of medieval Europe. Rama's devotion to God and honor, his steadfast love for his wife, and his unfailing loyalty to his father, brothers, and allies—the monkeys and other animals—as well as his desire to serve by freeing the world from the menace of the demons all show his heroic nature. As a typical hero he demonstrates great feats of strength and skill, which in this case are accomplished with the bow and arrow, "God's Shaft." Like the Greek Theseus and the Celtic King Arthur, Rama passes an early test of strength, the stringing of Shiva's great bow, which identifies him as the only man worthy of Sita. Typical too of the hero, he must go on a quest before he can assume his rightful place as king: He must rescue Sita who has been abducted by Ravana, and he must free humankind from the ravages of the demons. Finally, also typical of the hero, Rama, as a human avatar, is neither perfect nor superhuman. Nor are all of Rama's acts admirable. Though his love for Sita is unswerving, on freeing her he suddenly loses faith in her loyalty and makes her go through a test of which even the gods disapprove (O'Flaherty, 1975, pp. 202–203). By the time he realizes that such proof is not needed, Sita has walked through fire unscathed, thus proving her perfect loyalty.

One of the most popular figures in *The Ramayana* is the monkey general Hanuman, chief among those who fought Ravana. Hanuman, the only one among the monkeys who as an incarnation of the son of the wind god was able to fly and to change size, is rewarded for his courage and loyalty at the end by remaining immortal. In 1930 Dhan Gopal Mukerji wrote that athletic society gymnasiums and swimming clubs in India still carried as their emblem the image of Hanuman, the god of athletics.

The Ramayana, as a great adventure story with ideal love between husband and wife and loyalty between brothers and friends, whether they be human or animal, continues to be immensely popular. The chapter included here shows Hanuman's magical powers and devotion to Rama and Sita and the animals' love of Rama as they help to build a bridge between the southern tip of India and the island of Sri Lanka.

After all the monkeys had assembled in Kishkindha under King Sugriva, Rama, Hanuman, Angada, Lakshmana made inspiring speeches to them and exactly described their coming march to Lanka. Last of all spoke Sugriva, urging them to uphold the honour of the monkey race no matter where or how.

"On the morrow," the King concluded, "we march to Kanya Kumari (Cape Comorin) the southernmost point of India. Now go home and say farewell properly to your families. Report for duty before the first sunwing rises again above the gloom in the east!"

And the following day just as the eagle of dawn had begun to preen his golden pinions, with the clamor of a thousand storms the monkeys set out for Lanka. They leaped over many trees with the agility of hawks. They cleared the rolling hills as goats clear broken fences. They drank, bathed, and swam tawny rivers. They passed as locusts spread over autumn fields. Distances vanished under their feet like sugar into the mouth of a child. Rama and Lakshmana were carried on the backs of large monkeys who worked in relays.

And ere the first day was done they had covered a twentieth part of their journey.

No sooner had the sun risen and set seven times three than the cohorts of Rama stood like clamorous forests on the edge of Cape Comorin. They roared and shouted so loudly with joy that the "surge and thunder" of the Indian Ocean was drowned as a sparrow's chirp is stilled by the wind whistling in an eagle's wing. There they stood, two men surrounded by untold apes and baboons. Before them mile upon mile unfurled the blue banners of the sea. Wherever they peered the waste of waters stretched into forbidding immensity.

After sunset as soon as the bivouacs had been lighted and all the soldiers had comfortably settled in their separate camps Rama, Lakshmana, Sugriva, Jambuban, Angada, and Hanuman held a council of war. "How to span the ocean?" they questioned one another again and again. Rama said, "We cannot leap over the ocean like thee, Hanuman. Only a few tree-dwellers have thy skill and strength. There is naught for us to do but to build a bridge."

"A bridge on a vast ocean!" exclaimed Jambuban and Sugriva. But the young, such as Angada and Lakshmana, said, "It will take a long time to make. By the time it is completed Sita and most of us will have grown old and died."

Hanuman cried, "Why do I not leap over to Sita and bring her back on my neck. That will rescue her quickly and save us a long task of bridge-making." Rama smiled at them all and said, "It is not only for Sita's rescue that we have come, but also to put an end to Ravana and his demon-race. Sita is but one woman amongst many who are exposed to attack by the Rakshasas. It is not enough that we rescue her alone. We must destroy all Lanka and free all womanhood from the menace of Ravana. In order to do our task completely we must have a vast army at Lanka's door. Sita must wait until we build a bridge on which our cohorts can cross and annihilate the Rakshasas utterly."

"Sadhoo, well spoken," shouted all his listeners. But Jambuban the bear-headed monkey who was Sugriva's Dewan (prime minister) counselled, "With all the monkeys working every day every hour it will take ten years to build that bridge to Lanka. Ten years without fighting will undermine the heart of every soldier.

Bridge-building will make pacifists of our warriors. O Rama, set not out on thy plan to span the sea."

A somber and profound pause followed. As if it were unbearable Sugriva broke the silence. "I have pledged you, O Rama, that we shall rescue Sita for you. But I see no reason why we should toil to free all humanity from the menace of Ravana."

Lakshmana answered, "King Sugriva, it is your head, not your heart that speaks so. Prudence is a dweller in the house of reason, a miserly tenant in a narrow home. But what Rama wishes is the truth. We should slay Ravana. Let us save not only Sita but all womanhood by slaughtering the demon vipers no matter how long it takes."

Then shouted Angada and Hanuman, "Thy words have converted us, O Lakshmana. We are devotees at the shrine of thy truth. Let the bridge be built."

"But ten years of civilian work will dry off the spring of our enthusiasm," reiterated Jambuban. "An army of civilians cannot fight demons. Ferocious soldiers are needed for that."

Another pause more depressing that the previous one followed. The monkeys turned their faces toward Rama. Their instinct told them that he had a noble idea in his mind. That tiger-silencing one spoke softly like a mother to her children:

"The bridge can be built in two years. We may have to besiege Lanka for at least ten years after that."

Sugriva grumbled, "How canst thou say that?"

"I have that means by which to do it," rejoined Dasaratha's eldest-born. "Let us rest for the night with perfect peace. On the morrow, friends, we shall commence the building of the bridge."

The force behind Rama's simple words was so great that the meeting broke up without further discussion, and each monkey softly walked away to his camp to bed. Only the two men stayed together. Then, without speaking, Rama signed Lakshmana to meditate.

The two princes folded their legs and sat still praying and meditating. The stars strode across the sky and faded. The giants of the jungle roamed and clamoured while the vast army of tree-dwellers slept. But the two men prayed for the help of Heaven, for the aid of all four-footed beasts, and for the cooperation of birds. They sought also the assistance of the Sun, the moon, and the seasons. Each by each the souls of the sleep-

ing birds and beasts answered, "Yes, we will help." The heavenly bodies, too, answered, "We come, Rama, to aid you as you ask." So while the world slept, its waking soul pledged Rama its support. Such is the power that prayer and meditation can create! And because Rama was fighting to save not only his own bride but all humanity the whole universe was glad to espouse his cause.

Thus that memorable night was spent. And long before the red wheel of the Sun had churned the ocean into scudding gold, purple, and amber birds were swarming with stones in their beaks, leopards and lions were flinging skulls and bones of their prey into the deep, monkeys row upon row were pulling down trees and rocks, elephants were plowing up earth with their tusks and flinging it with their trunks, even Makara (Leviathan) and his sea-concealed family rose to assist Rama in his bridge-building.

Last of all came the chipmunks. They begged to be of service. Rama with sweet thanks said, "Dip your bodies in the sea, roll yourselves in the sand, then go and shake the sand between the stones that the apes are joining together. Go make mortar for me." The chipmunks busied themselves at once. Lo, hardly a few minutes passed when their chief crawled up to Rama's lap and said, "Some monkey flung a rock the wrong way and hit me. O Rama, I am dying." But Rama said, "I will heal you," and he stroked the chipmunk three times with his hand. The previous night's meditation had given Rama so much power that healing passed out of him and made the little beast whole in a trice. But Rama's fingers left their marks on his body so that even now India's chipmunks wear coats of three stripes. Those are the finger marks that their ancestors received at the building of the Rama-setu or Rama-causeway to Lanka.

The sea rose and fell but it was no longer heard; the sharp chirp of stones falling from bird-beaks, the crash and smash of rock and timber, the hissing of the surf, the hammering of boulder on boulder, the sinking of mammoth granite shafts in the deep, and the singing of those who worked and enjoyed work because they could sing, drowned all else. Thus toil became joy, and joy a serenity of the soul.

The day ended the night was no less like the day, for the moon poured effulgence from above in answer to the prayer of Rama. So the beasts of night toiled as hard as had done those of the day. Hammering of stone on stone rang louder than the storm smiting the "sapphire-silver" sea. So numerous were the beasts at work that they wrought with "thunder-stilling" fury. Though Rama slumbered his friends toiled at night.

Since they did this from their own free will they forged the stone chain on the sea without regard to his presence or his absence. Toil became their joy. They loved him, hence they toiled, not lashed by overseers, not cursed by leaders. ■

 # The Sword in the Stone

Europe: England

Almost nothing is known about the historic Arthur, except that he was a Romanized Briton who, after the collapse of the Roman Empire in 410 C.E., briefly restored Roman civilization in Britain. For 50 years he stopped the onslaught of "barbarians" from all sides, most notably the Germanic tribes the Angles (English) and Saxons, who would afterwards become the rulers of England.

The earliest historical records mention the battles at the end of the fifth century in which Arthur was thought to have played a leading role, but there are no records of him by name until 300 years later (Morris, 1973; Ashe, 1998). There is no dearth, however, of legends, romances, ballads, poems, novels, plays, operas, films, picture books, computer games, and Internet discussion groups about Arthur and his knights (Masson, 1999). Each era had its ideal Arthur and reasons for telling the Arthurian tales. Geoffrey of Monmouth's *History of the Kings of Britain* in 1138, written after the Norman conquest, provided legitimacy to the new rulers of England by tying them to Britain's glorious beginnings, all the way back to its legendary founder Brutus from Troy and including King Arthur. In this early legendary history Arthur is depicted as a war leader, and emphasis is still on his campaigns

against the Saxons, Picts, and Irish and against the barbarians on the European continent (MacColl, 1999). Legends about Arthur and most of the people associated with him (Uther, Guinevere, Merlin, Owen, Gawain, Mordred, Bedivere, Kay, and Yvain) had been part of the oral repertoire of the Welsh bards, but the international craze began only after Geoffrey's *History* was written.

Interest in the stories of King Arthur and his knights began to flower during the thirteenth century, the age of chivalry, when the French patron of the arts Countess Marie de Champaign and her courtiers began to invest King Arthur's court with their new chivalric ideals (Masson, 1999). The knight now not only was courageous and tough but also protected the weak and innocent, fought for high ideals, displayed chivalric honor during combat, and met all tests of courtesy to his lady, who was placed on a pedestal of love and veneration. It was through the French poet Chretien de Troyes that the Arthurian romances became best known throughout Europe, while it was through the German Wolfram von Eschenbach's story of Parzival that the quest for the Holy Grail became popularized as a Christian allegory (Comfort, 1914; Littleton and Malcor, 1996). The version of King Arthur that made him popular with English speakers, however, was Thomas Malory's *Mort d'Arthur* (1484). There was little interest in King Arthur during the seventeenth and eighteenth centuries, but after a few hundred years of neglect, the romance of Arthur and his

Source: "The Sword in the Stone" from *Stories of King Arthur and His Knights* by Barbara Leonie Picard. Wood Engravings by Roy Morgan. Oxford University Press, 1955. Reprinted by permission of the author. pp. 1–8.

knights was revived in the nineteenth century, most notably through the "Idylls of the King" by Tennyson and the operas of Wagner.

The stories continue to be retold and rewritten for our own age not only in popular musicals such as *Camelot* and spoofs such as the film *Monty Python and the Holy Grail,* but also by feminist writers such as Marion Zimmer Bradley, whose book *Mists of Avalon* (1982) presents a whole new view of the villain Morgan le Fay (Morgaine in the book). What has endured through the ages is the idea of a just and good king who once inspired his men to fight for what was right, protecting the weak and innocent, and whose world of peace and justice might yet come again. Of particular appeal in our democratic world is the round table, which signified the meeting of equals, where one seat was reserved for the perfect knight who earned it through merit. Sir Galahad was the only knight who was ever allowed to occupy this special seat, which was called Siege Perilous because it dumped off all unworthy knights.

Picard's version, told below, begins with the testing of the **culture hero**, Arthur. Merlin, who in earlier eras was considered a Druid (a Celtic seer), became a wizard in nineteenth century versions.

In the old days, as it is told, there was a king in Britain named Uther Pendragon. He was a good king and mighty, and much of his strength he owed to his chief counselor Merlin. For Merlin was an enchanter who could read the stars and hold converse with the fairy world; Merlin knew the secrets of nature and the hearts of men; to him the future was as clear as the past, and of either he could speak when he chose; and he could change his shape at will. So that it was small wonder King Uther prospered with such a counselor.

Now, at that time, the duke of Tintagel, in Cornwall, made war on his overlord, King Uther, and came against him with an army. In the fighting the duke was slain and his men yielded, all save those in his castle of Tintagel which was held by his lady, Igraine. And because she was a brave and noble lady, King Uther's lords pleaded with him that he would make peace with her, and to this Uther agreed. When he saw the Lady Igraine, how fair she was and of how great dignity, he loved her; and because, though of middle age, he had no queen, he took her for his wife, and there was great rejoicing in the land. At the same time he gave in marriage the two young daughters of Igraine and the dead duke, Margawse and Morgan le Fay. Margawse was wedded to King Lot of Orkney in Scotland; and Morgan le Fay, who, for all her youth, was as skilled in sorcery as any witch of thrice her years, was wedded to good King Uriens of Gore.

Soon after this Merlin came to Uther and said, "On a certain day, a son will be born to your queen, and because there are things which are hidden from other men yet not from me, I know that it would be well if you were to give me the child when he is born, that I may take him secretly to a good knight whom I know, and so shall he grow up in safety."

And because he ever trusted Merlin's counsel, King Uther agreed to this.

The months passed and there came a day when a son was born to Uther and Igraine, and the little child was wrapped in cloth of gold and given to Merlin, who carried him swiftly away from the castle of the king to the home of a knight named Sir Ector. And Sir Ector's lady took the babe as her foster child, and he was christened Arthur and reared as brother to her own son, Kay.

Two years later that which Merlin had foreseen took place, and King Uther fell sick and lay dying, with his good Queen Igraine weeping at his bedside. Then Merlin came to the king at the head of all the nobles of the realm and asked, "Is it your wish that Arthur, your son, should be king when you are gone?" And before all the great lords gathered there, King Uther said, "That is my wish and my command." After that he spoke no more, but died. And soon Queen Igraine was also dead, for she did not long survive her lord. And again as Merlin had foreseen, once the land was without a strong man to rule it, the nobles fell to quarreling amongst themselves and gathering each of them his own army and marching against his neighbour; and in the heart of each one was the thought, "Wherever he is, what is this child Arthur to me? Surely I myself am more fitted to be a king than any other in the land?" And so it went on for many years with all Britain in great turmoil and distress.

But in the home of Sir Ector, young Arthur grew into a handsome lad, courteous and brave; skilled in horsemanship and all knightly feats, obeying and honouring those whom he thought his parents, and ever loving his supposed brother, Kay. Often Merlin would come to Ector's house and talk with Arthur, telling him strange and marvelous things and teaching him much that a king should know; though Arthur guessed not why he was thus favoured by one whose wisdom had been so respected by a monarch.

When Arthur was some fourteen years old, Merlin caused, by his enchantments, a large stone to appear before the great church in London. Upon this stone was an anvil, and thrust into the anvil was a sword, and on the anvil was written in letters of gold, "He who draws forth this sword is the rightful king of Britain."

When the people saw this they all marveled, and many tried to draw forth the sword, but they all failed. Therefore ten knights were chosen to guard the stone and anvil day and night, that they might keep watch for him who was to be their king.

Soon after, a great tournament and jousting were proclaimed in London for New Year's day, and knights came from all over the land to try their skill at arms, and there were many among them who hoped also to draw the sword from the anvil.

Now Kay, Sir Ector's son, had but lately been ordained knight, and he was eager to show his skill before strangers and wished to test his courage in the tourneying, so he begged that his father might permit him to travel to London and take part in the great gathering. To this Sir Ector agreed, and one morning he and Kay set forth; and with them went Arthur as squire to the new-made knight, to carry his shield and his lance for him and to look to his horse.

They rode across the wintry fields and along the frosty roads until they were close to London, and there they lodged at an inn, close by the great church. Although he said nothing of it to his father or to Arthur, Kay had determined in his heart to try to draw the sword out from the anvil. "For," he thought, "why might it not be I who shall be king as well as any other man?" But Arthur was too eagerly watching and hearing all the sights and sounds of London to have any other thoughts in his head.

On the first day of the jousting, the three of them rode to the place where the contests were to be held, a wide field beyond the city walls. Arthur carried Kay's lance and his shield which he had polished until it shone; but in his eagerness Kay had forgotten his sword and left it at the inn, and it was not until they were in sight of the gay colored pavilions which had been set up in the tourney field that he missed it, and exclaimed in annoyance.

"What has happened?" asked Arthur.

"I have forgotten my sword," said Kay. "Ride back to the inn and fetch it for me."

Arthur did as he was bidden and Kay called after him impatiently, urging him to make haste. But when Arthur came to the inn he found the door locked and the windows shuttered fast and the hostess and all her servants gone to watch the jousting.

He rode along the streets looking for someone from whom he might borrow a sword, but he saw no one at all, for everyone had gone to the fields beyond the city walls. Just as Arthur was despairing, he saw before him the great church, and there, in front of it, the stone with the anvil and the sword.

"I will try to draw out the sword from the anvil," he thought, "for it seems there is no other sword left in all the city, and it shall never be said that my brother Kay lacked a sword at his first jousting."

Even the ten knights who guarded the stone were gone to the tourneying, so that no one saw Arthur when he dismounted and walked up to the stone. He took hold of the hilt of the sword and made to give it a mighty pull, but to his surprise the sword came out of the anvil easily, as thought it had never been held fast. Yet Arthur wasted no time marveling at this; he mounted his horse and galloped back to where Kay waited for him at the entrance to the tourney-ground. "Here is a sword for you, brother," he said.

Kay looked at the sword and knew at once that it was the sword from the anvil, for he had stared long at it the day before, wondering whether he dared try to draw it forth. He glanced at Arthur, but Arthur was tightening the girths of his saddle and did not notice him. On an impulse, Kay went to Sir Ector and held out the sword. "Here is the sword from the anvil, father. Am I to be king of all Britain?"

With wonder Sir Ector asked him, "How did you come by it?"

And Kay stared at the ground and said slowly, "My brother Arthur gave it to me."

Sir Ector called to Arthur and questioned him, and Arthur said, "I drew it out from the anvil that my brother might not lack a sword. Have I done wrong?"

The three of them rode back to the church, and there Sir Ector put the sword back in the anvil. Then he tried to draw it forth himself, but it would not move an inch. "Now do you try, Kay," he said. But though he too tried with all his strength, neither could Kay release it.

"Now shall Arthur try," said Sir Ector. And when Arthur set his hand to the hilt of the sword, he drew it forth with no effort.

Marveling, Sir Ector said, "You shall be king of Britain, Arthur."

"For what reason should I be king, father?"

Sir Ector pointed to the letters of gold that were graven on the anvil. "Because it is so decreed," he said. And he knelt before Arthur and Kay knelt beside him.

"Do not kneel to me, father," pleaded Arthur with distress.

"I am not your father, lord," said Ector. And he told Arthur of how Merlin had brought a little child to him, wrapped in cloth of gold. "And I thought then, and have thought ever since, that you came of nobler blood that I or mine," he said.

But when Arthur knew that he was not Sir Ector's son, and that Kay was not his brother, he wept and said, "You and your lady have ever been kind to me, and I could not have loved you more had you been my own parents, nor could I love Kay more were he truly my brother, and now must I lose you all?"

"You must be king," said Sir Ector gently, "for so it is decreed and only one who was a coward and worthless, would shirk a duty God had set on him."

Yet Arthur still wept. "I shall never forget all you have done for me. When I am indeed king, ask what you will of me, and it shall be yours."

"I am an old man," said Sir Ector, "and for myself I ask nothing. But there is Kay. If you would make him seneschal of all your household, then should I be well content."

"It shall be so," promised Arthur.

Afterwards, Arthur had to replace the sword in the anvil, and then once again, in full sight of all the people gathered there, he had to draw it forth; and with one accord they called to him as their rightful king. And the lords who were wearied of their quarreling made peace and swore to follow Arthur, so that all the land was his.

His first deed when he was crowned was to fulfill his promise to Sir Ector, and make Kay his seneschal, the chief lord of all his household.

Good Sir Ector and his lady died soon after, but Sir Kay the Seneschal grew up to have a bitter tongue which he took no pains to curb. He was quick to anger, and his ungracious ways lost him many a friend; but Arthur always loved him, and for himself, not merely for the remembrance of the childhood they had passed together. And for his part, Kay loved Arthur jealously, serving him with devotion even while he criticized what he chose to regard as folly: the king's rashness in danger, his unfailing generosity, and the trust he showed to all. ∎

Gawain and the Lady Ragnell

Europe: England

Sir Gawain, Arthur's nephew and bravest knight (until Lancelot came along), featured in the Celtic legends of

Source: "Gawain and the Lady Ragnell" from *The Maid of the North: Feminist Folktales from Around the World* by Ethel Johnston Phelps, © 1981 by Ethel Johnston Phelps. Reprinted by permission of Henry Holt and Company, LLC. pp. 35–44.

Arthur long before the high Middle Ages. His most famous test is told in the poem *Sir Gawain and the Green Knight,* written by a fourteenth century contemporary of Chaucer. The poem begins with a test of courage, an offer by a mysterious Green Knight, arriving at King Arthur's court, to swap a head for a head. This part of the Green Knight story retells a far older legend, a version of which was recorded in the story cycle about the Irish hero Cuchulain from the first century C.E. (Fleming et al., 1996). Following the chivalric ideals of the high Middle Ages, however, Gawain is tested not only for courage but also for courtesy and honor; he must spend three days with the Green Knight's wife without succumbing to her charms. He passes the test and retains his honor. In the following story he is even more sympathetic, as he not only retains his own honor but also treats his wife with real respect.

The story on which Ethel Phelps based the following retelling was written by an anonymous poet who was a contemporary of Chaucer (late 1300s). Apparently, this romance was well known at the time, as Chaucer told a related version through the tale of the Wife of Bath, and still another version was written by the poet John Gower as "Tale of Florent" (Sands, 1966).

Long ago, in the days of King Arthur, the finest knight in all Britain was the king's nephew Gawain. He was, by reputation, the bravest in battle, the wisest, the most courteous, the most compassionate, and the most loyal to his king.

One day in late summer, Gawain was with Arthur and the knights of the court at Carlisle in the north. The King returned from the day's hunting looking so pale and shaken that Gawain followed him at once to his chamber.

"What has happened, my lord?" asked Gawain with concern.

Arthur sat down heavily. "I had a very strange encounter in Inglewood forest . . . I hardly know what to make of it." And he related to Gawain what had occurred.

"Today I hunted a great white stag," said Arthur. "The stag at last escaped me and I was alone, some distance from my men. Suddenly a tall, powerful man appeared before me with sword upraised."

"And you were unarmed!"

"Yes. I had only my bow and a dagger in my belt. He threatened to kill me," Arthur went on. "And he swung his sword as though he meant to cut me down on the spot! Then he laughed horribly and said he would give me one chance to save my life."

"Who was this man?" cried Gawain. "Why should he want to kill you?"

"He said his name was Sir Gromer, and he sought revenge for the loss of his northern lands."

"A chieftain from the north!" exclaimed Gawain. "But what is this one chance he spoke of?"

"I gave him my word I would meet him one year from today, unarmed, at the same spot, with the answer to a question!" said Arthur.

Gawain started to laugh, but stopped at once when he saw Arthur's face. "A question! Is it a riddle? And one year to find the answer? That should not be hard!"

"If I can bring the true answer to the question, 'What is it that women most desire, above all else?' my life will be spared." Arthur scowled. "He is sure I will fail. It must be a foolish riddle that no one can answer."

"My lord, we have one year to search the kingdom for answers," said Gawain confidently. "I will help you. Surely one of the answers will be the right one."

"No doubt you are right—someone will know the answer," Arthur looked more cheerful. "The man is mad, but a chieftain will keep his word."

For the next twelve months, Arthur and Gawain asked the question from one corner of the kingdom to the other. Then at last the appointed day drew near. Although they had many answers, Arthur was worried.

"With so many answers to choose from, how do we know which is the right one?" he asked in despair. "Not one of them has the ring of truth."

A few days before he was to meet Sir Gromer, Arthur rode out alone through the golden gorse and purple heather. The track led upward toward a grove of great oaks. Arthur, deep in thought, did not look up until he reached the edge of the oak wood. When he raised his head, he pulled up suddenly in astonishment.

Before him was a grotesque woman. She was almost as wide as she was high, her skin was mottled green, and spikes of weedlike hair covered her head. Her face seemed more animal than human.

The woman's eyes met Arthur's fearlessly. "You are Arthur the king," she said in a harsh, croaking voice. "In two days time you must meet Sir Gromer with the answer to a question."

Arthur turned cold with fear. He stammered, "Yes . . . yes . . . that is true. Who are you? How did you know of this?"

"I am the lady Ragnell. Sir Gromer is my stepbrother. You haven't found the true answer, have you?"

"I have many answers," Arthur replied curtly. "I do not see how my business concerns you." He gathered up the reins, eager to be gone.

"You do not have the right answer." Her certainty filled him with a sense of doom. The harsh voice went on, "But I know the answer to Sir Gromer's question."

Arthur turned back in hope and disbelief. "You do? Tell me the true answer to his question, and I will give you a large bag of gold."

"I have no use for gold," she said coldly.

"Nonsense, my good woman. With gold you can buy anything you want!" He hesitated a moment, for the huge, grotesque face with the cool, steady eyes unnerved him. He went on hurriedly, "What is it you want? Jewelry? Land? Whatever you want I will pay you—that is, if you truly have the right answer."

"I know the answer. I promise you that!" She paused. "What I demand in return is that the knight Gawain become my husband."

There was a moment of shocked silence. Then Arthur cried, "Impossible! You ask the impossible, woman!"

She shrugged and turned to leave.

"Wait, wait a moment!" Rage and panic overwhelmed him, but he tried to speak reasonably.

"I offer you gold, land, jewels. I cannot give you my nephew. He is his own man. He is not mine to give!"

"I did not ask you to *give* me the knight Gawain," she rebuked him. "If Gawain himself agrees to marry me, I will give you the answer. Those are my terms."

"Impossible!" he sputtered. "I could not bring him such a proposal."

"If you should change your mind, I will be here tomorrow," said she and disappeared into the oak woods.

Shaken from the weird encounter, Arthur rode homeward at a slow pace.

"Save my own life at Gawain's expense? Never!" he thought. "Loathsome woman! I could not even speak of it to Gawain."

But the afternoon air was soft and sweet with birdsong, and the fateful meeting with Sir Gromer weighed on him heavily. He was torn by the terrible choice facing him.

Gawain rode out from the castle to meet the king. Seeing Arthur's pale, strained face, he exclaimed, "My lord! Are you ill? What has happened?"

"Nothing . . . nothing at all." But he could not keep silent long. "The colossal impudence of the woman! A monster, that's what she is! That creature, daring to give me terms!"

"Calm yourself, uncle." Gawain said patiently. "What woman? Terms for what?"

Arthur sighed. "She knows the answer to the question. I didn't intend to tell you."

"Why not? Surely that's good news! What is the answer?"

"She will not tell me until her terms are met," said the king heavily. "But I assure you, I refuse to consider her proposal!"

Gawain smiled, "You talk in riddles yourself, uncle. Who is this woman who claims to know the answer? What is her proposal?"

Seeing Gawain's smiling, expectant face, Arthur at first could not speak. With his eyes averted, the king told Gawain the whole story, leaving out no detail.

"The lady Ragnell is Sir Gromer's stepsister? Yes, I think she would know the right answer," Gawain said thoughtfully. "How fortunate that I will be able to save your life!"

"No! I will not let you sacrifice yourself!" Arthur cried.

"It is my choice and my decision," Gawain answered. "I will return with you tomorrow and agree to the marriage—on condition that the answer she supplies is the right one to save your life."

Early the following day, Gawain rode out with Arthur. But not even meeting the loathsome lady face to face could shake his resolve. Her proposal was accepted.

Gawain bowed courteously. "If on the morrow your answer saves the king's life, we will be wed."

On the fateful morning, Gawain watched the king stow a parchment in his saddlebag. "I'll try all these answers first," said Arthur.

They rode together for the first part of the journey. Then Arthur, unarmed as agreed, rode on alone to Inglewood to meet Sir Gromer.

There the powerful chieftain was waiting, his broadsword glinting in the sun.

Arthur read off one answer, then another, and another. Sir Gromer shook his head in satisfaction.

"No, you have not the right answer!" he said raising his sword high. "You've failed, and now—"

"Wait!" Arthur cried. "I have one more answer. What a woman desires above all else is the power of sovereignty—the right to exercise her own will."

With a loud oath the man dropped his sword. "You did not find that answer by yourself!" he shouted. "My cursed stepsister, Ragnell, gave it to you. Bold, interfering hussy! I'll run her through with my sword . . . I'll lop off her head . . . " Turning, he plunged into the forest a string of horrid curses echoing behind him.

Arthur rode back to where Gawain waited with the monstrous Ragnell. They returned to the castle in silence. Only the grotesque lady Ragnell seemed in good spirits.

The news spread quickly throughout the castle. Gawain, the finest knight in the land, was to marry this monstrous creature! Some tittered and laughed at the spectacle; others said the lady Ragnell must possess very great lands and estates, but mostly there was stunned silence.

Arthur took his nephew aside nervously. "Must you go through with it at once? A postponement perhaps?"

Gawain looked at him steadily. "I gave my promise, my lord. The lady Ragnell's answer saved your life. Would you have me—"

"Your loyalty makes me ashamed! Of course you cannot break your word." And Arthur turned away.

The marriage took place in the abbey. Afterward, with Gawain and the lady Ragnell sitting at the high dais table beside the king and queen, the strange wedding feast began.

"She takes the space of two women on the chair," muttered the knight Gareth. "Poor Gawain!"

"I would not marry such a creature for all the land in Christendom!" answered his companion.

An uneasy silence settled on the hall. Only the monstrous Lady Ragnell displayed good spirits and good appetite. Throughout the long day and evening, Gawain remained pleasant and courteous. In no way did his manner toward his strange bride show other than kind attention.

The wedding feast drew to a close, Gawain and his bride were conducted to their chamber and were at last alone.

The lady Ragnell gazed at her husband thoughtfully.

"You have kept your promise well and faithfully," she observed.

Gawain inclined his head. "I could not do less, my lady."

"You've shown neither revulsion nor pity, she said. After a pause she went on, "Come now, we are wedded! I am waiting to be kissed."

Gawain went to her at once and kissed her. When he stepped back, there stood before him a slender young woman with gray eyes and a serene, smiling face.

His scalp tingled in shock. "What manner of sorcery is this?" he cried hoarsely.

"Do you prefer me in this form?" she smiled and turned slowly in a full circle.

But Gawain backed away warily, "I . . . yes . . . of course . . . but . . . I don't understand . . . " For this sudden evidence of sorcery with its unknown powers, made him confused and uneasy.

"My stepbrother, Sir Gromer, had always hated me," said the lady Ragnell. "Unfortunately, through his mother, he has a knowledge of sorcery, and so he changed me into a monstrous creature. He said I must live in that shape until I could persuade the greatest knight in Britain to willingly choose me for his bride. He said it would be an impossible condition to meet!"

"Why did he hate you so cruelly?"

Her lips curled in amusement. "He thought me bold and unwomanly because I defied him. I refused his commands both for my property and my person."

Gawain said with admiration. "You won the 'impossible' condition he set, and now his evil spell is broken!"

"Only in part." Her clear gray eyes held his. "You have a choice, my dear Gawain, which way I will be. Would you have me in this, my own shape, at night and my former ugly shape by day? Or would you have me grotesque at night in our chamber, and my own shape in the castle by day? Think carefully before you choose."

Gawain was silent only a moment. He knelt before her and touched her hand.

"It is a choice I cannot make, my dear Ragnell. It concerns you. Whatever you choose to be—fair by day or fair by night—I will willingly abide by it."

Ragnell released a long deep breath. The radiance in her face overwhelmed him.

"You have answered well, dearest Gawain, for your answer has broken Gromer's evil spell completely. The last condition he set has been met! For he said that if, after marriage to the greatest knight in Britain, my hus-band freely gave me the power of choice, the power to exercise my own free will, the wicked enchantment would be broken forever."

Thus, in wonder and in joy, began the marriage of Gawain and the lady Ragnell. ■

Robin Hood and the Bishop of Hereford

Europe: England

Robin Hood is a perennial favorite. The first known reference to the popularity of his legend is in William Langland's 1377 *Piers Plowman,* in which a lazy priest named Sloth admits that he doesn't really know the Mass, "But I can [know] rymes of Robyn Hood" (cited in Leach, 1955, p. 13; Barber, 1999, p. 504). Since then ballads, pageants, plays, poems, children's books, Looney Tunes cartoons, television series, computer games, and films have celebrated the legend. Robin Hood was a thirteenth or fourteenth century outlaw, described in John Mair's fifteenth century chronicle as one who "would allow no woman to suffer injustice, nor would he spoil the poor, but rather enrich them from the plunder taken from abbots" (cited in Leach, 1955, p. 13).

But what made Robin so popular during the late Middle Ages and for hundreds of years thereafter is not simply that he robbed the rich and gave to the poor, but that he stood for the yeoman's love of freedom and resistance to oppressive laws (Singman, 1998; Theis, 2001). Some of the most irksome of the laws, referred to in the stories, were the forest laws instituted after the Norman conquest, which could get a person hanged for hunting in the king's forests. Because the king's forests included much of England and extended to towns and fields, these laws also prevented people from keeping the deer out of their fields or from cutting wood (Theis, 2001). It was easy to become an outlaw under such harsh conditions. Several ballads, or story poems sung to a tune, relate how a free landholder might become a beggar or a serf for defaulting on a loan by even one day. The Sheriff of Nottingham, the main representative of authority in most of the Robin Hood legends, and the clergy, who were often more interested in amassing wealth than in caring for their parishioners, are two of Robin and his men's most frequent targets. Robin, however, is shown to be a religious man, who in at least one story, "Robin Hood and the Monk," risks his life to go to church.

Robin, his men, and in the later ballads Maid Marian also stood for the joyful freedom of the green forest as compared with the confining civilization of town. In some of the stories, such as "Robin and the Butcher" Robin or Little John acts as an unsuccessful merchant or derides town life (Knight and Ohlgren, 1997). Nature and the coming of summer were celebrated in the fifteenth and sixteenth centuries, with Maying festivities that included pageants and parades featuring Robin Hood as King of the May and Maid Marian as Queen (Knight and Ohlgren, 1997).

Frances James Child, a nineteenth century folklorist, collected English and Scottish ballads in the

Source: "Robin Hood and the Bishop of Hereford" from *The English and Scottish Popular Ballads* by Francis James Child. Child Ballad 144. New York: Cooper Square, 1962. Reprint of 1889 edition. pp. 195–196.

Appalachians, where many of the descendants of English and Scottish immigrants continued to sing and tell the old folktales (1962). Robin Hood ballads were among those he collected.

Besides the version below, there is at least one other variant told in "Robin Hood and the Bishop," in which Robin does not even provoke the bishop but must hide from him as he approaches the forest. Robin accomplishes this by changing outfits with an old woman who is happy to help him as she recalls his earlier kindness to her. Although the high ranking clergy are often shown as heartless in the medieval ballads, having the bishop act like the sheriff is a bit unusual but not implausible, as bishops were members of the aristocracy and could engage in military action (Knight and Ohlgren, 1997).

One of the earliest set of adventures of Robin Hood written for children was by the American artist and writer Howard Pyle at the end of the nineteenth century. In his *Merry Adventures of Robin Hood of Great Renown of Nottinghamshire* Pyle celebrated the outdoors and emphasized the robust, rough-and-tumble life of Robin and his merry men. Since then numerous other children's versions have been written, from picture books to Robin McKinley's psychologically probling novel *Outlaws of Sherwood* (1988).

Some they will talk of bold Robin Hood,
And some of barons bold,
But I'll tell you how he served the Bishop of Hereford
When he robbed him of his gold.

As it befel in merry Barnsdale,
And under the green-wood tree,
The Bishop of Hereford was to come by,
With all his company.

"Come, kill a venson," said bold Robin Hood,
"Come kill me a good fat deer;
The Bishop of Hereford is to dine with me today,
And he shall pay well for his cheer.

"We'll kill a fat venson," said bold Robin Hood,
"And dress it by the highway-side;
And we will watch the Bishop narrowly,
Lest some other way he should ride."

Robin Hood dressed himself in shepherd's attire,
With six of his men also;
And, when the Bishop of Hereford came by,
They about the fire did go.

"O what is the matter?" then said the Bishop,
"Or for whom do make this ado?
Or why do you kill the king's venson,
When your company is so few?"

"We are shepherds," said bold Robin Hood,
"And we keep sheep all the year,
And we are disposed to be merry this day,
And to kill of the king's fat deer."

"You are brave fellows," said the Bishop,
"And the king of your doings shall know;
Therefore make hast and come along with me,
For before the king you shall go."

"O pardon, O pardon," said bold Robin Hood,
"O pardon, I thee pray!
For it becomes not your lordship's coat
To take so many lives away."

"No pardon, no pardon," says the Bishop,
"No pardon I thee owe;
Therefore make haste, and come along with me,
For before the king you shall go."

Then Robin set his back against a tree,
And his foot against a thorn,
And from underneath his shepherd's coat
He pull'd out a bugle-horn.

He put the little end to his mouth,
And a loud blast he did blow,
Till threescore and ten of bold Robin's men
Came running all on a row;

All making obeysance to bold Robin Hood;
'T was a comely sight for to see:
"What is the matter, master," said Little John,
"That you blow so hastily?"

"O here is the Bishop of Hereford,
And no pardon we shall have."
"Cut off his head, master," said Little John,
"And throw him in his grave."

"O pardon, O pardon," said the Bishop,
"O pardon, I thee pray!
For if I had known it had been you,
I'd have gone some other way."

"No pardon, no pardon," said Robin Hood,
"No pardon I thee owe;
Therefore make haste and come along with me,
For to merry Barnsdale you shall go."

Then Robin he took the Bishop by the hand,
And led him to merry Barnsdale;
He makd him to stay and sup with him that night,
And drink wine, beer, and ale.

"Call in the reckoning," said the Bishop,
"For methinks it grows wondrous high."

"Lend me your purse, Bishop," said Little John,
"And I'll tell you bye and bye."

Then Little John took the bishop's cloak,
And spread it on the ground,
And out of the bishop's portmantua
He told three hundred pound.

"Here's money enough, master," said Little John,
"And a comely sight 't is to see;
It makes me in charity with the Bishop,
Tho he heartily loveth not me."

Robin Hood took the Bishop by the hand,
And he caused the music to play,
And he made the Bishop dance in his boots
And glad he could get so away. ◾

The Singing Contest

Europe: Finland

Kalevala, or land of heroes, is both a place and the title of an epic created by a nineteenth century Finnish physician and folklorist, Elias Lönnrot, out of Finnish narrative folk poetry, also referred to as runes, that he heard during 20 years of collecting in what was then eastern Finland (Keralia). Today the region is part of Russia, but the culture and language are Finnish. Lönnrot was clear about the fact that his epic was an artificially constructed narrative, created from many disparate runes that might never have been sung together and that included not only narrative poems but also wedding songs and a great many charms collected by Lönnrot. Foreign scholars of folklore such as the German Jacob Grimm, however, hailed it as a newly discovered epic. The stories about old Vainamoinen (Calm-water Man), Ilmarinen, and

Lemminkainen (accent always on the first syllable), all heroes who traveled from Kalevala to the north country of Pohjola (Poh-yo-la), were likened to the wanderings of Odysseus (Pentikäinen, 1989). Lönnrot structured the epic around the quest for a magical object, a kind of horn of plenty, the Sampo. Louhi, the Mistress of Pohjola, had ordered Vainamoinen to forge it in return for his freedom after she had saved him from the primordial sea. She even offered her daughter into the bargain. Since Vainamoinen was not a blacksmith, he got Ilmarinen, another hero of the Kalevala, to go to the north country and forge it. Ilmarinen succeeded and got his bride, but years later, Vainamoinen, Ilmarinen, and Lemminkainen set off for the north again to steal the Sampo. It shattered as Louhi tried to recapture it. The fragments of the Sampo resulted in all the salt in the ocean (a valuable resource) and the growth of grain on land. The nature of the Sampo has never been fully identified, but it seems to represent nature's bounty.

Source: "The Singing Contest" from *Heroes of the Kalevala: Finland's Saga* by Babette Deutsch, © 1949. Reprinted by permission of Pearson Education, Inc., Upper Saddle River, NJ. pp. 16–29.

Although Lönnrot created the structure of the epic and edited the folk poems or **runes**, only two percent of the Kalevala was actually invented by him. The rest of the story was represented in runes of varying degrees of antiquity. Folklorists and archeologists believe that some of the runes reflect the **shamanistic** religion, myths, and customs of the Central Asian ancestors of the Finnish people and date back as far as 3000 years, while other runes were influenced by medieval Catholicism. The more recent runes present Vainamoinen as human, whereas the earlier runes seem to reflect his mythic nature. Vainamoinen has been called "first man" and was seen as a creative force who, as he floated in the ocean, created life. In earlier versions of *The Kalevala* Lönnrot presented him in mythic terms:

> . . . where his head rose,
> there he ordered islands;
> where he turned his hand,
> there he named a cape;
> where his foot stepped,
> there pike were provided;
> when he went near the land,
> there he built beaches;
> rested his head upon the ground,
> there a bay was prepared;
> turned his side upon the ground,
> there a smooth shore . . . (Pentikäinen, 1989,
>   pp. 134)

The great singing contest described in the selection below between Vainamoinen and Joukahainen was placed early in *The Kalevala* by Lönnrot because he felt that it reflected an early part of the myth/legend, with the two contestants using shamanistic chants to affect the world. (Pentikäinen, 1989). Vainamoinen's taunt that Joukahainen has only women's knowledge may refer to the different styles of singing performed by the sexes: Men sang narrative songs, and women sang lyrical songs (Bosley, 1989). Lönnrot preserved the trochaic rhythm (one strong and one weak syllable per beat), along with alliteration and parallelism, which are the hallmarks of the Kalevala runes (Bosley, 1989; Pentikäinen, 1989). Most children's versions of *The Kalevala* are told in prose.

Long and long ago there lived in the North Country, which is called Pohjola, a clever youth. His name was Joukahainen and he thought himself even cleverer than he was.

In those days, when the world was new and cold, the power of a man lay not only in the strength of his arms. He must also have knowledge of many things and a fine voice. For to know the names of things and to sing well was a way of making magic. Now one thing Joukahainan was sure of, and this was that he could sing better than any maker of songs who ever lived.

One day Joukahainen made a trip to the village. There he found the old men and the girls and the old women and the young men all talking about another singer, who lived in Kalevala, the Land of Heroes. He was the oldest magician, born of the Mother of Waters, and he had all the wisdom of the world. Lusty old Vainamoinen, they called him, and the fame of his singing had gone forth until it reached as far as the North Country.

"He can sing, oh, how he can sing!" said the young girls.

"Better songs than you know how to make, Joukahainen," said the young men.

"Better songs than your father taught you, Joukahainen," said the old men and the old women.

This made Joukahainen very angry.

He went home to his mother and told her what he had heard.

"I must go to the Land of Heroes, mother, and challenge this Vainamoinen. There is no doubt but that I shall come off best, and then everyone in the North Country will know that there is no singer greater than your son Joukahainen."

"Oh, no," said his mother.

"No, indeed!" said his father. "Vainamoinen is a most mighty singer. He will sing against you. He will sing your mouth into a snow-drift. He will sing your hands and feet into ice."

"My mother is wise," answered Joukahainen. "And my father is very wise. But I know better. I will defy this Vainamoinen. I will sing my own songs. I will sing him into stone shoes. I will sing him into wooden trousers.

I will sing a rock onto his shoulders and a stone onto his heart. I will sing his hands into stone gloves and his head into a helmet of stone."

Then Joukahainen went to the stable and fetched his horse. It was a wonderful horse whose mouth breathed flame and whose hooves struck sparks when he stirred. Joukahainen harnessed his horse to a golden sledge, mounted the seat, brandished his beaded whip, and thundered away.

He drove for a day, and he drove for a second day, and he drove for a third day, and on the third day he came to the sweet fields and broad heaths of the Land of Heroes.

Now it happened that lusty Vainamoinen, the oldest magician, was also driving there and on the same road. Joukahainen saw him coming but did not stop. He drove on and he drove fast. Suddenly the sledges jammed. The shafts were wedged together and the collars of the horses were wedged together, and the reins were all tangled, and the runners were dashed to pieces. The shafts sent forth steam like smoke, and the runners dripped snow-water like sweat.

So the two stopped, and looked at each other, considering.

"Who are you?" asked old Vainamoinen. "And how were you brought up, that you drive on without thinking? The horses' collars are broken and the wooden runners are broken. My sledge is smashed to pieces."

"My name is Joukahainen," answered the young man. "But you ought to tell me who you are too. To what race do you belong? From what low stock do you come?"

"Young man," said the other, "if you are Joukahainen, you should move aside, for remember, you are the younger."

"Who is younger and who is older is no concern of mine," said Joukahainen. "All that matters is who is wiser. Let him who knows most keep to the road, and let the stupid yield. If you are Vainamoinen, the oldest magician, then let us set ourselves to singing. We shall see who can teach the other, and who is the greater master of song."

"What sort of knowledge have I?" said Vainamoinen. "What sort of songs can I sing? I have lived all my life quietly among these moors, listening to the cuckoo calling on the border of my own fields. But never

mind that. Be so good, young man, as to tell me all that you know. Relate the sum of your wisdom."

"I know this," answered Joukahainen. "The smoke-hole is in the roof, and the fire is on the hearth. The seal leads a pleasant life, feeding on salmon and herring. The pike spawns in frosty weather and the perch in the summer season.

"If this is not enough for you, I can tell you other weighty matters. In the north they plow with reindeer, and in the south with mares, and in far-off Lapland they use elk.

"I know the tall trees on Mount Pisa and the fir trees on Horna Rock.

"I know three great waterfalls and three broad lakes and three tall mountains."

"These are stories for children," said old Vainamoinen. "This is the learning of women. It is not suited to bearded men. Tell me words of deep wisdom, tell me of everlasting things."

"Very well," answered Joukahainen. "I will tell you more. I know that the titmouse is a bird and that the viper is a snake and that the ruff is a fish. I know that iron is hard and that black mud is bitter. I know that boiling water is painful, and that scorching fire hurts. I know that water is the oldest medicine, and the foam of the cataract is a magic potion. I know that the Creator of the World is a sorcerer.

"Indeed, I will tell you more. I know that water springs from the rock and that fire falls from heaven. I know that we get iron from ore, and find copper in the hills.

"And I will tell you more. I know that marshy country is oldest and that the willow is the first of trees. I know that in the ancient days men made houses of pine-roots, and pots of stone."

"Is this all that you can tell me?" asked lusty old Vainamoinen, "or is it the end of your nonsense?"

"Oh, I can tell you many little things," said Joukahainen. "Well I remember the time when I plowed the ocean and hollowed out its depths. I dug caves for the fishes, I sank deep caverns in the sea. It was I who made the lakes and heaped up the high hills and formed the rocky mountains. When the earth was created it was I who planted the pillars of the sky and reared the arch of the heavens. I sent the moon on its journey and taught the sun its path and fixed a place for the Great Bear, and it was I who sprinkled the heavens with stars."

"You are a liar," said old Vainamoinen. "You have no shame. Certainly you were not present when the depths of the ocean were hollowed out and the high hills heaped up. No one had ever seen you when the pillars of the sky were planted; no one had even heard of you when the moon was sent on its journey and the sun was taught its path and a place was fixed for the Great Bear and the sky was sprinkled with stars.

"If I am ignorant," retorted Joukahainen, "I will look for knowledge at the sword's point. Let us measure swords, old Vainamoinen. Let the blade decide between us, you broad-mouthed singer!"

"I am not afraid of your blade or of your knowledge," said old Vainamoinen. "I will not draw my sword on such a weakling."

This made Joukahainen angrier than ever.

"The man who will not fight," he said, "I will sing into a swine. I have overcome heroes before this. Such a man I will sing into a snouted swine and pitch him onto the dunghill in the corner of the cow-shed."

Then Vainamoinen was filled with rage. And out of his rage he began to sing.

Vainamoinen sang and the lakes swelled up and the earth shook. The hills full of copper trembled and the rocks resounded with thunder. He sang till the mountains cracked and the stones broke on the shore.

He sang of Joukahainen and of his sledge and of his horse. He sang the runners into saplings, the horse-collar into a willow tree and the reins to branches of alder. He sang the gilded sledge into a lake among the rushes. He sang the beaded whip into a reed beside the water. He sang Joukahainen's horse to a stone.

He went on singing. He sang the golden-hilted sword to a flash of lightning. He sang the bright cross-bow into a rainbow. He sang the feathered arrows into hawks in the sky. And when Joukahainen's dog lifted its muzzle he sang him into a stone.

He went on singing. He sang Joukahainen's cap into a mist and his gloves into water-lilies, and his blue coat into a fleecy cloud and his shining belt into scattered stars.

He went on singing. And as he sang Joukahainen sank into a swamp, up to his hips into a marsh, up to his armpits into a quicksand.

Then Joukahainen knew that the contest was ended, that his journey was over, and that he was beaten in song by the oldest magician.

He struggled to raise one foot but he could not lift it. He tried to raise the other but it was shod with stone.

"Oh, wisest Vainamoinen!" he cried. "Reverse your magic! Sing your songs backwards! Release me from torment! Loose me from this place of terror! Oh, oldest of magicians, only set me free and I will pay whatever ransom you ask."

"What will you give me," asked Vainamoinen, "if I reverse my magic, if I sing my song backwards and set you free?"

"I could give you two splendid cross-bows, one swift as the wind, the other sure to hit the mark. You have only to choose between them."

"I do not want your wretched bows," said Vainamoinen. "I have plenty of them myself. All my walls are covered with cross-bows, there are cross-bows on every peg. My cross-bows go hunting in the woods all alone without any man's help."

And he sang Joukahainen deeper into the swamp.

"I could give you two splendid boats," cried Joukahainen. "One is a light racer and the other bears the heaviest loads. You have only to choose between them."

"I do not want your boats," said old Vainamoinen. "I have plenty of them myself. All the creeks are crowded with them, boats to face the gale and boats that travel against the wind."

And he sang Joukahainen deeper into the swamp.

"I have two noble stallions," cried Joukahainen. "One of them cannot be matched for speed and the other is beautiful in harness. You have only to choose between them."

"I do not want your horses," said old Vainamoinen. "I have plenty of them myself. There is a tenant for every stall in my stables. Their backs glisten like water, their haunches wear lakes of fat."

And he sang Joukahainen deeper into the swamp.

"Oh, old Vainamoinen, reverse your magic words, sing your songs backwards!" pleaded Joukahainen. "I will give you a golden hat, I will give you a helmet filled with silver that my father won in battle."

"I do not want your silver," said old Vainamoinen. "I have no use for your gold. I have plenty of both myself. Every store-room is crammed with treasure. Every chest overflows with gold as old as the moonlight and silver as old as the sun."

And he sang Joukahainen yet deeper into the swamp.

"Oh, old Vainamoinen, loose me from this place of terror!" cried Joukahainen. "Free me from torment, and I will give you all the corn stacked in my barns and the yield of all my fields."

"I do not want the corn in your barns," said old Vainamoinen, "and your fields are beneath my notice. I have plenty of them myself. I have fields on every side, and all are rich with stacks. My corn is the finest that grows."

And he sang young Joukahainen deeper into the swamp.

Now Joukahainen was in great misery. He was in the swamp up to his chin. His newly grown beard was bedraggled with mud, his mouth was sunk in the moss and his teeth bit on the roots of trees.

"Oh, wisest Vainamoinen," he mumbled, "oldest of magicians, reverse your magic, sing your songs backward, grant me my life, free me from this prison. My feet are sunk in the streams, my eyes smart with sand. Sing your songs backward and break the spell!

"I will give you my sister Aino. She will dust your room for you and sweep your floor, and keep the milkpots clean. And she will wash your clothes. She will weave you golden cloth and bake you cakes of honey."

Old Vainamoinen was pleased by these words. It would be a good thing to have little Aino, Joukahainen's lovely sister, to care for him in his old age. He sat down on a stone rejoicing and rested and sang. He sang for an hour, and he sang for yet another hour, and then he sang for a third hour. And he reversed the magic words and sang the songs backward and broke the spell.

Joukahainen lifted his chin out of the mud and disentangled his newly grown beard. He led his horse down from the rock and drew his sledge out of the bushes and loosed his beaded whip from the reeds. Then he mounted his sledge and hurried home to his mother.

He was full of gloomy thoughts. He clattered along with mad speed and crashed the sledge to pieces at the door.

His mother was frightened by the noise. His father was angry.

"You are a reckless fellow!" he said. "Did you break the shafts on purpose? Why do you drive so wildly and come crashing home like this?"

Young Joukahainen could not keep back his tears. He shifted his cap without a word. His lips were dry and stiff. His nose drooped sadly.

"What is wrong?" asked his mother. "Why are there tears in your eyes? Why is your mouth so stiff? Why does your nose droop?"

"There is good reason for me to be sad, mother," said young Joukahainen. "The oldest magician has beaten me. How can I keep back the tears? I must mourn all the rest of my life. I have been beaten by Vainamoinen, and what is more, I have pledged him my little sister Aino to be his wife. I have promised him my mother's darling daughter Aino, to care for him in his old age and wait on him always."

At this his mother clapped her hands.

"What are you grieving about?" she cried. "This is no cause for tears. All my life I have wished that we were kin to that high-born hero! All my days I have hoped that the great singer Vainamoinen might take my daughter Aino for his wife!"

But when Joukahainen's sister Aino heard his story, she did not clap her hands for joy. She began to cry. She wept for a whole day and she wept all of the next day as well.

"What are you crying about, my little Aino?" her mother asked her. "You are a lucky girl to have won such a noble bridegroom. Vainamoinen is the greatest of singers and he is the oldest magician."

"Yes, he is an old man," said Aino sadly, and went on crying. She did not wish to marry an old man, even if he were Vainamoinen, the magician.

"Stop crying, foolish girl," said her mother. "The sun shines on other doors and windows than those of your father's house. There are strawberries growing in meadows that are not your father's meadows."

But Aino went on crying.

Still crying, she wandered away into the wood, to gather twigs from which she could make bath whisks, one for her father, one for her mother, and one for her brother, young Joukahainen.

And what strange things happened in the wood you shall hear. ■

Legends About People, Places, Animals and Plants

 The Golden Earth

Ethiopia, located on the Horn of Africa, the portion of the continent that juts into the Red Sea and is closest to Asia, was for thousands of years a crossroads for nomadic tribes, traders, explorers, invaders, religious crusaders (often several of these rolled into one) from Arabia, Europe, and other parts of Africa. The earliest humans might have come from its Rift Valley, and it is one of the oldest countries in the world. Ethiopian emperors traced their ancestry to King Solomon and the Queen of Sheba up to the time of the last emperor, Haile Selassie (*Encarta Africana,* 2000). Its varied land includes high mountains, narrow valleys, and open grasslands that provide good grazing in the winter, though they become parched in the summer, when the few watering holes become gathering places for different tribes (Courlander and Leslau, 1950). As a crossroads of civilizations, Ethiopia established one of the earliest Christian churches, the Coptic Church, and acquired a large Muslim population after the Islamic invasions in 1529. Ethiopia experienced an attempt by the Portuguese to establish Roman Catholicism in the 1600s, but the Turks helped to expel the Jesuit missionaries. Ethiopia also experienced incursions by Oromo-speaking herdsmen from the south in the sixteenth and seventeenth centuries, the overthrow of their emperor by the British in 1868 after a diplomatic slight, invasions by the Sudanese, and colonization by the Italians later in the nineteenth century. In 1896, however, the Ethiopians succeeded in over-

throwing the Italian rule and were the only nation in Africa to retain their sovereignty in the face of European colonialism (Munro-Hay "Ethiopia" in *Encarta Africana,* 2000).

The story "The Golden Earth" speaks of the Ethiopians' desire for independence and love of their land. The emperor referred to in this story, which Wolf Leslau, a folklorist, heard from a north Ethiopian in the province of Tigray, was probably Kassa, who unified Ethiopia after a period of disunity in the middle of the nineteenth century and who renamed himself Thewodros II (Courlander and Leslau, 1950). The theme of foreigners taking the measure of the country, recording their observations of the different peoples, plants, animals, political affairs, religious issues, opportunities for trade, and so on, seems to have occurred on a number of occasions, starting with the Portuguese Jesuits of the 1600s (Munro-Hay, "Ethiopia" in *Encarta Africana,* 2000).

The people say that once two European explorers came to Ethiopia. They were seen going north to south, visiting every corner of the vast country. Everywhere they went they made maps of its mountains, roads, and rivers.

Word came to the Negus, or Emperor. After hearing about the men who were making maps, the Emperor sent a guide to help them. When, after several years, the Europeans were through with their task, the guide went back to Addis Ababa and reported to the Emperor what he had seen.

"Everything they have seen, they have written down," the guide said. "They have looked at the beginnings of the Nile at Lake Tana and followed the river down from the mountains. They have surveyed the rocks for gold and silver. They have charted the roads and trails."

The Emperor reflected on the work the Europeans were doing. At last he sent for them so that he might see them before their departure from the country. When they came he greeted them, fed them, and gave them valuable gifts. And when they went to the seashore to board their ship, he sent an escort with them.

As the explorers were about to leave, the Emperor's servants stopped them and removed their shoes. They scrubbed the shoes carefully and returned them to the Europeans.

The Europeans were perplexed, thinking it was a strange Ethiopian custom.

"Why do you do this?" they asked.

And the Emperor's messengers replied: "Our Emperor has told us to wish you a safe voyage homeward, and to say this to you:

"You came from a far-off and powerful country. You have seen with your own eyes that Ethiopia is the most beautiful of all lands. Its earth is dear to us. In it we plant our seed and bury our dead. We lie on it to rest when we are weary, and graze our cattle on its fields. The trails you have seen from the valleys to the mountains, and from the plains to the forests, they have been made by the feet of our ancestors, our own feet, and the feet of our children. The earth and Ethiopia is our father, our mother, and our brother. We have given you hospitality and valuable gifts. But the earth of Ethiopia is the most precious thing we own, and therefore we cannot spare even a single grain of it." ∎

Sasabonsam Meets His Match

Africa: Ghana—Sefwi

When foreigners think of West African stock characters, they think of tricksters. West Africans, however, have other frequently recurring stock characters such as the three appearing in "Sasabonsam's Match": the precocious child with magical powers who speaks, or in this story springs, from his mother's womb; the hunter who in many stories defeats Sasabonsam and other monsters; and cannibalistic monsters such as Sasabonsam. He is a forest monster of the silk-cotton tree (a tropical tree related to the more familiar cotton plant).

The fact that Sasabonsam almost reaches heaven and addresses the Sky God as he rears up before dying

and the fact that he is transformed into a great river suggest the mythic nature of this story. Because the infant hero is human, however, in spite of his magical attributes, the story is closer to being a legend than a myth, perhaps along the lines of hero tales about Theseus and Perseus in Greek mythology, both of whom had divine fathers and slew monsters but acted as humans rather than gods.

In West African folk narratives, oral formulas and storytelling devices include formula openings and closings, repetition of entire phrases or of all but a key word in a phrase, and a stock of fixed metaphors that are familiar to both the teller and the audience. Most important, however, is audience participation that involves encouraging responses to the story (Berry, 1991). In fact, according to folklorist Jack Berry, if there is no response by the audience for a long time, the storyteller himself interjects a response such as

Source: "Sasabonsam Meets his Match" from *West African Folktales* collected and translated by Jack Berry. Edited with an introduction by Richard Spears. Copyright © 1991 by Northwestern University Press. pp. 28–29.

"good." The formula opening and closing of this story are typical among the Sefwi. Other West African ethnic groups use different formulas. Another storytelling device is to withhold the name of an important character until after the main action has been outlined, probably to increase suspense (Berry, 1991). In this story Sasabonsam's name is not mentioned until halfway through the story. As editor, I added it in parentheses at his first appearance to help readers match the title of the story with the character.

Storyteller: Now this story—I didn't make it up!
Audience: Who did then?

A hunter went hunting. He wandered all day without firing a shot. He decided to give it up, but just as he was turning for home he saw an antelope that he shot and killed. He found some vines and started to tie the carcass up when he heard a voice behind him.

"Hunter, cut off the animal's legs."

The hunter turned around and was horrified to see a man as tall as a silk cotton tree. His limbs were thin, and his hair reached down to his knees. His eyes were huge balls of fire, and his teeth were like red-hot spears. The hunter was so terrified that he could neither move nor speak. Once more he was told to cut off the animal's legs. He managed to do as he was told. The monster [whose name was Sasabonsam] picked up the rest of the carcass, swallowed it whole, and without another word, vanished. The hunter went home with what was left of the antelope.

On the following day he went to another part of the forest, and the same thing happened. And the next day, too. And the day after that. And so it went on for several weeks until the hunter's wife, who was pregnant, decided to find out why her husband only brought home legs, and what he did with the rest of the meat.

She made a tiny hole in her husband's powder box and filled the box with ashes. Early the next morning when the hunter set off from his village he left a trail of ashes. His wife followed him to his usual hunting grounds. She hid behind a tree. Presently, along came a black duiker [antelope]. The hunter lifted his gun. *Bam!* The duiker fell dead.

"Hunter, cut off the animal's legs."

The hunter, by now, had no will of his own left, and he did what he was told. Sasabonsam swallowed the animal and shouted again, "Hunter, cut off the animal's legs," this time pointing to the tree behind which the wife was hiding. Thinking that a stray bullet had killed some other animal, the hunter went to do as Sasabonsam ordered. What do you think he found, there? Of course, his wife. She fainted from fright. Sasabonsam stood there, his eyes flashing—his mouth pouring smoke. "Cut off the animal's legs!" he ordered. The hunter couldn't move. Sasabonsam became angry and picked up the woman to swallow her. But as soon as he got hold of her, her belly opened and out jumped a baby that grew at tremendous speed. It was soon as big as Sasabonsam himself, and only then did it stop growing. The child blew fire and smoke from its mouth and nostrils.

These two giants now began to fight over the woman's body. They howled and roared. They tore up tall trees by the roots and used them to club each other. The dust from their feet, as they stamped, rose high into the sky. All the animals in the forest ran away. The fight was fierce and lasted a long time and neither seemed to be winning. They were so evenly matched the fight could not go on much longer. They both lay down on the ground gasping for breath. But as the wonder child lay watching Sasabonsam he saw a little hammer hanging from his belt. Quick as lightning, he grabbed it and hit Sasabonsam on the head with it three times. Sasabonsam reared up and stretched high into heaven to tell the Sky God Nana Nyamee Kwame that one of his children had wounded him. But he couldn't reach the Sky God. He fell full-length on the ground and turned into a great river. His arms and legs became the streams that flow into the river. As for Akokoaa Kwasi Gyinamoa—for that was the child's name—he went back to his mother womb and lay there waiting to be born. ∎

Storyteller: This is my story which I have now told you, whether it is sweet or whether it is not sweet, take a bit of it and keep the rest under your pillow.

A Merry Prank of Pa-Leng-Ts'ang

Asia: Mongolia

The verbal arts are, according to Mongolian folklorist Pureviin Khorloo (1996), the oldest of the arts in Mongolia. Until recently, the Mongols were a nomadic people. Folktales, proverbs, epics, and songs were highly developed arts. Because storytelling was such an important part of daily life, anyone could and did tell tales, but long epics and orally rendered versions of Chinese literature, often accompanied by a lute-like instrument called the horsehead fiddle, were performed by elders who had developed their skill to a high art.

Although this brief anecdote is probably the kind anyone might tell, it highlights the value placed on verbal expression and on using one's head (Khorloo, 1996).

Up and down around the open steppes and sandy deserts of Mongolia, on the north of vast China, Pa-leng-ts'ang traveled without end. Wherever he went he brought happy laughter, silver sayings, funny tricks, and wise thoughts. For that reason folks old and young, rich and poor, were happy to see him in their midst.

One hot dusty day Pa-leng-ts'ang trundled along the road singing dancing and thinking of a clever tale to

Source: "A Merry Prank of Pa-Leng-Ts'ang" from *The Magic Boat and Other Chinese Folk Stories* by M. A. Jagendorf and Virginia Weng. Copyright © 1980 by M. A. Jagendorf and Virginia Weng. Used by permission of Vanguard Press, a division of Random House, Inc. pp. 159–160.

tell in the next camp. Suddenly he saw coming toward him an important official and his followers on high horses. They recognized the famous trickster at once.

"Ha," said the official, "there goes that braggart Pa-leng-ts'ang, who thinks himself the cleverest fellow in all Mongolia! I'll show you how I can outtrick him and make a fool of him." He stopped his horse and shouted, "Ho there, Pa-leng-ts'ang, you think you are the cleverest trickster in all our land. Well, show me you can get me off my horse if I do not want to get off!"

Pa-leng-ts'ang was silent for a while. Then, with a smile on his face, he said, "I agree with you. I cannot get you off your horse if you don't want to. But if you were standing on the ground, I could make you get on your horse whether you like it or not."

The stupid official leaped out of his saddle, "Show me," he cried. "Put me back on my horse!"

Pa-leng-ts'ang answered, "You see, I got you off your horse, didn't I?"

Now the official knew he had been tricked, so, grumbling, he climbed on his horse to continue his trip. But Pa-leng-ts'ang laughed, "What do you say? Haven't I just made you get on your horse again, too? I have done both of the things you said I could not do!"

Everyone else laughed too as the official sheepishly rode off while Pa-leng-ts'ang walked on lightly, a smile on his face, thinking of the next merry prank. ■

Saint Bridget

Europe: Ireland

After St. Patrick, St. Bridget is Ireland's best-loved and most widely celebrated saint. Both saints are associated with the founding of Christianity in Ireland in the

fifth century (St. Bridget was said to have met St. Patrick.) Both saints represented a pastoral, rural ministry, the first in the Roman Catholic world, which in its early days focused on the large cities with a hierarchy that closely paralleled the structure of the Roman Empire (Morris, 1973). St. Bridget founded a church and convent, which as abbess she ruled at Kildare (Cill Dara, "cell of the oak"), 40 miles southwest of Dublin. According to *Butler's Lives of the Saints* (1998), several features set St. Bridget apart from her sister abbesses on the European continent. Following pre-Christian Celtic tradition, St. Bridget had more power than European abbesses, and her convent housed both men and women. She also had a great deal more influence than did European holy women, being able to administer Holy Communion and other priestly functions and having (according to some biographers) been named bishop. Whereas St. Jerome and other biographers of female saints within the Roman Empire depicted their virtues primarily as domestic and seldom recorded their having performed miracles, St. Bridget's Irish biographers show her life to have paralleled far more closely the life and ministry of Jesus, including the performing of miracles (*Butler's Lives of the Saints,* 1998; Clark, 1998). St. Bridget was powerful and influential, but most of her legends emphasize her kindness and mercy, which she valued above following rigid religious rules. Her charity, especially her giving away her father's sword to a poor man, is symbolic of her choosing kindness over aggression (and perhaps valuing spiritual power over worldly power). Eleanor Farjeon's (1936) version of her legends reflects many of the characteristics and spiritual symbols associated with Bridget. Kindness, miracles used to alleviate human suffering as in the story of the condemned man who had killed the king's wolf (in other versions the animal is a fox), her association with livestock (the cows with clothes on their horns come to her), and her association with light and fire are all part of her legend as a saint. These characteristics also tie her to her pre-Christian namesake, the goddess Bridget, who was associated with fertility in livestock, with blessing the hearth, with inspiring poetry (she was the goddess of poetry), and with the sacred fire that was tended by her

Source: "Saint Bridget" from *Ten Saints* by Eleanor Farjeon. Helen Sewell, illustrator. London: Oxford University Press, 1936. Reprinted with permission by David Highham Associates Limited. pp. 35–43.

druidesses at the same spot where St. Bridget founded her church. February 1, St. Bridget's feast day, is the day spring began with the pagan celebration of Imbolg, when the goddess blessed hearths and ensured the well being of the new lambs. "In many ways she [St. Bridget] marks the transitional point between paganism and Christianity, taking over much of the old religion without intolerance or persecution, incorporating its roots in the land and the seasons" (*Butler's Lives of the Saints,* 1998 February, vol. 2, p. 4)

Into the hall of the King strode Dubtach his friend, full of temper.

The King, a wise man, asked: "Well, Dubtach, what brings you from your lands to me today?"

The nobleman replied: "It is that daughter of mine, the one we call Bridget."

"They say she is beautiful."

"She is as beautiful as the dawn, and I will not have her in my house another day!"

"Why will you not, Dubtach?"

"Because if I keep her I shall soon have no house left! She gives everything away, everything! whether it is hers to give or not."

The King began to smile. "To whom does she give?"

"To beggars. She has only to see man, woman, or child holding out a hand at the door, and she puts into the hand whatever is nearest. It was always so! When she was small she gave away her cake, her doll, the shoes off her feet—and then she gave her sister's doll and her brother's shoes. Now she is grown she clears the board of food for anyone who is hungry, and tells him to keep the silver dish she heaped it on. Or she snatches up a gold goblet and fills it with drink, and gives some thirsty wretch both drink and goblet! When she has no money or jewels of her own left, a tale of misery sends her running for anybody's money and jewels. She does not even ask. She simply gives! My doors are beset with beggars who know her ways. I cannot afford to keep my daughter any more. So I have brought her to you."

"What do you want me to do?" asked the King.

"I want you to buy her," said Dubtach.

"Where is the girl?"

"Sitting in my chariot without."

"Let us go and look at her," said the King.

They went to the door, and there in Dubtach's chariot sat the maiden, as beautiful as hearsay. She was calm and radiant as the summer sea. Her hair was like a field of corn, her eyes were blue as flowers, and she had as little thought of herself as a meadow has.

It seemed to the King he might do worse than buy her. Before he could say so, Dubtach roared a question at his daughter: "Girl! where is the royal sword, my gift from the King?"

"Father," said Bridget, "while you were within, such a poor man came by. Your heart would have ached to see him. He was sick and starving. He could scarcely walk. His clothes were falling to pieces. He was in need. I gave him your sword."

"My sword to a beggar!"

"There was nothing else to give him," said Bridget simply.

Dubtach was dumb with wrath. The King stepped forward, and hiding another smile he said to Bridget: "You had no right, my child, to give away the royal sword."

"But he was hungry. He can change it into bread."

"Still, the sword was not yours to give."

The maiden, with a look of wonder, said: "Sir, if a beggar came and showed me his need, I would give away my father and my king."

The King, a wise man, decided not to buy her. He said to Dubtach: "The best thing you can do is to get her a husband."

"There's a young lord in our parts who pesters me for her," growled Dubtach, "but she will have none of him."

Then Bridget said: "I will not make my vow to a man. I will only make it to God."

"How old are you, child?"

"King, I am fourteen."

"Then you are too young to know what is best for you." Turning to his friend, the King said: "If any young man is willing to wed her, let him."

Dubtach mounted his chariot and drove his daughter back the way the they had come. As they drove, she pleaded with him: "Father, do not compel me to this. Let me go to Usny, where the Bishop is, and let me take the veil."

"It is your wedding-veil you must wear, you wilful girl," said Dubtach.

On reaching his house he sent a message to the young nobleman and bade Bridget make ready to receive him. She went to her chamber but not to adorn herself; she knelt and prayed God to take her beauty from her. "It stands between Thee and me, O Lord," said she, "therefore destroy it, that no man will look upon me."

Word was brought that her bridegroom was below. The young man, who thought of her beauty by day and dreamed of it by night, had ridden eagerly to greet her. What cared he about her charities? Let her only be the mistress of his house, and he was ready to lay all he had at her feet, to do with as she pleased. He could hardly wait for her to come to him.

But when she came, he started from her, dismayed. Her face was drawn, her hair had lost its lustre. Where were those two blue eyes he had loved to look on? She now had only one, the other was sealed and shrunken, and all her bloom was withered.

"Bridget, is it indeed yourself?" he faltered.

"Yes," she said, "and I pray you not to urge this marriage on. I will be for ever grateful if you do not."

It was he who was grateful now to be released. He went to Dubtach and told him that a blight had fallen on his daughter; and her father, when he looked upon the child, knew that no man would wish to have her in his house. So he let the young lord go away without her.

Then Bridget said: "Father, I must go to Usny. The holy Bishop Maccail will not turn me away." And Dubtach no longer denied her.

With three other young virgins, Bridget went to Usny and knelt before the altar in the church. The Bishop received the profession of the maidens and put white habits on them. No sooner was the ceremony ended than Bridget's beauty flowed back to her again. She bowed her head and put her sweet lips to the dry foot of the altar, and the sap flowed back again to the seasoned wood, and it turned as green as a tree when Spring is come.

Then Bridget went out with her maidens and journeyed a long way till she came to a place that pleased her. A mighty oak-tree spread its shade over a grassy plain, and in its shelter Bridget built her cell. Now she could live according to her heart, with none to scold if she gave her all away. It was not long before the people of those parts came to know of the fair young nun who lived under a tree and never denied a beggar; and they called it Kil-Dara, the Cell of the Oak.

"She gives you the bread out of her mouth with a smile of beauty," they said, "and it tastes the like of no other bread at all. There is none so pure as she is."

"How would there be? She was christened in new milk as soon as she saw the light, for a pitcher warm from the cow was spilled on her as she lay whimpering on the threshold."

"Was it on the threshold she was born? Small wonder she has the smile of joy on her face. Did not the Bard say, 'Happy is the child that is born neither in the house nor out of the house!'"

The name of her and the fame of her ran like a sweet breath of wind round Ireland, and not only beggars flocked to the Holy Oak, but many young maidens, all eager to live her life. One after another Bridget habited them in white like herself, till the green plain seemed peopled with a flock of angels. Soon there were so many that dwellings began to spring up in the neighbourhood of the oak; one was added to another till a city was formed, and they called it Kildare.

Not only holy women, but holy men also were drawn to Kildare, and before long Bridget had to divide her church into three parts, one for the sacred virgins, one for the monks, and one for the lay people. She prayed St. Conlaeth to come and be bishop of the city, and the monks' father; while she herself was Abbess, and the mother of them all. And of those, too, who came from a distance to ask her advice, and attend the festivals of her church.

A peasant's family once came to such a festival from beyond the River Liffey, leaving their cattle and their farm unguarded. During that day a great to-do brought Bridget to the Convent gates, and she saw a herd of cows with garments tied to their horns coming at a gallop along the road. As soon as they saw her the cows lay down at the gates, and everybody assembled to look at them. Suddenly the peasant from over the river exclaimed: "God bless us! these cows are ours!"

"Are the clothes yours too?" asked Bridget.

"I couldn't say whose they are," said the peasant, but his child cried pointing: "Maybe they belong to those men there, da!" And now a band of naked men was seen coming at a run along the same road. When they beheld the crowd they stopped abashed, but Brid-

get, seeing only men that needed to be clothed, called from the gates: "Are these your garments, poor fellows?"

"Yes," they said.

"How come they to be tied to the horns of the cows?"

"The Liffey was swollen and we had to swim, and thought our garments would come dry so. But the cows ran off and left us as you see, bad luck to them."

"The cows, however, were not yours at all," said Bridget. "It seems you stole them in their owners' absence."

"It does seem so," they agreed.

"Now was not that a very bad thing to do!" cried Bridget, her blue eyes shining reproaches on the men. "It is very wrong to take what is not yours. Did you never think of these poor ones you were robbing? And did you never think you had only to come and ask me for cows if you wanted them? Oh, you have not been good!" she said severely. Then she undid the garments from the cattle, and gave them to the thieves, and bade them clothe themselves and come in to be fed. And at the end of the day the peasants went home driving their cows before them, and all were satisfied.

Another time she heard of a poor man in trouble, for he had killed a wolf running free near the palace of the King, and brought it in, expecting a fee for its head. But the wolf was the King's own creature, as tame as a dog, so the King pronounced death on him, and cast him into prison. The tale was brought to Bridget, who sprang at once into her chariot and drove by the bog-side to go and plead for the man. And over the bog a great wild beast came leaping, outracing her horses, and with a bound it seated itself beside her in the chariot. When Bridget saw that it was a noble wolf, "Heaven sent you surely!" said she, fondling his ear. The wolf put his chin on her shoulder, and when she alighted walked beside her into the King's presence.

"Is it yourself, Bridget?" said the King.

"It is," said she, "and King, you must spare the poor rustic in your prison, for no man ought to suffer for a mistake, and besides that I have brought you a grander wolf than the one that was killed unwittingly."

The King without more ado took the wolf in exchange for the man; and maybe he knew it was useless to argue with Bridget anyhow. All things were fain to give in to her, from the King on the earth to the sun in the sky.

For one day, sprinkled with an April shower, she came quickly into her cell, and flung her wet mantle over a sunbeam shining through her window-bars to the floor. In her haste she mistook it for a beam of wood, and the sunbeam was glad to bear the virgin's mantle, but she herself went about her duties and forgot it. So the mantle hung there till after the sun went down. Presently one of the nuns peeped into the cell to see what light was shining there; and the sunbeam meekly begged her to remind Bridget that he was waiting to follow his master. But not till she came and lifted the mantle off him did the ray retire into the night to find the sun.

To her the sunlight was the best of God's gifts to earth; she would sit in the twilight watching it depart from the sky while she talked with her maidens of the joys of paradise. One evening the blind girl Dara sat beside her, and as the sun went down they spoke of God's love which is inexhaustible, and when the sun rose again they were speaking still. It rose behind Wicklow mountains, and first the peaks were gold, and then the light spread down the face of the hills to the plain, and the leaves on the trees and the blades of grass were gold with glittering dew. And Bridget sighed with bliss and then with grief, because blind Dara could not see what she saw. She breathed a prayer and touched the sightless eyes, and instantly Dara opened them, and saw. For a little while she looked on the world in silence; then she said softly: "Close my eyes again, mother! while my eyes behold the world, I cannot see God with

my soul." Then Bridget breathed a second prayer, and earth's vision passed away from Dara's eyes.

Maybe Bridget thought of this, when the time was come for it to pass from hers. Maybe she thought of a vision she had had long ago when she heard the old Saint Patrick preach a sermon, and while he preached she slept. He came to her afterwards, when she was awake, and gently rebuked her: "Bridget, why did you sleep when the Word of Christ was being spoken?"

"Forgive me, father," she said, "I was sent a dream."

"Tell me the dream," said Saint Patrick; and Bridget said:

"I saw, and behold the land was ploughed far and wide, and sowers went forth in white raiment and sowed good seed. And it sprang up a white and goodly harvest. Then came other ploughers and sowers in black, and they hacked and tore up and destroyed that beauteous harvest, and strewed tares far and wide. And I saw again, and behold, the island was full of sheep and swine and dogs and wolves, striving with one another and rending each other."

"Alas, my daughter!" said Patrick. "In the latter days will come false teachers, who shall lead away many, and the good harvest sprung from the Gospel-seed we have sown will be trodden under foot. And there shall be controversies in the faith, between the faithful and the bringers-in of false doctrine."

But this had not come to pass when Bridget died. All her life she had looked on a golden world, and she only gave up that vision to behold one brighter. ∎

Legend of the Corn Beads

North America: United States—Cherokee

Legends are frequently short, their significance lying not in an elaborate storyline but in the retelling of historic events that strengthen the identity of the group through shared triumph or grief. In 1838 the Cherokee Nation was forcibly removed from its native lands in Georgia, North Carolina, Tennessee, and North Alabama to Oklahoma. The removal constituted a great betrayal of treaties and trust; in 1830 the Supreme Court had upheld the status of the Cherokee as a nation in Georgia, and the Cherokee had adopted European-American ways. The Cherokee lived on farms, had a constitution, developed a writing system, published a newspaper, and in general chose to live as neighbors with, rather than opponents of, the white settlers. The move in the winter resulted in the death of at least 4000 people and another 4000–6000 in casualties before the march and during the first year of settlement in Oklahoma, earning the event the name "Trail of Tears" (Duncan, 1998).

Not all Cherokee were removed. A sizable number hid in the mountains, others returned from Oklahoma, and a few were allowed to stay in North Carolina. These were the ancestors of the Eastern Band of the Cherokee in North Carolina.

Storytelling is a living art among the Cherokee. Edna Chekelelee, whose story is reprinted here, visits schools and tells four types of stories, which she classifies as happy stories (about animals and other folktales), sad stories (which tell of sad events such as the one included here), bad stories (about people who did bad things), and legends (stories from a very long time ago, including myths).

Told by Edna Chekelelee

Source: "Legend of the Corn Beads" from *Living Stories of the Cherokee* edited by Barbara R. Duncan. Copyright © 1998 by the University of North Carolina Press. Used by permission of the publisher. pp. 131–132.

Cherokee women
    wear the legendary necklace made of corn beads.
It is a gift
    from the Great Spirit
    in the shape of a teardrop.
This is the Cherokee legend of the corn beads.
In the 1800s
    during the Trail of Tears,
    the corn stalks were eight feet tall,
    and corn was twelve to eighteen inches long.
The corn stood back and watched
    as the Indian people were getting pushed and shoved
    by the white soldiers.
And the corn cried and cried.
And the teardrop landed on the corn fodder,
    and the corn dropped down to three feet tall.
That's why it's called teardrop,
    our mother of corn.
The Cherokee women used these teardrops,
    our mother of corn,
    to make beautiful cornbeads,
    but to me this is sad.
But it is a way to remember
    the Trail of Tears. ■

Legend of the Swift Wind (The Roadrunner)

North America: United States—Apache

The theme of the hero who is alone, both when low and despised as well as when performing the supremely heroic act that saves his community, is given unique expression in this legend of the origin of the roadrunner. Lou Cuevas learned the songs, chants, and stories that his Apache medicine man grandfather

Source: "Legend of the Swift Wind (The Roadrunner)" from *Apache Legends: Sons of the Wind Dancer.* Copyright © 1991 by Lou Cuevas. Reprinted with permission by Naturegraph Publisher, Inc. pp. 23–31.

passed on to him when he was a child. A **medicine man** is someone who is in touch with the spirit world and who often uses chants of the myths and legends to reach the spirit world. It was the myths of the origins of different spirit animals, the animals that lived before the time the world became populated by ordinary animals and people, that Cuevas liked the best. Like many other Native Americans today, Cuevas wants to reinforce his people's traditional identification by retelling the stories his grandfather told. Cuevas says that it is at his grandmother's request that he has become a storyteller. "[Apache] storytellers are honored people purposely selected by the spirit of living things to chant atop special mountains, near rivers, waterfalls, and open campfires. . . . The spirit song, which varies from tribe to tribe, is like a prayer, and the more reverent the location, the more the spirits will aid in the chant" (Cuevas, 1991, pp. 7–8). It is important to remember, says Cuevas, that these animal spirit stories are not merely entertainment but have a sacred character.

Many ages ago, when the land belonged to the ancient Ndee, later known as the Apache, the Swift Wind story came into being. Since then, some have forgotten the tale, some do not understand it. Even today, among many clans, there are few who know of it. During ancient times it was forbidden for anyone except the Ndee to possess spirit knowledge. Yet now, as the yellow flames of time dance before you, I will speak the legend as it was related to me by my grandfather. It is a story about a wondrous creature whom the ancient ones called the Swift Wind.

Late in the summer, at the time of the Golden Moon, during the year of the Mating Wolf, when the boys of the Ndee tribe came to maturity, a great feast was called for. It was a time of harvest, a time of thanks, and a time known to them as the Choosing. The tribal elders were grateful that the Giver of Life, also called the Great or Sky Spirit, had blessed them during the year. Further, they knew that if theirs was to be a remembered nation, the youth of the tribe would have to win favor in a ceremonial dance. From it, the Great Spirit would choose the destiny of the boys.

Since the choosing was made from among the elder sons of the tribe, to them were made available the ornaments made by the young women. The girls brought them beaded jewelry, decorative paints, silver and gold bells, brightly embroidered deer skins, string belts, colorful moccasin boots, and very impressive war bonnets, all of which went into costumes that would please the Sky Spirit. Then an enormous bonfire was made ready in the center of the camp, a large number of drums were formed into a circle and finally, when all was ready, an offering of food and drink which was to be shared by the entire tribe was brought and the celebration began.

Displayed in their colorful costumes, the young men were cheered as they paraded into the camp center. Soon after, the drums created a beat and the boys began to dance, fashioning a festive mood as they chanted and encircled the great bonfire. As the celebration went on, the tribe moved to the rhythmic sounds of the booming drums which spoke of the Great Spirit. Eventually, everyone began singing praises to their great protector for their gifts, their health, and their joy. Hour after hour, the lively feasting continued while the sun set and the moon rose.

The hidden valley of the Ndee shook with a tremendous echo which reached high up into the night sky. There, in the shadow of the earth, watching his people, stood the Great Spirit. As he listened to their voices, he became pleased and smiled. So moved was the Sky Father by the mention of his name in their many songs that he took from his medicine pouch magic sky crystals and gently sprinkled them on the chosen boys.

Down in the valley, the elders of the tribe were pleased with their young men and admired them for their songs, their spirit, and their bright array. As the chief looked on the dancers, he saw not the boys but future hunters, guardians, and warriors of the tribe. In these same youths, the elders saw their replacements. The eyes of the tribal women saw their sons, their brothers, and, for many, their future husbands. This filled them with great pride. The joy in their hearts brought tears of happiness. Then all at once, they saw the black sky open up. and it began to rain. But it was a strange sort of rain; it did not feel wet.

The tribe was amazed. Still the drums continued to beat and the boys continued to chant and dance. Faster and faster they went. As their bodies were ducking and bowing, their arms made gestures as if they were in flight. The flames of the fire began to grow and grow, and then, unexpectedly, to the utter astonishment of everyone who looked on, the brightly painted bodies of the boys started changing.

There were several thousand pairs of eyes in the valley that night. Before these eyes, the bodies of the boys began to grow feathers. Out from beneath their painted skin grew white, gold, brown, and black feathers changing them from boys into golden eagles. The transformation continued, with the decorated faces of the boys turning into the beaked faces of birds. Their small feet changed into the powerful claws of the famed fliers. Finally, the change was completed when the arms of each boy became the powerful wings of the bird of prey.

The drummers of the tribe had stopped their beat when they saw what was happening, yet by some unseen power the drums continued to send out a magical sound. As the drums played, the flames grew higher and higher until all at once, they exploded in a huge column of flame which shot the eagles high up into the sky. While all this was going on, no one gave much notice to one boy who, although he had grown feathers, did not look like an eagle and still danced round the fire all by himself. He was a bird, but he did not resemble the others.

The elders of the tribe and the rest of the people were in awe as they saw their young men flying in the full-moon night. From the eagles came a high shrill cry of joy and the people down below were filled with great pride. However, the chief of the tribe and then, soon after, the rest of the people noticed that one boy, a lad named Quo-Qui, meaning Swift Wind, was not flying above the fire. Indeed, he still continued to dance around the flaming circle completely unaware of anything or anyone around him. Everyone was puzzled.

Unaware as he was of their questioning stares, Quo-Qui remained on the ground oblivious to the other boys flying above him in the night sky. Saddened by the sight, the parents of Quo-Qui could not believe what they had witnessed. The elders were disappointed and the women were confused. The chief decided to consult with the medicine man. With the fire dying out, the boys who had changed into eagles came floating down and, once on the ground, ran triumphantly into their proud parents' arms. There was much happiness in their hearts. Yet in the eyes of Quo-Qui's parents, there was only doubt. Something was very wrong.

From that eventful day onward, the Ndee began to gossip about Quo-Qui and his disgrace. It was not bad enough that the boy felt ashamed and alone; to make him feel worse, there were many in the tribe who began to call him Runt Bird. Some believed that he had been cursed and should be driven out. Others suggested that perhaps Quo-Qui was not yet a man and, therefore, could not turn into an eagle. Numerous voices argued that Quo-Qui was outcast by the Great Spirit and

should not be allowed to participate in any future ceremonial dances.

Whatever the views of the tribe, only one man had the power to change the law and that was the tribal chief. He more than anyone had heard the talk of his people and knew that he had to decide what was to be done. After consulting with the medicine man and the tribal elders, the chief informed his people that it had been the decision of the Great Spirit to turn Quo-Qui into a bird. Because he had feathers like the others, his people would have to be patient and wait for the Sky Father to show them why he had chosen Quo-Qui to be what he was. Only time would tell, he told them. Yet deep within his heart, the chief, too, had grave doubts, but he said nothing lest it change the future.

During the days which followed, the parents of Quo-Qui sat down with the boy and asked him if there was anything in his heart which would cause the Great Spirit to be angry with him. His mother cried and asked if there was some secret disgrace of which he had not told them. Quo-Qui's heart was heavy knowing that his own parents doubted his courage and honor. Did they not know their son well enough to realize that there was nothing for which he was ashamed? Still, seeing their grief, he explained that he could not remember anything that night except that he was touched by the Great Spirit. He was unable to explain why he could not fly. Thereafter, his parents were sorry that they had ever doubted their son and asked his forgiveness. Quo-Qui understood their concern and set out to solve his problem. But first he needed to hunt and this he did. With a fine prize in hand, he went to visit the only man who might explain the puzzle to him.

Quo-Qui's father had felt the sorrow carried by his son and advised him to seek out an explanation from the tribal medicine man. It would be he who could tell Quo-Qui what purpose the Great Spirit had for him. Following his father's counsel, the boy, with the gift in hand, went to see the mysterious but very wise medicine chief. Placing his catch before the tepee, he asked permission to speak to the holy man. The wife of the medicine man took the boy's offering and prepared a meal. After the two had eaten, the woman left them alone to talk.

The medicine man built a small fire in the center of the tepee. As the fire grew to its limits and then died out, the strangely painted man sang to the spirits who then whispered into his ears what they had heard about Quo-Qui. At the end of his song, the medicine man looked at the troubled Quo-Qui and told him what the spirits in the fire had said.

"There are those who seek to be great," the old man declared, "but in so doing, they become small. I see in the ashes that you are small, but in time you will be great."

"How can I be great, Holy One?" Quo-Qui questioned in disbelief. "I cannot fly! I am not made to look like my brothers! I am troubled by my people's laughter and, except for my parents, I am alone. There is a great weight in my heart. I do not understand."

"The Great Spirit guides your fate," the old man told him. "But he cannot control your heart. You have courage. Let it serve you now! The ashes tell me that you have been chosen. Nothing can change that. Your destiny awaits the moon; do not fight it."

"I do not doubt my courage, Holy One," replied Quo-Qui confidently. "I await my destiny. All I ask now is, have I dishonored myself? This I must know so that I may cleanse my spirit."

"Your fate is now in the wooded hills north of our camp," the medicine man advised. "There, within the empty bellies of our brothers who cry out in the wind, lies your future. But do not seek it, for even now it approaches. You have not been dishonored, but will bring honor. If you are now alone, it is because on the day of trial you will be alone. Go my son. Allow your heart to remember that true courage is the greatest shield."

Days passed and the boy endured all the laughter which came to him. Quo-Qui's parents were proud of their son who still walked tall through the camp. Soon a new moon rose and the day of trial arrived.

Since the first celebration of the Choosing there had been other celebrations. Each was a ceremony to give thanks or to ask the Great Spirit for something. During the Eagle Dance in which the chosen were seen, the result was always the same. The other boys were magically changed into great eagles except for Quo-Qui. So discouraged did he become that he told the others that he would not join in any longer. No one argued otherwise. Quo-Qui's spirit was in deep despair, even

on the day when the chief sent all of his hunters on a five-day hunt for game.

Left behind in the camp were the women, the children, and the aged who could not fend for themselves. The chosen boys of the Eagle were given the task of guarding the camp against intruders. All of them eagerly took their assigned positions throughout the camp. Yet when Quo-Qui asked the oldest boy where he should go to stand guard, he received only laughs and jeers and was told to go and hide with the women and children where his little feathers would not show his disgrace. Quo-Qui became very angry, but he said nothing as he turned and walked away. Behind him he could hear the others call him names. He felt completely alone.

So loud was the growing laughter that few heard the frightful howl of starvation coming down from the nearby woodlands. It was the terrible cry of a great timber wolf. Joining the awful whine came the added growls of many other wolves, all of which sounded terribly close. Down in the camp, the people recognized the cry of the silver wolf and knew it meant they were searching for food. They also remembered that, when wolves went on the prowl, nothing short of death would keep them from their prey. The camp people grew horrified as certain destruction came closer and ever closer.

Numbering fifty in all, the silver-grey forms with their black manes came charging out from the thicket. They looked lean and savage. Their blood-red eyes glittered in the noonday sun. The entire camp panicked and everyone scattered for the shelter of their tents. As fear gripped the people, the Eagle boys looked at the howling pack and saw their long, sharp teeth. For a moment, they were hypnotized by the fearful sight.

Throughout the Ndee camp, the screams of frightened women and the wail of little children created a great din. Hearing it, the Eagle boys quickly gathered themselves to prepare a plan of defense. It was obvious that they were all that stood between the wolves and their people. Although the boys did not lack courage, they lacked a plan of action.

"What shall we do?" asked one.

"We must go for help!" suggested a second.

"We will all be dead by the time it arrives!" shouted another.

"We were given the task of defending the camp!" said the bravest of the boys. "It is clear, we must die to save our people."

"Our brother, the wolf, does not understand who we are," announced the eldest of the group. "Therefore, we shall perform our sacred Eagle dance and change into our Eagle form, proving that we are the chosen of the Great Spirit. Then, they will be too frightened to do any harm!"

"Yes!" encouraged another. "When they see us fly above them, they will become fearful and run away! Let's hurry, because our campfire burns low!"

All the boys agreed and were too busy to notice that Quo-Qui had joined the dance as well. The chanting began while the murderous wolves were moving steadily into the camp. Once inside, the wolves immediately stopped. There before them was a strange sight. Instead of running for their lives, the boys had chosen to dance. Despite their hunger, the wolves waited suspecting a trap. Then, when nothing happened, the wolves again bounded forward toward the group. All at once, the boys changed into eagles and shot up into the sky above them.

However, instead of being impressed, the wolves only became annoyed that some of their prey had gotten away. They did not understand the dance and what was more important, they were not frightened by the magical transformation. Ironically, the boys had not realized that once in the air, the eagles could do little against the wolves except to cry out in their high shrill voices and distract them with their claws. The people in the camp saw that Quo-Qui, the boy they had ridiculed, alone remained to save them. The wolves readied themselves to devour the remaining people hiding in their tents. Then, they noticed a curious looking little bird still dancing on the ground in front of them.

Quo-Qui, who had changed into a bird, had not flown into the air. He remained and was still circling the fire with his dance. Round and round he went, creating such a distraction that the wolves decided he should be the first to die. Turning aside from the women and children, the great timber wolves regrouped and at-tacked the tiny bird in the center of the camp. That was what Quo-Qui was waiting for.

Peering though the flaps in their tents, the frightened people saw the silver horde chasing the agile bird round and round the fire. With his little gray wings firmly outstretched, Quo-Qui kept himself just out of reach by shooting himself forward each time the wolves lunged at him. Finally, the tiny gray bird with the soft brown feathers turned away from the fire and headed away from the camp. The wolves, determined to catch him, were fast on his heels.

Each time the leader and the rest of the pack thought they were just within reach, they opened their powerful jaws and sprang for him. But each time the pack attacked, the little bird turned to the right or to the left and glided along the air to land a few yards ahead of the surprised predators. The wolves became furious and increased their speed, sure that they could catch the tiny form. Little did they realize that the clever bird had by this time led them miles away from the camp.

At last, in one final desperate charge, the entire wolf pack formed into a wide semicircle and forced the streaking bird to smaller and smaller turns. Then, when they were sure that Quo-Qui could not turn, they all sprang forward in one massive leap, unaware that a sharp cliff lay ahead.

As before, when the pack sprang toward him, the speedy bird shot forward into the air. Unknowingly, the entire group vaulted into a great open canyon. Flying out into the immense gorge, the timber wolves fell quickly to their death on the rocks below, while Quo-Qui shooting farther, eventually glided slowly and softly to the canyon floor on the same tiny wings which had changed into the fastest little bird in the Southwest.

The flying eagles, who had been following the chase, saw that their brother had been transformed into a magical bird that all men would forever after recognize as the Roadrunner.

Today, in memory of that event, the Apache look upon the story of the Roadrunner as a good example to pass on to their children. If one looks for greatness in size, one tends to overlook it. ■

A Woman's Fight ⭑

North America: United States—Crow

In her introduction to *Spider Woman's Granddaughters: Traditional Tales and Contemporary Writing by Native American Women,* editor Paula Gunn Allen (1983) stated that "War stories . . . capture all the traditional themes of Indian women's narratives: the themes of love and separation, loss, and most of all, continuance" (p. 21). She reminds the reader that for the past five centuries Indian women have lived in a "war zone," because the displacement of Native Americans and destruction of both people and culture had been an ongoing experience since the arrival of the Europeans and continues in places in Latin America to this day. But, Gunn says, the women's stories tell not only about defeat and captivity but also about resistance and endurance.

In the following account Pretty Shield, who was a well-known Crow medicine woman, told about a raid by a rival Native American tribe that she experienced as a child (in the late 1800s). The introduction of the horse and guns in North America by the Spanish created a new climate of rivalry among the tribes of the Great Plains. Horses were highly valued because they made hunting buffalo much easier than was the case traditionally, when hunting had to be done on foot, and horse raids became a way of life. The horse also changed the face of the plains, allowing people to build larger tepees, since the horses could carry them better and farther than could the dogs that had been used for pulling the poles and skins needed for the tepees. People had to move with the seasons to find more sheltered ground and more abundant hunting areas. The Crow acted as middlemen, trading horses, shirts, featherwork, and bows with village Indians for guns, which they carried to the

Shoshone in the Rocky Mountains. As the story makes apparent, it was the women who built the tepees.

Rivalries and warfare among the Crow and other Plains tribes followed a set code of rules. The goal of skirmishes was to capture horses, capture the enemy, and count coup, that is, show how good a warrior you were by striking the enemy with a stick, not by killing him. To be ranked a chief among the Crow, a man also had to lead a war party without loss of life. According to Allen, the point of these fights was primarily to develop competence, including spiritual competence, not all-out war against another group. This kind of ritualized warfare was a way of life for the Crow men.

Women too had to have courage, but they showed it in other ways. One can recognize, for instance, the role of courageous women to inspire resistance to an enemy. Allen's point is that the same kind of courage shown by the women in this story is what Indian women have had to demonstrate continually to keep going and resisting "even though all hope, all chance of survival, of dignity, of happiness and liberty to live in their chosen way seems lost" (1983, p. 21).

Storyteller: Pretty Shield

Once, when I was eight years old, we moved our village from The-mountain-lion's lodge [Pompey's Pillar] to the place where the white man's town of Huntley now stands. There were not many of us in this band. Sixteen men were with us when the women began to set up their lodges, and one man named Covered-with-grass was sent out as a wolf. I could see him on the hill when my mother was setting up her lodge-poles. I was dragging the poles of my play-lodge to a nice place that I had selected when I saw Covered-with-grass, the wolf on the hill, signal, "The enemy is coming."

Instantly two men leaped upon the backs of horses, their war-horses, that were always kept tied

Source: "A Woman's Fight" from *Pretty Shield: Medicine Woman of the Crows* by Frank B. Linderman. Copyright 1932 by Frank B. Linderman, renewed © 1960 by Norma Waller, Verne Linderman and Wilda Linderman. Reprinted by permission of Harper-Collins Publishers, Inc. pp. 200–209.

near lodges, and rode out on the plains to drive the other horses into camp.

There was great excitement, much running about by the women, who left their lodges just as they happened to be when the signal came. Some of the lodges had but a few poles up. Others, whose owners were quicker, had their lodge-skins tied, hanging loosely from the skin-poles.

Men, watching the hills, stationed themselves, one between every two lodges. Mothers, piling packs and parfleches into breast-works, called their children; and horses whinnied. Then I saw the horses that had been out on the plains coming fast, their hoofs making a great noise and much dust. I must get out of the way.

Dragging my poles, a load beneath each arm, I ran between two lodges whose lodge-skins were flapping in the wind, my own little lodge yet on my back. In came the horses, more than a hundred, sweeping into the camp between two lodges that were far apart, too far apart, I thought. And this thought gave me an idea. Why not close that wide gap between those two lodges? Why not set up my little lodge between the two big ones, and shut this wide place up?

While yet the horses were running around within the circle of the camp I dragged my poles to the spot, and quickly pitched my lodge there. I heard my mother calling me. I had to work very fast to shut up that wide place, believing that my little lodge would keep our horses from getting out, and the Lacota from getting in; but I did not finish pegging down my lodge-skin, not quite. Corn-woman found me. "Ho! Ho!" she cried out, "here is a brave little woman! She has shut the wide gap with her lodge. Ho! Ho!"

But just the same she picked me up in her arms and carried me to my mother, as though I were a baby. Corn-woman told this story every year until she died.

Now I shall have to tell you about the fighting, a little, because it was a woman's fight. A woman won it. The men never tell about it. They do not like to hear about it, but I am going to tell you what happened. I was there to see. And my eyes were good, too. [. . .]

Yes [. . .] a woman won that fight, and the men never tell about it. There was shooting by the time my play-lodge was pitched. A Lacota bullet struck one of its poles, and whined. Arrows were coming among the lodges, and bullets, when Corn-woman carried me to my mother, who made me lie down behind a pack. I saw what went on there.

Several horses were wounded and were screaming with their pain. One of them fell down near my mother's lodge that was not yet half pitched. Lying there behind that pack I did not cover my eyes. I was looking all the time, and listening to everything. I saw Strikes-two, a woman sixty years old, riding around the camp on a gray horse. She carried only her root-digger, and she was singing her medicine-song, as though Lacota bullets and arrows were not flying around her. I heard her say, "Now all of you sing, 'They are whipped. They are running away,' and keep singing those words until I come back."

When the men and even the women began to sing as Strikes-two told them, she rode out straight at the Lacota, waving her root-digger and singing that song. I *saw* her, I *heard* her, and my heart swelled, because she was a woman.

The Lacota, afraid of her medicine, turned and ran away. The fight was won, and by a woman. ■

 ## Seeds of Faith

North America: United States—New Mexico—Hispanic

Introduced to the rest of the world by the Spanish explorers, chili peppers—and all other green and red peppers—come from the Americas and were culti- vated by Native Americans of Mexico and Central America. The Spanish and Mexican settlers first came to New Mexico, which was at that time the northern part of Mexico, in 1598, and their culture and folklore became a blend of Spanish and Pueblo traditions (Anaya, 1999). Atencio, a storyteller, grew up in Northern New Mexico and still lives there. She tells her stories in a New Mexican Spanish dialect to schoolchildren, senior citizens, business groups, and other audiences. She learned these stories from her mother, who had learned them from her godmother (Atencio, 1991). Some of the stories she tells, such as "La Llorona" ("The Weeping Woman"), are told in many parts of Latin America and are a blend of stories from Native American and Hispanic cultures (Dorson, 1970). Legends, such as "Seeds of Faith," however, are more regional. Northern New Mexico is famous for its hot chili dishes, and Catholicism is the dominant religion throughout Latin America; many of the Hispanic folktales and legends from the Southwest include religious elements (Anaya, 1999).

There are relatively few English language collections of Latin American and Hispanic folktales and legends for children. Most of the translations are of Indian cultures but not of the Hispanic sources according to folklorist John Bierhorst. John Bierhorst's new translation, *Latin American Folktales* (2002), is a good resource for adults and young adults to learn about the range of Latin American folktales and legends from Argentina to Mexico, as well as Hispanic and immigrant Latino cultures in the United States.

One warm and sunny summer morning, an elderly man named Angelico went outside to breathe in the clean mountain air. He sat down in his favorite rocking chair and slowly sipped his coffee. He admired his unique surroundings—the rugged foothills and the fertile valley of his birthplace. The sounds of birds singing and the rushing of the river sent him into a state of daydreaming. His thoughts took him back to the years when his great-grandfather, Bernardo, would spend many nights telling stories to his grandchildren and neighbors. He recalled one of his favorite stories told

Source: "Seeds of Faith" from *Cuentos from My Childhood: Legends and Folktales of Northern New Mexico* by Paulette Atencio. Santa Fe: Museum of New Mexico Press, 1991. Reprinted with permission by Museum of New Mexico Press, Santa Fe, New Mexico. pp. 26–28.

by Don Bernardo—that of the chili seeds, or seeds of faith.

Don Bernardo's garden had been doing poorly for a few years. Feeling depressed, he decided to make a visit to the *morada* (a Catholic meeting place for a group of religious men). Since he was of Mexican descent, his prayers were made directly to the Baby Jesus, also known al *El Nino de Atocha*. He prayed that his luck would change and that his garden would improve.

A few days later, while hoeing his plants, he noticed some strange weeds growing. He assumed they were weeds, but after each watering, he noticed tiny, freshly made footprints next to the strange plants. He returned to the *morada,* as he often did, and lit a candle. He sang his favorite *alabado,* a religious hymn, and had started his prayers when he noticed that the shoes of the Baby Jesus statue were covered with mud. Don Bernardo decided that the strange weeds he had seen in the garden must be gifts from the Baby Jesus. He took off running and didn't stop until he got to the garden. When he arrived there, Don Bernardo was disappointed. The weeds had wilted and he could no longer see the footprints. He spent two hours sitting there chewing tobacco and came to the conclusion that it was not the end but rather the beginning of these remarkable plants.

He took special care of the so-called weeds until they began to flower. After what seemed a lifetime, the plant produced long, firm, green stems. Don Bernardo felt it was time to cut them. Later he would decide what to do with them. He took them home, examining them with interest. When he decided to taste them, he had the surprise of his life! He discovered they were very hot! They burned his mouth, so he drank a gallon of water and was forced to eat some sugar.

Don Bernardo was accustomed to swearing, but since the priest was nearby, he began to shout, "Chi, chi, chi!" Finally, he said, "Chili," which is how the hot, green plant got its name. He believed with all his heart that the Baby Jesus had blessed him with this gift because of his prayers. After many years of replanting the chili seeds, Don Bernardo became quite proficient at cultivating the wonderful plant, which became an important ingredient in many traditional dishes.

Years later, on his dying bed, he recounted the story of the seeds of faith and how to grow them properly. He explained the whole process, from saving the seeds, planting, making *ristras* and chili powder to the different uses of chili in preparing food.

Don Bernardo had been a poor farmer. The only inheritance he left his family was the discovery of the chili seeds. Little did he know that he would become a local legend spreading throughout the world. The religious significance and delicious taste of the chili will hopefully live forever. ■

Legends of the Supernatural

La Llorona

One of the best-known Hispanic tales from the Southwestern United States, "La Llorona" ("The Weeping Woman") is equally well known in Mexico. Mexican-born writer Francisco Jimenez grew up hearing it, as did New Mexican writer Rodolfo Anaya (Anaya, 1999; Jimenez, 2001). Although the tale type is international, appearing, for example, in stories from Germany and from Hawaii (Atencio, 1991, p. xi), the weeping woman is the best-known character in the Latino oral tradition (Anaya, 1999). "La Llorona" is a living legend that has kept generations of children from wandering too close to rivers. The death of the children and the connection with rivers, however, is also associated with a pre-Columbian Aztec goddess who sacrificed babies and, shrieking, disappeared into lakes or rivers. According to folklorist Richard Dorson (1970) the two traditions, Hispanic and Aztec, merged in this story, the Aztec goddess having become a young woman killing her children. Atencio's reference at the beginning of the story to Marina la Malinche, the "faithful (Aztec) companion" of Her-nando Cortez, the Spanish conquistador, also suggests a Hispanic-Aztec connection. The legend is used as a means of social control, not only to keep children from rivers and staying out too late at night but also to warn young girls about being headstrong and going against their family's advice. *Booooo!*

The story took place in the town of Sante Fe, New Mexico, sometime in the early 1800s. A beautiful baby came into the world. She was welcomed with open arms and received the best of everything. Maria was her name. Her parents were very wealthy. They lived in a huge two-story house.

As the years passed, she was blessed with a beauty possessed by few, if any, of the local girls. She had dark skin, eyes like a pair of sapphires, and jet black hair that cascaded past her fragile shoulders all the way down to her waist. She was given many lovely clothes, toys, and a collection of dolls, which she placed on top of her canopy bed. But she was nothing but a spoiled brat! Some of the little girls would go to her house and say, "Maria! Maria! Do you want to play with us, Maria?" Maria would answer in a very brattish tone of voice, "I don't want to play with you because I don't have to! My mommy buys me pretty clothes but your clothes are nothing but rags!"

Source: "La Llorona" from *Cuentos from My Childhood: Legends and Folktales of Northern New Mexico* by Paulette Atencio. Santa Fe: Museum of New Mexico Press, 1991. Reprinted with permission by Museum of New Mexico Press, Santa Fe, New Mexico. pp. 3–6.

"La Llorona." Illustrated by Vicky Trego Hill.

Copyright © 1987 by Vicky Trego Hill. From: *La Llorona.* © Joe Hayes and Vicky Trego Hill, 1987. Reproduced with permission by Cinco Punto Press.

Soon Maria grew older and more beautiful. By this time, none of the girls liked her. But what did it matter! The boys did! They were all in love with her and wanted to marry her, yet Maria wouldn't even give them the time of day. She didn't think they were good enough for her.

One afternoon, she went for a walk with her grandmother. She explained to the older woman that she wished to marry the most handsome and strongest man in all of Sante Fe. Her grandmother, in return, advised her to find an honest, kind man who would care for her and a family. Maria laughed and thought her grandmother was just too old and didn't know any better.

Not long after this conversation, the man of her dreams arrived in town. His name was Gregorio Ventura. He came all the way from El Paso, Texas. He was a very good-looking man but was as wild as they come. He loved to drink, gamble, and womanize. When they met, though, it was love at first sight, but both were stubborn and played hard to get. Eventually they married, despite her family's disapproval.

Things were fine for a few years. They were blessed with a beautiful daughter and handsome son. Unfortunately, Gregorio soon became restless. He returned to his wild ways. Maria was left behind and became very lonely. It was hard for her. Throughout her life, she had received everything her heart desired, but now she could not have the man she loved. She also knew that many people were talking behind her back.

One evening, Maria and her children were sitting out on the porch. Gregorio drove up with another woman by his side. He got down, talking to his children and gave them some gifts, but didn't even look at Maria. Then he drove away. Maria started crying hysterically until she was out of control. No one can say what really happened. Maria dragged her children to the river. She yelled at them and told them that if she hadn't had them that maybe Gregorio would still love her. She then pushed her children into the water. The current was very strong. The children had never learned how to swim and they drowned! At that moment, Maria came to her senses and began to scream for help, but no one could hear. She ran along the riverbank trying to reverse her horrible action. She fell and hit her head on a rock. Death came swiftly for her.

The following day, Maria's parents and a few other people went in search of her body. When they found it, they took it back to Sante Fe. Sacred burial ground was denied her by the local priest, so Maria was buried on the bank of the river where she had perished along with her innocent children. Such a tragedy had never happened before and the community was deeply affected. No one wanted to go home. All the people just stayed outside talking.

That night, people began to hear anguished sounds of crying. Some said it was just the wind, yet most feared it was Maria continuing to cry over her lost children. In fact, they felt certain they could make out the words, which seemed to get closer and closer: "Ay,

Ay, Ay! Where oh where are my children!" she cried. From that night on, no one ever called her Maria anymore. They called her *la llorona*. All the mothers warned their children to be home before dark because *la llorona* was out looking for her children and might take one of them away.

There was one boy who refused to listen. One night, he disobeyed and walked toward the riverbank where *la llorona* was often heard. As he got closer to the river, he heard a woman crying and calling out for her children. Soon he could make out a draped figure coming toward him with outstretched arms! She came closer and closer to where the young boy was standing. He was so terrified that he couldn't move. *La llorona* picked him up and was about to fling him into the river when the church bells started to ring! She dropped him and, in a flash, disappeared from view. The young boy's heart was beating fast, his mouth was dry, and he couldn't stop shaking. Finally, he began to run and did not stop until he reached his house. He was crying and talking at the same time—trying to inform his mother what *la llorona* had done to him. His mother did not believe him and was about to spank him for being late and disobeying. It was then that she saw the boy's torn shirt was stained with blood. She also found fingernail markings imprinted deeply into his skin.

The following day, the mother took her son all over Sante Fe and showed the people what *la llorona* had done. Years have gone by since the story of *"La Llorona"* was told. Many people say *la llorona* is just make-believe. Others say that if you listen closely at night, you will still hear her crying, "Ay, Ay, Ay! Where oh where are my children!" ◼

Spearfinger

North America: United States—Cherokee

When Kathi Smith Littlejohn tells stories to children in schools, whether they are Cherokee or not, the one story they most frequently request is "Spearfinger." Freeman Owle, another Cherokee storyteller, also says that as a teacher he found that his students liked ghost stories the best, although when he was a child, as soon as his family began telling ghost stories, he would hide his head under a pillow. Frightening yet intriguing, legends about such anomalous beings as haunts, ghosts, witches, and ogres seem to have universal appeal. Perhaps by giving concrete form to and talking about our unnamed terrors, we can conquer them, as does the small boy in this story. Kathi Smith Littlejohn grew up learning only a few of the stories of her Cherokee ancestors, but when she moved back to western North Carolina and began working as Director of Health and Human Services, she began to hear traditional stories from her colleagues and soon started to add these to her repertoire. Her primary audience is schoolchildren, which is evident from her style. Because this story was recorded at a live telling (at the Cherokee Elementary School) and was rendered into text using breaks to reflect the teller's oral rhythm, it is best to read the story aloud (Duncan, 1998).

Storyteller: Kathi Smith Littlejohn

Okay.
We've got time for one more.
Have you ever watched a real scary movie?
Were you scared?
No.
What about when you went to bed and turned off the lights,
    did you look under the bed for monsters?

Source: "Spearfinger" from *Living Stories of the Cherokee* edited by Barbara R. Duncan. Copyright © 1998 by the University of North Carolina Press. Used by permission of the publisher. pp. 62–66.

No.

How 'bout your closet?

Did you hear your dog outside and think Jason had
   come to kill you?

Well, you have to remember that those monsters are
   not real.

You can turn off the VCR any time.

You can walk out of the movie theater any time.

Turn on your light at any time, and the monsters are
   gone.

It's just in our imagination.

But a long long long time ago,
   those monsters were real.

And the worst one
   that the Cherokee people had
   was called
   Spearfinger.

She was awful.

She was forty feet tall,
   and she was covered with this rock-like skin
   that no bullet, no weapon could penetrate.

And she was bloodthirsty.

She had one long,
   razor-sharp,
   spear finger,
   that she would slip up behind you,
   slip it through your back,
   pull out your liver,
   and eat it in one gulp.

She was covered with dried blood
   and snot, and gore dripped from her teeth.

She had razor-sharp teeth,
   she was vicious,
   and she was always coming around.

She loved to eat the flesh of young children
   more than anything.

And to get close to the children,
   she could change her shape.

She could turn and look just like your sister,
   just like your granny.

And as you were out picking blackberries
   or fishing or playing,
   your friend could disappear,
   and she would take his place,
   and you'd never know it until it was too late.

One day
   this village not far from here

knew that Spearfinger was getting close to them
And they just panicked.

   "What are we gonna do? Just let her walk in here
      and eat everybody?"

   "Well, I think we ought to fight her."

And they argued back and forth,
   "No, not me, I think we ought to run."

So they finally came up with a plan,
   that they would dig this huge pit
   all the way around the outside of the village
   and cover it over with branches and trees and
      brushes,
   and when she fell into it,
   then they would kill her.

Everybody started helping.

They started digging,
   and everybody started helping,
   and moving rocks and getting the bushes.

And a young man
   about your age,
   was really trying to help.

He was a little bit clumsy,
   'cause he was real excited.

He was trying to help,
   and he'd go to pull this, and he'd fall down.

He'd run to get a big bucket of mud,
   and he'd spill it.

Finally,
   his dad got real aggravated with him
   and said,
   "Just go over there and sit.
   If you can't do any better than that, just get out of
      the way."

Oh, this really hurt his feelings,
   'cause he was just trying to help.
   "Golly, those little babies there, nobody's yelling at
      them, they fall down."

And went over,
   sat underneath the bushes,
   and he was just very upset.

He thought,
   "Spearfinger's coming,
   we all need to help,
   and nobody even wants to talk to me."

He felt real sorry for himself.

And he noticed
   that there was a little bird

that was stuck in a honeysuckle vine
and couldn't get loose.
But he was still real upset,
and not even thinking about the bird,
he just gently let it loose,
and was very surprised when the bird didn't fly off.
Instead,
the bird came right on his shoulder
and said,
"I really thank you for helping me,
and I'm gonna tell you a secret about Spearfinger.
I know where her heart is."
"She doesn't have a heart.
You can't shoot her through the heart because it's
all covered with rocks.
Even our strongest warrior can't shoot through that."
"No," she said,
"The birds follow Spearfinger, and we know all of
her secrets.
We know where she hides,
we know where her heart is
'cause she doesn't fool with trying to eat us, we're
too small.
Look at the tip of her spear finger,
and that's where her heart is.
Shoot her there."
Oh, he was so excited,
and he ran, and he said,
"Dad, Dad, Dad, I know where her heart is."
The dad said,
"I told you to get over there and sit down.
I don't want to hear it."
And he ran over,
and he tried to tell his mom,

but before he could even tell anybody,
they heard a horrible scream through the forest.
And it was Spearfinger.
And she was coming fast,
and she was ravenously hungry.
Oh, she was screaming,
and they ran and hid,
and she fell into the pit,
and they ran,
and they started trying to kill her,
threw rocks at her,
and she was just clawing her way up to the top.
Blood was just foaming at her mouth.
She was nasty.
And she was awful.
They knew that if she got loose she would kill
everybody.
So they were trying to shoot her,
shoot with bows and arrows,
and they were screaming and running and trying
to hide.
The little boy ran up to the strongest warrior and said,
"Look at the tip of her spear finger."
And he looked,
and it was just about as big as that,
just tiny, just tiny.
He drew back
and shot her through the heart,
and she fell over dead.
And after that the little boy was a great hero.
Everybody listened to him after that day.
Thank you. ∎

White House Ghosts

North America: United States

Stories of haunted houses are one of the six most frequently collected types of American legends. The others are legends about buried treasures, tricksters (these are often outlaws who evade the authorities and are seen as defending individual freedom against repressive laws), heroes (mostly personal anecdotes about famous people), healers, and the origins of place names (Dorson, 1971a).

American newspapers have always played an important role in spreading legends, but in the nineteenth century many a legends was not only repeated but even created by newspapers writers. The latter are "literary" legends, which differ from traditional legends by their lack of variant versions, their smooth styles, and the development of the characters' personalities. Today tabloid newspapers carry on the tradition of creating legends, but newspapers of all kinds pass them on.

Traditional American legends, which can be found in newspapers, books of regional lore, and local travel booklets and Web sites, typically come in many variants, are told in fragmentary fashion, and lack character development. Before the Civil War, family and sporting magazines also regularly printed legends. If the legend is local, members of a community know at least parts of it and will understand allusions to it.

For her telling of the legends about the White House ghosts, Maria Leach, a popular reteller of American folklore, scoured books of folklore, as well as folklore journals, which in turn cited newspapers as sources, such the legends cited in the article "Folklore in the News: Ghosts in the White House" from *Western Folklore* (1958). The same stories have been retold in *National Parks* magazine, vol. 68, no. 11/12 (1994) and in a *New York Times* article on March 2, 1997, which described both the history of the Lincoln Bedroom, and lore about the ghost of President Lincoln.

In the following account the ghosts seem to be closely related to the personality or interests of the individual about whom it is told. The stories reflect some of the most frequently reported types of ghostly phenomena: rapping noise made by ghost, ghost plays musical instruments, ghost hunting for something lost, ghost of a cat, and ghost identifying himself or herself (Leach, 1974).

The White House must be the most thoroughly haunted house in the United States. Eight ghosts are

Source: "White House Ghosts" from *Whistle in the Graveyard: Folktales to Chill Your Bones* by Maria Leach. Copyright © by Maria Leach 1974. Used by permission of Viking Publishing a division of Penguin Putnam, Inc. pp. 17–19.

well known, and many strange things have been seen or heard. President Truman, for instance, opened his bedroom door two or three times to insistent rappings, and there was nobody there.

Probably the oldest ghost in the White House is Abigail Adams, wife of John Adams, second president of the United States. Although the cornerstone of the White House was laid in 1792, the first tenants, John and Abigail Adams did not move in until 1800.

The famous East Room was not finished even then. So Abigail used to hang her wash up to dry there. Several people have seen her going in or coming out of the East Room in her quaint colonial dress, but no one evidently has ever looked to see if the ghost of a clothesline were there or if any of John Adams' shirts were hanging on it.

The most famous of the White House ghosts is Abraham Lincoln. Lincoln paces the floor of the bedroom on the second floor, they say, on the *night before* any threatened great calamity to the United States actually happens. This worried tread was heard on the night before the United States entered World War I and again on the eve of World War II.

Several people have seen Lincoln's back standing in the window of his bedroom, looking out over the Potomac River toward Virginia, just as he used to when some battle was at stake over there between the Union and Confederate armies. Eleanor Roosevelt saw Lincoln sitting on the edge of his bed pulling on his boots one day as she passed his bedroom door. Queen Wilhelmina of the Netherlands said she met Lincoln one evening in the hall while she was visiting in the White House.

One afternoon the whole household was in a flurry because Dolly Madison had been seen in the garden. She was walking distractedly from flower bed to flower bed, looking for something. Then someone remembered that Dolly Madison had planted the first rose beds at the White House. "She is looking for her own roses," someone said—and true enough! That very morning the rose beds had been dug up and transplanted. Once Dolly found them, safe and growing in another spot, she went away and had not been seen since.

Dolly Madison's little cat is a famous ghost, too. It had often been seen curled up in the sun on a window seat or just running around somewhere.

Other famous and recorded stories are that Andrew Jackson has been heard laughing in bed! Abe Lincoln's wife, Mary Todd Lincoln, said she heard Andrew Jackson swearing. Thomas Jefferson has been heard playing the violin. Even an old janitor named Jerry Smith has been seen wandering through the White House with his feather duster.

Occasionally a Mr. Burns (who donated the eighteen acres of land for the White House in 1790) announces himself, unseen, out of the air. "I'm Mister Burns!" he says, "I'm Mister Burns!" Somebody should do something for Mr. Burns to put his soul to rest. They should put up a plaque for him or hold a memorial service, or something. He deserves it. ■

Web Supplement Stories

Web supplement stories are located at **www.ablongman.com/lechner.**

Hero Tales and Epics

Odysseus
The Cyclops
The Island of Aeolus, the Laestrygons, Circe

Europe: Greece

Use of the word *odyssey* has become ubiquitous in our culture. A Web search on the word turned up over a million Web sites. The first two pages alone included such varied uses of the word as the name of an automobile, an educational travel tour agent, an audio components business, a golf putting equipment business, a magazine, an e-commerce Web development company, a bicycle components and accessories business, a scientific project (NASA's Mars Odyssey), a science fiction film (*2001: A Space Odyssey*), a program for students from kindergarten through college designed to foster their creativity and problem-solving abilities (Odyssey of the Mind), a Library of Congress exhibit entitled "African American Odyssey," Web sites for such diverse purposes as interactive science activities for young people, conferences on global information systems, and Internet-based social studies projects for classes doing cultural studies. And that was only the first two pages! There were also many sites devoted to the classic itself, including a full-text copy of a translation by Samuel Butler and a breezy, illustrated pop

retelling created just for the Internet. Besides the many uses of the word for the names of businesses and projects, we also use the word metaphorically to mean a journey of exploration, especially of the self.

Homer, the poet who first immortalized this name, wrote probably some time in the eighth century B.C.E., drawing on folkloric material but creating an epic that celebrated the heroic attributes the Greeks of his time valued. Odysseus exhibits the virtues of physical courage and strength; ingenuity (he was often referred to as wily) where strength was not enough; restraint, patience, tact, self-control, and perseverance to return home in spite of all odds and temptations (Lattimore, 1965). To this list one could add practicality. Over and over Odysseus uses practical arguments rather than emotional ones to appeal to his men. On the island of Circe, for instance, when he wants to explore, against the advice of his men, who are afraid, he says that because they have no idea where they are, they must try to find some way of getting their bearings.

Besides the tests of courage, strength, and intelligence that he readily passes, Odysseus must also pass tests of restraint, patience, and self-control. He is not quite so successful at these, but ultimately he shows great capacity for each of these virtues. He is able to restrain himself from eating the Lotus Eaters' dream-inducing fruit, from opening the wind bag of Aeolus, from eating the cattle of Helios, the god of the sun, and from pleasures of the flesh when he chooses to give up two goddesses (Circe and Kalypso) to return home to his wife. Like a true epic hero, Odysseus is not perfect. He succumbs to pride in the face of prudent advice when he insists on taunting Polyphemus; he loses sight of his goal when he enjoys the charms and comforts of Circe and her palace for a year; and he falls asleep at crucial moments such as at the helm while approaching Ithaca the first time as well as on the island of Helios.

Although Homer's epic is the work of a known poet or poets, it is based on oral tales, some of which are readily recognized for their folkloric motifs. The story of Polyphemus has many variants, including a Celtic one. In the Celtic myth a one-eyed giant, Balor, must be defeated by the champion of light and knowledge, Lugh, just as Odysseus must defeat this cannibalistic giant, one of the one eyed Cyclopes, whose dark cave means death and whose world is ignorance and an uncivilized life (Powell, 1998).

Though there are mythic elements in *The Odyssey,* it is Odysseus' human side, his endurance and ultimate triumph when he is happily united with his wife, combined with the exciting adventures he encounters along the way, that have made this a popular legend throughout the centuries, though not in all eras and places. The Romans, claiming descent from the Trojans through Aeneas, considered Odysseus a villain, and Dante, the thirteenth century Italian poet, placed him in one of the circles of Hell in the *Inferno.* As a man whose quest for adventure and knowledge pushed him ever into unknown and possibly dangerous territory, however, Odysseus has been a hero for the Western world since the beginning of the age of exploration (Powell, 1998).

The Odyssey has been translated many times. It is said that each generation needs its own translation. Two from the 1960s are interesting to compare for the difference in their tone. Richmond Lattimore's translation (1965), using hexameters (six beats to each line) and multisyllabic words derived from Latin or Greek, has a mellifluous sound, while Fitzgerald's translation (1961) with its pentameters (five beats to each line) and shorter words has a stronger, more strident sound. Notice the difference between the following two descriptions of the verdant, abundant island off Polyphemus' coast, which the Greeks feel that with their

knowledge of farming and sailing they could easily develop while the uncivilized Cyclops race is unable to make good use of it. Lattimore's translation:

> From there, grieving still at heart, we sailed on
>   further
> along, and reached the country of the lawless
>   outrageous
> Cyclopes who, putting all their trust in the im-
>   mortal
> gods, neither plow with their hands nor plant
>   anything,
> but all grows for them without seed planting,
>   without cultivation,
> wheat and barley and also the grapevines,
>   which yield for them
> wine of strength, and it is Zeus' rain that waters
>   it for them.

The Odyssey of Homer translated by Richard Lattimore. Harper and Row, 1965, p. 140.

Fitzgerald's translation:

> In the next land we found were Kyclopês,
> giants, louts, without a law to bless them.
> In ignorance leaving the fruitage of the earth in
>   mystery
> to the immortal gods, they neither plow
> nor sow by hand, nor till the ground, though
>   grain—
> wild wheat and barley—grows untended, and
> wine-grapes, in clusters, ripen in heaven's rain.

The Odyssey of Homer, translated by Robert Fitzgerald. Doubleday, 1961, p. 148.

From: *Stories from Homer* by Alfred J. Church. New York: Thomas Y. Crowell, 1901. "The Cyclops" pp. 145–157 and "The Island of Aeolus, the Laestrygons, Circe" pp. 158–167.

The Story of the Children of Lir

Europe: Ireland

It is fortunate for us that the bards of Ireland had preserved their ancient legends through poetry and song into the era of monastic scholarship. Irish monks, though skeptical about the truth of the stories of the previous inhabitants of Ireland, did record them, even if at times under protest: "I like not to have the labour of writing this section imposed upon me: wherefore I beseech you . . . not to reproach me for it," wrote an eleventh or twelfth century monk (Morris, 1973, p. 147).

Archeology, however, backs up many of the events in ancient Ireland's *Book of Invasions,* which is part of the story cycle that has been classified as the Mythological Cycle. Not all of the accounts were part of the oral tradition, because the monks connected Ireland to biblical history, making the first man to come to Ireland a son of Noah.

Starting with the stories about the Fir Bolgs, whom the legends credit with introducing agriculture, however, the stories begin to have archeological support. It is thought that a Stone Age people settled in Ireland around 2000 B.C.E. who practiced agriculture. They created stone barrows as burial chambers that the Celts found when they migrated to Ireland. A more recent migration, sometime before 1000 B.C.E. and remembered vividly in the stories, was that of a Bronze Age Celtic group that arrived on the island from Greece by way of Scandinavia. These people brought bronze cauldrons, the sword and spear, smiths, wrights, carpenters, doctors, and druids.

A later group of Celts, arriving in Ireland sometime between 1000 and 600 B.C.E., were Iron Age people who called themselves the Milesians, after Mil of Spain, and called the earlier Celts the Tuatha de Danann, or the tribe of the goddess Dana (Morris, 1973; Fleming et al., 1996). They credited the Tuatha de Danann with skills in a wide range of crafts as well as with great magical knowledge and referred to their rulers by the names of Celtic gods. Thus the Dagda, identified as the mightiest of the Danns, in "The Story of the Children of Lir," was the ancestral deity of the Celts, also called "Good Father" (Fleming et al., 1996). Lir himself was the god of the Sea, and his son Manannan, after whom the Isle of Man was named, was god of the sea as well. The children changing into swans is also part of the Celtic mythic tradition associating swans with the Otherworld (Fleming et al., 1996; MacRaois, 1997).

"The Story of the Children of Lir" is the beautiful and sad tale of four enchanted children flying for 900 years as swans, only to miss the Tuatha de Dananns' departure for the Invisible World, also known as the Otherworld, leaving the visible world to the conquering Milesians. The later Celts called the abandoned homes of the Tuatha de Dananns *sidhs.* The earlier Celtic people did build round stone burial mounds; the one at New Grange was one of the biggest and is still an impressive site near Dublin. Though in later centuries the Tuatha de Dananns came to be known as the Fairies, they were not imagined as little. They were tall and beautiful, with beautiful clothes, and they presided over an Otherworld that was as lovely as a dream, where an unending supply of food came from a magic cauldron.

The ending of the story links the pre-Christian Celts with Christian Ireland, as the Children of Lir, though sad to have missed their folks, were happy to be released from their enchantment and to be baptized by St. Patrick.

From: *The High Deeds of Finn and Other Bardic Romances of Ancient Ireland* by T. W. Rolleston. London: George G. Harrap, 1922. pp. 3–21.

The Chase of the Gilla Dacar

Europe: Ireland

Finn Mac Cumhal, spelled *Finn Mac Cool* or *Coul* in English, one of the great legendary Celtic heroes of pre-Christian Ireland, was thought to have lived during the reign of the High King Cormac mac Art in the third century C.E. Legends about Finn and the Fianna, a forest-dwelling troop of hunter-warriors, were passed on orally by bards and learned men called *filidh.* The stories were first recorded by Christian monks, perhaps as early as the seventh century, though the most extensive written sources come from the twelfth century (MacCana, 1987). As protectors of Ireland from invaders and as keepers of the peace within the land, the Fianna had to pass a test of skill and endurance and swear to live by a code of conduct: (1) never to take cattle by force, (2) never to refuse a request for money, (3) never to retreat if outnumbered by less than ten to one, (4) and never to avenge any harm done to a kinsman. Generosity and exceptional courage, the second and third points, were two of the most important Celtic values, while the first and last points were important if the Fianna were to keep the peace among rival provinces and families (Morris, 1973; Cahill, 1994). The Fianna were greatly honored in their time and were paid well by a grateful king and people. Though they lived in the woods, they had their own druids, poets, musicians, doctors, and even seamstresses to make them beautiful clothes. (MacCana, 1987; Fleming et al., 1996). Still, by living in the woods, Finn and his men kept close to the natural world and even to the Otherworld, the world of the Tuatha de Danann, or Immortals. According to legend, these beings, also referred to as the Fairy Folk in later times, ruled Ireland before the Celts.

Though Finn, whose name meant "Fair" or "Light," was closely allied with the historic king Cormac mac Art, his character might be more mythic than historical. Born to a mother who was descended from both the king of the Tuatha de Danann and the king of the Fomorians, their monster enemies, he began life under a cloud. His true identity had to be hidden at birth, as his father, the leader of the Fianna, had just been murdered by a rival group. His mother, fearing for Finn's life, took him to be raised in the woods by a female Druid and a female warrior, who taught him all the skills of survival. At an early age he could outrun deer and hare. Once, happening on a group of boys at a mansion, he single-handedly beat them all in a hurling match (a hockey-like ball game played with sticks). Afraid of recognition by his enemies, he went into the world under an alias and became apprenticed to a poet; poetry was as highly regarded in Celtic society as skill in battle. Here he also accidentally gained supernatural knowledge. As he was cooking a fish for the poet, he burned his thumb on the Salmon of Knowledge (Fleming et al., 1996). Finally, the young Finn earned the right to be the leader of the Finneans by killing Aillen, a being from the Otherworld, who every year during the end of summer–start of winter holiday, Samhain (pronounced Sowen), burnt the High King's castle to the ground. (The Catholic Church later adapted Samhain as All Hallows Eve, or Halloween.)

In the story "The Chase of the Gilla Dacar" Rolleston retells a typical adventure from the cycle of tales about Finn and the Fianna. It starts out in the natural world but ends in the rescue of the Immortals of the Otherworld, who had lured Finn's men to their world for that purpose. Most of the children's versions of the adventures of Finn Mac Cool seem to be more tall tales developed from the legends than the legends themselves. In these humorous stories Finn and Cuchulain, Ireland's greatest legendary hero, actually meet, although the semihistorical legends set them 200 years apart. In the tall tale versions Finn's grandmother is the one who raises him secretly, along with his beloved hound Bran, inside a tree trunk, and she is the one who teaches him to run faster than anyone else by playing a wild game of tag up and down hills with him. His wife Ooghnah plays an important role in helping him outsmart the even tougher and bigger Cuchulain, and the two heroes build the Giant's Causeway, a natural landmark on the coast of Northern Ireland.

From: *The High Deeds of Finn and Other Bardic Romances of Ancient Ireland* by T. W. Rolleston. London: George G. Harrap, 1922. pp. 134–148.

Robin Hood and Little John

Europe: England

The life-affirming, merry tone of most of the Robin Hood stories is one of the reasons they continue in popularity. Even in the stories in which Robin Hood meets his match, the tone is joyful, if rough: Robin meets someone who challenges him to a fight; the two men fight fairly and in the end become friends. Two companions whom he acquired in this manner are Little John and Friar Tuck. According to Jeffrey Singman, a Robin Hood scholar (1998), the challenge and ensuing fight were a way of testing each other's mettle and ability to handle themselves as free commoners without the status and weapons of the nobility yet with courage and skill showing personal worth.

Howard Pyle, a turn of the twentieth-century American artist and writer, created out of many ballads a prose version for children, *The Merry Adventures of Robin Hood of Great Renown in Nottinghamshire* (1946). It is an understatement to say that Robin Hood continues to intrigue writers as shown by the many retellings for children.

From: *The Merry Adventures of Robin Hood of Great Renown in Nottinghamshire* by Howard Pyle. New York: Grosset & Dunlap. 1946. Pp. 20–28.

Classroom and Library Applications

The following classroom applications are provided as examples of the types of applications that are possible using traditional literature with children. The suggested applications will take advantage of each genre's unique characteristics, but there is a great deal of overlap among the genres in themes, characters, and story elements, so an application that is suggested under one genre might well work with other genres as well.

The sample applications below are arranged to correspond to the sections in the *Allyn & Bacon Anthology of Traditional Literature*. These applications could be used similarly with the other stories in the same section. For picture book versions of the stories, see the web supplement based "Picture Books Related to the Stories" at www.ablongman.com/lechner for specific stories. The Web site www.ablongman.com/lechner also includes further stories in each genre (Web Supplement), as well as a searchable *Bibliographic Database of Fables, Folktales, Myths, and Legends in Picture Books and Story Collections*. Other Web-based sources of full-text stories are listed under "Fables and Pourquoi Tales, Folktales, Fairy Tales, and Myths and Legends" in the Appendix.

▧ Fables and Pourquoi (Why) Tales

Because fables are brief and have distinct morals, they provide a convenient vehicle for character education. Many pourquoi tales also teach lessons in socially acceptable behavior. Their simple plots and limited number of characters make them also convenient for practicing oral expression through reader's theater and creative writing. Fables can also provide an opportunity for older children to practice critical thinking.

Character Education

Fables and pourquoi tales function as a more palatable way to teach positive social values than direct lecture does. Once children understand that fables are designed to teach specific lessons, they are often eager to find the "moral" in the stories they hear. Identifying the moral of a story, however, can be a challenge. Two approaches for identifying morals follow.

In the first approach, read and discuss several related fables with similar morals. The following is an example of the way similar fables can be used for identifying the morals of stories:

- Read aloud (or have children read) "The Lion and the Mouse," an Aesop fable, and "The Mice that Set the Elephants Free," a Panchatantra fable.
- Have children compare the stories using a Venn diagram. Draw a circle for each story, with the circles overlapping in the middle. Differences are placed in the nonoverlapping parts of the circles, and the similarities are placed in the overlapping portion. Because Aesop fables typically spell out the moral of the story, this can also help children make connections between the two stories. "Little friends may prove great friends" applies to both stories, even though the Panchatantra tale does not spell out this moral. See Figure 6.1.

In the second approach, have children identify the moral of these two stories by omitting Aesop's moral and having them, as a class, come up with a moral based on a comparison of the two fables.

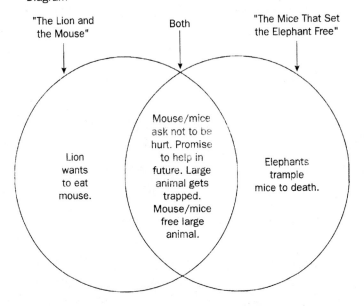

FIGURE 6.1

Similarities and Differences between "The Lion and the Mouse" and "The Mice That Set the Elephants Free" Using a Venn Diagram

- Have children list the different and similar elements of the stories.

- Let children suggest morals, and have them explain their reasoning. Susan Lehr (1991), who worked with kindergarten and first graders, found this to be important when discussing theme. Frequently, the themes that young children draw from stories are different from those of adults; listening to children explain their rationales is helpful both to encourage children to create their own meanings from the stories they hear and read and to enable the teacher or other adult to understand children's perspectives.

Oral Expression

Reader's Theater   The brevity and simple structure of fables and pourquoi tales make them ideal for creating reader's theater with children, giving children an opportunity to write scripts and to practice oral expression. The idea behind reader's theater is to have children read their parts, not to memorize them, thus freeing them to focus on the text and its interpretation rather than on memorizing. All children can participate, and none need feel embarrassed about reading aloud, as practice reading will allow each child to read smoothly.

For detailed instructions, see the resources by Mildred Laughlin and Kathy Latrobe, and by Judy Sierra listed at the end of this chapter. For free scripts for the classroom, see Aaron Shepard's Reader's Theater home page at http://www.aaronshep.com/rt/index.html.

Creative Writing   Because pourquoi tales are so fanciful, they capture children's imagination. After reading several pourquoi tales, children can write their own. The following are suggestions for brainstorming preceding a pourquoi tale writing assignment:

- Discuss the use of animal characters to represent human behavioral traits.
- Discuss story structure: characters are introduced in first sentence; a problem is introduced; the problem is elaborated on through several situa-

tions; a solution is found; there is social reward or punishment; an observed phenomenon is "explained."

- Let children brainstorm social-behavioral problems they have observed (fighting, teasing, not sharing, etc.).
- Have children in small groups select a problem and animal characters that would represent different behaviors and discuss how observed nature phenomena might be explained as a reward or punishment for the character's behavior relating to the identified problem.
- Have each group write a pourquoi tale to fit the group's determined problem, characters, and explanation for observed phenomenon.

Critical Thinking

African dilemma tales can be used in the same way that they are used in African villages: to have students discuss alternative solutions and judgments to the problems presented in the fables. Both "The Girl and the Python" and "Mirror, Airplane, and Ivory Trumpet" from Zaire present a challenge in fairness. Early elementary school children are concerned about issues of fairness and would find the dilemma of who did the most in each story to save the victim an interesting problem to discuss. When the fables' solutions are not revealed, children are invited to consider the problem of fair rewards themselves.

- List all suggestions for who in these stories did the most to help, along with each student's reasoning. At this point all suggestions should be accepted.
- Once each suggestion is on the board, have children discuss which arguments have the greatest merit.

Did the punishment fit the crime? In many pourquoi tales specific animals' characteristics change because of undesirable or antisocial acts they commit. In the Cherokee story "How the Possum Lost His Tail" Possum permanently loses his lovely bushy tail because he is such a show-off. Have children consider the reason for and appropriateness of the outcome. For example:

- Read "Cat and Dog and the Return of the Dead" from Haiti.
- Have an alternative ending in which Dog too gets his "Day in Court."
- Have Dog and Cat both argue their case.

Because this story has larger philosophical implications about life and death, this would be a more appropriate lesson to do with older children. Most pourquoi tales, however, would work with younger children too. "Why Bats Fly by Night and Birds by Day" and "Why Hens Scratch the Ground" from South Africa present values of cooperation and being careful with each other's property, respectively.

Folktales

Cumulative Tales

The repetitive nature of cumulative tales make them favorites with younger children. In collecting stories, it is often the children that supply the folklorists with the cumulative tales. These stories provide an ideal vehicle for having children practice oral expression through storytelling, as well as for recognizing the story structures of formula tales. "The Cat and Mouse" from England and "Talk" from Ghana are both relatively short and suitable for this exercise. These stories are examples of two different kinds of formula stories. "The Cat and the Mouse" is a circular chain story that ends up where it began. "Talk" is a cumulative story. One character is added to the next until the surprise ending, when all are dispersed. The stories also provide a contrast in the kinds of people, animals, and foods mentioned, affording an opportunity to discuss the similarities and differences between traditional village lives in the two countries.

Read both of the stories aloud to the class. Have children identify each of the characters in the stories and create a chart of characters on poster board for each story. This chart can be kept up to help cue children about the sequence of characters in the story.

- Discuss whether the story is a chain story or a cumulative story to help children become aware of story structure.

- Discuss the wording: what new words are added as character(s) meet a new person and which words repeat.
- Model and have children practice the "voices" for each character in each of the stories.
- Children can also create masks or poster board puppets to hold while telling the stories.
- Small groups can collaboratively retell one of the two formula tales, using voices and puppets or masks to help distinguish characters.

For a longer cumulative tale that children can compare to the familiar "Gingerbread Man," see "The Pancake" on the Web Supplement: www.ablongman.com/lechner.

Fairy Tales

Fairy tales, with their well-developed plots, stock characters, descriptive and often fanciful language, and distinct themes, provide many different opportunities for classroom application in language arts as well as in social studies. Some applications include creating a plot map; recognizing storytelling styles; identifying recurrent motifs among variants of a story; identifying and comparing themes in different variants of a story from the same culture or across cultures; comparing characters and their motivations; comparing culturally specific details of variants of a story across cultures; creative writing using traditional story structures, characters, motifs, and themes; and critical thinking about characters' motivations and stereotypes used in traditional stories. Below is a description of three applications: creating a plot map, identifying Recurrent motifs, and critical thinking.

Creating a Plot Map   Creating a plot map can help children identify a sequence of events, look for cause and effect, and notice typical patterns in traditional (and other) literature with a linear plot sequence and a progressive plot. (The initiating event begins the rising action toward the climax of the story). Because character and theme are often conveyed through action rather than dialog or description in traditional tales, a plot map can also help children notice similarities and differences between characters and identify differing thematic emphases of versions of a story.

As children practice analyzing plot structure, they learn to identify the main problem of the story, separating it from the basic, general problem; the initiating event and other events and actions, such as the trials of the hero; the climax of the rising action; and the resolution of the problem.

Table 6.1 is a comparison between Charles Perrault's 1697 French "Cinderella" (the version made familiar in the United States through Disney) and the story of "Vasilisa the Fair," a Russian story retold by Alexandr Afanas'ev and found in the *Allyn & Bacon Anthology*. This comparison provides an example of how plot structures can be mapped with children and how this activity helps children identify the concepts mentioned above. The contrast between Cinderella's and Vasilisa's actions can help children to also consider different ways story heroes respond to the problems they face.

Other Cinderella tale type (AT 510A) variants within this anthology that could be compared to these two are "Tattercoats" from England (on the Web Supplement) and "La Estrellita" from the southwestern United States.

Identifying Recurrent Motifs   Motifs are elements within traditional stories that occur in various combinations across stories and cultures. In "The Beauty and the Beast" variants, which in the *Allyn & Bacon Anthology* include not only "The Black Bull of Norroway" but also "The Stepdaughter and the Black Serpent" from Turkey and the Greek myth "Cupid and Psyche," some typical motifs include the animal or invisible husband, the bride's journey, the temporary loss of the husband, and the magical objects needed to tame or regain him. Other motifs can include magic numbers, tests of courage, tests of kindness or respectfulness, riddles, and transformations (from human to animal or animal to human). Children can identify the motifs in several stories and create a **motif chart.** The example in Table 6.2 compares motifs in four variants of the "Beauty and the Beast" tale type (AT 410). "Beauty and the Beast" stories, the best-known versions of which are literary fairy tales, share the folkloric theme and basic plot structure of the hero's journey, tests of courage and/or love, and final disenchantment of the beast. Because "Beauty and the Beast" is so well known, it will be used as a basis for this cross-cultural comparison of motifs.

Creating a Plot Map

Story	Cinderella	Vasilisa
Background and Setting:	• Middle-class city home • Father and mother "absent" (mother dead, father weak) • Stepmother and two stepsisters cruel to Cinderella (hero) • Deprive her of her status, overwork her.	• Middle-class country home • Father and mother "absent" (mother dead, father away on trip) • Stepmother and two stepsisters cruel to Vasilisa (hero) • Deprive her of food, overwork her
Main Problem	Cinderella is not allowed to go to ball	Baba Yaga will probably eat Vasilisa
Initiating Event	Invitation to the Prince's ball	Stepsisters let fire go out and send Vasilisa to Baba Yaga
Other Events— Trials of Hero's Character	• C. does all her chores cheerfully • C. helps sisters get ready for ball • C. left behind, cries • C. helped by Fairy Godmother, is grateful • C. goes to ball, acts kind • C. follows rules • C. waits to be recognized	• V. does all the chores, stays healthy, pretty • V. remembers mother's blessing/feeds doll • V. goes to Baba Yaga • V. and doll do all chores at Baba Yaga's • V. bravely asks questions • V. knows when not to talk • V. moves in with old woman • V. weaves, sews, sends old woman to czar to catch his eye • Expresses gratitude
Climax of Story	C. is found to fit the shoe	Two climaxes: • Baba Yaga sends V. home safely and house burns down with step's in it • Czar recognizes quality of V.'s workmanship and discovers her beauty
Resolution	• C. marries prince • Stepsisters become court ladies	• Stepsisters die • V. marries czar • Old lady is cared for by royal family

After having created such a chart, children can be asked to compare elements that relate to theme. For instance, the "How the Beast Is Almost Lost" and "How the Beast Is Won" categories suggest the central themes of the stories. Other categories can be added, or for a constructivist approach, categories can be devised together with children after several variants of a story in this anthology and in picture book versions have been read.

Comparing Culturally Specific Details in International Variants of a Tale One important reason for introducing international fairy tales is that both similarities and differences among cultures can be explored. Creating a chart of culturally specific details with children can be used as a jumping-off point for exploring specific cultures in depth through small group projects or as individual research projects. Creating such a chart also makes one more aware of cultural objects and

▓ **TABLE 6.2**
A Motif Chart for "Beauty and the Beast" Variants

Story	Beauty and the Beast	The Red Bull of Norroway
Country	France	Scotland
Hero	Beauty—most beautiful daughter	No name—youngest princess
Family of Hero	Merchant father, two sisters—jealous, greedy; three brothers—good (in some)	Royal father, mother, two sisters—proud
Beast	Beast—enchanted prince	Bull—enchanted Duke of Norroway
Enchanter	Fairy	Enchantress
Why Enchanted	In some versions jealous, in others punishment for vanity, cruelty	Unknown
Helpers	Dream fairy, invisible or animal servants	Old wife
Setting	City, cottage, wild woods, garden, palace	Palace, Countryside, Palace
Magical Objects, Transport Animals, Numbers	Rose, treasure chest, ring, key, horse, mirror (not all of these appear in each version), three sisters; three (or 30 or seven) days she may stay away	Pin—Princess pulls it out of bull, three nuts with "wee wifie" characters, three nights in Duke's room
How Beast Is Almost Lost	Beauty breaks promise to return on time (unable to commit to beast over own family)	Princess is late, enchantress almost gets Duke of Norroway to marry her
How Beast Is Won	Beauty declares her love for beast	Princess stays in Duke's room at night and wakes him

practices that one takes for granted in one's own culture. The chart could be similar to the motif chart, but instead, culturally specific details might be emphasized by comparing the kinds of foods, jobs, artifacts, animals, plants, geographical features, and so forth that characters use or encounter, along with possible examples of customs, such as greetings, gifts, and the form tests take. For instance, in "Mother Holle" from Germany the sisters are tested by having to take bread from the oven and shaking out Mother Holle's feather bed, whereas in "Kumba the Orphan Girl" from Gambia the sisters have to greet two coconuts along the way and make a dish from a single rice and an old bone.

Critical Thinking Critical thinking can be applied as children learn to identify stock characters and the stereotypes traditional storytellers draw on (e.g. stepmother, old woman as wicked witch, helpless princess, handsome young man as also brave) and the way these stereotypes do or do not work in real life.

■ TABLE 6.2
Continued

Story	The Stepdaughter and the Black Serpent	Cupid and Psyche
Country	Turkey	Ancient Greece
Hero	No name—Stepdaughter	Psyche—Most beautiful princess
Family of Hero	Poor Stepmother	Royal father, mother two sisters—jealous
Beast	Serpent—Enchanted son of Padishah (Sultan)	Invisible—Cupid, god of love
Enchanter	Allah	None
Why Enchanted	In response to Padishah's prayer for a son, even a serpent	As a god he must stay invisible to mortal Psyche
Helpers	Mother's spirit	Invisible servants, ants, nymphs, Cupid
Setting	Palace, cottage, grave, palace	Palace, wild mountaintop, palace, Venus's, journey into wilderness and underground, palace
Magical Objects, Transport Animals, Numbers	Golden box with seven holes for milk from seven cows, diamond cradle, branches of rosebush and holly, 40 nights, serpent kills 40 brides, 40 hedgehog and snake skins	Zephyr for transportation, ants, untamable golden sheep, beauty powder of the gods, three sisters, three tasks
How Beast Is Almost Lost	For the final trial the stepdaughter must be the one to rise to the challenge or someone else will get the Sultan's son as husband	Psyche breaks taboo against looking at husband (lack of trust)
How Beast Is Won	Stepdaughter nurses him, teaches him, forces him to shed serpent exterior	Cupid forgives and rescues Psyche

- Have children write down and then discuss their images of witches, stepmothers, fairy tale heroes, and so on.
- Then have them compare these characters to real people in their own experience.
- Discuss the function of stereotypes in folklore—as a fast way to communicate a type rather than trying to develop realistic characters.
- Compare fairy tale characters with characters in picture storybooks or fiction. Do the character types show up in these genres? Are the characters better developed? Are some of the characters in these genres just as stereotyped or flat as fairy tale characters?

Children can also identify stories in which the stereotypes do not hold. In the "Beauty and the Beast" stories mentioned above, for instance, the girls are brave and perseverant seekers, not passive or helpless.

Other critical thinking activities can include finding different solutions from those of the protagonists for a problem, such as finding a peaceful rather than a violent solution, or thinking of other rewards and punishments than those offered in the story.

Noodlehead Tales, Tall Tales, and Other Humorous Tales

Literary Devices Humorous tales depend a great deal on the way in which they are presented. This genre can be used to teach the literary devices of exaggeration, understatement, and irony. Because younger children lack both real-world experience and reading experience to be able to readily identify and utilize these devices, classroom discussion about what is realistic and what is exaggerated will be essential before reading noodlehead tales and tall tales. For the most part, the stories in this section are developmentally more appropriate to use with older children. Tall tales, which rely on exaggeration and often also on understatement, are popular with third and fourth graders, whereas stories which rely on irony are more appropriate with fifth grade and up.

Exaggeration and Understatement in Tall Tales American tall tales depend on understatement as much as on exaggeration for their humorous effect. Esther Shepard's *Paul Bunyan,* from which a chapter is included in the *Allyn & Bacon Anthology* demonstrates these techniques.

- Have students read the "Paul Bunyan" selection in this *anthology.*
- Students should underline statements that seem to minimize the enormity of an object or feat. For instance, at the end of the second paragraph the narrator says, "all he had to cook em on was one of them there drumhead stoves they used to have." It seems as if this were a very small type of stove until you read the rest of the sentence: "and he couldn't only cook but sixty-four drippin' pans full at a time."
- Next have students underline exaggerations such as "And even so the cook used to have to get up twenty-six hours before daylight to get the biscuits cooked in time."

In some tall tales the teller begins with realistic descriptions, so when the exaggerations begin, listeners or readers are inclined at first to believe the story, and only after a while do they realize that they're listening to a whopper. In stories of this nature students can also identify the point at which a realistic adventure turns into a tall tale.

Once children become adept at identifying the devices of understatement and exaggeration, they can write their own tall tales about an adventure or a character. Children can write about actual people, giving them larger-than-life qualities, or they can take an everyday situation, such as walking home from school or the problems they had getting their homework done, and create a tall tale around these themes.

Irony Irony is defined as the contrast between expectations and reality, or between appearances and reality. Three types of irony found in literature are verbal irony, situational irony, and dramatic irony. *Verbal irony* is used when a narrator or a character says the opposite of what he or she means. A famous instance of verbal irony is Mark Antony's praise of Brutus in Shakespeare's *Julius Caesar,* when he keeps reiterating that "Brutus is an honorable man" while it becomes more and more apparent that he means the opposite. In *situational irony* an event turns out opposite of what is expected by character and reader. In *dramatic irony* a character does not realize that his or her actions will lead to the opposite results of what he or she expects, but the reader is aware that the character's greed, selfishness, foolishness, or dishonesty is likely to lead to trouble for the character. Folktales tend to use the last two types more than verbal irony.

Several stories in the *Allyn & Bacon Anthology* make use of irony. In "The Storyteller" from Ethiopia the king who can't get enough of stories finally begs for the story to end. In "How the Animals Kept the Lion Away" from Algeria the smaller animals are able to scare away the lion by making him think they had killed many lions as they kept bringing out the same lion skin three times. The irony in "The Talking Skull" takes a deadly turn when the hunter learns too late the meaning of the skull's words "talking brought me here."

In a lesson on irony:

- Define the term and discuss familiar stories and situations in which things turned out differently from what students expected. "The Story of the Three Pigs," which is familiar to most children, is a good example. The wolf expects to eat all three pigs; instead, he ends up in the pot of hot water.
- Read the Scottish "Get Up and Bar the Door" and the Japanese "The Silence Match" as examples of stories in which the characters' stubbornness results in a problem that outweighs any gain they might have received by "winning" their contests. The minimal stakes in the contest(s) add to the irony in showing how silly the couple(s) are, while the final irony is that even after all that happened, the contest is still more important to these couples than anything else.
- After reading one or both of the stories, have children identify what the characters' expectations were and why things turned out the way they did.
- Discuss with students situations in which a contest or desire to have their own way got out of hand, leading to negative results. What were these negative results?
- After reading and identifying several stories with irony, try having students dramatize one, emphasizing the irony.
- As a creative writing extension to the lesson on irony, students could write scripts for a "local news" story relating the rice cake robbery incident, having each member of the couple as well as the robber tell their versions of the story. The same thing could be done with "Get Up and Bar the Door."

Other noodlehead stories, such as "Lazy Jack," and "Hans in Luck," both Web Supplement stories, provide extended dramatic irony as the characters keep thinking that they are doing the right thing with each foolish decision.

Trickster Tales

The multifaceted nature of the trickster makes trickster tales more complex and challenging to teach than fables and pourquoi tales, with their explicit lessons, or fairy tales, which express hopes and dreams of a happy life. When teaching trickster tales, one can look

at both those elements that unite the trickster character globally and those that make him (or sometimes her) unique in each culture. Critical thinking, regional or cultural studies, and geography are three ways in which one can use trickster tales.

Critical Thinking As a result of the multifaceted nature of the trickster as well as the fact that many culture heroes act as tricksters, stories about these types of characters, though concentrated in the chapter on trickster tales, can also be found in the chapters on fables, noodlehead tales, myths, and legends. "What Spider Learned from Frog" among the fables, "Juan Bobo" among the noodlehead tales, "Prometheus," "Coyote Fights Some Monsters," (Web Supplement), "Thrym Steals Mjollnir," and both the Native American (Hitchiti) and the Pacific Island (Tonga) stories of "The Theft of Fire" among the myths have trickster heroes, whereas among the legends "The Cyclops" (on Web Supplement) and "Robin Hood and the Bishop of Hereford" feature two legendary tricksters, Odysseus and Robin Hood.

- To demonstrate the multifaceted nature of the trickster, have students read five or six trickster tales and have them respond in their journals as to how they feel about each of the tricksters in the stories. Do they feel the trickster's actions are justified, funny, satisfying, reprehensible, or what?
- Have each student create a chart categorizing the tricksters they had read about into four categories: approved/liked, neutral, disapproved but could see their point of view, wholly disapproved.
- Create a class chart with students based on individual responses. Once patterns become apparent, discuss reasons for students' judgments. The discussion is an important way for students to discover alternative points of view and interpretations of the tricksters' actions, and they should therefore be encouraged to be respectful of, and open-minded about, others' opinions. The summary of class opinions should include both majority and alternate perspectives.
- Select one type of trickster, such as trickster as underdog or resistor of oppression, and find

examples of this type of trickster across cultures. (Juan Bobo among the noodleheads and Robin Hood among the legends also belong in this category.)

- Have students research the social and historical context that might have given rise to this type of trickster in their culture.

History, Geography, and Culture Study Both tricksters and their stories are wanderers. Migrations, forced removal from native homes to a new place, trade, and military conquests have carried stories across continents. Coyote stories are found throughout the western United States and Mexico, wherever Native American tribes have migrated and have come into contact with each other. The Hoca stories traveled with the conquering Ottoman Empire, whereas the Hoca's Arabic counterpart, Goha (see the first story among the noodlehead tales in the anthology) is found throughout Arabic-speaking countries in North Africa and the Middle East. The Anansi stories came from Africa to the Americas with African slaves and can be found from the eastern United States (mainly the Sea Islands off the Georgia coast) to the Caribbean and Central America. Other African tricksters, such as Hare/Rabbit and Tortoise, have found their way to the United States; Brer Rabbit does many of the same tricks as the different tricksters do in Africa. Studying the migrations of trickster stories can be part of a culture study as it relates to historical events. The stories were often adapted to the new environments and therefore provide an opportunity for cultural studies and global connections.

Comparing the tricksters of Africa (Anansi, Rabbit/Hare, Tortoise) with their American counterparts can be used to look at the different physical environments and social contexts in which the stories were told.

Locating African trickster stories and their American counterparts is not difficult. Besides the three Anansi stories from Africa in the *Allyn & Bacon Anthology*, "The Fantastic Lying Contest," "The Master Trickster," and "What Spider Learned from Frog" in the fables chapter, there are many picture books that tell Anansi stories from Africa (see the "Picture Books Related to the Stories" for lists as well as the *Bibliographic Database of Fables, etc.*, both on the Web Supplement at www.ablongman.com/lechner.

For Caribbean Annancy stories, see James Berry's *Spiderman Anancy* (Holt, 1989). The latter includes 20 stories about Anancy from Jamaica. For a large folkloric collection (i.e., not recorded with children in mind) on the Web, see Martha Warren Beckwith's *Jamaican Anansi Stories* at www.sacred.texts.com/afr/jas/. One would have to select and print out appropriate stories for children. The dialect is challenging but readable and would add to the cultural study.

For African American trickster stories, start with those in the *Allyn & Bacon Anthology*, that is, "Brer Tiger and the Big Wind," and "The Moon in the Pond," and follow up with collections and picture books listed on the Web Supplement. Virginia Hamilton's *Ring of Tricksters* is especially helpful in identifying African and African-derived tricksters in the Americas.

Illustrations and other sources on cultures: Kente cloth from Ghana can be located on the Web; well-researched picture books, especially by artists such as Baba Wagué Diakité and Leo and Diane Dillon, are good sources for clothing and housing in West Africa; encyclopedias of art as well as general encyclopedias will help students relate the visuals they find in picture books to actual art works, housing, clothing; magazines such as *National Geographic, National Geographic Kids, Cobble Stones,* and *Muse* (from Cricket Magazine Group and the Smithsonian) can also be excellent supplementary resources for visuals as well as other cultural information.

- Have students locate on a map of the world the places where Anansi and other African trickster stories are told. (Anansi is originally from Ghana, while Hare and Tortoise can be found in other West African countries.)
- Students should read a variety of Anansi and other African, Caribbean, and African American trickster stories.
- Have students note similarities and differences between the people, deities, animals, and situations that the tricksters encounter.
- In small groups, have students research the regions where the stories were told (geography, climate, agriculture, traditional (historic) social structure).
- Students can create illustrated booklets or multimedia presentations covering their regions. Be-

sides the topics mentioned above, they can include illustrations of traditional clothing and art.

For applications for **pourquoi (why) tales,** see applications for fables above.

▨ Myths

Themes and Cross-Cultural Studies

Myths are stories about questions of origins and explanations for the way life is. There are many creative ways to study myths with children, but one that lends itself to cross-cultural study is to focus on one type of myth:

- Identify one type of myth. Creation myths or myths about the obtaining of fire are two examples. Other frequently recurring themes in many cultures include the idea of a world flood, why people have to labor for a living, where bad things such as disease or warfare come from, how good people are rewarded or bad people are punished, and why people die.
- After identifying a type of myth, have students read stories relating to the same theme from different cultures. For instance, there are several myths relating to the obtaining of fire in this anthology: "Prometheus" from ancient Greece, "The Theft of Fire" from the Hitchiti Indians of Alabama and Oklahoma, "The Obtaining of Fire" by the Gé Indians of Brazil, and "The Theft of Fire" from the South Pacific Island of Tonga.
- Have students create a comparison chart for the different characters, their motivations, and their specific actions in bringing fire to the world.
- After reading the stories, students can research the history, geography, and social and religious organization of each culture.
- Have individuals or groups create a PowerPoint slide show presenting the culture they researched and the way the story of the obtaining of fire, as told in that culture, relates to other myths from the culture. (For example, did the same character bring other benefits to humankind? Was the character who brought fire rewarded or punished?)
- Students can compare visual representations of myths in different picture book versions of the same myth. Picture book retellings often leave out important elements of myths or change the tone from serious to lighthearted.

Looking for Allusions

Another popular activity that works especially well with Greek myths is to have children find allusions to the myths or mythical characters in everyday vocabulary, art, advertising, scientific and medical terms, and literature.

Introducing Science Units

Science units are often introduced or paired with readings of myths. Michael Caduto and Joseph Bruchac's books (see "Resources for Activities Using Traditional Literature in the Classroom or Library" below) pair Native American myths with science lessons on the environment, wildlife, and astronomy.

▨ Legends

Because legends are based loosely on historical people or events, this genre lends itself to social studies applications involving cultural values, history, and geography. One application is to have students reflect on what is a hero.

Developing Concepts of the Hero

We use the term, "hero" quite loosely, frequently applying it to people we might more accurately label as celebrities. Conversely we often define the term narrowly, associating it with physical strength and courage in combat. Having students define the concept of the hero can help them expand and clarify their thinking about who can be a hero.

- Students can identify characteristics they consider important in a hero through brainstorming.
- After reading traditional hero tales from different cultures, students can begin to list characteristics of the traditional hero using a comparative chart. Certain traits, such as perseverance, are likely to show up for every hero; others, such as physical strength or being shrewd, might not.
- Have students list names of modern heroes and explain what makes their heroes heroic.

- Have students compare characteristics of their modern heroes with those of traditional heroes. What characteristics match? Which characteristics are different? How do the characteristics of the traditional hero and those of the modern hero compare with their original list?

Some ideas to consider are the following: What are heroic traits that were more important in the past than today? What heroic characteristics that women were and are likely to exhibit, such as courage needed to endure hardships while nurturing or even sacrificing for family, are not usually found in hero tales? Why not? What are heroic traits that are equally important no matter when or where you live? What are new demands on people that call for new types of heroes? This can be a discussion topic in social studies that can lead into reading of biographies, newspapers, and magazine articles.

Creative and Expository Writing

Some possibilities for creative or expository writing relating to heroes follow:

- Classroom hero: Write a description of a classroom hero and convince others that this person deserves the title of hero.
- Create a hero tale: Either select a real person and create a fictional situation in which he or she act as a hero or create a hero tale about a fantasy character that you made up. Write it in the form of a nonfiction biography.

▨ Resources of Activities Using Traditional Literature in the Classroom and Library

Web Sites

AskERIC, of the Educational Resources Information Center: http://www.askeric.org/. This site has lesson plans for all school subjects; fairy tales and folklore lesson plans are found through a site search.

Carol Hurst's Home Page: www.carolhurst.com. Provides reviews of children's books and lesson plans in curriculum-related areas. They have an excellent, multi-layered lesson plan around Greek myths involving art, children's books, and traditional versions of such stories as "Icarus and Daedalus."

MarcoPolo Internet Content for the Classroom: http://www.marcopolo-education.org. A well-organized, high-quality searchable site of Web-based teacher resources, including lesson plans on fables, folktales, mythology, and legends. Lesson plans are tied to national standards.

Books

Bosma, Bette. (1992). *Fairy Tales, Fables, Legends, and Myths: Using Folk Literature in Your Classroom.* New York: Teacher's College Press.

Buss, Kathleen, and Karnowski, Lee. (2000). *Reading and Writing Literary Genres.* Newark, DE: International Reading Association.

Caduto, Michael, and Bruchac, Joseph. (1988). *Keepers of the Earth: Native American Stories and Environmental Activities for Children.* Golden, CO: Fulcrum Press.

Caduto, Michael, and Bruchac, Joseph. (1991). *Keepers of the Animals: Native American Stories and Wildlife Activities for Children.* Golden, CO: Fulcrum Press.

Caduto, Michael, and Bruchac, Joseph. (1994). *Keepers of the Night: Native American Stories and Nocturnal Activities for Children.* Golden, CO: Fulcrum Press.

Goforth, Frances S., and Spillman, Carolyn V. (1994). *Using Folk Literature in the Classroom: Encouraging Children to Read and Write.* Phoenix, AZ: Oryx Press.

Hancock, Marjorie R. (1999). *A Celebration of Literature and Response: Children, Books, and Teachers in K–8 Classrooms.* Upper Saddle River, NJ: Merrill/Prentice Hall.

Laughlin, Mildred K., and Latrobe, Kathy H. (1990). *Reader's Theater for Children: Scripts and Script Development.* Littleton, CO: Teacher Idea Press/Libraries Unlimited.

Lehr, Susan. (1991). *The Child's Developing Sense of Theme: Responses to Literature.* New York: Teacher's College Press, Columbia University.

National Storytelling Association, The. (1994). *Tales as Tools: The Power of Story in the Classroom.* Jonesboro, TN: National Storytelling Press.

Sierra, Judy. (1996). *Multicultural Folktales for the Feltboard and Reader's Theater.* Phoenix, AZ: Oryx Press.

Susag, Dorothea M. (1998). *Roots and Branches: A Resource of Native American Literature—Themes, Lessons, and Bibliographies.* Urbana, IL: NCTE.

Web-Based Sources of Traditional Literature

The following is a selective list of Web site sources of fables, folktales, myths, and legends that will help teachers and librarians extend their print collections. These sites were selected for the reliability of their sources and the stability of the site. The list is by no means comprehensive, but in this volatile environment stability seems more important. A search for specific titles (e.g., Cinderella) using the search engine http://www.google.com will turn up many more sites. Searches on legends and an ethnic group or geographical area will also yield a great many hits.

Fables and Pourquoi Tales

Aesop's Fables Online Collection: AesopFables.com

India Parenting for a few more Panchatantra and Jataka tales: www.indiaparenting.com/panchatantra/index.shtml

Indian Why Stories: http://www.1-language.com/library/fiction/indianwhy/

Windsor Castle: http://oaks.nvg.org/. This eclectic site includes sets of fables, fairy tales, and other folktales. Under Norwegian tales one can find the cumulative tale "The Pancake."

For other pourquoi tales a search of http://www.google.com using the search statement: "why tales" OR "pourquoi tales," yields many sites with one or two tales and lesson plans.

Folktales in General, Including Cumulative Tales

Professor D. L. Ashliman: http://www.pitt.edu/~dash/ashliman.html. The texts on this site are reliable. They include Folklore and Mythology—electronic texts; German Myths, Legends and Sagas; and Indo-European Folk- and Fairy Tales.

Project Gutenberg: http://promo.net.pg. Project Gutenberg has over 6000 books entered as full-text electronic books. To find books of folktales, enter the word "folktales" in the subject search. You will also need to search under "fairy tales" and "mythology" separately for those genres.

University of Virginia Library Electronic Text Center: http://etext.lib.virginia.edu/. This site provides full text to a wide range of books, among them folktales. At the e-text center home page, click on "e books for Microsoft Reader and Palm Pilot."

Fairy Tales

Cinderella Project: http://www-dept.usm.edu/~engdept/cinderella/cinderella.html. This is a University of Southern Mississippi project that reproduces the stories and shows the images of English language Cinderella stories from historic books in the DeGrummond Children's Literature Research Collection.

Project Gutenberg: http://promo.net/pg. Project Gutenberg has over 6000 books entered as full-text electronic books. To find books of fairy tales enter the word "fairy tales" in the subject search. This retrieves both literary and folk fairy tales.

SurLaLune Fairy Tale Pages: http://www.surlalunefairytales.com/ Edited by Heidi Anne

Heiner, this site gives full-text versions and Ms. Heiner's annotations, as well as book covers with links to Amazon.com, for 26 popular folk and fairy tales such as "The Beauty and the Beast" and "The Gingerbread Man."

Myths and Legends

Project Gutenberg: http://promo.net/pg. Project Gutenberg has over 6000 books entered as full-text electronic books. Among these are the full text of Bulfinch's *Mythology*.

Myths and Legends: http://members. bellatlantic.net/~vze33gpz/myth.html. This is an incredible resource for locating links to myths and legends resources ranging from encyclopedias to actual stories. Each link is annotated. Egyptian and Mesopotamian myths as well as Greek myths can be located through this site.

Sacred Texts: Internet Sacred Text Archive: http://www.sacred-texts.com/index.htm. This is the place to go for texts of myths and other sacred texts from cultures other than ancient Greece and Rome. Links take you to actual stories as well as scholarly articles and books. Annotated.

Glossary

Aarne-Thompson Tale Types: A classification system for folktales. *See also* Tale Type Index.

Aesir: In Norse myths the name for the gods.

Allegory: A form of narrative that uses concrete images of objects, characters, and actions to stand for abstract concepts outside of the narrative. An allegory is an extended metaphor. In an allegory the plot of the narrative as well as the abstract ideas are of interest. Allegories include John Bunyan's *Pilgrim's Progress* (a Christian allegory) and the Parables in the New Testament.

Animal tales: Also referred to as beast tales, these stories have animals as protagonists. Fables are often animal tales, but other types of folktales, such as "The Three Little Pigs," are also animal tales.

Archetype: A set of recurrent symbols stored in humanity's "collective unconscious." According to Carl Jung, a twentieth century psychoanalyst, all humans share unconscious memories of our past as a species consisting of primordial images expressed through myth, religion, dreams, fantasies, and literature.

AT number: Refers to Aarne-Thompson Tale Types. *See also* Tale Type Index.

Avatar: An incarnation or manifestation of a Hindu god as a human hero. Two of the god Vishnu's human avatars were said to be kings, Krishna and Rama.

Bard: Historically, an oral poet, often a court poet, whose function was to glorify the deeds of heroes or leaders. Technically, the word *bard* referred to Celtic oral poets in general. In France they were called *trouvères* in the north and *troubadours* in the south; in Scandinavia they were called *skalds*. Today the word is used generically to mean poet.

B.C.E.: Before the Common Era. This is the international designation for B.C. (Before Christ).

Beast epic: A medieval literary form consisting of a linked set of animal tales revolving around the same characters. Beast epics were especially popular in France. Stories about Reynard the Fox and the animals with whom he interacted were frequently the subjects of these tales.

Atman: In Hinduism the concept of the individual's soul. This is in contrast to Brahman, the universal soul of which everyone is a part.

Bodhisatta: Often spelled *Bodhisattva*. In Buddhism, an enlightened person who chooses not to enter nirvana (escape the cycle of rebirths) but instead remains within the cycle as a guide and teacher for others.

Brahman: In Hinduism the universal soul of which all are a part. Each individual also has a unique soul, Atman.

Brahmin: A member of the priest cast in India.

Burlesque: A form of comedy that makes light of serious situations or treats light situations in a serious manner (displays a discrepancy between content and style of presentation). The term has also been applied to include raucous stage entertainment with songs and skits.

C.E.: Common Era. This is the international designation for A.D. (Anno Domini, or Year of the Lord).

Chapbooks: Inexpensive books containing ballads, poems, tales, and religious tracts.

Comedy: A form of drama or, more generally, literature that is designed to provoke smiles or laughter using wit and humor. The comic effect is achieved by allowing the viewer, listener, or reader to recognize an incongruity in speech or action.

Cosmogony: A theory or model of the origins and evolution of the universe. Cosmogonic stories relate the origins of the universe.

Cultural evolution: Also known as *unilinear theory*, a nineteenth century theory of culture that postulated that all human societies go through the same evolutionary stages, with different societies being at different stages. Thus studying a "primitive" society's beliefs, stories, and institutions can tell researchers what more "advanced" societies were like in the past. Cultural evolutionists also believed that modern societies retain some customs as survivals of their primitive past. This theory is no longer held by anthropologists.

Culture hero: A hero (often male) who brings great gifts to his community through acts of creation such as bringing fire, through fighting for the community's safety against outside foes from dragons to human oppressors, or through providing inspiration for noble or courageous behavior. The last function is also often demonstrated by women.

Cumulative tales: Tales with formulaic plot structures using an additive formula which involves numerous characters each repeating the actions or words of previous characters until the story's sudden climax. See also **Formula tales.**

Cuneiform writing: Sumerian, Assyrian, Babylonian, and ancient Persian writing made up of wedge-shaped characters imprinted in soft clay with a pointed stick.

Demon: A powerful supernatural spirit. In common usage in the West demons are considered evil, but in other cultures, especially in Hindu mythology, demons are chaotic rather than evil. They can be worshipful toward the gods and they can even show generosity, but they can also easily become evil.

Dharma: Right conduct in Hinduism, which involves acting with patience, self-control, selflessness, and truthfulness.

Dialect: The speech of two or more groups that speak the same language but with marked differences in grammar, pronunciation, and vocabulary. Dialects can be regional or social.

Diffusionists: Anthropologists and folklorists in the nineteenth century who believed that all cultural traits (including tales) were developed in a few centers of culture, from which they spread.

Enlightenment: In Buddhism the state a person reaches after following an eightfold path of correct attitudes, ethical behavior, and meditation.

Epics: Long, narrative poem that tells of the deeds of a hero or heroes.

Ethnographer: A social scientist who studies and systematically describes a society's culture.

Etiological tales: Tales that explains the origin of something. Pourquoi tales are often labeled as etiological, as are many myths.

Fables: Usually brief folktales told with the express purpose of teaching a lesson or moral, frequently employing animals as characters.

Fairy tales: Frequently also called wonder tales or Märchen, these tales involve magic or enchantment. They can be folktales or literary tales (i.e. created by a known author).

First People: The creatures populating the earth before the establishment of the world as we know it in Native American myths. The First People had attributes like today's humans and animals but were more powerful and larger. All the animals spoke like humans and many, such as Coyote, were instrumental in helping to establish the order of the present world.

Folk literature: Literature created by anonymous author(s) and transmitted orally by other members of the community. *See also* Fables; Folktales; Legends; Myths; Oral literature.

Folktales: Imaginative tales that are transmitted mainly orally, with various tellers over time shaping the story. In this anthology folktales are limited to stories about humans and animals acting like humans, as distinct from both myths, which involve sacred stories of a cosmic nature, and legends, which purport to be nonfictional. Folktales include many genres, such as animal tales, fairy tales, and pourquoi tales.

Formula tales: In folk narratives, tales with a repeating plot structure. Two of the most common types are cumulative and chain structures. See also **Cumulative tales.**

Friend of a friend: A typical source for unverifiable urban legends.

Functionalism: An anthropological theory of the early twentieth century whose proponents considered all beliefs, myths, and customs to have a function in maintaining the social systems of which they are a part.

Golden Age: A mythical age described by the Greek writer Hesiod who lived around 700 B.C.E. It was one of four (or five) ages, each succeeding one being worse than the previous. During the Golden Age humans were noble, their life span far exceeded anything known today, the season was always spring, and the earth gave forth its bounty without being forced by humans. The concept of the Golden Age was similar to the concept of the biblical Garden of Eden.

Griot: An oral singing poet in West African countries, frequently the official court genealogist and historian.

Ideophones: Onomatopoic words in Bantu (African) languages that represent sounds or concepts, such as "yolee, yolee, yolee" for "quietly, quietly, quietly," as used by Baba Wagué Diakité in *The Hatseller and the Monkeys*.

Irony: A deliberate discrepancy between what one says and what one means (verbal irony), between what one expects and what actually occurs (situational irony), and what a character expects and what the listener or reader knows will actually happen (dramatic irony).

Jinn: Plural of *jinni* or *djinni*. In Islamic belief jinn are spirits that can take human or animal form and can be good or evil. Good jinn accept the teachings of Mohammed.

Jotunheim: Land of the giants. Jotun are giants.

Jump tales: Suspenseful, scary stories whose sudden endings make listeners jump.

Karma: In Hinduism and Buddhism the total effect of an individual's actions (good and bad) over multiple reincarnations. Happy and unhappy lives and rebirth as lower or higher animals (in Hinduism this includes changes in casts) are manifestations individual Karma.

Legends: Stories of a semihistorical nature that are told as true, though they may include fictitious elements.

Lunar calendar: A calendar based on the cycles of the moon. Festivals are tied to specific lunar months and phases of the moon, as, for instance the Chinese New Year begins at the second new moon after the winter solstice. The Islamic and Jewish calendars are also lunar based.

Märchen: The German word for fairy tales.

Medicine: In Native American religions this refers to a mystic power. A medicine bundle, worn on a belt in a pouch, will have various plant pollens and animal parts, such as a tooth or claw, that are thought to impart their sacred power or protection to the wearer.

Medicine man: In Native American societies a healer who is in touch with the spiritual world. A medicine man helps individual as well as the community. See also **Shaman.**

Moksha: In Hinduism a state of perfection in which the soul resides after liberation from the cycle of rebirths. The more familiar term is the Buddhist Nirvana.

Motif: In literature a simple story element out of which an entire narrative may be woven, such as a princess being abducted by a dragon or sorcerer. In folklore a motif is a recurrent story element such as an incident, character, or theme. Folkloric motifs recur in diverse stories from many different cultures (e.g., identifying the true hero or heroine by a specific sign or test such as Cinderella's slipper test).

Motif index: Developed by the American folklorist Stith Thompson, this multivolume index leads readers to stories in collections where specific motifs can be found.

Myth: A sacred story told as part of a world view or religious belief system and used to make concrete abstract concepts about cosmic and societal origins.

Mythology: A complex network of myths that, taken together, constitute the stories that explain the belief system of a people.

Nirvana: In Buddhism a state of perfection in which the soul resides after liberation from the cycle of rebirths through enlightenment. In Hinduism this state is called *Moksha.*

Noodlehead tales: Humorous stories about impractical, foolish people.

Oral literature: Material composed by unknown author(s) and transmitted by word of mouth. It includes narratives, epic poems, ballads, nursery rhymes, proverbs, and dramatic material with multiple variants. It is a convenient collective term for the various genres of orally transmitted material; the term 'literature" is usually reserved for written materials.

Parody: A comic literary form that presents another, more serious work in a humorous fashion.

Pourquoi tales: Also known as *Why tales,* these stories are both etiological tales that claim to explain the origins of an observed nature or social phenomenon, and didactic tales which teach social values.

Psychoanalytical theory: A psychological theory first developed by Sigmund Freud, which states that people go through stages of development, each with its own tasks and potential for unresolved conflict, starting with infancy—the oral stage. Conflicts arise when the child's desires and the need for maturing (for example, giving up the breast/pacifier) are not resolved and are expressed in the unconscious. Dreams and stories are symbolic representations of this conflict that are not normally available to individuals in the conscious state. In literary criticism scholars look for these symbolic representations for explanation of the material's underlying meaning or character's unexpressed motivations.

Rishi: The Hindi word for a sage.

Runes: Characters incorporated into the alphabet developed by the Germanic tribes of Europe in the third century. Runes came to be used for magical incantations and charms. In the nineteenth century the term was applied by Emerson to poetry, song, or verse. The folk poems from which the Finnish Kalevala was created are also referred to as runes.

Samsara: The cycle of rebirth in which all humans and animals are trapped until they are able to reach enlightenment, according to Buddhist teachings.

Satire: A literary work that uses humor to highlight a human or societal failing with the intention of inspiring improvements.

Shaman: A spiritual leader, most notably among Siberian, Central Asian, and Native American peoples, who is able to heal the sick and communicate with the world beyond. Among Native Americans he is also called a Medicine man.

Sikh: A member of the Sikh religious group which was formed in the fifteenth century from Hinduism and Islam in north India, in the Punjab region.

Skald: An oral poet in medieval Norway, Denmark, and Iceland. See also **Bard.**

Stock characters: Conventional story characters within a literary or folk tradition. The Appalachian trickster Jack and the African American trickster Brer Rabbit are two examples of stock characters. Others include the Russian witch Baba Yaga, the Norwegian youngest son Boots, and the Puerto Rican noodlehead Juan Bobo.

Structuralism: A theory of myths that proposes that myths are formed of significant opposites, named "binary opposites" by Claude Levi Strauss. The resolutions of these opposites demonstrate the beliefs of the culture that tell the myths. Binary opposites include male/female, young/old, and home/exile.

Sweat lodge or sweat house: A sacred building for spiritual renewal in many Native American religions. It is aligned with the four sacred directions: north, east, south, west.

Tale Type Index: A classification system for folktales developed by Antti Aarne, the nineteenth century Finnish folklorist edited and published in 1928 by the American folklorist Stith Thompson in *The Types of the Folk-tale: A Classification and Bibliography*. Classification is based on recurrent plots, characters, and component elements (motifs). characters. This system allows for the identification of variants of the same tale and supports cross cultural folktale research.

Tall tales: Humorous tales that relate impossible events or a larger-than-life character's exploits, giving realistic but hugely exaggerated details. Tall tales are considered an American genre.

Toast: An African American genre of oral narrative poetry consisting of rhymed couplets, often with four stresses to a line. It was popular from the early twentieth century through the 1970s, when it gave way to rap. The subjects of toasts were usually humorously exaggerated tricksters and "bad men." The latter represented the resistance of African Americans against the economic and social inequities of the pre–Civil Rights era.

Traditional literature: Literature that has been handed down from generation to generation. Most traditional literature is oral, but some literature, such as a culture's great epics, might be written. *See also* Oral literature.

Trickster: A character who frequently outwits others, especially those who are more powerful, thus achieving personal gain, avoiding work, getting out of trouble, or saving the community. Mythic tricksters may also bring gifts to the community.

Trickster tales: Stories about stock characters who use their wits rather than brawn to gain their ends or get out of trouble.

Urban legend: Unverifiable story or rumor spread orally, via newspapers, or via the internet. The settings and concerns are contemporary.

Wonder tales: Another term for fairy tales. This term is considered more accurate than *fairy tale,* because it encapsulates the essence of this story type, which involves magic or enchantment, while fairies seldom appear in "fairy tales."

Why tales: *See* Pourquoi tales.

Ziggurat: A Mesopotamian temple tower in the shape of a pyramid with stepped, rather than smooth sides. Both Assyrians and Babylonians built ziggurats.

References

Chapter 1 An Introduction

Bascom, William. (1992). *African Folktales in the New World.* Bloomington, IN: Indiana University Press.

Bettelheim, Bruno. (1976). *The Uses of Enchantment: The Meaning and Importance of Fairy Tales.* New York: Knopf.

Bottigheimer, Ruth. (1993). "The Publishing History of Grimm's Tales: Reception at the Cash Register." In Donald Haase (Ed.), *The Reception of Grimm's Fairy Tales: Responses, Reactions, Revisions* (pp. 78–101). Detroit: Wayne State University.

Briggs, Katharine, and Ruth L. Tongue. (1965). *Folktales of England.* London: Routledge & Kegan Paul.

Bruchac, Joseph. (1985). *Iroquois Stories: Heroes and Heroines Monsters and Magic.* Freedom, CA: The Crossing Press.

Bruchac, Joseph. (1996). "The Continuing Circle: Native American Storytelling Past and Present." In Carol L. Birch and Caroline A. Heckler (Eds.), *Who Says: Essays on Pivotal Issues in Contemporary Storytelling.* (pp. 91–105). Little Rock, AK: August House.

Brunvand, Jan Harold. (1978). *The Study of American Folklore: An Introduction* (2nd ed.). New York: Norton.

Buss, Kathleen, and Lee Karnowski. (2000). *Reading and Writing Literary Genres.* Newark, DE: International Reading Association.

Campbell, Joseph. (1968). *The Hero with the Thousand Faces* (Bollingen Series XVII). Princeton, NJ: Princeton University Press.

Cashdan, Sheldon. (1999). *The Witch Must Die: How Fairy Tales Shape Our Lives.* New York: Basic Books.

Dorris, Michael. (1992). "For Indians, No Thanksgiving." In B. Slapin and D. Seale (Eds.), *Through Indian Eyes.* Also reprinted in Lawana Trout, (Ed.), *Native American Literature: An Anthology* (pp. 16–18). Lincolnwood, IL: National Textbook Co., 1999.

Dorson, Richard. (1965). Introduction to Wolfram Eberhard (Ed.), *Folktales of China.* Chicago: University of Chicago Press.

Dorson, Richard. (1973). *America in Legend: Folklore from the Colonial Period to the Present.* New York: Pantheon.

Doty, William. (1986). *Mythography: The Study of Myths and Rituals.* Tuscaloosa, AL: University of Alabama Press.

Dundes, Alan. (1989). *Folklore Matters.* Knoxville, TN: University of Tennessee.

Dundes, Alan. (1992). "Foreword." In William Bascom, *African Folktales in the New World* (pp. vii–xx). Bloomington, IN: Indiana University Press.

Esbensen, Barbara J. (1992). "Retelling the Told Tales of Kah-ge-gah-ge-bowh and Arthur Parker." In Gary D. Schmidt and Donald R. Hettinga, (Eds.), *Sitting at the Feet of the Past: Retelling the North American Folktale for Children* (pp. 21–24). New York: Greenwood.

Gág, Wanda. (1936). *Tales from Grimm.* New York: Coward-McCann.

Georges, Robert A., and Jones, Michael O. (1995). *Folkloristics: An Introduction.* Bloomington, IN: Indiana University Press.

Goble, Paul. (1992). "On Beaded Dresses and the Blazing Sun." In Gary D. Schmidt and Donald R. Hettinga (Eds.), *Sitting at the Feet of the Past: Retelling the North American Folktale for Children* (pp. 5–14). New York: Greenwood.

Haase, Donald. (1993). "Response and Responsibility in Reading Grimm's Fairy Tales." In Donald Haase (Ed.), *The Reception of the Grimms' Fairy Tales* (pp. 230–249). Detroit: Wayne State University Press.

Hearne, Betsy. (1993, July). "Cite the Source: Reducing Cultural Chaos in Picture Books, Part One," *School Library Journal 39*(7):22–27.

Hearne, Betsy. (1993, August). "Respect the Source: Reducing Cultural Chaos in Picture Books, Part Two," *School Library Journal, 39*(8):33–38.

Hearne, Betsy. (1999, Winter). "Swapping Tales and Stealing Stories: The Ethics and Aesthetics of Folklore in Children's Literature," *Library Trends, 47*(3):509–528.

Jackson, Mary V. (1989). *Engines of Instruction, Mischief, and Magic: Children's Literature in England from Its Beginnings to 1839.* Lincoln, NE: University of Nebraska Press.

Jung, Carl G. (1969). *The Archetypes and the Collective Unconscious* (2nd ed., Bollingen Series XX). Princeton, NJ: Princeton University Press.

Keeler, Ward (1992). *Javanese Shadow Puppets.* Oxford: Oxford University Press.

Kimmel, Eric. (1994, December). "The Author as Storyteller: My Opinion." *The Texas Teller, 8*(3):1–2.

Lester, Julius. (1987). "Foreword," *Tales of Uncle Remus: The Adventures of Brer Rabbit* (pp. xiii–xxi). New York: Dial.

Lüthi, Max. (1982). *The European Folktale: Form and Nature* (Translated by John D. Niles). (Translations in

Folklore Studies). Philadelphia: Institute for the Study of Human Issues.

MacDonald, Margaret Read. (1999). *Traditional Story Telling Today: An International Sourcebook*. Chicago: Fitzroy Dearborn.

Montejo, Victor. (1999). *Popol Vuh: A Sacred Book of the Maya*. Toronto: Groundwood, 1999.

Neumann, Siegfried. (1993). "The Brothers Grimm as Collectors and Editors of German Folktales." In Donald Haase (Ed.), *The Reception of Grimm's Fairy Tales: Responses, Reactions, Revisions* (pp. 24–40). Detroit: Wayne State University.

Nodelman, Perry. (1992). *The Pleasures of Children's Literature*. New York: Longman.

Norton, Donna E. (2001). *Multicultural Literature: Through the Eyes of Many Children*. Upper Saddle River, NJ: Prentice Hall.

Okpewho, Isidore. (1983). *Myth in Africa: A Study of Its Aesthetic and Cultural Relevance*. London: Cambridge University Press.

Okpewho, Isidore. (1992). *African Oral Literature: Background, Character, and Continuity*. Bloomington, IN: Indiana University Press.

Pentikäinen, Juha Y. (1989). *Kalevala Mythology* (Translated and edited by Ritva Poom). Bloomington, IN: Indiana University Press.

Powell, Barry B. (1998). *Classical Myth* (2nd ed.). Upper Saddle River, NJ: Prentice Hall.

Propp, Vladimir. (1968). *Morphology of the Folktale*. Austin, TX: University of Texas Press.

Stone, Kay. (1986). "Oral Narration in Contemporary North America." In Ruth Bottigheimer (Ed.), *Fairy Tale and Society: Illusion, Allusion, and Paradigm* (pp. 13–31). Philadelphia: University of Pennsylvania.

Stone, Kay. (1993). "Once Upon a Time Today: Grimm Tales for Contemporary Performers." In Donald Haase, (Ed.), *The Reception of Grimm's Fairy Tales: Responses, Reactions, Revisions* (pp. 250–268). Detroit, MI: Wayne State University.

Stone, Kay. (1996). "And They Lived Happily Ever After: Fairytale Stories as Narrated by Carol McGirr and Susan Gordon." *Women and Language, 19*(1):14–20.

Temple, Charles; Miriam Martinez, Junko Yokota, and Alice Naylor. (2002). *Children's Books in Children's Hands: An Introduction to Their Literature* (2nd ed.). Boston: Allyn and Bacon.

Toelken, Barre. (1996). "The Icebergs of Folktale: Misconception, Misuse, Abuse." In Carol L. Birch and Caroline A. Heckler (Eds.), *Who Says: Essays on Pivotal Issues in Contemporary Storytelling* (pp. 35–63). Little Rock, AK: August House.

Yolen, Jane. (1986). *Favorite Folktales from Around the World*. New York: Pantheon.

Zipes, Jack. (1983). *The Trials and Tribulations of Little Red Riding Hood: Versions of the Tale in Sociocultural Context*. South Hadley, MA: Bergin & Garvey.

Zipes, Jack. (1988). *The Brothers Grimm and Folktale: From Enchanted Forest to Modern Worlds*. New York: Routledge.

Zipes, Jack. (1989). *Beauties, Beasts and Enchantment: Classic French Fairy Tales*. New York: Penguin.

Zipes, Jack. (1993). "The Struggle for the Grimms' Throne: The Legacy of the Grimms' Tales in the FRG and GDR Since 1945." In Donald Haase (Ed.), *The Reception of Grimm's Fairy Tales: Responses, Reactions, Revisions* (pp. 167–206). Detroit: Wayne State University.

Chapter 2 Fables

Abrahams, Roger. (1983). *African Folktales: Traditional Stories of the Black World*. New York: Pantheon.

Alembi, Ezekiel B. (1999). "Narrative Performance in a Changing World: The Case of the "Storytellers in Kenya." In Margaret Read MacDonald (Ed.), *Traditional Storytelling Today: An International Sourcebook*. Chicago: Fitzroy Dearborn Publishers. pp. 68–70.

Bascom, William. (1975). *African Dilemma Tales*. The Hague: Mouton Publishers. [World Anthropology]

Ben Amos, Dan. (1972). "Two Benin Storytellers." In Richard M. Dorson (Ed.), *African Folklore*, pp. 103–114. New York: Doubleday.

Berry, Jack. (1991). *West African Folktales*. Chicago: Northwestern University Press.

Bierhorst, John. (2002). *Latin American Folktales: Stories from Hispanic and Indian Traditions*. New York: Pantheon.

Bodhi, Bhikkhu. (1994). *The Noble Eightfold Path: The Way to the End of Suffering*. Buddhist Publication Society. Accessed on April 14, 2002, on the Web at www.accesstoinsight.org/lib/bps/misc/waytoend. html (also available as a book by the same title)

Bottigheimer, Ruth. (1996). "Fairy Tales and Folk-tales." In Peter Hunt (Ed.), *International Encyclopedia of Children's Literature*. London: Routledge.

Bruchac, Joseph. (1996). "The Continuing Circle: Native American Storytelling, Past and Present." In Carol L. Birch and Melissa A. Hacker (Eds.), *Who Says? Essays on Pivotal Issues in Contemporary Storytelling*, Little Rock, AR: August House.

Courlander, Harold and Wolf Leslau. (1950). *Fire on the Mountain and Other Ethiopian Stories*. Henry Holt.

Du Toit, Brian M. (1976). *Content and Context of Zulu Folk Narratives*. Gainsville, FL: University Presses of Florida.

Gonda, Jan. (1987). "Indian Religion: An Overview." In *Encyclopedia of Religion,* Vol. 7, pp. 168–176. New York: Macmillan.

Hafner, Dorinda. (1996). *I Was Never Here and This Never Happened.* Berkeley: Ten Speed Press.

Jacobs, Joseph. (1894, 1920). *The Fables of Aesop.* London: Macmillan.

Jones, John Garrett. (1979). *Tales and Teachings of the Buddha: The Jataka Stories in Relation to the Pali Canon.* London: George Allen & Unwin.

Lenaghan, R. T. (1967). "Introduction." In Aesopus, *Caxton's Aesop.* Cambridge, MA: Harvard University Press (pp. 3–21).

MacDonald, Margaret Read, Ed. (1999). *Traditional Storytelling Today: An International Sourcebook.* Chicago: Fitzroy Dearborn Publishers.

Odaga, Asenath Bole. (1984). *Yesterday's Today, the Study of Oral Literature.* Kisumu, Kenya: Lake Publishers.

Ogede, Ode. (1999). "The Storytelling event Among the Igede of Nigeria." In Margaret Read MacDonald (Ed.), *Traditional Storytelling Today: An International Sourcebook* (pp. 54–58). Chicago: Fitzroy Dearborn.

Patterson, Annabel. (1991). *Fables of Power: Aesopian Writing and Political History.* Durham, NC: Duke University Press.

Ryder, Arthur. (1925). *The Panchatantra.* Chicago, IL: The University of Chicago Press.

Singano, E. and A. A. Roscoe. (1980). *Tales of Old Malawi.* Limbe, Malawi: Popular Publications.

Chapter 3 Folktales

Aarne, Antti, and Stith Thompson. (1961). *The Types of the Folktale: A Classification and Bibliography.* Helsinki, Finland: Suomalainen Tiedeakatemia.

Abrahams, Roger. (1985). *Afro-American Folktales: Stories from Black Traditions in the New World.* New York: Pantheon.

Anderson, Rachel, and David Bradby. (1986). *Renard the Fox.* Illustrated by Bob Dewar. Oxford: Oxford University Press.

Applebee, Arthur. (1978). *The Child's Concept of Story: Ages Two to Seventeen.* Chicago: University of Chicago Press.

Atencio, Paulette. (1991). *Cuentos From My Childhood: Legends and Folktales from Northern New Mexico.* Santa Fe, NM: Museum of New Mexico Press.

Baker, Augusta. (1987). "Introduction." In Julius Lester, *The Tales of Uncle Remus, the Adventures of Brer Rabbit,* Illustrated by Jerry Pinkney (pp. vii–x). New York: Dial Books.

Bascomb, William. (1992). *African Folktales in the New World.* Bloomington, IN: Indiana University Press.

Bass, Ramona. (1989). "Why Rooster Catches Roach." In Linda Goss and Marian E. Barnes (Eds.), *Talk That Talk: An Anthology of African-American Storytelling.* New York: Simon & Schuster.

Bennett, Louise. (1966). "Me and Annancy." In Walter Jekyll (Ed.), *Jamaican Song and Story: Annancy Stories, Digging Sings, Dancing Tunes, and Ring Tunes* (pp. viii–xi). New York: Dover.

Berry, Jack. (1991). "Introduction." In *West African Folktales.* Chicago, IL: Northwestern University Press.

Bierhorst, John. (1976). *Black Rainbow: Legends of the Incas and Myths of Ancient Peru.* New York: Farrar, Straus, & Giroux.

Bierhorst, John. (2002). *Latin American Folktales: Stories from Hispanic and Indian Traditions.* New York: Pantheon.

Bolden, Anthony. (1998). *All Blues: A Study in African American Resistance Poetry.* Doctoral dissertation. Louisiana State University.

Bolte, Johannes, and Georg Polívka. (1963). *Anmerkungen zu den Kinder-U. Hausmärchen der Brüder Grimm.* [Notes on the Children and Household Tales of the Brothers Grimm]. Hildesheim: Georg Olms Verlagsbuchhandlung.

Botkin, B. A. (Ed.). (1944). *A Treasury of American Folklore: Stories, Ballads, and Traditions of the People.* New York: Crown.

Bottigheimer, Ruth. (1996). "Fairy Tales and Folk-tales" In Peter Hunt (Ed.), *International Encyclopedia of Children's Literature.* London: Routledge.

Bright, William. (1993). *The Coyote Reader.* Berkeley, CA: The University of California Press.

Bruchac, Joseph. (1966). "The Continuing Circle: Native American Storytelling Past and Present." In Carol L. Birch, and Caroline A. Heckler (Eds.), *Who Says: Essays on Pivotal Issues in Contemporary Storytelling* (pp. 91–105). Little Rock, AK: August House.

Bullchild, Percy. (1985). *The Sun Came Down.* San Francisco: Harper & Row.

Bushnaq, Inea. (1986). *Arab Folk-Tales.* New York: Pantheon.

Calame-Griaule, Genevieve. (1984). "The Father's Bowl: Analysis of a Dogon Version of AT 480." *Research in African Literatures 15:*168–184.

Campbell, Marie. (1958). *Tales from the Cloud Walking Country.* Bloomington, IN: Indiana University Press.

Cart, Michael. (1995). *What's So Funny? Wit and Humor in American Children's Literature.* New York: HarperCollins.

Cashdan, Sheldon. (1999). *The Witch Must Die: How Fairy Tales Shape Our Lives.* New York: Basic Books.

Courlander, Harold and George Herzog. (1974). The Cow-Tail Switch and Other West African Stories. New York: Henry Holt.

Courlander, Harold, and Wolf Leslau. (1950). *Fire on the Mountain and Other Ethiopian Stories.* New York: Henry Holt.

Dégh, Linda. (1994). *American Folklore and the Mass Media.* Bloomington, IN: Indiana University Press.

Dégh, Linda. (1995). *Hungarian Folktales: The Art of Mrs. Zsuzsanna Palko.* New York: Garland.

Delacre, Lulu. (1996). *Golden Tales: Myths, Legends, and Folktales From Latin America.* New York: Scholastic.

Dentan, Robert Knox. (1999). "Enduring Scars: Cautionary Tales among the Senoi Semai, a Peaceable People of West Malaysia." In Margaret Read MacDonald (Ed.), *Traditional Storytelling Today: An International Sourcebook* (pp. 130–133). Chicago: Fitzroy Dearborn.

Dorson, Richard. (1965). "Foreword" In Briggs, Katharine. *Folktales of England.* London: Routledge and Kegan Paul. (Folktales of the World Series, University of Chicago.)

Dorson, Richard. (1970). "Foreword" In Americo Paredes (Ed.), *Folktales of Mexico.* Chicago: University of Chicago Press, pp. xi–xvi.

Dorson, Richard. (1972). *African Folklore.* New York: Doubleday.

Dorson, Richard. (1976). *Folklore and Fakelore.* New York: Harvard University Press.

Dorson, Richard. (1977). *America in Legend.* New York: Pantheon.

Duncan, Barbara. (1998). *Living Stories of the Cherokee.* Chapel Hill, NC: University of North Carolina Press.

Dundes, Alan (Ed.). (1973). *Mother Wit from the Laughing Barrel: Readings in the Interpretation of Afro-American Folklore.* Englewood Cliffs, NJ: Prentice-Hall.

Dundes, Alan (Ed.). (1982). *Cinderella: A Folklore Casebook.* New York: Garland.

Du Toit, Brian M. (1976). *Content and Context of Zulu Folk Narratives.* Gainesville, FL: University Presses of Florida.

El-Shamy, Hasan M. (1980). *Folktales of Egypt.* Chicago: University of Chicago Press.

Erdoes, Richard, and Alfonso Ortiz. (1998). *American Indian Trickster Tales.* New York: Viking.

Faulkner, William J. (1977). *The Days When the Animals Talked.* Chicago: Follett.

Fine, Elizabeth. (1999). "Lazy Jack": Coding and Contextualizing Resistance in Appalachian Women's Narratives." *NWSA Journal 11*(3):112–137. Accessed through Project Muse on 04/06/2002.

Geertz, Clifford. (1983). *Local Knowledge: Further Essays in Interpretive Anthropology.* New York: Basic Books.

Girardot, N. J. (1987). "Chinese Religion: Mythic Times." In *Encyclopedia of Religion* (vol. 3, pp. 296–305). New York: Macmillan.

Goble, Paul. (1990). *Iktomi and the Buffalo Skull: A Plains Indian Story.* New York: Orchard Books.

Gonzalez, Lucia M. (1997). *Señor Cat's Romance and Other Favorite Stories from Latin America.* Illustrated by Lulu Delacre. New York: Scholastic.

Hafner, Dorinda. (1996). *I Was Never There and This Never Happened.* Berkeley, CA: Ten Speed Press.

Halliwell, James Orchard. (1970; original 1849). *Popular Rhymes & Nursery Tales of England.* London: The Bodley Head.

Hamilton, Virginia. (1995). *Her Stories: African American Folktales, Fairy Tales, and True Tales.* Illustrated by Leo and Diane Dillon. New York: Blue Sky Press/Scholastic.

Hamilton, Virginia. (1985). *The People Could Fly: American Black Folktales.* Illustrated by Leo and Diane Dillon. New York: Knopf.

Hamilton, Virginia. (1997). *A Ring of Tricksters: Animal Tales from America, the West Indies, and Africa.* Illustrated by Barry Moser. New York: Blue Sky Press/Scholastic.

Harris, Joel Chandler. (1880). *Uncle Remus, His Songs and His Sayings; The Folk-lore of the Old Plantation.* New York: D. Appleton.

Hearne, Betsy. (2000). "Ruth Sawyer: A Woman's Journey from Folklore to Children's Literature," *The Lion and the Unicorn 24*(2):279–307.

Huck, Charlotte S., Susan Hepler, Janet Hickman, and Barbara Kiefer. (2001). *Children's Literature in the Elementary School.* Boston: McGraw-Hill.

Hurston, Zora Neale. (1935; 1963). *Mules and Men.* Bloomington, IN: Indiana University Press.

Jagendorf, M. A., and R. S. Boggs. (1960). *The King of the Mountains: A Treasury of Latin American Folk Stories.* New York: Vanguard Press.

Jakobson, Roman. (1945). "Commentary." In *Russian Fairy Tales.* Collected by Aleksandr Afanas'ev. Translated by Norbert Guterman. New York: Pantheon, 1945.

Jekyll, Walter. (1907). *Jamaican Song and Story: Annancy Stories, Digging Sings, Dancing Tunes, and Ring Tunes.* London: David Nutt.

Johnston, Basil. (1995). *The Manitous: The Spiritual World of the Ojibway.* New York: HarperCollins.

Jones, Steven S. (1986). The Structure of "Snow White." In Ruth B. Bottigheimer (Ed.), *Fairy Tales and Society: Illusion, Allusion, and Paradigm* (pp. 165–186). Philadelphia: University of Pennsylvania Press.

Jurich, Marilyn. (1998). *Scheherazade's Sisters: Trickster Heroines and Their Stories in World Literature.* New York: Greenwood Press.

Kennedy, X. J. (1991). "Strict and Loose Nonsense: Two Worlds of Children's Verse." *School Library Journal* 37(3):108–112.

Khorloo, Pureviin. (1996). "Introduction." In Hilary Roe Metternich, *Mongolian Folktales.* Boulder, CO: Avery Press in association with University of Washington Press.

Lastra, Sarai. (1999). "Juan Bobo: A Folkloric Information System" *Library Trend, 47*(3):529–555.

Leach, Maria. (1958). *The Rainbow Book of American Folktales and Legends.* Cleveland, OH: World Publishers.

Leach, Maria. (1961). *Noodles, Nitwits, and Numskulls.* Illustrated by Kurt Werth. Cleveland, OH: Collins and World.

Leach, Maria (Ed.). (1972). *Funk & Wagnall's Standard Dictionary of Folklore, Mythology, and Legend.* Maria Leach, Ed. San Francisco: Harper & Row.

Lester, Julius. (1987). "Foreword." In *The Tales of Uncle Remus, the Adventures of Brer Rabbit.* (pp. xiii–xxi). Illustrated by Jerry Pinkney. New York: Dial Books.

Lewis, Paul. (1989). *Comic Effects: Interdisciplinary Approaches to Humor in Literature.* Albany, NY: State University of New York Press.

MacDonald, Margaret Read. (1982). *The Storyteller's Sourcebook: A Subject, Title, and Motif Index to Folklore Collections for Children.* Detroit: Neal-Schuman Publishers in association with Gale Research.

Magel, Emil. (1984). *Folktales from the Gambia: Wolof Fictional Narratives.* Washington. DC: Three Continents Press.

Massignon, Genevieve. (1968). *Folktales from France.* Chicago: University of Chicago Press.

Mayer, Fanny Hagin. (1984). *Ancient Tales in Modern Japan: An Anthology of Japanese Folktales.* Bloomington, IN: Indiana University Press.

Mueller, Gerhard O. W. (1986). "The Criminological Significance of the Grimms' Fairy Tales." In Ruth Bottigheimer (Ed.), *Fairy Tales and Society: Illusion, Allusion, and Paradigm* (pp. 217–228). Philadelphia: University of Pennsylvania Press.

Norton, Donna E. (1999). *Through the Eyes of a Child: An Introduction to Children's Literature* (5th ed.). Upper Saddle, NJ: Prentice Hall.

Odaga, Asenath Bole. (1984). *Yesterday's Today, the Study of Oral Literature.* Nairobi, Kenya: Lake Publishers.

Okpewho, Isidore. (1983). *Myth in Africa: A Study of Its Cultural Relevance.* New York: Cambridge University Press.

Okpewho, Isidore. (1992). *African Oral Literature.* Bloomington, IN: Indiana University Press.

Opie, Iona, and Opie, Peter. (1974). *The Classic Fairy Tales.* London: Oxford University Press.

Oppenheimer, Paul. (1991). *Till Eulenspiegel: His Adventures.* New York: Garland.

Owen, D. D. R. (1994). *The Romance of Reynard the Fox.* Oxford, England: Oxford University Press.

Owomoyela, Oyekan. (1997). *Yoruba Trickster Tales.* Lincoln, NE: University of Nebraska Press.

Paredes, Americo. (1970). *Folktales of Mexico.* Chicago: University of Chicago Press.

Pavonetti, Linda M., and Christine M. Combs. (1999). "American Hyperbole: The Tall Tale," *JOYS: Journal of Youth Services in Libraries* 12(2):37–42.

Pellowski, Ann. (1990). *The World of Storytelling.* New York: H. W. Wilson.

Pelton, Robert D. (1980). *Tricksters in West Africa: A Study of Mythic Irony and Sacred Delight.* Berkeley, CA: University of California Press.

Philip, Neil. (1992). *English Folktales.* London: Penguin Books.

Philip, Neil. (2001). *The Great Mystery: Myths of Native America.* New York: Clarion.

Propp, Vladimir. (1968). *Morphology of the Folktale.* Translated by Laurence Scott. Austin, TX: University of Texas Press.

Roberts, John W. (1989). *From Trickster to Badman: The Black Folk Hero in Slavery and Freedom* (p. 233). Philadelphia: University of Philadelphia.

Ross, Gayle. (1994). *How Rabbit Tricked Otter and Other Cherokee Trickster Stories.* Illustrated by Murv Jacobs. New York: HarperCollins.

Scott, Dorothea H. (1980). *Chinese Popular Literature and the Child.* Chicago: American Library Association.

Seki, Keigo. (1963). *Folktales of Japan.* Chicago: University of Chicago Press.

Senkoro, FEMK. (1996). "The Structural and Social Significance of the Journey in Children's Folktales from Zanzibar." In M. Machet, S. Olën, and Thomas van der Walt (Eds.), *Other Worlds Other Lives: Children's Literature Experiences: Proceedings of the International Conference on Children's Literature, Pretoria, 4–6 April 1995* (Vol. 3, pp. 46–77). Pretoria, South Africa: University of South Africa, 1996.

Sierra, Judy. (1996). *Wiley and the Hairy Man.* Illustrated by Brian Pinkney. New York: Lodestar.

Solomon, Jack, and Olivia Solomon. (1994). *Ghosts and Goosebumps: Ghost Stories, Tall Tales, and Superstitions from Alabama.* Athens, GA: University of Georgia Press.

Sprug, Joseph W. (Comp.). (1994). *Index to Fairy Tales, 1987–1992: Including 310 Collections of Fairy Tales, Folktales, Myths, and Legends: With Significant Pre-1987 Titles Not Previously Indexed.* Methuchen, NJ: Scarecrow Press.

Steel, Flora Annie, and R. C. Temple. (1983; original 1894). "Preface." In Flora Annie Steel, *Tales of the Punjab: Folklore of India.* New York: Greenwich House.

Stone, Kay. (1986). "Feminist Approaches to the Interpretation of Fairy Tales." In Ruth B. Bottigheimer (Ed.), *Fairy Tales and Society: Illusion, Allusion, and Paradigm* (pp. 229–236). Philadelphia: University of Pennsylvania Press.

Thompson, Stith. (1989). *Motif Index of Folk Literature: A Classification of Narrative Elements in Folktales, Ballads, Myths, Fables, Medieval Romances, Exempla, Fabliaux, Jest Books, and Local Legends.* Bloomington, IN: Indiana University Press.

Tyler, Royall. (1987). *Japanese Tales.* New York: Pantheon.

Van Sertima, Ivan. (1989). "Trickster, the Revolutionary Hero." In Linda Goss and Marian E. Barnes (Eds.), *Talk That Talk: An Anthology of African-American Storytelling* (pp. 103–111). New York: Simon and Schuster.

Walker, Barbara K. (1990). *The Art of the Turkish Tale* (vol. 1). Lubbock, TX: Texas Tech University.

Walker, Barbara K. (1993). *The Art of the Turkish Tale* (vol. 2). Lubbock, TX: Texas Tech University.

Walker, Warren S. (2000). *Some Tales Behind the Tales.* Archive of Turkish Oral Narrative. Occasional Papers: 3. Lubbock, TX: Texas Tech University.

Warner, Marina. (1995). *From the Beast to the Blonde: On Fairy Tales and Their Tellers.* New York: Farrar, Straus and Giroux.

Wolfenstein, Martha. (1978). *Children's Humor: A Psychological Analysis.* Bloomington, IN: Indiana University Press.

Wolkstein, Diane. (1978). *The Magic Orange Tree and Other Folk Tales.* New York: Knopf.

The Yanagita Kunio Guide to the Japanese Folktale [Nihon mukashibanashi meii]. (1986). Translated and edited by Fanny Hagin Mayer. Bloomington, IN: Indiana University Press.

Zipes, Jack. (1988). *The Brothers Grimm: From Enchanted Forests to the Modern World.* New York: Routledge.

Zipes, Jack. (1993). "The Struggle for the Grimms' Throne: The Legacy of the Grimms' Tales in the FRG and GDR since 1945. In Donald Haase (Ed.), *The Reception of Grimm's Fairy Tales: Responses, Reactions, Revisions.* pp. 167–206. Detroit: Wayne State University.

Zipes, Jack. (2001). *The Great Fairy Tale Tradition: From Straparola and Basile to the Brothers Grimm.* New York: Norton.

Ziv, Avner. (1988). *National Styles of Humor.* New York: Greenwood Press.

Zong In Sob. (1982). *Folk-tales from Korea* (3rd ed.). Elizabeth, NJ: Hollym International.

Chapter 4 Myths

Aarne, Antti. (1961). *The Types of the Folk-tale.* Translated and enlarged by Stith Thompson. Helsinki, Finland: Soumalainen Tiedeakatemia.

American Heritage Dictionary of the English Language, 4th ed. (2000). Boston: Houghton Mifflin.

Beier, Ulli. (1966). *The Origin of Life and Death: African Creation Myths.* London: Heinemann.

Bierhorst, John. (1988). *The Mythology of South America.* New York: William Morrow.

Bolle, Kees W. (1986/87). "Myth: An Overview." In *The Encyclopedia of Religion* (vol. 10, pp. 261–273). New York: Macmillan.

Brown, Virginia Pounds, and Owens, Laurella. (1985). *Southern Indian Myths and Legends.* Leeds, AL: Beechwood Books.

Bruchac, Joseph. (1986). *Iroquois Stories: Heroes and Heroines Monsters and Magic.* Freedom, CA: The Crossing Press.

Bruchac, Joseph. (1996). "The Continuing Circle: Native American Storytelling Past and Present." In Carol L. Birch and Melissa A. Heckler (Eds.), *Who Says: Essays on Pivotal Issues in Contemporary Storytelling* (pp. 91–105). Little Rock, AR: August House.

Caduto, Michael, and Bruchac, Joseph. (1989). *Keepers of the Earth: Native American Stories and Environmental Activities for Children.* Golden, CO: Fulcrum.

Chatterjee, Debjani. (1992). *The Elephant-Headed God and Other Hindu Tales.* New York: Oxford University Press.

Christie, Anthony. (1985). *Chinese Mythology.* New York: Peter Bedrick. [Library of the World's Myths and Legends.]

Colum, Padraic. (1937). *Orpheus Myths of the World.* New York, Macmillan.

Converse, Harriet, and Parker, Arthur. (1908). "Myths and Legends of the New York State Iroquois." *New York State Museum Bulletin* no. 125.

Coolidge, Olivia. (1949). *Greek Myths.* Boston: Houghton Mifflin.

Davidson, H. R. Ellis. (1964). *Gods and Myths of Northern Europe.* Harmondsworth, England: Penguin.

Doty, William G. (1986). *Mythography: the Study of Myths and Rituals.* Tuscaloosa, AL: University of Alabama Press.

Duncan, Barbara R. (1998). *Living Stories of the Cherokee.* Chapel Hill, NC: University of North Carolina Press.

Eliade, Mircea. (1963). *Myth and Reality.* New York: Harper and Row.

Encarta Africana, CD-ROM. (2000). Redmond, WA: Microsoft.

Encyclopedia Britannica: Ultimate Reference Suite, CD-ROM. (2000). Chicago: Encyclopedia Britannica.

Fenton, William N. (1962). "This Island on Turtle's Back." *Journal of American Folklore 75*(298): 283–300.

Fenton, William N. (1998). *The Great Law and the Longhouse: A Political History of the Iroquois Confederacy.* Norman: University of Oklahoma Press.

Fitzhugh, William W. (1997, Winter). "Global Culture Change: New Views of Circumpolar Lands and Peoples." *Anthro Notes: National Museum of Natural History Bulletin for Teachers.* 19(1). Accessed March 8, 2002, http://nmnhwww.si.edu/anthro/outreach/anthnote/winter97/anthnote.htm.

Giese, Paula. (1996). "Native American Books: Reviews." A link from *Native American Indian Resources.* http://www.kstrom.net/isk/ Last updated 1997. Accessed 7/7/2003.

Girardot, N. J. (1987). "Chinese Religion: Mythic Themes." In *Encyclopedia of Religion* (vol. 3, pp. 296–305). New York: Macmillan.

Green, Roger Lancelyn. (1968). *Tales of Ancient Egypt.* New York: Henry Z. Walck.

Hamilton, Edith. (1942). *Mythology.* Boston: Little, Brown.

Ha-yen-doh-nees. (Leo Cooper). (1995). *Seneca Indian Stories* (Illustrated by Beth Ann Clark). Greenfield Center, NY: Greenfield Review Press.

Hearne, Betsy. (1993a). "Cite the Source: Reducing Cultural Chaos in Picture Books. Part One." *School Library Journal 39*(7): 22–27.

Hearne, Betsy. (1993b). "Respect the Source: Reducing Cultural Chaos in Picture Books. Part Two." *School Library Journal 39*(8): 33–37.

Hultkrantz, Åke. (1987). "Arctic Religions" *Encyclopedia of Religion* (vol. 1, pp. 393–399). New York, Macmillan.

Ions, Veronica. (1983). *Indian Mythology.* New York: Peter Bedrick. [Library of the World's Myths and Legends.]

Johnston, Basil. (1995). *The Manitous: The Spiritual World of the Ojibway.* New York: HarperCollins.

Kawbawgam, Charles. (1994). *Ojibwa Narratives of Charles and Charlotte Kawbawgam and Jacques lePique, 1893–1895.* Recorded with notes by Homer H. Kidder. Edited by Arthur P. Bourgeois. Detroit: Wayne State University Press.

King, Winston L. (1986/87) "Religion." In *The Encyclopedia of Religion* (vol. 12, pp. 282–293). New York: Macmillan.

Kirk, G. S. (1970). *Myth: Its Meaning and Functions.* Berkeley: University of California.

Leeming, David, and Page, Jake. (1997). *Mythology of Native North America.* Norman, OK: University of Oklahoma Press.

Levy, Jerrold. (1998). *In the Beginning: Navajo Genesis.* Berkeley: University of California.

Lindow, John. (1991). "Interpreting Baldr, the Dying God." In G. Barnes, M. C. Ross, and J. Quinn (Eds.), *Old Norse Studies in the New World: A Collection of Essays to Celebrate the Jubilee of the Teaching of Old Norse at the University of Sydney 1943–1993* (pp. 71–83). Sydney, Australia: Department of English, University of Sydney.

Lindow, John. (1994). "Thor's 'Hamarr.' " *The Journal of English and German Philology 93*(4): 485–505.

Lindow, John. (1997). *Murder and Vengeance among the Gods: Baldr and Scandinavian Mythology.* FF Communications, no. 262. Helsinki, Finland: Suomalainen Tiedeakatemia.

Mourning Dove. (Humishuma). (1933). *Coyote Stories.* Caldwell, ID: The Caxton Printers.

O'Bryan, Aileen. (1953). *The Dine: Origin Myths of the Navaho Indian.* Smithsonian Institution Bureau of American Ethnology. Bulletin no. 163. Washington, DC: U.S. Government Printing Office.

O'Flaherty, Wendy D. (1975). *Hindu Myths: A Sourcebook Translated from the Sanskrit.* Harmondsworth, England: Penguin.

Oliver, Louis Littlecoon. (1990). *Chasers of the Sun: Creek Indian Thoughts.* Greenfield Center, NY: Greenfield Review Press.

Parker, Arthur. (1908). "Introduction" and Footnotes to "Myths and Legends of New York State Iroquois," by Converse, Harriet and Arthur Parker. *New York State Museum Bulletin* no. 125.

Parker, Arthur. (1923, 1989). *Seneca Myths and Folktales.* Lincoln, NE: University of Nebraska Press. [Buffalo Historical Society Publication, vol. 27.]

Philip, Neil. (2001). *The Great Mystery: Myths of Native America.* New York: Clarion.

Powell, Barry B. (1998). *Classical Myths* (2nd ed.). Upper Saddle River, NJ: Prentice Hall.

Reed, Alexander W. (1974). *Myths and Legends of Polynesia* (Illustrated by Roger Hart). Wellington, New Zealand: A. H. & A. W. Reed.

Ricoeur, Paul. (1986/87). "Myth: Myth and History." In *The Encyclopedia of Religion* (vol. 10, pp. 273–282). New York: Macmillan.

Riordan, James. (1990). "Introduction." In *The Sun Maiden and the Crescent Moon: Siberian Folk Tales.* New York: Interlink.

Scott, Dorothea Hayward. (1980). *Chinese Popular Literature and the Child.* Chicago, IL: American Library Association.

Schnurbein, Stefanie von. (2000). "The Function of Loki in Snorri Sturluson's Edda." *History of Religions 40*(2): pp. 109–124. Retrieved February 22, 2002 InfoTrac One File.

Sen, Kshiti Mohan. (1961). *Hinduism.* Harmondsworth, England: Penguin.

Simpkinson, Anne A. (1997, July). "Sacred Stories." *Storytelling Magazine 9*(4): 24–27.

Swanton, John R. (1929). *Myths and Tales of the Southeastern Indians.* [Smithsonian Institution Bureau of American Ethnology Bulletin 88.] Washington, DC: U.S. Government Printing Office.

Turville-Petre, E. O. G. (1964). *Myths and Religion of the North: The Religion of Ancient Scandinavia.* Westport, CT: Greenwood Press.

Wilbert, Johannes, and Karin Simoneau (Eds.). (1978). *Folk Literature of the Gé Indians.* Los Angeles, CA: UCLA Latin American Center Publications.

Wilbert, Johannes, and Karin Simoneau (Eds.). (1989). *Folk Literature of the Caduveo Indians.* Los Angeles, CA: UCLA Latin American Center Publications.

Wyman, Leland C. (1970). *Blessingway* with Three Versions of the Myth. Recorded from the Navajo by Father Berard Haile. Tucson, AZ: The University of Arizona Press.

Chapter 5 Legends, Hero Tales, and Epics

Alexander, Caroline. (1996, February). "A Pilgrim's Search for Relics of the Once and Future King." *Smithsonian 26*(11):32–43.

Allen, Paula Gunn. (1983). *The Woman Who Fell from the Sky.* San Francisco: Aunt Lute.

Anaya, Rodolfo. (1999). *My Land Sings: Stories from the Río Grande.* New York: HarperCollins.

Ashe, Geoffrey. (1998, March). "The Saxon Advent." *British Heritage 19*(3):16–25. Online, accessed on July 7, 2001, through EBSCOhost.

Atencio, Paulette. (1991). "Introduction." In *Cuentos from My Childhood: Legends and Folktales of Northern New Mexico.* Santa Fe, NM: Museum of New Mexico Press.

Barber, Richard. (1999). *Myths and Legends of the British Isles.* Woodbridge, Suffolk: Boydell Press.

Berry, Jack. (1991). *West African Folktales.* Chicago: Northwestern University Press.

Bierhorst, John. (2002). *Latin American Folktales: Stories from Hispanic and Indian Traditions.* New York: Pantheon.

Bosley, Keith (Transl.). (1989). "Introduction." In Elias Lönnrot, *The Kalevala: An Epic Poem after Oral Tradition.* Oxford, England: Oxford University Press.

Brunvand, Jan Harold. (1984). *The Choking Doberman.* New York: Norton.

Butler's Lives of the Saints. (1998). Revised by Paul Burns. Collegeville, MN: Burns and Oates/The Liturgical Press.

Cahill, Thomas. (1994). *How the Irish Saved Civilization.* New York: Doubleday.

Cavendish, Richard. (1982). *Legends of the World.* New York: Schocken.

Child, Francis J. (1962). *The English and Scottish Popular Ballads* (5 vols.). New York: Cooper Square.

Clark, Elizabeth A. (1998). "Holy Women, Holy Words: Early Christian Women, Social History, and the 'Linguistic Turn.'" *Journal of Early Christian Studies 6*(3): 413–430. Online, accessed on July 21, 2001, through Project Muse.

Comfort, W. W. (Transl.). (1914). "Introduction." In Chrétien le Troyes, *Arthurian Romances.* London: Everyman Library.

Coon, Lynda L. (1997). *Sacred Fictions: Holy Women and Hagiography in Late Antiquity.* Philadelphia: University of Pennsylvania.

Courlander, Harold, and Leslau, Wolf. (1950). *Fire on the Mountain and Other Ethiopian Stories.* New York: Henry Holt.

Cuevas, Lou. (1991). *Apache Legends: Sons of the Wind Dancer.* Happy Camp, CA: Naturegraph.

Deutsch, Babette. (1949). *Heroes of the Kalevala: Finland's Saga* (Illustrated by Fritz Eichenberg). New York: Julian Messner.

Dorson, Richard. (1965). "Foreword." In Katharine M. Briggs and Ruth L. Tongue (Eds.), *Folktales of England.* London: Routledge, WA: Mircosoft.

Dorson, Richard M. (1970). "Foreword." In Americo Paredes (Ed.), *Folktales of Mexico.* Chicago University Press.

Dorson, Richard M. (1971a). *American Folklore and the Historian.* Chicago: University of Chicago Press.

Dorson, Richard M. (1971b). *America in Legend: Folklore from the Colonial Period to the Present.* New York: Pantheon.

Duncan, Barbara R. (1998). *Living Stories of the Cherokee.* Chapel Hill, NC: University of North Carolina Press.

Encarta Africana, CD-ROM. (2000). Redmond, W.A: Microsoft

Farjeon, Eleanor. (1936). *Ten Saints.* London: Oxford University Press.

Ferguson, A. (2001, August 13). "The Myth Machine." *Time Magazine.* pp 34–38.

Fernandez, James. (1986). "Folklorists as Agents of Nationalism: Asturiori Legend and the Problem of Identity." In Ruth Bottingheimer (Ed.), *Fairytales and Society.* Philadelphia: University of Pennsylvania Press. pp. 133–146.

Fitzgerald, Robert, translator. (1961). *The Odyssey of Homer.* New York: Doubleday.

Fleming, Fergus, et al. (1996). *Heroes of the Dawn: Celtic Myth.* London: Duncan Baird Publishers and Time Life.

Jansen, Jan. (2001). "The Sunjata Epic: The Ultimate Version." *Research in African Literatures 32*(1):14–46.

Jimenez, Francisco. (2001). *Breaking Through.* Boston: Houghton Mifflin.

Khorana, Meena. (1999, Fall). "From the Margins to the Mainstream?" *Children's Literature Association 24*(3): 148–151.

Khorloo, Pureviin. (1996). "Introduction." In Hilary Roe Metternich, *Mongolian Folktales.* Boulder, CO: Avery Press in Association with University of Washington Press.

Kieval, Hillel J. (1997). "Pursuing the Golem of Prague: Jewish Culture and the Invention of a Tradition." *Modern Judaism 17*(1):1–20. Online, accessed on July 21, 2001 through Project Muse.

Knight, Stephen, and Ohlgren, Thomas H. (1997). *Robin Hood and Other Outlaw Tales.* Kalamazoo, MI: Western Michigan University for TEAMS. Accessed from the Web on July 20, 2001: http://www.lib.rochester.edu/camelot/teams/.

Kovacs, Maureen Gallery. (1989). *The Epic of Gilgamesh.* Stanford, CA: Stanford University.

Lattimore, Richmond (translation and introduction by). (1965). *The Odyssey of Homer.* New York: Harper & Row.

Leach, MacEdward. (1955). *The Ballad Book.* New York: A. S. Barnes.

Leach, Maria. (1974). *Whistle in the Graveyard: Folktales to Chill Your Bones* (Illustrated by Ken Rinciari). New York: The Viking Press.

Littleton, C. Scott, and Malcor, Linda A. (1996). "Legends of Arthur." In Fleming, Fergus, et al. (Eds.), *Heroes of the Dawn: Celtic Myth* (pp. 103–133). London: Duncan Baird Publishers and Time-Life.

MacCana, Proinsias. (1987). "Celtic Religion." *Encyclopedia of Religion* (vol. 3, pp. 148–166). New York: Macmillan.

MacColl, Alan. (1999, March). "King Arthur and the Making of an English Britain." *History Today 49*(3):

7–14. Online, accessed on July 7, 2001, through EBSCOhost.

MacRaois, Cormac. (1997). "Old Tales for New People: Irish Mythology Retold for Children." *The Lion and the Unicorn 21*(3):330–340. Online, accessed on Sept. 21, 1999, through Project Muse.

Masson, Sophie. (1999). "The Age of Arthur." *Quadrant 43*(3):65. Online, accessed on July 8, 2001, through Infotrac.

Mayer, Marianna. (1999). *Women Warriors: Myths and Legends of Heroic Women* (Illustrated by Julek Heller). New York: Morrow.

Morris, John. (1973). *The Age of Arthur: A History of the British Isles from 350 to 650.* New York: Scribner's.

Mukerji, Dhan Gopal. (1930). *Rama, the Hero of India.* New York: Dutton.

Niane, Djibril Tamsir. (1965/1986). *Sundiata: An Epic of Old Mali.* Essex, England: Longman.

O'Flaherty, Wendy D. (1975). *Hindu Myths: A Sourcebook Translated from the Sanskrit.* Harmondsworth, England: Penguin.

Pentikäinen, Juha Y. (1989). *Kalevala Mythology* (Translated and edited by Ritva Poom). Bloomington, IN: Indiana University Press.

Powell, Barry. (1998) *Classical Myth* (2nd ed.). Upper Saddle River, NJ: Prentice Hall.

Pyle, Howard. (1946). *The Merry Adventures of Robin Hood of Great Renown in Nottinghamshire.* New York: Grosset & Dunlap.

Sandars, Nancy K. (1960). *The Epic of Gilgamesh.* London: Penguin Classics.

Sands, Donald (Ed.). (1966). *Middle English Verse Romances.* New York: Holt, Rinehart and Winston.

Sen, Kshiti Mohan. (1961). *Hinduism.* Harmondsworth, England: Penguin.

Singman, Jeffrey L. (1998). *Robin Hood: The Shaping of the Legend.* New York: Greenwood Press.

Theis, Jeffrey. (2001). "The 'ill kill'd' Deer: Poaching and Social Order in *The Merry Wives of Windsor.*" *Texas Studies in Literature and Language 43*(1):46–73. Online, accessed on July 20, 2001, through Project Muse.

Yurko, Chris. (1996, December 23). "This Computer Cookie Crumbles," *Daily Hampshire Gazette.*

Index

Note: Page numbers followed by *f, i,* and *t,* indicate figures, illustrations, and tables, respectively.